The Gun Digest Book Of

TRAP & SKEET SHOOTING

3rd Edition

by
Chris Christian

DBI BOOKS, INC.

Editorial Staff

Senior Staff Editors
Harold A. Murtz
Ray Ordorica

Production Manager
John Duoba

Editorial/Production Associate
Jamie L. Puffpaff

Editorial/Production Assistant
Holly J. Porter

Assistant to the Editors
Deana L. Walker

Electronic Publishing Manager
Nancy J. Mellem

Electronic Publishing Associate
Robert M. Fuentes

Electronic Publishing Assistant
Edward B. Hartigan

Cover Photography
John Hanusin

Managing Editor
Pamela J. Johnson

Publisher
Sheldon L. Factor

ABOUT OUR COVERS

Trap, Skeet and Sporting Clays are much more than games of chance. All three are challenging athletic events demanding the best from both shooter and equipment, and Ruger has a good part of that equation down pat.

Sturm, Ruger & Co. has long been involved in Sporting Clays and sponsors a team that is rated among the best in the world. Using this experience, Ruger produced the excellent 12-gauge Sporting Clays shotgun (rear), and now has the new 20-gauge Sporting Clays model seen in the foreground.

Both models feature reduced-weight 30-inch barrels, which allow faster target acquisition, while the extra two inches of length promote smooth and necessary follow-through on those far-flying targets. To help with sighting, these competition shotguns have both front and mid-rib gold beads. Four interchangeable screw-in choke tubes come with each Sporting Clays gun—Modified, Improved Cylinder and two Skeet tubes.

Like the other fine Ruger Red Label shotguns, the Clays guns are made with 400-series stainless steel receiver, trigger and forend iron. The stock and semi-beavertail forend are of straight-grain American walnut with 20-lpi checkering.

The barrels are hammer-forged, chrome-moly steel that are stress relieved, contour ground, precisely fitted and silver-soldered (not soft soldered) to the finished monoblock. To give more uniform patterns and "softer" recoil, the barrels are back-bored and accept longer stainless steel choke tubes. Factory steel shot loads can be used without damage.

Both Sporting Clays shotguns measure 47 inches overall, and have the same stock dimensions—$14^1/_8$x$1^1/_2$x$2^1/_2$ inches. Weight of the 12-gauge gun is $7^3/_4$ pounds, while the new 20-gauge model scales an even 7 pounds.

There's no doubt about it—Sporting Clays is a tough game, but Ruger's purpose-built over/unders will help to even the odds if you're up to the challenge.

Photo by John Hanusin.

ISBN 0-87349-163-7   **Library of Congress Catalog Card #83-070143**

Contents

Introduction **5**

Section I: Trap **7**

Chapter One: The Art of Wingshooting **8**

Chapter Two: Trap: The Oldest Shotgunning Game **12**

Chapter Three: Trap's Top Guns **17**

Chapter Four: Trap Loads Are Simple **26**

Chapter Five: Trap's Fundamentals **32**

Chapter Six: Handling Handicaps **39**

Chapter Seven: Dealing with Doubles **44**

Chapter Eight: International Trap **49**

Chapter Nine: Tips from a Champ **55**

Section II: Skeet **59**

Chapter Ten: The Evolution of Skeet **60**

Chapter Eleven: Today's Winning Skeet Guns **66**

Chapter Twelve: Top Loads for Skeet **73**

Chapter Thirteen: Skeet Simplified **79**

Chapter Fourteen: The Doubles Game **89**

Chapter Fifteen: International Skeet **95**

Chapter Sixteen: Skeet's Finer Points **102**

Section III: Sporting Clays **109**

Chapter Seventeen: Sporting Clays: The New Game in Town **110**

Chapter Eighteen: Sporting's Top Guns **119**

Contents

Chapter Nineteen: Loads for Sporting Aren't Simple **127**

Chapter Twenty: Starting In Sporting **134**

Chapter Twenty-One: Sporting's Smaller Side **146**

Chapter Twenty-Two: Semi-Autos vs. Over/Unders **153**

Chapter Twenty-Three: Sporting's Toughest Shots **162**

Chapter Twenty-Four: Sporting's Newer Side **172**

Chapter Twenty-Five: Sporting Tips from the Top **179**

Section IV: Fine Tuning **187**

Chapter Twenty-Six: Hotrodding Your Smoothbore **188**

Chapter Twenty-Seven: Shotgun Fitting Is Easy **197**

Chapter Twenty-Eight: Women and Shotgun Sports **209**

Chapter Twenty-Nine: Do You Need To Reload **218**

Chapter Thirty: The Non-Toxic Alternative **232**

Chapter Thirty-One: What It Takes To Win **241**

Chapter Thirty-Two: Accessories You'll Find Useful **246**

Section V: Appendices **255**

Official Rules
    Trap **256**
    Skeet **265**
    Sporting Clays **276**

Manufacturers' Directory **280**

Introduction

Author Chris Christian has tried alll shotgun games and one of his favorites is Sporting Clays. Here he's about to practice what he preaches at a Sporting stand near his Florida home.

I GOT A PRESS release the other day from the National Shooting Sports Foundation that said clay target games experienced record growth in 1993. They based that fact on the number of clay targets sold throughout the country, sales figures from the major ammo makers, and on the input of clay target range operators who stated that first-time visitors are coming back as repeat customers in record numbers.

What might be surprising to some is that a growing number of new shooters are women. In fact, it is estimated that over 1.5 million women now regularly participate in clay target games.

I wasn't surprised by the growth figures. I guess people are finally discovering that smoking a clay target isn't just something to do with your shotgun when bird seasons are closed. It's a lot of fun in its own right, and a sport the entire family can enjoy in a congenial, safe and environmentally friendly way. I mean, it's not like clay targets are some sort of endangered species. They are made of pitch and resin and if we run short of them we'll just make more!

I won't be so presumptuous as to say that this book will make you a champion at any shotgun game. Reaching that level requires the keen reflexes, visual acuity and hand/eye coordination that are the hallmark of any successful athlete.

Some people have it and some don't. However, if you are a novice or intermediate shooter I am firmly convinced that you will find the information you need on these pages to improve. I wouldn't be surprised if some expert shooters find a nugget or two within this text to help them get that all-important "one more bird,"—often the difference between the winner and the runner-up.

It was my decision to break this book into sharply defined sections covering trap, Skeet, and Sporting Clays separately. I did that to simplify the information one needs to understand the differences between the games. I hope this doesn't give readers the impression that these games are so radically different as to be exclusive of one another. Nothing could be further from the truth.

An aerial target is an aerial target. Regardless of its distance, angle, speed and direction, the shooter must have the gun properly positioned on his shoulder, must have his body properly oriented to the target, and must keep the gun moving while he triggers the shot. Other major assets are a properly fitted shotgun, the correct choke for the job, and quality loads that will get the job done. Poor equipment selection will hurt your scores; good equipment will improve them. You'll find a lot of discussion about these factors in this book, and understanding their importance will benefit shooters at any game.

There has always been a friendly disagreement among shooters over the various differences in the skill levels required to achieve success in the array of shotgun games. Naturally, the most difficult game usually happens to be the one the individual at the podium happens to shoot best!

Having shot all the games covered in this book (some more successfully than others), I have formed my own opinions on them and have decided to add my two cents to the fray.

The easiest game to learn initially is 16-Yard ATA trap. You don't have to think. You just point the gun at the trap house and react to whatever target comes out.

The easiest game to master is American-style Skeet. It may look complicated at first, but once you learn the required position and lead for each target it becomes the easiest game in which to run twenty-five straight.

The most physically challenging game is International Skeet. The extreme low gun position and speed of the targets will test your physical skills to the limit. It makes the other games look easy!

When it comes to the game I consider most fun, it's a toss-up between Doubles trap and Bunker trap. Both are fast-paced, and I haven't quite decided whether I have more fun chasing down a pair of targets in Doubles or using those two shots to nail one really nasty target in Bunker.

The game requiring the greatest overall skill level? I'd have to say FITASC/Sporting Clays. No two courses are alike and shooters have to adjust quickly to tremendously varied target presentations, each possibly requiring the shooter to change not only his load, but choke, stance and shooting technique as well. The best way to learn these challenging games? Shoot trap and Skeet from a low gun position. You'll see all of those targets on the Sporting fields!

An aerial target is an aerial target, no matter what game you are shooting. This book will start you down the right path to master them.

Chris Christian
Georgetown, Florida

Acknowledgements

No book of this size and scope gets done entirely on the efforts of one person. This one is no exception and I had some help from a number of folks who deserve both thanks and mention.

To Skeet masters Keith Otero, Roy Dear and Mary Beverly...Sporting Clays champions Bill Whitehurst and Bonnie McLaurin...and trap experts Jim Pettengill and Mark & Lisa Sever, I offer my sincere thanks for the knowledge you shared.

A special thanks to shotgun coach Lloyd Woodhouse of the United States Shooting Team for his invaluable insights into the more subtle aspects of successful clay target shooting.

To Jack Baier of Turkey Run Sporting Clays course and Wayne Pearce of the Gator Skeet & Trap Club for allowing me free run of the facilities. A special thanks to all my friends at the Palatka Skeet Club and to Skeet shooter Bob Lee for spelling me at the camera.

To those industry experts... Larry Nailon at Clearview Products, Dave Fackler at Ballistic Products, master stock fitter Jack West, Chuck Webb at Briley, Doug Engh of Hornady, Becky Bowen and Marty Fajen of Bec-Mar, and David Feldman at El Gavilan, I thank you all for your cooperation and support.

To Mike Larsen of Federal Cartridge Company and Mike Jordan of Winchester and Neil Chadwick of Victory USA. Thanks as well to the folks at ACTIV, Remington and Fiocchi.

A special thank you to Staff Sergeant Joseph J. Johnson of the Public Affairs Office of the United States Army Marksmanship Unit.

Section I
Trap

chapter one

The Art Of Wingshooting

REDUCING AN AERIAL TARGET to a puff of dust, or a ball of feathers, has been called a combination of art and science. That's about as succinct a definition of wingshooting as I have ever heard. It applies regardless of whether the target is made of pitch and resin, or feathers and bone.

The scientific aspects of wingshooting will be addressed in later chapters of this book. As we go along, we'll discuss effective loads, proper barrel and stock work, chokes, patterns and the other invaluable aids that play such a large role in wingshooting success.

But for now, the artistic side is worthy of consideration on its own. If you have ever watched a master wingshooter crumple aerial targets with a consistent combination of fluid grace and blazing speed, I think you'll agree that it is true artistry. Yet, a fact that may surprise some people is that no two shooters will execute that artistry in precisely the same way. The reason is that it is extremely rare to be able to shoot directly at a moving target with a stationary gun and score a hit. Simply put, one must deliver the shot charge to the place where the target will be when the shot charge arrives. That requires the gun to be moving at the moment the shot is triggered, and most often pointed somewhere other than directly at the target.

In that respect, connecting with an aerial target is no different from an NFL quarterback tossing a deep pass to a sprinting receiver down the field. The quarterback certainly can't throw the ball directly at the target, but must place it at a point where the receiver and ball will meet. The Joe Montanas of the world have developed the uncanny ability to accomplish that feat without making the receiver break stride. The journeymen of the game also get the job done, although not quite as impressively, and perhaps not in the same manner. The same is true of wingshooting.

Basics of Lead

There are a number of shooting techniques that will, usually, result in the shot charge and target arriving at the same place at the same time. Each entails the shooter being able to

U.S. Shooting Team competitor Chris Pearce prepares to call for a low house eight International Skeet target—one of the toughest in any shotgunning game. Notice the "controlled aggression" in his stance. He has .41-second to react on this shot!

Veteran wingshooters know that they may have to adjust their basic stance for unusual conditions. You don't get much room to swing on a target at this Sporting Clays station, and the shooter must make body position changes to adjust to that situation.

The upright stance of this shooter is a good choice for trap, but may not give him the lateral movement required for other games.

see a slightly different relationship between his muzzle and the target. Even shooters using the same technique may have different explanations of precisely what relationship they see at the instant their subconscious mind triggers the shot.

Market hunter Fred Kimble, who hunted during the 1800s and is considered by some shotgun historians to have been one of the greatest shots of all time, is quoted as stating that the most common lead he used on ducks crossing at 40 yards was one bird length. At 60 yards, the lead as increased to two bird lengths. That's not much lead! The average mallard duck, of which Kimble was speaking, measures about 24 inches in length. If we assume the average speed of a flying mallard to be 35 miles per hour, and a target range of 40 yards, computer figures indicate the lead required would be about $6\frac{1}{2}$ feet, with a shot charge velocity of 1235 fps. Yet, Kimble saw no more than 24 inches of lead.

According to the computers, Kimble could not have killed any ducks. Yet, he is considered to have been one of the finest wingshots to have ever lived. How did he do it? Here is where the individual artistry of the wingshooter surfaces.

There are a number of shooting techniques. Computer figures can be given for the sustained lead method, sometimes called the maintained lead by our British friends. As we'll see later, that is the only shooting system in which precise leads can be computed and will be relatively close for all shooters. Kimble could not have used that system with the leads he said he observed. Instead, he had to have been using one of the fast-swing/swing-through techniques.

Beginning with the gun mounted behind the target, the swing-through shooter will swing the muzzle through the target until he reaches a distance in front of it that his previous experience, and subconscious mental computer, tells him is the correct amount of forward allowance to bring the shot charge to the target. At that point, he triggers the shot. The gun is moving faster than the target, and there is a delay between thought and deed. That microsecond delay involves the body muscles and also the mechanical action of the gun. By the time both are overcome and the primer actually ignites the shell, the gun has continued to swing past the target and the true lead is actually greater than you perceive. Although Kimble may only have seen 2 feet of lead on a 40-yard crossing target, his shooting style actually gave him more than that.

You can test this for yourself. Pound a stake into the ground, back up 30 to 40 yards and swing your shotgun from left to right through the stake. Trigger a shot when your eyes tell you the gun muzzle is right on the stake. You won't hit it. Your shot charge will impact past the stake in the direction of your swing.

Repeat the exercise and vary the speed of your swing. You will quickly see that the faster you swing, the farther beyond the stake your shot charge strikes. The quicker your mind reads the "bird picture" (the relationship between muzzle and target) and the more consistently your mind perceives it and reacts to it, the more consistent the impact point of the shot charge will be.

This is why no two shooters can be taught in exactly the same manner. A slight change in swing speed or a minor dif-

Successful shooters have learned that there is no one correct way to bust aerial targets. Each must begin with the fundamentals and develop his own style. These Bunker trap shooters discuss some of the finer points of that demanding game.

ference in visual prowess or reflexes will cause two different gunners using the same fast-swing technique to steadfastly maintain that they use two totally different amounts of lead on two identical targets.

This is why it is virtually impossible to "clone" a shooter. Attempting to teach a shooter that there is only one correct way to shoot an aerial target is to deny the irrefutable fact that individuals are just that—individuals. Each shooter will have to be grounded in the fundamentals, and then develop his or her own personal style based upon them. There are some shooters who are perfectly comfortable with an extremely fast swing on close-range (under 20 yards) targets. They swing so quickly that they will tell you they see absolutely no lead—they shoot when the muzzle meets the bird. Double the distance and some shooters change their shooting style to more of a sustained lead or to a pullaway technique. Why abandon the fast swing just because target distance increases? They are not comfortable trying to quickly perceive the 2 to 3 feet of forward allowance they might require. However, they find that a different, more controlled technique is not only comfortable but effective. The reverse might be true for other shooters.

An Easy Stance

Savvy shooters will attempt to learn as many of the various shooting techniques as they can and determine which will work best for them under varying shooting conditions. One of the most basic techniques is achieving the proper shooting stance.

The purpose of the stance is to provide a platform for the gun to allow the shooter to place the load on the target. That's really all it does, yet this simplification is sometimes overlooked.

Consider this: A rifleman attempting to place a single bullet

(Above) Low house Skeet station seven is one of the very few clay target shots that can be broken with almost no gun movement. For other shots you'll have to move the gun, and sometimes vigorously.

(Left) No two shooters will have the exact same physical abilities. Many older shooters find that they must adjust their stance to allow for their physical limitations, but keep right on breaking targets!

Some instructors might consider this shooter's stance to be too exaggerated. However, he is a AAA Skeet shooter and handles Sporting Clays almost as well. He's found the style that works for him!

An appreciation of fine shotguns is inherent in those shooters who understand the art of wingshooting. They know that even a slight change of balance and handling can affect their scores—sometimes for the worse, other times for the better. Most shooters are on a perpetual search for the gun that will boost their ratings and are frequent visitors to Vendor's Row at major tournaments.

within a 5-inch circle at 200 yards from a standing position requires a rigid platform to execute that precise shot. Anything that can be done to remove body movement and tremors is an asset. Rifle shooting calls for the weight to be evenly distributed, with perhaps a slight emphasis on the rear foot. The arms holding the gun need to be brought as close to the central body mass as possible, with the leading hand in direct alignment with the body's long axis to support the gun. The entire objective is to "freeze" the gun long enough to allow the sights to find the center of the target and the shot to be triggered.

A shotgunner has totally different requirements. The shot must be triggered from a fluidly moving gun, and the body must be "loose" enough to swing the gun through what could be a considerable arc. A rifleman who moves his gun more than an inch or so will miss his mark, yet a shotgunner who is, for example, taking a high house station four target in International Skeet may need a swing arc covering as much as 90 degrees at 20 yards!

Obviously, the stance that works for the rifleman won't for the shotgunner. This is one of the biggest mistakes new shooters make—they bind themselves up with too rigid a stance.

The shotgunner needs a wide range of movement in both the horizontal and vertical plane because he may have to swing quickly on rising, falling or sharply angled targets. This is best accomplished with an emphasis on forward foot weight; some like a 60:40 ratio between that and the back foot, others like even more. The hips need to be free to pivot, and they are what actually starts to drive the body for the shot. Flex in the knees is desirable, but too much of it may contribute to erratic gun movement.

A rifleman's stance is rigid; a wingshooter's stance must be one of controlled aggression, a coiled spring ready to release upon command.

The stance that works best for a 6-foot 180-pound athletic male may not be the best for a shorter, stouter, more sedate shooter. Each will have to work from the fundamentals to establish the body position that allows him the best use of the physical characteristics at his disposal.

The result may be a noticeable difference in the way each individual assumes his basic position before calling for the target, yet their scores may be identical! As I said, you can't clone shooters.

Sometimes, individual shooters may alter their stance for different shooting situations. I have a tendency to do that. When I am shooting games from a pre-mounted gun (Doubles trap, Bunker trap and Handicap trap), I tend to put a little more flex in my knees and a bit more crouch in my body than I would if I were shooting from an unmounted position. The reason is that these targets are all rising targets, and the increased flex in the knees provides a little more energy to drive the gun through the target with the fast-swing technique I prefer in these games.

Change to Sporting Clays, International Skeet, Five Stand or other games, I will be shooting from a low (unmounted) gun. My upper body assumes a more upright position, with slightly straighter knees. The most important thing in low gun games is that the gun be mounted smoothly and consistently every time, and the more flex and body crouch I have, the more that critical shoulder pocket shifts as I move my body to the target. By keeping the body upright and relying on more pivoting from the hips, a more consistent gun mount is achieved. At least it is for me.

To learn the art of wingshooting, learn the fundamentals and apply them to your abilities. After that, it is simply a matter of seeing lots of targets at different speeds and different angles and learning to program your mental computer to execute the correct swing and lead.

chapter two

Trap: The Oldest Shotgunning Game

THE GAME OF trap has been around a long time. In fact, a *real* long time! One of the earliest mentions of the game in print was in 1793 in the English publication known as *Sporting Magazine*. Yes, they actually had outdoor magazines back then. The report stated that the sport was "...well established recreation." One would assume that it was primarily an English sport at that time. The targets were live pigeons, held in a box or "trap" as it later became called, and released via a string that lifted the lid when the shooter "called for the bird." The first known records of an organized version of trap in the United States (to the best of this writer's knowledge) are contained in the records of the Sportsman's Club of Cincinnati, Ohio, and date from 1831.

The game continued to be shot with live pigeons (a version that still exists today) until 1866, when Chas Portlock of Boston, Massachusetts, introduced a glass ball to American shooters. However, the balls met with limited success because the traps used to propel them were of such poor quality that many of the balls broke upon launching. That problem plagued American shooters until Portlock developed an effective trap design to throw his balls.

However, glass ball shooting began its decline when George Ligowsky invented the first clay pigeon, and the trap to throw it, about 1880. This was a significant step for shotgun games because the new, disc-shaped clay pigeon actually began to simulate the flight of a live bird, whereas the older glass balls were simply lobbed into the air.

These early clay pigeons were actually made of clay and baked in an oven. They were quite hard and it took a dead-on shot to bust one. Today, clay targets are made primarily of pitch and are much easier to break.

Trap Shooting Today

Trap shooting in the United States today is under the direction of the Amateur Trapshooting Association (ATA), and a full copy of their rules will be found in the Appendices.

A trap field consists of a single trap, located in a trap house partially buried in the ground. Five shooting positions are situ-

(Above) It is considered proper form not to load your gun on the line until the shooter two stations before you has called for his target. The middle shooter is preparing for his shot, while far right shooter has, quite correctly, not yet loaded.

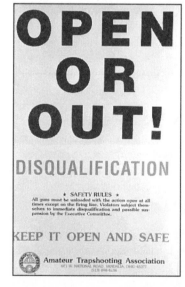

(Left) Safety rules are stressed on any clay target range. This rule reminds shooters that gun actions must be open and fresh or fired hulls removed from the gun before changing trap stations.

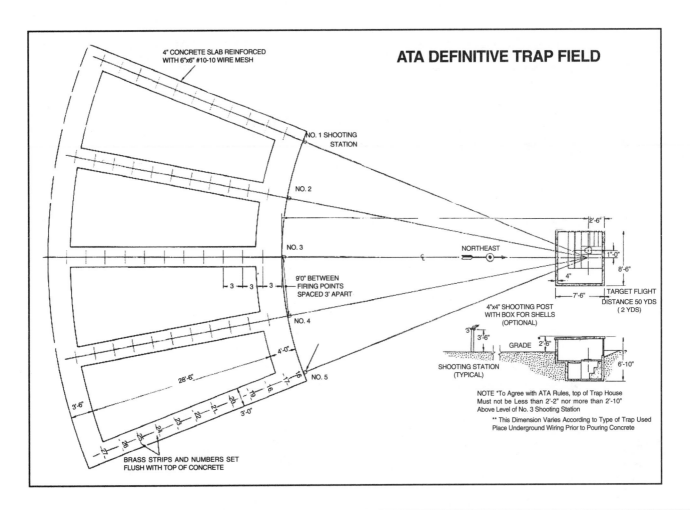

ATA DEFINITIVE TRAP FIELD

4" CONCRETE SLAB REINFORCED
WITH 6"x6" #10-10 WIRE MESH

NO. 1 SHOOTING
STATION

NO. 2

NO. 3

NORTHEAST

9'0" BETWEEN
FIRING POINTS
SPACED 3' APART

NO. 4

4'-0"

28'-6"

NO. 5

3'-6"

3'-0"

BRASS STRIPS AND NUMBERS SET
FLUSH WITH TOP OF CONCRETE

2'-6"

1'-0"

8'-6"

4"

7'-6"

TARGET FLIGHT
DISTANCE 50 YDS
(2 YDS)

4"x4" SHOOTING POST
WITH BOX FOR SHELLS
(OPTIONAL)

3'

3'-6"

GRADE   2'-6"

SHOOTING STATION
(TYPICAL)

6'-10"

NOTE *To Agree with ATA Rules, top of Trap House
Must not be Less than 2'-2" nor more than 2'-10"
Above Level of No. 3 Shooting Station

** This Dimension Varies According to Type of Trap Used
Place Underground Wiring Prior to Pouring Concrete

ated 16 yards behind the trap house and spaced 3 yards apart. The 16-Yard event, the most common trap game, is shot from these five positions.

From each of the 16-yard positions, a lane, marked in yardage increments, runs back to a point 27 yards behind the trap house. Handicap trap is fired from these various yardage markers.

The trap machine is required to launch clays at unknown angles for each station. The clays fly within 22 degrees of the right or left of the trap center. These special oscillating traps have built-in "interrupters" which break up any patterns and help prevent the shooter from "reading the trap." Thus the shooter is never really certain exactly where the bird will fly. The only guarantee is that it will be within a defined zone for each of the five stations.

Standard clay targets are used, and they may be any of a number of colors or color patterns. The machine should be calibrated to launch them at a speed of about 41 mph and produce a trajectory that puts the birds between 8 and 12 feet above the ground at 10 feet in front of the trap, propelling them out to a distance of no less than 48 yards and no more than 52 yards from the trap house.

This range spread is allowed under ATA rules and compensates for different wind and weather conditions. Most trap ranges set the bird height to about 10 feet under conditions of no wind or a very gentle breeze. Should a strong wind be blowing directly into the trap house, the target trajectory will be set lower to retard rapid climb of the bird so it will travel

Trap squads will be under the direction of a puller/scorer who will make certain everything functions as planned and that safety rules are adhered to.

Most trap ranges will have qualified instructors available to assist new shooters, and it is money well spent in getting started in this game.

the minimum distance. A head wind will make the target climb more quickly. A tail wind, on the other hand, keeps the target from climbing, and under these conditions the range personnel may have to set the target to the full 12-foot height in order to keep it in the air long enough to make the 48-yard distance.

If a wind shift during a match prevents the targets from falling within the prescribed height and distance parameters, a competitor is well within his rights to ask the referee to stop the match and reset the machine.

The 16-Yard event is the most popular. Shooters compete here under a class system based upon their previous scores, or known ability, to assure they are shooting against competitors of similar skill levels. Previous scores generally require a shooter to have engaged about 300 registered targets, and the percentage of those targets broken will be his average. There are usually five classes, but if shooter turnout is light, the ATA has provisions within the rules for reducing that figure to four, or even three classes. Here's the breakdown:

ATA 16-Yard Classification

Five Classes:

AA	97 percent or better
A	less than 97 to 94 percent
B	less than 94 to 91 percent
C	less than 91 to 88 percent
D	less than 88 percent

Four Classes:

A	95 percent or better
B	less than 95 to 92 percent
C	less than 92 to 89 percent
D	less than 89 percent

Three Classes:

A	95 percent or better
B	95 to 91 percent
C	less than 91 percent

Shooters fire five rounds at each station and change on the command of the puller/scorer who, in this case, is taking a respite from the summer Florida heat under his umbrella!

Shooters take a break between rounds at a Florida tournament. The gun in the foreground has the action locked open, as all guns should be when not actually on the shooting pad.

The rules specifically state that no shotgun larger than 12-gauge may be used. This allows competitors to shoot any of the smaller gauges, but few do because the decreased shot charge is simply too great a handicap for competition. If you are just shooting for fun, there is nothing wrong with using a smaller gauge. I have shot many a round of trap with both the 28-gauge and the 410-bore. It's fun—frustrating, but still fun!

Allowable ammunition is equally broad. The maximum shot charge that may be used in competition is a 3-dram equivalent load with no more than $1^1/_8$ ounces of shot. Only lead shot may be used in a match, ruling out copper- or nickel-plated shot. The largest shot size allowed is #$7^1/_2$. This has been carved in stone for so long that 3-dram, $1^1/_8$-ounce, 12-gauge loads containing premium hard black #$7^1/_2$ shot are generally referred to as "trap loads."

Many shooters today use lighter 12-gauge loads to reduce recoil, reserving the maximum loads for handicap rounds and the second shot in the Doubles match.

Many trap shooters favor guns with raised combs which elevate the shot charge above the point of aim to compensate for the sharply rising targets. This Jack West adjustable comb is a popular trap gun modification.

Etiquette and Procedures

A round of trap consists of twenty-five shots. A trap squad may contain up to five shooters.

Each shooter will take one of the five positions (stations), and the shooter on station one will lead off. Once he has fired his round, the shooter on station two may then call for his bird, with the following shooters calling for their birds in turn. This rotation will be repeated until each shooter has fired five rounds from his station.

At that time, the trap puller/scorer will call "Change," followed by a quick rundown of the number of birds each contestant hit at that station. It will sound something like this, "Change...1-3, 2-4, 3-5, 4-2, 5-1." Translated into English, that means it is time to change to the next station; station one broke three birds, the shooter on two got four, station three ran it clean (got all five), station four only hit two birds, and the shooter on station five needs some real help because he only managed to whack one of them.

The shooters will then move to the next station in a clockwise manner, station one moving to station two, etc., and the shooter on five now moving to station one. When everybody has reached their new positions, the shooter who originally began the round on station one, and is now on station two, will again lead off. He will be the first shooter at each new station regardless which it is.

Guns will not be loaded until the shooters are actually on their stations and the lead-off shooter has called for the first bird. It is considered proper etiquette to load your gun with only one round at a time, and only when the shooter two positions before you has called for his bird. When moving between stations, the gun must be unloaded and the action open.

It is common for the scorer to call missed birds as the competitors shoot, using the word "Lost" to denote a miss. In order to score a hit, the shooter must only knock a visible piece off the target, and this can sometimes create differences of opinion between scorer and shooter!

Many trap ranges incorporate other games. Author's favorite, the Gator Skeet & Trap Club in Gainesville, Florida also throws Skeet, International Skeet, Bunker trap, and Five Stand sporting! It's a scattergunner's version of Disney World!

The scorer is almost invariably right, at least if he has any experience at all. He is in position to do nothing but watch the bird as it leaves the house and is unencumbered by any of the pressures and decisions facing the shooter. Still, scorers are human, and an occasional mistake can be made. If you feel that you hit the bird, tell him. If one or more of your squad mates agree with you, the scorer will often change his call.

Trap is a fast-paced game. In fact, of all the shotgun games, a round of 16-Yard trap is usually completed the quickest—about twelve to fifteen minutes.

Trap shooters get used to that quick-paced rhythm, and a shooter that is slow, sluggish or constantly questioning the scorer's calls will disrupt it. Such shooters are not viewed in a very favorable light by their squad mates.

A courteous trap shooter will make every effort to fall into the shooting rhythm of the squad. It is important when you take your position that you be ready to shoot. Have all the shells you require, plus any other accessories you will need.

This rhythm is so important to many veteran shooters that they will make every possible attempt to shoot on squads composed of others with whom they have shot with in the past, and who provide the right rhythm!

That is not just for convenience's sake; a herky-jerky squad can disrupt a shooter's concentration and decrease his score. Conversely, a smooth-running squad that hits the zone can elevate a shooter's score! Trap is one of the few shooting games where the shooters around you can exert a positive or negative influence on your performance without any conscious effort on their part.

That is a factor about trap that must be understood by new shooters. And, it is one reason why trap shooters have gained the reputation for being somewhat close-mouthed and aloof. Whether that is totally true or not is an arguable point. However, there is no doubt that a trap squad will not display the same laid-back, gregarious nature that you will see among Skeet or Sporting Clays shooters. That doesn't make it bad or good—just different.

For this reason, you will not see a lot of conversation among squad members during a shoot, nor will advice and shooting pointers be freely offered while the round is in progress. The best trap squads are focused, business-like and quick-moving. That's the nature of the game. New trap shooters would do well to keep that in mind and attempt to emulate it. It can have a positive effect on your scores and on your progress as a trap shooter.

Shooting Accessories

There are a number of accessory items for this game, and you'll get a look at many of them in an upcoming chapter. To get started, however, you really need very few.

Eye protection is important in any shooting sport and should always be worn. Some ranges require it. Ear protection is also a plus. Not only does this help prevent permanent hearing loss, but it will also help reduce recoil fatigue and will go a long way in helping you to avoid developing a flinch.

Shooting vests and shell pouches are nice, and most shooters will want to obtain them, at some point. They are not really needed for trap, however, because there isn't much movement on the field. You have plenty of time to pick up the box of shells at your feet and haul it to the next station, and more than enough time to reach down and grab a shell from it when you need one. If you are saving your empty hulls to reload, you will need something to put them in, and an inexpensive belt pouch works well. Trap is not a complex game. It's a lot of fast-paced fun.

Every summer over 6000 shooters make the pilgrimage to Vandalia, Ohio, for the ATA's Grand American trap shoot. This event has been accurately described as the largest participant event held in the entire world of sports. The ATA, formed in 1923, has been headquartered in Vandalia since 1924, and today numbers more than 36,000 active shooters and more than 1100 affiliated clubs. Not bad for our oldest shotgunning game!

Trap's Top Guns

Two-time Florida State International Trap Champion Jim Pettengill takes this simple aproach to the game of trap, and his over/under reflects that outlook. It gives maximum reliability and lively handling qualities, and it's easy to keep clean.

LIKE VIRTUALLY ALL clay target games, trap originated as an attempt to duplicate field shots on actual game birds. To an extent, the current game will do that. However, that only applies to flushing birds moving quickly away from the gunner and rising as they do so. Birds having that flight pattern include pheasant, quail, sharptails, and, sometimes, chukar, among others. The fact that trap targets are launched at a speed far higher than any game bird can achieve on the flush actually makes modern trap an optical illusion. Real birds will rise, but they won't do it that quickly.

What a trapshooter gets when he calls for a bird is a target that appears to be moving away from him either as a straightaway, or at a quartering angle, yet is rising quite quickly.

This means that shooters need a gun that will place the shot charge above the actual point of hold, to compensate for the sharp climb of the target. If the gun shoots "flat," as we would want for a Skeet, Sporting Clays, or hunting gun, then the shooter must actually cover the target with the muzzle of the gun, swinging right up through the target and blocking it out. Since that causes the shooter to lose sight of the target at the critical moment he triggers the shot, it becomes a factor that will decrease the shooter's score.

As a result, the guns that win in trap are those that will place the center of their pattern well above the point of aim. In some cases, depending upon the shooter, that might be as little as 3 inches at 40 yards. Other shooters favor a much higher-shooting gun, and I have seen some that have a built-in elevation of over 18 inches at that range.

That can be achieved simply by installing a different rib on the barrel. I had an extra 28-inch barrel for my Franchi Prestige so fitted a number of years back by Simmons, who are probably the best-known custom rib makers, and it elevates the pattern 9 inches above my point of hold at 40 yards. I did not need to make any alterations to the stock. By switching back to the 26-inch barrel with its flat rib, I can use the gun for trap, Sporting Clays and Skeet. Some shooters get the gun to shoot high by having the barrel bent slightly upwards. It's not obvious to the naked eye, but this elevates the pattern.

The most common way to produce a high-shooting gun is to raise the comb height. This effectively raises your eye, which is the "rear sight," and the gun will then shoot higher. This can be done with either a detachable cheekpiece, or with a high-combed stock. Most guns marketed as trap guns will have a drop at comb of 1³/₈ inches, instead of the 1¹/₂ inches that is almost standard for field-grade guns.

Another factor that determines an effective trap gun is its handling quality. Stand behind a Skeet shooter addressing a mid-field crossing shot and you will see him swing his gun through a degree of lateral movement that will cover a range of up to 15 yards as he tracks and breaks the target. Stand behind a trap shooter, and you will see that even the most extreme bird angle won't cause him to move the gun more than about two feet from his starting position. That movement must be very quick and forceful, and must drive right through the target. That driving motion has proven to be best accomplished with a longer, heavier gun that tends to stay moving once it gets started. The most effective trap guns are those with barrels in excess of 30 inches in length, and with a weight of 8¹/₂ to 9¹/₂ pounds.

Trap shooters also favor tighter chokes than those pursuing Skeet and Sporting Clays. A fast trap shooter, shooting from the 16-yard line, might get onto a target when the bird is at a range of 25 yards. More likely, it'll be 30. If he is a little slower, the bird could be 35 to 40 yards away from him. A Modified choke is considered to be a relatively open choke for trap, although I feel it is about the best choice for the 16 Yard game if the shooter is using quality, hard-shot loads. The Handicap and Doubles games are best played with Improved Modified or Full choke.

A shooter engaging targets from the 27-yard handicap line is looking at shots of 40 to 50 yards, and many will opt for Extra-Full choking.

If a shooter plays the Doubles game or International trap, he needs a gun capable of firing two shots. If he just shoots 16 Yard and Handicap Singles, a single-barrel gun works fine. Those who play all the trap games sometimes use a two-barrel set: an over/under receiver that is fitted with a single barrel and also a set of double barrels.

The ardent trap shooter ends up with a gun that has a very limited application for any other shooting game, or actual field work. Long, heavy, and tightly choked, the trap gun is a specialized tool for a specialized game. If you want to win this game, you will need one.

Today's Trap Guns

With that said, however, I also need to point out that you do not need a specialized trap gun if you just want to go out and shoot a little trap for fun. An aerial target is an aerial target. It flies, you shoot it. That can be done quite nicely with any shotgun you happen to own, although it does get a little tough with the 410 and 28-gauge! I routinely shoot trap with my 28-inch-barreled 12-gauge Ruger Red Label, just to keep in practice for the outgoing targets that I often see in Sporting Clays. All I do is slip in a Modified or Light Modified tube instead of the Skeet 1 and Improved Cylinder tubes that nor-

No matter how good your gun is, you'll need to practice with it to do well. Corporal Theresa Wentzel of the U.S. Army Marksmanship Unit hones her technique at International, the toughest trap game. (U.S. Army photo by Joseph J. Johnson.)

mally occupy the gun when shooting Skeet or Clays. I make certain that I have loaded up with #8s, instead of 9s, and I'm ready to have some fun. With this flat-shooting gun I can't float the bird above the bead and have to make certain that I swing up and through the target, but that's what I would have to do on outgoing Sporting Clays targets anyway. I don't expect that I would ever win the Grand American with this gun, but I certainly carry a 90 percent average with it. Since I do not shoot trap on a serious competitive basis, this approach makes a lot more sense to me than investing anywhere from $800 to $25,000 for a specialized gun that is not particularly suited for anything but trap.

If you want to take your Mossberg, Winchester or Remington "huntin'" pump gun out to the trap range, do it! For that matter, try trap with any make or model of shotgun you happen to own. If it has only a fixed Improved Cylinder choke, don't worry about that either. Use a 1¹/₈-ounce 12-gauge trap load; if you miss the bird, don't blame the gun and choke! If at some later date you decide that you want to be a serious trap competitor, then you can consider a specialized trap gun, but you don't need it to start.

If you are ready right now for a specialized trap gun, here's a look at the best ones currently available. Unless otherwise noted, all are chambered for 12-gauge shells.

Remington

Once offering one of the better selections of high quality, yet lower-priced competitive shotguns, Remington seems to have abandoned the competitive market of late. Their 1994 catalog shows only two trap guns, the single-barrel **Model 90-T** and the semi-auto **11-87 Premier Trap**.

The Model 90-T is a classic break-action single barrel intended for 16-Yard and Handicap trap only. The 34-inch

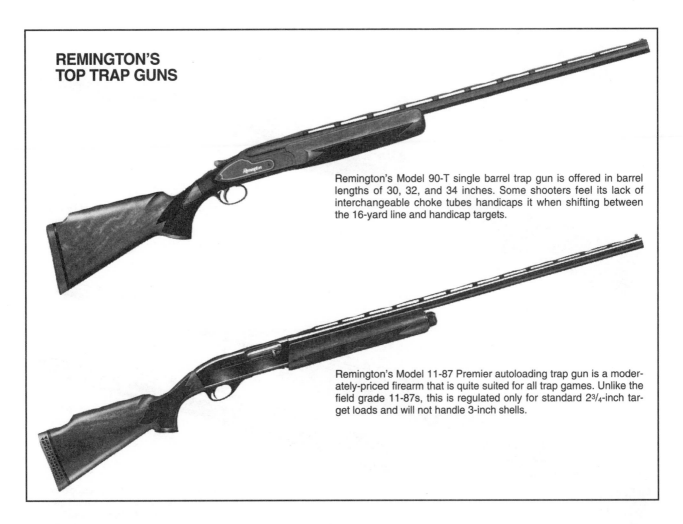

Remington's Model 90-T single barrel trap gun is offered in barrel lengths of 30, 32, and 34 inches. Some shooters feel its lack of interchangeable choke tubes handicaps it when shifting between the 16-yard line and handicap targets.

Remington's Model 11-87 Premier autoloading trap gun is a moderately-priced firearm that is quite suited for all trap games. Unlike the field grade 11-87s, this is regulated only for standard 2³/₄-inch target loads and will not handle 3-inch shells.

barrel is factory back-bored and available as a fixed Full choke only. Overall length is 51 inches, with a total weight of 8⁷/₈ pounds. Available in four stock configurations with varying drop at comb and a standard 14³/₈-inch length of pull, the gun can be had with a standard rib or with a special adjustable high rib.

Remington's 11-87 gas gun entry is available as a right- or left-hand model with 2³/₄-inch chamber only, and, unlike the field grade 11-87 model, is not pressure compensated for varying loads. It's strictly regulated to standard trap loads. The 30-inch barrel is threaded for REMChokes. The straight comb version offers a 14³/₈-inch length of pull; 1³/₈-inch drop at comb; and a 1³/₄-inch drop at heel. The Monte Carlo stocked gun features the same dimensions except for a 1⁷/₈-inch drop at heel. Both models tip the scales at 8³/₈ pounds.

Browning

Offering one of the most extensive lines of modestly-priced quality trap guns, Browning has become the leading player in this area.

Citori Trap: Available in Grades I, III, and Golden Clays, this proven over/under can be had with either a conventional sloping comb stock or straight Monte Carlo, and in barrel lengths of 30 or 32 inches. Barrels are back-bored for reduced recoil and improved pattern density and are threaded for their competition model Invector-Plus choke tubes. A high-post ventilated rib with the popular ivory colored twin bead setup is standard. Critical dimensions on both stock types are: length of pull, 14³/₈ inches; drop at comb, 1³/₈ inches; drop at heel, 2 inches. The 32-inch-barreled models measure 49 inches in overall length and weigh 8 pounds, 11 ounces, while the 30-inch-tube gun measures 47 inches and tips the scales at 8 pounds, 7 ounces.

Citori Plus: Browning bills this upgrade of the basic Citori model as the "...most advanced production-made trap gun," and they may well be right. As with all Browning competition guns, the barrels are back-bored and fitted for the Invector-Plus choke tube system; Full, Improved Modified and Modified are supplied. The barrels are also ported to help reduce muzzle rise, with a non-ported barrel option available for those who shoot the International version of the game where porting is not allowed. The high-step rib is adjustable from 3 to 12 inches above point of aim at 40 yards. Available barrel lengths are 30 or 32 inches.

A very practical feature is the adjustable stock, allowing for changes to length of pull, comb height, angle of buttplate, and cast-on/off of comb. The buttpad also incorporates a built-in recoil reducer that Browning claims cuts perceived recoil by up to 45 percent. Overall weight is about 9 pounds, 7 ounces.

For those who enjoy a single-barrel gun for 16 Yard and Handicap games, the Citori Plus is available as a combo package that adds a separate single barrel of either 32 or 34 inches.

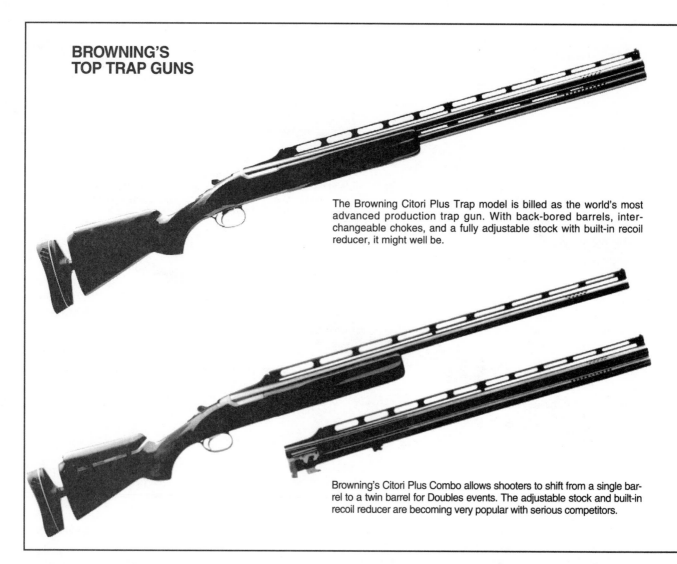

The Browning Citori Plus Trap model is billed as the world's most advanced production trap gun. With back-bored barrels, interchangeable chokes, and a fully adjustable stock with built-in recoil reducer, it might well be.

Browning's Citori Plus Combo allows shooters to shift from a single barrel to a twin barrel for Doubles events. The adjustable stock and built-in recoil reducer are becoming very popular with serious competitors.

BT-99: The single-barrel trap gun by which many others are judged, it has earned an enviable reputation over the last 20 years. Available with either 32- or 34-inch barrels, with a high-step $11/32$-inch-wide floating rib, they are back-bored and fitted for the Invector-Plus choke tube system with Full, Improved Modified, and Modified tubes supplied. Stock configuration is offered as conventional or Monte Carlo comb styles, with a length of pull of $14^3/8$ inches, drop at comb $1^7/16$ (conventional), or $1^3/8$ inches (Monte Carlo), and a drop at heel of $1^5/8$ and 2 inches, respectively.

The BT-99 Plus is essentially the same gun with the adjustable stock and high-step adjustable rib found on the Citori Plus package.

Recoilless Single Barrel Trap: This unusual gun features a bolt-operated design with what can only be described as a "movable inner mass." That mass is the inner bolt, barrel and receiver. This collection of parts actually moves forward at the moment of recoil. The inertia of this moving mass cancels out most of the cartridge's energy. Browning says this recoilless system reduces actual recoil from a standard trap load by 54 percent, and by a whopping 72 percent with the lighter 1-ounce, $2^3/4$-dram loads favored by a growing number of 16 Yard competitors.

The ventilated rib is adjustable for point of impact to place the shot 3, 6, or 9 inches high at 40 yards. Drop at comb and length of pull can also be adjusted via interchangeable spacers between the recoil pad and stock. Available in barrel lengths of 27 or 30 inches, the gun weighs about 9 pounds. Full, Improved Modified, and Modified choke tubes come with the gun.

One indication of Browning's success in the trap game is the number of them you see on the line... there are a lot of them!

Beretta

One of the oldest gun makers in the world, if not the oldest, Beretta is well represented in both the U.S. and international competition.

A390 Sport Trap: This semi-auto, gas-operated model features your choice of ported or non-ported barrel, and a stock fully adjustable for length of pull, comb height and cast. Available in barrel lengths of 28 (special order) 30 and 32 inches, with fixed or interchangeable chokes, Beretta's newest gas gun tips the scales at $8^1/4$ pounds and has already earned a solid reputation for reliability.

Gold Trap: This over/under offers a lighter overall weight

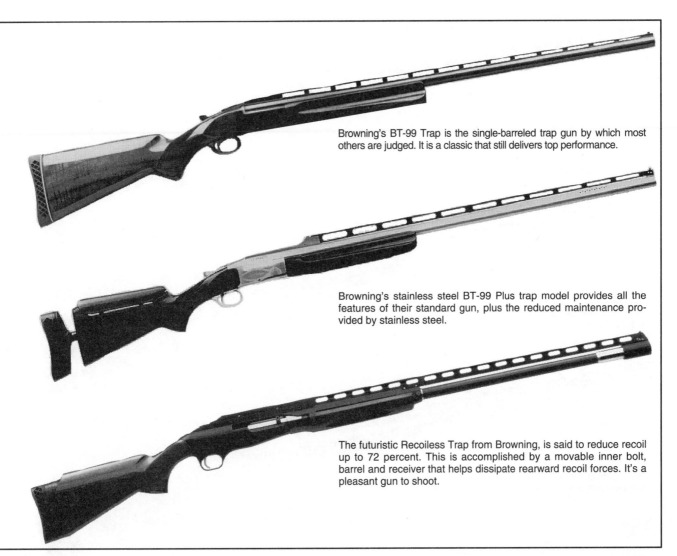

Browning's BT-99 Trap is the single-barreled trap gun by which most others are judged. It is a classic that still delivers top performance.

Browning's stainless steel BT-99 Plus trap model provides all the features of their standard gun, plus the reduced maintenance provided by stainless steel.

The futuristic Recoiless Trap from Browning, is said to reduce recoil up to 72 percent. This is accomplished by a movable inner bolt, barrel and receiver that helps dissipate rearward recoil forces. It's a pleasant gun to shoot.

BERETTA'S TOP TRAP GUNS

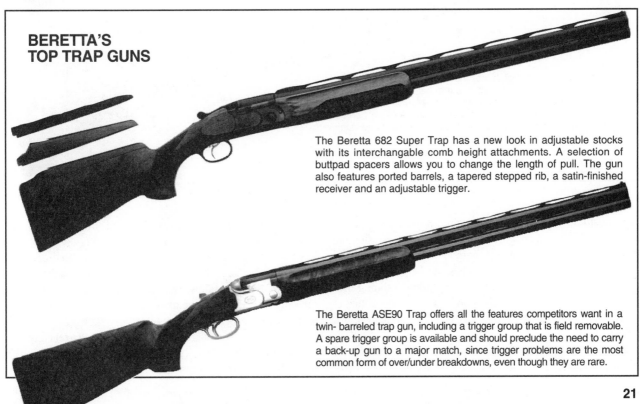

The Beretta 682 Super Trap has a new look in adjustable stocks with its interchangable comb height attachments. A selection of buttpad spacers allows you to change the length of pull. The gun also features ported barrels, a tapered stepped rib, a satin-finished receiver and an adjustable trigger.

The Beretta ASE90 Trap offers all the features competitors want in a twin-barreled trap gun, including a trigger group that is field removable. A spare trigger group is available and should preclude the need to carry a back-up gun to a major match, since trigger problems are the most common form of over/under breakdowns, even though they are rare.

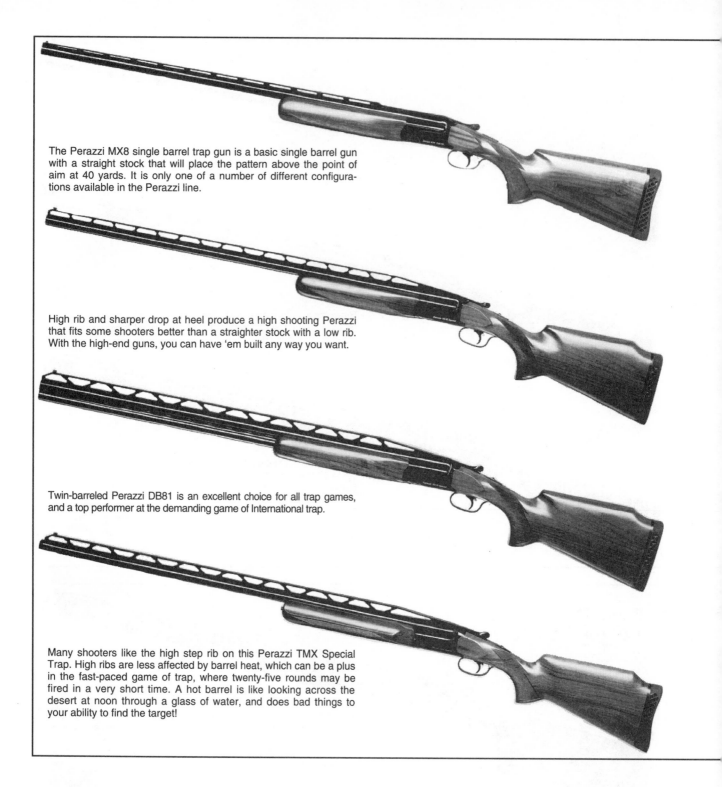

The Perazzi MX8 single barrel trap gun is a basic single barrel gun with a straight stock that will place the pattern above the point of aim at 40 yards. It is only one of a number of different configurations available in the Perazzi line.

High rib and sharper drop at heel produce a high shooting Perazzi that fits some shooters better than a straighter stock with a low rib. With the high-end guns, you can have 'em built any way you want.

Twin-barreled Perazzi DB81 is an excellent choice for all trap games, and a top performer at the demanding game of International trap.

Many shooters like the high step rib on this Perazzi TMX Special Trap. High ribs are less affected by barrel heat, which can be a plus in the fast-paced game of trap, where twenty-five rounds may be fired in a very short time. A hot barrel is like looking across the desert at noon through a glass of water, and does bad things to your ability to find the target!

than most trap guns, a factor that some shooters find appealing. Available in 12 gauge, or 20 gauge on request, the gun tips the scales at just 8 pounds. Barrels of 30 inches are standard, although 28- and 32-inch tubes can be ordered. Fixed chokes are also standard. The Gold Trap offers a sliding-trigger length of pull adjustment and comes with two interchangeable triggers, one canted for right-hand shooters and one for lefties.

S682 Gold X Super Trap: A serious over/under gun for serious shooters, this model is built for versatility and durabili-

ty, right down to replaceable bearing shoulders on the monobloc and hinge pins. The 30-inch barrel is standard (with 28- and 32-inch tubes on request) with either fixed or interchangeable chokes. The Super Gold Trap models have ported barrels and a fully-adjustable stock. The trigger is adjustable for length of pull. Total weight on the various offerings in this model varies from 8.8 to 9.2 pounds.

This gun is also available as a single-double-barrel combo.

ASE 90 Gold Trap: This new over/under has a receiver machined from a solid block of nickel-chromium-molybde-

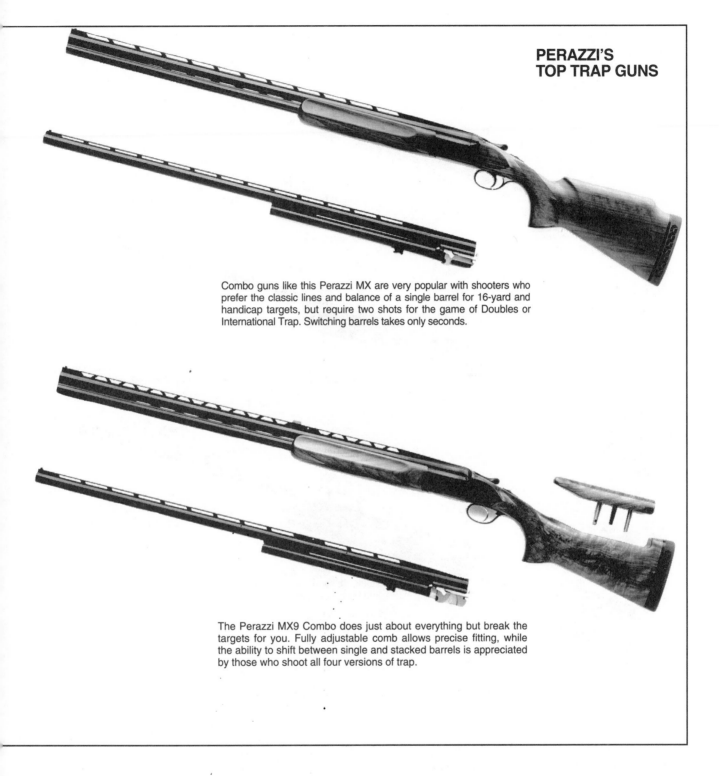

Combo guns like this Perazzi MX are very popular with shooters who prefer the classic lines and balance of a single barrel for 16-yard and handicap targets, but require two shots for the game of Doubles or International Trap. Switching barrels takes only seconds.

The Perazzi MX9 Combo does just about everything but break the targets for you. Fully adjustable comb allows precise fitting, while the ability to shift between single and stacked barrels is appreciated by those who shoot all four versions of trap.

num steel and is heat-treated for strength and durability. Replaceable hinge pins and barrel bearing shoulders give it the longest possible life. The trigger group assembly is field removable for cleaning and inspection, and a spare trigger group is available, to preclude the need to carry a backup gun to a major shoot. The trigger is adjustable for three different length of pull positions.

Stock and forearm are easily removable and a wide variety of stock measurement combinations is available. This, essentially, allows the gun to be custom fitted to the shooter. Bar-

rels are available in 30 and 32 inches, with fixed or interchangeable choke tubes, and a separate single barrel is available in the Gold X Trap combo package. All-up weight is $8^{1}/_{4}$ pounds.

SO5: Beretta's top-of-the-line trap gun is the exquisite S05. This can be individually fitted to the shooter and is available with barrel lengths from 28 to 32 inches. The average weight is $8^{1}/_{4}$ pounds, and the list of options is extensive.

With the exception of the upper-end Berettas, all of the

LJUTIC'S TOP TRAP GUNS

Ljutic's classic Mono Gun is considered one of the most durable and reliable single barrel trap guns made. More than a few of these guns have been on the trap lines for over thirty years without repair.

This low rib Monte Carlo version of the Ljutic Mono Gun is very popular with shooters who prefer a slightly flatter shooting, more conventionally-stocked, gun.

Like other high-end trap guns, the Ljutic can be had in a variety of stock, rib, and barrel configurations. Defining a standard Ljutic is impossible because of that.

previously discussed shotguns fall into the moderately-priced class and are essentially mass-produced guns using modern manufacturing techniques that allow parts to be made to certain tight tolerances. When a technician on the assembly line puts a gun together, he or she does so by pulling a part out of a parts bin and installing it. If it fits, and is within specification, it stays. If not, it goes back into the bin and another part is selected. Such modern production methods allow a quality product to be assembled with a minimum of costly hand-fitting, and without the need to employ highly trained and very expensive assemblers. One might consider these guns to be the Fords and Chevys of the smoothbore family, and this description applies to those shotguns you will find listed in the Skeet and Sporting Clays sections as well. There is noth-

ing wrong with that. I drive a Ford pickup truck and shoot Rugers.

Some shooters, however, aren't Ford and Chevy kinda folks. They are more comfortable with a Mercedes or a Ferrari, and they can afford them. They don't mind paying five to ten times what my Ford cost as long as they feel they are getting a premium product. That same philosophy holds true for shotguns as well, and the last three gun makers discussed here fall into that class.

Krieghoff, Perazzi and Ljutic can be considered the Mercedes and Ferraris of the competitive shotgun world. The reason for that, other then their hefty price tag (to $20,000, sometimes more) is the high degree of hand fitting involved. Unlike mass-production guns with interchangeable parts,

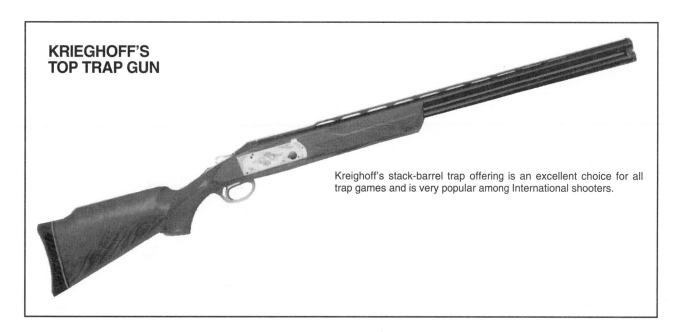

KRIEGHOFF'S TOP TRAP GUN

Kreighoff's stack-barrel trap offering is an excellent choice for all trap games and is very popular among International shooters.

these guns consist of parts that are hand fitted and hand formed. All critical components like sears, the trigger system, lugs, receivers, etc., are machined in rough form and then hand fitted and finished by highly skilled craftsmen to produce an individual gun. Once the basic gun is complete, the same care extends to fitting the gun to the customer. Mass-market guns come with standard stock dimensions, but not these. The customer can determine exactly what stock dimensions are needed in terms of length of pull, pitch, drop at comb and heel, cast, rib height and width. The end result is a hand-crafted shotgun precisely tailored to the shooter. This is one reason why you rarely see a new Krieghoff, Perazzi or Ljutic on the shelf at your local gun dealer. Only rarely are these models made with "standard" stock dimensions for off-the-rack sales. On those occasions when it does happen, the customer will have the option of selecting a buttstock with different dimensions, or an adjustable buttstock, if he desires. Generally, however, when you see one of these guns on a gun dealer's rack it is a used model. And you won't see a lot of those. Folks who favor these upper-end guns tend to hang onto them for quite awhile! These guns are generally purchased through an authorized distributor or sales representative who will assist the customer in ordering the measurements and features he requires. While each of these makers offers a number of different models, the only real difference among them is in barrel, rib and stock configurations. The heart of the gun, the action, is essentially the same. The various model designations are simply a brief way to describe the different features.

Krieghoff

The **K-80** model is considered one of the premier trap guns in the world today. Available in an almost endless array of barrel lengths, stock measurement options and various rib designs, the K-80 is literally a custom proposition. The options include being able to specify the point of impact of each barrel in a set of over/under barrels. The trigger is adjustable for length of pull, and one basic K-80 receiver can handle anything from a 410 over/under barrel to a 34-inch 12-gauge single barrel. Combo sets are also available.

The variety of options offered make it virtually impossible to describe an "average" Krieghoff.

Perazzi

Like the Krieghoff, the Perazzi is available with many, many options. This maker offers world class models in single barrel, double barrel, and combo sets. Options include adjustable-impact ribs, adjustable stocks, and a wide variety of barrel and choke options. The Krieghoff and the Perazzi are considered to be the preeminent shotguns on the international competition circuit, and are among the favorites of top-ranked U.S. competitors.

Ljutic

The only American gunmaker offering a competitive shotgun in the same class as the Krieghoff and Perazzi is Ljutic Industries, based in Washington state. Their single-barrel **Mono Gun** has earned a world class reputation for precision and durability. In fact, some Ljutics built in the early 1960s are still in active competition today.

While their single barrel has been most popular, Ljutic's new over/under **LM6** may unseat it. This gun, like all of the company's models, is virtually custom fit to the shooter and is available with a variety of options including: pull or release triggers; multiple-barrel sets; screw-in choke tubes; lightweight or standard-weight models; a diverse selection of rib widths and heights; and single-double-barrel combo sets. Like the popular fast-food ad says, "You can have it your way!" That puts Ljutic right up there with the elite gunmakers in the shotgun game.

Whether it's an off-the-rack model or a top-of-the-line custom-fit model, there are plenty of effective trap guns to choose from. If you want to win at trap, you'll probably end up with one of the above makes.

Trap Loads Are Simple

OF ALL THE clay target games, trap is by far the easiest for which to select highly effective loads, whether you opt for factory fodder or roll your own. In fact, there aren't more than a few load combinations that are really suitable.

The heaviest load allowable under ATA rules is a 12-gauge, 3-dram, $1^1/_8$-ounce load of #$7^1/_2$ shot. This has become such a standard that loads in this combination are invariably referred to as "trap loads," and every ammo maker worth his salt offers them. They are also some of the most highly refined shotshells in the game. Any reloader who thinks he can beat the performance of factory trap loads, and stay within the rules, is kidding himself. The best one can hope to do is equal their performance.

These loads have the power to break any target on a trap field—even the 50-yard-plus birds you'll see from the 27-yard handicap positions. If a shooter wanted to standardize on one load and one load only for this game, he couldn't go wrong with this one.

All that power and recoil, however, is not always needed. In fact, a number of shooters have found that switching to lighter loads and, sometimes, smaller shot, can help their scores.

Number 8 shot will reliably break any clay target out to about 35 yards. By the time the target gets to 40 yards, the breaking power starts to get a bit "iffy." Since virtually any shooter on the 16-yard line will break his target inside 35 yards, there is no reason not to use #8 shot for that event, and some very good reasons why you might want to.

A $1^1/_8$-ounce load of #$7^1/_2$ shot will contain about 393 individual pellets. The same charge of #8 will have about 461. This puts a significantly larger number of pellets in the pattern. Shooters can take advantage of this by using a slightly more open choke, which will increase the size of the gun's pattern. If you are not scoring as well as you would like at the 16-yard line with a Full-choked gun and a #$7^1/_2$ load, shifting to an Improved Modified or even Modified choke and #8 loads can give you a few more birds. You have a larger usable pattern and the individual pellets still have enough energy to break the target.

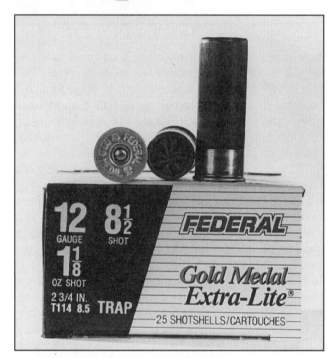

(Above) Author likes the Federal #$8^1/_2$ load for 16-yard and the first shot in doubles. When mated with an Improved Cylinder or light Modified (Skeet II) choke, it benefits a quick shooter with larger useful patterns.

(Left) All trap loads are not created equal, and shooters are advised to try as many different types as possible to find the one that works best.

Even a quick shooter will have trouble breaking targets from the 27-yard line within 40 yards of the gun. Most favor the heaviest load allowed, the 3 dram 1$^1/_8$-ounce #7$^1/_2$ load, for these long shots.

Lighter Loads

Another option with #8 shot is to drop to a lighter load. A 1-ounce load of #8s will contain about 410 pellets, or just slightly more than a 1$^1/_8$-ounce load of 7$^1/_2$s. The lighter shot charge will, if the powder charge is the same, result in less felt recoil, yet will put the same number of pellets in the air. A number of savvy shooters will shift to 1-ounce loads of #8s for 16-yard work simply to reduce the cumulative effects of recoil over an extended match. That can pay dividends by keeping them a bit fresher at the end of they day, and they are not really sacrificing pellet count or pattern size over the heavier 1$^1/_8$-ounce #7$^1/_2$ load.

While the 3-dram load is fairly standard in trap, there has been a shift lately to lighter, 2$^3/_4$-dram loads with the same 1$^1/_8$-ounce shot charge. The heavier dram load moves at about 1235 fps, and the 2$^3/_4$-dram gets about 1120 to 1165 fps, depending upon the powder used. It is my opinion that, from the 16-yard line, the slight reduction in velocity makes no difference in a shooter's score, just in the recoil he will absorb. The lighter loads are softer shooting. When moving back to longer handicap distances, however, I do tend to favor the full 3-dram, 1$^1/_8$, #7$^1/_2$ load.

Another load option is a 1-ounce, 2$^3/_4$-dram load of #8$^1/_2$ shot. This one moves at about 1180 fps, and 1-ounce of #8$^1/_2$ shot carries about 480 pellets. This is as soft a 12-gauge load as you can shoot that still has enough energy to get the job done. In fact, in an 8$^1/_2$- or 9-pound gun, this load will produce less recoil than most 7-pound 20-gauge guns, or 5$^1/_2$- to 6-pound 28-gauge guns!

The drawback to this load is that #8$^1/_2$ pellets start to run out of target breaking power at a range of just over thirty yards. However, a quick shooter will break 16-yard targets at under that range. The increased pellet count allows the use of a Modified choke, to increase pattern size, with a significant—and I do mean significant—reduction in recoil.

Some of the best scores I have ever shot from the 16-yard line have come with this shell in a Modified-choked gun. However, you can't ride the target and take your time. This load works well when you get on the bird quickly and don't mess around! Still, the incredibly soft-shooting qualities of this (or any other 2$^3/_4$-dram 1-ounce package) make it worth the time it takes to experiment with it from the 16-yard line. You might find it does good things for your scores and your shoulder.

I know some shooters who have attempted to use #9 shot with an open choke and shoot quickly. I have yet to see that tactic be successful. Number 9 shot runs out of consistent target-breaking power right around 25 yards, and that is an awfully close range at which to break all your 16-yard targets. Some days it works, some days it doesn't.

My own trap load selection runs like this: Anything beyond the 20-yard handicap line calls for the full 3-dram, 1$^1/_8$-ounce load of #7$^1/_2$ shot; inside that, I feel comfortable with the 2$^3/_4$-dram, 1$^1/_8$-ounce loads. At the 16-yard line I have no problem with a 1-ounce load of #8 shot, or the same load of #8$^1/_2$s.

Factory Ammunition

Here's a look at what the major ammunition makers offer in 12-gauge trap loads.

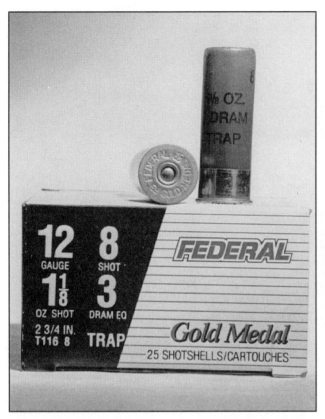

This 3 dram load of #8 shot offers an increased pellet count over #7½ shot, for extra pattern density, and is favored by many shooters for the mid-handicap ranges.

Federal

For maximum yardage shooting, Federal offers two "Handicap Loads," featuring 1⅛ ounces of #7½ or #8 shot, that provide a bit more velocity and slightly tighter patterns, both pluses from the 27-yard line.

While paper shells might seem obsolete in today's world, top level competitors simply won't allow Federal to discontinue their offerings. Many savvy shooters prefer them because they not only seem to shoot a bit softer than plastic hulls, but they do not leave plastic fouling in the chamber.

Federal's quality control is second to none, and they offer one of the most complete lines of trap loads in the industry.

FEDERAL CARTRIDGE CO.					
Load	Dram Equiv.	Shot Ozs.	Shot Size	Velocity FPS	Comment
T113	2¾	1	8	1180	
T114	2¾	1⅛	7½, 8	1145	
T115	2¾	1⅛	7½, 8,8½	1125	Light
T117	2¾	1⅛	7½, 8	1145	Paper
T172	2¾	1⅛	7½, 8	1145	Paper
T116	3	1⅛	7½, 8	1200	
T118	3	1⅛	7½, 8	1200	Paper

Remington

Remington Duplex shells use two different shot sizes based on the theory that the heavier pellets will provide breaking power at long range, while the lighter pellets help add pattern

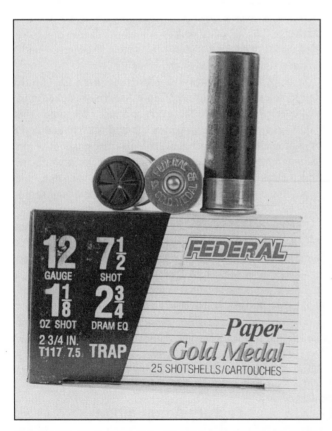

Federal's 2¾ dram paper hull load in either #7½ or #8 shot is popular with many shooters due to its lower recoil and excellent patterns.

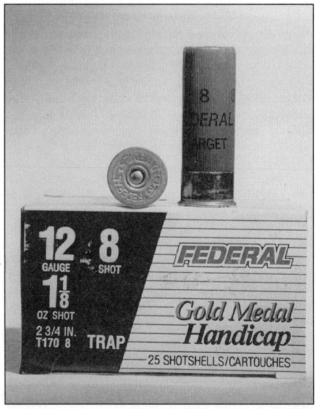

Federal's Handicap load offers a bit more velocity than their standard 3 dram load to increase target breaking power at longer range.

density. Some shooters, myself included, question the ballistic efficiency of using two different shot sizes in the same shell. One would logically conclude that the different weight and density of the shot would not allow them to maintain the same velocity, and thus mixing sizes would create a shell that encourages a longer than normal shot string. Whether this is a benefit or a disadvantage is best determined by the shooter himself.

Duplex loads are another of those items that seem to discourage a middle-of-the road opinion: shooters either love 'em or leave 'em.

REMINGTON					
Load	Dram Equiv.	Shot Ozs.	Shot Size	Velocity FPS	Comments
RTL12M	3	1⅛	7½, 8, 9	1200	
RTL12L	2¾	1⅛	7½, 8, 8½, 9	1145	
LRTL	2¾	1⅛	7½, 8, 9	1100	Rem-Lite
MRTL12M	3	1⅛	7½x8	1200	Duplex
MRTL12L	2¾	1⅛	7½x8; 7½x8½	1145	Duplex

Winchester

Though the line is not as extensive as Federal or Remington, Winchester's Double A target loads are some of the most respected in the game.

WINCHESTER "DOUBLE A"					
Load	Dram Equiv.	Shot Ozs.	Shot Size	Velocity FPS	Comments
AAL12	2¾	1	7½, 8, 9	1180	Xtra-lite
AASL12	2¾	1⅛	7½, 8, 8½, 9	1125	Super-lite
AA12	2¾	1⅛	7½, 8, 9	1145	
AAH12	3	1⅛	7½, 8, 9	1200	Handicap
AAM12	3	1⅛	7½, 8, 9	1200	Heavy

ACTIV

One of the more unusual shells on the market, the ACTIV offerings have no brass head. Made via the Reiwelin Process, the hulls are all plastic with a steel insert in the base to reinforce the head, rim and primer pocket. The all-plastic ACTIV hulls are about the slickest-feeding shells I have ever used. With no brass to collect corrosion, they pop in and out with ease. This also makes reloading an easier chore because they require almost no effort in the resizing die. Some folks originally questioned the loading life of non-brass shells, but I have used them for years and love them.

ACTIV					
Load	Dram Equiv.	Shot Ozs.	Shot Size	Velocity FPS	Comments
ATG12G	3	1⅛	7½,8,9	1200	
ATG12GL	2¾	1⅛	7½,8,9	1145	
ATG12UL	Lite	1⅛	7½,8,9	1100	Lite
ATG12H	2¾	1	7½,8,9	1180	

Remington's Duplex loads have not caught on with many trap shooters, but they are reliable target breakers.

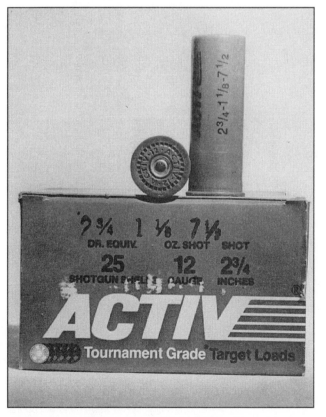

ACTIV shells are quite popular and very reloadable. Their large internal volume will allow reloaders good velocity at lower than normal pressure.

Victory's 3 dram #7½ heavy Sporting Clays load makes a fine handicap trap load.

The light recoil of this 1-ounce load belies the target breaking power of its #7½ payload. Many recoil sensitive shooters favor 1-ounce loads, especially for practice.

Fiocchi's high-speed target load is popular with many shooters who want a fast shell with a full 1⅛-ounce shot charge.

Victory USA

If you're not familiar with this company, it's not surprising. They are relatively new to this country, but not to competitive shooting. Made in Cyprus, Victory shotshells earned an outstanding reputation among International and Sporting Clays shooters for their consistency, high velocity and modest recoil. Imported into this country by Victory USA, their quality rivals that of the "big three" and are priced competitively. Although systemized for Sporting Clays use, there are several offerings that make superb trap shells.

VICTORY USA

Load	Dram Equiv.	Shot Ozs.	Shot Size	Velocity FPS	Comments
Challenger	2¾	1	7½, 8	1300	
Super Sporting	3	1⅛	7½, 8	1270	
V1 Sonic	3	1	7½, 8	1400	

Fiocchi of America

This full-line European ammunition maker offers a good range of target shotshells loaded with hard shot and are well respected by shooters around the globe.

FIOCCHI

Load	Dram Equiv.	Shot Ozs.	Shot Size	Velocity FPS	Comments
12TL	NA	1	7½, 8, 8½	1150	
12TH	NA	1	7½, 8, 8½	1200	
12F-Lite	2⅞	1⅛	7½, 8, 9	1175	
12VIPLT	2¾	1⅛	7½, 8, 9	1150	
12VIPHV	3	1⅛	7½, 8, 9	1210	

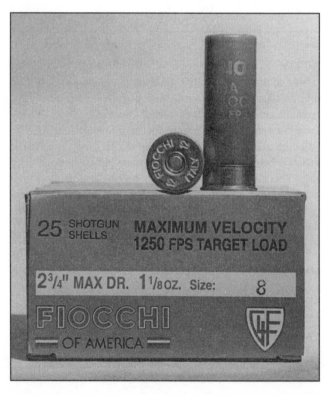

A fast shooter can break 16-yard targets at no more than 30 yards from the muzzle. Shot size #8$\frac{1}{2}$ has plenty of target breaking power at that range, and the increased pellet count in a 1$\frac{1}{8}$-ounce load allows for more open chokes that produce a wider, yet sufficiently dense pattern at that range. Shooters who are not blazingly quick usually opt for loads in #8 shot to be sure of enough target breaking power at longer range.

Trap Reloads

Shooters who prefer to load their own shells will find a wealth of good load recipes in any number of loading manuals. Federal, Winchester and ACTIV offer very informative pamphlets on loading data for their components. A few observations on trap reloads are in order, however.

It is an accepted and proven fact that, all other factors being equal, the harder the lead shot (higher antimony content) the tighter the load will pattern, the more uniform and evenly-distributed the pattern will be, and the shorter the shot string. This is because hard shot suffers less deformation in the barrel as it is fired. Round, undeformed pellets fly true and maintain a more consistent velocity. Soft pellets (low antimony, or chilled shot) don't make it out of the barrel in a perfectly round condition. This causes a number of pellets in the load to veer away from the main pattern (becoming "fliers") and offer greater resistance to the atmosphere, resulting in their losing velocity faster than the round pellets. This causes them to fall behind the main shot charge, which extends the shot string. The farther the shot has to travel to the target, the more the pattern falls apart.

Trap is not a close-range game: 20 yards is a very short shot and it takes a real expert to get onto a bird that quickly. From the 27-yard handicap line, shots of 50 or more yards are com-

mon. Trap shooters cannot afford fliers, patchy patterns or long shot strings! If you load your own trap shells, use top quality, high-antimony shot. It costs a little more, but it is the quickest way I know for a shooter to increase his score.

Powder selection for trap loads is rather wide, and a number of powders of different burning rates will work quite well. I tend to avoid quick-burning powders like 700-X, Red Dot and Trap 100. My experience has been that they tend to provide a slight increase in recoil, more of a sharp rap than the softer push I prefer, and some of them can be rather dirty-burning, leaving lots of powder residue in the gun. Owners of semi-auto shotguns who use these powders may find that they need to clean their guns more frequently. Powders with a slightly slower burn rate, like IMR PB and Green Dot, will deliver the same velocities at slightly lower pressures, and are easier on the shoulder. You may not notice the difference in recoil immediately, but it will become apparent after a couple of boxes of shells. My favorite powder is IMR PB. It meters very consistently, burns very cleanly (I shoot several gas guns where this is an asset), and provides what I feel is superior performance over other commonly used powders in this application.

Whether you buy 'em or load 'em, contemporary trap loads are simple to select. The key is to try as many as possible and use the one that works best for you.

chapter **five**

Trap's Fundamentals

AT THE RISK of offending some veteran trapshooters, I will say that trap is probably the easiest clay target game to learn initially. That's because it does not require complex thought. One does not think his or her way through a round of trap; indeed, thinking can get you into trouble! Instead, one "reacts" his way through a round.

In effect, trap is not much different from someone's suddenly tossing a baseball at your face. You don't do a lot of thinking about the ball—your hands automatically come up to intercept it. If you have good reactions and are in the proper body position you will catch it. If not, you may just knock it out of the way. If you are really a maladroit, you'll take one in the chops.

That pretty well sums up trap. The only difference is that instead of intercepting an incoming baseball with your hands, you are intercepting an outgoing clay target with a shot charge. In both cases, that task is best accomplished if the shooter has assumed the proper body position to allow his reflexes to take over. Here's a step-by-step look at getting started in trap, and much of the advice on basic body position and gun handling will apply to every other clay target game described in this book.

Proper Gun Hold

Unlike a rifle, which must be held steady to hit a target, the shotgun must move. It must flow to and through the target as the shot is triggered if the charge is to intercept the target. One of the biggest causes of missed clay targets—at any game—is stopping the movement of the gun as the shot is fired. Some new shooters encourage that by holding the gun incorrectly.

The gun touches the body at four different places: at both hands, the cheek, and in the shoulder pocket. It must make contact in a consistent manner every time the gun is shouldered or the point of impact of the shot charge can change. In addition, the gun position must be comfortable enough to allow the shooter to smoothly and quickly move the gun in both the horizontal and vertical plane. A tight, contorted, locked-in gun mount might be just fine for a rifleman, but it's

(Above) ATA trap shooter and stockfitter Jack West demonstrates an effective gun hold. Note the inside angle of his leading arm elbow and the angle his arm makes with the gun. The 90-degree elbow on his trigger arm forms a solid shoulder pocket which helps keep the butt in the proper position. Notice the weight-forward stance. This allows him to swing the gun properly.

Trap is the only clay target game where pump-action shotguns are still competitive. This shooter cradles the Winchester Model 12.

Getting some basic instruction is a wise move for new trap shooters. Coaches understand the subtleties of body position and proper gun hold, and can save new shooters much time in discovering the importance of these factors on their own.

a disaster for a shotgunner. If this seems basic, it is. However, it has been my experience that gun mounting is the biggest problem for new shooters, especially those who have had any rifle shooting experience. They often assume a gun mount and body position that does not offer them the freedom of movement they require.

The leading hand, the one holding the forend, plays a far larger role than just being a gun support. Consider it like the steering wheel of an automobile because that's what it does—it drives the gun in the vertical and horizontal plane. If the hand is improperly positioned on the forend, you will lose some of that control.

Putting the hand too far back toward the receiver offers good biomechanical leverage for moving the gun up and down, but very little for moving it side to side. Too far forward is the reverse—it robs power to quickly move the gun up and down.

Top coaches recommend that the leading hand be placed on the forend at a point that will allow the elbow to form a 90- to 100-degree angle between forearm and upper arm. The leading arm should then form a 45-degree angle to the side of the gun. This 45-degree angle is the best compromise for both vertical and horizontal movement. More than 45 degrees inhibits vertical movement, and less than that restricts the horizontal. Trap shooters need unrestricted movement in both planes.

Since shooters are built differently, this should simply be considered a starting point from which the shooter can build

his stance. However, many top shooters have found a different forend hold works best for them.

The arm angle of the trigger hand is a different matter. If the elbow is too low it can reduce the shoulder pocket area that the gun butt must lock into, and can actually cause the gun butt to shift position as it recoils. If the elbow is too high it will create a large shoulder pocket, but a high arm position puts a lot of strain on the muscles. Most shooters will find the best arm position for them somewhere between these two extremes.

Another variable that can affect scores is the position of the shooter's head. Simply put, the head should be as erect as possible. When mounting the gun, bring the gun to the face instead of the other way around.

Stance and Weight Distribution

A shotgunner should consider his body to be like a tank. Everything below the hips is the chassis that provides support, and everything above the hips is the turret that pivots to swing the gun. A correct stance allows this to happen.

The feet should be spread a comfortable 9 to 12 inches. Too wide a stance inhibits upper body movement, and too narrow a stance can decrease the shooter's balance. Weight distribution should favor the leading leg (left leg for right-handers) with about a 65:35 ratio. Some shooters favor keeping the back leg straight with a bit of flex in the leading knee. Others want both knees slightly bent, but you should avoid any exaggerated crouch.

The shooting rhythm of a squad can aid or hinder a shooter's score. Many veteran shooters try to shoot with those whom they have shot with in the past and whose rhythm is in tune with theirs.

This fast-swing shooter favors a slight crouch that allows the stored energy in his flexed knees to help drive his upper body and generate the speed required for effective shooting.

Those who prefer a more deliberate shooting style often stand more upright. Fast and instinctive shooters (like this writer) want both knees slightly flexed and use that stored energy to help drive the upper body to achieve the gun speed needed for this style of shooting.

Natural Point of Aim

This is a term you will read throughout this book, so let's define it right now.

The natural point of aim is the position at which the gun points when the shooter brings his gun to the firing position with no further body movement. When the shot is fired and the gun recoils, it will come right back down to that position.

Natural point of aim is equally important for riflemen, pistol shooters and shotgunners because, once that position is found, the shooter has the best body position for the target he has selected and the widest area of body movement to either side of the target.

Finding your natural point of aim for any given target is easy: take your normal shooting position and focus on the aiming spot, bring the gun to the firing position and close your eyes. Raise the gun up to the recoil position and then lower it back down to the original position. Now, open your eyes.

If the gun is back on target, you are there. Chances are it will be to one side or the other. Correct this by moving your leading foot in the direction you want the gun barrel to move, while shifting your back foot appropriately to maintain your basic stance. Adjustments to natural point of aim are always made with the feet, never with the upper body. The upper body remains in its set position while the feet are moved to aim the gun where you want it. The procedure is the same whether you are shooting a rifle, pistol or shotgun.

Understanding the natural point of aim is critical for a shotgunner because it will determine your swing arc. If the arc is not sufficient to drive through the target, you'll lose the bird.

One Eye or Two?

Human vision operates on the binocular principle: two eyes working in concert to establish depth perception through the ability to focus both of them on a single object. For most people, one eye—the master eye—will be more dominant and will serve to sharply define the target, while the "off eye" provides the second opinion needed for depth perception. See Chapter 27: "Shotgun Fitting Is Easy" for an explanation on determining the master eye.

Trap targets are carefully regulated as to height, angle and speed. These two "trappers" are setting target angles for a major Florida tournament. After a shooter sees enough targets, effective trap shooting is merely a matter of reacting quickly and properly to them.

Savvy shotgun shooters take advantage of this principle and shoot with both eyes open. The master eye looks right down the rib, and the off eye looks past the barrel, confirming depth perceptiuon. With a little practice this is very easy to do in Skeet and Sporting Clays. In fact, many shooters do it without conscious thought because this is the only real way to track these extreme angle targets.

It's a little tougher for many trap shooters because of the natural tendency to sight down the barrel as they wait for the bird. Because the targets are primarily outgoing, they can be picked up easily with just one eye. Sometimes the off eye just naturally closes as you sight down the rib. I know it happens to me, despite the fact that I shoot a lot more Skeet and Sporting Clays than trap, and have absolutely no trouble keeping both eyes open at those games. Sometimes I have to consciously remind myself to open both eyes at trap. This usually happens after I miss two targets in a row!

If you do not shoot trap with both eyes open, you tend to concentrate too much on the rib and bead and not enough on the target. You must quickly acquire the target as it comes out of the house and determine its exact course. If you don't, the bird gets a big jump on you and throws your timing off. With two eyes in operation you can maintain the proper rib picture, and quickly pick up the bird.

One of the most important things any shotgunner can do to improve his score at any clay target game is to make "both eyes open" a consistent part of the mental checklist he runs through before calling for the bird.

Muzzle Position

When calling for the target, you have to start with the gun muzzle in some position when calling for a trap target. Contrary to the opinions of some experts, there is no one right position for every shooter. There are two techniques that can be effective, "high gun" and "low gun." In this case, these terms do not refer to whether the gun butt is on or off the

Some deliberate shooters favor a more erect stance than those who shoot a faster, more instinctive, style. This shooter has long arms and has found that a forward position with his leading hand works best for him. There is no one right gun hold for all shooters.

shoulder, but to how high above the trap house a shooter points the gun before the target emerges.

All ATA trap targets will emerge from a point near the center of the trap house and on a rising angle. High gun shooters prefer to position the muzzle at a point about 4 feet above the house and let the bird rise upward and through the barrel. If a shooter is using both eyes, he can pick up the bird up quite well with this system, since the off eye will "look through" the barrel and will have no problem finding the bird. A shooter who uses only one eye is going to have real problems!

Most high gun shooters also tend to favor high-shooting guns, those that place their pattern anywhere from 6 to 18 inches above the bead. Combined with a high gun hold and binocular vision, this will let a shooter acquire the target and break it quickly with a relatively small degree of gun movement. High gun shooters will also tend to focus their eyes farther from the trap house—about 15 to 17 yards—and break the birds a bit farther onto the field. This is what I call a "deliberate" shooting style—almost rifle shooting with a shotgun.

The high gun hold is probably the most popular technique among veteran shooters. However, it may not be the best way for new shooters to develop their skills.

It is my opinion that new shooters will gain skill more quickly if they start with the low gun hold, with the muzzle pointed right at the back edge of the trap house, or just slightly below it. There are three reasons why I feel this way.

First, with the gun pointed at the top of the house, the bird will always emerge over the muzzle, with both bird and muzzle within the shooter's vision. For those who cannot shoot with both eyes open, this low hold is one of the few ways they can achieve success in trap. Instant target acquisition combined with a clear muzzle picture makes maintaining a proper sight picture easy. With this technique your eyes are focused right where the bird will first appear. This aids the shooter in acquiring the bird quickly, which is necessary for a low gun hold to be effective.

Second, the low gun technique requires the shooter to do the most important thing any shotgunner can learn—swing the gun! The bird will emerge as an orange streak past the gun muzzle and the shooter cannot be lazy in going after it. The

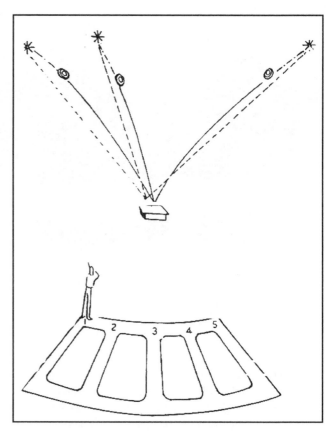

Station One: Target array on station one requires that right-handed shooters fudge their natural point of aim to the left in order to have the swing room required for the extreme left-hand target.

Drawings Courtesy Winchester News Bureau

shooter will have to swing quickly to catch it. This builds shooting speed that allows the shooter to get onto the bird while it is still climbing at high speed and has not yet been affected by the wind. It is a more consistent target, and the shooter doesn't have to make changes in his sight picture to accommodate environmental extremes. You drill 'em and kill 'em the same way every time. This is truly the "fast-swing" technique in action, and it has an additional benefit in that your lead is greatly reduced because of the speed of your swing!

The target requiring the greatest lead in trap is the extreme 22-degree angled shot on stations one and five. Some deliberate shooters tell me they are using anywhere from 18 inches to 3 feet of lead on these targets, and breaking them at about 35 to 39 yards. Shooting the low gun hold and the fast swing, I seriously doubt if I see a lead greater than two target lengths, or about 8 inches. I break those targets at about 30 yards, where I have a dense, yet optimum pattern from an Improved Cylinder or Light Modified choke with either #8 or #8½ loads. On the more gently-angled shots I am shooting at the leading edge of the bird. Lead is not something I spend much time thinking about— I just swing, pull the trigger and smile!

The final advantage is that, because of the speed of the swing—flowing directly through the bird—and the closer break range, you can shoot trap with the low gun technique using a standard field-stocked, flat-shooting gun. I use the

Handicap targets require extreme precision in the point and swing. A good instructor can often see where a shooter is going wrong and get him onto the right track.

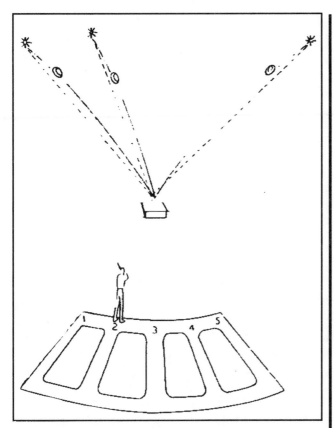

Station Two: Moving one station to the right shrinks the target angles and allows shooters to shift their body position more towards the trap house center.

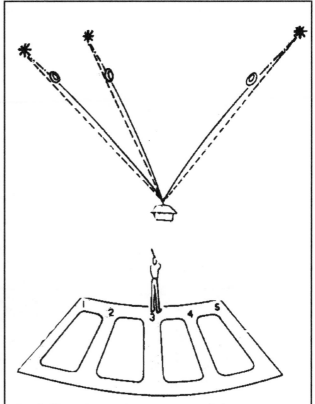

Station Three: Here the shooter sees even-angled targets on either side of center, which requires that he be prepared to react quickly in either direction.

same Ruger Red Label on trap that I do for Skeet and Sporting Clays. I just slip in a different Briley choke tube.

For all of these reasons, I think the low gun technique is better for a new shooter than the more rigid, deliberate high gun technique. Once a shooter begins with this, and learns the basics, it is not hard to change to a high-shooting gun and the higher hold, should he choose to use it.

Station Shooting Positions

The last thing a new trap shooter needs to learn is where to put his natural point of aim for each station. That will vary depending upon whether the shooter is right- or left-handed, using a deliberate or fast swing, shooting one-eyed or two, and uses a high gun or low gun. Let's sort out all these options.

Station One

The toughest target on this station is the extreme left angle. All shooters will have to move their natural point of aim to the left in order to have the swing-room to get it. For right-handed shooters that means establishing the natural point of aim near the left corner of the trap house. Lefties may have to go a bit outside the house since they will not have as much swing to the left as a right-hander. Low gun, fast-swing shooters will then shift the gun back to the rear center of the trap house, just below the edge. Regardless of which angle the target takes, it

will come out right over the muzzle. This center-back trap house hold will be the same for a low hold, fast-swing shooter on all five stations.

High gun shooters should place the muzzle at a point above the left-hand corner of the house, although there are some, generally those with Bunker trap experience, who will also use a high-center-back hold for all houses. We'll explain why when we get to the chapter on International trap.

Station Two

The angles decrease here and the natural point of aim is moved back toward the center of the house: about two-thirds of the way to center house from the left edge for right-handed shooters, and a little farther left for lefties. High gun shooters will want to position the gun above the house, midway between center and left edge.

Station Three

The angles are even here, and most right-handed shooters tend to take a natural point of aim about 6 inches right of center house, with lefties about 6 inches to the left. This gives each of them a built-in fudge toward their weak swing side. High gun shooters shift the gun about the same distance to the side of center to prevent a straightaway target from hiding under the barrel.

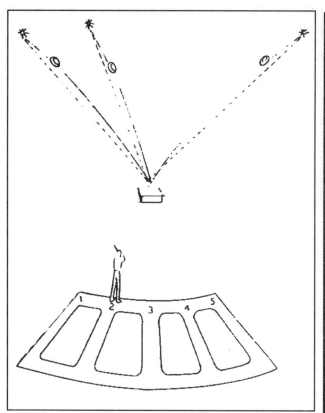

Station 4: Right-handed shooters begin to have problems when they reach station four, because of the restricted swing range to their right side. They will have to fudge their natural body position to the right if they intend to hit many extreme right-angled targets.

Station 5: This is the toughest station for right-handed shooters. The extreme right-angled target can get away from a shooter if he doesn't fudge his body position to it. The left-hand targets don't require a lot of swing arc because they appear to the shooter more as straightaways. Set up for the greater angled target, and you'll improve your score on this station.

Station Four

This is a mirror image of station two. Right-handed shooters begin fudging their natural point of aim to the right, almost to the edge of the trap house, to accommodate their restricted right-side swing, while lefties stay a bit closer to center trap. The high hold is midway between center and right trap house edge.

Getting the gun properly mounted to the body is a key to consistent shooting. This shooter takes his time moving his gun into the proper position. Some shooters even have a three- or four-step ritual to make sure they get it done right.

Station Five

This is the mirror image of station one and is one of the toughest shots for right-handed shooters. It's best to take a natural point of aim about a foot or so past the right edge of the trap house. Lefties should aim close to the edge of the house.

If right-handed shooters don't take that hard left-to-right angle into account and turn their body position with it, they will lose the bird. On station one, lefties have to do the same thing with the extreme left-angle bird.

Trap Reading

The last matter that needs addressing is the phenomenon called "reading the trap." Some shooters think they can figure out what target angle is coming next and be ready for it. Experts will tell you that you can't—at least not all the time. Anticipating targets is a very good way to get caught with your pants down and lose a target. It's a bad habit to get into.

Once a shooter has the right body position—those detailed here will serve as *starting* points—trap becomes a fairly easy game to learn. When the target appears, you just react; don't think, don't try to outsmart the target, just drill the one in front of you. What makes trap a challenging game to master is to force the body to make that correct reaction each and every time a target appears.

Handling Handicaps

DURING THE EARLY days of trap, all shooters were basically on the same footing; they competed on a head-to-head basis.

As with any competitive event, it soon became apparent that all contestants are not created equal, and it wasn't long before the same names kept appearing at the top of the leader board match after match. Since trap has always been more financially-oriented than other clay target games, this was not good for attendance. I mean, why would a shooter of only modest skill plunk down his hard-earned money to engage in a competitive event in an attempt to win some of it back when he knows that another shooter is going to walk away with it all?

It didn't take a Rhodes scholar to deduce that if only five shooters have a realistic chance to win, then that's about as big as your match is going to get after the other shooters figure out who they are!

The separate Handicap event was the match organizers'

way of encouraging more than a half-dozen shooters to show up.

Handicap trap is a Singles event shot in the same manner as the standard ATA 16 Yard match—in the same order, at the same targets, and on the same field. The difference is that individual competitors are moved back from the 16-yard line based upon their individual scores and averages. The minimum move is to 17 yards (for juniors), and the maximum to 27 yards. Increments in between are in half-yards. Thus a shooter might be assigned to shoot from the 23½-yard line, and his score competes directly against those shot by all other competitors, no matter what their handicap yardage.

The purpose is to assign each shooter his own handicap, as is done in golf and other games, in an attempt to put all shooters on an equal footing. Like many handicap systems, it hasn't worked all that well.

In the last few years it has become apparent that those shooters whose skill has earned them a spot on the 27-yard

Long-range Handicap targets provide the shooter with a different look than do the 16-yard targets, although they are traveling at the same speed. Shooters must overcome this apparent illusion if they are to shoot good scores.

(Left) Shooters are normally paired by their handicap yardages during a match in order to keep competitors on a fairly even line, for safety reasons.

(Below) A variety of guns can be used in 16 Yard trap, but once one moves back to the 27-yard line in handicaps, the proper firearm becomes very important.

Federal's 3 dram paper-hulled #7½ is a favorite with many 27-yard competitors. It takes a lot of punch to nail a 50-yard target, yet the paper hull seems to do it with a bit less recoil.

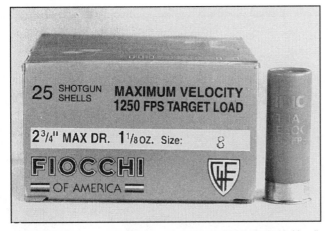

High-speed #8 loads like this Fiocchi are a popular choice with Handicap shooters in the mid-range (up to 24 yards) area. The #8 shot maintains excellent pattern density and the increased velocity gives it a bit more target-breaking power than the standard 2¾ dram load.

handicap line are still the ones to beat. It is extremely rare for a 23-yard shooter to beat a 27-yard shooter—despite the 4-yard difference in target distance. The 27-yard shooters are still superior, their skill and reflexes making them the ones to beat. The 27-yard shooters also tend to win because they understand the critical differences between the game as it is shot from the 16-yard line, and that played from the handicap ranges. There are some serious differences—both obvious and very subtle!

Loads and Chokes

The most obvious difference is the distance to the target. A quick 16-yard shooter will break his birds about 30 yards from his shooting position. This is a very comfortable range regarding pattern control. An Improved Cylinder choke is actually quite adequate when combined with a 1⅛-ounce load of #8½ shot. That shot size has enough target-breaking power, and provides almost as many pellets in the load as would a 1⅛-ounce #9 Skeet load. Number 8½ shot fills out an Improved Cylinder pattern very well, giving the shooter more than enough pattern density and a nice margin for error.

Slower 16-yard shooters often rely on a Light Modified (also called Skeet 2), or Modified choke and the same load with #8 shot. They find this combination works very well in the 33- to 37-yard range at which these leisurely shooters usually break their birds.

Start moving shooters back from the 16-yard line, however, and the whole game changes. You can forget #8½ shot, in any load, at any range past 33-35 yards; that shot size is not heavy enough to consistently break birds with a proper hold. You will lose some targets that heavier shot pellets would have broken. These shooters must now opt for #8s and tighten the choke to maintain effective pattern density. There goes some margin for error—even for a fast shooter if he is shooting much beyond the 20-yard handicap line. Slower shooters at the same range now find they break their targets at about 40 yards, and that requires a denser pattern than a Light Modified or Modified choke will produce. They must increase their choke to decrease the pattern size.

When you shoot your way back to the 27-yard line, it really gets tough! Quick shooters have a target break point somewhere between 40 and 50 yards and for leisurely gunners that point is over 50 yards. You still have only 1⅛ ounces of shot to do the job even with maximum loads.

The demands upon the load and choke at this range are so severe that, for a period of time, it was automatically assumed that no 27-yard shooter could break 100 straight targets because the loads wouldn't be up to the task! Obviously, that didn't remain the case for long, as shot quality and wad development rose to the task.

What it does point out, however, is that the game gets much more precise the farther one gets from the comfortable confines of the 16-yard line. Shot size must be increased to maintain target-breaking power and that results in a decrease in pattern density over smaller shot. Pattern density must be maintained by using tighter chokes that throw smaller patterns, because the larger the shot size the fewer pellets there are in a given load to make up the pattern.

Your margin for error goes right into the toilet.

"Any small error at 27 yards is a miss," says Florida shooter Lisa Sever, who "earned" her 27-yard handicap while still a college shooter. "One minute mistake is all it takes. At the 16-yard line, you could recover from that and get at least a piece of the bird. Not at the 27-yard line. You must have much more polish in your swing and point."

Shooting from the farther handicap ranges, as Lisa does, requires some serious changes in equipment and mental attitude from those required at 16 yards.

The most notable change is in the firearm used. The majority of top Handicap shooters prefer a single-barrel gun with a long sighting radius. This is why we see the graceful 32- and 34-inch-barreled guns so often on the trap line. The longer barrel, yet slightly lighter muzzle weight inherent in such guns (compared to a double gun), provides a more precise aim and greater muzzle control than what can be achieved with the over/unders that dominate the Doubles game. Many top-quality trap guns are offered as a two-barrel set with both a single barrel and over/under barrels fitted to the same receiver.

You can also bet that the single-barrel will be choked tighter than a banker's heart. While Modified and Improved Modified are commonly seen on the 16-yard line (with slightly more open chokes being popular in Doubles), Full (.035-inch constriction) and even Extra-Full (.040-inch+) are the rule from 27 yards.

While some shooters do quite well with relatively flat-shooting guns, many of the top Handicap shooters want a high-shooting gun. This allows the shooter to stay under the bird for a more precise target picture than that achieved with a "flat" gun that must be swung up and through the bird to "cover" it. The higher shooting gun also helps compensate for the fact that the shot charge will be losing velocity and actually be starting to drop in its trajectory as the 40-yard-plus mark is reached.

Shot size normally is confined to #7 1/2, although some shooters will try to stretch #8 shot in an attempt to maintain a dense pattern. Loads will run the gamut from "light" to full 3-dram-equivalent, depending upon the shooter's preference and confidence level in them.

Even with the proper equipment, Handicap shooters must develop the proper mental attitude. One of the first things they must do is beat the "illusion."

A target at the 16-yard line appears to be moving fast, and the shooter realizes he must move quickly to catch it. The target seems to leap from the trap and rapidly move out of the shooter's field of view because of his proximity. It makes the shooter go after it.

Move back the 11-yard difference to the 27-yard line and the picture changes. The shooter's field of view is now noticeably much wider. The 27-yard bird now emerges in this wider field of view (looking smaller, of course) and it appears to be moving slower. Also, it doesn't seem to require the immediate "now" movement to catch it.

Single barrel guns with tight chokes dominate the Handicap game. Lisa Sever favors an over/under for all other trap games, but opts for her venerable Winchester Model 12 for the 27-yard line.

Although no longer made, the Winchester Model 12 is still one of the odds-on favorites among top Handicap shooters. One has to wonder how they can still find parts for these old guns.

Handicap trap from the 27-yard line requires the most precision of any shotgun game. It takes a lot of practice.

The Handicap Illusion

This visual illusion, based solely on an 11-yard difference, gives the shooter the impression that he has all the time in the world to get on the target. In fact, there is much less physical gun movement required at the 27-yard line than at the 16-yard mark.

That's the illusion. While gun movement is reduced, it must be moved as quickly, or more quickly, than it was when shooting from the 16-yard line if the target is to be hit within any reasonable break range.

A slow shooter on the 27-yard line is "raw meat" here. Of course, those who have shot their way back to trap's toughest position are well aware of that, and any tendency toward laggardly shooting behavior would have been put behind them long ago.

"You have to get to that 27-yard target just as quickly as you would at 16 yards," notes Sever. "The appearance of more time is just an illusion, but it fools a lot of newer Handicap shooters. For me, one of the keys to handicap shooting is to realize that I do not have the time the visual appearance of the target tells me I do, but to also realize that I can't anticipate the target, or rush it. I have to make myself wait until I can acquire and read the target before I make my move, then move smoothly and precisely—and without hesitation—to the bird. There is no real change in body or foot position, and only the slightest increase in lead on the angled targets. The mental aspect of beating the illusion of more time yet not getting in a big hurry is important to dealing with handicap targets."

For those who want to become great handicap shooters, there is one additional piece of advice that was offered by the late shooting great Frank Little. His philosophy was that all 16 Yard trap should be considered to be nothing more than practice for the 27-yard line. He advocated using the same tight, full choke, #7$\frac{1}{2}$ load at the 16-yard line that you would at the 27-yard line. His reasoning was simple: with that choke and load any target that does not become a small puff of black smoke at 16 yards was not pointed well enough to have been hit at 27 yards. If you can hit 16-yard targets with that combo, 27-yard birds will be a lot easier. That is getting very precise.

chapter seven

Dealing With Doubles

DOUBLES TRAP WAS introduced into the tournament format about 1911 in order to spice up the game, and it's safe to say it has succeeded quite admirably at that goal.

As the name implies, Doubles trap consists of two birds released simultaneously on two separate flight paths: one bird is set to fly at the extreme 22-degree angle to the right, and the other is set for the same angle to the left. Since both birds are launched from the same trap, their velocity is slightly less than that of a singles target from the same machine because the added weight of the extra bird robs just a touch of speed from the throwing arm.

The game is shot from the 16-yard line in a standard five-shooter squad. A full round consists of twenty-five pairs (fifty birds). Shooters fire at five pairs from each station. Thirteen pairs are presented on the first walk through the stations. This is followed by a very short break, then the remaining twelve pairs are presented on the next walk-through.

At each station the shooter loads two shells and fires one shell at each target. The trapper moves the shooters through the five stations, making certain that the proper shooting order is maintained.

Many shooters consider Doubles trap to be the toughest ATA trap game. It is not quite as popular as Singles or Handicap trap. One reason is Doubles requires shooters to have a gun capable of firing two rounds, and some shooters refuse to put down their single-barrel guns. Another reason, however, is the intimidation factor: A number of trap shooters have trouble dealing with the concept of two targets in the air simultaneously. A lot of that, I believe, is mental.

I recently watched a shooter who was a competent Skeet and Sporting Clays gunner step up in a squad of veteran ATA trap shooters for the very first round of Doubles trap he had ever fired. This shooter didn't even own a "trap gun," so he just took his Sporting Clays gun and slipped in Skeet 2 and Improved Modified tubes. Treating the targets just like Sporting Clays birds, he broke forty out of fifty the first time he ever shot the game! The trap shooters on the squad, who knew he had never shot that game before, were quite surprised at

Doubles trap requires two shots and that is one reason it is not popular with shooters who can't put down their single-shot trap guns. Here's a rack of O/Us and gas guns that would work for Doubles.

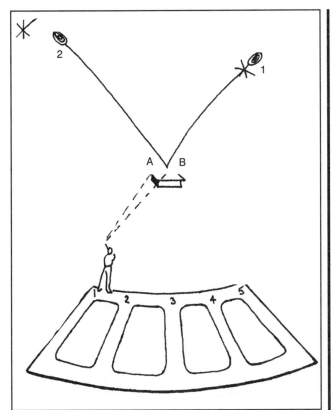

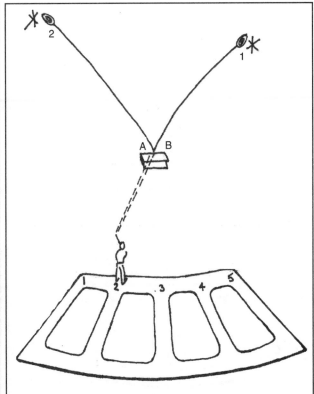

Station one: Line A shows proper natural point of aim to left-hand corner of the front of the house for a right-handed shooter (left handers will want to move further left). Line B shows the gun hold moved back to the center of trap house. Target #1 now becomes a straightaway that can be taken quickly with the shooter having enough swing room to catch and drive through target #2.

Station two: Right-handers shift their natural point of aim back to a point halfway between the corner and the center of the house. Target #1 is a very slight-angled target that most fast-swing shooters will break by shooting at the leading side of the bird. Target #2 requires less lead here than it did from station one.

Drawings Courtesy Winchester News Bureau

how well he picked up this "tough" game. The shooter, however, wasn't surprised. He didn't think it was that difficult. He wasn't intimidated by seeing two targets in the air at the same time because in Sporting Clays he sees that all the time!

Simultaneous targets are common in Skeet and Sporting Clays. In fact, Skeet shooters regularly deal with two targets that are not only traveling slightly faster than Doubles trap birds, but also are flying in opposite directions! They find nothing out of the ordinary with seeing two targets at once, and don't allow that to intimidate them.

I think some trap shooters who don't perform as well in Doubles as they do in Singles and Handicap have talked themselves into being intimated by seeing two targets in the air. It's not that tough of a game.

As mentioned earlier, the targets not only fly a bit slower in Doubles, but they are locked into one flight path. In sharp contrast to Singles trap games, where the bird may take one of a number of different flight paths and requires the shooter to identify the flight angle very quickly, in Doubles the shooter already knows precisely where both birds will be. The angle will not vary throughout the round. The angle to the shooter will change as he moves to each different station, but it will always be the same for that station.

This means the shooter can set up for a very quick shot on whichever bird he desires to shoot first, and then swing right

over for the second. Any shooter who has had experience at Skeet doubles will find this quite familiar.

Doubles Strategies

Here's a station-by-station look at how some of the best shooters approach this game:

Station One

The right-hand bird will be virtually a dead straight-away shot, while the left-hand bird will be an extreme right-to-left quartering shot. The most effective procedure is to set up the initial gun hold to put you dead-on the straightaway, take it just as fast as you can, and then swing quickly over to the out-going angled target.

The reason for taking the straightaway bird first is simple: it takes less gun movement, and as soon as the gun fires, the shooter can give all his attention to the tougher, angling bird. If the angling bird is shot first, the shooter is left with a long, and possibly falling, straightaway shot that is very easy to swing past and miss. In fact, if the straightaway is taken as the second bird the shooter will actually have to stop his swing and aim deliberately at the bird. That's bad form with a smoothbore. For that reason, veteran Doubles shooters advise that the straightest-flying bird always ought to be taken first.

Right-handed shooters won't find this particularly difficult

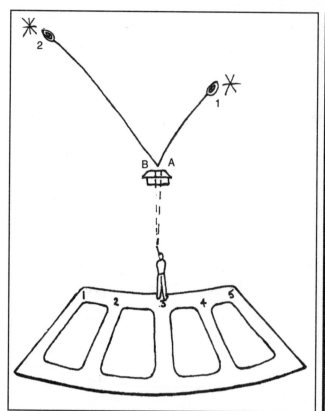 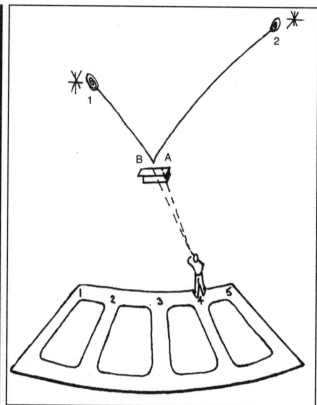

Station three: Equal angle on both targets means the natural point of aim is brought 6 inches to the right of traphouse center, with the gun hold shifted to traphouse center. Target #1 is taken quickly and target #2 requires shooting at the leading edge. Left-handed shooters will want to take target #2 first, since they will have a greater swing arc to the right side.

Station four: The reverse of station two. A right-handed shooter will want a point of aim midway between the house center and right-hand front edge, and a gun hold at traphouse center. The left-hand bird is taken first here.

from station one because they can swing more easily to the left than they can to the right. If a shooter takes his natural point of aim about 6 inches to the left of the center of the trap house, and then moves the gun back to dead center, he should then have all the body movement the shots require. Left-handed shooters may have to fudge more to the left.

Station Two

The angle on the left bird is now decreased, while the right-hand bird gains a slight amount of angle to the right. It is no longer a true straightaway. Still, it is the straighter target and should be taken first. It will require shooting at the leading edge of the bird, but the lead is not much for a fast-swinging shooter. Right-handed shooters can position their natural point of aim at the center of the trap house, and most shooters will then have plenty of swing room left for the angled bird. Left-handed shooters may still have to fudge that position a bit to the left of the center of the trap house.

Station Three

This is considered the toughest shot in this game and really intimidates a lot of shooters. Neither bird is more straightaway than the other, and both leave the trap house diverging at a 45-degree angle. Here is where the known course of the target can really pay off.

One of the birds has to be shot first, of course, and many right-handed shooters find they will do better by taking the right-hand bird first—actually fudging their natural point of aim toward it. Their greater left-side swing arc will still give them plenty of time to take the left bird with the second shot. Neither bird will have a great degree of angle to its flight path and little lead is required. Knowing the exact flight path, the shooter can jump his first bird very quickly. Left-handed shooters often do better taking the left bird first.

All of this, however, is not carved in stone. Some shooters find that reversing the above procedure pays off because they happen to do better on long shots that have only a slight quartering angle on them. The shooter must experiment and see what works best for him.

Station Four

We've now come to the reverse of station two. The left-hand bird becomes the more straightaway and should be taken first. Left-handed shooters can usually set up right on the center of the trap house, but right-handed shooters will likely have to shift their natural point of aim about 6 inches right of center to have the swing-room needed for the second bird.

Station Five

This becomes the mirror image of station one with the left-

46

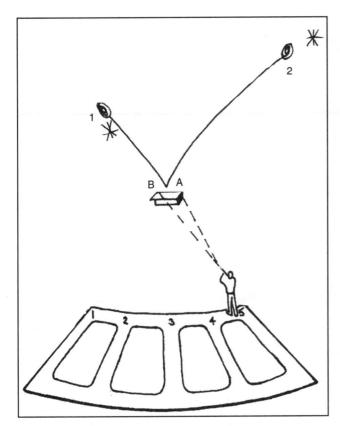

Station five: This is one of the toughest shots for a right-handed shooter. He will want to take a point of aim on the right-front edge of the house, or maybe even a few feet outside, in order to have the swing room for the right-hand bird. Gun hold is on center of the house. The left side bird is broken quickly as a dead straightaway target. Left-handed shooters won't need as much fudging to the right side of the trap house.

hand bird being a true straightaway, and the right bird flying at an extreme angle. Right-handed shooters often have problems with this station because they don't shift their natural point of aim far enough to the right to allow them to keep their cheek on the stock for the right-hand bird. I often shift my natural point of aim all the way to the right-hand corner of the trap house just for that reason. You don't need a perfect body position on the first bird because it has no angle on it, but the second bird will get away if you run out of swing room. Left-handers often have this same problem on station one.

When a shooter sets up for the shots in the above manner, gun movement for all shots becomes consistent. In essence, you square a corner with the gun—straight up on a vertical line for the first bird, and straight across (with just a slight upward angle) for the second bird. There is no confusion, and with a little practice, you will find your gun automatically goes to the second bird unerringly, just like in Skeet doubles.

The faster you can shoot the first target the better off you are, because you will be able to catch the second bird at a consistent spot on its flight path where it is still rising. Having a consistent second target is important because you don't have time to aim at it! The shot must be swung through and fired quickly, and if you catch the bird at a consistent point, you will have a an easy time breaking it consistently.

Shooting the first target quickly is easy in this game because you know exactly where it will appear. Some top shooters who opt for high-shooting guns have refined their initial gun hold on the first target so well that they can break it with almost no gun movement! It becomes much like a Skeet low house seven, in that respect.

One problem shooters often have with the first target is that they are thinking about the second one. They try to rush the first bird and often subconsciously start swinging the gun toward the second bird before they trigger the shot on the first. That kind of mistake will lose that first bird for you every time! One way to avoid that problem is to shoot a practice round of Doubles, but only load a shell in the first barrel. Once you realize you can't possibly get the second bird because there is no shell for it, the natural tendency is to make sure you get the first. Then swing the gun through the second bird and trigger your imaginary shot.

It sounds somewhat simple, and maybe a bit unorthodox, but it will program your subconscious to make certain you get the first bird. For shooters who consistently have trouble with the first bird, this is a good way to get that on-board computer properly programmed. It doesn't do any good to hit every second bird if you miss all the first shots; your score is still only 25x50. You get the same score if you hit all the first birds and miss all the second shots. In either case, it's not a great score. It helps if you can whack both birds in a pair.

Some very good Singles shooters often have trouble with the second bird. They fail to realize that the swing they must use to get from the first to the second bird is faster than the same swing they would use to take that bird as a single. If they use the same bird picture, they may well be shooting in front of that bird. A shooter who is consistently missing the second bird should not automatically assume he is behind it. Often, the reverse is true.

Loads and Chokes

Loads and chokes for Doubles trap are strictly a matter of personal choice, but it is my experience that many shooters are overchoked for the first bird. Modified is commonly considered

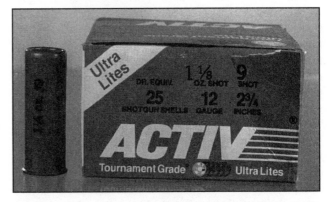

Doubles trap may be the only time you'll ever see #9 shot on the line. Quick shooters can get on the first bird in plenty of time for the smaller shot to be effective, and the increased pattern density from the larger number of pellets allows more open chokes, and a little more room for error. A tighter choke and heavier shot is definitely required for the second bird.

This shooter's natural point of aim is too close to the center of the trap house to allow him the swing room he will need on the right-angled station five target. For a right-handed shooter, the position at station five must be taken for the angled target. This does not compromise the left bird because that one is virtually a dead straightaway that requires little body movement.

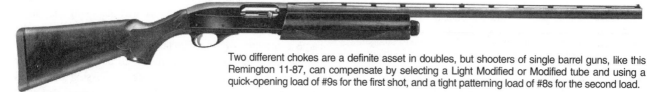

Two different chokes are a definite asset in doubles, but shooters of single barrel guns, like this Remington 11-87, can compensate by selecting a Light Modified or Modified tube and using a quick-opening load of #9s for the first shot, and a tight patterning load of #8s for the second load.

to be the best choice for 16 Yard Singles, and many shooters select it for their first shot on Doubles. However, you have to consider that because you know exactly where that first bird will be, and because you are making a conscious effort to shoot it quickly, you may be taking that target significantly closer to the gun than you would in 16 Yard Singles.

When I shoot Doubles, I doubt seriously if the first bird gets any farther than 27 yards from the muzzle before I fire. That's almost in the range of a Skeet 1 choke and a load of #9s! In fact, I know several shooters who use just that combination for their first shot. My first choice for the first barrel is a $1^{1}/_{8}$-ounce Federal #8$^{1}/_{2}$ trap load from an Improved Cylinder choke. There is plenty of target-breaking power in that combo out to about 35 yards, and I'm not going to let the first target get that far away. The larger pattern, however, will get me some extra birds if I'm having a "sloppy" day. If I am shooting 1-ounce loads (either #8$^{1}/_{2}$ or #8s) I will tighten down to a Skeet 2 choke, but that's as tight as I will go on the first barrel in Doubles.

A Modified choke and #8 shot is much more powerful than one needs for the first target in Doubles, and the tighter pattern can cost you a slightly mis-pointed bird that a more open pattern would have caught.

The second bird is a different story.

This target will generally be farther out than would be the case in Singles. I normally use a Skeet 2 choke for Singles with a load of either #8$^{1}/_{2}$ or 8s, because I am a fast shooter. That is not enough performance for my second bird in Doubles, even though I am trying to get there as quickly as I can. In Doubles, I shift to an Improved Modified choke with a full $1^{1}/_{8}$-ounce 3-dram load of #8s. For the second bird, most shooters find they need at least one choke tighter than they would in Singles.

If you are shooting Doubles with a single-barreled repeater having only one choke option, consider a Modified choke with a $1^{1}/_{8}$-ounce #9 Skeet load for the first shot. This load will open up a bit faster than larger shot sizes, giving what amounts to an Improved Cylinder pattern. You'll have enough power to break targets to a bit beyond 30 yards. Go with a 3-dram $1^{1}/_{8}$-ounce trap load for the second shot. If you reload, consider using softer chilled shot for those #9s to open the pattern a bit more for that first shot, but do stick to premium hard shot for the second load.

Doubles trap may be a bit more challenging than other trap games, but in my opinion it is a lot more fun. I have also found it to be excellent practice for Sporting Clays because you will see many of those kinds of shots on the Sporting fields. It's a game well worth playing, especially if you want to shoot other games.

chapter eight

International Trap

International clay targets are constructed more strongly than conventional clays in order to reduce the risk of target breakage at the increased launching velocity. Shooters favor higher velocity shells to increase striking energy from the #7½ pellets commonly used. (U.S. Army photo by Joseph J. Johnson)

Bunker traps are complex and not common. PFC Danny White and PFC David Alcoriza service one of the United States Army Marksmanship Unit's bunkers at Fort Benning, Georgia, where many of our top International shooters train. (U.S. Army photo by Joseph J. Johnson)

THE INTERNATIONAL COMPETITIVE shooting community seldom embraces the shooting games that we enjoy in this country. They seem to regard the American versions as rather rigid, somewhat staid, and so easy that top shooters can regularly make perfect scores. I have to admit that I tend to agree with that.

The result is that competitive shooting events held under the banner of the U.I.T. (Union International de Tir, the governing body for international shooting sports) have been modified to increase the level of difficulty and make them far more challenging. That is certainly true for the International version of trap, or as it is sometimes called, Bunker or Trench trap.

Trap Machines

The difference starts with the machines used to throw the targets. American-style trap, or ATA trap, as it will be referred to from here on, uses one clay bird machine set to vary the target spread. The machine is placed at ground level and throws targets within a 45-degree arc. The speed of each ATA target is fixed at about 41 mph.

International trap uses fifteen separate machines, all placed below ground level. Each one is adjusted to throw at a specific angle. There are five shooting stations, as in ATA trap, and three machines are used for each station. For example, a shooter on station three will take targets only from traps seven, eight, and nine. The left-hand trap (the number seven trap) will throw birds at an angle to the right, and the right-hand trap (number nine) throws them off to the left. Instead of the maximum ATA angle of 22 degrees from center, the International angle can be as much as 45 degrees. The center trap throws a straightaway bird.

The elevation of the targets is also much more varied, and can be extreme. ATA targets are all fixed to throw at a single elevation of about 30 degrees. International targets may be launched anywhere within a window of 3.0 to 3.5 meters above ground at a point measured 10 meters in front of the trap house. Targets from a trap set to the lowest elevation may

49

INTERNATIONAL CLAY PIGEON FIELD

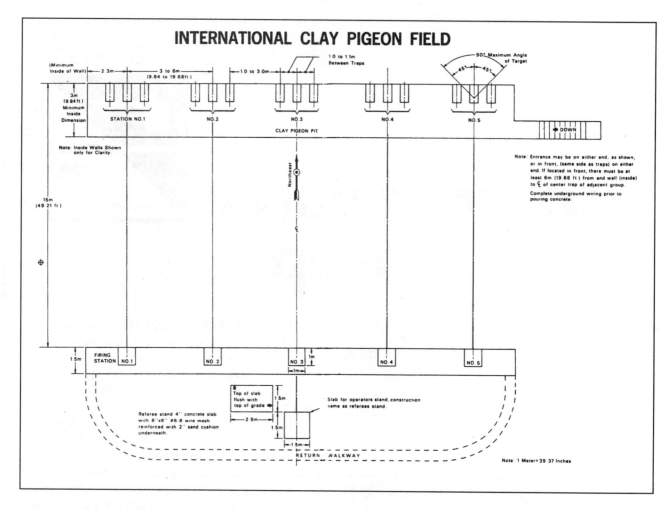

travel 70 yards and never rise more than 1 meter off the ground. The next target thrown may skyrocket almost straight up!

The same variation also exists in target speed. A low target that travels 70 meters may reach a speed of 60 mph, and it flies away from the shooter. That is one of the fastest clay targets you will see in any game. A target thrown at a more vertical angle, that covers only 60 to 65 meters, will be significantly slower.

In a nutshell, International targets travel farther, faster, and at angles twice as extreme as anything seen on an ATA trap field.

The allowed loads make things just a touch more difficult. The 12-gauge is standard, and the maximum allowable shot charge is 24 grams, or about 7/8-ounce. ATA shooters are allowed to use up to 1 1/8 ounces of shot.

A round of International Trap consists of the same twenty-five targets as ATA, but shooters get a break here. They are allowed to fire twice at any target and it scores just as dead if it is hit with the first or second shot.

In ATA trap, you fire five rounds per station and rotate to the next station. Not so in this game. The shooter fires one round and then rotates immediately to the next station. It is a game of constant motion, with the shooter making five full passes down the line. During the course of the round, the shooter receives two targets from the right-hand trap machine,

two from the left, and one from the center machine, at each numbered station. They come in random order and the shooter doesn't know what is coming next. Some shooters, however, try to remember what has been thrown (much like a blackjack player counting cards). They feel this gives them a slight edge near the end of the round when they may know (or think they know) what target is left that must be thrown from a specific station.

Of course, if they make a mistake and are waiting intently for a target that has already been thrown, they are dog meat!

Over/unders dominate this game. Most shooters favor a choke in the .018- to .022-inch constriction range (about Modified) for the first barrel and will often use the same #8 1/2 shot size favored by International Skeet shooters. A fast shooter will generally get onto the target with the first barrel at a range of 25 to 30 yards, and #8 1/2 pellets have plenty of target-breaking power at that range. Given the increase in pellet count in the load and the more open choke, the gun will throw a wider pattern. The second barrel, however, will be choked down to the Full range (.028- to .032-inch) and stuffed with a #7 1/2-size load, in the event the shooter misses with the first barrel, because the bird must then be broken at a greater range.

Changes in Technique

The International version of trap is a good bit more challenging than the ATA version, and requires a change in tech-

International competition requires a lot of officials. This June 1994 event at Colorado Springs shows at least five officials for a single five-man trap squad! All of them watch for target breaks. (U.S. Army photo by Joseph J. Johnson)

nique to shoot well. Few people understand the differences (and the changes required) as well as Lloyd Woodhouse, the coach of our U.S. Olympic shotgun team.

"The first change an ATA shooter will need to make," Woodhouse notes, "is in his initial gun hold. The ATA version will allow them to hold at a higher point over the trap house because all of those targets will always come up from under the gun. In the International game you cannot do that, because a low target will run right underneath your barrel and be blocked from your vision. You may not even see the target until it is way out in the field and about ready to hit the ground."

The philosophy of holding a lower gun is, as we'll see later, the same as that used in Sporting Clays to prevent the barrel from blocking one's visual acquisition of the bird. Woodhouse recommends shooters adjust in the following manner.

"There are five marks on the front of the trap house, facing the shooter," he explains. "Each mark gives the location of the center trap for that particular station, and it also marks the point at which the targets from the right- and left-hand traps will cross on the field. This is a physical mark, and most successful shooters will hold their muzzle right on that mark to make sure that the target always comes out above the gun."

The extreme angles that can be thrown also require that shooters adjust their foot position, or natural point of aim as well.

International trap allows two shots and most shooters train themselves to fire both barrels, even if the target is hit by the first. USAMU shooter, PFC Danny White, pops a pair of empties at a recent event in Colorado Springs, home of the USST. (U.S. Army photo by Joseph J. Johnson)

Bunker trap targets are launched from below shooter level and have a wider permissible angle and higher speed than ATA targets. Note microphone in front of each shooting stand. They voice-actuate the target release and remove any chance of inconsistency that might plague a human target puller.

Bunker trap requires a shooter to be fast and aggressive. The increased target speed and wider angles will not allow a shooter to be as deliberate as would the more leisurely game of ATA trap.

"Most shooters will have a wider swing range to their off side (swinging to the left for a right-hander) and still be able to stay with the gun, meaning keeping their cheek firmly on the stock and their head down. A long swing to the strong side (right swing for a right-hander) will often cause the gun and shooter to separate," states Woodhouse. "For this reason I recommend that the natural point of aim be moved slightly to the strong side. I would suggest that a right-handed shooter take a natural point of aim 6 inches to the right of the house mark, and then swing the gun back to the mark when calling for the target. The reverse would be true for a left-handed shooter. This helps increase the swing range to the strong side to accommodate the severe angles in International trap."

Second Shots

Another factor that must be addressed is the allowance of firing a second shot, should the first one miss. This is, believe it or not, a difficult habit to get used to for ATA-style trap shooters. When the shot is fired in that game, whether the bird is hit or missed, most shooters dismount their gun. It's an ingrained, subconscious response that can be very difficult to change. The second shot in International trap must be a subconscious response, in and of itself, and that has to be learned through practice.

The gaping maw of the bunker trap at the Gator Skeet & Trap club provides room for fifteen separate trap machines. This complex layout is one reason why full International bunker traps are not overly common. They take a lot of room and are expensive.

Many International shooters train to make themselves fire a second shot, even if the first hits. This way the second shot becomes as automatic as the first. Here's how Coach Woodhouse suggests that be done.

"I encourage shooters to fire both barrels, even if the first barrel scores," he explains, "but only under certain conditions."

"If you get into the habit of breaking the target with the first shot," he continues, "and not shooting the second (because there is no reason to), then you get into the habit of becoming complacent and you start coming out of the gun, pulling the gun away from the cheek after the first shot. If you miss the target with the first barrel, then you are doomed because you're coming off the gun and the target will get away from you. However, just triggering the second shot after you break the target with the first is no good because it conditions your subconscious to shoot at nothing— you don't have a target. I tell my shooters to do one of two things: if you hit the target with the first barrel, then pick a piece of that broken target and follow it with your eyes and gun until it hits the ground; if you are in a good position, and feel very confident that you can break that piece of target, then shoot it. If not, and you don't feel confident, then just follow it."

"Either way," Woodhouse feels, "the shooter is now alert,

'with' the gun, and still following targets in the target zone. If you ever require a second shot, this becomes a perfect rehearsal for those times, because it makes you keep the gun alive and the shooter ready to shoot. Lastly, breaking a little piece of target the size of a quarter at 40-plus yards is a tremendous confidence-booster. It's a very positive thing for the shooter."

Double Trap

If International trap sounds like a tough game, there is an even tougher version that has recently been introduced called Double Trap. This game is now incorporated into International competition for both men and women.

Double Trap uses the same fifteen trap layout as the singles game, but only the three traps on station three (traps, seven, eight and nine) are used. As the competitors change stations, the angle at which they are shown the targets from the center machines will change the nature of the shots.

Three basic setups, or schemes, can be used in this game. Each will use only two of the three traps, with a pair of birds launched simultaneously.

The "A Scheme" uses traps seven and eight. Trap seven is fixed at an angle 5 degrees to the left of dead center with station three, and at a height of 3.5 meters, at a point measured 10 meters in front of the trap house. Trap eight is set at zero degrees (a dead straightaway from station three) at a 3-meter height. Both targets will travel 50 meters, which means their speeds are slower than International trap. They more resemble an ATA target as far as speed goes, and their speeds will be constant throughout the round.

The "B Scheme" uses traps eight and nine. The number eight trap is a dead straightaway at a 3.5-meter height, while the number nine trap is set at a 3-meter height and 5 degrees to the right.

The last scheme uses traps seven and nine, with a setting of 5 degrees left and right, respectively, and at a 3-meter height.

The speed of Double Trap targets is the same, regardless of the scheme.

A round of Double Trap consists of twenty-five pairs, or fifty targets. In competition, that is repeated three times for a total of 150 birds, which is followed by a twenty-five pair shoot-off round for the top shooters.

"Although this game is relatively new," says Coach Woodhouse, "it is here to stay in International competition."

Double Trap Tactics

Double Trap also requires a slight change in tactics, as compared to those used in standard International trap.

Since all targets come out of the trap house at a rising angle, a shooter can use the higher gun hold favored by ATA shooters. Since the speeds are slower, and the angles and target order known to the competitors, the first bird can be jumped upon very quickly. Most shooters opt for a relatively open

Florida shooter Lisa Sever shows the proper low gun hold that prevents targets from hiding below the barrel. Note her aggressive, flexed stance. This is a game for fast shooters.

Many shooters like the Federal paper hull, copper-plated International load because it seems to produce a bit less recoil than the plastic-hulled versions. Despite the small (7/8-ounce) shot charge, this one will reach out and crush a 40-plus-yard target.

Modified choking with the #8½-shot International load for the first barrel. The second barrel will be choked tighter, with a #7½-shot load.

"In all schemes," Woodhouse explains, "the targets will appear essentially as leading and trailing birds. Just as in Sporting Clays, I advise my shooters to take the trailing target first and then swing through to the leading target. This avoids the shooter standing there with a "dead gun," or having to make complicated changes in gun direction and speed."

Although that sounds somewhat uncomplicated and straight-forward, Double Trap is not easy. In fact, if you compare the score percentages that are used to rank shotgun competitors into various classes for the different games, you will see that a shooter can miss a lot more Double Trap targets and still be classed as a Master (AA) class shooter, than at any other game.

That's what makes Double Trap so challenging.

International Trap

Master (AA)	93.00 percent and up
A	87.00 - 92.99 percent
B	80.00 - 86.99 percent
C	73.00 - 79.99 percent
D	below 73.00 percent

Double Trap

Master (AA)	90.00 percent and up
A	80.00 - 89.99 percent
B	70.00 - 79.99 percent
C	60.00 - 69.99 percent
D	below 60 percent

Tips From A Champ

Two-time Florida State International Trap Champion Jim Pettengill has found that using a single foot position for each of the five trap shooting stations, "squaring himself" (aligning his natural point of aim) with the trap house, works better for him than adopting a different position for each station as some advocate. This facility has both trap and Skeet houses sharing the same range.

TRAP IS SOMETIMES characterized as a simple game of reflexes that requires the shooter to do nothing more than react quickly to a target. Others refer to it as "rifle shooting with a shotgun" and point out the need for rigid, dogmatic precision if one would master the game. As is often the case with widely differing opinions, the truth lies somewhere between those extremes, and few shooters of this writer's acquaintance understand that better than Jim Pettengill.

Although Pettengill is an accomplished AA trap shooter and a two-time Florida State International Trap Champion, he doesn't consider himself to be a "trap shooter." He prefers to describe himself as simply a shotgunner, and he is equally at home on the Skeet field, either American or International, and enjoys Sporting Clays as much as the next gunner.

This diverse shooting background gives Pettengill an interesting perspective on the game of trap, and one that is not locked into the traditional dogma that often states, "There is only one correct way to shoot trap." Here is his refreshing appraisal of winning trap techniques, which should provide plenty of food for thought for novice and expert alike.

Beginners' Biggest Mistakes

"Trap targets are an illusion," he states. "Many of the angles look like they are moving straight away from the shooter and that they can be 'aimed' at. Many new trap shooters do just that. They compound the problem by adopting an upright rifleman's stance with most of the weight on the back foot, the leading hand slid back on the gun almost to the receiver, and the arms locked in close to the body. It's almost like they are shooting at a tin can, and naturally they don't hit much.

"It is sometimes very difficult, initially," he continues, "to get new shooters to accept the fact that they must actually swing smoothly and fluidly through the target and keep the gun moving. You don't often have this problem with Skeet shooters, because the extreme angle on Skeet targets forces the shooter to move the gun. It is somewhat common with new trap shooters because of the illusion the targets create. Yet, the same moving gun is required to hit targets in either game; there is just less gun movement in trap."

As with any shotgun game, proper stance, with enough flex in the knees to provide lateral mobility, and a leading hand position that allows that hand to drive the gun is important. After the shooter achieves the proper stance, he can then adjust his body position in relation to the trap house.

Many trap shooters are of the opinion that the natural point of aim should be adjusted for each of the five shooting stations in order to allow the shooter to "fudge" toward his weakest swing side. This, they say, assures them of enough swing room on the extreme-angled targets. Pettengill doesn't find that works for him.

"I use the same basic body position for each station," he explains, "and that is to align my natural point of aim with the center of the trap house. This is a direct result of my experience in International trap where the target angles are twice as extreme and the targets fly at much greater speed. In this game, if you fudge your body position too much to one side, a target in the opposite direction can get away from you. Once I learned this at International trap, I found I had no trouble incorporating the body position into ATA trap and have never had a problem running out of swing room. This 'squared stance' gives me equal mobility to either side."

Proper Hold

Another commonly taught trap technique is that the gun hold (ready) position should also be different for each station. Pettengill doesn't buy this either.

"When I first began shooting trap in the early 1970s," he says, "I began with the standard technique of shifting the gun hold according to the station I was on. On station one, that would put my muzzle on the left-hand corner of the house, a right-hand gun hold for station five, and splitting the difference in between. This worked fine for the extreme-angled shots, but I was having some trouble I couldn't understand

with the gentle angles. I continued to shoot this way until it dawned on me that the off-center gun hold was causing me to misread some of the slight-angle targets. The result was that I would be on one of the extreme stations with a gun hold on the corner of the trap house, get a target with a little quartering angle on it and read it as a straightaway. That would cause me to shoot behind it just because I misread it.

"I have since discovered that this is not uncommon," he notes. "In fact, a lot of good shooters will tell you that the toughest targets for them aren't the hard angles, but the slight angles. I think that is due to nothing more than an off-line gun hold causing a misread. When I started shooting International trap, it became quickly apparent that a center-trap hold gave me the quickest and best target read for those tougher targets, yet didn't hurt me at all on the extreme angles. You will read those hard-angled targets quickly and correctly, regardless of the gun hold you use. There is no mistaking them. It is the slight quartering angles that cause the problems with target reads and that is compounded with an off-line gun."

"A shooter who holds an off-center gun is holding to gain an advantage on the one target that is almost impossible to misread," he notes, "and causing himself problems with the targets that are easiest to misread. I would rather hold for the hard-to-read targets, and the center-trap hold works best for me. I suspect that a lot of newer shooters will find it works for them as well. You must correctly read the target before you go after it, and a center-trap hold gives you the quickest read."

Pettengill is convinced that a center-trap gun hold is the quickest way for a new shooter to start shooting scores in the high 80s and low 90s. When it comes to the question of how high above the trap house the shooter should point the muzzle as he waits for the bird, Pettengill is a lot more flexible.

"In Bunker trap," he explains, "we find a very low gun hold—right on the back edge of the trap house—works best. In ATA trap, I will often hold about 18 inches above that, and that is a lower gun position than many shooters use or recom-

This shooter's aggressive stance marks him as a fast shooter. Getting onto targets quickly is important in trap, and the mark of an experienced shooter.

A smooth, weight-forward stance that allows the shooter to achieve proper gun movement in both a horizontal and vertical plane is necessary for trap, as Pettengill demonstrates here. Some shooters bind themselves up with an improper stance.

mend. There are some shooters who hold what amounts to a parallel gun, the gun barrel high enough to actually be parallel to the ground. This has never worked for me because the barrel can hide a target that comes out low, and this makes it difficult to read quickly. It is much easier to bring a gun up to a target than it is to bring it down to a target. A lower gun hold

means you are always going upward and, since the targets are rising, that is an asset."

That gun hold position is not carved in stone, however. Pettengill points out that gun elevation can, and should, be altered if conditions demand it. Sometimes an individual trap may be set a bit higher or lower than normal. The higher the target angle, the higher the gun should be held in order to allow the shooter to get onto the faster-rising target, within his own shooting rhythm. A lower target will require a slight drop in gun hold.

Tricks

A bigger problem, though, is the wind.

"A wind blowing toward the trap will make the targets rise quickly," says Pettengill, "and a good shooter will realize this and raise his initial gun hold point to accommodate it. A wind on the shooter's back will flatten targets and require a much lower gun hold. A wind from the side will raise one of the extreme-angled targets and knock the other down. This also requires adjustments to gun hold. There is no one correct muzzle elevation for trap. This is one area where a shooter must be able to adjust to changing conditions if he wants to be able to maintain his normal shooting rhythm."

Wind is also one of the reasons that Pettengill favors a high-shooting gun for trap. His Perazzi MX-8 shoots almost a full pattern high. This, he maintains, allows him to float the bird above the bead and keep it in full view during the entire shooting process. If the wind suddenly causes the target to drop, he is able to see it happen and react to it. Those shooters who opt for flat-shooting guns (and some of the greatest trap shooters in history have used them) must cover the bird with the muzzle, which causes them to lose sight of it at the moment the shot is triggered. Most of the good shooters who favor flat-shooting guns are very fast shooters and get on the target quickly while it is still under the primary launch influence of the trap. Pettengill could be described as a moderate-speed

Pettengill finds that a relatively low gun hold on the center of the trap house gives him the fastest "read" of a target and helps prevent misreading some gentle-angle shots.

Shooter on the left displays common errors of stance and gun hold for trap. His upright and rigid position, with his weight on the back foot, encourages "aiming" instead of swinging through the target. Instructors say this is a common mistake among new shooters.

shooter, and he firmly believes that trap targets should be shot while they are still rising.

"The longer you leave that target out there," he explains, "the farther away from you it is getting, and the greater the chance of it changing direction due to the wind. Both of those things just make it tougher to hit."

Load Selection

When it comes to load selection, Pettengill does not believe that bigger is always better.

"A few years back," he remembers, "the U.I.T. changed the allowable load for International trap from $1^1/_8$ ounces (32 grams) to 1 ounce (28 grams). Like most shooters, I thought the smaller shot charge would make my scores go down, but it didn't. In fact, my scores went up, and so did those of a lot of other shooters. I can only conclude that the lighter recoil level inherent in those shells had a positive effect. I figured that if those little 1-ounce loads would handle those more stoutly constructed International targets then they should certainly work on the ATA birds. I began using them for ATA and my scores went up there as well."

While Pettengill favors the 1-ounce loads for Singles and Doubles, he admits that he seems to shoot the longer handicap targets better with the standard $1^1/_8$-ounce load. He is also firmly convinced that #$7^1/_2$ shot is the only choice, and he uses $2^3/_4$-dram loads.

"One #$7^1/_2$ pellet can crack a target and get you a visible piece," he states, "but I don't believe one #8 pellet will do that. I don't mess with size 8 shot for trap."

Practice is Important

When it comes to improving your skills through a regular practice regime, there are a number of theories as to the best practice techniques. Pettengill's favorite is to shoot International trap!

"I feel Bunker trap is the best practice for shooters who want to build their skill and shooting speed at ATA trap. I know that a lot of ATA shooters are hesitant to shoot Bunker trap because they think it will mess up their 'delicate' timing, and that's bull! Most of the guys who start shooting Bunker trap find their ATA scores going up. After you have gotten used to the faster, more extremely angled targets you get in Bunker, the ATA targets look bigger and slower. They're a lot easier because Bunker will teach you to read and react to targets more quickly and precisely. I think Bunker trap is a greatly overlooked training aid for ATA shooters. Just ask any ATA shooter who has spent any time shooting Bunker; they will agree."

Pettengill's most useful advice for newer shooters, however, concerns attitude, not technique.

"It is a lot easier to get a novice shooter to the point where he can break twenty-one to twenty-two birds per round in ATA trap than it is to teach him Skeet or any other shotgun game," he opines. "The learning curve for most people will get them there pretty quickly. After that, though, they must expect to hit a flat spot on that learning curve. This is normal, and inevitable, yet it tends to discourage new shooters who are encouraged by the initial progress they have made but are not prepared for the inevitable flattening of the curve.

"When you hit this flat spot on the curve," he concludes, "have patience. Seek out the advice of a competent coach or instructor. Don't get discouraged or start making radical changes in your equipment and shooting style. Usually that flat spot is something minor. If a shooter is prepared for this and doesn't let it disrupt him, he will discover what that minor thing is and conquer it."

Section II
Skeet

chapter ten

The Evolution Of Skeet

THE CLAY TARGET game we now call Skeet got its start shortly after the turn of the century when three Massachuetts wingshooters got tired of missing game birds in the field.

You could probably win a trivia bet on this one, but it was C.E. Davies, his son Henry, and shooting buddy William Foster who originated the game that ultimately grew into contemporary Skeet. Being avid and skilled wingshooters, they realized that the game of trap would not duplicate the angles and flight patterns of all game birds. They bolted a trap machine to a plank, and by altering their position in relation to the trap and setting it at high and low elevations, they found they could recreate the flight of virtually any bird, and have a heckuva lot of fun in the process!

The original layout was a full circle with a 25-yard radius. The circle was marked off like the face of a clock, with shooting stations located at each hour. The trap was positioned at 12 o'clock and threw the targets at 6 o'clock. Two rounds were fired from each of the twelve stations, with the twenty-fifth shot fired from the middle of the field and the target flying right over the shooter's head. This original version of Skeet was referred to as "shooting around the clock" and lasted in that form for a couple of years.

The obvious drawback to a 360-degree shot fall zone (it does play hob with spectators!) was overcome in 1923 when Foster, then editor of the bygone *National Sportsman* magazine, conceived the idea of two traps set within a semi-circle rather than a full circle. Not only did this allow the game to be played on much less land, but it also earned the undying gratitude of all who drove automobiles to the shoots.

Unfortunately, the new game didn't have a name, so Foster sponsored a contest to create one. Here's another trivia bet winner: Out of the over 10,000 entries, the name "Skeet," a derivative of the Scandinavian word for "shoot," won. Mrs. Gertrude Hurbutt, of Dayton, Montana, submitted the name and won $100 for her effort.

Skeet was originally developed as a hunter's game, and it even required a low gun position when calling for the bird. It has evolved into a formalized competitive event, and winning

(Above) Skeet developed as a hunter's game and will give many of the kinds of shots you are likely to see in the hunting fields. High house station one (shown here) should be familiar to any dove hunter.

(Left) Skeet machines throw a single target at a fixed angle and speed. They hold only enough targets for a maximum of five shooters in a squad.

A shooter never loads his gun on a Skeet range until he actually steps up onto the shooting pad to take his turn. Violation of this rule is not tolerated.

Skeet targets fly toward the shooter, and, once broken, the pieces are dangerous. Eye protection is very important in this game, because even a small piece of target at 45-plus mph can cost you an eye.

Any gun that will fire two rounds is acceptable for Skeet, but over/unders tend to dominate the game.

has gotten tougher. In the first National Championship match held in 1927, the winning team missed eight targets out of 125. Today, a top-ranked shooter who misses eight targets out of 1000 might seriously consider taking up golf!

This level of perfection often intimidates new shooters, but it shouldn't. I certainly don't intend to take anything away from those steely-eyed AAA and AA Class shooters who run 100 straight targets and consider it to be nothing more than a warm-up exercise. They are true masters of the game and their form and timing approaches perfection. However, to be brutally honest, Skeet does lend itself to that type of performance. Of all the clay target games available today, Skeet is by far the easiest. A look at a Skeet field will reveal why.

Field Layout

A Skeet field is laid out in a semi-circle with trap houses located at both ends at 3 o'clock and 9 o'clock. The left-hand house is called the high house and launches the bird from a distance of 10 feet above the ground, and at a slight upward angle. The right-hand house is the low house and sends the bird out at a more abrupt upward angle from a position 3 feet above the ground.

The traps are locked into a fixed position and throw the bird to the exact same spot every time. When properly regulated, they will launch the bird at about 42 to 45 mph and the bird must travel between 55 and 65 yards through the air, landing at a predetermined spot under "no wind conditions."

Seven shooting stations are set in a semi-circle around the outside of the field. Station one is directly under the high house, with the following stations moved 26 feet, 8 inches to the right of the previous station. The last station, number eight, is located in the center of the field, midway between the two houses.

Ten feet forward of station eight is a white stake called the Eight Post. The traps are regulated to send the bird directly over the top of this stake.

The speed and flight path of the bird are fixed. The shooter knows precisely where it will come from, where it will go,

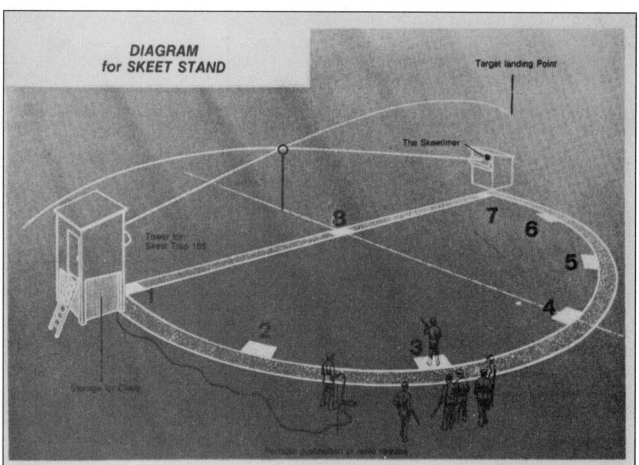

DIAGRAM
for SKEET STAND

Target landing Point

The Skeetimer

Tower for
Skeet Trap 185

8   7   6

5

4

1

2   3

Storage for Clays

Portable gunshelter or rated remote

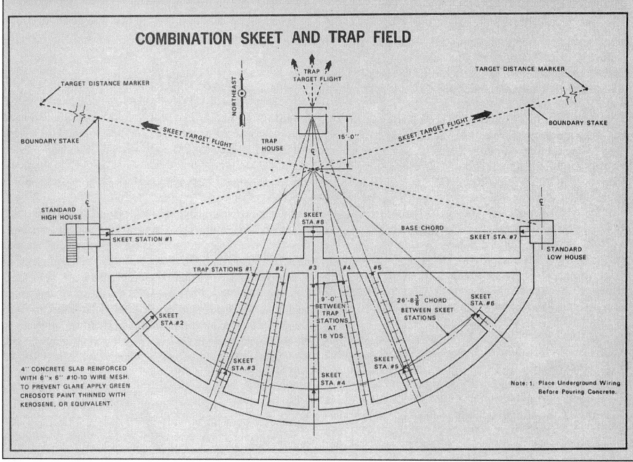

COMBINATION SKEET AND TRAP FIELD

TARGET DISTANCE MARKER

TARGET DISTANCE MARKER

TRAP
TARGET FLIGHT

NORTHEAST

BOUNDARY STAKE

SKEET TARGET FLIGHT

SKEET TARGET FLIGHT

BOUNDARY STAKE

TRAP
HOUSE

15'-0"

STANDARD
HIGH HOUSE

SKEET
STA #8

BASE CHORD

SKEET STATION #1

SKEET STA #7

STANDARD
LOW HOUSE

TRAP STATIONS #1   #2   #3   #4   #5

SKEET
STA.#2

9'-0"
BETWEEN
TRAP
STATIONS
AT
16 YDS

26'-8 3/8" CHORD
BETWEEN SKEET
STATIONS

SKEET
STA #6

SKEET
STA.#3

SKEET
STA #5

4" CONCRETE SLAB REINFORCED
WITH 6"x 6" #10-10 WIRE MESH.
TO PREVENT GLARE APPLY GREEN
CREOSOTE PAINT THINNED WITH
KEROSENE, OR EQUIVALENT.

SKEET
STA #4

Note: 1. Place Underground Wiring
Before Pouring Concrete.

Finding the proper gun hold position for each shooting station is an important part of learning the game. This shooter prepares to call for the high house three target, and has his gun far enough in front of the house that the target will not run away from him.

how fast it will be traveling and when it will be launched. The shooting positions are fixed and each shooter will see the same speed and angle of the bird for each presentation from that station.

Each shooting position will show the shooter a different angle, but once the shooter learns the proper lead and technique for each of the stations he has all the information he needs to break every target consistently.

The shooting format for standard Skeet is simple. The squad, composed of up to five shooters, starts at station one and works around the field to station eight. At stations one, two, six and seven, each shooter is given four targets—a single bird from the high house, a single from the low house, and one pair of doubles where both the high and low house birds are launched simultaneously. When shooting singles, the high house target always comes first. In doubles, the outgoing target (regardless of which house it came from) must be shot first, then the shooter swings back to pick up the incoming bird. At stations three, four and five, the shooter will get only a single target from each house (no doubles), with the high house coming first. At station eight, he will shoot the high house, then the low.

Four Gauges

Competitive Skeet is shot as a four-gauge event. In a Registered match, where scores are kept for classification purposes, the 12-gauge event will be open to all gauges 12 or smaller, using shot loads not exceeding $1\frac{1}{8}$ ounces of shot. The 20-gauge event is open to all guns of 20 gauge or smaller, with a shot charge not to exceed $\frac{7}{8}$-ounce. The 28-gauge event can be shot with either the 28 or the 410-bore and a shot load of

Florida Skeet shooter Bob Lee is ready for low house station seven, the only target on a Skeet field that can be broken consistently without moving the gun from the initial mounting position.

not more than $3/4$-ounce. The 410 event requires the 410 with no more than $1/2$-ounce of shot. Regardless of the gauge actually used, all scores will be recorded under the gauge in which the event is fired.

The only restriction on shot size is that no shot smaller than #9 (2mm) may be used. However, some ranges will have individual restrictions on shot size, based upon the size of their shot fall area.

This does not mean that in order to shoot Skeet one must have four gauges. You are quite free to enter only a specific gauge event, if you desire, and to shoot non-registered practice rounds with whatever you want.

Nor does it mean that if you are an inexperienced shooter that you must go head-to-head with the experts. There is a classification system (as in any shooting sport) that pits shooters against those of similar abilities. In Skeet, that system is based on the percentage of registered targets you have broken.

Individual Skeet Classification

Class	12-gauge	20-gauge
AAA	98.5% and over	N/A
AA	97.5% to 98.49%	96% and over
A	95% to 97.49%	93% to 95.99%
B	93% to 94.99%	90% to 92.99%
C	90% to 92.99%	86% to 89.99%
D	86% to 89.99%	under 86%
E	under 86%	only five classes

Class	28-gauge	410-bore
AA	95% and over	93.5% and over
A	92% to 94.99%	89.5% to 93.49%
B	89% to 91.99%	84.5% to 89.49%
C	85% to 88.99%	81% to 84.49%
D	under 85%	under 81%

Etiquette and Procedures

A round of Skeet consists of twenty-five shots. However, it is advisable to have an extra half-dozen shells with you. It is possible to break both birds during a doubles presentation with one shot, in which case you have to shoot them over again. It is also common to get a broken bird ("no bird") out of a house in doubles and not be able to stop yourself from shooting in time. "No birds" are also reshot. You can use more than twenty-five shells in a round and nothing is more irritating to those waiting their turn to shoot than to have a shooter run back to his car for more shells.

A Skeet squad consists of up to five shooters. The reason for limiting it to five is that most traps won't hold enough birds for any more than that. Your shooting rotation is determined by the sign-up sheet and it is your responsibility to know which shooter you are to follow.

On the Skeet field, a gun is never, repeat *never* loaded until the shooter actually steps onto the 3-foot-square shooting pad to take his turn. The rest of the time the gun must be visibly unloaded. With pumps and semi-autos, rack the action open and lock it there. Break open double guns. This is only common sense that not only guarantees the gun is unable to fire,

Skeet is a game that is popular with both men and women shooters. Many women can outshoot a lot of men!

High house one is a deceptive target. It looks like a straightaway but it is not. The shooter must lead this bird by actually shooting below it. The proper initial gun position, shown here, allows the gun to be swung down and through the target to achieve the proper lead.

but lets everyone else in the squad confirm that at a glance. Skeet shooters are among the friendliest and most gregarious members of the shooting community, and I have yet to see an experienced Skeet shooter who did not genuinely want to see everybody have a good time, and do all he could to help inexperienced shooters learn the game. However, nothing will turn this shooter into a rampaging demon faster than discovering that one of his squad mates is wandering around behind him with a loaded gun.

Skeet shooting is one of the safest participant sports there is. In fact, more people are injured while bowling, playing golf, jogging, swimming, etc. than are ever hurt on a Skeet field. Strict adherence to the safety rules keeps it that way.

While awaiting your turn to shoot, don't crowd the shooter already on the pad. Be in line and prepared to take your place when the time comes, but the only person who should be within 10 feet of the shooter on the pad is the target puller/referee.

Some Skeet ranges have a rule that as soon as a fired shell hits the ground it becomes the property of the range. It is advisable to check to see if that rule is in effect before you start a round. If it is, abide by it. Most of these clubs collect those shells and sell them to reloaders to help offset their costs of operation. If there is no such rule, it is perfectly permissible for the shooter to pick up his empties as he leaves the shooting station, as long as it is done expeditiously. The only time on the Skeet field that is truly "yours" is the time you are on the pad shooting. Causing delays at other times is infringing on the time another shooter has paid for.

When you step up onto the pad to shoot, it is generally accepted that the target puller will release the target at the first sound from you. If you are not prepared for the target, it's a good idea not to say anything! When you do call for the bird, do so in a loud enough voice that the puller can clearly hear it. It makes little difference what command you give: "Pull," "Yaaah!," "Now!"—whatever you are comfortable with is perfectly acceptable. Just be consistent in the command you

give and you'll help yourself by making the puller's job easier.

With a smooth functioning squad, a round of Skeet should be completed in no more than 20 minutes, and often less.

Accessories You'll Need

Savvy shooters wear eye protection as a matter of course. In Skeet, if it is not a range rule, you should consider it mandatory. Many shots in Skeet are incoming birds and when the shooter breaks the bird, the pieces can keep coming. A piece of broken bird traveling at almost 45 mph can cost you an eye, and it is not at all uncommon to get pelted with a few shards during the course of the round, whether from birds you have broken, or from birds others have shot; maybe even from the next field. Any shooter not wearing eye protection on a Skeet field is taking a big chance with his vision.

Hearing protection is also an excellent idea. Not only does it protect your hearing, but it will also go a long way toward guarding you from recoil fatigue and flinching brought on by continued exposure to high noise levels. A jumpy, tired shooter will not perform well. Muff-type protectors can be uncomfortable for some, but there are a number of excellent moulded plugs that fit inside the ear that work very well and do not interfere with cheeking the gun. Even an inexpensive set of throw-away foam plugs is better than nothing.

You will also need some effective way to carry your shells as you move around the field, and if you are saving the hulls for reloading, you'll need a place to put those empties. Many shooters favor a shooting vest with pockets to hold both. These also can be had with a bit of padding in the shoulder area to dampen recoil. There are also belt pouches available with divided compartments that perform quite well and are inexpensive and comfortable. Either is preferable to lugging a box of shells around in your hand, or trying to stuff thirty 12-gauge shells into your Levis.

Gun breakdowns can occur on the range but most are not quickly repairable, so there really isn't much point in lugging a tool kit with you.

There is one little item, however, that can help—a shell knocker. It is quite possible for a fired shell to hang up in the chamber or a squib load (either a reload or a fresh factory round—it happens with both) to leave a wad stuck in the barrel. A cleaning rod will remove either, but they are cumbersome to tote. A simple solution is a piece of brass rod about 6 inches long. If you shoot all four gauges, its diameter should allow it to slip down a 410-bore tube. Pushed forcefully down the barrel it will dislodge most such obstructions and can be carried easily in a back pocket. It can be very annoying for a squad member to have a jammed chamber or an obstructed barrel when it is his turn to shoot, and not have anything handy with which to clear it. Toting a shell knocker will make you a very popular shooter!

The governing body for Skeet in America is the National Skeet Shooting Association (NSSA). You will find a full copy of their rules in the Appendix of this book.

Skeet is a simple game, and best of all, most shooters will have an easy time finding a Skeet range where they can enjoy it.

Veteran Skeet competitors have developed some interesting ways to tote their gear. This home-made gun cart was photographed many years ago. A similar type is now being made by a number of companies catering to Sporting Clays shooters.

chapter eleven

Today's Winning Skeet Guns

SKEET WAS ORIGINALLY created by hunters, as a hunter's game. Since the inventors were, essentially, northeastern upland bird shooters who occasionally dabbled in ducks, the game reflected that in the quick and close nature of the shots, similar to those one would commonly see on grouse, woodcock and small pond mallards. In fact, the longest shot you will see on a Skeet field is about 27 yards, and that length only rarely. The closest shot will be less than 4 yards, and most will range from that to about 20 yards.

The way the original game was shot, it more closely resembled Sporting Clays than contemporary Skeet. The gun was required to be off the shoulder when the bird was called for—low gun position, as it is called today. Given the nature and range of the targets, a light, fast-handling smoothbore with a wide-open choke was a distinct asset.

In fact, a specific degree of choke—called Skeet 1—was developed for this game. For a 12-gauge, that is a constriction of .004-.005-inch and is intended to place the entire shot charge within a 30-inch circle at 25 yards. An additional choking, called Skeet 2 (or as it is more commonly called today "Light Modified"), is about .012-.014-inch and was intended to provide a slightly denser pattern for the longer second shot on Skeet doubles. A gun choked Skeet 1 and Skeet 2, by the way, is an extremely effective upland gun. For all practical purposes, however, a standard Improved Cylinder choke (.009-inch constriction in a 12-gauge) will deliver just about the same performance on a Skeet field as either of the Skeet chokes. If you have a gun that is choked Improved Cylinder and want to shoot some informal Skeet, use it. It'll do the job well. I know that for a fact, because during my early years in competitive Skeet I only shot a 12-gauge (all I could afford) and it was a gas gun with a single barrel choked Improved Cylinder. I shot my way into 12-gauge AA class with it.

The Modern Skeet Gun

Today, Skeet is shot from a pre-mounted gun, which removes the requirement for serious gun handling ability, and the radiused buttpads commonly found on Sporting Clays guns. This practice has also encouraged the use of longer barrels, with more muzzle weight, that will promote a smoother swing. As recently as 5 or 6 years ago, a 26-inch barrel was considered standard for an over/under. Today, 28 inches is about as short as many want to go, and a number of shooters opt for barrels in the 30- to 32-inch range. Interestingly, the shift to longer barrels is a direct result of the knowledge gained on the Sporting Clays fields.

If you want to use the Skeet range as a means to tune up for the fall hunting season, just use an open-choked hunting gun that will deliver two shots. That much still applies. If you want to win a major Skeet tournament, however, you've got problems.

Skeet has become as ritualized, and stylized, as any clay target game in the world, and as one might suspect, there is a very specialized breed of gun that wins.

Competitive Skeet is shot as a four-gauge event—12, 20, 28 and 410-bore. You can shoot in only one of those gauges (I did for a number of years) but you will be confined to winning (or losing) in that class only. The High Overall match winner will have to shoot all four.

The four-gauge ability can be accomplished in a number of ways.

In years past, competitors might simply show up with four different guns, and they might have been a somewhat unusual mix of pumps, semi-autos and double-barreled smoothbores. Others might have selected what could be termed a "matched" four gun set. Remington offered its excellent Model 1100 semi-auto in that manner for a number of years, and even

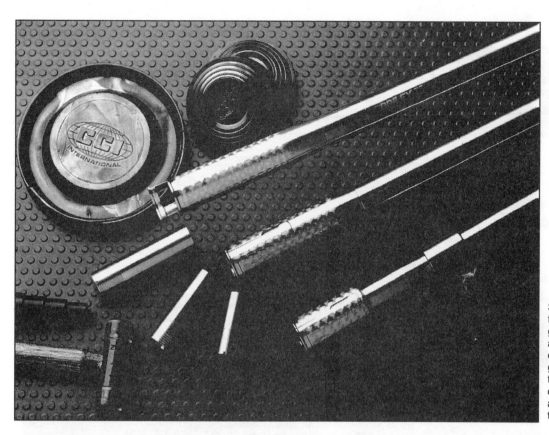

Sub-gauge insert tubes dominate the game of Skeet and allow shooters to use one gun for all four gauges. These Briley tubes have interchangeable chokes and will last the life of the gun.

included barrel weights for the smaller gauges that would give all of the guns the same weight and, some said, the same feel. Winchester offered its over/under Model 101 as a four-gun set, and other makers followed suit. However, that approach has fallen out of favor today.

Another method that still enjoys some popularity is an over/under with four barrel sets.

Barrel Tubes

Still another approach, which has been used by past champions, was to opt for a lighter-recoiling 12-gauge gas-operated semi-auto for that class, and use an over/under with interchangeable sub-gauge tubes (a 20-gauge gun with 28 and 410 tubes) in the remaining classes.

Contemporary masters, however, have a totally new approach. They use a 12-gauge over/under with 20, 28 and 410 tubes, and omit the 12-gauge shell entirely. They have found that a shooter of reasonable skill does not require the full $1^1/_8$-ounce 12-gauge shot charge to break a Skeet target, and elect to use the 20-gauge (usually with 1-ounce loads) in the 12-gauge event, shifting to the legal 20-gauge $^7/_8$-ounce load for the 20-gauge event, and using the 28 and 410 tubes for those events.

What they get with that approach is a three-gauge capability where each gauge has the exact same balance, weight and feel as the others. There is an old adage that goes, "Beware of the man with one gun because he probably knows how to use it." That applies here, and it is true. The only difference in gun feel between the different gauges, when set up in this manner, is the recoil generated by the different gauges.

Sporting Clays shooters who opt to shoot in the newly introduced sub-gauge classes are beginning to use the same system.

That requires an explanation of sub-gauge insert tubes. For that, I'll go to Chuck Webb of Briley Mfg., Inc., probably the largest and most respected maker of these tube sets.

"Insert tube sets have come to dominate the Skeet market in the last 8 or 9 years," he states, "and they are now becoming popular with Sporting Clays shooters.

"The tubes," he continues, "or, at least the ones we make, are constructed of 6061 aircraft aluminum, with the chambers made from titanium and secured to the barrel via threading. We can make these tubes with a fixed choke, but normally supply them with interchangeable stainless steel choke tubes with four choke tubes per gauge, although you can certainly order additional tubes—we make one of the widest selections of constrictions in the industry. The interior and exterior aluminum surfaces of the barrel are hard-anodized, and if the tubes are used properly, they will last the life of the gun."

What you have with insert tubes are interchangeable barrels-within-a-barrel, complete with their own extractors and interchangeable chokes.

Fitting these tubes requires that the gun be sent to Briley. That's because the tubes are precisely fitted to the barrel they will be used with. In most cases, the fit is so close that a tube for the top barrel will not go into the bottom barrel of the gun.

While Skeet and Sporting Clays shooters using over/unders are the biggest customers for these specialized accessories, they can be fitted to any break-action shotgun (side-by-sides and single shots).

According to Webb, Briley has tested their tubes with target-sized steel shot and found no problems with their use. If there is a way to damage the tubes, it is when a shooter

Though no longer made, the Remington 3200 is still commonly encountered on many Skeet ranges. Note the slick plastic tape around the buttpad of this gun—it's owner is an international competitor and finds it promotes a smoother gun mount.

Beretta's Pintail is intended as a field gun, but has all the required features to make a good 12-gauge skeet gun. It is a fitting companion to the venerable and well-respected A303 model that has graced clay target ranges for years.

The Beretta 682 is their basic competition gun, available in a staggering array of configurations. The 28-inch-barreled-skeet version is a popular choice for those shooters who want a gun that will have interchangeable sub-gauge tubes added.

Standard Skeet guns can also work well for the demanding game of International Skeet, but many competitors in that game are exploring sporting clays models for their better handling qualities.

attempts to insert them into a gun for which they were not fitted. For shooters of even minimal intelligence, that shouldn't be a problem, because the tubes are serial-numbered to the gun.

"If the 20-gauge tubes are inserted into a different 12-gauge shotgun," Webb says, "you might possibly split the tube on firing; there will be no chance of injury to the shooter, just the tube. The 28-gauge and 410-bore tubes (because of the smaller inside diameter and greater amount of metal) could probably be shot on their own as individual barrels, but the 20-gauge does need the support of the barrel to which it was fitted. That's about the only way you can mess up a tube set."

Sub-gauge tubes will add 10 to 14 ounces of weight to the barrels of the gun, and many shooters find the added muzzle weight an advantage when it comes to executing a smooth swing.

Knowledgeable shooters who know they will "tube" a gun often opt for a model with a weight of around 8 pounds. By the time the tubes are installed, this brings the total gun weight to a bit less than 9 pounds, and makes a comfortable package. If the tubes are added to an already heavy gun, the additional weight might be uncomfortable. A shooting buddy of mine has a tubed Remington 3200 (which, although no longer made, is an excellent but heavy gun) and finds he shoots it better without tubes in 12-gauge. He finds the additional weight fatiguing.

While tubes are the way to go if you want to win, shooters who just want to enjoy the game on an informal basis can get by very nicely with just one gun and gauge. In fact, my advice to that type of shooter would be to stop reading here and turn to the chapter on guns for Sporting Clays. Any one of those in 12- or 20-gauge will be an ideal choice, and also a great performer on the Sporting fields and the autumn bird fields.

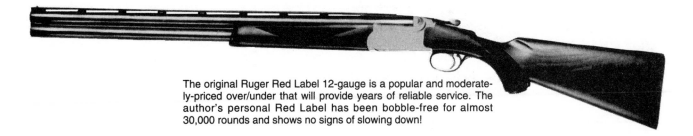

The original Ruger Red Label 12-gauge is a popular and moderately-priced over/under that will provide years of reliable service. The author's personal Red Label has been bobble-free for almost 30,000 rounds and shows no signs of slowing down!

Skeet's Top Guns

Competitive Skeet shooters will also find the Sporting Clays over/unders to be excellent choices as the basis for a tubed Skeet gun set. If a wider range of choices is required, here's what the major makers offer in their Skeet models.

Ruger

Red Label: The standard 12-gauge model has become a popular choice with Skeet shooters looking to compete with quality equipment, but without the big price tag of the high grade imported guns. In 1994, Ruger made two basic changes in their existing models: all 12- and 20-gauge shotguns now feature back-bored barrels (.743-inch in 12-gauge, .633-inch for 20) and are fitted to accept only the new, longer choke tubes used in the Sporting Clays model. These changes will reduce recoil and improve patterns.

The 20-gauge model offers an interesting alternative to small-framed shooters who find the weight of a tubed 12-gauge to be excessive. With a weight of only 7 pounds, the little 20 can be tubed for 28 and 410 and keep the weight under 8 pounds—about a pound lighter than many 12-gauges with tubes. With the 20-gauge rapidly replacing the 12 in the 12-gauge class, it's an option many are considering.

Beretta

This Italian gun maker has a richly deserved reputation in the competition arena, and offers four basic models in their Skeet gun line:

A390 Sport Skeet: This new gas-operated semi-auto essentially replaces the older, highly-regarded A303. The gun is also available in the Sport Super Skeet version, which has a ported barrel, adjustable cast and length of pull via three different (supplied) rubber recoil pads, and adjustable drop by means of two different stock inserts supplied with the gun. A rough-shaped insert to allow shooters to precisely fit the drop themselves is available on request.

Both models are available in 12-gauge only with either $2^3/_4$- or 3-inch chamber and a fixed Skeet choke. A 28-inch barrel with wide tapered rib is standard. Overall length is 47.5 inches, weight 8.1 pounds.

Another semi-auto option from Beretta is the recoil-operated **Pintail**. Capable of handling all $2^3/_4$- and 3-inch 12-gauge loads, it is a fine choice for the shooter who wants to shoot Skeet on an informal basis and use the same gun for hunting. With a weight of only 7 pounds, it makes a handy hunting gun and a lively swinger on clay birds.

S682 Gold Skeet: This over/under has a low-profile boxlock action, ventilated side ribs, and a special matte black finish on the barrels. An interchangeable leather-covered rubber recoil pad is standard. The 12-gauge barrels are 28 inches long with $2^3/_4$-inch chambers and a fixed Skeet choke. **Gold Super Skeet** version has the same adjustable stock capability and ported barrels as the Gold Super Skeet A390. For all-gauge shooters, the gun is available as a four-barrel set.

A more finely-appointed version, the **S687 Diamond Pigeon Skeet**, offers high-grade wood and engraving.

ASE 90 Gold Skeet: This new-for-1994 model has a nickel-chromium-molybdenum receiver machined from a single block of steel, and is hardened for extra durability. A fully interchangeable trigger lock assembly can be easily removed and replaced with a spare lock, eliminating the need to carry a back-up gun to competitive events. Available in 12-gauge only with 28-inch barrels, $2^3/_4$-inch chamber and a fixed Skeet choke, it is 45.3 inches in overall length and weighs 7.6 pounds. The lighter weight on this model makes it an excellent choice for fitting a tube set.

S05 Gold Skeet: Beretta's top-of-the-line model has a true sidelock action. The premium walnut stock can be made to the customer's supplied dimensions. Available in 12-gauge, with $2^3/_4$-inch chambers, 28 inch barrels, and with fixed Skeet chokes.

Krieghoff

The **K-80** series has earned a reputation as one of the top competitive shotguns in the game. Their Skeet gun array is one of the top performers, and one of the most innovative.

Shooters who favor a full four-barrel set will find the K-80 version an excellent choice. The set consists of four barrels (12, 20, 28 and 410) fitting one receiver. All barrels are evenly weighted and balanced for consistent performance. Sub-gauge barrels have standard Skeet chokes. The 12-gauge barrels use Tula chokes (a slightly faster-opening choke than standard Skeet constriction) and are ported. Average weight of the gun with each 28-inch barrel set is $8^1/_4$ pounds.

Those who like tubed guns have several options based on the K-80 two-barrel set. This innovative approach provides one 12-gauge barrel set of normal construction, 28 or 30 inches long with fixed Skeet chokes or interchangeable tubes. A second 12-gauge barrel set, fitted to the same receiver, is called the "carrier" barrel; it is of thinner construction and not intended to be fired without insert tubes. Once tubes (from a number of makers) are installed, the lighter initial barrel weight now becomes a perfect match for the other 12-gauge barrel.

This allows a shooter to set up his 12-gauge for both Skeet

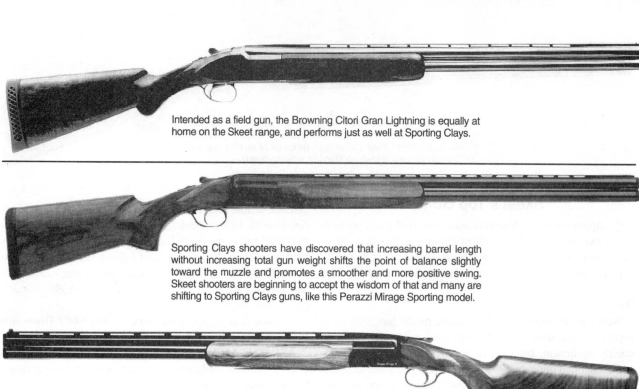

Intended as a field gun, the Browning Citori Gran Lightning is equally at home on the Skeet range, and performs just as well at Sporting Clays.

Sporting Clays shooters have discovered that increasing barrel length without increasing total gun weight shifts the point of balance slightly toward the muzzle and promotes a smoother and more positive swing. Skeet shooters are beginning to accept the wisdom of that and many are shifting to Sporting Clays guns, like this Perazzi Mirage Sporting model.

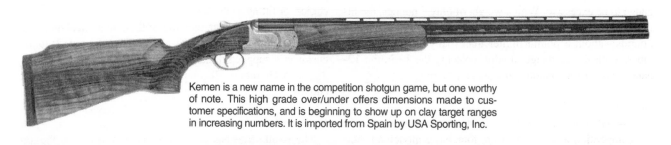

This top of the line Perazzi can be ordered with a number of options, including flat or parallel ribs, different stock dimensions and custom choke boring. The hallmark of the Perazzi line is a gun custom-fitted to the shooter.

Kemen is a new name in the competition shotgun game, but one worthy of note. This high grade over/under offers dimensions made to customer specifications, and is beginning to show up on clay target ranges in increasing numbers. It is imported from Spain by USA Sporting, Inc.

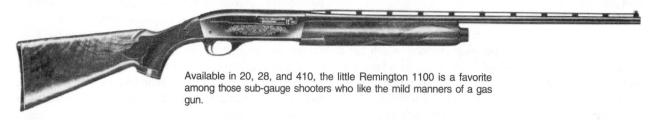

Available in 20, 28, and 410, the little Remington 1100 is a favorite among those sub-gauge shooters who like the mild manners of a gas gun.

and Sporting Clays, and shift to the carrier barrel for sub-gauge events with insert tubes. Very slick!

This version is available as a standard weight (8$\frac{1}{4}$ pounds) or a lightweight version (7$\frac{3}{4}$ pounds) and, as with all Krieghoff guns, offers a variety of stock fitting options and rib configurations.

Browning

Offering one of the largest product lines in the shotgun game, a shooter should have no trouble finding a 12-gauge Skeet gun that can be very nicely tubed. Specific Skeet models are offered in all four gauges (12, 20, 28 and 410) and, as of 1994, all are offered with Browning's Invector choke tube system. Critical dimensions for all Skeet guns are: length of pull, 14$\frac{3}{8}$ inches; drop at comb, 1$\frac{1}{2}$ inches; drop at heel, 2 inches. All are available with either 26- or 28-inch barrels with the following weights per gun, by gauge: 12-gauge—8 pounds; 20-gauge—7 pounds, 4 ounces; 28-gauge—6 pounds, 15 ounces; 410-bore—7 pounds, 6 ounces.

All 12- and 20-gauge models have back-bored barrels and chrome-lined chambers.

Some shooters find the stock dimensions on the Skeet

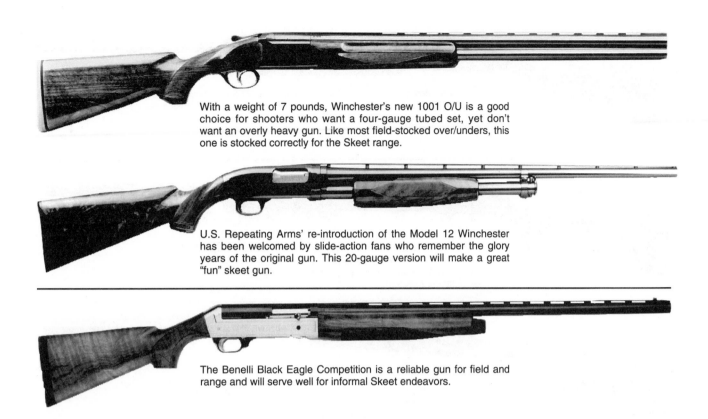

With a weight of 7 pounds, Winchester's new 1001 O/U is a good choice for shooters who want a four-gauge tubed set, yet don't want an overly heavy gun. Like most field-stocked over/unders, this one is stocked correctly for the Skeet range.

U.S. Repeating Arms' re-introduction of the Model 12 Winchester has been welcomed by slide-action fans who remember the glory years of the original gun. This 20-gauge version will make a great "fun" skeet gun.

The Benelli Black Eagle Competition is a reliable gun for field and range and will serve well for informal Skeet endeavors.

guns a bit longer and higher than they like. The solution is to opt for one of the field grade models. Their stock dimensions are: length of pull, 14 1/4 inches; drop at comb, 1 1/2 inches; and drop at heel, 2 3/8 inches. I find my 28-gauge Lightning model with field stock dimensions to be a fine performer on both the Skeet and Sporting Clays fields. Some shooters may find that one of the different stock dimensions perform better for them, and the fine performance exhibited by the Browning **Citori** line of over/unders is available in both the Skeet and field models.

Perazzi

On the International Skeet fields of the world, this high-grade Italian gun maker enjoys a true world class reputation. American-style Skeet shooters will find the handling qualities and legendary reliability will benefit them as well. Perazzi does not offer multi-barrel sets, but the guns can be easily tubed. The most popular models on the Skeet fields are the **MX7, MX8** and **Mirage**. All differ slightly in weight and balance, but with the Perazzi line that is simple to change, since all have interchangeable stocks that allow a shooter to virtually custom fit the gun to himself, and to whatever clay target game is pursued. Each gun is available with a detachable trigger group, interchangeable or fixed chokes (in one or both barrels), a number of different rib configurations, and barrel lengths from 26 to 28 inches.

One of the more interesting models is the newer **MX10**. This top-of-the-line over/under has a comb adjustable for drop and cast, and a special high-step rib that allows the shooter to adjust the actual point of impact of the barrels via the rib, not the buttstock. Barrel lengths range from 28 to 29.5 inches. Chokes are available as fixed or interchangeable.

Critical dimensions on the Perazzi line are just about whatever a shooter wants them to be, and overall weight will vary with barrel and stock dimension changes.

Kemen

Similar to the Perazzi is the **Kemen KM-4**. This is also a high-end shotgun featuring a drop-out trigger assembly, various rib options including flat or stepped, high-grade walnut, and stock dimensions made to the customer's specifications. The barrels, forend and trigger parts are interchangeable with the Perazzi guns. The Kemen is imported from Spain by USA Sporting, Inc.

SKB

Series 85: These over/unders are offered in a number of Skeet models, as both four-gun sets, single gauges, and a three-barrel set consisting of a 20-gauge gun with 28 and 410 barrels and matching forends.

The three-barrel set has 28-inch barrels with interchangeable tubes in the 20- and 28-gauges and fixed Skeet 1 chokes in the 410. Overall weight, with each barrel, is right at 7 pounds per gun in the **585** model, 7.4 pounds in **685** and 7.5 pounds in the **885**.

The 12-gauge SKBs are available in both 28- and 30-inch barrels and make excellent guns to tube.

Remington

There was a time when the Remington four-gun 1100 Tournament Skeet series was a popular item on the Skeet fields, but I can't remember the last time I saw a full set being used. In fact, according to Remington's latest catalog, the 12-gauge version is no longer even being made, leaving just the 20, 28 and

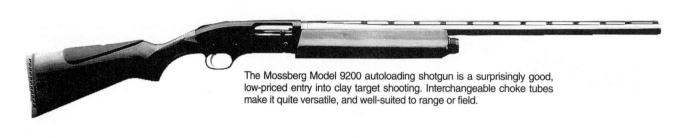

The Mossberg Model 9200 autoloading shotgun is a surprisingly good, low-priced entry into clay target shooting. Interchangeable choke tubes make it quite versatile, and well-suited to range or field.

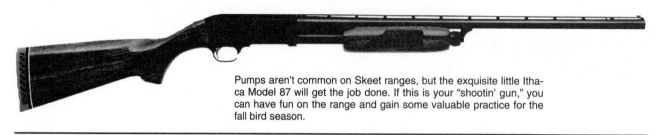

Pumps aren't common on Skeet ranges, but the exquisite little Ithaca Model 87 will get the job done. If this is your "shootin' gun," you can have fun on the range and gain some valuable practice for the fall bird season.

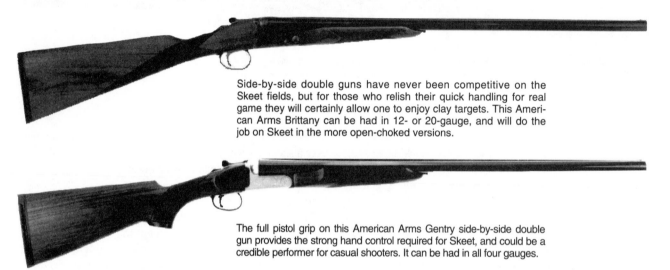

Side-by-side double guns have never been competitive on the Skeet fields, but for those who relish their quick handling for real game they will certainly allow one to enjoy clay targets. This American Arms Brittany can be had in 12- or 20-gauge, and will do the job on Skeet in the more open-choked versions.

The full pistol grip on this American Arms Gentry side-by-side double gun provides the strong hand control required for Skeet, and could be a credible performer for casual shooters. It can be had in all four gauges.

410 models in the line as individual guns. Critical dimensions on those are 14-inch length of pull, $1\frac{1}{2}$-inch drop at comb, and $2\frac{1}{2}$-inch drop at heel. The 20-gauge offers a 26-inch barrel and a weight of $6\frac{3}{4}$ pounds. The 28 and 410 models have 25-inch barrels and weights of $6\frac{1}{2}$ and 7 pounds respectively.

The **Model 11-87** has taken over 12-gauge chores, with the same stock dimensions and a weight of $8\frac{1}{2}$ pounds with a 26-inch barrel.

Winchester

Winchester fans will find the **Model 1001** field model an effective Skeet gun. With a weight of only 7 pounds, this over/under is a good choice for shooters looking for a lightweight, tubed, four-gauge gun. Critical dimensions are $14\frac{1}{4}$-inch length of pull, $1\frac{1}{2}$-inch drop at comb, and 2-inch drop at heel. The gun features back-bored barrels, single selective trigger and automatic ejectors.

While the above-mentioned guns are all suitable for competitive Skeet, they are not the only choices available. As stated earlier, all you really need is an open-choked gun that will fire two rounds, and with the wide availability of factory guns

fitted with interchangeable choke tubes, it is quite easy to find a quality hunting shotgun that can do informal double duty on the Skeet fields. Some fine choices are the **Benelli** short-recoil-operated **Black Eagle Competition** model available with 26- or 28-inch barrel with interchangeable choke tubes. This gun has a drop adjustment kit option that allows the stock dimensions to be changed to fit the shooter without modifying the stock. The inexpensive **Mossberg Model 9200** is an affordable gas-operated 12-gauge semi-auto that will handle both $2\frac{3}{4}$- and 3-inch shells and features barrel interchangeability. Those who favor pump-action shotguns for both field and range will find the **Winchester Model 12**, in either 12- or 20-gauge, to be a reliable performer, as is the **Ithaca Model 87 Supreme.**

Though side-by-side doubles are seldom seen on the Skeet range in the hands of competitive shooters, you will see them toted by a number of bird hunters warming up for the fall season each year. If you happen to own a fine SxS like the **Merkel Model 200E**, or the **American Arms Brittany** or **Gentry** models, there is no reason not to spend an afternoon on the Skeet field with it. If you do, you'll find afternoons in the fall bird fields much more productive.

chapter twelve

Top Loads For Skeet

Number 9 shot is the most popular size for Skeet loads and will reliably break targets inside 25 yards. There are a few places where #8½ shot could be handy, however.

LIKE TRAP, SKEET does not require a diversified selection of loads. While competitors will be required to obtain loads for four different gauges, the maximum permissible shot weight per gauge is tightly defined and, with the exception of the 12-gauge and one application of the 20-gauge, nothing is to be gained by deviating from that.

The 12-gauge is allowed a maximum of 1⅛ ounces of shot, with the 20-gauge carrying ⅞-, the 28 holding ¾- and the 410 having only ½-ounce.

Shooters are allowed a latitude in shot size, but again, the nature of the game pretty well dictates that nothing is gained by using any shot size other than #9.

Skeet is a close-range game. In fact, the farthest shot a shooter will see on a Skeet field will be about 27 yards. In standard Skeet, this would only occur if the shooter really hesitated on an outgoing target and let it get so far out that such poor form would likely dictate a miss anyway. In the Doubles game, it is possible to see longer shots on the second bird at stations three, four and five than one would see when shooting them as singles. These birds can often be "shot out of position" and may present longer than normal shots, but they don't approach the range at which trap targets are routinely broken. In contrast, many shots will be quite close—low house eight is commonly broken only 3 yards off the muzzle, and the majority of the shots on the remaining stations do not exceed 20 yards.

Since #9 shot will reliably break any target inside 25 yards, it has become the almost universal choice for Skeet. With a pellet count of about 585 pellets per ounce, that gives a 1⅛-ounce 12-gauge load a pellet count of over 650 individual pellets! The 20-gauge will pack 510, with the 28 gauge and 410 carrying 435 and 292, respectively.

That means the ¾-ounce #9 load in the 28-gauge is packing a lot more pellets than a full 1⅛-ounce load of #7½s, which carries only 390 of them.

Number 9 shot will do the job, but there are two instances where shifting to #8½ shot can help. The first is on the second shot in the regular Doubles game. These targets can get out far

Skeet is a close-range game, with the longest shot being about 25 yards, and some as close as 3 or 4 yards. This makes #9 shot the perfect choice for all except the longer second shots on some doubles stations. Many shooters opt for #8$\frac{1}{2}$ shot there.

enough that they verge on being close to the outer limits of #9 shot's reliable break range. I find that a few #8$\frac{1}{2}$ loads in my pocket are real confidence boosters, since I know they will consistently break targets 5 to 10 yards farther than #9 shot. I generally use #9s for standard Skeet, and the first bird in Doubles, with the #8$\frac{1}{2}$ load reserved for the second shot. Other shooters opt for a lighter load of #9s for the first shot and a heavier load of the same size shot for the second, theorizing that the increased pellet count provides multiple hits to add striking energy at those outer range limits. I wouldn't argue with that approach, either. I do know that my Doubles scores have improved and become more consistent after switching to the larger shot size for the second shot. I'll be the first to admit that it may be strictly psychological—I know the shells will break the target in any legal position, so I'm not inclined to hurry, or change my rhythm. Maybe #9s would work just as well, but the mental game is every bit as important as the physical game, and if the larger shot makes me feel better, there's no reason I shouldn't use it in that situation. The decrease in pellet count between #9 and #8$\frac{1}{2}$ isn't significant enough to make a difference.

The second situation where I favor #8$\frac{1}{2}$ shot is in the $\frac{1}{2}$-ounce 410 loading. This little rascal needs all the help it can get!

Early in my shooting career, when I was searching for the "magic load," a veteran shooter advised me not to even bother

patterning the 410. "It's too frustrating," he stated. After ignoring his advice and running many test patterns, I have to admit he was right.

My experience with the $\frac{1}{2}$-ounce 410 load indicates that consistent patterns are rare. Even the best factory loads will occasionally throw one with a few holes that a bird could slip through, or maybe be struck by only one or two pellets. That may not be enough to give the shooter that all-important "visible piece." My solution to that has been to increase the shot size to provide more striking energy per pellet. By going to #8$\frac{1}{2}$ shot for the 410, I decrease overall pellet count from about 290 to around 240, but each individual pellet packs more punch. It takes fewer #8$\frac{1}{2}$ pellets to break a bird than it does with #9s. Since I can't control the pattern density, the only thing I can do is get more punch from each individual pellet, and #8$\frac{1}{2}$ gives that to me.

That increase in pellet size is not something that will be a night-and-day difference, but it will get me an extra bird or two, and that is more than enough reason to use it. I tend to think of it like chicken soup for a cold—it can't hurt. Interestingly, a few manufacturers are now beginning to make specific 410 loads for sub-gauge Sporting Clays. Guess what shot size they are loading? You got it, #8$\frac{1}{2}$!

Though shot weights for the 20, 28 and 410 are pretty much carved in stone (nobody in his right mind opts for lighter loads with these), a number of shooters find that lighter 12-gauge

Skeet is shot as a four-gauge competitive event in (left to right) 12-, 20- and 28-gauge and 410-bore. Many knowledgeable shooters feel that Skeet is responsible for keeping the 28-gauge shell alive.

Most serious Skeet shooters are reloaders simply because of the economics of the game, but also for the ability to tailor loads for the small gauges. The 410-bore, in particular, needs all the help it can get.

loads are a plus. The less recoil one absorbs during the day makes him or her a better shooter at the end of the day. Many shooters find the 1-ounce load to be as much shell as is required. Others opt for the security of the full $1^1/_8$-ounce load, but select one of the $2^3/_4$-dram "Lite" versions. At my own club, I don't know of a single experienced shooter who uses a 3-dram, $1^1/_8$-ounce load. It's not needed. In fact, some top

shooters don't even bother with the 12-gauge at all—they shoot the 12-gauge event with their 20-gauge gun. One obvious reason is the decreased recoil. Skilled shooters don't need more than $^7/_8$-ounce of #9s to break a Skeet target anyway.

Another reason is convenience. Most of the top shooters today shoot over/unders fitted with sub-gauge tubes. In order for the tubes to fit properly, the barrel must be clean. If a shooter has a good score in the 20, 28 or 410 event in the morning segment of a tournament, he knows he faces the possibility of a shoot-off in the same gauge at the end of the day. If he pulls the tubes and starts running 12-gauge rounds through the gun he will have to scrub the barrel in order to reinsert the appropriate tubes later.

Thus, the 12-gauge has somewhat disappeared from the Skeet fields, at least in the hands of skilled shooters. Instead, an "illegal" Skeet load is becoming perfectly legal—the 1-ounce 20-gauge. It is legal to use in a 12-gauge event because even though the shooter may be using a 20-gauge, he is still allowed the 12-gauge maximum shot charge of $1^1/_8$ ounces.

Here's what the ammo makers offer for those who favor factory fodder.

Factory Ammunition

Federal

The softest shooting 12-gauge Skeet load in the line-up is the S114 "Extra-Lite" with $1^1/_8$ ounces of shot. The T113 (1-ounce #$8^1/_2$ load, mentioned in the trap load chapter) is also a very good Skeet shell, and even softer shooting than the S114.

Standard $2^3/_4$-dram loads in $1^1/_8$ ounces are represented by the S115 (plastic) and S117 (paper), both advertised at 1145 fps and carrying #9 shot. Their full-powered 3-dram loads are the S116 (plastic) and S118 (paper). The $1^1/_8$-ounce #9 payloads clock 1200 fps.

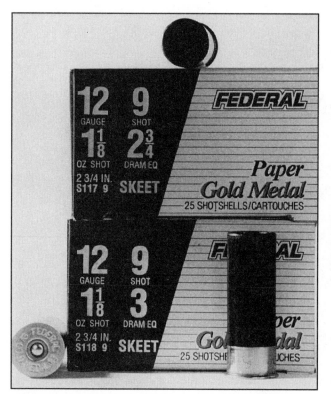

Many shooters feel the $^3/_4$-ounce, 28-gauge Skeet load is every bit as effective as the full $1^1/_8$-ounce, 12-gauge load on Skeet targets.

Federal's paper-hulled loads are offered in both $2^3/_4$- and 3-dram versions. They are popular with many shooters who feel the paper hull produces less recoil than plastic shells.

Winchester's 410-bore AA target load is representative of the breed. The maximum allowable shot charge for the 410 is only $^1/_2$-ounce.

Sub-gauge loads consist of the 20-gauge S206 ($7/8$-ounce #9s at 1200 fps), the 28-gauge S280 ($3/4$-ounce #9s at 1230 fps), and the 410 S412 ($1/2$-ounce #9s at 1230 fps). Federal also offers a $1/2$-ounce 410 load with #8$1/2$ shot (a favorite of mine), the SC412.

Winchester

All of the Winchester load designations listed in the trap load section (Chapter 4) are available in #9 shot. One load in the 12-gauge arena that is worth mentioning is their AAL12 "Xtra-Lite" 1-ounce number in #9 shot. This is a thoroughly delightful and soft-recoiling Skeet load, and I burn a lot of them.

Winchester also offers the basics in sub-gauge loads that have been good performers on the Skeet fields for years.

WINCHESTER "DOUBLE A"

Load	Dram Equiv.	Shot Ozs.	Shot Size	Velocity FPS	Comments
AAL12	2$3/4$	1	7$1/2$,8,9	1180	Xtra-lite
AASL12	2$3/4$	1$1/8$	7$1/2$,8,8$1/2$,9	1125	Super-lite
AA12	2$3/4$	1$1/8$	7$1/2$,8,9	1145	
AAH12	3	1$1/8$	7$1/2$,8,9	1200	
AAM12	3	1$1/8$	7$1/2$,8,9	1200	Heavy
AA20	2$1/2$	7/8	8,9	1200	
AA28	2	3/4	9	1200	
AA410	Max.	1/2	9	1200	

Victory USA

Recoil-conscious shooters may want to check out Victory's Stryker Series International 12-gauge load using only $7/8$-ounce of #9 shot. It is the softest-shooting 12-gauge shell I have found and has more than enough payload to run 100

straight. Their Challenger series (1-ounce at 1320 fps) and the Super Sporting series (1$1/8$ ounces at 1270 fps) are both available in #9 shot and do an excellent job on the Skeet range.

Another useful shell is their Challenger Felt Wad with 1-ounce of #9 shot. The felt wad tends to open patterns a bit more quickly, and some shooters find this can boost their score.

Victory does not, at this time, offer a 28-gauge shell, but they do provide Skeet-legal loads in the 20 and 410.

Remington

All 12-gauge loads (except Duplex) listed in the trap chapter are available in #9 shot and are excellent choices for Skeet.

Sub-gauge loads are well represented and include a new Sporting Clays shell for the 410.

REMINGTON SKEET LOADS

Load	Dram Equiv.	Shot Ozs.	Shot Size	Velocity FPS	Comments
RTL12M	3	1$1/8$	7$1/2$,8,9	1200	
RTL12L	2$3/4$	1$1/8$	7$1/2$,8,8$1/2$,9	1145	
LRTL12	2$3/4$	1$1/8$	7$1/2$,8,9	1100	REM-Lite
MRTL12M	3	1$1/8$	7$1/2$x8	1200	Duplex
MRTL12L	2$3/4$	1$1/8$	7$1/2$x8,7$1/2$x8$1/2$	1145	Duplex
RTL20	2$1/2$	7/8	8,9	1200	
RTL28	2	3/4	9	1200	
SP410	Max.	1/2	9	1200	
SP410SC	Max.	1/2	8$1/2$	1200	Sporting Clays

Fiocchi of America

The 1-ounce loads listed elsewhere in the trap chapter are not available with #9 shot, something I find difficult to understand since the 12TL at 1150 fps, while an acceptable 1-ounce Skeet load with size #8$1/2$ shot, would be an excellent one with

Remington offers a complete line of Skeet loads in 12-, 20- and 28-gauge and 410-bore. Thier loaded ammo and components are very popular.

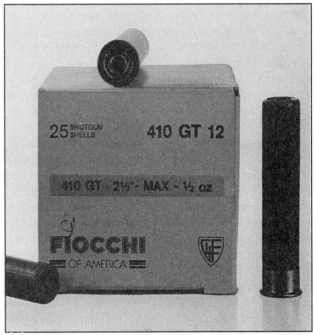

The Fiocchi 410 GT12 Skeet load can be used for both feathered and clay birds. The brand is very popular in both the U.S. and Europe.

#9s. The remaining listed 12-gauge loads are all available in #9 shot.

Sub-gauge loads are pretty standard and cover Skeet uses very well.

FIOCCHI

Load	Dram Equiv.	Shot Ozs.	Shot Size	Velocity FPS	Comments
12 F-Lite	$2^7/_8$	$1^1/_8$	$7^1/_2,8,9$	1175	
12 VIPLT	$2^3/_4$	$1^1/_8$	$7^1/_2,8,9$	1150	
12 VIPHV	3	$1^1/_8$	$7^1/_2,8,9$	1210	
20 VIP78	$2^1/_2$	$^7/_8$	8,9	1200	
28 GT34	2	$^3/_4$	9	1200	
410 GT12	Max.	$^1/_2$	9	1200	

ACTIV

The selection of Skeet shells available from ACTIV consists only of the 12- and 20-gauge. All of the 12-gauge shells mentioned in the trap load chapter are available in #9 shot and do a fine job on the Skeet range. The 20-gauge number is a Skeet-legal $^7/_8$-ounce #9 load and denoted as A201.

ACTIV

Load	Dram Equiv.	Shot Ozs.	Shot Size	Velocity FPS	Comments
ATG12G	3	$1^1/_8$	$7^1/_2,8,9$	NA	
ATG12GL	$2^3/_4$	$1^1/_8$	$7^1/_2,8,9$	NA	
ATG12UL	Lite	$1^1/_8$	$7^1/_2,8,9$	NA	Lite
ATG12H	$2^3/_4$	1	$7^1/_2,8,9$	NA	
A201	$2^1/_2$	$^7/_8$	$7^1/_2,8,9$	NA	

Reloads

The majority of serious Skeet shooters are reloaders, and the reason is simple economy. If you do a "best buy" by case-lot of the four different gauges, you will find that the 12, 20 and 410 cost virtually the same, while the 28-gauge generally runs about 20 bucks more. Considering that the 410 carries less than half the shot of the 12-gauge (with the 28-gauge running about 65 percent) and that both use less powder, it becomes somewhat difficult to explain why they should cost as much as or more than a larger 12-gauge shell, but they do.

Skeet shooters who load their own can realize a savings of about fifty to sixty percent on the smaller shells, and around forty percent on the 12- and 20-gauges!

Shot selection for Skeet loads isn't quite as critical as for trap. I favor hard shot for everything in trap, but don't mind the less expensive chilled shot for the 12- and 20-gauge loads. In fact, novice shooters might actually be helped by soft shot in these two gauges. You have more than enough #9 pellets in even the $^7/_8$-ounce 20-gauge load to break the close-range targets. The drawback is that it's difficult to get the load to open up. Soft shot does that better than hard shot.

When I get down to the 28-gauge I tend to revert to Lawrence Brand Magnum shot. This under-appreciated little jewel (the 28-gauge) is such an efficient shell that good hard shot can make it every bit as effective as a $1^1/_8$-ounce 12-

Victory's Challenger 1-ounce #9 load is a top choice for Skeet shooters who want less recoil and is becoming very popular.

gauge load. Indeed, a number of shooters find they can carry the same average with both. Not surprisingly, many shooters opt for the 28-gauge as their practice load because it is truly an effective Skeet shell. Inside 30 yards, it will break anything the heavier 12- and 20-gauge will, and with softer manners. It just makes sense to give it the best.

With the 410-bore loading, hard shot becomes mandatory. While I do like the miniscule shell (and even do some bird hunting with it), I can't praise its inherent design and efficiency as highly as the lovely 28-gauge. It needs help and can't really tolerate soft shot even though many budget-conscious shooters do load it with that. I've already mentioned my preference for #$8^1/_2$ shot in this shell, although I know some Skeeters who can whip my tail when using standard #9 shot 410 loads.

When it comes to powders, I still favor IMR PB for the few 12-gauge loads I burn on the Skeet range just for its soft-recoiling and clean-burning nature. In the 20- and 28-gauges, I have developed a strong liking for 800X, Unique and Herco. They tend to keep pressures below 10,000 LUP (Lead Units of Pressure), and I shoot in steamy Florida where the high heat can raise shotshell pressures. In the 410, H-110 is the powder of choice, although WW296 will work.

While handling the loading chores for four different gauges may seem like a complex endeavor, it is not—two sizes of shot, two different grades in size #9 if you prefer, the appropriate wads, and just a couple of different powders are all it takes to give you your best shot.

Skeet Simplified

A belted shell pouch and slip-on shoulder pad are adequate for starters, but many shooters will opt for a shooting vest as they gain more interest in the game of Skeet.

OF ALL THE clay target games, Skeet is without a doubt the easiest to learn. Unlike trap and Sporting Clays, where targets may take varying trajectories when released, the path of every Skeet target is fixed. Shooters know precisely when the target will be launched, what path it will take and how fast it will be going.

Once the shooter learns the proper body and gun position for each station, along with the required lead, he has all the information required to break every target consistently. This chapter will provide that information, but before that, let's take a moment to look at the two most effective shooting techniques: fast-swing and sustained lead.

Lead Techniques

With the fast-swing technique, the shooter begins with the gun behind the target. The barrel is then swung quickly through the target, at a speed faster than the target is moving. One shotgunner described it as "painting the bird out of the sky with the muzzle." As the muzzle catches, then overtakes, the target, the shot is triggered when the shooter sees the required amount of lead.

The advantage to the fast-swing technique is that it is the most effective way to handle almost any aerial target, including trap, Sporting Clays and feathered game. Because the gun must be moving much faster than the target, the shooter has an almost automatic, built-in means of compensating for targets moving at varying speeds: the faster the target is going, the faster the gun must be swung to catch it. On the Skeet field, the fast-swing shooter has the specific advantage of getting onto the target more quickly than the sustained lead shooter. This is a plus on windy days when targets sometimes dance to their own tune. The faster you can break it, the better off you are.

The disadvantage, if it could be called such, is that it is impossible to precisely explain what length of lead is required for each station because no two fast-swing shooters will see the same lead. Individual reaction times and swing speeds will vary. One shooter may swear he sees only 2 feet of lead at station four, while the next may claim it takes 4 feet. Mastering the fast-swing technique requires practice and repetition in order to program your own mental computer. It is, however, time well spent because it will make you a better and more versatile shot. It will also be to your advantage should you take up trap or Sporting Clays, and will certainly increase your gamebird average in the field.

The sustained lead requires that the gun muzzle start ahead of the bird and never get behind it. Once there, the gun and target speed are matched while the shooter seeks a precise lead before triggering the shot.

This works out very well in Skeet because every lead is known in advance. The disadvantage (other than being a poor choice for targets of varying speeds whose precise lead is not known) is that it requires a bit more time to get onto the target than the fast swing. This doesn't at all hurt the shooter on the easy, lazy incoming targets and, indeed, many fast-swing shooters will revert to the sustained lead technique on them. It can result in the shooters' "riding" an outgoing target too long and may cause problems if there is a stout breeze. In doubles, this technique can't be used because you will have to fast-swing through the second bird.

If Skeet is the only shotgunning you will do, the sustained lead technique can make you a AAA-ranked shooter. I know, because I started with that method. Unfortunately, it caused problems in other wingshooting areas, and I had to go through the traumatic experience of "unlearning" this technique. Today, I shoot fast-swing for virtually everything except close-range incoming targets, where the sustained lead technique works very well.

With that said, I will now state that all of the leads given in this chapter dealing with the fundamentals of Skeet will be sustained leads, since those are the only leads that will be essentially the same for every shooter. For those wishing to learn the more effective fast-swing technique, just cut those leads in half as a starting point. You will quickly see if your body rhythm needs to be increased or decreased.

A Station-By-Station Look at Skeet

Station One

This station positions the shooter directly under the high house. Four targets are presented at this station, high and low house singles, and one pair of doubles (one bird from each house).

The high house target is easy but deceptive. It appears to be a straightaway shot, but because it is launched from above the shooter, and has a slight upward angle, it is not. You must actually lead this target by shooting underneath it. If you shoot it like a straightaway, you will miss it by going over and behind it every time!

To break this target, take a comfortable shooting position that aligns gun and body on the Eight Post. This advice will hold for virtually every station on the field, because it is advantageous to have your body set for the best shooting position at the point at which you will actually break the target. Since every target on the field is calibrated (if the trap machines are properly adjusted) to send the bird directly over

High house one requires the initial gun position to be at an upward angle so the barrel can be swung down and through the bird. The shooter fires when the muzzle is about six inches below the target.

the Eight Post, it makes sense for this to become your focal point. If the Eight Post is where you set up, you will be in position to break every station, with the possible exceptions of high house two and three, low house five and six, and station eight, which will all be explained as we reach them.

Once you are positioned, bring the muzzle up to about a 30-degree angle above horizontal and call for the bird. As soon as the bird appears over the muzzle, swing down and through the bird, triggering the shot when you see a 6-inch lead below it. Take this bird as quickly as you can, because if it is allowed to get beyond the Eight Post, it starts to drop rapidly and becomes a much tougher shot. "Riding" this bird will cause you to occasionally break the low house bird also, with the one shot, when shooting doubles at this station.

If you are having trouble with high house one, increase the gun angle to 45 degrees. This will cause you to swing faster to catch the bird, and often helps.

Low house one is easy. Again, align your body on the Eight Post and then bring the gun back to a point about four feet to the outside (left) of the house. On any incoming Skeet target, never align the gun directly on the trap house opening where the bird will emerge—it will temporarily blot out the

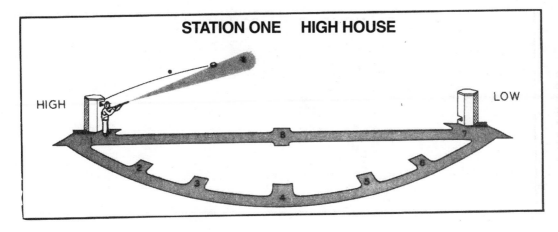

STATION ONE   HIGH HOUSE

HIGH

LOW

This deceptive target looks like a straightaway, but shooters must actually trigger the shot with the barrel below the target if they are to score.

Drawings Courtesy Winchester News Bureau

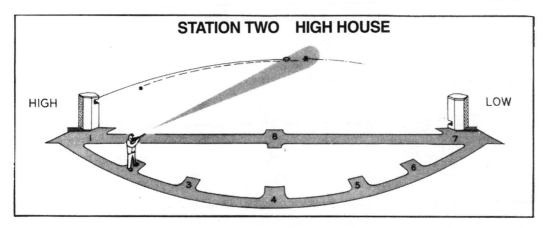

STATION ONE   LOW HOUSE

HIGH

LOW

Smart shooters are in no hurry to break this easy shot and allow it to reach the same point where they will shoot it as a double. It's easier to find it when you always look for it in the same place.

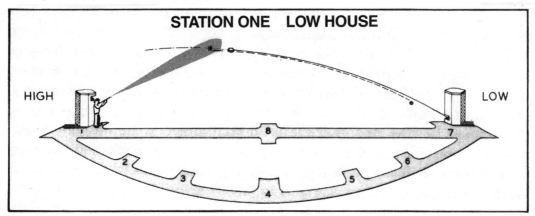

STATION TWO   HIGH HOUSE

HIGH

LOW

A tough shot for right-handed shooters, this requires a lot of lateral body movement and the shooter must drive forcefully through the target. Get sluggish here and you'll miss.

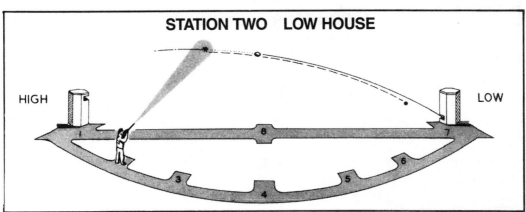

STATION TWO   LOW HOUSE

HIGH

LOW

This is very similar to the low house target from station one. Shoot it in the same place with just a slight increase in lead.

An easier angle than station two high house, this requires another foot of lead, but gives the shooter more time to get onto the bird.

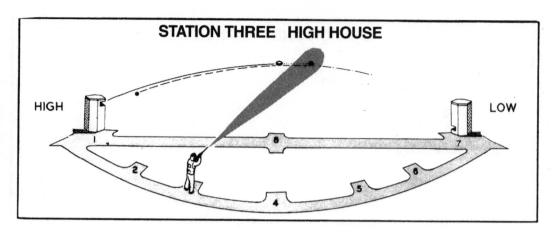

STATION THREE   HIGH HOUSE

This is one of the easier targets on the field when taken as a single. The shooter has plenty of time to find it and establish the correct lead.

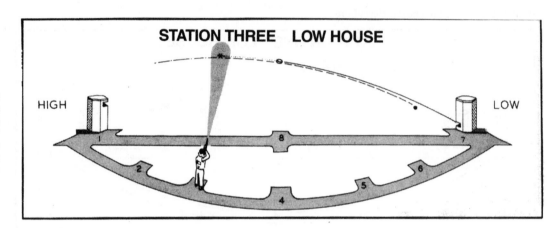

STATION THREE   LOW HOUSE

This is one of the longest shots you'll see on a Skeet field and tricks many sustained lead shooters who do not believe they need a 4-foot lead on a 21-yard target. Fast-swing shooters can cut that lead in half.

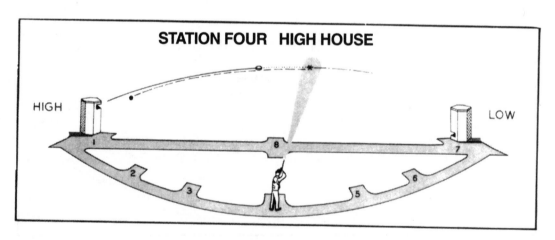

STATION FOUR   HIGH HOUSE

Virtually the same shot as from the high house, but in a different direction. If you break both station four targets near the Eight Post, you don't even have to change foot position.

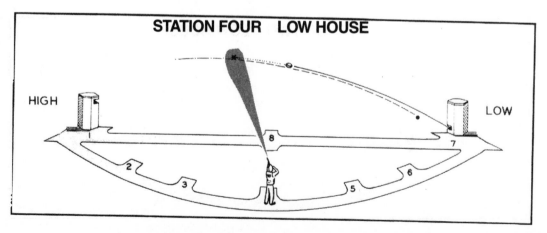

STATION FOUR   LOW HOUSE

bird as it emerges and will interfere with your ability to quickly pick it up.

Once the bird is released, swing smoothly with it, yet don't be in a hurry to break it. Veteran Skeet shooters want to break this target (along with low house two and high houses six and seven) in the same place they will break it during doubles. Let the target reach a point about 45 degrees off your left shoulder and take it there. The lead for this target is one foot.

If you get into the habit of shooting station one singles in this manner, doubles are a snap: take the high house quickly and when you come back for the low house you will find it right where you normally break it as a single.

ot the body to bring the gun about two-thirds the way back to the house. If you come too far back toward the house, you may not catch this target. Put the gun at the same elevation at which the bird will appear. Once the bird comes out, get onto it quickly with about 2½ feet of lead. You must follow through on this shot. Any slowing or stopping of the swing will result in a miss. That's true of any Skeet target, but especially so on high house two!

Low house two is much easier. Treat it just like low house one, and extend the lead to 18 to 24 inches. Let the bird get to a point almost equal with your position—that's where it will be during doubles.

This is a good starting position for the high house two target. Initial gun position should not be too close to the house. If so, the shooter may have trouble smoothly catching the bird.

Station Two

Four targets are again presented: high and low house singles and one set of doubles. This station, however, is not as easy as one.

The high house shot is, at least for me, one of the toughest targets on the field. It is a vicious quartering angle that must be taken quickly, and with a lot of lateral body movement. Right-handed shooters have trouble with this station because the body does not swing as well to the right as it does to the left.

Start by positioning on the Eight Post, or maybe just a bit to the right of it to give yourself a little more room to uncoil. Piv-

Doubles are the same as at the last station. Get on the outgoing target (high house) quickly, and come back to find the incoming low house right where you normally break it as a single.

If you are having a problem with high house two, the answer is to swing faster and shoot quicker. You have to be aggressive on this target.

Station Three

During a standard round of Skeet, only two targets are taken at this station, both singles, one each from the high house (first) and the low house. The high house is an outgoing quartering shot similar to high house two, but you have more time and it is an easier shot. Position on the Eight Post or a bit to the right of it, and give the bird 3 feet of lead.

The low house is an incomer, similar to low house two, but becomes more of a crossing shot due to the distance. Position as with low house two and give this target $3\frac{1}{2}$ feet of lead.

One problem with station three (along with four and five) is wind. If there is a breeze, these targets can do some serious dancing! It pays to develop the habit of getting onto these birds quickly. That will also help you when you play the Doubles game and find yourself taking doubles at these stations.

Station Four

Like station three, the shooter is presented with two singles. Both are direct crossing shots and are the longest one will see on a Skeet field. These birds are 21 yards away from the shooter when they cross the Eight Post. The lead for both houses is 4 feet.

I prefer to position on the Eight Post for both houses and try to break them as they cross the post. Some shooters use a different foot position for the high and low houses at this station (as well as three and five), but I do not concur because it causes problems when you shoot these stations in the Doubles game. As long as you are positioned on the Eight Post, you have all the range of movement you require for both singles and doubles.

Up to this point, shooters have been seeing new angles and shots at each station. As we move to station five, however, things begin to become familiar.

Station Five

This is nothing more than station three in reverse, with the high house becoming the incomer (and still shot first) and the low house becoming the outgoing target.

The high house is taken using the same $3\frac{1}{2}$-foot lead that was used on low house three. The low house is taken with the same 3-foot lead as high house three. Positioning on the Eight Post is the same.

The biggest difference is that the low house takes a more abrupt upward angle because of your proximity to it, and you must rise with it. Other than that, every bit of practice you take at station three helps you with station five, and vice versa.

Station Six

This is a reversed image of station two. The high house is shot first and is a gentle incomer, just like low house two. Body position is the same, as is the 18- to 24-inch lead used on low house two.

Low house six becomes the outgoing target and is a sharp and rapidly rising target. For right-handers, however, it is easier than the "Demon High House Two" because the body uncoils better to the left. Shoot it the same way, using the same body position and $2\frac{1}{2}$-foot lead.

For doubles, the outgoing low house is shot first, with the incoming high house taken as it draws in to a 45-degree angle to the shooter's right.

Shoot station six the same way you shot station two.

Station Seven

This is the easiest station on the field. The high house is shot first, but let it get close, and use a 1-foot lead.

The low house looks like a dead straightaway and, if you have a little upward angle in your initial gun position, it is. This target can be broken with no gun movement—position the gun and body on the Eight Post, elevate the gun barrel to a point about 8 feet above it, and if the trap is regulated properly the target will "appear" right over your front bead.

Pull the trigger—dead bird.

Doubles at this station are so easy one wonders why they even bother. Take the outgoing house with no gun movement and let the recoil ride the gun up to perfectly pick up the incoming bird. Piece of cake.

If you are looking to introduce a new shooter to Skeet and you want to build their confidence quickly, take them to station seven first.

Station Eight

Having completed our trip around the outside of the field, it is now time to step inside and face two of what seem to be the most intimidating targets on the field.

The high and low house eight targets are not "gimmees,"

All Skeet targets are directed to fly over the center stake, or "Eight Post." This is normally where a shooter will want to take his natural point of aim on all stations except eight.

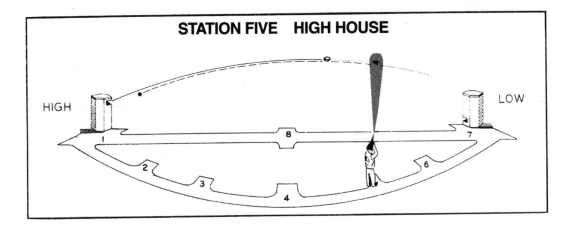

STATION FIVE HIGH HOUSE

This is almost the mirror image of the station three low house. The lead is the same.

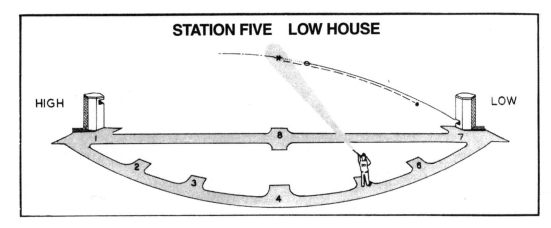

STATION FIVE LOW HOUSE

Very similar to the station three high house except the target is usually climbing a little more. The leads are the same and the shooter must concentrate on swinging up and through the target.

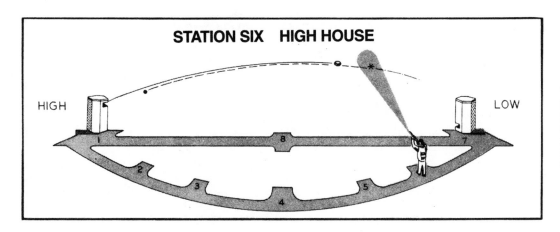

STATION SIX HIGH HOUSE

This is as easy as the station two low house, although the target is often falling slightly, depending upon the wind direction.

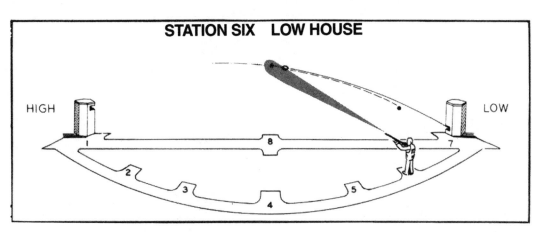

STATION SIX LOW HOUSE

Left-handed shooters have the same problem with this target that right-handers do on the station two high house. You must swing quickly through this target and trigger the shot as soon as you have your lead. If you hesitate, you'll lose this bird.

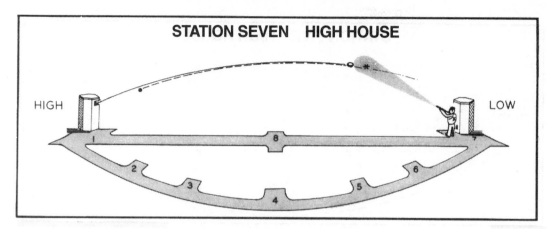

STATION SEVEN HIGH HOUSE

One of the easiest shots on the field, this target should be broken in the same place you will see it as a double.

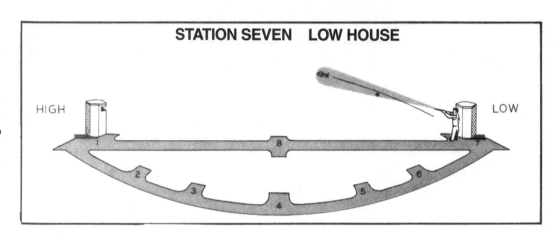

STATION SEVEN LOW HOUSE

This is the only target on a Skeet field that can consistently be broken with no gun movement. It's a true "gimmee!"

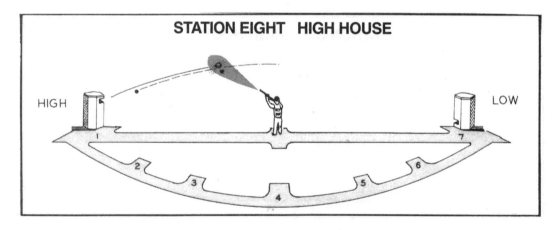

STATION EIGHT HIGH HOUSE

More intimidating than it looks, shooters should swing fast through this target and trigger the shot as soon as the muzzle reaches the leading edge of the bird.

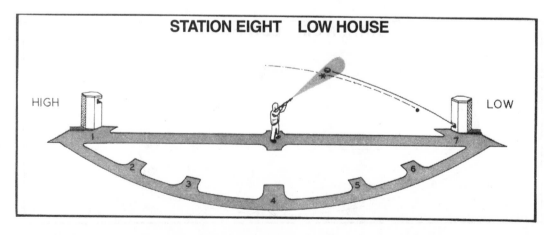

STATION EIGHT LOW HOUSE

The closest shot on a Skeet field, with many birds broken 4 yards off the muzzle. Fast-swing through the target and trigger the shot as soon as the muzzle blots out the bird.

Low house seven is the only station on the field where the target can be consistently broken without gun movement. This shooter shows the proper gun hold angle to allow the bird to magically appear over the bead. Pull the trigger and it's dead!

Beginning shooters often place the gun muzzle right in the house window on station eight, but this will block out the initial visual acquisition of the bird. As Bob Lee demonstrates, the gun hold should be to the outside of the window, and at the same elevation. This lets him quickly see the bird and swing through it.

but they are not nearly as tough as they look and you have more time to shoot them than you might think.

The reason these two targets are so intimidating is because they are so close. In years past, some shooters even used special "spreader" loads to handle them. Once shooters found out how easy these targets were to break, however, the station eight birds lost their intimidation factor.

High house eight is taken by positioning gun and body right on the trap house opening, then moving the gun 4 feet to the right of the trap house. As the bird comes out, swing quickly up and through it, triggering the shot just as the gun muzzle passes the bird and shows just a hint of daylight between bird and muzzle.

The low house is shot by positioning on the opening and then moving the barrel 3 feet to the left of the house. When the bird comes at you, swing up and through and break the shot the moment the muzzle blots out the bird.

These targets are that simple.

If you have been counting shells, you will know that we have only fired twenty-four of our twenty-five rounds. The last round is called the "option round" and is fired at the first target missed during the round. If you get to low house eight without a miss, the last round is fired as a second shot on that station.

If you have never run 25 straight before, it is the toughest shot on the field. If you make it, it is also the most satisfying.

Getting to that point, however, takes proper equipment and intelligent practice.

All-Important Practice

The foregoing angles, leads and body positions provide all the information required to consistently break every target on the field. In order to make use of that information, though, a shooter must see enough of those targets, and break them, in order to build the positive subconscious images needed for success. There are good and bad ways to do that.

The worst, in my opinion, is for a new shooter to simply fall in with a squad and start shooting. This is because the new shooter will see new angles and shots at each station. Before he can begin to understand and master them, he is whisked off to the next station where the "new" starts all over again. Along the way he, or she, will get a lot of well-intentioned advice from the other shooters on the squad, yet much of it will be confusing and sometimes contradictory. That makes for a very poor learning environment in any situation.

The most effective way to teach (or learn) Skeet, and the most efficient in terms of time and ammunition spent, is to start on one particular shot and keep on working with it until it is burned into the subconscious. Then move to the next.

My preferred system is to begin working on the easy incoming shots and ignore everything else for a while. This builds a shooter's confidence and begins to demonstrate the symmetrical nature of the game.

I start teaching at station one and work on the low house until the shooter has that down pat. It sometimes takes as few as four or five shells! Once the shooter has a solid feel for that target, I move to low house two. It is virtually identical, except for the lead, and the positive experience with low house one is a plus at low house two. Then we go to low house three and do it again.

Shifting to stations five, six and seven, we now work on the incoming high houses until the shooter has a firm grasp of all these shots.

When this point is reached, I move to station four to work on both high and low houses. The leads are identical, and these shots are similar to those the student has already learned at stations three and five. This also gets the student used to swinging quickly on fast-moving targets, because until now all shots have been lazy incomers. Station four is, in my mind, the perfect spot to make the shift from deliberately taking incomers to aggressively pursuing outgoing birds.

After that it is back around to stations three, two and one, and then over to five, six and seven for work on the outgoing targets. Station eight comes next, and the final lesson is putting it all together with doubles.

Using this approach, the time required to give a new shooter a solid, working knowledge of the game can be reduced from months to weeks. I have seen some students expend as little as ten boxes of shells in practice, and then go out and pop twenty-one to twenty-three birds the first time they shoot a complete round!

Instruction like this, assuming a competent instructor, can also prevent the shooter from acquiring bad habits at the start, which can do some serious damage to a shooter's scores.

Common Errors

Even with this, however, a shooter must still execute the fundamentals properly in order to score. Sometimes this does not happen. There are three very common ways to miss even the easiest Skeet target and they will, on occasion, plague shooters at almost any level of skill.

The most common, in all likelihood, is lifting the head from the stock. Not surprisingly, this seems to be the bane of new shooters and those who have taken a lot of time off from the game. Under these conditions the targets will seem to be the size of aspirin tablets moving at about the speed of a Patriot missile! New shooters often pop their heads off the stock to get "a better look" or to just find the target. When the head comes off the stock, the shot charge goes high every time.

There is no quick and easy cure for this, other than to constantly remind yourself to "Love Thy Wood." Take plenty of care when mounting the gun to assure a proper cheek weld with the stock. That cheek weld is critical to success in any wingshooting endeavor, and a shooting basic that must be constantly worked on and reinforced.

Stopping the swing is another quick way to blow a target and, surprisingly, this often seems to affect mid-level shooters the most. It can be especially prevalent among shooters who rely completely on the sustained lead technique, since this can, at times, encourage indecision and hesitation.

New shooters see targets moving so swiftly that they must swing very quickly to catch them, and this forces them to swing through the target. Once a shooter gains some experi-ence, however, two things seem to happen at the same time: the targets suddenly grow much larger and they seem to slow down a lot.

The shooter now knows he has plenty of time and becomes more concerned with getting "just the right lead." The gun swings through the target, the correct lead is obtained, analyzed, trimmed up a bit, and then the subconscious says "We've got it!"

Then, just as the trigger gets slapped the gun gets stopped, and the shot charge sails harmlessly behind the target.

The best way to avoid that is to think of wingshooting in the same light as many other sports: *one must follow through.*

Think of it this way: If a golfer stops his swing the moment his club makes contact with the ball; or a bowler stops his arm movement when he lays the ball down on the alley; or a tennis player quits when the racket strikes the ball; what would the results be? Nothing. Zip. *Nada.* No follow through equals no results.

Shotgun shooting isn't any different. In order to hit an aerial target, the gun must be moving at the moment the shot is triggered, and it must continue to follow right on through the target. If you are troubled by stopping your swing, try following the broken pieces and mentally take a second shot. If you develop the habit of staying with the broken pieces after the shot, even if for just a fraction of a second, you won't have to worry about stopping your swing.

The last of the common problems is simply not being ready when you call for the bird. Believe it or not, this can often sneak up on experienced shooters without warning.

What happens is this: you've broken that target hundreds, maybe even thousands of times; you could do it in your sleep, and with one hand. You never miss that bird. Then you step to the shooting pad, let your mind drift, and when the bird comes out you are totally unprepared. Your timing is completely off and the bird sails away unscathed.

I watched a world class shooter do this at a national championship one time, and he cheerfully admitted his gaffe afterward. He stepped to the shooting pad, took a moment to admire an airplane flying overhead, called for the bird, and found his mind was still on the airplane. He missed.

Everyone will develop his own little routine when he steps onto the pad. Some squiggle around. Some adjust their shooting vest or glasses. I sweep all the little bits of broken targets off the pad with my foot. The point is, we all do it. While it may look a little quirky to others, it is actually a very important part of our shooting game—it is the subconscious mind's way of preparing us to execute the shot. Let the subconscious do its job. If you have a comfortable "pad routine," don't deviate from it or you'll short-circuit your own success.

When you are about to conduct an evolution that requires a number of complicated body movements and mental decisions that must happen in about 1.2 seconds, your subconscious mind is the best friend you've got. Don't get in its way.

Combine that with an understanding of the proper leads and angles, and an effective practice regime that lets your subconscious absorb them, and you'll find that Skeet can indeed be simple.

The Doubles Game

Many shooters use a slightly heavier load or heavier shot for the second bird on doubles at the mid-field stations, because these targets are often taken at longer than normal ranges.

THERE WAS A time when this wasn't true, but if you want to win a trophy in Skeet today, you will have to survive a shoot-off, and it will be the doubles version of the game. For that matter, if you are looking for the "High Overall" trophy, you'll have to shoot Doubles anyway, so you may as well start preparing for it now.

There are stations in regular Skeet where doubles (a pair of targets launched simultaneously from the high and low house) are shot. This is a normal part of the game, and one that any shooter will learn to handle simply by shooting Skeet. When you get to the actual game of Doubles, however, you will find that it is slightly different and that you will shoot two different variations of it: regular Doubles and shoot-off doubles. We'll start discussing how different they are with the first version.

Regular Doubles is a scheduled event in any Skeet tournament. It will usually be written into the program as "25 pairs" or "50 pairs." The former means it is a fifty-round match, while the latter listing calls for 100 rounds. It is shot as a 12-gauge event, although that does not stop shooters from using gauges smaller than that. In fact, the 20-gauge gun is currently the tool of choice among top shooters, for reasons that have been explained in a previous chapter.

Regular Doubles

Regular Doubles is played as follows: shooters start at station one and are presented with the same pair of doubles they will see in standard Skeet. You shoot the high house bird first, and you only shoot the one pair at this station. Moving to station two the shooter sees the same thing—basic Skeet doubles, with the high house again shot first. By now you have fired four shots. Then you move on to station three, where the game starts to change.

In standard Skeet, station three is a pair of singles from the high and low house. In the Doubles game, you get both at once, with the high house taken first. Move to station four and the situation repeats itself.

On station five you again have two birds at once, but this

time the outgoing bird (now the low house) should be taken first. Stations six and seven offer one pair of doubles, just the same as in a standard Skeet round.

Of course, we haven't fired all of our shells yet, so we now make a reverse trip around the field. From station seven we go back to six and repeat the doubles presentation there, then we go back to five and do it again.

When we reach station four on the return swing (for the second time) a major change takes place. Now the rules require the low house bird be taken first, and this can be one of the toughest shots on the Skeet field. The reason is simple: This is the only time you will ever shoot the low bird first on station four and it does terrible things to your subconscious computer.

Moving back to three, things get normal again and we shoot the high house first, as we do at station two.

That completes the first half of a Doubles round and requires twenty-four shells. The second half is identical to the first, except that we now finish on station one, instead of two, in order to get rid of those last two rounds.

Shoot-Off Doubles

Shoot-off doubles is a condensed version of this game. Here, shooters move between stations three, four and five with the order of the targets the same: high house always first at three, low house always first at five, and alternating between high and low house at four. This will continue until one shooter has not missed. He wins.

Shoot-off doubles was created when Skeet scores began to become so perfect that a standard 100-bird match would see several shooters with the same upper level score. It was simply a way to decrease the amount of time it would take to conduct a shoot-off and determine a winner in that event. What makes shoot-off doubles so tough is the fact that they are shot in the gauge class the shooters used to get to the shoot-off.

If several shooters tie in the 410 class, they will have to shoot doubles with the 410, although some clubs will run a standard round of Doubles first, and then shoot-off doubles for any shooters who survive that. In the 12-, 20- and 28-gauge events, you can expect to go directly to shoot-off doubles in those gauges.

How to Shoot Doubles

Doubles intimidates many shooters, but it shouldn't. In fact, regardless of the doubles game you are shooting—shoot-off or regular—there are only three stations that offer anything different from what you've already seen in standard Skeet: stations three, four and five. For that reason, there is no purpose served by making any alterations to your shooting style for stations one, two, six and seven—shoot them like you always do. You will want to make some changes for three, four and five, and here's how to adjust for the different presentations you'll see on those.

Station three: the normal foot position on the three mid-field crossing stations (three, four and five) would have the body aligned to break both birds right over the center stake. Some top shooters, when shooting these stations as singles in the regular round, will shift their foot position for each of the two birds, but I don't recommend that unless you have shot long enough to positively know it benefits you.

With the body aligned on the Eight Post (stake), you are in

Two targets traveling in opposite directions at high speed make
Doubles from stations three, four and five extremely challenging.

Any shooter who intends to win should begin practicing Doubles from stations three, four, and five, as soon as possible. Most class and match wins are determined in a shoot-off from these three stations.

position to utilize your full range of body movement to break each single over the stake. Unfortunately, in Doubles, this foot position can hinder you. There aren't more than a handful of shooters that I have seen who can shoot fast enough to take both the first bird and the second with their body aligned on the stake. The second (low house bird) is invariably going to get beyond the stake, and if the stake is where your body is aligned you may have trouble picking the target up and catching it.

This is a situation where you know the second bird is going to be tough, and experienced shooters will usually fudge their body position to favor that bird.

It becomes a matter of individual reaction time and shooting style, but every shooter will benefit by shifting his basic station three position in the Doubles round toward the high house side of the stake. I normally start new shooters out with an alignment position almost halfway back to the high house, and see where we might want to fine tune it from there. This will bind the body up slightly on the outgoing first bird (high house), but gives perfect position on the second. Some shooters can handle the slightly restricted swing on the high house and some can't. Those who have trouble catching the high house bird may have to start easing their gun position back toward the stake.

You don't have to wait to shoot a Doubles round to find out if this is the case with your shooting rhythm. You can practice this while shooting standard Skeet. Simply adjust the initial gun position back toward the high house on singles at station three until you find the point at which you are too bound up to take high house three. Once you find what your own body's limitations are, you can begin adjusting your gun position to give you the best shot.

Station four Doubles will show shooters the longest shots seen on a Skeet field, and is one of the greatest challenges of the game.

The first time we visit station four we have a similar situation, wherein the high house is shot first and the low house can get away from you. The same readjustment of the body to the high house side of the field is recommended.

The second time we see station four it's a different situation. Now the low house is first. If you discount the subcon-

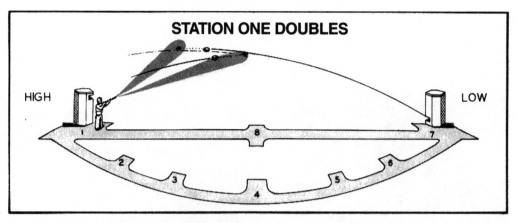

STATION ONE DOUBLES

The high house target is taken first with normal lead and the gun is swung back to break the low house target at an angle of about 45 degrees to the shooter's left.

Drawings Courtesy Winchester News Bureau

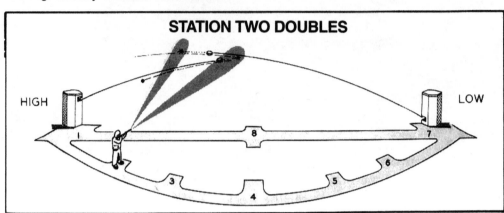

STATION TWO DOUBLES

High house target first, with low house target broken at the same point as it would be taken during singles.

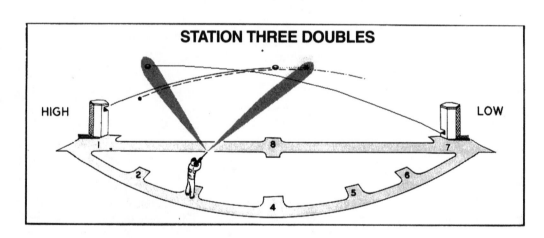

STATION THREE DOUBLES

The high house target must be taken quickly in order to get the gun back to the low house target. Shooters often fudge their natural point of aim to the high house side of the field in order to have sufficient swing room for the low house target, which is usually taken beyond its normal position when shot as a single.

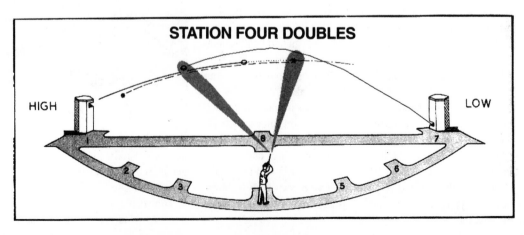

STATION FOUR DOUBLES

This is considered the most difficult station in doubles since the high house is taken first the first time the station is shot, and the low house taken first the second time through.

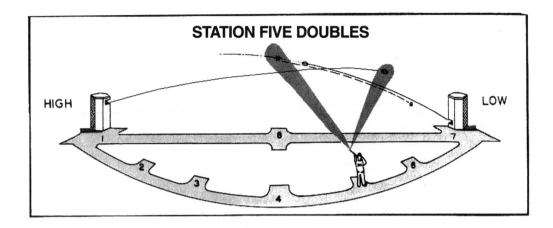

STATION FIVE DOUBLES

HIGH   LOW

The low house is taken first, and many shooters will shift their natural point of aim to the low house side of the field to increase the swing distance on the second bird. A tail wind will cause the high house bird to hunt the ground quickly, requiring the shooter to speed up his timing.

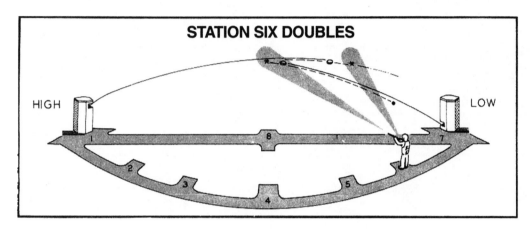

STATION SIX DOUBLES

HIGH   LOW

The low house target is taken first and the incoming high house broken at about a 45-degree angle to the shooter's right. This can be a difficult shot for left-handed shooters.

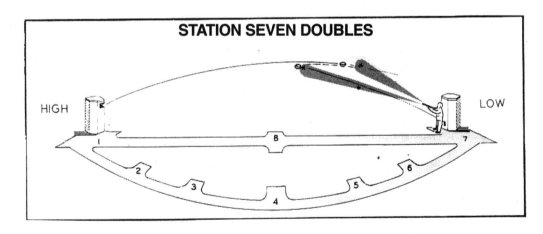

STATION SEVEN DOUBLES

HIGH   LOW

This is the easiest Double shot on the field. With proper gun hold position the low house bird can be taken without moving the gun, and the recoil will lift the gun into the perfect position to pick up the high house target.

scious reaction to shooting the low house bird first, this is actually not as tough a shot as shooting the high house bird first. The reason is that when the high house is taken second its normally higher trajectory tends to keep it in the air a bit longer than the low bird. Many shooters find they can use a normal "align on the stake" position here and get away with it. Others find that only a slight fudging toward the low house is all that is needed to get back smoothly on high four for the second shot.

Station four is, however, one Skeet station where a heavier second load is a major asset. Regardless of where you catch the second bird at station four, it is going to be one of the longest shots you will see on a Skeet field. You are pushing

the range at which #9 shot will reliably break a target. I favor a 1 1/8-ounce 12-gauge load of #8 1/2 shot, or a 1-ounce load of the same if I am shooting the event with a tubed 20-gauge. The heavier shot pellets will get you an extra bird now and then, and that is sometimes enough to win.

A number of shooters who routinely opt for the 20-gauge in this event use a full 1-ounce load of #8 1/2 for all of their doubles shots, simply to remove the possibility of confusing different shot size loads during the pressure of a shoot-off. They know the importance of a heavier load for the second shot on the middle stations and don't want to take the chance of not getting one in the gun. For the same reason, it is not at all uncommon for experienced competitors to have a few #8 1/2

Station six is an easier shot for right-handed shooters than for left-ies, because they have a better swing to that side. It still requires a quick and aggressive swing.

loads made up for the 28-gauge and 410 as well. They may not use them in regular Skeet, but if they do have a good day in those gauges, they know they'll have to run them in the shoot-off, and the heavier loads can come in very handy.

Station five is similar to station four on the second swing. The high house becomes the second bird and its trajectory favors the shooter. You do not need to fudge as much toward the low house from a basic "align on the Eight Post" position, but some shooters find it does help to edge to the low house side slightly.

This shift in body position, as mentioned earlier, is a personal matter. There is no one correct foot position for every shooter because body shapes, swing speeds and reflexes are different. You accept the fact that favoring the second bird is a good idea, and then begin experimenting with your foot position until you find the one that works best for you.

One way you can definitely help yourself in the Doubles game is to change the way you shoot singles in regular Skeet. If you have ever watched a top shooter, you will see that he takes every mid-field crossing shot just as soon as he can. In fact, these competitors will try to break them before they get to the stake. This is obviously an asset in the Doubles game, because the faster you can break the first bird the more time you have for the second, and the less you have to fudge your gun position for it.

Fast shooting also becomes an asset on a windy day. It takes a very strong wind to affect the flight path of a Skeet target before it gets to the stake because it is still under the influence of the trap velocity. By the time it gets to the stake, however, the wind will catch it and you may find it does some terrible things to it. If you shoot Doubles in a laid back, "ride the target forever" mode, you'll get murdered if the wind comes up. You have to be a little excited and pumped up to shoot good Doubles.

Doubles is a different game, but not radically so. It isn't a great deal more difficult than standard Skeet. In fact, the classification scores show that over the course of 100 rounds, Doubles is only about one bird harder.

Doubles Classification 12-gauge only

Class	Average
AAA	97% and over
AA	95% to 96.99%
A	91% to 94.99%
B	85% to 90.99%
C	80% to 84.99%
D	under 80%

It is, however, a game one will have to master if he intends to advance to the upper levels of the sport. If you are going to win any trophies in Skeet today, you'll have to do it in a shoot-off, and Doubles will be the game.

International Skeet

International Skeet is one of the author's favorite shotgun sports and he regards it as one the most challenging games available to shotgunners.

THE GAME WE shoot as American Skeet has been called, and rightly so, the easiest of the various clay target games to master. That lack of real challenge hasn't rested very well with our English and European counterparts and, as a result, they have modified the game into a slightly different and infinitely more difficult version, for International competition. Here's a look at what our shooters face in World Cup and Olympic competition.

International Skeet is shot on the same field as the American version, with all distances and dimensions identical but the target order and speed different.

Firing Order

On station one, International shooters first take a high house single, and then a pair of doubles. As in American Skeet, the high house is shot first. There is no single target from the low house, which is considered to be one of the easiest shots in Skeet. Moving to station two, the same procedure is repeated with a single high house and a pair of doubles.

At station three, the shooter is presented with a single from each house, and then a pair of doubles, with the high house target taken first. On station four the procedure is the same. At station five, we again get a pair of singles, with the high house target taken first, and then a pair of doubles, with the low house taken first.

Moving to station six, we have a single from the low house, and a pair of doubles, with the low house taken first. At station seven, single targets are dispensed with entirely, and the shooter takes one pair of doubles, with the low house shot first.

On station eight, the shooter will load one shell and take a single from the high house. At that point the shooter will unload the gun, turn completely around to the low house (turning to the outside of the field in a clockwise direction), load a single shell, and take the low house single. There is no "option round" as there is in American Skeet.

What the course of fire does is delete the easiest shots in American Skeet (low houses one, two, seven and high houses six and seven) and replace them with the toughest shots on the

International Skeet is shot on the same field as the American version, but it is a totally different game. The complexity and target speeds require top-notch gun handling and the right mental attitude.

Competitors are allowed to bring the gun to their shoulder for a brief pre-target sight picture only at stations one and eight, and then must immediately return to the ready position before calling for the target.

Target Speed

International Skeet targets are also cranked up to a higher speed for their legal setting. They move about 5 mph faster than American targets. This requires that they be more stoutly constructed to take the higher launch velocity and, in addition to being made from harder materials, they also have a reinforcing ring on the throwing ring. How tough are they? Coach Lloyd Woodhouse, of the United States Shooting Team (USST) told me of a picture he has from a competition in Cuba that shows him standing with all of his 195 pounds on one foot atop a target, and the target is just fine!

It is not uncommon to find whole unbroken targets on an International field that have a few holes punched completely through them. It takes a solid, center-pattern hit to get that all-important "visible piece."

The last significant difference between the two Skeet games are the load and gauge. International Skeet is shot almost exclusively with the 12-gauge, while American Skeet uses the

USAMU shooter Sgt. Shawn Dulohery demonstrates proper low gun hold for International Skeet. Note contrasting strip on his vest at the hip. The gun must touch this until the bird actually appears. Moving the gun early results in a lost bird! (U.S. Army photo by Joseph J. Johnson)

field, which are doubles from three, four and five. In effect, it takes away the "gimmees" and incorporates shoot-off doubles into the basic round.

That alone tends to prevent a lot of perfect scores. But wait, it gets tougher!

Gun Position

International Skeet is shot from a low gun position, and when they say low they aren't kidding! Competitors must have a permanent contrasting strip (about 1 inch wide and 9³/₄ inches long) from the side to the front of the outer shooting garment placed at the top of the shooter's hip line. The stock of the gun must touch this line at the low gun "ready" position, and the gun cannot be moved from it until the target actually appears. You basically have the gun butt on the hip when you call for the target, and, as in Sporting Clays, the target release device is equipped with a variable delay of up to 3 seconds.

Compared to the ready position in Sporting Clays, International Skeet is much lower and requires more gun-handling skills.

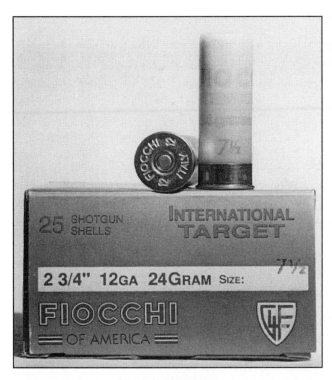

Some shooters favor the #7½, 24-gram International load for the second shot at doubles from the mid-field stations to increase target-breaking power on these longer targets.

Federal's #8½ International load was developed with input from the U.S. Shooting Team, and has become one of their favorites. Author likes it for many Sporting Clays shots as well.

12, 20, 28 and 410. The maximum allowable load for International is a mere 24 grams (about ⁷/₈-ounce) with a maximum shot size of #7½.

Most of the USST shooters favor loads in size #8½, and they use the excellent International loads made by Federal Cartridge Co. However, at least one shooter I know on the team opts for the #7½ load for the second shot on doubles from stations three, four and five. The #8½ shot, incidentally, is an excellent doubles load for American Skeet, as well as for many shots in Sporting Clays. Despite the rather diminutive shot charge, this Federal load is an awesome performer and will really crush a target. Recoil is light, and its 1330 fps velocity gets it to the target quickly. It's a real jewel!

Guns and Gear

Guns for International Skeet are little different from the 12-gauge guns used for our version of the game. One sees both over/unders and gas-operated semi-autos in competition, although the stackbarrel guns do predominate. The standard Skeet constriction of .004- to .005-inch is considered the best bet. The preferred barrel length for the over/unders falls right within the 28- to 32-inch range that we see on the Skeet fields in this country. One difference is that ported guns may not be used in International competition, but given the gentle recoil of the 24-gram load, they're not really much of an asset anyway.

The only significant difference is in the recoil pad. Because of the extreme low ready position, the pad must be smoothly radiused at the top to aid in a smoother gun mount. Most shooters also round off the inner edge. This is also common in

International targets are more stoutly constructed than their American counterparts in order to survive the higher launching velocity. They require a solid hit to break.

Sporting Clays. Some competitors go a bit farther and apply a slick-surfaced PVC tape to the sides, and sometimes to the top of the pad to remove that sticky "pencil eraser" feel that can cause drag on the shooting vest with some types of pads.

When it comes to selecting a shooting vest, the International style, which has a slick-faced shooting pad extending com-

97

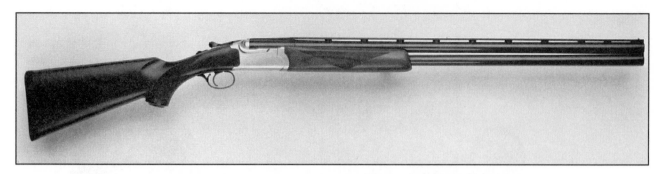

Many of the country's top International Skeet shooters are beginning to adopt some of the newer over/unders designed for Sporting Clays, like this Ruger, instead of more traditional Skeet guns. The increase in barrel length and improved balance are a plus on high-speed targets.

pletely down the gun-mount side, is the overwhelming favorite.

Eye and ear protection is mandatory and, as in American-style Skeet, is a fine idea because you can get pelted with an occasional target piece during a round. Some competitors are taking a page from their Sporting Clays counterparts and opting for electronic ear plugs. These contain an electronic cutoff circuit that shuts out noise levels above a certain decibel level, yet amplifies low-level sounds. Many instructors wear them because it makes their teaching job easier and allows better communication with their shooters. On the International and Sporting Clays fields, they have another advantage in that they can amplify sounds enough to actually let you hear most trap machines release the target. To my way of thinking, that is of no small importance!

The variable target delay of up to 3 seconds can result in a significant change in the timing of a shooter who is used to having the target appear immediately when he calls for it. The target may come immediately, or may be delayed long enough to bring on the jitters. With conventional ear plugs the only target acquisi-

tion device the shooter has is visual. In the real world, we tend to blend all of our senses into one system. With the amplification powers of electronic ear plugs, we can now use both sight and sound to acquire the target. These can be a significant advantage to some shooters, and they are now commonly accepted among Sporting Clays shooters. I suspect this new technology will work its way onto the International fields, as well.

Shooting Tips
for International Skeet

International Skeet is far more complex and challenging than the American version. Not surprisingly, it can create problems for those shooters used to the tamer American sport.

"The biggest problem for new shooters is getting the smooth and consistent gun mount down pat," says Lloyd Woodhouse, who has been teaching our Olympic shooters the finer points of scattergunning for almost a decade. "Gun handling is critical in this game, and it must become a subconscious learned response. That can take a lot of practice, and a lot of shooting."

Station seven is one of the easier shots on the International Skeet field—if one could consider any of them easy—because only a single pair of doubles is taken here, and the low house bird is a dead straightaway.

Doubles from the mid-field stations require very fast shooting to catch the second target because of the higher speed of International targets. If you lag you lose!

Interestingly, Woodhouse and his assistant coaches have developed a training system that is quite similar to the one I use to teach new shooters the American version of the game. It works on the principle of starting with the easy shots to build the shooter's confidence, and gradually progresses to the more difficult shots. Woodhouse calls it "stage training."

"The theory," Woodhouse explains, "is to set the stage for success, and this works well to develop gun handling skills. We would start a new shooter off with a pair of low house station one single targets. This is a very easy shot and gives the shooter 1.4 to 1.6 seconds to mount the gun. Then we move to station two and shoot low houses again. Once the shooter is comfortable with this, we move to stations six and seven and shoot the incoming high houses. All of these are easy targets that give the shooter the maximum amount of time to mount the gun. This insures that the shooter experiences success.

"Our next stage," he continues, "is to go back to station one and start working our way through the stations taking just the low houses. As we reach stations four through seven, we are now gradually decreasing the 'time look' at the targets and requiring the shooter to increase the speed of the gun mount, but we do start with the easy targets and build the shooter's confidence before we begin asking more of him, or her. There is a very significant difference in the time element for gun mounting between a low house one and a low house six.

"By slowly decreasing the amount of time the shooter has to consciously think out and execute the gun mount," he notes, "we get the mount so rigidly built that it does become a subconscious learned response. That lets the shooter keep the conscious mind on important things like acquiring the target, and executing a smooth swing and follow-through."

Sgt. Shawn Dulohery of the elite U.S. Army Marksmanship Unit (USAMU) is poised for a quick shot on station seven doubles. If the first bird is not taken quickly, the second bird will fly off the field before the shooter can get to it. (U.S. Army photo by Joseph J. Johnson)

The combination of a variable delay, increased target speed and low gun position makes International Skeet far more challenging than the American version. On station eight the shooter has about .4-second to react and break the target!

Developing a fluid gun mount is critical in this game, as well as in Sporting Clays. It is easier if one starts with the proper hand position on the gun. In that respect, regardless of the type of shotgunning you do, the following advice from our Olympic Team coach is well worth reading.

"Biomechanically," Woodhouse explains, "if you put the elbow of your leading hand directly below the gun, like a rifleman's stance, you have the greatest leverage for moving the gun up and down, but the weakest leverage for moving the gun from side to side. If you move that elbow out to a 90-degree angle from the gun, you now have the maximum leverage for side movement, but the weakest leverage for up and down movement. We find that an elbow position of 45 degrees gives us the best compromise for effective movement in both directions, and that is where we like to start a shooter. After that, we can fine tune the position over time.

"The same is true for moving the hand forward and back on the forearm," he continues. "If the hand is way out on the forearm, the elbow is almost straight. If you move it back almost to the trigger guard, then the elbow is bent too much. In that position your arm can support a lot of weight. If you move the hand forward and straighten your elbow, then you won't be able to hold as much weight. The farther back your hand is on the forearm, the heavier the muzzle seems and the more it has a tendency to whip. If the hand is moved way out on the forearm you have very positive control over the muzzle, but minimum strength to move it. By starting with the 45-degree elbow position, you automatically adjust the forearm hand to the best compromise position."

Woodhouse adds, "Many American-style Skeet shooters not only have the forearm elbow out to almost a 90-degree angle, but stick the trigger hand elbow out the same way also. They can get away with this because from a pre-mounted gun position they really only have to move the gun on a horizontal line, unless, of course, the wind is blowing and making the targets rise and fall above and below their normal track. When that happens, the wind eats these shooters up because they don't have the biomechanical leverage to quickly and precisely adjust their elevation."

Another problem many American-style shooters have with International Skeet is in their initial body position when calling for the target. As in American Skeet, the International shooter will take his natural point of aim where he expects to break the target. That will vary with the targets, although the center stake (Eight Post) is a good place to start for singles on stations one through seven. For doubles on stations three, four and five, it doesn't hurt to fudge that natural point of aim toward the more difficult target, which will be the second bird. The problem arises when the shooter pivots his upper body back to the house for his initial acquisition of the target.

"I have yet to see an American-style Skeet shooter who shoots a sustained lead, which is what I teach my shooters, who didn't have to make adjustments in that body position for the International game," says Coach Woodhouse. "Normally, you would adjust your visual acquisition point a little farther out from the house because the targets come out a little quicker. Many American shooters will take an initial gun hold position on a line just about parallel with the face of the house, or a little inside that. We recommend they increase that to about 10 to 20 degrees farther toward the center of the field."

Fast-swing shooters, like the author, will find that is not always necessary. They can often take their normal position.

The exception to that is station eight. This is one case where the increased target speed, combined with the low gun position, will require the shooter to compensate. Both the high and the low houses will send their targets to the boundary stake in about $^6/_{10}$-second. Shooters must take the target inside that, normally in about $^4/_{10}$-second. That is not much time to mount the gun, acquire the target and see the lead! Adjusting your foot position can help here.

The low house eight target in International skeet is one of the most intimidating targets a shooter will face in any game. Author's shooting partner, Bob Lee, takes a moment to compose himself before "facing the beast." The bird will fly nearly into his face from the low house window.

The only places on the field the shooter is allowed to raise his gun to the shoulder for a sight picture are stations one and eight. The gun must then be returned to the legal hold position before calling for the bird.

"One problem right-handed shooters often have with station eight," according to Woodhouse, "is that they often face too far into the house. Your natural point of aim comes into play big-time here, because these shots are subconscious—there is no real time for thought. If you were to take the distance from the center stake back to the house window and divide it into thirds, two-thirds of the way back to the stake is where most people will break those targets. That should be the natural point of aim, that circle of air two-thirds of the way back to the stake. The initial acquisition position should have the upper body pivoted back to a point just outside the house. Many shooters tend to look into these houses—crowding them—too much and it will hurt on these targets."

One area where shooters won't have to make many adjustments on is their leads. Despite the targets' increased speed, the leads remain virtually the same. The increased gun speed required to align with the target, whether the shooter uses the sustained lead or the fast-swing technique, will compensate for the increased target speed.

Surprisingly, one of the biggest factors that can adversely affect skilled shooters making the transition from American Skeet to International is not physical, it's mental.

"One of the most important things a shooter has to condition his mind to accept in this game is that he is not going to shoot many 100 straights," Woodhouse states. "In American Skeet, if you shoot a 99x100 in a major match, you can go home. There will be shooters who have shot perfect scores and they will settle things in a shoot-off, but not in International Skeet. You can miss a target and still win the match—even the best will miss. A shooter must accept that and then develop the mental discipline to miss a target and still maintain the focus. That shooter must realize the he or she is still in contention, and get right back down to business. I spend a lot of time working on just that mental aspect with our shooters, and it is very important if you want to win."

While International Skeet is not nearly as popular in this country as is our more sedate version, I much prefer it. This is a game that will truly test your skills.

International Skeet Classification

Class	Average
Master (AA)	95.00% and up
A	87.00 - 94.99%
B	81.00 - 86.99%
C	75.00 - 80.99%
D	below 75.00%

chapter sixteen

Skeet's Finer Points

SKEET IS A game that encourages, and indeed demands, virtual perfection if one is to win. Achieving that level of perfection requires proper training, equipment and practice. In previous chapters we've discussed equipment and basic training along with the proper techniques. Here, we'll let two of the South's top Skeet shooters explain how they put those factors together to win.

Roy Dear is a AAA-class shooter and as a perennial member of Florida's All-America team has achieved the enviable goal of shooting 400x400 (100 straight with each of the four gauges) in a registered match. Among his many wins are U.S. Open 20-Gauge Champ in 1992, Florida State 12-Gauge Champ 1991, and 28-Gauge Champion at the 1994 Great Southern Shoot in Savannah, Georgia.

Keith Otero, another AAA-class shooter, won the Florida State 28-Gauge Championship in the spring of 1991 and came back later that year to win the Fall State 28-Gauge Championship. Shortly after these victories, he suffered a severe injury that left him flat on his back with a broken neck for almost a year. Once he was able to return to shooting, he proved he was back in form by winning a major Southeastern match, the St. Augustine Octoberfest, with an impressive 396x400!

Other than the fact that I know both of these gentlemen well, and have shot with them for years, another reason for their inclusion in this chapter is that both display different styles that have achieved top-level results. Roy Dear is an extremely fast shooter who can break targets before many other shooters could even get their guns pointed in the vicinity. Otero, while quick, is a more deliberate shooter who will let his birds get farther into the field.

Their differing styles reflect their own utilization of their visual acuity, reflexes and shooting style, and further reinforce a concept made throughout this book: You cannot "clone" shooters because there is no one method that will be correct for every one. Far too much depends upon the physical abilities of the individual shooter. Here's how they have capitalized on their own abilities.

Good shooters can get into slumps if they practice alone. Having another skilled shooter there can help show you why you missed a target.

While many top shooters practice most with the smaller gauges, experts suggest finishing your session with the larger gauges in order to remain familiar with the increased recoil.

A smoothly functioning squad that arrives on time is a plus when it comes to posting better scores. A shooter who is consistently late and delays the squad can break the other shooters' concentration.

Keith Otero feels that mastering the 410 is one of the most important things a shooter can do, and spends much of his practice time with it.

Effective Practice

"Just getting out and shooting targets is practice, but it is not effective practice," says Dear. "A lot of shooters goof around, have fun and joke a lot. There's nothing wrong with that, unless you really want to improve your shooting.

"I'm a firm believer in serious practice," he continues. "I always try to practice with shooters whose ability equals or exceeds mine, and who take their practice as seriously as I do mine. I don't like to practice with people who clown around because it will affect my score in a match at some point."

Otero agrees strongly with Dear. Both shooters make certain that they take their practice as seriously as possible by shooting registered targets for their practice!

"Shooting registered targets will make you take your practice seriously and strive to break every target," Otero notes. "That mental discipline will pay off in a tournament."

Practice Guns

What they practice with is equally important.

The most used gauge in practice, at least according my observations over many years on a Skeet field, is the 28-gauge. On the surface, it seems a logical choice. It's a mild-mannered round that uses less powder and shot than the 20- or 12-gauge and thus cuts shooting expenses. It is also perceived as a "little gun," but in reality it is not. In fact, it has little handicap on the Skeet field over the 12-gauge. That is why both Dear and Otero do not consider it to be the best gauge to practice with.

"I do a lot of my practice with the 410," says Otero, "because that is the gauge that will kill you in a match, and the one that intimidates a lot of shooters. There was a time when it intimidated me badly enough that if a shoot started out with that gauge, I was mentally in trouble. If you shoot an 80 or so with it, then you are already down 20 birds for HOA (High Overall) and the best you can do is shoot 380x400 if you run the other three gauges straight. That won't win you much, and that realization will affect your shooting with the other gauges.

103

Practicing with skilled shooters who take their practice seriously is one way to improve your skills. This group of shooters registers their practice targets!

Conquering that 410 is, in my opinion, the most important thing a shooter can do because it will help you all across the board."

Otero started down that path by making himself shoot 6000 registered targets in one year with the 410. Today, the 410 is his primary practice gauge, but he makes certain that he finishes his practice with the 12-gauge.

"Practicing with the 410 is an excellent way to bring your scores up with all gauges," he says, "but don't neglect the larger gauges. Their increased recoil can throw your form and timing off slightly if all you shoot is the 410."

Dear practices in a similar manner.

"I start my practice with 100 rounds of 410," he says. "That gauge requires more precision and keeps me from getting sloppy. If you can hit them with the 410 you can hit them with any of the other gauges. After those 100 rounds of regular Skeet, I'll shift to the 28 or 20 and shoot a fifty-bird round of Doubles. The last thing I will do is shoot a box of shells on doubles from stations three, four and five. Practicing shoot-off doubles is a much overlooked aspect of the game by many shooters, especially newer shooters. I think they should begin practicing this as soon as possible because they will regret their lack of familiarity with it at some point."

Another overlooked shot is the second shot on low house eight.

"I think new shooters should practice taking two shots at low house eight," says Otero. "It's strictly a mental thing, but what you are doing out there is making sure you are good enough to take your option shot there—not at some previous miss back down the field. When many shooters do get that chance, the pressure of that shot is intense. In fact, when I am refereeing and pulling targets I will often see a shooter miss, and when I say 'option' he will say something like, "Well I

The two shooters at left have learned the fine art of relaxing between shots. Trying to maintain a high level of concentration during the entire round is very difficult, and ultimately hurts the shooter.

Making the second shot on low house eight can present some serious mental barriers to newer shooters. Otero recommends that they practice taking two shots on that station.

don't have to worry about that anymore," referring to that second shot on station eight. I guess it bothers some people to have to confront that shot so why don't they practice that one so it becomes less intimidating?

"The sign of a good Skeet shooter," he laughs, "is when you get to low house eight and are upset if you only get to shoot one round there. If you practice taking two shots there, it'll pay off with a much more confident attitude and you'll start finding out that you will get that opportunity more often."

Speaking from personal experience, the author can attest to the mental pressure of that second shot on low house eight if you have not had the opportunity to shoot it many times. Practicing two shots on low eight helped me tremendously during my early Skeet days when two shots on eight were a rarity.

Winning in the Wind

If there is one thing that can intimidate Skeet shooters more than the 410 or the second shot on low eight, it is the wind. It will make targets do some very strange things! Watch a high house four target launched into a head wind and it will climb like an International trap target. Send it out with a strong tail wind and it will hunt the ground like a rabbit! In gusty winds, it might go anywhere. Every shooter has his own philosophy for dealing with the wind, and this is where our two experts differ in their approach.

"I don't do anything differently in the wind," states Roy Dear. "I just concentrate on keeping my head down on the stock and visually acquiring the bird quickly, and staying focused on it so that if it dips or rises I can quickly move the gun to it."

One reason for that approach is that he has trained himself to shoot all targets very quickly. That can pay off in the wind for some shooters.

"The wind seldom affects the bird very much until it gets to the center stake," he says. "Before that, it is still primarily under the influence of the launching velocity. If you teach yourself to break the bird before it hits the stake all the time, you can solve a lot of those problems."

He adds, "If I make any change it all, it is in my mental prep for the shot. I force myself to think about cheeking the stock more firmly as I swing back on the second bird. You must stay with the gun for that target. Many newer shooters tend to lift their head off the stock just to find the bird, and that will lose it for you.

"Some shooters," he concludes, "think that you have to do things differently in the wind and I feel that is a mistake. If you start changing your natural timing to accommodate the wind, or other temporary conditions, you're going to get yourself in trouble."

Otero disagrees.

"I have attempted to increase my normal rhythm and timing to break targets closer to the stake," he says, "but that does not work for me, or for other more deliberate shooters. That means that I have to make some adjustments for the wind.

"One thing I do," he continues, "is to turn my foot position slightly more into the house so I can be a little more aggressive on the bird. I want to shoot it a little more quickly than I would under calm conditions. I would normally shoot the bird around the center stake, say 10 feet to either side of it. Shifting my body into the house lets me get on the bird a bit quicker, while it is still under the influence of the launching velocity."

Otero finds this simple adjustment is all that is required on singles target in the wind. Doubles require an additional adjustment.

"Shooting the first bird quicker will throw off your normal timing on the second bird in doubles, because it will not be as far to your side of the field after you break the first bird as it would if you shot with your normal rhythm. That can be a positive thing here, because you normally shoot that second bird well past the center stake, but in a wind, if you let it get that far, the bird will be doing some strange things. This changes my normal rhythm for doubles on stations one, two, six and seven, because I want to—in addition to breaking the first bird fast—break the second bird much closer to the stake. I like to practice in the wind and do practice this different timing."

Doubles on the mid-field stations (three, four and five) don't require as much adjustment, but do require a lot of concentration on the second bird. Sometimes, shooters concentrate on it too much!

"It's not at all uncommon," Otero notes "for shooters to become so worried about the second bird in a wind that they will rush their shot on the first and miss it. You've got to make certain that you get the first bird before you go after the second."

When it comes to training yourself to shoot faster all the time, in order to avoid problems in the wind, Otero has some interesting thoughts.

"There are some people who can train themselves to be really quick shots all the time, and it works for some shooters. It doesn't work for me because I did not start that way and it doesn't suit my shooting style. Each shooter has to determine what rhythm is best for him. One drawback to shooting quickly, however, is shooting what we call a 'bird on a string.' That's a bird that is perfectly regulated in its flight path and the shooter knows exactly where it will go. On windy days some shooters will have a hard time with that because the target isn't

going to be where you expect it, and the shooter's timing is so quick—two shots almost simultaneously on doubles—that they don't have the time or the timing to go after an out-of-line bird. That is one drawback to practicing breaking birds just as fast as you can: there will be times when you have to find a bird."

Surviving Shoot-Offs

Many new shooters feel that shoot-offs are only for the top shooters, but that's not true. Even a shooter with only six months' experience can find himself in a shoot-off in Class D. How well he handles it will determine his success. It can be a trying experience!

"Shoot-offs are a mental thing that can really intimidate new shooters," says Otero. "They get really wound up and nervous, when, in fact, they shouldn't be. When you stop to think about it, that shooter is in a much better position to win than if he didn't make the shoot-off! He should be thinking positively, but a lot of times he will beat himself by thinking negatively. The best way to handle the pressure of a shoot-off is to get into as many of them as you can. It's just a matter of experience and composure."

For Otero, his mental prep for surviving a shoot-off is simple: Get the first bird first!

"I want to see the first target I shoot at break before I even think about taking the second bird," he says. "That's what settles me down and gets me to work."

Dear has his own routine.

"I start preparing for the shoot-off the night before," he says. If that sounds somewhat overconfident, it is not, because, in this writer's experience, Dear is almost invariably going to be in at least one shoot-off in any match he enters. So, for that matter, will Otero.

Roy Dear (left) knows the advantages of pacing yourself in a long match in order to be as fresh for the all-important shoot-off as he was when the first round was fired.

"I like to get a good night's sleep, eat a light breakfast a couple of hours before I shoot, and maintain a good fluid intake during the actual match itself. I like something with caffeine in it, like soda or coffee. I feel the caffeine helps keep me pumped, but there are other shooters who avoid caffeine because it makes them jumpy. During the breaks in the match, I like to sit in the shade or in my motor home and just relax. I don't haunt the scoreboard. It's just something else to think about. I also don't watch the other shooters shoot. That's just something that will tire you out. Once the shoot-off is about to start, I always wash my face with cool water and just freshen up a bit. That puts me in a good frame of mind. After that, the shoot-off is nothing more than doing what got you there in the first place. You have to maintain your composure and not get excited. Just shoot."

Avoiding Beginners' Mistakes

While experts like Dear and Otero are already thinking toward the shoot-off before they even arrive at the match, there are many newer shooters wondering how to negotiate the field without missing all the targets! There are both physical and mental pitfalls that await them.

"I think one thing that affects new shooters the most, especially if they have some bird hunting experience, is that we count the misses in Skeet," Otero notes. "In the hunting fields, you don't count the empty hulls (unless you have some clay target experience), you just count the birds in the bag. A shooter who bagged a 12-bird limit of doves may feel he is a real good shot. He forgets it took him maybe 100 or more shells to get them. In Skeet, he is painfully reminded of each miss, and that can really bother a new shooter—especially when they watch a veteran run fifty targets without a miss, while the new shooter happens to get just a dozen or so. This can be a major

Mastering the game of Skeet requires a lot of practice. Like many top shooters, Keith Otero loads his own shells and buys his components in bulk. This is only a couple months' supply of powder.

Spending plenty of time on the stations that give you the most trouble, especially if another good shooter is along to watch your form, is an important part of improving your game.

Experts recommend staying away from the scoreboard until you've finished shooting. Worrying about other shooters does your game little good.

mind-mess for some shooters, and it can really affect their enjoyment of the game, and they may not come back."

"What new shooters need to do," Otero feels, "is to not equate their shooting ability with the number of targets they miss during their first few rounds. Consider it a new game, a learning experience, and accept the fact that they will have to gain some experience before they start breaking targets regu-

Roy Dear has trained himself to shoot quickly in order to avoid problems in the wind, but that approach does not work for every shooter if it doesn't fit his normal style.

larly, but that they will be able to do that with some practice and a few tips."

Dear offers a list of additional tips for new shooters:

1. "Many shooters don't pay enough attention to their initial foot position. There will be one foot position for each target that will give the optimal amount of swing to break it, and the shooter needs to find the position that works best for him. Many don't look for it."

2. "Look at the bird. Too many new shooters are focused on the barrel or their front bead, and this will not give them a clear view of the target. If the gun is mounted properly you don't need to see the bead, it will be right on the bird if your eyes are on the bird."

3. "Failure to follow through on a shot is a real killer for many new shooters. I recommend that new shooters develop follow-through by tracking a broken piece of the bird with their gun after they have broken it with the first shot. This will force them to swing the gun through the shot and follow through. It is also an excellent technique for a more experienced shooter who happens to be in a slight slump."

4. "Pick up the bird quickly as it leaves the house and don't let it run away from you. Have full visual control on the bird and you will be surprised how quickly it seems to slow down, and how much larger it looks."

5. "Work on problem stations, don't just shoot through them on a round. Take twenty-five shells, go to the station that gives you problems, and work on it. The game will come together much quicker if you break it down and work it out one station at a time. A lot of new shooters are hesitant to do that, though. They want to shoot a full round and see their score. Taking the stations, especially the ones that really give you problems, one at a time will do much more for your shooting than looking at your scores."

Lastly, both Dear and Otero are strongly in agreement that one of the biggest stumbling blocks to improving scores is listening to too many "advisers." When you get tips from a half-dozen different shooters, much of it will be contradictory. Pick one shooter who is good, and willing to help you, and listen to him. Too many cooks will spoil the soup, and that won't fine-tune your game.

Section III
Sporting Clays

chapter seventeen

Sporting Clays: The New Game In Town

SPORTING CLAYS, or Hunter Clays, as it is sometimes called, is not the rigidly-programmed, relatively predictable clay target game we find in trap and Skeet. Nor is it a game that lends itself to perfection. Even the world's greatest shots miss with surprising regularity, and a perfect score in a tournament is virtually unheard of.

This is a game where everybody will miss, laugh about it and go on to the next shot. That's probably why it is on its way to becoming the most popular shotgun game in the country.

That wasn't always the case. In fact, just a short decade ago Sporting Clays ranges were about as common as good manners at a punk rock concert. Although the sport was well established in Europe, it was only beginning to make its presence felt on these shores. Fortunately, that has changed quite a bit in the last 5 years, and it is safe to say that the majority of new shotgun ranges being constructed or those under re-construction, are either primarily Sporting Clays, or incorporate Sporting into their program.

For shotgunners bored with the unvarying fare of trap and Skeet, the first taste of Sporting Clays is a veritable smorgasbord! Targets zip by at speeds and angles previously unseen on American ranges. Sometimes it will be a single clay leaping from a hidden trap and disappearing behind a conveniently-placed tree before the surprised gunner can even react. Just about the time the gunner feels he has that target figured out, the boom of his shotgun can send another target speeding across the field. Or, two targets may pop up. They might be crossing, climbing, incoming, outgoing, quartering, streaking high overhead or even falling.

Just when the shooter starts to get comfortable with that selection, some sneaky range operator will change the speed or angle on the trap, or even move the shooting stand, leaving the hapless gunner to face an entirely new set of challenges.

For many wingshooters, this game is as much fun as you can legally have with a shotgun with your clothes on!

Sporting has its roots in the hunting fields, thus most stations will have a "critter" name, and targets will simulate the characteristic flight of that critter.

Sporting Clays uses a slightly different format than trap or Skeet, but gun safety rules are universal. Safety is something every shooter should take seriously.

Good Sporting courses utilize existing terrain features to create interesting and challenging shots. This duck pond station can have some very tough, long-range crossing shots. Note the shooting cage that severely restricts the shooter's movement. Restrictive cages are a standard feature of this game.

Sporting Clays Origins

Sporting Clays began its popular rise in England just about the same time that Skeet was becoming the favored new game in America, about the early 1920s. It would be incorrect to say that Sporting was an immediate success. It just sort of slowly grew into the most popular shooting game in England over the last 20 years or so.

The Orvis Company is generally credited with sponsoring the first Sporting Clays match to be held in the United States, in 1983. The game had been played here before that, however. Remington Farms, in Maryland, had a version of Hunter Clays in operation in the late 1960s. The firm imported British course designer Chris Craddock to these shores and, using the hilly, wooded terrain of Remington Farms, he was able to lay out a truly impressive course.

In 1985, the United States Sporting Clays Association was formed. In 1989, the National Sporting Clays Association, (affiliated with the National Skeet Shooting Association) became the dominant, governing body for this game in the United States.

How Sporting Is Played

Sporting Clays takes trap and Skeet several steps further. While a Sporting shooter will see some of the same angles here that he might on a trap or Skeet field, that is about as similar as the three games get.

There are significant differences between Sporting Clays and trap and Skeet. Here are the major ones:

1. Like other games, the bird is called for by the shooter. However, in Sporting, a delay of up to 3 seconds may be incorporated by the puller before he releases the target. Some launching controls have a built-in variable delay, similar to International Skeet.

2. When calling for the bird, the shooter must have the gun in a low position, meaning the entire buttstock must be visible below the armpit. In addition, the gun can be mounted only when the bird, or birds, become visible.

3. Other shotgunning games provide for "alibis"—if a gun or ammunition malfunction occurs, the shooter is allowed to reshoot the target. This is not always the case in Sporting Clays! Alibis are allowed, but are more limited and the rules applying them are stricter.

4. Shotguns of 12-gauge or smaller are allowed. Shooters are also allowed to use different guns at different stations, and guns fitted for multiple barrels with different length barrels and chokes are permitted. Shooters may change barrels, or choke tubes, between stations. Sporting Clays has often been referred to as "golf with a shotgun" and some shooters bring along a full bag of guns.

Sporting Clays stations often make use of intervening brush or trees to make the shooter's job a bit tougher. This station at Turkey Run Gun Club, in Alahcua, Florida, doesn't give shooters much time to catch this speeding target.

5. Trap and Skeet use one target. In Sporting, five different targets may be incorporated in a single round:

A. The standard trap clay bird;

B. A slightly smaller (90mm) bird, and thus travels faster;

C. A 60mm bird (about the size of a tennis ball) that really gets moving;

D. A Battue target, about ¼-inch thick and very flat, that takes some highly unpredictable paths during flight;

E. A thicker, tougher version of the standard clay target used as a ground-bouncing rabbit. This sturdier target takes a harder hit to break.

6. The targets may be presented as singles, true pairs (when

Innovative placement of traps can allow ranges to change angles and presentations on many stations. This constantly varying fare is one key to the game's popularity.

Sporting is the only clay target game where shooters will see a target bouncing along the ground. The little white "rabbit" in the center of this photo can be a tough target to break.

One of the challenges of the game is that sneaky course designers will often create only a narrow "window" between the trees in which the shooter must break the targets. Shooters not only need to know how to break the birds, but also, when and where to do so.

both targets are launched simultaneously), following pairs (the second target is launched behind the first, at the puller's discretion, and often with a time lag), and as report pairs, where the second target is launched at the sound of the shooter's first shot.

7. If that isn't confusing enough, there are also "poison birds," targets of a separate and clearly discernible appearance that may be inserted at random, anywhere in the match. Any shooter firing on this target will be rewarded with a miss. Shooters who refrain from shooting at these targets will score an automatic hit. You never know when or where one will pop up, except that they will never be thrown as true pairs.

Terrain Hazards

As you can imagine, these rules give course designers a tremendous amount of latitude, and they are encouraged to use it. It is common for courses to use existing terrain features to deliberately place obstructions in the path of a shooter. For example, some targets may fly through trees or brush and only give the shooter a very small window of visibility to break it. Or, there may be two or three windows available on a given shot and each option will change the basic nature of that shot. It is then up to the shooter to determine which might be to his best advantage.

The use of natural terrain features can also result in targets being presented below the shooter, as he stands on a hilltop, or targets that fly uphill from the shooter. In most cases, shooting cages are required and they may be designed to restrict the

shooter's range of movement and require him to break the target within a relatively confined area.

The result of this course latitude means that Sporting Clays courses, like golf courses, will differ across the county. No two will truly be the same.

Course managers are also encouraged to make frequent changes in their target presentations just to keep things interesting.

What results is one of the most challenging and enjoyable shotgunning experiences around.

Sporting Stations

Since courses will vary considerably, there is no "standard" Sporting Clays range as in trap and Skeet. Shooters will see a wide variety of target presentations, and this has made Sporting Clays a thinking shooter's game. You can't react your way around a Sporting course. You must think your way through it, analyzing each individual station as you come to it. Here are some of the target presentations you are likely to see.

The Rabbit Run

Sporting Clays traces its roots to the hunting field and that flavor lingers in the modern game. Virtually all of the various Sporting Clays target presentations are intended to represent a situation that will occur in the hunting fields and are invariably named after specific "critter" shots.

Sporting Clays courses around the world are often designed to reflect the local hunting traditions, as well as a geographical adaptation of the terrain. Many American wingshooters are taught from an early age not to shoot rabbits while bird hunting because they may run the risk of hitting one of the bird dogs, or teach the dogs bad habits. Not necessarily so in Europe. Rabbits are fair game in any "rough" or "walk-up" hunt, and, thus, the rabbit target has become a staple of many Sporting Clays courses.

The Rabbit is a ground-bouncing target using a sturdier, specially-made clay target. It is launched from a special machine so that its flat edge hits the ground and bounces across it. Sometimes a piece of carpet is placed at the first contact point the clay makes with the ground to help cushion that initial blow. These targets are not as easy to break as a standard clay because of their heavier construction. There is no way to predict precisely what path the target will take after it first hits the ground.

Course managers may create a short, narrow opening for the target to pass through, or may let it sweep across open ground. Sometimes this target is launched as a following target, or a report target, in conjunction with an aerial bird. The Rabbit may run partially on the ground and then "jump" or bounce smoothly into the air. The most common range to encounter this target is 15 to 40 yards.

This is a quick-sweeping shot that demands a strong follow-through, and last minute corrections to account for erratic movement. Not surprisingly, this is a tough target—even more so because many American shooters must overcome an ingrained mental block that prevents them from shooting a target on the ground.

Josh Miller, one of Florida's top junior shooters, displays perfect low gun form before he calls for the target. Note the gun butt is ready to mount, but still legally visible below his armpit.

Shooters will see a lot of unusual angles during a round of Sporting. This high, incoming "dove" can be very difficult if the shooter lets it get past directly overhead. This is one you can't relax on.

Woodcock

This is usually a low overhead or extremely hard crossing throw that gives the shooter just a quick glimpse of the targets. Doubles might be thrown here. The range is generally 20 yards and under.

Some ranges may throw these targets from multiple traps located at various positions in front of the shooter. This is quick, fast shooting with a wide-open choke.

Duck Tower

The Duck Tower is often a 40- to 70-foot tower with five stations laid out around its base. There may be fewer stations, with only a few presentation variations. The tower may be behind the shooter, with birds going away, or they may quarter away and fall off to the side. There is often one station where the target may be very much an incoming angle. The targets may be standards, 90mms, or 60mms. Unless, of course, you have a truly devious course manager, in which case who knows what you will get. Some of the truly sadistic managers will install an oscillating trap, add a "poison bird," or something even more radical. You can expect to shoot this one anywhere from 20 to over 60 yards.

Dove

Doves can be similar to the Duck Tower in that the birds are launched from a very elevated position. Often, however, they will be incoming angled shots. Unless, of course, Mr. Devious Course Manager puts out extra shooting stations along the flight path and thus creates overhead crossing targets. One of my favorite sporting stations is the incoming Dove Tower at Cherokee Rose, in Griffin, Georgia, where a cage limits the downward position of the gun. The target house is dead ahead of the shooter and throws what looks like a high house eight Skeet shot, except the birds are almost 15 yards up and traveling as true pairs. It is possible to start behind both birds, swing through and take the trailing bird first, then continue the swing to get the lead bird. You just have to do it real quick and there ain't much room for error!

Grouse Bluff

This is the most charitable name you will hear this ulcer-maker called. Most couldn't even be printed in an X-rated book!

This is generally a hillside shot, with the shooter looking down into a gully. Some stations may have crossing shots, and often stick a tree or two along the flight path to really make you think the shot through, while others may have a more "away" angle. Some stations combine both by putting in two different shooting platforms that will alter the angle from crossing to outgoing. Regardless, this writer has never seen an easy shot on a Sporting Clays course that had the word "Grouse" in the name!

Blue Bill Pass

This is very similar to a low-angle Duck Tower. The purpose, I suppose, is to simulate a passing shot on a lesser scaup bluebill duck. They often skim low and fly faster than hell. That's about what these targets do. Some shots may have a slight outgoing angle, but many will be hard crossers. If the course manager is a real sadist, there may be four or five shooting stations scattered along the flight path, each of which changes the angle, distance to the target, and the lead. This station may be shot from 20- to 50-plus yards, and the longer shots are some of the toughest you will ever see.

Duck Boat

Our favorite course designer has been drinking too much again, and this time dragged home an old boat. You get into it to shoot. Sometimes it actually floats in water, other times it lays on a bed of very wobbly truck tires. Just getting a steady shooting position in the boat is tough enough, but hitting the targets, which may be incoming, crossing, or outgoing at 15 to 40 yards, is even tougher.

Springing Teal

The trap is angled skyward and the birds go almost straight up. You'll get the full range of presentations here—singles, true pairs, report and following doubles. Do you try to hit them on the climb at relatively short range, or wait until they peak out, or try to hit them as they fall? If you wait too long you may have a 60-plus-yard shot!

Rising Sharptail

This event often uses the little 60mm target and throws it away from the shooter at a rising angle. Because of the speed and the small size of the target, this can often call for a Full choke and a high velocity load, even though the birds may be taken inside 40 yards.

Whistlin' Bobs

This simulates the close range flush of a quail with the target heading quickly away from the shooter, and, just like its

Quick counts in Sporting Clays. You don't always have a lot of time to dally on a target before it finds the safety of the trees!

Safety is heavily stressed in this game, since many traps are manually operated and may require the trapper to move forward of the shooting stand to reach the trap house. Guns are never loaded until the trapper is safely inside.

Guns are loaded only when the shooter steps into the cage to take his turn. Violating this rule will get you thrown off any course in the country, and rightly so.

All Sporting Clays shots begin from a low gun position, and the proper position can vary depending upon the angle of the shot. Outdoor writer Larry Weishuhn shows the proper low gun position for a high incoming shot. Note the trigger finger is outside the trigger guard until the gun is mounted—that's safe gun handling.

namesake, heading quickly to cover. Fast shootin' with an open choke!

Sneaky Snipe

This can be similar to the Rising Sharptail, except the targets may not achieve a great deal of height. The window on this station can be quite small, with the target often starting out against a wooded background, zipping across a small patch of open sky, and then back across the background.

Duck Pond

Another favorite of mine from Cherokee Rose, this station has three strategically-placed traps that can throw incomers, outgoers and settling crossing shots to a shooter on a small stand that juts out into a pond. You don't know what you're going to get when you call for a bird.

Rising Ringnecks

A very steep-climbing bird, similar to Springing Teal, but at a shorter range. Often there is another bird, quartering away, that joins the first.

Modified Dove Tower

Sometimes seen as a component of a standard Dove Tower, this has the targets coming from behind the shooter on a high

going away angle. It looks a lot like a Skeet high house one on steroids.

The foregoing can be considered a basic look at some of the presentations offered on courses around the country, but it can not be considered all-inclusive. Sporting Clays isn't like that, nor do veteran shooters want it to be. If course design and target presentations ever reach the point where shooters begin to run clean scores, things will change. That's the nature of the game. In fact, I'm convinced that some course managers stay up nights just thinking about new ways to drive more Sporting Clays shooters to drink.

Etiquette and Procedures

Sporting Clays is a very laid-back game, and the procedures are very similar to Skeet. A squad will be assembled containing two to five shooters, and from there they will wander through the course with a course guide/puller. The shooting rotation within the squad may be set by the course guide or left up to the shooters. If the shooters would like to change the rotation of that shooting order, there is nothing in the rules to stop them.

Like Skeet, each shooter steps onto the shooting station as his turn comes. The first shooter to take the shooting station at each field has the right to "see" the targets—to call for birds to be thrown without firing—in order that he and the other mem-

You don't need a fancy gun or equally fancy equipment to have a good time at Sporting Clays. You old huntin' gun can do the job adequately, and provide some valuable practice for the fall bird season.

bers of the squad can actually see what they are going to get.

This is an important step, and if you are in a squad where the first shooter has ignored this factor, please remind him between stations. The first shooter has the responsibility to call for the birds to be shown, and every shooter on the squad will benefit from this. If he continually forgets, change his rotation and get somebody in the first spot who is a little more considerate of the others.

Targets will be scored as hit when a visible piece is knocked off them by the shooter. On a doubles presentation, if the shooter manages to break both birds with one shot, he is credited with both and saves a shell.

When shooting doubles or pairs, if the shooter misses the first target, he has the right to fire his second shell at it, or try to get both targets with the second shell. If the shooter breaks both targets with either the first or second shell, he gets credit for both.

If a target in the air is broken by pieces of another target, it shall be treated as a "no bird." When this happens, the shooter shall receive whatever score he got on the first shot, and the doubles will be thrown again. The shooter must make an attempt to hit the first target, but he will already have that scored. It is only the second target he is shooting for score.

Scorers will call missed birds as "lost." If the shooter disagrees with the call, he must make his protest before firing another shot. The scorer will then poll the other shooters, and even spectators, and can change his call based upon that input. If he doesn't change it, his call stands.

In the event a gun is acting up, the shooter can ask the puller/referee for permission to test-fire it. Other than that, every round fired will be for score.

Like Skeet, know your rotation order in the squad; be ready to step to the shooting pad when your turn comes; and don't crowd the shooter currently on the pad. Other than that, enjoy!

Accessories You'll Need

Given the fact that a good Sporting Clays course is like a golf course, you will do a lot of walking. Some ranges have golf carts available, and you will have to tote all your necessary items with you. There are some items you'll definitely need.

Sporting is a pretty laid-back game. For some shooters, it's as much a pleasant walk in the woods as a shootin' match!

Sporting is a laid-back game, and a fifty-bird round can take most of an afternoon. Smart shooters make certain they are well prepared with all the equipment they might require for that length of time.

A shooting vest is an excellent idea. You will want some place to put the five to fifteen shells you will use on each station. And, you may want divided pockets on that vest to hold #7¹/₂, #8 and #9 shot separately. As we will see in later chapters, changing loads for different targets can be a big plus. Since Sporting Clays requires a low gun starting position, you will also want a vest of International style. These do not have a distinct shoulder pad which can catch the recoil pad during the mount. Instead, they have a smooth face, often with padding on the shooting side to allow a sloppy gun mount to still get the buttstock where it belongs.

Those vests made for Sporting Clays shooters will often have loop-type holders, or small pockets, to hold extra choke tubes and a suitable tube wrench. You will most likely have to change tubes as well as shot loads during an event. A good Sporting Clays vest will keep it all where you can find it in a hurry.

A standard round of Sporting is either fifty or 100 birds, and that's a lot of shotshells to lug around. Add to that the fact that experienced shooters will be carrying between three and five or even more different loads, and it is easy to see that stuffing them all in your vest pockets is going to leave you exhausted by the end of the round. That's a lot of weight to wear constantly. Instead, get a tote bag to carry your shells, shell knocker, choke tube lube, spare eye and ear protection, maybe a

plastic bottle of water, lens cleaning paper and other items you may need.

The only time you will have to lug a separate shell bag is between stations. The rest of the time you can toss it on the ground and let Mother Earth pack the load for awhile.

You would be surprised what a difference that can make by the end of the day. Four or five boxes of shotshells weighs a bunch!

If you are on a course that doesn't offer golf cart transportation between stations, consider the shoes you will wear. There can be a lot of walking involved, and toting a shotgun and lots of shells means you are wandering around, up hill and down, dragging 20 or more pounds. Jogging-type shoes are not a bad idea. The more comfortable your shoes, the better you'll feel.

A round of Sporting takes a lot longer than a round of trap or Skeet, and there is more physical exertion involved. You might want to tote some type of quick energy snack with you. Dried fruit is great, since its sugar gets to work quickly and doesn't give you false energy like the refined sugar in candy does.

That's a pretty lengthy list, but Sporting Clays is a rather complex game. It is a thinking shooter's game, and one that will test the versatility of both your equipment and technique.

It's also a heckuva lot of fun and can become very addictive!

Sporting's Top Guns

Most shooters who favor over/unders do so for their reliability and ease of maintenance. They are far more convenient than gas guns. The new crop of Sporting Clays guns have proven so effective that a number of top Olympic International Skeet shooters are beginning to use them at that game. Designed for ease of mounting and a smooth swing, Clays guns work very well there!

SPORTING CLAYS IS a game with its roots firmly planted in the hunting fields, so one would assume that any field-grade shotgun would be an acceptable choice. That assumption is correct, but it relies heavily on one's definition of the term "acceptable."

If your reason for shooting "Sporting" is to tune up for the fall season, then by all means use the gun you intend to tote afield. If you want to learn the capabilities and limitations of your favorite smoothbore, there is no better way to do it than by spending a few summer weekends on a Sporting Clays range. It makes no difference what gauge it is, or what action type: if it'll spit out two shells, it becomes an acceptable choice.

If your goal is to play the game for the game's sake, however, you might be disappointed with your favorite field gun.

Gun Requirements

Sporting Clays is a demanding game, and a varied one. You will see targets, distances, angles, and presentations that appear in no other clay target sport. To master this game, if such a thing is possible, will require a smoothbore equal to the challenge. Fortunately, the game has been in existence long enough that top competitors are beginning to figure out just what combination of factors will characterize an effective gun for Sporting. Here's a butt-to-muzzle look at what the experts think works best today.

The first concern is getting the gun mounted quickly to your shoulder, since all Sporting Clays shots begin with the gun butt clearly visible below the armpit. A recoil pad with sharp edges or a lot of deep serrations on the face is going to inhibit fast mounting by catching and dragging on your clothing. If you fumble a gun mount and don't lock it in, you can pretty well kiss that target goodbye! For that reason, a radiused pad with a relatively smooth face is a major asset. So, too, is having the buttstock properly fitted to your individual build. If you can't snap the gun into a smooth and consistent mount, then everything else becomes uncertain.

Although the actual "bird picture" over the barrel is a matter of individual preference, most Sporting Clays shooters want a relatively flat-shooting gun that has its pattern impacting equally above and below the bead.

The rib and bead arrangement is another matter of personal preference. I know some excellent shooters who don't want any beads on their rib. Their contention is that if the gun is fitted properly, beads become nothing more than a distraction. Other shooters fare well with a step in the rear of the rib and a single front bead. Some prefer a large bright bead, while others favor a smaller, more subdued model. I find that I shoot best with a flat rib and double gold bead arrangement. This may sound like nitpicking, but the picture you see over the sighting plane is a critical part of your subconscious triggering mechanism. When you find the setup with which you are comfortable, you will shoot better. Changing bead arrangements is a relatively simple matter, and worthy of experimentation.

When Sporting first became popular, those opting for over/unders often settled on relatively short barrels of 25 to 26 inches on the theory that the lighter guns, with a more between-the-hands balance, would get on targets faster. Time

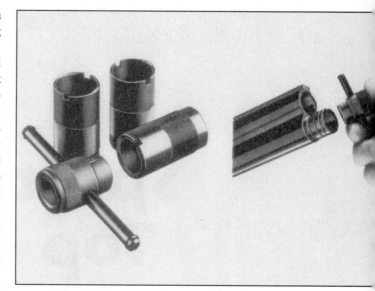

Trap and Skeet shooters can get by with fixed chokes, but Sporting Clays shooters require interchangeable tubes. While flush mounted tubes like these are effective, many shooters prefer protruding tubes that can be quickly changed without a choke tube wrench.

Sporting Clays shooters want their guns to shoot relatively "flat," (center the pattern where the bead looks). This tower shot at Space Port Gun Club drops pretty quickly.

and experience have shown that not to be the case. Stack-barrel shooters today invariably opt for barrels in the 28- to 32-inch range, and even longer, because the additional weight forward promotes a stronger, smoother swing with less chance of stopping the gun. I find that I shoot the 30-inch-barreled Ruger Sporting Clays Red Label noticeably better than my standard Red Label with 28-inch tubes. That 2 inches of barrel may not sound like much, and both guns have the same overall weight, but the longer-barreled gun balances 3/8-inch forward of the hinge pin, while my standard gun balances right at the hinge pin. That small difference is worth a few extra birds per round.

Those who favor semi-autos or pumps find the 28-inch barrel a bit more effective than 26-inch tubes.

Given the need for a quick follow-up shot, many shooters have found barrel porting to be an aid because it reduces muzzle jump and gets them back on target a bit faster.

The ability to gain improved pattern control over the widely varying ranges one sees in Sporting has given rise to a serious interest in custom barrel work designed to enhance shotshell performance. That's covered in a later chapter so we won't spend time on it here, but many of today's current crop of Sporting Clays guns have lengthened forcing cones, back-bored barrels and long chokes.

Given the need for frequent choke tube changes, some makers are producing tubes with knurled ends that protrude from the barrel, allowing them to be quickly changed without a wrench. A very nice touch on any interchangeable tube intended for Sporting is an identifying system that allows the shooter to determine what tubes are in the gun by simply looking at the muzzle, instead of having to remove the tube to find out. It's a nice convenience that I wish more makers would offer. It is not hard to forget what tubes you have in the gun in the heat of battle.

Sporting Clays Guns

Guns with any of the above features were not very common in years past. Today, however, Sporting Clays is the hottest thing in shooting, and virtually every shotgun maker worth his salt is introducing models specially designed for this game—and those same "competition" guns make excellent field guns! Here's a look at who's doing what.

Many Sporting shooters opt for the supposedly softer recoil of a gas-operated semi-auto, and overcome the single choke handicap by shifting to a heavier load when they need to extend the range on a second shot.

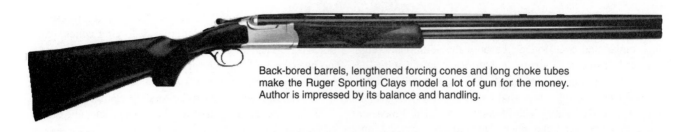

Back-bored barrels, lengthened forcing cones and long choke tubes make the Ruger Sporting Clays model a lot of gun for the money. Author is impressed by its balance and handling.

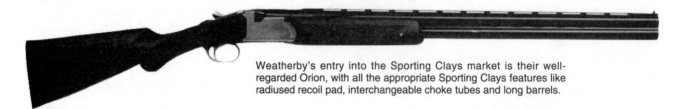

Weatherby's entry into the Sporting Clays market is their well-regarded Orion, with all the appropriate Sporting Clays features like radiused recoil pad, interchangeable choke tubes and long barrels.

Ruger

Ruger's standard model makes a pretty good Sporting gun, but their new Sporting Clays model goes it one better. The 12-gauge over/under has 30-inch barrels, without the solid filler strips between the barrels as found on the standard version. The barrels are back-bored to an interior diameter of .741-.745-inch, and have lengthened forcing cones. Choke tubes are a new item for Ruger, and these are $2^7/_{16}$ inches in length. They will not interchange with standard Red Label tubes. The older tubes used identifying notches on the muzzle end, but the new longer tubes sadly do not. The gun is supplied with four tubes: two Skeet 1s, and one each in Improved Cylinder and Modified. Full and Extra-Full tubes are also available, and all tubes are etched with standard markings on the side of the tube. Topping the barrel is a flat, serrated ventilated rib with a double gold bead sighting system. The gun is chambered for the 3-inch 12-gauge shell.

The Sporting Clays model comes with a single selective trigger controlled by Ruger's tang-mounted safety/barrel selector system, and has automatic ejectors. Competitive shooters can have the ejectors converted to extractors (a nice feature if you happen to reload) and the automatic safety converted to manual, by the factory. Critical dimensions are: overall length, 47 inches; weight, 7.7 pounds; length of pull, $14^1/_8$ inches; drop at comb, $1^1/_2$ inches; and drop at heel, $2^1/_2$ inches.

I've had a considerable amount of hands-on experience with this particular gun and I rate it as one of my favorites for this game, as well as for the Skeet field.

In 1994 Ruger introduced a 20-gauge version of this gun, which is identical in all features and stock dimensions, but with a weight of 7 pounds.

Weatherby

Weatherby's original **Orion Grade II Sporting** model with 28- or 30-inch barrels proved a popular choice. This year, however, they have introduced an upgraded version called the Orion Grade II Classic Sporting. Available with a 28-inch barrel, the stock dimensions are identical to the original model: overall length, 45 inches; length of pull, $14^1/_4$ inches; drop at comb $1^1/_2$ inches; drop at heel $2^1/_2$ inches; with a weight of $7^1/_2$ pounds. Both are chambered for $2^3/_4$-inch 12-gauge shells.

The new model has a rounded pistol grip, more slender forend, a Broadway-type rib with a white front bead and subdued mid-point bead, and a radiused recoil pad. Internally, the forcing cones are lengthened, and the barrels are back-bored to .735-inch.

The gun is supplied with five interchangeable choke tubes (Skeet 1, Sporting Clays 1, Improved Cylinder, Sporting Clays 2, and Modified) with Improved Modified, Full and Extra Full also available. The tubes are marked with standard choke abbreviations on the bodies, and end-notched for convenient in-gun identification. The choke designation "SC 1" (Sporting Clays 1) is a .007-inch constriction (falling between Skeet 1 and Improved Cylinder) with SC 2 being .016-inch (about a Skeet 2 constriction) and falling just below Modified. It is doubtful that even the most discerning Sporting shooter would require a wider choke tube selection than this!

Perazzi

One of the most respected names in top-end competitive shotguns, Perazzi offers what amounts to custom fitting in their basic Sporting Clay models—**the MX7, MX8, Mirage,** and the **MX10** with adjustable stock. Barrel lengths are available from $27^9/_{16}$ to $31^1/_2$ inches, with interchangeable chokes optional in one or both barrels. Perazzi choke tubes are marked on the tube in numerals ranging from 0 to 11, the first being a straight Cylinder tube, with successive tubes each having .004-inch greater constriction.

Critical stock dimensions on the Perazzi are whatever you want them to be. The guns have interchangeable buttstocks that can be ordered in a wide range of pull lengths, drop at comb and heel, with cast-on or cast-off, or straight comb with sloping field stock, or with Monte Carlo. In effect, you are custom-fitting the gun to yourself when you buy it. Overall length and weight vary with barrel and stock selection. Perazzis aren't the kind of gun you buy off the rack at the local firearms emporium, but those who can afford them swear by them.

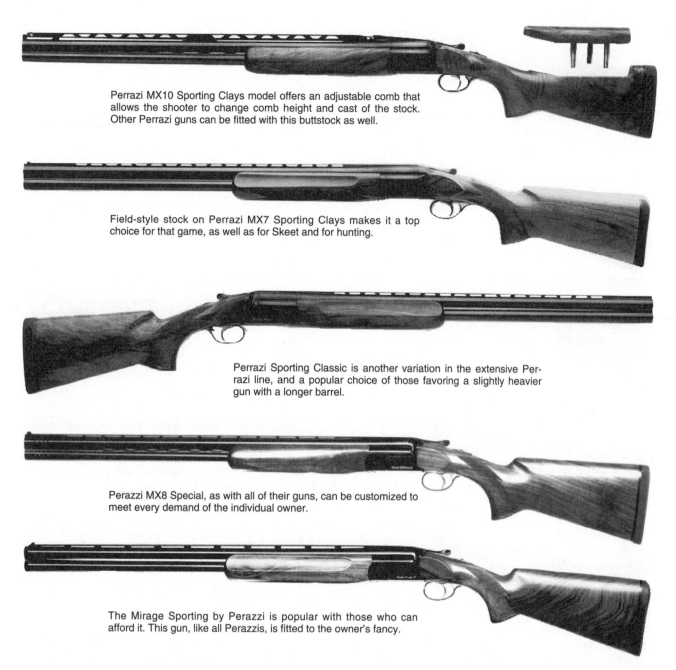

Perrazi MX10 Sporting Clays model offers an adjustable comb that allows the shooter to change comb height and cast of the stock. Other Perrazi guns can be fitted with this buttstock as well.

Field-style stock on Perrazi MX7 Sporting Clays makes it a top choice for that game, as well as for Skeet and for hunting.

Perrazi Sporting Classic is another variation in the extensive Perrazi line, and a popular choice of those favoring a slightly heavier gun with a longer barrel.

Perazzi MX8 Special, as with all of their guns, can be customized to meet every demand of the individual owner.

The Mirage Sporting by Perazzi is popular with those who can afford it. This gun, like all Perazzis, is fitted to the owner's fancy.

Winchester/U.S. Repeating Arms Co.

New to the line is their 12-gauge over/under **Model 1001**, pronounced "ten-oh-one." It has a single selective trigger, automatic ejectors, a 10mm flat ventilated rib, back-bored barrels and a new long choke tube system. A white front bead and mid-rib metal bead comprise the sighting system. The gun is available with either 28- or 30-inch barrels. Standard choke tubes supplied consist of Skeet 1, Improved Cylinder, Modified, and Improved Modified, with standard choke abbreviations etched on the side of the tube near the muzzle. The gun is chambered for 2³/₄-inch 12-gauge shells.

Critical dimensions are: length of pull, 14³/₈ inches; drop at comb, 1³/₈ inches; drop at heel, 2¹/₈ inches; weight, 7³/₄ pounds. Another feature worth noting, the recoil pad is nicely radiused.

Those favoring the softer recoil of a gas-operated semi-auto will find excellent raw material in the **Winchester Model 1400**. Its four-lug rotary bolt assures a solid lockup and reliable operation. You will need to radius the recoil pad and add some choke tubes to augment its basic selection of Improved Cylinder, Modified, and Full. However, it has the potential to make into a fine Sporting gun at a price that makes custom work an attractive option. The gun is available in both 12- and 20-gauge, with a 28-inch barrel.

Critical dimensions are: length of pull, 14 inches in 12-gauge and 13¹/₂ in 20; drop at comb, 1¹/₂ inches; drop at heel, 2¹/₂ inches; weight, 7³/₄ pounds for the 12-gauge or 7¹/₂ pounds for the 20. This is a reliable gun that doesn't cost an arm and a leg and can be "tricked up" to break as many targets as a $10,000 shotgun.

Browning

The folks in Utah have a number of Sporting Clays models in their line and all now have their new Invector Plus long

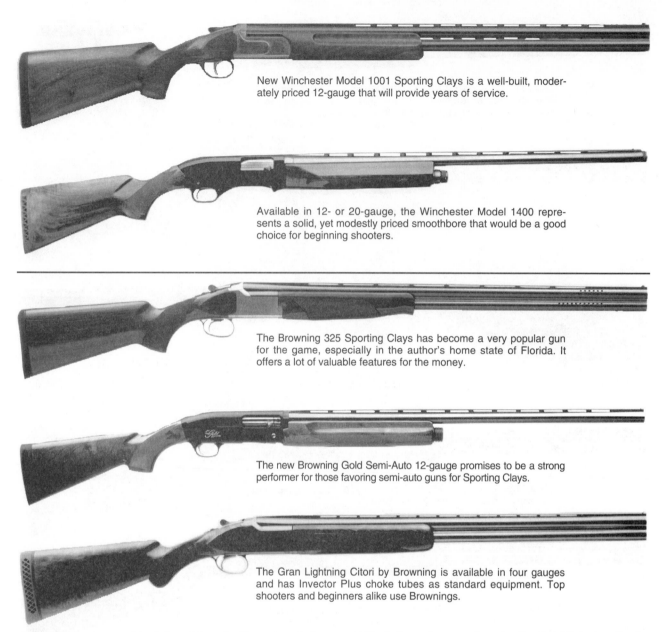

New Winchester Model 1001 Sporting Clays is a well-built, moderately priced 12-gauge that will provide years of service.

Available in 12- or 20-gauge, the Winchester Model 1400 represents a solid, yet modestly priced smoothbore that would be a good choice for beginning shooters.

The Browning 325 Sporting Clays has become a very popular gun for the game, especially in the author's home state of Florida. It offers a lot of valuable features for the money.

The new Browning Gold Semi-Auto 12-gauge promises to be a strong performer for those favoring semi-auto guns for Sporting Clays.

The Gran Lightning Citori by Browning is available in four gauges and has Invector Plus choke tubes as standard equipment. Top shooters and beginners alike use Brownings.

choke tube system and back-bored barrels. Browning choke tubes are etched with the choke denomination, and notched on the muzzle end for easy in-gun identification.

The Browning 12-gauge Sporting Clays over/unders are primarily chambered for the 2³/₄-inch shell (although the **Lightning Sporting** model can be had with 3-inch chambers) and a number of them are offered with factory barrel porting. Stock dimensions vary by model, and several have adjustable length of pull. Space does not permit a full cataloging of their entire line, but it is extensive enough to please any shooter. Barrel lengths in different models are available from 28 to 32 inches. Their **Model 325**, with 32-inch barrels, has proven to be very popular with those playing the demanding game of FITASC.

Browning has not ignored the gas gun shooter, and is offering their **Browning Gold** in 12- and 20-gauge with back-bored barrels that have what they term "a self-cleaning gas system." Both use the Invector Plus choke tube system. Both the 12 and 20 are chambered for the 3-inch shell.

Critical dimensions are: length of pull, 14¹/₄ inches for the 12-gauge and 14 inches for the 20; with the drop at comb 1¹/₂ inches and the drop at heel 2¹/₃ inches for both. The 12 weighs 7¹/₂ pounds, and the 20 tips the scales at 6 pounds, 14 ounces. The 12 is available with 26-, 28- and 30-inch barrels, and the 20 in 26- and 28-inch tubes. Either gun has the potential to be an effective and soft-shooting Sporting gun.

Browning also offers their standard **Citori** line in 12, 20, 28 and 410, with Invector Plus interchangeable choke tubes standard in all gauges, and the 12 and 20 with back-boring. The Browning lineup is one of the most extensive in the industry.

Beretta

Another well-known brand in the high-end shotgun market, this Italian firm has recently introduced new models designed to appeal to both Sporting shooters and those who take their competition guns into the game fields: the **686** and **687 Silver Perdiz Sporting** and the **686 Onyx Sporting**.

These over/unders have a 12.5mm competition rib that is

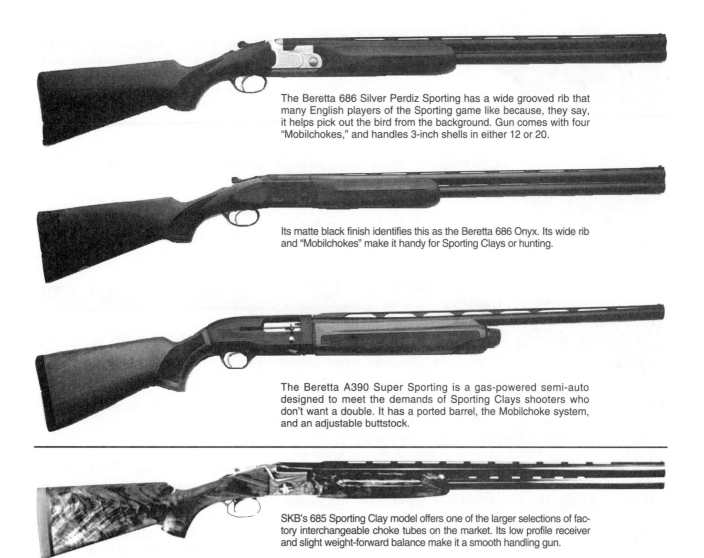

The Beretta 686 Silver Perdiz Sporting has a wide grooved rib that many English players of the Sporting game like because, they say, it helps pick out the bird from the background. Gun comes with four "Mobilchokes," and handles 3-inch shells in either 12 or 20.

Its matte black finish identifies this as the Beretta 686 Onyx. Its wide rib and "Mobilchokes" make it handy for Sporting Clays or hunting.

The Beretta A390 Super Sporting is a gas-powered semi-auto designed to meet the demands of Sporting Clays shooters who don't want a double. It has a ported barrel, the Mobilchoke system, and an adjustable buttstock.

SKB's 685 Sporting Clay model offers one of the larger selections of factory interchangeable choke tubes on the market. Its low profile receiver and slight weight-forward balance make it a smooth handling gun.

very popular among English Sporting shooters. Some feel a wider rib helps pick a target out quickly against the often-cluttered background common to Sporting Clays ranges. This extra-wide rib has a 2.5mm groove in the center and a target front bead for quick acquisition. The guns are supplied with four Mobilchoke tubes for Full, Modified, Improved Cylinder and Skeet 1 constrictions, with additional tubes available. Both guns also have 3-inch 12- or 20-gauge chambers.

The Onyx has a classic matte black receiver highlighted with a gold-filled "P. Beretta" signature. It's available with 28- or 30-inch barrels. The Silver Perdiz offers scroll engraving on a silver receiver and is available in 28- or 30-inch barrels in the 12 gauge; 28-inch barrels in 20 gauge; or in a 12-gauge combo set with both 28- and 30-inch barrels. Critical dimensions on both guns are: drop at comb, 1.4 inches; drop at heel, 2.2 inches; length of pull, 14.7 inches; weight, 7.7 pounds; with an overall length of 45.9 inches with the 28-inch barrels.

Gas gun shooters haven't been forgotten. Beretta's A303 earned an excellent reputation on the competition fields, and continuing that tradition is the firm's new **A390 Super Sporting**, one of the few semi-autos available that was designed especially for the game. The 12-gauge autoloader has ported barrels in 28- or 30-inch lengths, the Mobilchoke system, and a unique factory buttstock that provides adjustments for length of pull, comb height and cast. With a weight of 8 pounds, this should be one of the most comfortable factory-offered autoloaders around, and should be ready to go right out of the box.

SKB Shotguns

The new **Series 85 SKB** over/unders offer eighteen different models in 12-, 20- and 28-gauge designed for the Sporting Clays game. The two smaller gauges come equipped with SKB's standard short choke tube system in Full, Improved Modified, Modified, Improved Cylinder and Skeet 1. The 12-gauge "Competition" long choke tube system is offered in seven different constrictions with muzzle notches for quick in-gun identification. Critical dimensions for all SKB Sporting Clays models are: length of pull, $14^{1}/_{4}$ inches; drop at comb, $1^{7}/_{16}$ inches; and drop at heel, $1^{7}/_{8}$ inches. Barrel length in 20- and 28-gauge is 28 inches, with 28-, 30- and 32-inch tubes offered in the 12-gauge. Average weight for the 12-gauge is 8 pounds, 6 ounces, or 7 pounds, 4 ounces in 20; and 7 pounds, 2 ounces in 28-gauge. All have a low profile receiver, wide, stepped target-style rib, and radiused recoil pad.

Remington's new Peerless over/under has all the required features to make it an excellent choice for Sporting Clays or the game fields.

The Remington Model 11-87 "Premiere" Sporting Clays is a worthy successor to the company's now-discontinued Model 1100 and has all the features needed for success in a variety of clay target games.

The Sporting Clays version of the Kreighoff K-80 offers all the features of the K-80 model in a quick handling package. It is considered state of the art in competition shotguns.

Remington

Although not offering a specific O/U in a Sporting Clays model, the company's new **Peerless** 12-gauge has plenty of potential. It's supplied with Remington's standard Rem-Chokes, but a full set of special Sporting Clays tubes are available options. These have knurled, protruding ends that make fast tube changes easy. They are available in five constrictions with tube designations clearly marked on the tube. Also available are a number of Full and Extra Full accessory tubes, making the RemChoke lineup one of the most complete choke offerings from any major maker.

The Peerless is available with 26-, 28- and 30-inch barrels, the latter likely to find most favor. Critical dimensions are length of pull, $14^{3}/_{16}$ inches; drop at comb, $1^{1}/_{2}$ inches; drop at heel, $2^{1}/_{4}$ inches; and weight of $7^{1}/_{2}$ pounds with the 30-inch barrels.

Gas gun shooters will find Remington's **Model 11-87** a thoroughly reliable choice. Available in 12-gauge, it will handle $2^{3}/_{4}$- or 3-inch shells, and is offered with barrels of 26, 28 and 30 inches. Barrels are fully interchangeable and threaded for the full line of RemChokes. Critical dimensions are length of pull, 14 inches; drop at comb, $1^{1}/_{2}$ inches; and drop at heel, $2^{1}/_{2}$ inches. Weight, with the 30-inch barrel is $7^{7}/_{8}$ pounds.

Rottweil

The Rottweil **Paragon** is an interesting concept in shotgun design that has detachable and interchangeable trigger groups, user-selected automatic ejectors or extractor system, and replaceable firing pins without disassembly of the gun. The trigger is adjustable in three directions. The 12-gauge over/under is a modular system with full interchangeability of receiver, barrels, buttstocks, forends and trigger groups, with no additional fitting required. Screw-in choke tubes are available. No further technical information on the gun was available at the time of writing. It's being imported by Dynamit Nobel-RWS, Inc.

Ljutic

Well known on the trap circuit, the firm's new **LM6** series over/under will likely be seen in the hands of discerning Sporting shooters in the future. Ljutic guns are built to individual customer specifications, resulting in whatever critical stock dimensions you require. Barrels are available in 28- to 32-inch lengths and interchangeable choke tubes are available. Total gun weight is about $8^{3}/_{4}$ pounds; many Sporting competitors favor such heavy guns, both for their smoother swing and lessened recoil. Multiple barrel sets are offered as an option. One of Ljutic's more interesting options is in the trigger mechanism. It can be supplied in pull/pull, release/pull, or release/release fashion.

Krieghoff

The firm's **K-80** has earned an excellent reputation in trap and Skeet, and their new Sporting series should do the same. This 12-gauge over/under has a host of options including a trigger adjustable for length of pull, point of impact adjustment for the bottom barrel, removable trigger group, and interchangeable buttstocks, including a model adjustable for drop at comb and cast. It also uses a safety that can be locked into the off-safe position for competition.

The K-80 Sporting series is available with 3-inch chambers and barrel lengths of 28, 30 and 32 inches. Two rib options (12-8mm tapered and 8mm parallel) are available. Factory choke tubes consist of five models from Cylinder to Super Full. The standard model has an average weight of $8^{1}/_{4}$ pounds, while the Lightweight version tips the scales at $7^{3}/_{4}$.

Shooters looking for an effective Sporting Clays gun have a wide variety to choose from that will fit nearly every budget.

chapter
nineteen

Loads For Sporting Aren't Simple

Top shooters, like three-time National Women's Champion Bonnie McLaurin, pay particular attention to their shell selection. Sometimes the difference between winning and being runner-up is the one target you shot with the wrong shell.

SPORTING CLAYS HAS been referred to as "golf with a shotgun," and the description is an apt one. No other shotgun game can match the diversity of shots one will be presented with in Sporting Clays, nor, for that matter, will the speeds and distances at which those targets are encountered be found anywhere else.

For that reason, there is no such thing as the "ideal Sporting Clays load." When one stops to consider that the shot being addressed at the moment may be broken 10 yards off the gun, and the presentations at the next station could be 50 yards out, it becomes obvious that one load can't do it all.

The best choice in a 50-yard load could easily be the worst for a 10-yard shot. The longer bird will require heavier shot pellets to maintain striking power, plus a dense pattern and a very short shot string to get the pellets concentrated at the target. At 10 yards, the shooter will be best served with a very fast-opening load, and shot size is unimportant. Even the smallest shot will smoke a clay target at that range, assuming the pattern can find it.

Change that scenario to a 25- or 30-yard shot, and either of the above "ideal" loads would be a poor choice!

Load Selection Is Important

Most Sporting Clays shooters are well aware of the need to be equipped with a selection of interchangeable choke tubes to handle varying distances. The knowledgeable shooters are also becoming aware that they must give equal thought to the selection of shells they carry. In fact, many experienced shooters feel that a minimum of three different loads—short-, medium- and long-range—would be a bare bones approach. Most favor five distinctly different loads, varying in shot size, payload weight, velocity and even shot hardness.

Here's a look at why a varied selection of 12-gauge shells is an excellent idea, and how you can achieve it.

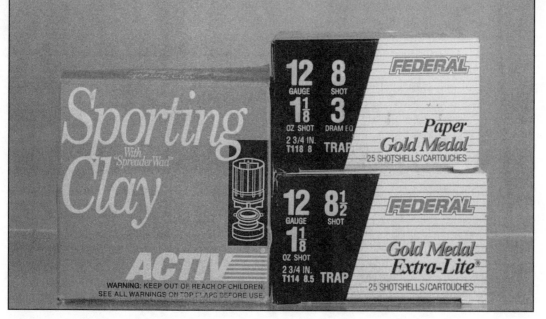

This is one of the author's favorite factory load selections for Sporting fields in the Southeast, where few targets are thrown beyond 35 yards. The ACTIV load handles the close shots, Federal's Extra-Lite #8½ load provides a mild-shooting load for targets in the 20- to 35-yard range, and the heavy 3-dram Federal load of #8s will crush targets to 45 yards with a Modified choke.

Ultra-Short Range

Although extremely close-range shots (under 10 yards) are not as common in Sporting Clays as they are in Skeet, they certainly occur, and the most effective shell is not hard to define. You need one that opens the pattern quickly. A shooter with a 12-inch pattern will have considerably more chance to break a tight target than one with a 5-inch pattern. Shot size is not a critical requirement here: any size target pellet will do. Since #9 shot packs the largest pellet count per load, it's the odds-on favorite. This size shot also exhibits the tendency to pattern less tightly than larger, sturdier pellets, making it a doubly good choice.

Regardless of the choke in use, and without resorting to custom "spreader" wads, there are three basic ways to increase close-range pattern spread: use soft shot, which tends to deform under firing pressures and produces a lot of out-of-round pellets that become fliers; increase velocity, which results in essentially the same thing if less than ultra-hard shot is used, and will even encourage some pattern spreading with #9 shot, regardless of its hardness; or opt for shells with fiber wads instead of modern one-piece plastic shotcups. These will also open patterns. Any one of these factors alone can increase pattern size. Combine a couple of them, and it can make a noticeable difference at close range.

One easy way to accomplish this is to stock up on the ubiquitous promotional ("Dove & Quail") loads that dot the discount stores at the beginning of each fall season. These generally toss a 1-ounce charge of shot that is not as hard or as precisely formed as the premium target loads, at velocities around 1300 fps. Their inability to deliver tight patterns is legendary and that makes them an excellent and inexpensive choice for ultra-close Sporting targets. The fact that they only carry a 1-ounce charge makes no difference, because there are more #9 pellets in a 1-ounce load than you need at that range anyway. All you have to do is get the pattern to open quickly and these are some of the fastest-opening factory-loaded shells available. Their patterns may be as full of holes as a rusty bucket at 30 yards, but they work very well up close.

Another option would be any of the high velocity (1300-plus fps) target loads carrying 1-ounce or less of plain lead

shot. Not as effective as Dove & Quail loads, these are a much better bet than premium target loads that are intended to throw dense, uniform patterns.

Close Range

A lot of shots on a Sporting range will fall within 10 to 20 yards, and effective shells are easy to find—pick any good #9 Skeet load because this is precisely what they were designed to do.

Medium Range

Twenty to 30 yards probably represents the majority of the shots found on a Sporting range and good shells are equally easy to find. Trap loads are ideal. This is the range at which the #8 loads were designed to operate at their best. On the shorter shots, some feel a 1- or 1 1/8-ounce load of #8½ shot is hard to beat. They have plenty of target breaking power to a range approaching 35 yards. On the longer shots, consider switching to #8 shot. It'll do the job out to about 40 yards. In either case, one benefits from the increased pellet count over loads using #7½. Some ammo makers offer #8 loads with a fiber wad, and they are also effective within this area.

Long Range

We're getting into Handicap trap ranges at 40 to 45 yards, so it only makes sense that a heavy 3-dram #7½ trap load would be an excellent choice, and it is. On the shorter side of the range, the 2 3/4-dram, "Lite" 1 1/8-ounce, #7½ loads will also work very well.

Ultra-Long Range

The 45-plus-yard shots are some of the toughest shots one will see on a Sporting Clays range, and not just because distant targets take a good punch to break. They also take a fast load to catch! While the heavy Handicap trap loads in #7½ are still a good bet, some shooters are finding that the International trap loads are a better choice. Although they start with only 24 grams of #7½ shot (about 7/8-ounce), their special shotcups and plated shot pellets give them a very tight-patterning ability at extreme range. Since most of them are moving at 1300-plus fps, they are also an aid in cutting down the long leads required for those extreme distances. In addition, they normally exhibit very short shot strings that get the most out of their smaller shot charge. They are gaining a lot of favor among Sporting Clays shooters when the targets get "way out there."

When it comes to breaking distant targets, the most effective shells will generally be those with nickel-plated shot. These are noticeably more expensive than shells containing other types of shot, but you won't need many of them in a round. They are well worth the extra cost when you need them.

Factory Ammo

For shooters looking to build a versatile shell selection, you can certainly find it represented within the selections offered by the various ammo makers. Often, however, for the reasons explained above, simply buying someone's "Sporting Clays" load may not give you the best shell for the job. Here's what's available from the factory folks.

Federal

Not listed in the Federal catalog are their "Game Loads," the promotional loads described previously. They would be this writer's choice for ultra-close-range work. For close-range work, you would be hard put to beat any of their various #9 Skeet loads, which are listed in the Skeet chapter. Ditto for their trap loads for medium range.

Federal also makes several loads specifically marked as being for Sporting Clays: SC116 (3 dram, $1^1/_8$-ounce, #$7^1/_2$ and 8, at 1200 fps) is a good choice for medium-range shots in #8, and the #$7^1/_2$ size works well for slightly longer shots. SC114 is, essentially, their "Extra-Lite" shell (in #$7^1/_2$ and #8) with a wad that encourages slightly quicker-opening patterns. I like the #8 version for medium shots as well. Their Gold Medal Special Plastic Sporting Clays load, SC170 (size #$7^1/_2$ and #8) offers a high-velocity shell that, in the heavier size, does good long-range work. Some of my favored Sporting Clays loads from Federal are their International Trap loads— N110 is plastic, N119 is paper. Both toss a 24-gram plated load of #$7^1/_2$ shot at 1325 fps and do lovely things beyond 40 yards. The same loads in shot size #$8^1/_2$ are very effective at close range, being designed for the fast-paced game of International Skeet.

Winchester

As with Federal, this company's uncataloged promotional loads are fine ultra-close-range loads, and their previously listed Skeet and trap loads perform well at close and medium ranges.

Their version of the 24-gram International load in sizes #$7^1/_2$, #8 and #9 works quite well. For long shots use #$7^1/_2$ and close shots, size #9.

Victory USA

This innovative ammo maker truly shines in Sporting Clays, and one reason is that each individual size and type of shell in their well-thought-out line carries its own distinctive color. For

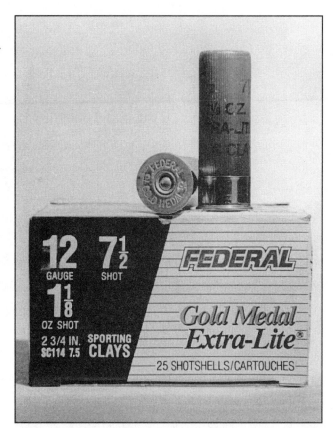

Federal's Sporting Clays loads use wads that open a bit quicker than their standard target loads. That's often an asset on Sporting ranges. Author finds this load to be a top-notch dove and quail load, as well.

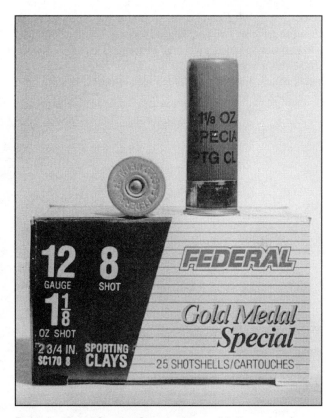

Federal's #8 shot Sporting Clays load is a solid all-round performer, and a top choice for 20- to 35-yard targets.

The 1994 Florida State Sporting Clays Champion Bill Whitehurst favors these 1-ounce Winchester loads for practice and smaller tournaments. There's plenty of target breaking power here, combined with light recoil.

shooters trying to keep five different loads separated, that is of no small importance! That factor alone has helped this new brand gain a quick and loyal following among American Sporting Clays shooters. In fact, you could safely call it the "in" shell.

Victory offers the most extensive 12-gauge Sporting Clays line-up in the industry. Their Stryker International series has the 24-gram International shot charge in #7, #8 and #9, with a velocity of 1460 fps. The #9 version is an excellent ultra-close-range load and its range can be stretched. The Challenger series ups the shot charge to 1 ounce in the same three sizes with a velocity of 1320 fps, while the Super Sporting series offers the three shot sizes as $1\frac{1}{8}$-ounce loads with a

velocity of 1270 fps. The Sonic series gives shooters the option of a full 1-ounce charge at about 1400 fps.

Four shell models, four different velocities, and three different shot charge weights give them the ability to handle just about any shot on the Sporting Clays field.

If more versatility is required, there is the faster-opening Challenger felt wad series in sizes #6 through #9, and their tight-patterning Challenger Nickel Sporting load in #7$\frac{1}{2}$ and #8.

Any Sporting Clays shooter who relies totally on factory ammunition, which is required at major NSCA matches, really needs to look no further than the Victory line-up. This writer is quite impressed with them.

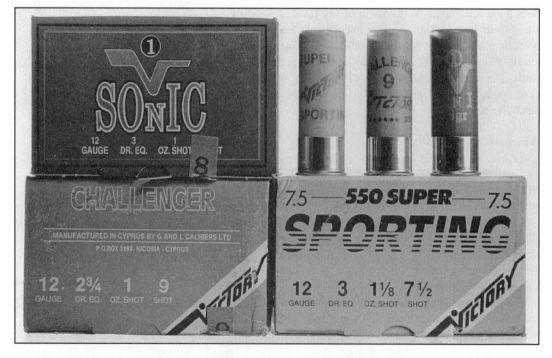

Victory offers a comprehensive line of shotshells designed expressly for Sporting Clays, and color codes the shells so shooters can keep various loads separated in their vest pockets. A very neat idea!

Many shooters looking for a single load for shots inside 40 yards will find a light load of #8s, like this Remington offering, to be a good choice.

For those who insist on shooting an entire round of Sporting Clays with just one shell, author feels the Remington 7½x8½ Duplex load is one of the best choices.

Remington

As with the other two members of the Big Three, Remington's excellent line of trap and Skeet shells will serve well as a basic selection to handle close, medium and long shots. They also offer a 24-gram International load in sizes #7½ (long range) and #9 (short range) that hits 1325 fps.

For those who favor Duplex loads, they offer two Sporting Clays models in addition to their already-listed trap and Skeet loads. They are the SC12L (2¾-dram, 1145 fps, #7½x8), and the SC12M (3-dram, 1200 fps, size #7½x8½). Although I am not a fan of Duplex loads, I do feel that if one were bound and determined to shoot a round of Sporting with only a single load, the latter Duplex number would be about as good a choice as one could get, with the possible exception of a 3-dram #8 trap load.

Fiocchi of America

As with the others, Fiocchi's previously listed trap and Skeet loads have a role on the Sporting Clays field. I really like their 12TX load, which throws an ounce of 8½s at 1250 fps. Of special interest, however, are their two International loads: 12IN24 (24 gram, 1400 fps, size #7½, #8 and #9) and the 12IN28 (1 ounce, 1290 fps, in the same three sizes). The latter would make a pretty fair three-shell selection, while shooters looking for high speed on distant targets would likely find it with the 1400 fps load in #7½. Fiocchi's International loads have a good reputation for tight patterns at long range, due to their use of high-antimony lead shot,

This heavier (3-dram) version of the Remington Duplex load offers a little more reach than their 2¾-dram offering.

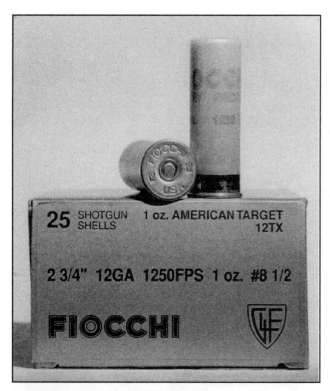

Fiocchi's 1-ounce high-speed #8½ is one of the author's favorites for targets in the 15- to 30-yard range. It's a real jewel that crushes targets, but not your shoulder.

although they probably won't equal the performance of nickel-plated shot.

ACTIV

Similar to the other makers, ACTIV has a number of loads in their trap and Skeet line that are ideal for Sporting Clays. They've been listed in those appropriate sections, so we won't repeat them here. They do fine work within the conventional close, medium, and long-range venues. Of special interest from this maker are their nickel-plated International Trap loads (see chart). They are quite superb when a target gets out past 45 yards.

The two Sporting Clays loads, SCL12G and SCL12GL, use wads that open the pattern a bit faster than conventional shotcups.

ACTIV					
Load	Dram Equiv.	Shot Ozs.	Shot Size	Velocity FPS	Comments
A12FL	3¼	1⅛	7½,8,9	1235	—
A12HH	3¼	1	7½,8,9	1320	—
A12TH	3	28 gram	7½,8,9	1290	—
SCL12G	3	1⅛	7½,8,9	1200	—
SCL12GL	2¾	1⅛	7½,8,9	1145	—

Reloads and Components

While NSCA rules prohibit reloads at major matches, they allow them to be used at the club level, at the discretion of the club. The individual club rules on reloaded shells will, understandably, vary, and shooters will certainly want to inquire about them before taking the time to roll their own.

If your club allows them, handloads can allow the Sporting shooter to create some specialty loads that he will not find readily available from the major makers. Dave Fackler of Ballistic Products Inc., an enthusiastic Sporting Clays shooter himself, has come up with a number of interesting wad designs, and has found a few more that he imports from Europe. They allow the reloader to craft some extremely effective custom loads. Here are a few of the specialty wads available and where they are best used.

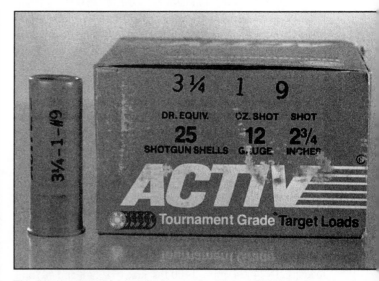

This light-recoiling, high-speed 1-ounce load from ACTIV is serious clay target medicine to about 30 yards.

ACTIV offers a special Sporting Clays shell loaded with the Italian Gualandi wad. These open faster than any other factory load the author has tried. He likes to keep a few of these in a pocket for those real "in your face shots."

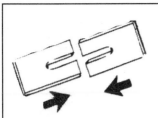

The Spreader-X from Ballistic Products is a two-piece cardboard insert that forms four chambers. It can be used with any wad, and opens patterns remarkably for effective Sporting loads.

The Ballistic Products 12-gauge G/BP Dispersor X-12 was has an integral X-spreader, which makes loading easy.

Ballistic Products' G/BP Brush Wad is a standard wad without the protective shotcup. Like the X-12 above, it can be loaded with 1 to 1⅛ ounces of shot.

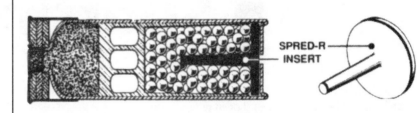

SPRED-R INSERT

The BPI Spreader Wad Insert is shaped like a thumbtack and can be used with any wad and size shot. It opens the pattern one degree.

For ultra-close-range shots, even the soft-shot promotional loads aren't going to give a large pattern inside 10 yards, although they will open up a good deal more than hard-shot target loads. Getting a pattern to open up very quickly, actually scatter the shot, is an advantage here. If you double the diameter of your pattern you don't just double your chances of getting the shot on target, you increase it by a factor of four. That's well worth the time spent making up some special "spreader loads."

In years past, creating these required inserting a separate component, either a cardboard X-spreader, or a spreader post, into a standard wad during the loading process. One can also cut the shot-protecting petals on a standard target wad back to about a quarter of their original length. These methods will still work, but there are easier ways to do it today, thanks to Fackler.

The Ballistic Products 12-gauge G/BP Dispersor X-12 wad is a one-piece, easy-to-load wad with an integral X-spreader moulded right into the shotcup. As the wad leaves the muzzle, the specially-designed petals fold back and allow the spreader to really get the pattern open quickly.

Another option is the G/BP 12-gauge Brush Wad, which is nothing more than a standard plastic wad without a protective shotcup. This was created to counter the rules some clubs have against wads with an X-spreader. Either of these wads can be loaded with 1 to 1⅛ ounces of shot, at various velocities. If softer grades of #9 shot are used they will more than double the pattern size of conventional loads. The Dispersor is at its best under 15 yards, while the Brush

Wad works well out to 20 yards.

Another option that is particularly useful in the close-range area is the G/BP Piston Skeet wad. This is a conventional one-piece target wad, but uses a unique petal arrangement to promote fast-opening patterns in the 10- to 25-yard range. It is very popular with European International Skeet shooters for that reason. This can be used with standard American components and also makes a great Skeet load. It's at its best with harder grades of shot and will throw some very wide yet uniform patterns from an open-choked gun. When loaded with #8 shot, it becomes a very useful shell for longer shots in the 20- to 30-yard range.

Mid-range shots can be handled quite well with standard trap load recipes, and they will be discussed in our reloading chapter.

Effective extra-long-range loads (45-plus yards) can be difficult to assemble from conventional target components, so Fackler has imported a special International trap wad commonly used in Europe, called the G/BP International Target Driver. This will handle shot charges from 1 to 1⅛ ounces and is designed to produce maximum pattern density at extreme range. When loaded with #7½ nickel shot, it becomes one of the best extra-long-range loads available to the reloader. It will break 60-yard birds.

While toting a large and varied selection of shotshells may seem like a lot of trouble, it is one of the best ways to give yourself an edge on any Sporting Clays course. If you are going to "play golf with a shotgun," it makes sense to have all the clubs in your bag!

chapter twenty

Starting In Sporting

UNLIKE TRAP AND Skeet, Sporting Clays is not a game that can be learned by rote and then shot on reflexes. The variation in target speeds, distances, angles, target sizes, and the different multiple target presentations inherent in Sporting make that impossible.

For example, it is easy to tell a Skeet student what the best foot position and the proper lead are for the station four target. That target will essentially be the same whether you shoot it in Maine or California—its speed, flight path and distance are rigidly prescribed by rules.

Ain't no such thing in Sporting!

You might find one course's rabbit target a rather simple shot, thrown from a slow-speed manual trap, and at a modest 15 yards from the gun. The next course may zip a rabbit target from a higher-speed electronic trap at a range of 40 yards! You can't even use the same choke for the two shots, let alone the same lead and technique. That's what makes Sporting Clays such a challenge.

The successful Sporting shooter doesn't necessarily "learn" to shoot this game. Instead, he learns a well-rounded selection of shotgun techniques, and then applies the correct technique for the particular target presentation he is facing on that station. It's a thinking shooter's game. Here's how to start getting your mind in tune.

Gun Position and Handling

Sporting Clays begins with the gun in a low gun position before the bird is called for. In standard Sporting, the butt must be visible below the shooter's armpit, and cannot be shouldered until the bird actually leaves the trap.

In my opinion, this is one of the most overlooked areas of Sporting Clays instruction, especially if the shooter has had some experience at trap and Skeet where the targets are called for from a mounted gun position. It is also one of the most important aspects of good shooting, and the reason should be obvious: Unless the gun is mounted to the same position each time, it will not shoot where you are looking each time. If that happens, your body position, target lead and shooting tech-

One of the most overlooked aspects of learning Sporting Clays is the need to develop a smooth and consistent gun mount. In terms of time and money, that is best done through both "dry practice" at home (with an empty gun, of course) and on a Skeet or trap range.

nique become moot points because you won't be on the bird even if you do all of them correctly.

If you doubt the truth in those words, just watch what happens to a Skeet shooter who has some skill (B Class and above) the first time he tries to shoot a round of Skeet from a Sporting Clays low gun position. His score will drop markedly. Trap shooters will likely fare even worse. Yet, every one of those shots and angles are ones he will have seen many times before. He knows the leads and techniques. It's just a question of mastering gun handling skills.

Gun handling is a skill that must be learned and practiced. It also helps if your equipment is properly set up for the task at hand.

A well-fitted shotgun is a tremendous asset, and one reason why experienced Sporting Clays shooters will go to the time and trouble to have it done correctly. It also helps if the heel of the recoil pad is smoothly radiused to prevent snagging as the gun comes up. Some shooters also put a slight radius on the

Author demonstrates that there is no one right initial gun hold position on a Sporting Clays range, with this one for a high incoming target. Compare it to the lower gun hold for the rabbit, and it's apparent that Sporting Clays is a thinking man's game.

inside edge of the recoil pad to further reduce drag. The toe of the pad also gets a smoothing. This aids in a smooth dismount of the gun, because, as we will see later, good shooters will sometimes dismount the gun between shots on some target pairs.

When selecting a vest or shooting shirt for Sporting, you will want one with an International-style shoulder pad that extends down the front of the vest. Those made for conventional trap and Skeet have a small pad that often catches the gun's recoil pad and makes a mess of the gun mount. The fewer things you have on your vest or gun to snag, the smoother and more consistent your gun mount will be.

Stance also plays a role. I have seen some of the most uncomfortable and exaggerated stances one could imagine among trap and Skeet shooters. Some of the semi-crouch-feet-stuck-together-body-wound-up-like-a-spring stances make a consistent gun mount a real feat!

I much prefer a student to stand up straight with the feet opened to about shoulder width. There should be no exaggerated crouch, but the knees should not be locked. Some shoot-

High overhead targets require a weight shift to the back foot. This is one of the few times that an effective shot would have the majority of the weight on the back foot.

This forend hand position may work for shooters in games where the gun can be mounted before the bird appears, but might be too far forward to allow a smooth mount in Sporting Clays.

ers are more comfortable with their weight spread evenly, while others like just a touch more weight on the leading foot. This provides better balance, a smoother swing and wider swing arc. Novice shooters often tend to take a "rifleman's" stance, with weight on the back foot. This is not good because it restricts the swing. The only time back foot weight is good form in Sporting is when you are presented a high incoming target that must be taken almost directly overhead.

The shooter's grip on the forend is another overlooked point. I like to move the student's hand around on the forend until he finds the point where he can mount, and dismount, the gun without strain using the forend (leading) hand only. That point is usually a bit farther back than the shooter started with, especially if he has been shooting trap or Skeet from a pre-mounted position. This will alter the weight distribution between the shooter's hands and make for a much smoother and more consistent gun mount.

Additionally, there is the matter of the erect head. When mounting the gun, it is always brought to the face—never bring the face to the gun! To do so is to encourage a lot of bobbing and weaving of the head, and since your eye is essentially the rear sight on your shotgun, you can imagine what it does to your score.

Proper gun handling techniques will allow the shooter a comfortable stance with a maximum range of movement. The eyes can be locked onto the bird and the gun will come smoothly to the bird without a great deal of conscious thought, and in a very consistent manner.

Master the gun mount and you are well on your way to becoming a good Sporting shooter. Neglect it and you'll have a helluva time!

One final matter concerns where to position the barrel before calling for the bird. In my opinion, there are only two hard and fast rules: (1) The muzzle should be within your

Sliding the hand rearward on the forend will help most shooters execute a smoother mount because of the basic biomechanical advantage of a hand position that puts the gun's balance more between the hands. Shooters should experiment with their leading hand position.

The proper initial gun hold position will vary with the angle of the target being presented, but it should never be so high that it will put the target below the gun barrel when it emerges. This shooter's hold is a bit high for the rabbit target he is about to engage.

range of vision so that it and the bird can be viewed simultaneously before the mount is begun; (2) The muzzle should never be held above the flight path of the target. If the bird leaves the trap and ducks under the barrel, you will temporarily lose sight of it, and your focus on it. You then have to re-acquire it and that wastes time you don't have to waste.

This, obviously, means that there is no one correct gun hold position. A ground-bouncing rabbit will require a much lower gun hold than a high, incoming dove. In pairs involving different targets, like a rabbit and a snipe, the hold should be correct for the first target you will engage.

Body Position

In the Skeet section, the importance of aligning the body to its natural point of aim was discussed. For most Skeet targets that will be near the Eight Post, since all targets are directed toward it. The principle of natural point of aim is still valid in Sporting, but it is much tougher to define and will change with the shot.

Determining body position starts with figuring out where you want to, or can, break the target. Every target will have an ideal break point on its flight path where it fairly screams "Kill me!" Not surprisingly, this is referred to as the kill zone. Given differing abilities and reaction times among different shooters, the best kill zone for each shot may vary among shooters. You have to figure out where it is for you, and position your shooting stance to it. This, in effect, becomes the Sporting Clays shooter's Eight Post. It may be nothing more than a small circle of air.

Multiple targets can complicate that, since a perfect position for one target may not be so for the other. Because lifting the feet to shift position while a bird is in the air is virtually guaranteed to cause a miss, you'll have to do the same type of fudging that occurs during Skeet doubles. Give yourself enough swing room to break the first target, and fudge your body position toward the second. This is one reason why an upright, fluid stance is so important in Sporting.

Author shows proper position to engage a ground-bouncing rabbit. The gun muzzle is within his field of vision and below the path of the target. Mounting the gun is quick and simple from this position.

The rabbit can be a tough station for many shooters because of the mental block a lot of shooters have when it comes to shooting a target on the ground.

Equally important is the point to which you pivot your upper body to get your "first look"—the point on the flight path where you first visually acquire the target. New shooters tend to come back much too far toward the trap. This often causes the bird to get by them, and then they have to really unwind to catch it.

Given the variety of target presentations, there is no hard and fast rule here, either. I prefer to come back to the trap hard enough to put some coil in the body and make me unwind a bit when moving to the bird. This generates gun speed during the mount. If the bird is consistently outrunning you, however, you may have to position yourself even more toward the kill zone.

Exceptions to that are some extremely fast and close crossing shots. Sometimes it can be to the shooter's advantage to take a first look point close to the house because it will make you swing like hell to catch it. At times that's exactly what is needed to break that target!

Time and experience will also alter your first look point.

The more proficient you become, the more you can fudge to the kill zone. Your first look point can also be altered by the shooting technique you use.

Shooting Techniques

Sustained lead and fast-swing were both explained in Chapter 13, "Skeet Simplified," and there is not much point in rehashing them here. Both have their uses in Sporting, and they pretty much parallel those in Skeet. Sustained lead is a good way to handle incoming targets that have a little angle away from the shooter, while the fast-swing is generally a superior technique for crossers, outgoers and quartering shots.

The biggest disadvantage to the sustained lead in Sporting is that it requires the lead to be known. You must have handled that distance and angle successfully in the past, and have filed the amount of daylight you see between muzzle and target away in your little on-board computer. Some experienced shooters who have virtually seen every shot can make good use of the sustained lead in a far wider variety of presentations than most shooters. The technique does not work nearly as well for me in this game as it does in Skeet. The problem is that we are all seeing new leads and angles on each new course.

Another factor is target speed. Skeet and trap targets have their velocities fixed. Sporting targets use machines that throw at different speeds, and the size and shape of the targets will also produce different speeds among them. All of this complicates things for a shooter using a technique that requires the exact lead to be known, and is relatively unforgiving if target speed and distance are misjudged. With the fast-swing, the speed of the target will tend to accelerate your gun speed and that, in itself, can help compensate for varying target speeds.

In my opinion, that makes the fast-swing the bread-and-butter technique for Sporting. The faster the target is moving, the faster you have to move to nail it. There is, however, another technique that can be extremely useful. The individual who explained it to me called it the "pullaway," and I will use the same explanation here, although I'm certain some shooters might pick nits with this definition.

The pullaway came about as a direct result of the low gun position used in Sporting Clays. It is not very effective from a pre-mounted position, nor is it easy to accomplish. It works because of the body's natural tendency to lock eyes upon an

Developing the ability to analyze a station, and determine how you are going to handle it, is critical for success. These shooters are paying special attention to how other shooters handle the target, and that is one approach.

aerial target while the upper body uncoils to track it in flight. If the proper gun mount technique is executed, the eyes never leave the target and the gun comes up to look exactly where the eyes are looking. Since the body is moving as the gun is being mounted, gun speed has already been generated. Once the gun is mounted, it is still moving at body speed, which is moving at target speed. At that point, the gun speed is quickly increased and the shot triggered.

In practice it works like this: Take your natural point of aim in the kill zone, pivot the upper body to the first look point, call for the bird and, as it appears, swing with it as the gun comes up. When the gun hits the cheek and shoulder, it is on the bird, not at a point behind it as with the fast-swing. As soon as the bird picture is seen, the body accelerates the swing and triggers the shot as soon as the lead is seen. For all practical purposes, the shot is triggered within milliseconds of the gun mount.

This particular technique results in two very positive things for the Sporting Clays shooter.

The first is a reduction in lead. The sudden acceleration of the gun, which is already, essentially, moving at target speed, creates a faster swing than possible with other techniques. Going back to the Skeet field, I find from a low gun position that I require about 4 feet of lead to break a station four crossing shot with the sustained lead. With the fast-swing, the lead decreases to a bit more than 2 feet. With the pullaway, it is cut even further, to about what appears to be 18 inches. It's worth remembering that this is a 21-yard direct crossing shot on a 45 mph bird. Some of the closer, slower targets on a Sporting range can be broken by virtually shooting at the bird.

The reduction in lead is primarily why the pullaway technique achieved its popularity.

Sporting Clays will use both electric traps (like this Skeet machine) and manual traps on the same range. Shooters must realize that electric machines throw targets at a higher velocity than manual traps, and that can affect your lead.

It's not uncommon in Sporting to be presented with crossing shots in the 40-plus-yard range. If you shoot a sustained lead, you will need over 10 feet at 40 yards. That's too much for most human brains to accurately compute and hold because you have no real frame of reference. The pullaway cuts those long leads down to something we can be more comfortable and consistent with.

Another factor enters into the picture with sustained leads that are long, and that is which way the target is crossing. A right-handed shooter will have the gun to the right cheek and the right eye looking down the rib. The left eye, assuming the proper "both eyes open" technique, will be looking down the left side of the barrels. If the target is crossing from the left, both eyes can easily see and track it. This provides the binocular vision we humans require for accurate depth perception.

If the target is a right-to-left crosser, however, the left eye can be blocked from seeing it by the gun. Holding a precise lead is extremely difficult with only one eye if the lead exceeds more than a couple of feet, and doubly tough if the target is rising.

There are some outstanding Sporting Clays instructors who recommend that right-handed shooters use the pullaway on all right to left crossing shots (the reverse being true for left-handers) just because of this, and teach the fast-swing or sustained lead for targets going the other way.

Regardless of the circumstance it is used in, the pullaway can greatly reduce the lead required on a target. Another advantage is the control it gives a shooter over where he breaks his targets.

Because the pullaway is fired almost simultaneously with the mounting of the gun, the only restriction on how quickly you can break the target is how fast you can mount the gun. Conversely, by delaying the mount, you can comfortably break targets at different ranges.

Going back to Skeet station four, a standard shot that any shooter can duplicate, I find that from a low gun position I cannot break the target with a sustained lead in a consistent manner until it has gone 10 to 15 feet past the Eight Post. The fast-swing lets me take it on the Post, and the pullaway lets me break it 10 to 15 feet in front of the Post. Or, I can break it anywhere along the flight path I choose just by delaying the gun mount. Some of that control can be had with the fast-swing, but the pullaway offers a larger degree of control. When you have to break a bird in a narrow window in trees or brush, or take one bird in a pair very quickly in order to get a reasonable shot on the second, the pullaway is worth its weight in gold. When a shot has to be made quickly, regardless of the speed, distance or angle, the pullaway can be lightning fast.

Multiple Targets

Once a shooter has a handle on the above techniques of gun mount, stance, body position and shooting techniques, he now must consider how to handle the gun on multiple targets.

A single target is just that. Shoot the thing, reload and call for the next presentation. Pairs, however, require some thought as to how they will be dealt with.

Following pairs are one bird launched within 3 seconds of

Experienced shooters will often discuss the finer points of a particular station and share their observations. The ability to think your way through a Sporting Clays course is important.

the shooter's command, and a second bird launched at some time within 3 seconds of that, at the puller's discretion. When shooting from a fluid, low gun position, experienced shooters find the act of mounting the gun itself to be an integral part of the shot-making process. So what do you do after you have broken the first bird and are waiting on the second? The smart shooters drop the gun from their shoulder! This makes both shots the same. That's also why these shooters radius the toe on their recoil pad. It makes the dismount as smooth as the mount.

You don't have to drop the gun back to the original starting position. It's easier to just push it slightly away from the shoulder, and drop the butt slightly to unlock the cheek.

Once a shooter becomes accustomed to this, he will find it also works on report pairs, where the second bird is launched at the sound of the shot fired at the first. You don't have as much time, but you don't need it. You're not going back to a rigid low gun position, merely dropping the buttstock. You don't have far to go to remount the gun, and with a bit of practice the partial dismount becomes as smooth as the mount.

In both cases, it beats the heck out of smoking the first target with a fluid gun mount and then standing there with a dead gun locked into your shoulder while you try to find, and then re-establish, swing speed on the second target.

Simultaneous pairs present a totally different challenge. If they are different targets (Fur & Feathers, for example), some skilled shooters still do a slight dismount after the first bird. If they are true pairs, there are a very few shooters skilled enough to do it. Most of us can't, at least not if we want to shoot the second bird in the same county as the first. You have to analyze the flight path of the birds and determine how you can best swing through the first to get the second, without having to slow the gun.

Sometimes that means taking the trailing bird first, and then accelerating to catch the lead bird. It works on some stations. Other times, you may have to take the lead bird first, recover from recoil, and catch the second with a classic Skeet shooter's pre-mounted fast-swing.

Every now and then, if the Good Lord is smiling on you and the course designer had an off day, you may find one point in the flight of that pair where both can be taken with one shot. This usually happens after they have gotten out a bit. If you happen to miss, well... you've now got an even longer shot on the second bird. It's a gamble, but sometimes it can be worth it. Smart shooters will watch the targets at viewing to see if it is feasible. If you can pull it off, it impresses the heck out of the other shooters.

These gun handling techniques are markedly different from those used in conventional trap or Skeet. However, trap and Skeet ranges are the best place to learn them. The reasons are purely time and money.

Most shooters have to travel a good bit farther to find a Sporting Clays range than a trap or Skeet setup. Sporting also takes a lot longer to shoot. A round of fifty birds can take a squad most of the afternoon. A round of Sporting Clays also costs a lot more than trap or Skeet. At my Skeet club, a member's fee for twenty-five birds is $2.50, or $5.00 for fifty. A

You are never too young to start at Sporting. This young shooter made a great showing in his age class at the 1994 NSCA Florida State Championships.

141

It may get you some funny looks from other trap shooters, but shooting 16-yard trap from a low gun position will aid Sporting Clays shooters on many of the targets they will see.

Gainesville, Florida shooter Chris Pearce prepares to engage a high-speed International Skeet target. Author feels this game, above all others, can provide some of the best practice for Sporting Clays shooters.

fifty-bird round of Sporting will run between $15 and $50, depending on the range.

Cross Training Practice

To learn fluid gun handling and the various shooting techniques, a shooter needs to see a lot of targets and a variety of angles. It's fast and cheap to do it on a Skeet or trap range. It is also very valid practice, because you'll find virtually every angle presented to you in trap or Skeet at some point on a Sporting field.

At my Skeet club, it is not uncommon for a few Sporting Clays aficionados to just open their own field and play their own games. We shoot between the existing stations to look at new angles, and frequently back up 10 or 15 yards from the mid-field stations to practice long crossers.

I have also practiced on a trap range by starting at the 16-yard line, then moving progressively forward until I was standing right behind the trap house. When you get on a Sporting field, you'll see those same shots represented as quail, pheasants, rising sharptails, etc., and you'll have a far better handle on them than you would if your experience with those angles has been limited to a few expensive rounds of Sporting.

Because you will see more targets in less time, your gun mounting technique will also be honed more quickly. There's nothing in anybody's trap or Skeet range rules that says you can't call for a target from a low gun position, so why not take advantage of that fact to fine-tune your gun handling skills?

For that matter, why not take advantage of cross training to master shots that are giving you fits on the Sporting Clays fields? Bonnie McLaurin remarked to me once, "Shooting

Many smaller clubs will allow shooters to alter the target presentations on standard trap and Skeet ranges and actually set up shots that duplicate those that shooters are having problems with in Sporting Clays. It's well worth the time and effort!

Sporting Clays is a lot like fighting a forest fire. Just when you get a problem solved in one spot, something flares up in another area."

That sort of thing happens to me all the time! A perfect example is one particular tower shot on a local Sporting range. It is not a difficult shot. I've been looking at Skeet targets like that for years. Essentially, the target comes off a 20-foot tower to the right and angles out into the field to the left at about 45 degrees. The target is very visible and is normally broken at about 20 yards, slightly to the shooter's right side.

It's a simple shot, and one I didn't think needed to be rushed—at least, not until they threw a true pair, with the birds in trail. Then the smooth rhythm I had been using to take the singles resulted in my second shot being at a 30-yard falling bird. Not my cup of tea!

The singles were easy, but the pairs were killing me. So I decided to speed up my shot rhythm, and promptly screwed everything up! Now they were all eating my lunch.

I solved the problem at a Skeet range. I backed up about 10 yards from a point midway between stations two and three to duplicate the angle and distance on the shot, and began practicing what could be called a slight variation of the pullaway shot. Upon seeing the bird, I'd mount the gun, get spot-on the bird, and immediately accelerate forward. The amount of lead was nothing. I triggered the shot as soon as the acceleration began. It didn't take a full box of shells to get the timing right. With pairs, all I had to do was mount on the trailing bird, fire, and swing smoothly through the first.

I invariably run that station now, and it only took 15 minutes on a Skeet range to figure out how to do it!

Another station that was giving me fits was also deceptively simple. The trap was located behind and to the right of the shooter, and three singles would come out at angles varying from a moderate quartering angle to a dead straightaway. Pairs were launched at the moderate right-to-left angle. The shot was not difficult. The problem was the lack of time because the birds were in the bushes within 25 yards.

I first started shooting this station by screwing my body all the way around to the right to stare right at the trap house, but I found I didn't have time to catch the birds, and was missing

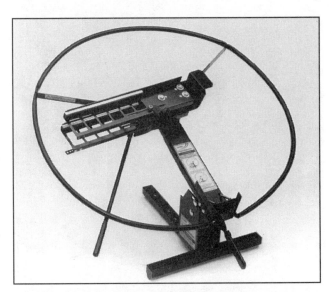

A portable trap can be a great training aid for new shooters because it will allow you to duplicate the flight of many targets that are killing you on the field, yet may not be adequately duplicated on trap or Skeet ranges. The current National Ladies Champion and the men's Florida State Champion use portable traps for just that reason!

Shooting standard Skeet targets out of their proper order on doubles, and from the low gun position, is an excellent form of practice for Sporting Clays. In addition, it's a lot less expensive than practicing on a Sporting range.

Author finds the Skeet range to be great practice for Sporting Clays. It's a lot cheaper, and you can see more targets in less time.

some easy singles because of it. I adjusted by moving my first look point farther out into the field, but found that caused me to shoot as soon as the gun hit my shoulder—almost spot or snap shooting. This resulted in my shooting behind birds with any angle on them.

That took four boxes of shells shooting from low gun from the 16-yard trap line to correct, and it was quite an interesting experience. I think I broke only eleven birds my first round. I had no problems with the extreme angled shots; it was the *gentle* angles I was missing. I found that I was rushing the shot and shooting behind the birds. Once I altered my timing to mount the gun slightly behind the bird and then move smoothly, and unhurriedly, through it, I started popping twenty-two to twenty-three per round.

That slight bit of practice and a little change in timing was all it took, and I now run that Sporting station regularly, as well. I have no idea how long it would have taken me to discover that solution by just shooting that one Sporting Clays station until I got it right, but four rounds of trap cost less than one round of Sporting Clays! That, I do know.

Another problem area that cross training has aided me greatly in is the building of speed on those close, quick, "in-your-face" targets that many Southeastern Sporting Clays ranges love to throw. If you measure distance and angle, a lot

Traps in Sporting are often hidden and may not give the shooter the opportunity to actually see the bird leave the trap. Shooters must develop the ability to pick up a bird emerging from "the bushes" if they are to be successful.

If a shooter can handle a low house eight Skeet target from the low gun position, he needn't worry about being too slow on the Sporting Clays ranges. Skeet, shot from the low gun, is good training for Sporting Clays shooters.

of these targets aren't that tough. Add increased speed, and stick some trees and bushes on the field for them to duck behind periodically, and things get a bit more complicated.

You have to jump these birds quickly, and having learned my clay target style as a sustained-lead American Skeet shooter, I just wasn't getting the job done.

Swearing off the slower American Skeet targets for awhile, and shifting over to the International Skeet range worked wonders on my speed. In fact, if I had to pick one clay target game that would benefit Sporting Clays shooters the most, that would be it! If you are just out to practice, there is nothing carved in stone that says you must adopt the gun-on-the-hip starting position: use your normal Sporting Clays low gun position. The faster speed of the International targets will certainly improve your speed.

Combine that with a few rounds of trap, maybe some selected Skeet station shots, and you will find lovely things happening to your scores at Sporting.

You can even practice your techniques for following and report pairs simply by telling the puller what you want him to pull.

The only realistic Sporting practice you can't get on a trap or Skeet range is trailing true pairs. Nothing in life is perfect.

With this "intensified" training regime, however, the first time you do step onto a Sporting field you will have a working knowledge of the various techniques you will need. Here's the way to go about applying them.

As you step up to a new station, view the target presentation and then analyze the shots with the following factors in mind. (1) What is the range at which you will be engaging the targets? This will determine your choke and load selection for that station; (2) If pairs are presented, which bird will you take first? Which shooting technique will be most effective for each? This isn't something you should try to figure out after the birds are in the air!

Sometimes you will have no choice in the order. At other times you may have wide latitude, including taking a trailing bird first and driving through to the lead bird, or, taking the lead bird first and then executing a fast swing on the trailer— or maybe even taking both with one shot. Planning how you will shoot them is very important because it will determine your kill zone, and that will determine your initial stance and gun hold position. Also note the flight path of the first bird you will shoot, and make sure your gun hold is correct for it.

After that, it's just a matter of properly executing your shot plan. Now, that's often easier said than done, and is one reason why Sporting Clays is the most challenging shotgun game around.

Sporting's Smaller Side

MOST OF WHAT one sees or hears about Sporting Clays centers around the 12-gauge gun. That's understandable. It has been the dominant gauge in competition since the sport's inception, and will continue to hold that position, but it's certainly not the only bore size seen on the Sporting fields.

There are a lot of folks who shoot Sporting Clays strictly for fun, and have no real interest in registered competition. As many are discovering, you can have just as much fun with the smaller gauges as you can with the big 12, and each passing year sees more sub-gauges making their way to the Sporting courses. This has not gone unnoticed by course managers. In fact, many are now utilizing bits of extra land to set up shorter, less demanding courses that not only allow shooters to use smaller gauges, but serve a second purpose in providing a slightly less challenging course to introduce new shooters to the game.

The interest in sub-gauges hasn't escaped the notice of the ammo makers, either. In fact, in a move that should clearly demonstrate how strong that interest actually is, many are bringing out special Sporting Clays loads for the 20, 28 and 410 guns. These folks don't create new loads just because they think someone might buy a box or two! They make them only when there is a demonstrated market, and it's obvious one exists here.

In fact, there is enough interest in sub-gauge sporting that the NSCA has future plans to incorporate gauge classes into registered competition, as has long been done in Skeet.

No, sub-gauge Sporting isn't a passing fad or fancy. It's here to stay and is certain to grow in popularity. This is amply demonstrated by the fact that a number of insert tube makers tell me that Sporting Clays shooters are now starting to have their 12-gauge guns "tubed" to smaller gauges in the same manner as Skeet shooters.

How effective can the little gauges be at this demanding game? To be perfectly honest, the 12-gauge will always be the best choice if breaking the maximum number of targets is your goal. The smaller gauges can't match the load versatility and long-range power of the bigger bore—they just can't car-

Author often shoots his Browning Citori Lightning on the Sporting Clays ranges. The little 28-gauge is a joy on the field, and can be quite effective if you handload for it.

Sub-gauge guns are not as big a handicap as many might suppose, especially in the Southeast and East, where most Sporting Clays shots are under 35 yards.

ry the shot to do it. With that obvious statement out of the way, however, it must also be said that the sub-gauges can offer surprising performance when target distances are kept under 35 yards. Many of the shorter, sub-gauge courses do just that.

Getting the most out of sub-gauges isn't quite as easy as with the 12. The load selection, whether you buy them or roll your own, is so varied in that gauge that many shooters no longer do much in the way of choke tube changes, they just change their shells to adjust patterns. That approach is less effective in the smaller gauges. Pattern control becomes more important and it is best achieved by balancing both load and choke. If your favorite 20, 28 or 410 isn't fitted for interchangeable choke tubes, the biggest favor you can do yourself is to have it done. Hastings, Briley, Clearview, etc., can all perform such work. Though I don't use a large selection of chokes tubes in the 12-gauge, when I head out with a 28-gauge or 410 I want to be carrying Skeet, Improved Cylinder, Modified and Full tubes. They *will* be needed.

You will also want to fit the gun to yourself with the same care you would apply to your favorite competition 12-gauge—maybe more. The smaller gauges just don't give you much margin for error, and good gun fit is critical.

On the plus side, both of these additions will make the gun a much better performer in the game fields. Also, a few rounds of Sporting Clays before bird season won't hurt your ability to bust feathers instead of clays!

Here's a look at how you can wring a little more performance from the smaller gauges:

20-Gauge

Although the 20 does qualify as a sub-gauge, I really don't think a reasonably skilled shooter is handicapping himself

Sub-gauge Sporting Clays matches are a reality now, and their popularity will only increase in the future. Many shooters are already tubing their guns in the same manner as Skeet shooters have for years.

very much on any targets inside the 35-yard mark. The 20 is plenty under those conditions, and its lower recoil level and lighter weight are often an asset to small-framed shooters.

There is a wealth of top-quality 20-gauge over/unders on the market. Many have recently been introduced specifically for Sporting Clays, with back-bored barrels, long choke tubes, and barrels in the preferred 28- to 30-inch range. The new Ruger Red Label Sporting Clays and Browning 325 are excellent examples. Beretta, Perazzi, SKB and Weatherby, along with others, also have top-quality O/Us on the market.

For maximum recoil control it would be hard to beat the popular Remington 1100, Winchester 1400, or the Browning Gold. Their gas-operated actions alter the recoil impulse noticeably and produce a very soft-shooting smoothbore. Have one of them properly fitted to the individual shooter, add a basic selection of choke tubes, and you will have a fine tool for Sporting.

Experienced 12-gauge shooters have learned that care in selecting the right load for the target distance can boost their scores. The same approach is even more important with the sub-gauges.

For ultra-close ranges (10 yards and under), any 7/8-ounce load of #9 shot that will open quickly is an asset. Victory offers a felt-wad 20-gauge that opens a bit faster than plastic shotcups. ACTIV offers the G201 field load, with slightly softer shot, that does the same. If you are a reloader, the Ballistics Products "Brush Wad" is available in 20-gauge and creates the best short-range load available when stuffed with an ounce of soft #9 shot. Another alternative is any of the soft-shot promotional loads. Generally, they are available in size #8 as the smallest 20-gauge offering, but they spread pretty quickly and that's what counts here.

Moving into the 15- to 25-yard range, it is hard to argue with any 20-gauge #9 Skeet load. This is exactly the range where they were designed to offer optimum performance. Remington offers a special 1-ounce Skeet load in #9, the RTL20M. Intended for those Skeet shooters who use the 20 in 12-gauge events, it would be my top choice for 20-gauge Sporting in a factory load for this range. If they would offer this same load with their premium hard target shot in sizes #7½, #8, and #8½ as well, they would probably have the best Sporting Clays lineup for the 20-gauge. It would be hard to think of a more complete load selection.

Moving beyond 25 yards, we start to see a decrease in the breaking ability of #9 shot. A proven way to increase that power, while maintaining as much pattern density as possible, is to shift to #8½ shot. A 1-ounce load in this size becomes my first choice for shots in the 20- to 30-yard range, but it is a combo you'll have to load yourself. Factory loads in 20-gauge

don't offer it. Instead, they provide #8 shot in a number of 7/8-ounce target loads, and some 1-ounce field loads in the same shot size. The target loads, by virtue of their harder shot, generally produce better results, despite carrying fewer pellets per shell. Results can also depend on how well your individual barrel handles the full 1-ounce load. It's worth taking the time to do some test patterning here. A good 1-ounce load of quality #8 shot is a consistent target-breaker out to 35 yards. Some very smart shooters handload a 1-ounce nickel-plated #8 shot load for over-30-yard shots, and they do marvelous work beyond 35 yards. The ability of nickel shot to maintain tight patterns and short shot strings improves 20-gauge performance at this range.

Beyond 40 yards, the 20-gauge starts to become marginal. Reloaders have the option of going to #7½ nickel shot in either 7/8-ounce or 1-ounce loads, depending upon which patterns best in their barrel. In factory offerings, one of the best long-range choices is the ACTIV nickel-plated "Supershot High Velocity Load" (N20HH). This is a 1-ounce load that provides as much long-range performance as you will find in a factory 20-gauge target load. If your gun has a 3-inch chamber, they have a magnum version of this load available that packs 1 1/8 ounces of nickel #7½. Other long-range alternatives are any of the premi-

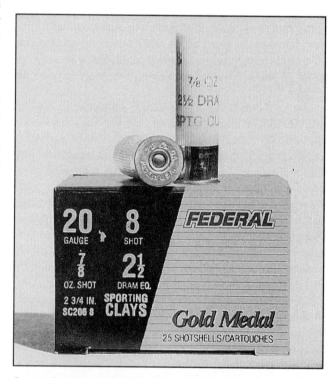

Special Sporting Clays loads for the 20-gauge are already making their way onto the market, proof that more than a few shooters are taking up the challenge of sub-gauge Sporting.

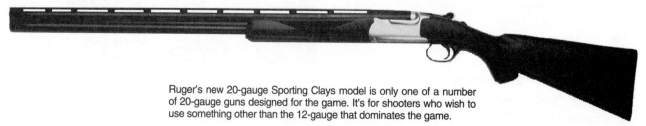

Ruger's new 20-gauge Sporting Clays model is only one of a number of 20-gauge guns designed for the game. It's for shooters who wish to use something other than the 12-gauge that dominates the game.

um copper-plated, buffered field loads offered by Remington, Federal and Winchester in size #7$\frac{1}{2}$.

28-Gauge

Inside 30 yards this little jewel doesn't really take a back seat to the bigger gauges. Between 30 and 40 yards it does need some help (read that to mean nickel shot) and beyond 40 yards it does help if a shooter has a sense of humor. That's not a knock of the 28-gauge. It's my second-favorite gauge, right behind the 12. It just points out that there's a limit to what you can expect from $\frac{3}{4}$-ounce of shot, no matter how efficient the shell, or how carefully crafted the load.

Moderately-priced 28-gauge guns of the clay target persuasion aren't exactly common. In fact, depending upon how you define the term "moderately priced," about the only one I can think of is the lovely little Remington 1100 Skeet gun, because it is a sweet little shooter. Remington has also chambered their 870 pump for the 28, and if you like pumps you'll like this one. Browning offers a 28-gauge pump in their BPS line, and these are quality guns, as well.

Moving up in price we find the Browning Citori, and by early 1995, it should be joined in that niche by the new Ruger Red Label 28-gauge. That gun has just been announced and I

have no information on it. However, knowing how Bill Ruger does things, my guess is that it will be a jewel. I already have my order in for one. Beyond that, 28-gauge guns get a bit pricey, yet they are certainly exquisite.

The lack of affordable guns is almost matched by the availability and price of ammunition. For some inexplicable reason, 28-gauge shells run about $20 a case more than 12-gauge. You'll also find a rather limited selection of shells, and this is one situation where it can really pay to reload. Not only can you save a significant amount of money on your shells, but you can greatly expand the versatility of this small round.

In the ultra-close-range area, the best choice among factory rounds are the standard $\frac{3}{4}$-ounce, 1200 fps, #9 Skeet loads offered by everybody that makes a 28-gauge load. A better choice by a wide margin is the Ballistic Products 28-gauge "Brush Wad" with $\frac{3}{4}$-ounce of soft #9 shot atop it. It's strictly the province of handloaders, but inside 15 yards you would think you were shooting a 12-gauge.

From that range out to almost 25 yards, you will be well served with a standard Skeet load using good hard shot. The little 28 is an extremely efficient shell and will break under-25-yard targets just as well as a 12- or 20-gauge. In fact, many

The smaller gauges are an excellent way to introduce new shooters to the sport. Even a shooter as small as this one won't be intimidated by the 28-gauge.

Skeet shooters carry as good an average with the 28 as they do with the 12-gauge.

Beyond 25 yards, out to almost 35 yards, #8½ shot becomes the best choice. In factory shells, this is available from Federal as the ¾-ounce SC280 Sporting Clays load. Remington also offers a 28-gauge Sporting load, but in #8 shot. I prefer the Federal until the range starts to creep out to 35 yards, and then I'd favor the Remington 28SC load. For reloaders, shifting to hard target-grade #8 or #8½ shot in your standard Skeet load recipe will accomplish the same thing for less than half the cost of factory shells.

Pushing the 28-gauge beyond 35 yards isn't easy, because you really don't have enough shot to work with. Winchester offers a 1-ounce load (X28H) in sizes #7½ and #8. For factory ammo shooters, whichever load patterns best in your gun is your best option. My solution is to go to a 1200 fps, ¾-ounce handload of #8 nickel shot. I've mentioned nickel-plated shot quite a bit, and that's because it simply gives the best pattern performance at extended range, in any gauge. I get mine from Ballistic Products Inc., but it is available from other sources. It is more expensive than lead shot, but in the case of the 28-gauge it is money well spent. When you factor the cost of nickel shot reloads against the cost of factory rounds, the nickel shot loads are not only cheaper, but more effective. If you develop the affection for the 28-gauge that I have, and you really want to wring the most out of it, becoming a reloader is the way to go.

410-Bore

Whoever designed the 410-bore (or 36-gauge, as it is often called in Europe) was either extremely drunk at the time or had a wickedly twisted sense of humor. In fact, no one even seems to want to own up to creating this load. The best I have been able to find in any reference work is the fact that the shell "just sort of appeared" at some point in history!

I don't blame the historians. I wouldn't take credit for it either, because it is one poorly designed shot launching platform.

The big problem is the extremely small diameter of the hull in relation to the shot column length. This encourages a lot of pellet deformation and long shot strings. Even with a Full choke and hard shot, the 410 patterns fall apart by the time they reach 35 yards, and they start to get noticeably patchy as close as 20 yards. This shell also operates at higher pressures than its larger cousins, which aggravates the shot deformation problem even further. Getting consistently smooth and even patterns from a 410 is tougher than getting the President to lower taxes, or admit that the average citizen should be allowed to own a firearm.

With that said, I have to admit that there is a certain appeal to this miserable little rascal.

Inexpensive 410 shotguns are common. Even the heaviest loads have recoil levels that could only be described as minuscule, and a pretty fair selection of shells can be found virtually anywhere ammunition is sold. A knowledgeable shooter would conclude that if the 28-gauge was as readily available in affordable guns and ammo as the 410, the latter

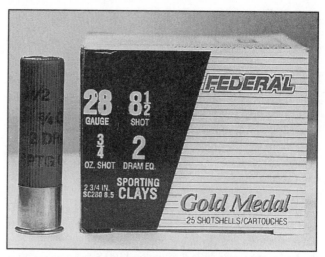

Federal's #8½ Sporting Clays load will give the 28-gauge a longer positive target-breaking range over the standard #9 Skeet load.

Not a legal load for 28-gauge sporting competition (NSCA rules restrict the 28-gauge to ¾-ounce of shot in registered matches), this Winchester offering can certainly be used for informal shooting and is an excellent choice when it comes to stretching the 28-gauge past the 35-yard mark.

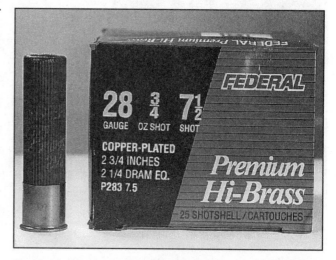

Shooters looking for a legal match load that stretches the 28-gauge to the max will find few better than this copper-plated, buffered offering from Federal.

Browning now offers their 28-gauge and 410 over/unders with their Invector choke tube system. It's well worth having!

These Briley choke tubes for the author's 410 Mossberg extend the potential of that little gun significantly. Assuming there is enough barrel wall thickness, any gun can be fitted for interchangeable choke tubes, and it greatly expands the effectiveness of the sub-gauges, both on the range and in the bird fields.

would probably fade from the scene, but they aren't, and it isn't going to!

Although I am not a fan of pumps, nor a real devotee of the 410, I have to admit that one of my favorite fun guns is a well-worn Mossberg 500 pump. It's light, cute and fun to shoot. A few years ago, Hastings installed interchangeable choke tubes in that gun, and the subsequent experiments with loads and chokes were remarkable.

When it comes to spreading a pattern quickly at close range, the 410 has no peer, unless the other guns are loaded with spreader wads. Using the basic Skeet choke tube, this gun will produce a circular pattern of about 25 inches at 15 yards with a 3-inch #9 shot load. By comparison, a soft-shot 20-gauge field load from a similar choke will create a pattern of about 19 or 20 inches at that range. That 410 pattern will be uniform enough to consistently get the job done. The pattern will go completely to hell by 20 yards, but inside 15 yards it is a clay-busting little fool! I load my own shells and use Lawrence Brand Magnum shot, but the factory Remington SP4103 load (a 3-inch #9 shell) will do just about as well. Victory also has a 410 load in size #10 shot as well as in sizes #5 through #11. It will work well inside 15 yards and the patterns from those shells are impressive. Clay targets just don't get through it in one piece.

Once the range increases beyond about 15 yards, I am through with the Skeet or Improved Cylinder tubes. The patterns are too patchy with any load. This is where the .009-inch Modified tube makes a big difference. Even though it is

technically a Modified choke in the 410, it does the best patterning job from 15 to about 25 yards. In fact, custom gunsmiths in the Skeet game have come to the almost universal conclusion that the most effective 410 constriction for Skeet shooters is .008-.009-inch. Anytime you can get a half-dozen top gunsmiths to agree on the same thing you can consider it a Universal Truth!

With the .009-inch tube in place, I like the standard #9, $1/2$-ounce Skeet load out to just beyond 20 yards, and shift to the same load in good hard #$8^1/_2$ shot for birds out to 30 yards. This is one case where less is better, as these $1/2$-ounce loads will generally deliver better patterns than most 3-inch loads. The short shot column and hard, target-grade shot produce less pellet deformation than the longer shot column in the 3-inch load. (Substituting nickel shot for lead can change that, though.) These loads are readily available from the factory in the Skeet lines from Remington, Winchester and Federal, with the $1/2$-ounce #$8^1/_2$ loads being found in the newer 410 Sporting Clays numbers from Federal (the SC412) and Remington (SP410SC). If a shooter confines his 410 endeavors to ranges under the 30-yard mark, he can get by quite nicely with these three different loads and a pair of choke tubes.

Beyond 30 yards the going gets tough with the 410. Choking the #$8^1/_2$ loads down through a Full tube will produce a fairly tight center core pattern at 30-plus-yards, with little margin for error. If you don't point it like a rifle, you're dead meat! Even if you do, you start to run out of power to break targets at about 35 yards. Shifting to hard #8 shot in a $1/2$-ounce load will

These three shell selections are about as good as you will get in factory ammunition for the 410 on the Sporting range. In fact, it might be difficult to reload a more effective selection of loads for ranges out to 35 yards.

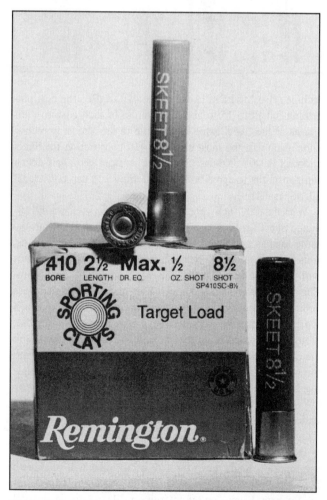

Remington's 410 Sporting Clays load will break targets about 7 to 10 yards farther than the standard 410 #9 Skeet load, and is a good choice for those who want to play 410 Sporting with just one load.

produce a pattern that looks acceptable on paper, but just does not seem to work in real life. There isn't enough shot in the charge to compensate for the inevitable effects of shot stringing, which don't show up on a stationary patterning board. Shot stringing will produce more than a few holes in actual practice. That often results in gaps in the pattern that cause the bird to be hit with just one or two pellets, and that may not be enough to get that "visible piece." Although #7$\frac{1}{2}$ shot works well with larger gauges because it increases the striking power of individual pellets, it doesn't seem to help here. You just don't have enough pellets in the load to do the job. The pattern density isn't there.

I've spent a lot of time looking for a 35-yard 410 load and will be the first to admit that, even with a Full choke tube, I haven't found one I like. All the 3-inch factory loads use shot that is just too soft to take the abuse it receives in that long, small-diameter shot column. If you are stuck with factory loads, the best bet is to pick a 3-inch #7$\frac{1}{2}$ load and hope you can get a couple of pellets onto the bird. Don't even bother to pattern the loads—it's too frustrating. Shoot for real. Alternate between a Modified and Full tube, and keep track of which performs best for you.

If you reload, you have a better option—3-inch loads of #8 nickel shot. It ain't perfect, but it is the best choice I have found when you have to push the 410 into the 30- to 40-yard range. You won't ever confuse this load with a 12-, 20- or even a 28-gauge load, but it will give you about as much as you can expect from a 410.

It helps to have an extremely well-developed sense of humor any time you take a 410 onto a Sporting Clays range. You'll need it.

Give the sub-gauge guns a try if you shoot for fun. They will provide that in spades.

Semi-Autos vs. Over-Unders

Over/unders have the reputation of being better handling smooth-bores than most semi-autos. However, you can balance out a gas gun just as well as an O/U, so it is a moot point.

IF YOUR GOAL in Sporting Clays is to improve your shooting skills in the bird fields and duck blinds, then by all means shoot the gun you hunt with. There is no better way to learn what to expect from your gun/choke/load combination than by actually putting it to the test in this demanding game.

If, however, you intend to pursue the game for the game's sake, you will very quickly discover that there are only two shotgun types that will take you into the winner's circle—the gas-operated semi-auto, and the over/under. That's not a knock on pumps or side-by-side doubles, just a simple statement of fact.

To excel in Sporting Clays a shooter needs a gun that will reliably fire two shots, while allowing total concentration on the target. Pumps require the shooter to manually chamber the second round, and while there are some scattergunners who can do that with remarkable alacrity, even the best will find that they will score a couple of targets less per round with a pump than they would with the gas gun or O/U. Side-by-side doubles can be lively-handling smoothbores and they'll get off two rounds very reliably. Unfortunately, the broad sighting plane offered by the twin barrels has been proven to give less precise leads on targets traveling on a largely horizontal plane, and that includes most clay targets.

Within the realm of semi-auto shotguns, there are also the recoil operated models, like the venerable Browning A-5. Their drawback, for most people, is that the long shuffling recoil action can be disconcerting when a fast second shot is required. If a shooter is used to a gas-operated semi-auto and he picks up a recoil-operated gun, the difference will become readily apparent.

That pretty much leaves us with gas guns and O/Us, and the debate over the relative merits of each action type can be a lengthy one. Often that debate will generate far more heat than light. Which is the best choice? Here's a comparison of the key factors that affect a competition shotgun, and the differences between the two types.

Recoil

Let's get to this point right away, because it is one of the two biggest reasons shooters select a gas-operated semi-auto in preference to an over/under. The gas gun is commonly believed to have less felt recoil. If you are talking about factory guns right out of the box, that statement is true.

When a gas-operated semi-auto is fired, a small amount of propellant gas is bled off from the barrel through one or more small holes drilled into the barrel. The gas acts to operate a piston mechanism within the forend that mechanically forces the bolt to the rear. An extractor mounted on the bolt grips the rim of the fired shell to pull it out of the chamber as the bolt recoils. When the bolt has drawn the shell back far enough to strike a fixed piece of metal called the ejector, the shell is kicked out of the gun. While all that is going on, a new shell is released from the tubular magazine onto the shell carrier below the bolt, and as the bolt moves forward under spring pressure the carrier rises to position the shell, and the bolt rams it into the chamber for the next shot.

That's a lot of "stuff" going on at one time.

The actual recoil is dependent upon the weight of the gun and the power of the shell. An 8-pound 12-gauge firing a $2^3/_4$-dram, $1^1/_8$-ounce load will have less recoil than the same gun firing a $3^1/_4$-dram, $1^1/_4$-ounce shell, your basic Issac Newton theory in action.

The gas gun does not necessarily reduce the actual recoil level. What it does is retard it, and spread it over a longer period of time. This makes a gas gun feel like it is a softer kicking gun. You get a shove instead of the sharp rap that would be produced by a fixed-breech gun of the same weight firing the same load.

With that said, I will now point out that my 12-gauge Ruger Red Label over/under delivers less recoil punishment *to me* than my 12-gauge Franchi Prestige gas gun, when firing the same loads. With the Franchi, which is a very soft shooting gas gun, 100 rounds in an afternoon will have me reaching for an aspirin bottle as I leave the range. With the Red Label, I don't need the aspirin. How can that be?

The reason is the difference between actual recoil (which can be measured in foot pounds of energy) and perceived—or "felt"—recoil, which is how our bodies react to recoil. The latter is the more important of the two, and is dependent on a number of factors, including how well the gun fits the shooter and what cushioning material is present between the shooter and the gun.

Put another way, a heavyweight boxer who delivers a solid left hook to your jaw with his naked hand would injure you severely, and possibly even result in your "assuming room temperature." If that boxer is wearing a 16-ounce boxing glove, however, he'll probably just knock you down and give you a headache. Yet the actual foot pounds of energy in the punch would be the same.

That's the case with my Red Label. It has been fitted precisely to me by stock fitter Jack West, and has a thick Kick-Eeze recoil pad and his padded comb. The Franchi has a Kick-Eeze pad as well, but no padded comb. The Franchi feels

Over/under shooters who are not enamored with recoil will find that they can reduce it noticeably by simply shooting any of the light loads like these REM-LITES by Remington. The magical recoil reducing properties of the gas-operated semi-auto are overstated. You can make an O/U into a very soft shooter!

slightly softer on firing, but the Ruger [...] long run.

Any shotgun can have its felt recoil [...] this manner. If the stock treatment is d[...] probably be a bit softer shooting than [...] can be made to produce less felt reco[...] box.

That's why the question of recoil bet[...] my mind, only comes into play if we are dealing w[...] tered factory guns. In that case, the gas gun wins the recoil war. However, that should not be the reason for selecting one over the other. Each can be made to shoot soft enough so that any shooter can enjoy them.

Balance and Handling

This is one area where over/unders have a perceived advantage. The twin barrels poking out past the forend give more forward weight than the single barrel on a gas gun, promoting a smoother swing, and one that is more difficult to stop once started. As a result, the targets are hit more often.

The balance and handling qualities of any shotgun are determined by the way the weight of the gun is distributed. If there is a bit more muzzle weight, the gun tends to swing more smoothly. If there is more weight in the butt, the gun seems to mount quicker, but can be a little more whippy on the swing. Over/unders tend to have a bit more muzzle weight and thus swing a bit more forcefully and positively.

You can alter the balance of a gas gun to give you the same swing characteristics of an over/under. It's not hard.

If you want to add a little more muzzle weight, fill an empty shotshell with shot, crimp it, seal it with duct tape, and stick it in the forward portion of the tubular magazine in place of the

Shooters looking for a very quick-handling smoothbore will find one of the 26-inch-barreled over/unders a good choice. It is difficult to get the same handling qualities in a gas gun without some custom work.

Over/unders can be had in multi-barrel sets that allow shooters to fire different gauges from the same basic gun. You can't do that with semi-autos.

Over/unders are comfortable for both north- and southpaws, but lefties will need to find those few semi-autos made especially for them, like this Remington 11-87.

wooden plug that is already there. A 12-gauge shell full of shot will weigh about 2½ ounces. This weight lies forward of the leading hand and will promote a smoother swing. You can add up to three.

Muzzle too heavy? Stick one or more of the shot-filled shells in the stock bolt hole in the buttstock. It's that simple.

You can change the balance and handling qualities of the over/under as well. Just add weight where you need it, and there are many products on the market to make that easy. Meadow Industries makes a neat little gizmo called the "Barrel Buddy" that attaches to the underside of the barrel. It gives you the option of adding up to 8 ounces of weight. It can't be used with a semi-auto because it prevents the forend from sliding off the gun in the normal manner during takedown, but works well for O/Us. Buttstock weight can always be added via shotshells (fired and shot-filled, not live shells) in the bolt hole of the stock.

Many shooters may not need to change the balance of their gas guns. I had the opportunity to shoot the Remington 11-87 Sporting Clays model awhile back, and I thought it handled well. The stock was a tad short for me, but the balance and swing compared very favorably to my Red Label, and I shot a very satisfactory round of Sporting with it. Many makers are adding a bit more muzzle weight to their gas guns as they bring out special "Sporting Clays" models.

If you don't like the way the gun balances as it comes from the factory, you don't have to live with it. It's so easy to change that the discussion of balance and handling between the two gun types becomes moot.

The One Choke Syndrome

If you shoot a gas gun, you have only one choke available. If you shoot an O/U, you have the choice of two. This is often touted as a major advantage of the stack-barrel. Again, there is some truth in that, but not as much as many might suppose.

There are a number of clay target games where having only one choke is no handicap, such as ATA 16 Yard trap, and Handicap trap. Every target is going to be broken within one relatively narrow range, and one choke is fine. Ditto for American Skeet.

Sporting Clays is a game where the ability to use different chokes is often cited as a reason for the twin-barreled gun's popularity in that game, but it is rare to find a station where the shots vary more than 10 yards in range difference. Regardless of whether they are singles, report pairs, true pairs, following pairs, or simultaneous pairs, once you know the range you can generally find one choke that will do.

One game where the shot array may present targets at wildly varying ranges from the same station is FITASC (acronym for the Federation Internationale de Tir aux Armes Sportives

de Chasse: one of two international governing bodies for shooting sports). Here, you step into a shooting station with your gun and loads, and must shoot whatever is presented with the chokes you have in the gun—you can't change them once you step up to shoot. You may get a target at 15 yards, and the next may be at 50. Yes, that game demands the versatility of two choke tubes. Or does it?

At the 1993 U.S. NSCA National FITASC Championships at Grinder's Switch, Tennessee, the winner used an over/under. The runner-up, however, used a Beretta gas gun! I'm sure he would be the first to admit that it was not the gun that kept him out of first place. He'll tell you he was beat by a better shooter, not by his equipment.

How does a shooter make one choke do the work of two? Easy. By changing shells. Many shooters assume that if they want the proper pattern for the range encountered, they must put the proper choke tube into the gun. That's not true. You can vary the pattern performance of your gun by simply changing your shells.

If that sounds confusing, consider this: in clay target games we do not grade the targets. All it takes to score a kill is to knock a visible piece off the target that the scorer can see. A target that is "inkballed" (powdered) counts no more than a target that is merely chipped.

If your load gives you that visible piece, no matter how small it may be, who cares what your actual pattern looks like?

A growing number of shooters are doing more shell changing than choke tube changing, even if they shoot an O/U.

For example, we are facing a Fur & Feathers presentation that gives us a rabbit target at about 15 yards, and a quartering away aerial target that will be broken around 25 yards. The ideal choke for this would be a straight Cylinder choke for the rabbit, and an Improved Cylinder for the bird. Or you can shoot them both with the Improved Cylinder, or Skeet 1, choke simply by using a quick-opening load of #9s in the first barrel and a 1⅛-ounce load of hard, target-grade #8s in the second barrel. The first load could be one of the inexpensive promotional loads with soft shot, a spreader reload using one of the Ballistic Products wads designed for that, or a factory ACTIV Sporting Clays load, which uses the Gualandi X-Spreader wad. Those quick-opening shells will give you as large a pattern as you're going to get at that range, regardless of the choke tube in the gun. The second load of hard #8s will provide plenty of pattern density and individual pellet target-breaking power for the longer shot—even if you shot them from a straight Cylinder choke!

To take a more extreme example, let's look at a FITASC shot where you might have one bird at a bit under 20 yards

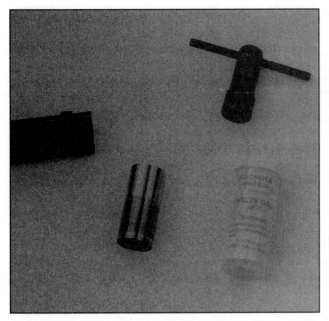

It is a common misconception that a single choke selection is a major handicap to semi-auto shooters. You can offset that by careful shell selection. Pick the right loads and one choke will not hurt your scores.

and a second at a little over 45. Many would choke Skeet 1 in the first barrel with a load of #9s, and slip a Full choke tube in the second barrel with a load of #7$^1/_2$s. The single choke shooter, however, can accomplish the same thing with a Full or Improved Modified choke (you have to choke for the longer bird) and then effectively open up that barrel to a Skeet 1 choke by using one of the fast-opening loads for the closer bird. The spreader-type loads will usually open a Full choke to about Improved Cylinder, and a Modified choke to about Skeet 1.

More subtle modifications can be made by altering the velocity and shot hardness of the loads. Soft shot at high velocity will usually pattern one complete choke wider than the tube you are using. Hard, target-grade shot at moderate velocity will often pattern a full choke tighter.

Many Sporting Clays ranges throw very few shots beyond 30 yards, and a shooter with a single barrel gun can do just as well as a shooter with an O/U. If a farther target is thrown, choke for it, and use a spreader load to open patterns for any closer target.

The usefulness of spreader loads is the reason I feel a gas gun shooter is not at a disadvantage because the gun offers only one choke.

That pretty well covers the three most common reasons for making the selection of either an O/U or a gas gun. From my point of view there is little real difference between them. Now, let's get down to the real differences.

Reliability

The over/under wins here. Period. No argument. In fact, the very best any gas gun shooter can do is to make his or her gun as reliable as the O/U, and that reliability factor is very important.

Many of the country's top shooters, like Florida Sporting Clays expert Bonnie McLaurin, favor the over/under because of its simplicity and reliability.

In some games, if you can't fire on the target for any reason, you lose it. Other games will give the shooter a certain number of "alibis" and allow targets to be reshot. Even then, a limit exists and beyond that you lose targets.

A gun malfunction can also be devastating to your confidence and adversely affect your subsequent performance. It is very difficult for the subconscious mind to perform the tasks required to break a target if it is wondering if the gun will go off! A gun malfunction early in the game, or in the key later stages of the match, can cause you to miss subsequent targets even if the malfunction never recurs. A mind is a terrible thing to mess up and a malfunction will do it.

Because of the large number of moving parts and mechanical operations required, a gas gun will never be as reliable as a fixed-breech O/U. That is the biggest single reason why top competitors show a marked preference for the stack-barrel guns. If you can stuff the shell in the gun and close the action, the primer will be struck when the trigger is pulled. If the shell is any good, it'll go off. Not so with gas guns. They can be working perfectly and still screw up!

The gas gun requires near-perfect ammunition, and the

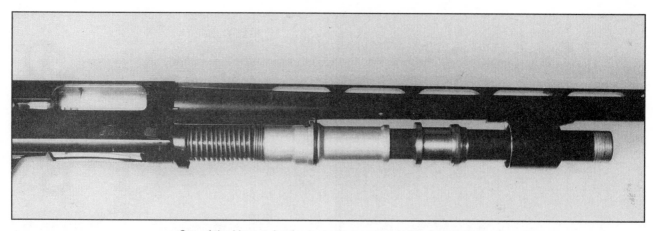

One of the biggest drawbacks to the gas gun is the complex gas operating system that makes it function. If it is not clean, or if the wrong lube or wrong powder is used, or the wrong load ...well, you get the idea! Gas guns can be finicky.

power level of the shell must be sufficient to operate the action, yet not so powerful that it generates too much gas energy. That can cycle the action too fast and result in a failure to feed a second shell. I have light target loads that will run 100 straight on the Skeet range in my Red Label, yet will not cycle the action on my Franchi.

If you reload, you must make certain that every shell is as perfect as a factory load. A hull that is worn, slightly out of round, or has a poor crimp may fail to feed and fire. Yet it'll run just fine in an O/U if it will fit into the chamber.

Gas guns must also be kept scrupulously clean if they are to even approach stack-barrel reliability, and that brings us to another factor:

Ease of Maintenance

Cleaning an over/under is simplicity in itself: unhook the forend, open the action, dismount the barrels, brush them out, reassemble and you're done. A little light lube on the ejector/extractor arms and the barrel hinge, and the gun is ready to shoot another tournament.

Virtually any shell you can shove into an O/U and have the primer go off will work in those guns, but semi-autos need near-perfect ammo to feed and extract. Reloaders must be careful.

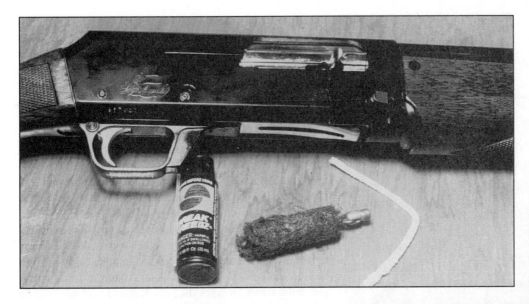

Many semi-auto shooters neglect to properly clean and lube the trigger assembly, and more importantly, scrub out the chamber. Failure to do either of these chores may result in your gas gun becoming a single shot!

Gas guns are more tedious. The forend must be removed, the barrel slid out of the receiver—with care taken not to lose any of the little O-rings found in most gas-operated systems—then the piston has to come off, and all the attendant parts laid out. And we're not done yet. Smart shooters also drift out the retaining pins that hold the trigger/shell carrier group in place (you do have a drift punch and small hammer, don't you?) and, for detailed cleaning, also remove the bolt.

Now that the gun is disassembled, here are some potential problem areas to attend to:

1. Trigger/shell carrier. Flush it out with something like Outer's Crud Cutter and allow it to dry. Spray the assembly lightly with Break-Free or any similar lube before reassembling. The reason this part must be cleaned is that unburned powder flakes can work their way into crevices and tie up the shell carrier. Some powders are notorious for this. When that happens, your gun becomes a single shot. It's a common problem, and an area many shooters neglect.

2. You'll scrub the barrel, naturally, but that doesn't finish that job. Pay particular attention to the gas ports. They can become clogged with carbon, reduce gas flow, and cause a feed malfunction. You will also need to remove plastic fouling from the chamber. This is left by the outer surface of the shell itself as a result of the heat generated upon firing. If allowed to build up, it will seriously impede the gun's ability to feed and extract shells. Standard bore cleaning solvents and brushes won't remove it. I use a bore brush wrapped with 0000 steel wool. Once you've scrubbed the chamber, leave it slick and dry! Oil in the chamber contributes to both feeding and extracting malfunctions.

3. Follow the manufacturer's instructions for cleaning the gas system. Some have certain lubrication do's and don'ts. Don't neglect to add some light lube to the action bars and the channels they ride in within the receiver. This is another area where unburned powder can mess you up.

That will handle routine cleaning. Every 10,000 rounds or so, it is advisable to take the gun to a good gunsmith for a thorough strip down and tank dunk cleaning.

Considering this, is it any surprise that many of those shoot-

An over/under breaks down into three basic components—barrel, receiver and forend. That makes them easy to store and transport, and makes cleaning a snap.

Author finds that sub-gauges require reloading to achieve their maximum performance, and it is much easier to load for an over/under than a gas gun. Also, you don't beat your hulls up nearly as much with an O/U and thus extend their reloading life.

Gas gun shooters need a flexible back because they will spend a lot of time bending over to pick up fired hulls. Most over/under shooters are understanding about that and don't normally mind the delay.

ers who fire 10,000 to 30,000 rounds per year prefer over/unders?

Durability

Another win for the O/U. At the risk of offending a few gas gun makers, the most expensive gas-operated semi-auto made won't even come close to the lifespan of even a moderately-

priced (but well-made) O/U. I won't get into predicting just how many rounds each will handle before it's ready for the scrap heap, but those top shooters who use gas guns in competition figure on replacing them yearly, and have one or more backup guns on hand.

Ease of Repair

As a rule, the gas gun wins this one. This is especially true if you are shooting a well-known model that has been around for awhile, like the Remington 1100 or the various Winchesters. You can likely find parts and service right from your local gunsmith. He knows what small parts routinely break or wear out, and tends to keep them in stock. Since gas guns are all designed for modern mass production with parts interchangeability, replacing parts is easy. When over/unders do need repairs, they are more complex, and I find it best to send them back to the factory. If the gun is an American-made model with solid repair facilities (like my Ruger) repair time can be quick. If you have an expensive European model, repair time can sometimes stretch into many months.

On the plus side, O/Us seldom require minor repairs. When a well-made example needs fixing it is generally after a lot of shooting—more than many shooters will do in two or three lifetimes!

Use of Reloads

The stack-barrel wins hands down on this one, for reasons that have already been discussed. Another factor that comes into play, however, is that the O/Us are easier on the shells and you can generally squeeze a few more reloads per hull from them. They don't ram the empties around and then toss them all over the ground—you just gently pluck them from the chambers and stick 'em in a pocket. That can be especially important if you are shooting on a range whose policy is, "When a shell hits the ground, it becomes the property of the club."

Since most serious competitive shooters are reloaders, this has become one of the strong points in the O/U's favor.

Cost

The second biggest reason shooters choose semi-autos over O/Us is that they cost less to acquire than a good quality stack-barrel.

The cost difference can be a significant factor for shooters on a budget, and that is something the shooter will have to decide for himself. However, in some cases, that difference can be deceiving.

There are a number of budget-priced over/unders on the market, and I generally ignore them. I find that in order to obtain an O/U with the quality needed to be a competitive gun, I'm looking at a suggested retail price of $1,100 to $1,500. A smart shopper can generally save a few hundred dollars if he looks for the best "street price." Guns in this bracket include the various Ruger Red Labels, the Browning Citori, Winchester 1001, and the Remington Peerless.

Quality gas guns like the Winchester 1400, Remington 1100 and 11-87, Browning Gold, and Beretta models will

The automatic ejection of gas guns can pose a problem in confined Sporting Clays stands. Fired shells may bounce off objects and come back at the shooter.

Gas guns offer the shooter an inexpensive means of barrel interchangeability. Over/unders can't match that.

have a retail price of a few hundred dollars less, and the "street price" philosophy will also apply to them.

If you are going to be in serious competition, the total difference in price of $400 to $600 may not be worth the increased inconvenience of the gas gun. That price difference is, after all, only about the equivalent of five to seven cases of shotshells. When you are talking about a gun you may want to keep, shoot, and possibly even invest a bit of money in for custom fitting, etc., that difference becomes a lot smaller. You're only talking about a five month supply of shells as the price difference on a quality gun you may well pass on to your children.

Over/unders also hold their value much better. If you decide you want to change guns after 20,000 or so rounds, you'll get a much larger percentage of your original purchase price back if the gun you are selling is a well-made O/U that has been cared for properly.

Try selling a gas gun that has gone 20,000 rounds and many knowledgeable shooters won't even look at it.

Those are the real reasons why over/unders, by and large, dominate competitive clay target games.

This is certainly not a put-down of gas guns. With the exception of the reliability factor, they will hold their own with the O/Us when it comes to busting clay targets. However, making a decision as to which type of shotgun to buy is more involved than that.

Many competitive shooters have their over/under ejectors converted to extractors that allow them to pluck the empties cleanly from the gun without worrying about their bouncing all over the ground. You can't do that with a gas gun and they are harder on hulls that you might want to reload.

chapter twenty-three

Sporting's Toughest Shots

HITTING AERIAL TARGETS is nothing more than matching their combination of speed, angle and altitude. That much holds true regardless of the clay target game one is engaged in at the moment. Veteran trap or Skeet shooters will see many of the angles they are familiar with the first time they step onto a Sporting Clays field, and the reverse is also true.

What separates Sporting Clays from other games, however, is that while you may be getting a familiar target speed, angle and altitude, you get those features in targets of widely varying size, weight and construction.

Launch two dissimilar targets from the same trap at the same angle, speed and altitude, and you will get two targets with dissimilar flight characteristics! That is something that is only seen in Sporting, because all other games use what is called a "standard" target. It exhibits standard and consistent flight characteristics, unless affected by a high wind.

The bottom line is that the Sporting Clay station you shot yesterday can be radically different today due to nothing more than a change in the targets loaded into the trap machine.

Another factor that separates Sporting from the other games is the array of target presentations available. When you factor in the mix of different targets, and combine that with the possibility of seeing those targets as singles, following or report pairs, and simultaneous (true) pairs, then you can have a tremendously varied shot presentation.

Sporting's Clays

That's why the game cannot be learned by rote and shot on reflex. Every station must be thought through, not only in regard to the flight path of the target(s), but also as to how different targets will fly from the same trap machine. Here's a look at the targets.

Standard

This is the same target used in trap and Skeet and is characterized by a relatively stable flight path. It is 110mm in diameter, and even casual shooters are familiar with its perfor-

Having your gear organized when you step onto the shooting station is important, especially if you may want to use different loads. It helps to be able to find them quickly.

Sporting Clays shooters face a variety of targets and each may have different flight characteristics. From left to right are the mini, midi, standard, and the stoutly constructed rabbit. The battue target shown on edge at top illustrates why it is called the "flying razor blade," and why shooters must wait for this target to turn on its edge before shooting it!

mance. We'll use it as a yardstick to measure the performance of the other clay targets commonly encountered in Sporting Clays.

Midi Target

This bird is of the same configuration as the standard, but is smaller in diameter at 90mm. It has the same flight characteristics as the standard, but can be one of the more frustrating targets on the field.

The reason is that determining the distance to the target is very important in figuring the lead required, as well as the choke and load that should be used. The midi target is often mixed in with standards, but because of its smaller size it can fool the shooter into thinking it is a standard target—just at longer range! It can be deceptive.

So can its speed. Because it is smaller and lighter, it will often leave the trap at a faster rate of speed, yet because it is lighter, it will slow down faster than a standard bird. If it is thrown with a standard target as a pair, as is often the case, this can sometimes result in its being the lead target for the first portion of the flight, and then being overtaken by the standard. This can play real hell with a shot plan! The challenge for the shooter here is to be able to quickly identify the target as a midi and understand the difference it will display in flight. It can require a different shot plan than when facing two standard targets as a pair.

Mini Targets

This 60mm saucer is the smallest target normally thrown in Sporting. Like the midi, it is just a scaled-down version of the standard. Unlike the midi, however, it is seldom misinterpreted. There is little doubt when one is thrown. It's like shooting at an aspirin tablet traveling at Mach 1.

Mastering a smooth gun mount is vital to Sporting Clays success, and some shooting stands require that you do it from a somewhat contorted position. Gun handling plays a key role in this game.

Targets moving through a screen of trees will produce a strobo-scopic effect and make tracking the target difficult. Compounding that is the fact that a tree may leap out and eat your shot charge before it finds the target!

One problem that plagues Sporting Clays shooters is contrasting light levels between shooting position and target. Shooting from shadow to bright light is not that difficult, but the reverse can hinder a shooter from picking up the target quickly.

The problem with minis is that their light weight really makes them zip out of a trap, and their small size can make it difficult to get an accurate fix on the range. Because of their size, they can also require a slightly denser pattern because they can slip through pattern gaps quite easily.

Another item to factor in with minis is that most of the time the target is colored completely black, and they are generally thrown as a part of a pair. The pair might be two minis, or a mini in combination with a midi or a standard. It is not hard to lose sight of this target and concentrate on the brighter one. They do tend to get out there fast and blend into any vegetation in the background. This means the shooter must concentrate on finding the best visual window to take the target as quickly as possible.

Range operators with a streak of sadism will generally throw this target in tight, tree-lined quarters. It can be a real bear!

Battue Targets

This is a totally different target than the three previous ones. This is a 110mm target, but only $3/8$-inch high, with a slight center dome. Its flight characteristics do not resemble any other target. Because of that, it is a very difficult bird to hit, and requires a lot of discipline on the part of the shooter. Not only will the target's unusual shape cause it to change attitude in flight, but it will also change profile.

Any time a rabbit target is part of the presentation the shooter must direct his gun mount to it, or risk not being able to pick that target up quickly. It is much easier to take a high bird from a low gun position than it is to take a low target from a high gun position.

The most common presentation for battues is as pairs, generally as crossing shots; sometimes with a very slight outgoing, or incoming, angle. As they are launched, they present a very slender profile to the shooter—they are edge-on flat! Some shooters call them "flying razor blades," and they can be very difficult to hit early in their flight. At a point somewhere around mid-flight, they begin to turn on their edge and present a fuller profile. This is referred to as "development," and the target now begins to become easier to find with a shot pattern. This "development" continues until the shooter now sees it as a round disc. Unfortunately, by the time the bird gets that far it is generally beginning to drop quickly and actually picking up a bit of speed as it falls.

The shooter must wait until enough of the target "develops" to be hit, yet not waste too much time. Since these are normally thrown as pairs, the second bird often presents a very difficult shot. Farther away and falling, it can be a very frustrating target.

Rabbit Target

This is a standard-size (110mm) target that is always presented as a ground-bouncer rolling on its edge. Since the ground is uneven, the target path may vary considerably as well. Some "rabbits" may zip across flat, some may bounce high and wild, and others may do both. No two targets will be perfectly alike in their running path. Because the target is

thrown into the ground, it is beefed up to avoid breakage. It often requires a shot charge heavier than the range would indicate in order to be certain of a break. Rabbits may be thrown as the only target on a station. They may come as singles, or as following or report pairs, but seldom as true pairs. They are often incorporated as the first target of a Fur & Feather presentation, with the second target (usually a standard) as an outgoing or quartering away target in about the same general distance range.

Reading the type of target being thrown, and understanding what it will do is only part of the process. You also must determine exactly what it is doing in relation to the actual shooting stand.

Terrain, trees, elevation changes, and the landscape in general can often paint a deceptive picture of what the target is really doing. Shadow and light can also play tricks on the shooter. Good range operators will use all of these to create some serious optical illusions. Some targets may look like they are true crossing shots, yet have some incoming or outgoing angle on them. A target launched downhill may appear to be rising when it is actually falling. One that appears to be rising, may actually be losing speed and falling.

An inventive range operator can create more illusions than David Copperfield. If you shoot the targets under that illusion, you will likely miss.

Skeet and Sporting Clays share many similarities, especially in the area of target presentation. Guns that work well for Sporting Clays are top choices for Skeet.

Developing Shot Plans

Another consideration is having a shot plan for true pairs. A lot of expert shooters are convinced that if the first target is missed, the shooter should fire at it again, instead of shifting to the second bird. This happens quite often among shooters with a hunting background or with experience in a game like International trap. There are some valid points to that argument.

A shooter firing at a target is already concentrating on that target. It has been acquired, tracked and engaged. If the shot is missed, the gun is already traveling with that target and it sometimes takes only a slight correction in point and hold to nail it with a follow-up shot. For some shooters, this is an effective way to salvage at least one bird out of a pair when the first shot misses.

Other shooters are not mentally geared to that. Skeet shooters (which is where I cut my competitive shotgun eyeteeth) are an excellent example. We shoot doubles as a regular part of the game and only get one shot per bird. Skeet Doubles invariably requires that the gun track be radically altered for the second bird. Shoot-off Doubles, for example, from stations three, four and five, demand that the gun direction be quickly reversed to acquire a target moving in the opposite direction. It becomes a fluid, learned subconscious response to leave the first target, whether it is hit or not, and immediately go after the second bird.

For shooters with this mindset, it may be well to stick with your shot plan to fire one round per bird, regardless of the results. Changing a preconceived plan that you have executed countless times before is very difficult to do in the millisecond you have to make the decision.

This impressive tower at Florida's Space Port Gun Club throws targets for several stations—all of them tough.

This unusual shot is an incoming tower presentation with an angle quartering toward the shooter. The target is launched at a slow speed to settle and drop. You have to think your way through this one because the high vegetation gives the shooter only a narrow window in which to break the target.

This shooter does not get much of a break on this outgoing tower shot because the overhead cage keeps him from taking a high gun position that would let him get on the target quickly. Range operators can be very "kind" to shooters this way but the good shooters know how to adjust.

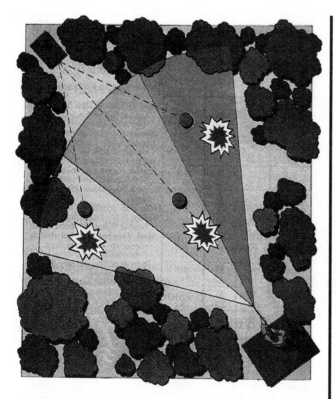

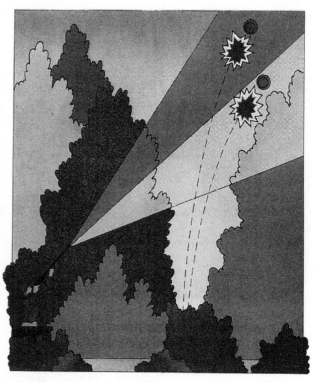

The "Driven Shot" simulates the flight of incoming birds from a low angle. Skeet station low house eight is excellent practice, especially if the shooter is able to move backward from the shooting pad for some of his shots. Angled birds may require a short lead, but direct incomers are best shot as the muzzle swings through and blots out the target.

Many shooters find the springing teal target best handled by allowing it to reach the apex of its flight and then shooting directly at it, or as shown here, slightly below it; all depends on the individual shooter's reaction time.

Illustrations courtesy Beretta: "Beretta Tips on Winning at Sporting Clays."

With the above in mind, here are some thoughts on developing "shot plans" for some of the more common target presentations we see on the sporting fields.

Incoming Tower Shot

This simulates incoming ducks, or doves, and the towers may be as high as 100 feet. This requires a little imagination.

On singles, the best bet is to be patient. Take a first look position at the first point you can visually acquire the target, and have some weight on the leading foot. But don't be in a hurry to take the target! Give the shot time to develop and wait until it approaches a direct overhead shot—don't mount the gun until you are just about ready to shoot. This gives you the largest possible target surface to shoot at, and makes the shot a relatively simple one. The shooter swings through the bird and triggers the shot as soon as the barrel passes the leading edge. A Skeet choke and #9 Skeet load are usually the best choice, as most of these shots are within 15 yards of the gun.

Following and report pairs are shot the same way, and the gun should be slightly dismounted between shots. True pairs are a little tougher. If the pairs are taking the same track, I prefer to shoot the trailing bird first and then continue the swing through the first bird. Leads are minimal, and the recoil of the gun will help move you from the trailing bird to the leader. That, of course, assumes the shooting cage gives you

enough room to get on the birds quickly, and that the birds are traveling within 5 or 6 feet of each other. If not, take the lead bird first, leave the gun mounted, and then fast-swing through the second target. Often when a shooter faces an incoming tower shot, he will find his gun angle restricted by the construction of the shooting cage to prevent his shooting the trap machine.

If the birds are launched on separate flight paths, take the most direct incoming bird first, and as quickly as you can. This gives you time to acquire the second bird, which will now be an incoming shot with some angle away from the shooter. I like to dismount the gun after the first shot and then remount for the second. Dismounting between shots gives you a better visual acquisition on the second target, and if you have worked on your gun handling skills, the remount and shot will be almost simultaneous. Leads are minimal in either case, since the targets are closing on you. I have never seen this shot presented where a Skeet choke and #9s were not the best bet.

Springing Teal

This target is thrown fast, almost straight up to a height of about 70 feet, and may be traveling slightly toward or away from the shooter.

This target intimidates a lot of shooters with trap or Skeet experience but, surprisingly, shooters with little shotgun expe-

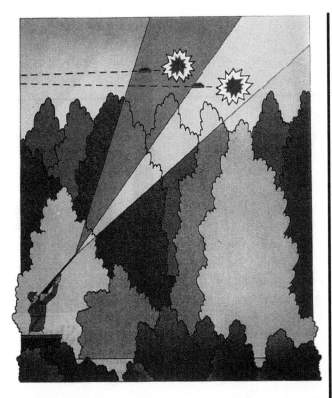

Outgoing tower targets must be broken by shooting underneath them. Skeet station high house one is excellent practice for this and shooters can vary the yardage on the shot by allowing the target to get farther from the house before shooting it.

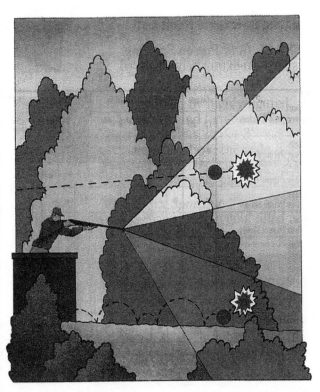

Fur & Feathers presentations require that the ground-hugging rabbit be taken first, followed by rapid upwards gun movement to get the aerial target. Fortunately, the air bird is usually going in the same direction as the rabbit—but not always!

rience find it easy! The reason is that they wait until the bird gets to the top of its flight, and then they shoot it as a stationary target as the bird just sort of hangs there. They forget all about any lead. That's the way to do it.

The gun hold point should be high, with weight on the front foot. The shooter should delay his mount until the target has almost reached its apex. At that point mount the gun, perch the bird on top of the bead and take it. When dealing with true pairs, take the target that hits the lower apex of its flight first, and then let the recoil swing you up to the second.

This presentation does, however, take some timing. If you are off, hitting the bird at the last portion of its upward flight is the better choice. Once it starts to fall, it becomes a very difficult target.

Outgoing Overhead Dropping Shot

This simulates a dove coming in from overhead and behind, and it confuses some shooters. If you are one of them, go to a Skeet range and spend a box of shells shooting the high house one target. That's all these basically are, although they do look like a high house one on steroids.

The first look point for this shot is almost directly overhead, with a little weight on the back foot. Shift your weight to the front foot as you acquire the target. The gun muzzle is high. Pick up the target as quickly as you can, mount the gun with the muzzle either spot-on or slightly behind the bird, then

swing down and through it. Trigger the shot when you see about 6 inches of daylight between the muzzle and the bird. Take this shot as quickly as you can because if you don't, it becomes a long-range dropping target that can be one of the toughest shots you will ever see! Hit it quick, and it is relatively easy. This shot will be handled well with an open choke and either #9s or #8$1/2$ shot.

This presentation is almost never seen as a true pair, but if you encounter it as such, take the trailing target first and drive through to the second, doubling the lead for the second bird. For following or report pairs, dismount the gun between shots and bring the upper body back to the initial first look point.

The Driven Shot

This is very similar to the Incoming Tower shot, except the birds start at a lower elevation and rise. The procedure, however, is not that different. You still need to swing quickly through the bird and trigger the shot when the muzzle passes it. If there is a difference, it is that the lead is a bit less. If the birds are close, you can nail this presentation as soon as the muzzle blots out the bird. A Skeet choke and #9 shot are the best bet. Spreader loads will help if the birds are within 20 yards.

If you are faced with simultaneous pairs in this presentation, you must acquire the targets as quickly as possible and nail the first bird fast. In this case, taking the leading bird first is the

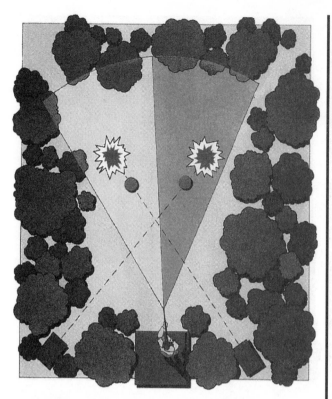

Outgoing targets with a slight quartering angle require very little lead. If the outgoing angle is 45 degrees or less, simply swing through the bird and trigger the shot at the leading edge.

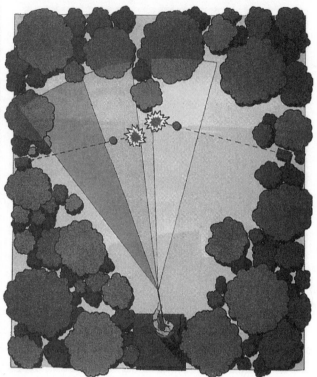

Close crossing targets often have the trap house shielded from the shooter, requiring that the bird be picked up and shot as soon as possible. Leads are normally short, due to the closeness of the target and the gun speed required to catch it.

best bet. You may not have time to take the trailer and then catch the lead bird. Let the recoil carry your gun to the following bird. Regardless of the pair presentation, this is fast and close shooting. It pays to be pumped up for this one!

Fur & Feather

This gives you a rabbit for the first target, followed (as a report, following or simultaneous pair) by an aerial target, which is usually a standard. The gun hold point on this must be for the rabbit, and the rabbit should be taken as early as is comfortable. Resist the temptation to rush the first shot to the point where you miss it. Make sure you get the rabbit, and then let the other target take care of itself. Rushing is the biggest mistake new shooters make on this presentation, and it costs them the rabbit. You won't get very far if you always miss the first target in a pair.

If there is one piece of advice that can be considered to be carved in stone regarding true pairs, it is, "Kill the first target every time!" The second target will, through practice and repetition, start breaking on its own!

On following and report pairs, dismount the gun after the rabbit. That gives you better visual ability to pick up the aerial bird. This is normally not a difficult shot, being usually a mild quartering away shot, or a gentle crosser. Open chokes, with #8½ for the rabbit, and #9s (maybe a spreader, because these are often close-range shots) for the bird, are good choices.

Going Away Shots

You will see these a lot, and most of the time there will be some quartering angle on any singles targets, and on one bird in a pair. The other bird in a pair will often be a dead straightaway that has some rising angle on it.

The range at which these targets may be engaged can vary considerably, from 10- to 35-plus yards. Regardless of the range, it is important to have weight on the front foot and pick up the first bird as soon as possible.

The choke and shot size will, of course, depend upon the range. This is generally Skeet 1 or Improved Cylinder territory, with shot in the #8½ to #8 range: the narrower profile of these targets will give you fewer pellet hits, and they need to be larger pellets to get a visible piece.

On a rising target, there will be a period where it levels out and flies almost straight for a second or so. That's the time to break it. If you wait too long and the target starts to drop, you have a much tougher shot.

On true pairs, take the straightaway as fast as you can. It may be a dead straightaway, or slightly rising. Then move to the quartering bird. It pays to fudge your natural point of aim to the second bird.

Crossing Shots

These can be some of the most varied shot presentations you'll see in Sporting Clays. You may get crossers at 12 yards, moving through a screen of trees or brush. You may get them at over 40 yards, sailing across a relatively open area. It's the same angle and target speed, but vastly different techniques are required to break them. Let's look at close targets first.

Many hard-crossers in Sporting Clays will be in the 15- to 25-yard range. These require a lot of lateral body movement, due to the closeness of the launching platform to the shooter. Some of the best possible practice you can get for these is to spend a day on a Skeet range working on the outgoing targets from stations two, three, five and six. You have to get the first look position close to the house, and then uncoil rapidly as you swing through the target.

The best shooting technique to use for these is the fast swing-through. Very few shooters can pinpoint the target quickly enough to execute a good pullaway shot.

Leads are often minimal. The faster the target is moving,

if you lay back, you've had it! It's pure reflex and speed of swing. The story is a little different on long crossing shots.

A target that makes you really coil up and unwind at close range gives you a lot more time at longer range, even if it is the same speed and angle. The increased distance between you and the target allows your field of view to become greater and acquire the target with less body movement. To me, there also seems to be a discrepancy between apparent speed of crossing targets at ranges inside 25 yards, and those beyond that. I know that I don't have to move as much to take a station five hard right-angle shot in trap from the 27-yard line as I do from the 16-yard line. The increased distance to the target means less body movement for the shooter, and the same holds true here in Sporting Clays.

Since I have that extra time, I tend to shoot all 30-plus-yard crossing shots with the "pullaway" technique, instead of the

Smart shooters will watch the flight of the target as many times as they can before it is their turn in the cage. The more you know about the bird the easier it should be to break.

the faster the gun has to swing to catch it. The faster the gun is moving, the less apparent lead is needed. Targets within 15 yards can often be broken, even by a somewhat lazy-swinging shooter, by triggering the shot as soon as the muzzle meets the bird.

With report and following pairs, a gun dismount between shots is the best bet. On true pairs, swing through and take the trailing target first, and then continue your gun movement to swing through the leading target. It is not a bad idea to fudge your natural point of aim a bit toward the direction of the second target (leading bird) when dealing with true pairs. You may need the extra swing room, because the second bird is likely to be taken out of the position where you would expect to break it under less strenuous presentations.

This is nothing more than very aggressive shooting. You have to aggressively go after any close-range crossing target;

fast swing. It works well for me, and gives me an apparent lead on a 40-yard crossing target of about 4 to 5 feet, as compared to the over 10-foot lead I would see with a sustained lead, or the 6- to 7-foot lead I would see with a swing-through. There is plenty of time to dismount the gun between shots on following or report pairs, and if you are using the pullaway, you will want to do so.

That's the procedure I would use for anything except true pairs. There, I would fudge my natural point of aim to the direction the target is traveling, take the trailing bird first with a pullaway, and then swing through the lead bird.

Should you be faced with battue targets on this presentation, you may have to fudge your body position even more to the target direction side, since experienced shooters wait longer for these targets to "develop" enough to be consistently broken.

No, it's not quite as simple as other clay target games.

Sporting's Newer Side

THERE IS NO doubt that Sporting Clays is the hottest shotgun game in America, and it is a rare clay target shooter who isn't itching to give it a try. Unfortunately, at the moment, that is often easier said than done.

A traditional Sporting Clays course takes a lot of land. In fact, it could require as much land as a nine-hole golf course. While the actual shooting stations don't require that much room, one has to plan for shot fall areas, and #7$\frac{1}{2}$ shot (the largest size allowed) can travel almost 340 yards through the air, and the areas where it lands can't really be used for anything else. That means a good Sporting Clays course can eat up a deceptively large amount of land, and land isn't cheap or, in some areas, readily available.

Another drawback is that the game is both time- and labor-intensive. As with golf, it takes a fair amount of time to negotiate a course, and the squad will require the services of a course guide/puller. If manual traps are used on any station, someone has to be paid to operate them.

No, Sporting Clays is not simple, inexpensive, or even feasible in some areas.

5-Stand Sporting

The brainchild of Scottish-born Raymond Forman, this new version is a computer-driven game that can be set up on existing trap or Skeet fields, even using some of the traps already in place. It can be run by one operator, and shooters can be cycled through in little more time than it takes to shoot a round of trap or Skeet. Yet the game can offer virtually every shot found on a full-sized Sporting Clays course. Some of the country's top range operators feel this may be one of the most significant things to happen to Sporting since it arrived on these shores.

"The game is a real money maker for us," one operator noted. "Our emphasis is on corporate/group entertainment, and we needed a game that could be shot day or night, rain or shine, 365 days a year. That is not feasible with Sporting Clays. You can't afford to cover walkways and shooting stations on a full-sized course, and lighting them up for night

Minimum personnel are required to keep a 5-Stand field operating. This is a boon to range operators because it cuts down overhead.

One reason for the growing popularity of the various 5-Stand Sporting games is physical size. They require no more room than a standard trap field and may even be able to utilize some of the installed trap machines.

shooting would take a bank of lights bigger than those that illuminate the Astro Dome.

"These new games," he continued, "use so little space that we can cover the shooting stations and light the field. We don't get weathered out like we do on our full-size Sporting course, and this has become a commercial range operator's dream."

To give you an idea of just how economically beneficial these games can be, Skeet Hall of Famer Danny Mitchell, who operates the Wolfe Creek Gun Club near Atlanta, Georgia, reported that on one recent weekend his range threw sixteen rounds of trap, 174 rounds of Skeet (which required opening six fields, with personnel to run them) and ninety-seven rounds of NSCA 5-Stand Sporting. All the Sporting rounds were handled by one man, on one field! That's a big reduction in costs.

While the new 5-Stand games have logistical and economic advantages for the range operator, don't be lulled into thinking they are just cheap, "fast-food" versions of the real game. They are not. In fact, they can be every bit as challenging as traditional Sporting Clays, or even harder.

There are a number of versions of the 5-Stand game. One is the original Raymond Forman version that is still seen on some ranges. This utilizes the "Birdbrain" computer to operate four to eight trap machines. The machine throws the same five shots for each shooter in random order. Five shots from each of the five stations makes a convenient twenty-five-target round. The shooter does not know what target will emerge when he calls for the bird. The game has three different levels, with three degrees of difficulty. On Level One, the shooter will see all singles. Level Two throws three singles and one simultaneous pair. Level Three presents two true pairs and one single.

Level Three, in the Forman version, is the toughest shotgun game this writer has ever tried!

Forman's game was never really standardized. The last time I shot it was at Cherokee Rose in Griffin, Georgia, and here is what was offered: As you stepped onto the field you were confronted with five shooting stations arrayed in a straight line, each with its own shooting cage. (Some clubs lay the shooting line out in a semi-circle, which can be dangerous.) Each shooter started at one station, received five targets, and moved to the next. As you changed stations, the angles changed, and the shots varied considerably. On the far left side of the field was trap 1 that launched a rabbit target across the middle of the field and a snipe target that took a similar crossing angle. Farther out from it was a grouse trap (trap 2) that launched a hard-angled shot that, depending where you were on the stations, could be a fast outgoing, quartering target or a long-range crossing shot. Trap 3 was located just forward and below shooting station three and was a wobble trap that simulated flushing quail on outgoing angles. Trap 4, located outside the edge of the field on the right-hand side, was a teal trap throwing high birds that settled into the middle of the field. Inside of that trap, on the right, was trap 5, a fast-climbing pheasant. Trap 6 was located on the roof and threw a high, outgoing dove.

Five-Stand traps are clearly numbered to be visible to the shooter.
This is important if the shot presentation is determined by a menu.

The NSCA 5-Stand Standardized game provides a target menu that allows the shooter to determine which traps will be thrown. Some games keep this a surprise, which makes them very tough!

These targets were tough to master with repeat practice, and what made that tougher was that they were thrown randomly, and you had to change stations every five rounds.

The only time you would know which target you would get was when the trap threw a broken target ("no bird"). It would then repeat that presentation. I often wished the trap had broken a few more targets!

That was one of the first mini-sporting games.

5-Stand Standardized

In 1992, the National Sporting Clays Association purchased the rights and trademark to NSCA 5-Stand Sporting, and made a few changes. The biggest was that the random order of the targets was dispensed with and the targets are now thrown in a known order that can be read from a menu posted at each shooting station. They also began a campaign to standardize the game, to an extent. That move has met with some controversy, but in reality it does make sense.

The purpose of some standardization is to establish NSCA 5-Stand Sporting as a game that can be shot anywhere in the country. This is important for future formalized competition with registered targets. If there is going to be any consistency in the future, at least one version of the game must become standard. But that is not to say it must be rigid.

The criteria for sanctioned NSCA 5-Stand Sporting are not tightly drawn. The field must have either six or eight individual traps, and except for one specialty trap, they must be automatic. Hand-set, manual traps can create a safety hazard on the small field where the same situation wouldn't exist on a larger Sporting Clays course.

To qualify as a sanctioned course, the following targets must be presented in the array: a tower outgoing bird, an incoming bird, a right-to-left crosser (or quartering away), a left-to-right crosser (or quartering away), a rabbit, and a vertical "teal-type" target. If the range is using eight traps instead of the minimum six, the extra two traps can greatly increase the options in target presentations.

The same three levels of difficulty are retained (Level One, singles; Level Two, three singles and a true pair; Level Three, one single and two true pairs), but the order is known and posted on a menu at the shooting station. That order, however, can be changed on a daily basis by changing the number of the

The game of 5-Stand Sporting Clays is almost as popular as the full-sized version and can be even more demanding. The balance and handling characteristics of contemporary Sporting Clays guns makes them winners here, as well.

trap, the angle of the trap, or even by moving the trap. For example, if a Level One shooter is going to get a single from trap 1 (all traps are clearly numbered and these numbers are visible to the shooter on each station), it might be a rabbit today and an outgoing tower tomorrow by simply changing the trap number. It allows a lot of variations in the basic field.

The field can also be set to play different games just by changing trap angles, although those changes will not be called sanctioned NSCA 5-Stand Sporting. One can even configure the traps to regular Sporting Clays rules and have a registered Sporting Clays match.

Although the NSCA-sanctioned version does have a set of criteria, there is a lot of versatility built into the equipment layout, and it can be quickly configured to a variety of other games.

Because of the cost and versatility and the small amount of space required, NSCA 5-Stand Sporting is growing rapidly in popularity. Many gun clubs that do not have the room for a full-sized range do have all the space required for this game. At the time of this writing, NSCA had over sixty sanctioned clubs, and others are seriously considering adding the course.

A number of ranges have what they refer to as a "5-Stand" range, although they don't meet NSCA requirements. These are often quite varied in their target fare and can be a lot of fun to shoot.

Because the targets and angles are known, the NSCA version is perfect for TV and spectator coverage. In fact, the game is under consideration for inclusion in the 1996 Olympics as an exhibition sport.

FITASC

While the new mini-games are ideal for ranges with limited space, there is another game that is beginning to make inroads onto the U.S. sporting scene: FITASC.

Some versions of the 5-Stand game can be more challenging than the full-sized game, because target angles on pairs presentations can be much more extreme.

175

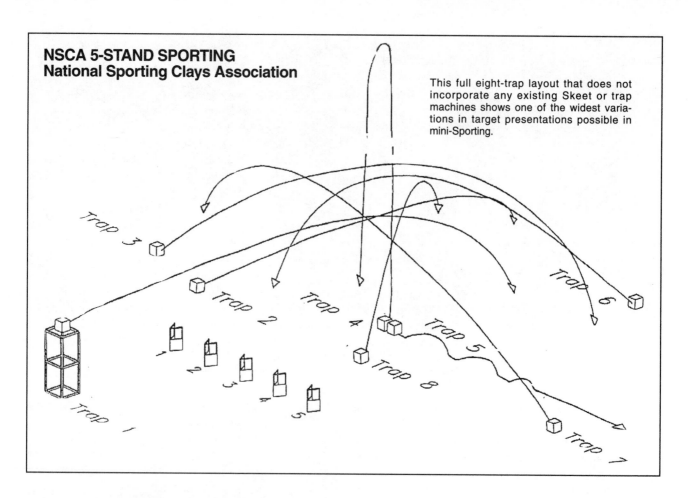

NSCA 5-STAND SPORTING
National Sporting Clays Association

This full eight-trap layout that does not incorporate any existing Skeet or trap machines shows one of the widest variations in target presentations possible in mini-Sporting.

Trap 3

Trap 2

Trap 4

Trap 6

Trap 5

Trap 8

Trap 1

Trap 7

1
2
3
4
5

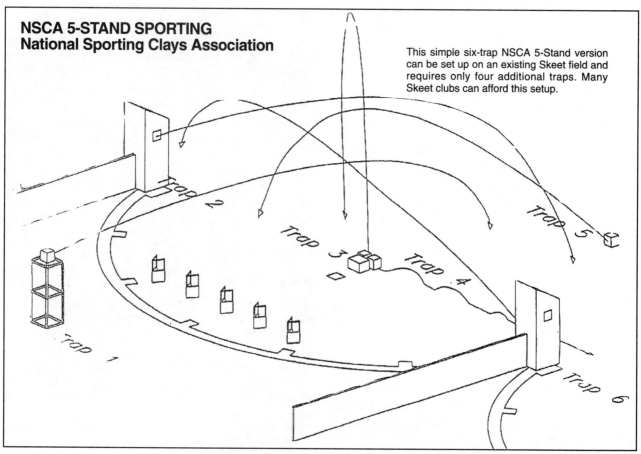

NSCA 5-STAND SPORTING
National Sporting Clays Association

This simple six-trap NSCA 5-Stand version can be set up on an existing Skeet field and requires only four additional traps. Many Skeet clubs can afford this setup.

Trap 2

Trap 3

Trap 4

Trap 5

Trap 1

Trap 6

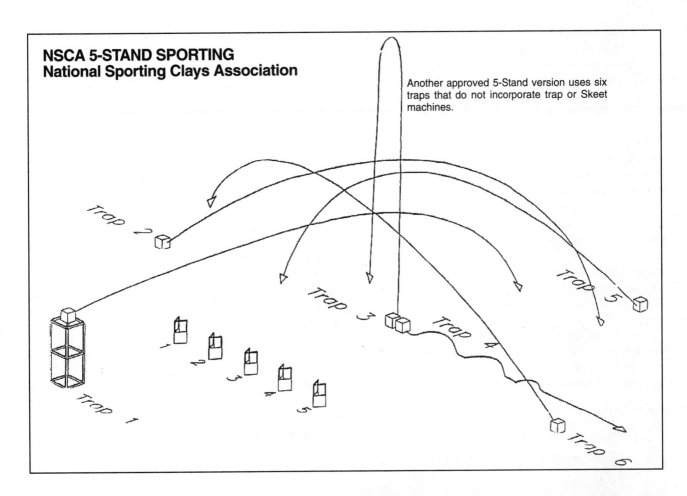

NSCA 5-STAND SPORTING
National Sporting Clays Association

Another approved 5-Stand version uses six traps that do not incorporate trap or Skeet machines.

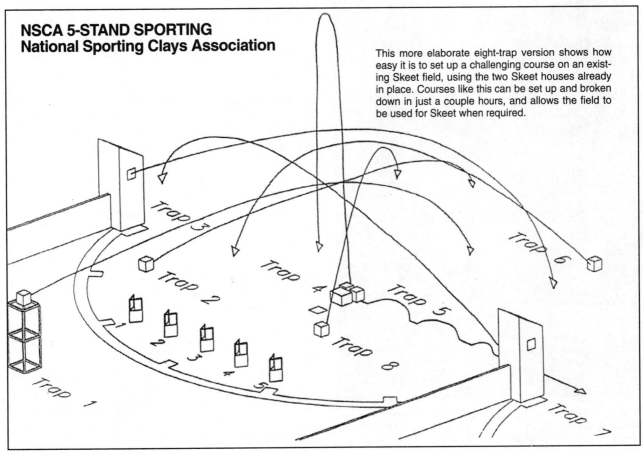

NSCA 5-STAND SPORTING
National Sporting Clays Association

This more elaborate eight-trap version shows how easy it is to set up a challenging course on an existing Skeet field, using the two Skeet houses already in place. Courses like this can be set up and broken down in just a couple hours, and allows the field to be used for Skeet when required.

FITASC stands for Federation Internationale de Tir aux Armes Sportives de Chasse and is one of the two world bodies (the other is the International Shooting Union, or "UIT") governing international shotgun sports. The FITASC version of Sporting Clays is to that game what International Skeet and trap are to the American versions of those games—more challenging!

This game centers on the Parcour, or layout. In traditional FITASC, a Parcour is a twenty-five target station with three different shooting positions for that station. In a 100-bird round, shooters visit four different Parcours.

There are no shooting cages in this game. There is a shooting pad, about a meter square in size. In the traditional version, targets are thrown in a 360-degree arc around the shooter. For obvious reasons, spectators are not encouraged to attend! The newer version deletes the 360-degree target arc, adds a fourth shooting position to the Parcour, and keeps shooters firing in more restricted directions. It is much more spectator-friendly.

In the Americanized version of Sporting Clays, each station may have a number of traps, but will throw only a few birds per trap. The English version uses fewer traps, but shifts shooters around the layout more and throws more targets from each

Proper gun hold position can be critical, given the wide target presentation angles one sees in the mini-Sporting games. It can change radically, depending upon which target is thrown first.

trap. Many English stations use only two traps, but keep things very interesting by presenting a lot of different angles. FITASC falls more in line with this.

The major difference between FITASC and Sporting is the degree of varied presentations a shooter will see as he moves to the different shooting positions on each Parcour. The shooter never sees the same shot more than twice. Generally, the first time it will be a single, and at the second presentation, the same target will be incorporated into a pair of doubles.

By moving shooting positions radically, the angle on the shots can change considerably, and what might be a relatively easy target from one position may be extremely difficult from another. The wide spectrum of target presentations includes greatly varying ranges. It is quite common to have targets as close as 10 yards and as far away as 60 yards from the same shooting position. This poses an interesting problem for the shooter, because once he steps onto the shooting position he cannot change his chokes! All shots must be handled with what is in the gun.

A varied load selection is far more important in FITASC than in standard Sporting, and some competitors carry as many as five or more different loads of varying shot sizes, weights and velocities. Since shooters may also shoot twice at any single, it is not uncommon for competitors to tote 100 or more rounds for a twenty-five bird shoot.

Another difference in this game is the gun position when calling for the bird. Traditional Sporting, and the various 5-Stand games, require the butt of the shotgun be off the shoulder and visible below the armpit. FITASC competitors are required to have a stripe on their shooting vest (usually tape) that extends 25 centimeters downward from the top of the shoulder toward the hip. The gun butt must be visible below the bottom of the line. In World Class matches, they measure the vest line!

Like NSCA 5-Stand Sporting, the trap order in FITASC is known and displayed on a menu at the shooting position. As the squad moves to a new position, the first shooter is allowed to have the targets thrown to be viewed. Once on the shooting pad, the shooter engages all his singles, and then he is followed by the next shooter. When the singles are done, the shooters return to the pad for doubles, and the second shooter in line now becomes the first. This rotation continues in order that every member of the six-man squad is required to shoot first for at least one new presentation.

This game requires about the same amount of land as a full-sized Sporting course, so it is not growing rapidly. It is growing in popularity, however, as many veteran Sporting shooters seek new challenges. A number of established Sporting Clays ranges have incorporated the game on available space.

In the U.S., the governing body for FITASC is the National Sporting Clays Association.

Though each of these various new games is similar enough to Sporting so that the same equipment and techniques can be used, each is different enough to increase the challenge to the shooter. The fresh new look of these games should ensure their popularity for years to come.

chapter

twenty-five

Sporting Tips From The Top

Some shooters try to get by with a set of relatively open choke tubes and change shells to tighten their patterns. Bill Whitehurst doesn't agree and thinks shooters should pay more attention to their chokes. He prefers to err on the side of too much choke, rather than too little.

BILL WHITEHURST VIVIDLY remembers the first round of Sporting Clays he ever shot. Having had some experience in competitive trap, and being an ardent bird hunter, he thought the "new game" wouldn't be much of a challenge. Armed with a lightweight 20-gauge, he went out to Big D Sporting Clays in Lake City, Florida, and gave it a whirl.

"I shot sixteen out of fifty," he laughs, "and was kind of depressed. Then, the manager told me there was a woman shooter out there who consistently shot in the forties, and that really did it to me. I wasn't going to let a woman beat me at something I'd been doing all my life, so I went to work to learn that game."

In 1994, Whitehurst won the NSCA Florida State Championship.

The woman Whitehurst referred to was Bonnie McLaurin, one of the premier Sporting Clays shooters in the country, and often called the "Chris Evert of Sporting Clays." Currently the captain of the NSCA Ladies All-America Team, she came by her shooting abilities quite honestly, having earned a berth on the U.S. Olympic International Skeet team from 1985 to 1990. Shifting to Sporting Clays, she won the National Ladies Championship three out of the last four years, and in 1994 won the Florida and Georgia State Ladies Championships, as well as the Zone 4 Southeastern Ladies Championship. She has also represented the United States in international FITASC competition. At the 1994 Florida State Championship, she was the runner-up to Bill Whitehurst for High Overall.

That one-two finish didn't surprise many shooters because for the last few years McLaurin and Whitehurst have been shooting and practicing partners, and undoubtably form one of the toughest couples teams in the country. Each brought certain talents to the team and each is quick to credit the other for helping them become more well-rounded shooters. Here are some of their thoughts on improving your game.

Loads, Chokes and Guns

McLaurin relies strictly on factory Winchester AA 2³/4-dram target loads in sizes #7¹/2, #8 and #9. During major matches, where factory loads are required, Whitehurst opts for the same loads. In practice, however, or in smaller matches where reloads are allowed, he rolls his own.

"I like a 1-ounce, 2³/₄-dram load," he says, "and I use one load formula with Winchester components and just change shot size. A lot of shooters like those killer 3-dram, 1¹/₈-ounce loads, but I don't. The increased recoil will wear you down. The lighter loads are very pleasant to shoot, and that does pay dividends in the later portions of a match."

Reducing recoil further was accomplished by the work done on his 32-inch-barreled Browning 325 by Phil Hughes at Seminole Chokes. The gun was back-bored, ported, properly custom fitted to him, and upgraded with a thick Kick-Eez recoil pad.

McLaurin also shoots a Browning 325 with similar work and Seminole choke tubes. Both shooters are adamant that one of the most important things any shooter can do is to have their gun properly fitted to them and fine-tuned.

"Many people don't realize it," says Whitehurst, "but a lot of over/under shotguns do not have their barrels regulated to the exact same point of impact. The top barrel on my Browning was shooting 6 inches to the right of the bottom barrel until Phil Hughes tuned them. Bonnie's gun did the same thing. Once a shooter gets his or her gun properly fitted and tuned, they will be more precise and won't require big loads that put a lot of shot in the air."

Whitehurst takes his quest for precision one step further by shooting a tighter choke than many other shooters.

"In my opinion," he says, "a lot of people are under-choked...they are using a choke that's too open. They will try to get through a round with just Cylinder or Skeet chokes, throw more shot out of them, and tighten down by going to larger shot. I don't like to do that. I'll use #9s and a Cylinder or Skeet choke only on targets inside 20 yards. Beyond that I'll go to an Improved Cylinder and #8s, reserving #7¹/₂s for long targets, or rabbits that are presented in an edge-on manner.

"I like to see a target crushed," Whitehurst continues, "not just a visible piece. It's a mental thing and that's why I tend to favor tighter chokes. If I'm not crushing the target, it can affect me."

McLaurin pays a lot of attention to chokes as well.

"I used to rely more on an open choke and just make shell changes for various distances," she says, "but the competition has gotten to the point where I now change both the choke and the shells. When the winning margin in a tournament may only be one or two birds, I want the optimum choke and load combination for each station.

"At the Alabama Governor's Cup," McLaurin remembers, "I had a pair of close targets, the kind that you can usually take with one shell. I had an Improved Cylinder tube in the gun and didn't change it. That cost me both of those targets because the pattern just wasn't big enough. Had I taken the time to slip in big Cylinder tubes and go to a load of #9s, I would have gotten one or both of them. I lost that event by one bird, and it does not take many lessons like that before you stop being lazy on the field."

Quality Practice is Vital

Shooting Sporting Clays is expensive, time consuming and often requires a fair bit of travel. Yet, serious shooters insist on a regular practice regime. McLaurin and Whitehurst solved that problem by resorting to standard Skeet fields, but with a twist.

"International Skeet was great training for me in Sporting Clays," McLaurin states, "because of the low gun position and the fast targets. Bill and I have carried that over to the Skeet fields and find that we can practice a great many of the shots we see on a Sporting field there. This is not only a lot less expensive, but takes less time."

Bill and Bonnie's Skeet field practice involves shooting from the legal Sporting Clays low gun position, and moving themselves around the field to see a wide variety of angles and target presentations. Doubles are a favored game, and they will often shoot one pair from a station in the correct Skeet order (outgoing target first), and then shoot another pair in the reverse order. This can be extremely effective practice for the long, dropping shots one often sees in Sporting.

Another tactic is to back away from the stations and shoot longer targets, sometimes as long as 70 yards. To add a bit more spice, they often back up a pickup truck to the shooting

The key to mastering the shotgun is to engage a lot of targets. Bill Whitehurst is convinced that trap and Skeet ranges are great training grounds for Sporting Clays shooters. You'll see all of those angles on the Sporting Clays fields.

point and shoot from the truck bed, which changes the angle even further.

"The advantage to practicing on a Skeet field," McLaurin claims, "is that you can duplicate many of the shots you will see in Sporting Clays and you can get a consistent target. On a Sporting range, the target may not be totally consistent because its flight will be dependent on exactly where the trapper places the bird on the throwing arm. If you are trying to figure out the precise lead and best technique to take a 50-yard quartering outgoing target, you want that target to be the same all the time, until you figure it out. On a Skeet field, it will be the same, and it will cost you less than a trip to a Sporting Clays range."

Another excellent source of practice is a dove tower, provided the shooter can vary his position around the tower without interfering with any other shooters that may be present. McLaurin and Whitehurst often time their visits to a nearby club to coincide with periods of low activity.

If certain shots cannot be duplicated by the above procedures, they take another route.

"I have a couple of portable trap throwers on my little farm, and Bonnie and I will get out there and set up any shots we want," Whitehurst notes. "If you've got the space to use one, an inexpensive portable trap can be a great practice aid."

(Above) Cross-training in other shotgun games is a big help to Sporting Clays gunners. USAMU PFC Danny White works out on the Bunker trap range, which is a great way to build speed for tough outgoing shots. (U.S. Army photo by Joseph J. Johnson)

Wobble trap is great practice for Sporting Clays gunners. The oscillating target angles will greatly improve a shooter's ability to handle quick outgoing targets.

Whitehurst favors 1-ounce loads and one choke degree tighter than normal for his practice. This builds precision that pays off when he shifts to the 1¹/₈-ounce load and slightly more open choke in a match. If you can hit them with an ounce, you can darned sure hit them with the heavier load!

Practicing with shooters who are as skilled and serious as you are is standard procedure for top shooters in Sporting Clays, as well as in every other shotgun game.

It's not uncommon for top Skeet shooters to do much of their practice with the diminutive 410-bore, on the theory that the smaller shell requires more precision, and if you can hit birds with that you can hit them with anything. Whitehurst has a similar philosophy.

"When I am practicing," he explains, "I will use one choke tighter than I normally would for a particular shot. For example, if I look at a shot and decide it is best handled with an Improved Cylinder choke, I will put in a Light Modified choke for practice. Combined with the 1-ounce loads I use, that makes me be more precise and keeps me from getting sloppy. If I can hit it with one choke tighter, I can darned sure hit it with the choke I would normally use."

When it comes to "quality practice," Whitehurst is a firm believer that you should practice with shooters whose skill level is equal to or exceeds your own, and who take their practice as seriously as you do. That's a common philosophy among top-level shooters in all clay target sports.

"Never take your practice for granted," Whitehurst states. "Always practice with the same determination that you would use to shoot a match. In fact, Bonnie and I now do a lot of our practicing by actually shooting the smaller local matches.

"An additional thing I feel is very important for shooters," he continues, "is to shoot at a variety of Sporting Clays ranges. Don't confine your shooting to just one course. You need to see as many different shots and angles as you can, and every course is a bit different. Shooting just one course all the time may make you a fine shooter on that course, but it will not help you as much in competition as will shooting a variety of courses on a regular basis. I consider this an essential form of practice."

Winning the Mental Game

"There are a lot of shooters who have made great progress on natural ability," McLaurin says, "but at some point in time that won't be enough to win a major match.

"The mental game is something that has to be addressed," she continues. "You cannot maintain a strong mental concentration level for more than the brief period of time it takes you to get up on the stand and shoot that particular bird. Some shooters don't accept that and try to stay keyed up the entire match. That alone will severely wear down a shooter. Mental exhaustion can be worse than physical exhaustion, and you can bring that on if you try to stay keyed and focused the en-tire match. I have learned to let down between stations, just let the mind drift and think of something totally different...even silly things. The atmosphere in Sporting Clays is very relaxed and it lends itself well to that. Yet, a lot of shooters hurt themselves by trying to force a high level of concentration for too long. The body can't do that."

The mental side of the game can beat shooters in other ways, as well.

"Shooting," notes McLaurin, "is an individual sport, just like golf. It is the shooter against the target, a matter of personal achievement. That can sometimes make us our own worst enemy when we become too involved with beating another shooter. That shouldn't be a factor. That shooter is not your competition, the target is. If you start thinking about the other shooters, your real competitor—the target—will beat you.

"I deal with this by setting personal goals that have nothing to do with the other shooters," she explains. "For example, in

Shooting a wide variety of Sporting Clays courses is considered essential training by experts McLaurin and Whitehurst. The more exposure you have to different shots and angles, the better you will shoot.

1994 one of my goals is to not shoot less than 80x100 in a tournament. I can't do anything about the other shooters, so why worry about them? If I get my eighty targets I'm happy. If I get beat, it doesn't bother me because I was just beat by a better shooter that day. If I mess up and don't get my eighty targets, especially if I did it because of stupid mistakes, then it will bother me because I beat myself. Having personal goals and striving to achieve them is far more important to your shooting success than how many other shooters you beat."

The mental game also extends to how you analyze and approach a particular station.

"One problem shooters have with Sporting Clays," says Whitehurst, "is the varied background and uneven terrain over which the targets appear. This can make it very difficult to properly estimate the distance to the point at which you intend to break the target, and that can cause you to select the wrong choke and load. That's one reason why I prefer a little tighter choke; generally when we improperly estimate the range we will underestimate it. The shot may look like 25 yards, but in reality it is 35. If I'm going to err, I would rather err on the side of too much pattern density than too little, for just that reason."

Whitehurst will often shoot an unfamiliar course, and then walk back through it to see how well he was estimating ranges. He does this by actually walking out onto the field and having the trapper throw targets over his head so he can accurately pace off the distance to the shooting stand. This exercise can greatly improve one's ability to properly estimate target ranges.

"Another problem newer shooters have," Whitehurst states, "is with pairs. Sometimes, especially with shooters who have had trap and Skeet experience, true pairs present a problem because the shooter has no experience with looking at them. He just doesn't see that presentation in other games. The key is to focus on one bird at a time, shoot it, and take the next. Normally, you would want to take the trailing bird first and then swing through to the lead bird, but there are always exceptions to that rule.

"If a pair is flying through a very small window," he continues, "you may have to take the lead bird first or it will get lost in the bushes before you can get to it. Another time when I take the lead bird first, usually, is in an overhead outgoing pair with one bird running directly behind the other."

When addressing pairs, there are times when it appears that both targets can be broken with just one shot. Some shooters look for these situations as a matter of course. Whitehurst doesn't.

"I heard Gen. Norman Schwarzkopf use the term 'club house shot' to describe both targets broken with one shell," he says, "and I think that trying for those will hurt you in the long run. I want to shoot two individual targets each time I shoot a pair, not count on both with one shell. On those occasions when I do get both with one shell—it happens and it is sometimes unavoidable—I always pick the biggest remaining piece and shoot it, just to keep myself geared to fire two shots on pairs. Early in my career I shot a pair and thought I had broken both with one shell, so I didn't fire the second. The scorer did not agree with me and I lost that bird. Now, I always shoot two shots at pairs. Period."

The ability to define two individual targets in a pair will come with more exposure to that presentation. One excellent way to get it is to shoot a round of pairs as a part of your practice routine. Many ranges will throw twenty-five pairs (fifty birds) instead of a standard round if you ask them.

Another mental problem that plagues many shooters is dealing with targets that are partially hidden by course terrain.

"Close shots among trees can bring on a difficult subconscious response," Bonnie McLaurin explains. "It's natural to want to avoid shooting a tree and that can make the shooter very hesitant, which guarantees a miss because these shots invariably require a fast swing at close range. Another factor that comes into play in Sporting that you won't see in other games is what I call the 'strobe effect.' This is what you get as a bird moves through trees and has very short periods of invisibility as it slips behind one every few feet. It can be very tough to acquire and follow. The same thing can also happen in deep woods as the bird passes through patches of light and shadow.

"Beating this illusion requires real concentration on the bird and the ability to pick it up quickly as it comes out of the house. The better you can see the target, the bigger and slower it will appear. When you can't see the target well it looks smaller and faster, and the uneven lighting, or intervening trees, creates the illusion of a much more difficult shot."

The ABCs

Confidence is one of the keys for any great shooter, and McLaurin has an unusual way of building it.

"I like to get out on a Skeet range and do things wrong," she says. "That may sound funny, but it is a great way to build confidence. For example, I know the proper foot position for low house one. So, I take the correct foot position, but take a completely incorrect gun position—point it way out onto the field beyond the stake. Then I close my eyes and call for the bird. When you open your eyes you have the right foot position but everything else is wrong—the gun is wrong, the bird is not where you would normally shoot it, and your timing is now way off. If you can recover and hit that bird you are well on your way to becoming a versatile shooter. It's a way of training your reflexes to adjust to abnormal circumstances. It's also a great way to boost your confidence because your brain will say, 'If I can hit it like this, how on earth could I miss it if I put everything in the right place to start!' "

Unfortunately, that can and does still happen. We all miss. Sometimes we fall into slumps and start missing a lot! Often we have no idea why this is happening. McLaurin does.

"The training I had with the U.S. Shooting Team gave me great insight into the actual mechanics of shooting," Bonnie explains, "and how those mechanics can get out of whack every now and then. Basically, everything we do is learned behavior—a sequence of events we learn in order to achieve an end. We don't consciously think about sticking a fork into a piece of food and then placing it precisely into our mouth. It is something we have done so many times before that it has now become a single act. But at some point there was a learning process: grip the fork, find the food, impale it properly, move it to the face without dropping it, find the mouth.... That is a sequence of actions. I use a sequence of actions that I call my ABCs when I prepare to shoot.

"When I step onto a shooting station," she continues, "the first thing I do is get my feet into the proper position to correctly address the target. I normally take a natural point of aim slightly beyond where I intend to break the target in order to have room for a good swing and follow-through. That becomes Step A. Next is the gun position. Where do I want to start my gun? Do I want to crowd the trap because this is a really quick target, or do I want to put the gun more into the field? What type of shooting style will I use on this target? That affects the gun position. That's B. The last step is C. Where do I put my eyes to find that first spot where I will pick up the bird? One thing I used to do when I first started shooting Sporting Clays was to crowd the trap (swivel right into the house) with both my gun and my eyes. What I have learned to do now is to get the gun out a little farther, but still crowd the trap with my eyes. I want to see the bird just as fast as I can, and if I can actually see it come out of the trap I am happy.

"What this does for me," she notes, "is to develop a pre-shot routine that I am happy with. Unfortunately, we sometimes get to the point where all this becomes habit, just like putting food in the mouth. Whenever I start having trouble with a particular shot, the way I sort it out is to go right back to those ABCs and consciously emphasize each one of them as a separate action instead of a single ingrained habit. When we start taking things for granted we start missing targets, and

Bonnie McLaurin believes the mental aspect of competition is ignored by many shooters, to their detriment. She perfected her mental game as a U.S. Olympic Team shooter, and credits it with her run of the National Championships.

that is often because we did a good A and a good C but skipped over B.

"It is not at all uncommon," she laughs, "for a shooter to suddenly start having trouble with a target they have been handling for years. When the mental game is working right, we normally do these things well. But, when we are struggling a bit, or when match pressure rears its ugly head, we can fall apart.

"Another thing you have to work hard to block out," McLaurin states, "may be the fact that the shooter in front of you, who you know to be a good shooter, didn't hit a single target on the station you're about to shoot. When that happens you can do one of two things: (1) go up and do the same thing—it's rather like a chain reaction; or (2) regroup mentally by putting yourself in a different state and blocking that out, then go up and shoot your birds. That can be a difficult thing to do after you watch a good shooter "zero" a station, but you can't play follow the leader, and that sort of thing does happen."

Whitehurst has a similar mental preparation before he shoots.

"I mentally visualize the shot," he says. "I actually imagine the bird coming out of the house, my gun moving to it, the lead develop, and the target breaking in the air. To me that is important. Then I get my foot and body position. I take a couple of deep breaths to help relieve any tension that might have

Sporting Clays lends itself to maintaining a relaxed atmosphere that experts believe can help a shooter with the mental aspect of the game.

Sporting Clays shooters can get good practice on incoming and crossing shots on a Skeet range. It saves time and money.

Anything that shooters can do to maintain a fresh and relaxed physical condition will help them during the course of a lengthy match. Many shooters now use pull carts or even golf carts to help prevent fatigue due to toting heavy guns and gear all day long.

built up and then execute the shot. It's just my way of letting the mind put the body to work."

Physical Conditioning

Letting the mind run the body is much easier if the body is ready, and both McLaurin and Whitehurst are convinced that physical conditioning is important for good performance at Sporting Clays.

"I shot one course in north Georgia back when I first started shooting Sporting," McLaurin remembers, "that was on very hilly ground, and by the end of the day I was exhausted. I made up my mind right then and there that if I was going to compete at a national level I was going to be in shape for it."

McLaurin now walks at least 5 miles, three times a week and works out regularly on an exercise machine, along with situps and pushups. Sporting Clays requires much more physical activity than other shotgun games. The shooter must carry 20 or more pounds of gun and ammo over several miles during the course of a day's shooting.

"Being in good physical shape will make you a better shooter," she feels, "and this is something many shooters neglect and they will pay for it at some time. I try to pace myself on the course and never get into a rush. I want to be as fresh and alert for the last targets as I was for the first ones."

Whitehurst is well aware of the need to maintain the "shooting platform."

"The night before a shoot," he says, "can be just as important as the day of the shoot. I try to eat a normal, nutritious meal, get to bed at my regular time, and go easy on the alco-

hol. One mixed drink the night before the shoot is my limit. I don't want to overindulge in anything. I just want to get a good night's rest.

"It also helps to understand your own body," he continues. "I am normally an early riser and up at 5:30 a.m. every day. But I have found that I do not shoot my best before about noon. If I have a choice of squadding times, I try to pick one from about 1 p.m. on. It's a little thing, but I know I shoot better in the afternoon and that might get me an extra bird or two. When I won the Florida State Championship, it was only by two birds. Those little things count!"

When it comes to advice for new shooters, McLaurin is quick to stress one key point.

"I hate to see people get discouraged early and base their opinion of their shooting abilities on just a brief number of outings," she says. "Have patience with yourself and work toward steady improvement, no matter how small that improvement might be. Shooters who are breaking twenty-five birds out of fifty should set a goal to break thirty. Then when that goal is met, increase it to thirty-two or thirty-three. Always look for upward movement. Some shooters feel that they can become great shots overnight just because they have some trap or Skeet experience, and that is not realistic. Sporting Clays is a different game, and a challenging one. But, don't get discouraged early. Time, experience and practice will improve your game."

For those who doubt the wisdom of those words, just remember that Bill Whitehurst's first round of Sporting was a sixteen!

Section IV
Fine Tuning

Hotrodding Your Smoothbore

"HIGH-PERFORMANCE SHOTGUN" is a term that can mean different things to different shooters. Some might define it as how smoothly and quickly the gun gets on fast-flushing grouse. Others might consider it an indication of how well it hits with heavy steel shot loads on a distant goose, or how "hard" it smokes clay targets.

Larry Nailon, however, has a different and much more succinct definition.

"When we speak about a high-performance shotgun," he explains, "what we are talking about is a gun that delivers the best down-range performance regardless of the load or distance. It is the combination of gun and load that delivers the maximum number of pellets in the load to the point of impact while simultaneously producing the largest useful pattern that has no gaps or holes a bird or clay target could slip through.

"High performance," he notes, "is simply down-range performance. To achieve that we must get every pellet, or as many as is humanly possible, out of the shell, through the bore and choke, and out the gun in a perfectly smooth, round and undeformed condition. Round pellets fly true and will arrive at the target together. Pellets that have been partially flattened or deformed will veer off course and even lag behind the main shot charge. Sometimes, they will be far enough away from or behind the main charge to be of absolutely no use. You may as well not even have fired them for all the good they will do you on that shot.

"It doesn't really matter how many pellets you start with in the load. What counts is how well you take care of what you start with. When we build a 'high-performance shotgun barrel,' our goal is to get as many pellets out of the gun in as undeformed a condition as possible."

Nailon does know a thing or two about tweaking a shotgun barrel for improved performance. As the president of Clearview Products, he has earned a highly respected reputation among top-notch competitive shooters in virtually every shotgun game for his custom barrel and choke work; yet, Nailon doesn't consider what he does to be new or earth-shaking.

Test patterning your barrel and load will show you what loads give the performance you require. You should pattern the gun at the range you intend to use that particular load. It does little good to pattern a spreader load intended to be fired at 15 yards at a range of 40 yards.

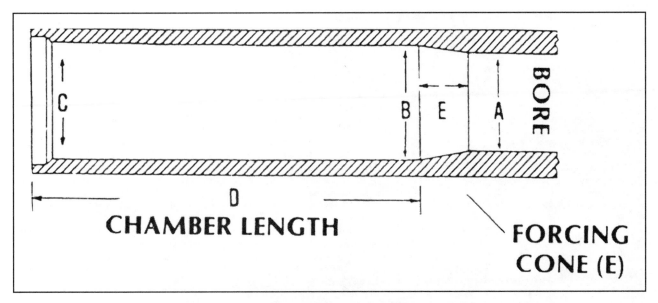

Chamber dimensions can have a significant effect on the ability of the shot charge to exit the shell and enter the bore without deforming shot. Larry Nailon makes certain that he tunes those dimensions to specification, something that not all gunmakers accomplish with each individual shotgun.

Critical Areas

"There are a number of modifications one can make to a shotgun barrel," he states, "that will result in a certain degree of performance enhancement. All I do is combine each of these proven enhancers into a total barrel work-over. Each of these modifications complements the others and results in a much greater increase in performance than you would get if you only opted for one or two of them."

When Nailon starts on a barrel, there are four key areas he is concerned with: chamber, forcing cone, bore and choke. Modifications to any one of them can improve performance. However, Nailon refines all four areas into perfect harmony to provide the maximum performance. Here's how he "tweaks" a barrel.

Chamber

Modern mass-production methods work because of manufacturing tolerances. As a result, measurements need only be "within spec." It is possible, although not common, to get a factory shotgun chamber having incorrect dimensions. Most commonly the chamber is shorter than required. The problem with a short chamber is that it may not allow the crimp to unfold fully without protruding into the forcing cone. If this happens, the wad and shot charge are restricted in their ability to exit the shell, and that occurs at the precise moment that maximum chamber pressure is reached. This causes shot pellets to deform and increases chamber pressure and recoil.

"Checking the chamber dimensions is a standard procedure for us," Nailon notes. "I also like to increase the length of the chamber to .060-inch longer than normal, especially if the shooter is a reloader. As a shell is reloaded and fired it tends to stretch just a bit, not unlike a brass cartridge case, and a slightly longer chamber becomes an asset."

Excessively long chambers, however, are not a benefit.

"We have found," explains Nailon, "that while 2³/₄-inch shells will function perfectly in a 3-inch chamber, the downrange performance of the load can sometimes suffer. The shot column/wad has an extra ¹/₄-inch run at its highest pressure point before it enters the forcing cone, and side pressure on the pellets at this point tends to beat up the pellets more than if they were fired in a chamber of the proper length for the shell."

Forcing Cone

Directly ahead of the chamber is the forcing cone, and as its name implies it acts as a funnel to guide the wad and shot charge from the chamber to the bore. The normal length of most factory forcing cones is between ¹/₂- and ⁵/₈-inch. Nailon doesn't like that either.

"The length of a shot column is about 1 inch in a light 12-gauge load and over 1¹/₂ inches in a heavy load. As the pellets at the bottom of the load are rammed into the upper pellets, outward pressure is tremendous. It is highest at the moment the shot charge moves from the chamber to the forcing cone. Since the shot column is moving through a constricting area (the forcing cone) that is only about half the length of the shot column, with as much as 10,000 psi behind it, it's pretty apparent that a significant number of pellets are being deformed before they even get into the barrel," he explains.

Nailon's solution is to lengthen the forcing cone.

"I feel a cone of 1¹/₂ inches is the minimum," he states. "My own patterning tests with our moving patterning board, where precise target speeds can be set and shot strings of up to 16 feet in length can be accurately measured, indicates that even a forcing cone length of over 2¹/₂ inches will help, not hurt."

Forcing cone lengthening is a custom technique that some

Long-range shooters aren't the only ones who can benefit from barrel tuning. Even the short-range patterns required by these Skeet shooters can be improved and made more uniform and consistent with proper barrel work.

major shotgun makers are now incorporating into their better grades of guns, often those intended for trap, Skeet and Sporting Clays shooters.

"The standard short forcing cone can be an asset if one uses the old fiber wad shells," Nailon claims, "but with modern one-piece plastic wads, it is obsolete. All a short forcing cone does here is raise pressure, increase recoil and deform shot."

Some of the biggest offenders in the short, tight forcing cone area are the low- and mid-priced Italian and Spanish imports, because many shooters in their original market area still rely on fiber wad shells.

Bore

Larry Nailon is a big believer in back-bored barrels, the process of deliberately boring the barrel out to a larger diameter than is industry standard for that particular gauge. To understand why that is so, an understanding of choke is required.

The term "choke" is used to describe two dissimilar, but related factors: (1) how the gun patterns and 2) the constriction at the muzzle of the gun.

The first definition is commonly understood. A gun that patterns 70 percent is considered to have a Full choke. A 60-percent pattern is Modified, while 50 percent is Improved Cylinder. A Cylinder choke runs about 40 percent. A Skeet choke is very close to Improved Cylinder in performance. In terms of measurement, a Skeet choke is intended to throw a 30-inch pattern at 25 yards.

The second definition is much less properly understood.

The actual muzzle constriction we refer to as choke is not totally dependent upon just the constriction at the muzzle. The actual choke achieved is the relationship between the constriction in the choke itself, and the inside diameter (ID) of the barrel.

The constriction is measured in thousandths of an inch. The British often refer to this as points of choke. For example, a measured constriction of .005-inch could be referred to as "five points of choke." A constriction of .019-inch would be nineteen points.

The degree of constriction required to produce different chokes varies from gauge to gauge, as can be seen in the nearby table of choke dimensions. With the 12-gauge, for example, no constriction gives Cylinder choke, .005-inch produces Skeet 1; .009 is Improved Cylinder; .012 equals Skeet 2; and so on. Extra-Full and Super-Full chokes run from .045- to .089-inch.

From the above it might seem that we could grab a choke tube marked Modified, screw it into our 12-gauge and get a 60-percent pattern. Maybe, maybe not.

If our 12-gauge has a bore diameter of .729-inch, and if we have a choke tube marked Modified that has an internal diam-

Back-boring a barrel allows improved choke performance through a bigger hole that deforms less shot. That results in improved downrange performance, as well as reduced pressure and recoil.

continues, "and you'll get the same pattern control. But with a back-bored barrel, you get it with a bigger hole in the muzzle for the shot to go through. Once the shot pellets enter the choke constriction they can do one of two things, if they are lead pellets: they can either reposition themselves (one pellet moving ahead of, or behind another) or they can be deformed. With a back-bored barrel and larger choke tube in use, the pellets have more room to reposition, and fewer are deformed."

With steel shot, especially the larger sizes, the situation changes. The pellets can either reposition, or damage the choke! Back-boring is even more important to waterfowlers than lead-shot users.

How much to over-bore depends on the individual barrel. Nailon feels most will take between .010- and .015-inch without difficulty. Going over .015-inch can produce a slight velocity loss, but often results in larger useful patterns. Nailon has one 12-gauge back-bored to .750-inch (.021-inch over industry standard) and reports that 1-ounce loads lack the pellets to fill the pattern, but that the gun shoots marvelously with 1¹/₈-ounce loads.

An additional advantage to back-boring is that Nailon and the customer now know precisely what that barrel's ID is, and that it is uniform from chamber to muzzle, without high spots. Back-boring will also reduce recoil to some extent.

One additional step Nailon takes on the bore is to burnish it. "If the bore isn't perfectly mirror smooth," he has found, "it tends to accumulate fouling, especially plastic fouling from the wad, at a much higher rate. This fouling acts to increase friction as successive wads and shot charges move through the barrel, decreasing velocity and increasing recoil. In extreme cases it can actually impede the performance of the wad and cause pellet deformation."

Most makers only finish a bore to "near smoothness." Complete polishing is a time-consuming job, and time is money in mass production. Even if the bore is chrome-lined, that's no guarantee it is smooth. Chrome is only as smooth as the surface over which it was applied, and if the bore wasn't polished mirror-smooth before the plating, you still have a rough bore.

Nailon polishes his bores with a set of specially designed hones running down to #800 grit. If you are one of those smart shotgunners who routinely cleans his barrel with a brush wrapped in 0000 steel wool, which is the best way to remove plastic fouling that solvents and brushes leave behind, you are doing a little burnishing every time you clean the gun. Nailon's method is just a lot quicker.

Choke

Once Nailon has tweaked the bore this far, all that remains are the choke tubes. Again, he disagrees with most manufacturers.

"Once the pellets enter the choke constriction they can either reposition or deform," he explains. "My goal is to give them the maximum opportunity to reposition before they begin to deform.

"Most factory choke tubes," he continues, "are about 1¹/₂

eter of .710-inch, then we do have 19 points of constriction between the two and will get a Modified pattern, assuming a decent load. Suppose, however, that the actual diameter of the barrel is .745-inch? If we insert our .710-inch tube, our real constriction is now .035-inch, or 35 points! Regardless of what is marked on the choke tube, we have a Full choke. Shot charges can't read, they can only respond.

If our 12-gauge barrel has a bore diameter of .720-inch, then our Modified, .710-inch tube is actually giving us only .010-inch constriction, 10 points, or about Improved Cylinder.

Sound farfetched? Not at all! In fact, every shotgun smith I have ever talked to tells me it is very common to get factory barrels above or below standard bore diameter. In fact, they may vary from .710- to .750-inch in guns coming off the same factory production line.

That in itself does not explain why Nailon favors back-boring barrels. This, however, will:

"The degree of pattern control you exercise is dependent upon the ID of both the barrel and the choke tube," he says. "If a 12-gauge barrel has an ID of .725 and you put a .715-inch tube in it, you have an Improved Cylinder choke. If you have a barrel with an ID of .750 and you want to install an Improved Cylinder choke, all you need to do is put in a tube with an ID of .740-inch.

"You have the same degree of constriction with either," he

inches long. That requires the shot to reposition in a limited amount of space. If you double the length of the choke tube, you double the time and distance they have to do that. All other factors being equal, longer choke tubes deform less shot and—remember—that is our ultimate goal with custom barrel work."

Nailon combines a 3-inch tube length with an inner taper that combines a cone with parallel surfaces, instead of the more commonly seen cone style that places the maximum constriction at one extremely short point. The addition of the parallel surfaces is a further aid in allowing the shot to reposition itself.

Making the longer, custom choke tubes is considerably more difficult than making factory-length tubes. It's more time-consuming and expensive because, as a machinist's rule of thumb, you can't hold precise tolerances in high-speed production when boring over two times the length of your diameter. To make his tubes, Nailon has to make a series of precise, fine cuts instead of getting it all done in one pass.

What the customer receives is a set of custom-made choke tubes sized precisely to the diameter of the gun's barrel. Nailon normally provides these in .005-inch increments, which assures a precise degree of pattern control. Lately, however, he has cut it even finer than that.

"We are finding that a number of competitive shooters, especially Sporting Clays gunners, want to go to half-step chokes to increase their ability to really fine-tune their patterns for whatever conditions exist in their area," he notes. "We

Gauge	Bore ID	Full	Imp Mod	Mod	SK2	Imp Cyl	SK1	Cyl
10	.775	.045	.035	.030				.000
12	.729	.035	.025	.019	.012	.009	.005	.000
16	.667	.028	.020	.015	.010	.007	.004	.000
20	.617	.025	.019	.014	.009	.006	.004	.000
28	.550	.022	.016	.012	.007	.005	.003	.000
410	.410	.017		.008		.004		.000

AMERICAN STANDARD BORE & CHOKE DIMENSIONS

All dimensions in inches. Note: The 10-bore and 410-bore are not ordianrily provided with those choke constrictions where data is missing. If you want those chokes you must use custom choke tubes.

have begun offering tubes in these half-step increments (i.e., .002-inch, 007-inch, etc.), and they really do make a difference. I have been shooting a .002-inch tube for close-range shots recently, and it does some amazing things. You'd be surprised the difference a simple .002-inch constriction can make over a straight Cylinder bore. That small difference, in the more open chokes, makes a much bigger change in pattern control than the same .002-inch difference does in the tighter chokes."

If a shooter does not want to go to the expense of a full-blown barrel make-over, he can still benefit from custom-fitted choke tubes.

Nailon will make choke tubes in whatever reasonable incre-

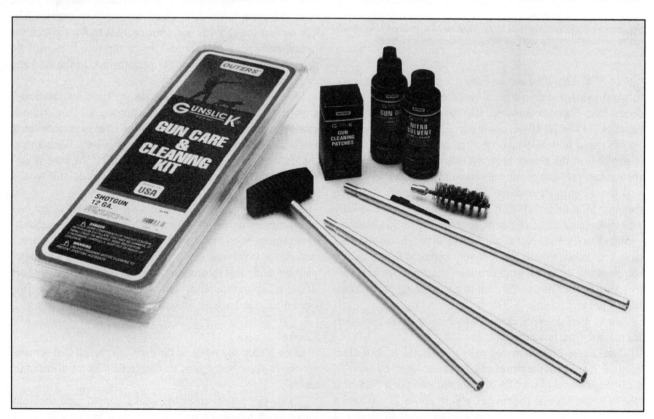

The most highly tuned barrel available will not produce the performance it is capable of giving if it is allowed to collect lead and plastic fouling. A stout cleaning rod and proper selection of brushes, plus some 0000 steel wool, will give you the performance you paid for.

mental series a shooter requests, in any one of the various popular thread systems. This does, however, require that the shooter either have the barrel ID measurements done by a competent gunsmith on a local level and supply them to Nailon, or simply send his barrel to Nailon, who would prefer to take those critical measurements himself.

Aftermarket Tubes

Another alternative to improved pattern control, albeit a less effective one, is for a shooter to simply add aftermarket choke tubes to his existing selection. However, factory-offered choke tubes are often rather limited in scope. Generally you can get Skeet 1, Improved Cylinder, Modified, Full and, sometimes, Extra-Full.

If you are not satisfied with the pattern control your choke selection allows you to achieve, then adding tubes in Skeet 2, Cylinder, Improved Modified or Extra-Full may help correct the situation. If your actual barrel ID is not .729-inch and, for example, your Modified tube is actually producing Improved Cylinder or Full patterns, going to some of the intermediate constrictions can help put those patterns back to where you want them.

There is, however, a pitfall with this approach if done incorrectly.

"There are a number of different choke tube systems on the market," explains Nailon. "More than one gun manufacturer may use the same system. For example, the Win-Choke system threads will fit a number of guns besides those made by U.S.R.A.C./Winchester. When you are talking abut different choke tube systems, you are basically talking about the thread pattern they use and the length of the choke tube.

"Just because a Win-Choke may screw into the barrel of your gun," he continues, "does not necessarily mean the total fit is exact. If the barrel diameter is not properly matched to

CHOKE STYLES

CONE PLUS PARALLEL

CONE

CYLINDER

SPREADER

The internal tapers and dimensions of choke styles vary. Most of the top choke makers in the world agree that the cone plus parallel-type will produce the most consistent and even patterns.

There is a wide variety of aftermarket choke tubes available for virtually any shotgun threaded to accept a particular system. All the tubes shown here are for use in the author's Red Label, and all perform well. The author supplied the barrel ID to the tube makers in order to assure a proper fit.

External choke tubes that can be quickly changed without the aid of a wrench, like the author's Briley tubes shown here on his Ruger Red Label, are very popular among Sporting Clays shooters who might change chokes at almost every shooting station.

193

Storing chokes tubes in a clean plastic container will prevent dirt and grit from getting into the threads and requiring the shooter to thoroughly clean them before they can be used again. Pockets are not good places to carry them!

Nearly any shotgun can be threaded to accept one of the many different interchangeable choke tube systems on today's market, and it is a modification that will only improve your scores.

External tubes allow shooters to change them quickly without a wrench. They are an asset for any shotgunner.

Hastings is just one company that provides aftermarket choke tubes for the different gunmakers' systems, and they work very well.

the choke tube, you won't get the pattern you expect. You can also have a problem with the fit at the base of the choke. A barrel will expand slightly upon firing. That expansion can range from about .002-inch to almost .010-inch. To accommodate this, there is a small step at the rear of the choke that allows for the expansion and helps guide the wad from the barrel into the choke. In effect, it acts almost like the forcing cone does at the chamber.

"If the barrel diameter varies too much from the diameter of the rear of the choke, then you get a ridge that the wad can hang up on. If that ridge is large enough, the wad can jam, the pressure will build, and you'll blow the choke tube out the end of the barrel. That's expensive to repair. Shuffling choke tubes around just because they have the same thread system and will fit into the gun is not a good idea," Nailon feels.

In a best-case scenario, you will not get the down-range performance you expect. In a worst-case scenario, you may seriously damage the barrel.

This, of course, does not mean that aftermarket choke tubes are dangerous, just that they can be, even if the thread systems are the same and the chart says they will interchange. For that reason I am not going to include a chart showing the compatibility of the various systems. Though there are some systems that will truly interchange, the majority of them are just different enough that problems can arise, even if the tube seems to fit the gun perfectly.

When you purchase aftermarket chokes tubes (and there is nothing wrong with that) you will do yourself a favor if you tell the supplier precisely what the make and model of your gun is; better yet, give him the barrel ID measurements, regardless of what the "chart" says your gun will take.

If your gun is not threaded to accept interchangeable choke tubes, then the best thing you can do for it is to send off the barrel off and have them fitted. It's not complex. A number of aftermarket companies do an outstanding job in this area, and it is not just limited to 12-gauge guns.

You can have tubes installed in any shotgun, right down to the diminutive 410. I know, because Hastings installed the Briley tube system on one of my 410 shotguns, and the difference in performance is hard to believe. What it does for the 28-gauge is beyond words!

The point is this: If your favorite smoothbore is not presently fitted to accept interchangeable tubes, you are wasting over half the gun's potential, regardless of gauge.

Interchangeable tubes can greatly increase your gun's performance, and there are no real mysteries to their use.

Tube Installation

One key is in the installation of the tube. It should be fully inserted into the gun, completely bottomed out in the threads, hand-tight and not over-torqued. If a tube begins to back out from the threads even slightly, there is a risk of gun damage.

Keeping a barrel clean of powder, lead and plastic fouling will produce more uniform patterns. Smart shooters clean their barrels with a 0000 steel wool-wrapped brush, since this will remove the plastic fouling that most solvents leave behind.

Interchangeable choke tubes are dependent on proper lubrication. Gun oil is not the best choice since it does not offer the threads any real support from the pressure generated upon firing. A heavy lube, like Colonial Arms' Choke Tube Lube, or B-Square's choke tube lube, will prevent a lot of problems.

It's an excellent idea to check the snugness of your tubes before any shooting session.

Tubes should *never* be installed in the barrel without lubrication on the tube threads. Standard gun-grade or machine oil is not the proper lubrication because it provides no support for the threads. Far better choices are Never-Seez, Lubriplate or any one of the many commercial choke tube lubes incorporating these ingredients. Improper lubrication is one of the biggest problems with interchangeable tubes. If you forget the lube, or use one that is inadequate, you may not be able to remove the tube from the barrel without the services of a gunsmith.

Also, barrels threaded for interchangeable tubes should *never* be fired without a tube in place. This is just about guaranteed to damage the threads and leave you with another costly repair bill.

It is also not a good idea to leave a choke tube in the barrel indefinitely, even with the best lube. Once a year, pull out the tube, clean it, re-lube it and stick it back in. If you forget about periodic maintenance, the tube may find a permanent home in that particular barrel.

It is worth pointing out that interchangeable choke tubes, lengthened forcing cones, back-boring and long choke tubes are not new developments. Custom smiths have been doing them for over twenty years. What should certainly be pointed out is that major gunmakers now include interchangeable tubes as standard equipment, and most are beginning to offer long choke tubes, lengthened forcing cones and long chokes on their top-of-the-line competition guns.

This only goes to prove that those "old-time" custom smiths and their discerning customers were more than right—they knew how to hotrod a smoothbore!

Shotgun Fitting Is Easy

Author makes a quick mount on the International Skeet range. An improperly fitted gun can do terrible things to your score here or on the Sporting Clays ranges.

FEW SHOOTERS GIVE it much thought when they see a handgunner or rifleman making careful adjustments to the sights on their firearms. Not only is this a perfectly normal operation, but also the sign of a shooter knowledgeable enough to realize that a gun that won't put it's payload where you aim it is relatively useless.

Yet, in what has to be one of the great unexplainable mysteries of the shooting world, let a shotgunner start fooling with the point of impact of his favorite smoothbore and many shooters are aghast! The unfortunate tinkerer is often branded as some sort of nitpicker dabbling in the black arts who will probably screw up a perfectly good shotgun.

Bull!

All the shooter is doing is demonstrating a thorough understanding of a basic Universal Truth. Regardless of the type of firearm you are using, if you and it aren't "lookin' in the same direction," it will require an act of Grand Cosmic Intervention to hit your target.

That's a pretty simple concept to embrace, and one reason why astute shooters want the best sights available on their rifles and handguns. Unfortunately, when you get around to considering shotguns in the same light, some shooters tend to become intimidated.

Fitting a shotgun to an individual shooter has, over the years, taken on the aura of magic. One journeys great distances to find "The Fitter," who then watches the shooter with detached interest, meditates a few minutes upon his observations, tosses a few chicken entrails upon the ground, studies those intently, and then maybe wanders off to consult an Oracle. At completion of the ritual, The Fitter will then rasp a bit of wood from the stock here and there, change the recoil pad, possibly add a new rib, and then pronounce the gun "Fit."

The shooter, now clutching his "Fitted" shotgun, makes the return journey to his homeland, secure in the knowledge that he will never miss another target.

Once home, our shooter now displays his prize to his fellow shooters, who "Ooh" and "Aah" appreciatively at his good fortune and fervently hope that one day they, too, can make

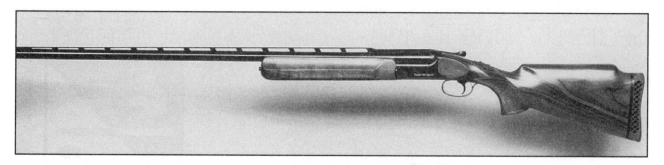

Even without the single barrel, this gun would be instantly identifiable as a trap gun due to the straight Monte Carlo stock and flared pistol grip. Trap is best played with a specialized gun, and a gun set up for that game would be a poor choice for Skeet or Sporting Clays.

Proper gun fit depends largely on the game for which it is intended. A gun fitted specifically for Handicap trap would be a poor choice for other tasks.

Games that require a low gun starting position, like Sporting Clays and International Skeet, require some special fitting to assure a smooth and consistent gun mount.

the pilgrimage to The Fitter. In the meantime, however, they accept the fact that they must continue to struggle with their "commoner" guns, because for a mere mortal to attempt such an act of wizardry on his own would surely bring the wrath of the gods upon him.

More bull!

There is no doubt that a shotgun properly fitted to an individual shooter can improve his score. Having that done by someone skilled and experienced in the operation is one way to go about it and will get the shooter started on the right path more quickly. In years past, it was considered the only way to do it right. Today, thanks to some recent innovations in adjustable combs and recoil pads, that is no longer true. In fact, due to these innovations, it now becomes an arguable point whether or not it is even the best way.

I am convinced that, because of adjustable combs and buttpads, the shooter who understands the basics of shotgun fitting, and what the various dimensions of a shotgun stock actually do, now becomes the best person to fit his own gun to himself. Not only will these accessories provide him or her with a properly fitted shotgun, but also the capability to alter that fit quickly to accommodate changing conditions.

Before I explain that point, let's take a look at exactly what a "fitted" shotgun is, and why any serious shooter will want one.

Why Fitting Works

Any individual with even average hand/eye coordination can stand on a trap, Skeet or Sporting Clays range, have a target thrown and, quite smoothly and without any real effort, raise an arm and track the target with a pointed finger. One does not have to consciously work the finger into position; you

A properly fitted stock places the eye dead center over the rib every time the gun is mounted. Consistent gun placement is mandatory for good shooting.

just focus on the target with the eyes and the finger will find it every time. Were that finger "loaded" you'd probably break that target darned near every time!

Swap that finger for a shotgun, however, and the picture changes considerably. Now you are struggling with a foreign object that must be placed against the body with proper—and consistent—contact at four different spots before you can even begin to track the target with it. And unless that shotgun exactly fits those four points the same way each time you bring it up into position, it will not be pointing at the same spot every time. If that happens, you won't hit the target every time.

Yet, switch back to your finger and you're right on the money. The purpose of fitting a shotgun is to turn it into a finger.

Fitting a shotgun is not difficult. It involves altering the basic dimensions of the stock to make the stock fit the basic dimensions of your body. The result is to have you and the shotgun looking at the exact same spot every time you throw it to your shoulder. The reason it is advantageous for shooters to fit the gun to themselves is that gun makers can't. They do not know whether the individual purchasing their guns will be 6½ feet tall with a 35-inch sleeve length or 5½ feet in height with a 30-inch sleeve. Or whether one has a very full, fleshy face or a thin, bony one. Or whether the shooter is a big, broad-shouldered NFL linebacker or a 5-foot tall female ballet dancer.

They cannot be expected to know the physical dimensions of the people who will purchase their guns. Yet, how well that shooter will do with that gun depends greatly upon how well the dimensions of the gun and shooter agree. As a result, mass-produced guns are built with "standard" stock dimensions intended to fit the "average" person.

Junior shooters often require custom fitting, but just shortening the butt stock often won't be enough. Some guns shoot high unless the comb height is also altered.

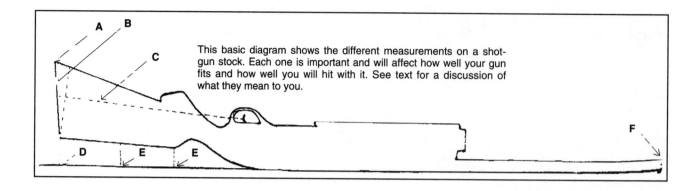

This basic diagram shows the different measurements on a shotgun stock. Each one is important and will affect how well your gun fits and how well you will hit with it. See text for a discussion of what they mean to you.

Many American shooters have learned to come to grips with this. They have, through trial and error, figured out how to crawl their body around on the stock to get everything lined up just perfectly. At least, most of the time. They have also learned that they shoot better with some makes of guns than with others. That's because manufacturers do not all adhere to the same stock dimensions.

When they do find a gun that truly fits them, the Big Light goes on! Shooting good scores becomes easier. Scores go up, and the world becomes a much nicer place in which to live!

Fitting Variables

You can keep searching for the Holy Grail, or just take the shotgun you now have and turn it into one. To do that, you will need to understand the basic measurements of a shotgun stock and what basic dimensions are built into it by the manufacturer. The figure above shows them, and if you are taking measurements on your own, be certain that any shotgun beads don't interfere with your measurements.

Drop at Comb

(The area between the Es.) This is where the cheek contacts the gun and largely determines whether the gun places its shot charge high or low. Consider your eye to be the rear sight on a shotgun, and the height of the comb to be the means for elevation adjustment.

The higher the comb height (less drop at comb) the higher your eye is above the barrel. This leaves you looking at lots of rib and actually pointing the barrel uphill. The higher the comb height, the greater the effect and the higher the gun will shoot. The lower the comb height (more drop at comb), the lower your eye is, the less rib you see, and the lower the gun will place its shot charge.

A change of about 1/8-inch in comb height will result in an elevation change of 8 to 10 inches at 40 yards. You can easily get that degree of change just by having a face that is fatter, or thinner, than "average."

The "universal" drop at comb for a flat-shooting field gun (50 percent of the pattern above and below the bead) is 1 1/2 inches. Trap guns, where a pattern impacting above the bead is desired, use a 1 3/8 drop at comb—about 1/8-inch more height than a field stock. This is often referred to as a high comb.

Length of Pull

This is the distance (dotted line C) from the face of the trigger to the center of the recoil pad. On factory guns it most commonly falls into the 14-to 14 1/2-inch length. If your sleeve length is around 32 inches and you usually shoot in light clothing, that length is about what you want. That's a big "IF," however. If you have longer or shorter arms, you probably need a different length of pull to shoot the gun effectively.

If you have a gun with a sloping comb (in contrast to a Monte Carlo-style comb that is level), a stock that is too short can often cause you to shoot high. This is because your cheek (and the eye above it) slides farther up the comb to a higher point. It can also cause you to bang your nose with the trigger hand and just make life miserable in general. A stock that is too long can cause problems in mounting the gun, and also makes it shoot low.

Pitch

This is the angle at which the buttstock meets the shoulder (dotted line B). You can measure the amount of pitch by standing the shotgun against a wall with the top of the receiver contacting the wall and the buttpad flat on the floor. If the barrel is away from the wall, you have down, or negative pitch. If the receiver and rib are in perfect contact with the wall, you have zero pitch. If the tip of the barrel contacts the wall before the receiver does, you have up, or positive pitch. Most shooters benefit from down pitch, and normal down pitch on a factory gun will place the barrel 2 to 2 1/2 inches away from the wall.

Cast at Toe

This is the angle at which the toe of the recoil pad (A) contacts the shooter's shoulder. One of the problems in making a smooth gun mount is that shotgun recoil pads run at a straight up and down angle, while the shoulder pocket they are supposed to fit into runs at a slight angle. The angle increases on a shooter with a heavy chest, and this person can benefit from an angled recoil pad. Dolly Parton would require a great deal more cast at toe than would Popeye's old girl friend, Olive Oyl.

Cast-On/Off

Cast-off is a slight lateral bend in the buttstock that moves the comb away from the shooter's face and positions the recoil

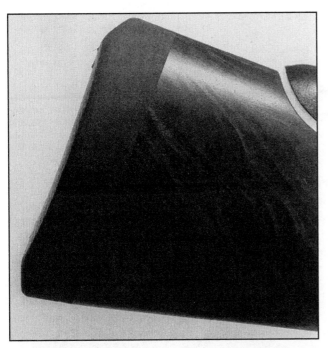

Guns used for low gun games, like International Skeet and Sporting Clays, require a radiused recoil pad to allow a smooth and consistent mount. Fumble the mount because of an ill-shaped pad and you've blown the shot.

pad farther out on the shoulder. Cast-on is the reverse. The primary purpose of either is to serve as a "windage adjustment" for the rear sight (the eye) and position the shooter's eye in perfect alignment with the center of the rib. If the eye is not perfectly centered on the rib, your patterns can impact to one side or the other.

Many English and European guns have some cast-off built in, on the theory that the shooter's eye should be moved into the comb to center the rib. American factory-made guns do not feature this.

Once the stock measurements, and what they accomplish, are understood, it is time to actually fit a shotgun to a shooter. While I have been fitting my own for years, I decided—for this book—to chicken out and actually make the pilgrimage to The Fitter.

The Fitter

For over thirty of his fifty-eight years, Jack L. West has been busting ATA registered trap targets. Since 1978, he has been fitting shotgun stocks for those who would like to do the same. All West does is fit stocks. He doesn't sell guns, do metal work, or teach shooting. He just fits stocks. And he's pretty good at it.

Among those shooters scattered across the country, and as far away as Japan and Australia, that are currently using West custom stocks are ATA High National Average shooter Daro Handy; ATA All-America gunners Larry Bumstead and Richard Musetti; and Skeet Hall of Fame member Danny Mitchell. Shooters at this level do not play with toys. They are serious shooters who rely on serious equipment. West provides that.

What West also provides is a very refreshing look at the fine art of stock fitting.

"The most important thing about getting a shotgun properly fitted to a shooter," West states, "is to keep it simple and make it comfortable."

That can be done with a traditional stock, through careful wood work that mates each critical dimension with the shooter's body. The drawback to that approach, however, is that the gun is properly fitted to the shooter only if the shooter doesn't change! Shift to thicker or thinner shooting clothes,

Jack West displays one of his synthetic-stocked Remington 1100 trap guns. This is an inexpensive way to achieve proper fit with very soft recoil.

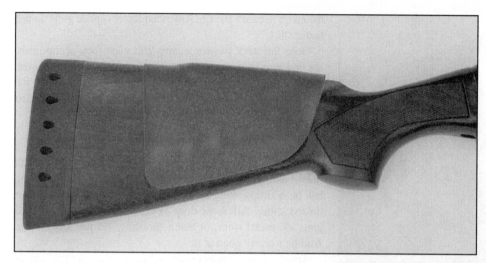

The Meadow Industries detachable cheekpiece is a simple and inexpensive way to increase comb height. It also provides some padding for the cheek.

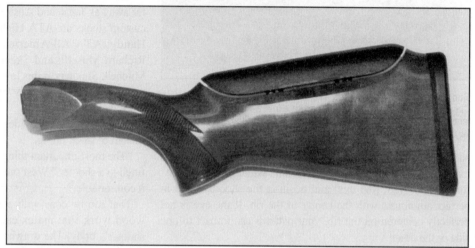

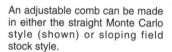

An adjustable comb can be made in either the straight Monte Carlo style (shown) or sloping field stock style.

gain or lose some weight, and the gun is no longer a perfect fit. West has a better solution.

"Adjustable combs and recoil pads are totally accepted now, even by the top shooters," he claims. "Five years ago they were considered a gimmick. I guess that goes to show how effective they are, because any time a new product or concept gains acceptance that fast, it's only because it works very well. The advantage of these adjustable stocks is that they not only make it very easy for the shooter to fit the gun to himself, but they also allow him to alter fit to meet existing conditions."

There are times when having the ability to quickly adjust a stock can be an advantage. A trap shooter, for example, shooting into a strong wind knows it will make the target rise more quickly. Increasing the comb height slightly will raise the point of impact to compensate for the wind without the shooter having to alter his point of hold. In short, adjustable stocks give the shotgunner the same degree of control that finely adjustable sights give riflemen and handgunners.

West makes his adjustable stocks from new wood, if the customer requests it, or from the customer's old stock, if the drawbolt hole provides enough room for it. In conjunction with Trico Plastics, West has designed an injection-moulded composite stock that is strong and durable. Available as a "drop-in" installation of buttstock and matching forend, the

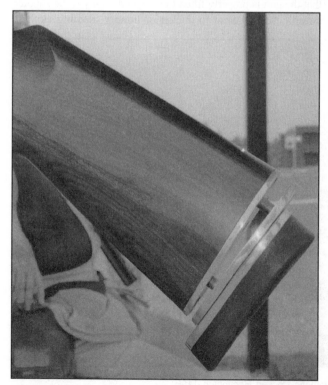

Adjustable recoil pads allow shooters to custom tune the critical gun-to-shoulder pocket fit.

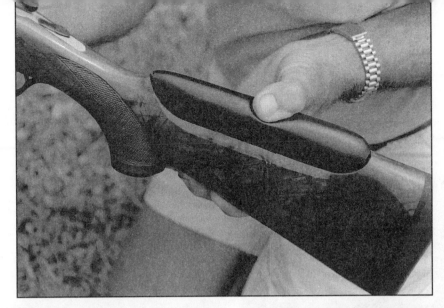

The Jack West padded comb is more than firm enough to allow consistent cheek placement, yet soft enough to keep that cheek happy. Note the thick Kick-Eez recoil pad on the author's Ruger Red Label. That and the padded comb make this a very soft shooting gun.

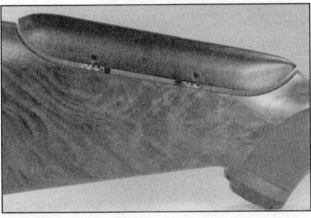

The adjustable comb is held in place by two sturdy Allen screws. Loosening them allows the comb to be removed for height and cast adjustments.

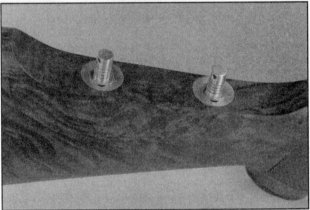

The Jack West padded comb rests on metal studs that can be adjusted for both height and cast.

Trico-West adjustable stock is available for the popular Remington 1100, 11-87 and 870 family of competition guns.

The adjustable stocks (wood or composite) utilize a level, Monte-Carlo comb and give a 1⅝-inch drop at comb at the lowest point, and will raise that ⅜-inch at the highest. Side movement (cast-on or cast-off) is 3/16-inch. One of West's most popular models is the padded comb. This is dense, vinyl-covered foam that provides a very smooth, padded surface and does a great job of cushioning the shooter's cheek from the abrasions and pounding caused by recoil. I have one on my favorite Ruger Red Label and absolutely love it.

The range of comb movement is considerable on a West adjustable stock. In fact, over 90 percent of shooters should be able to get all the windage and elevation adjustment they require from it, with no further stock work. Combine that with an adjustable recoil pad like the excellent Reinhart Fajen Adjustable Recoil Pad (available, as are a wide range of custom accessories, from Brownells, Inc.) and you have a wide range of adjustment that will allow you to fit your gun to virtually any shotgunning chore.

Here's how West works a shooter into an adjustable stock.

"Most of the shooters who opt for an adjustable stock," he explains, "are either experienced shooters who know what they want to do in the first place, or new shooters who have done the smart thing and gone to a professional shooting instructor who recommends the adjustable stock and will help them adjust it when it arrives. When a shooter actually comes into my shop for a personal fit, I will get the stock roughly adjusted, and then stand in front of the muzzle while the shooter mounts the gun to make the final adjustment. What I am doing is watching the shooter shoulder the gun and looking right into his pupil as he looks down the rib. You can get the gun very close to 'on' this way, but the real final test is to watch the shooter break targets with it—watch how the targets break—and fine tune from there.

"My rule of thumb for length of pull is whatever is comfortable for the shooter," he continues. "Since we are using a level comb, the length of pull has no real effect on the impact point of the shot charge, like it would with a sloping comb. I like to get the nose of the shooter no closer than 1 inch from the shooting hand, and not a lot farther back than that, either."

Determining the proper pitch for the stock is also not a difficult process.

"All the pitch angle does is distribute the recoil forces evenly on the shoulder pocket," he states. "If the pitch angle is not correct it will send the majority of the recoil force either to the top or the bottom of the shoulder and make the shooter uncomfortable. Pitch has no effect on point of impact with an adjustable stock, so you just make certain the angle is proper to let the pad lie evenly within the shoulder pocket. A heavy-

This is the traditional method of determining a shooter's correct length of pull, but it is not the best method. Many shooters find they will shoot better with a longer buttstock than this test indicates.

Recoil pads are an often overlooked consideration, but in a demanding game like Sporting Clays, a pad that will mount smoothly yet stay put on the shoulder for two shots is an asset.

set shooter may be most comfortable with more negative pitch than would a very slender shooter.

"The point of adjusting comb height," West says, "is to make the gun shoot where the eyes go and allow the shooter to adjust his mental 'bird picture' to the point of impact of the shot charge. This is a very individual thing, because different shooters may have a different subconscious bird picture ingrained over the years. Some shooters want the barrel covering the target, some want to see it just below the bird, and some may want to float the bird above it. Regardless of how much adjusting you do in the shop, this is something that must really be finished by actually shooting. That's the big advantage to an adjustable stock because the shooter can fine tune it himself."

Lateral impact of the pattern, which used to be adjusted with cast-on and cast-off within the stock, can now be more precisely adjusted with the lateral adjustment of the comb. West will, using the "look down the rib into the eye" technique, get things as centered as possible, but again, this is something the shooter will have to finish on his own.

"The real beauty of an adjustable stock," West grins, "is that the shooter does not have to go to The Fitter. I have sent stocks all over the world and 'fitted' the shooter over the phone."

Bed Sheet Test

Determining what degree of adjustment is needed requires that the gunner actually see where the shot charge is presently

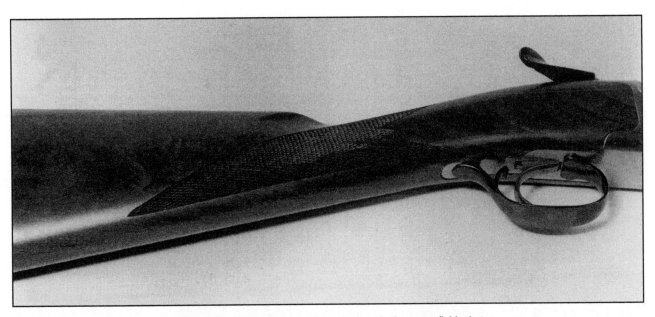

The straight English-style grip has its place in the game fields, but clay target gunners are wise to avoid it because it doesn't offer consistent hand placement.

hitting. One of the easiest ways to do that is with an old bed sheet. I would like to be able to take credit for this simple system, but I can't. I learned it from fellow shotgunner Bob Brister. I call it the "Brister Bed Sheet Shoot-Out."

To perform this test, get an old bed sheet. If your spouse is reluctant to part with any that are in present service, you can get some inexpensive ones at Wal-Mart. Smoothly tack up one over a safe backstop. Use a felt-tip marker or can of spray paint to mark a 6-inch circle in the middle, and back off 25 yards. Put a Full or Improved Modified choke tube in your gun and grab a handful of your favorite target loads. With the gun in a low gun position, get your body set on the circle, just as if you were aligning it on a target range to break a bird at a specific spot. Focus on the dot. Mount the gun smoothly and quickly, and fire as soon as the gun comes into position and you can see the circle over the barrel. Do not aim the gun or wiggle around on the stock. To do so totally defeats this exercise.

The reason for using a bed sheet is because it will take a number of rounds to punch a clearly defined hole into it. Fire as many rounds as it takes to get one. The reason for using a Full choke tube at 25 yards is that it will punch a compact hole. The center of that hole is where your gun is looking when you have made a smooth mount, while your eyes are looking at the "bird."

Once you have punched a hole in the sheet it is a simple matter to raise or lower the comb, move it a bit right or left, until you and the gun are looking at the same bird. You can also use this bed sheet test to determine if both barrels of an over/under or side-by-side are shooting to the same point of impact.

Once gun and shooter are singing from the same page in the hymnal, there are a few other things one can do in the area of comfort and control.

"Pistol grip fit is something that is totally ignored by the manufacturers," West feels. "It should fit the shooter. If you have small hands you will probably be better off with a narrow grip that lets you lock onto it. If you have a hand like a bear paw, you will need a thicker grip. A palm swell can also be a help. The only drawback is that if it is not in the proper position—so that it falls right into the perfect pocket of your hand—it can be a detriment."

"Another thing that I feel is important on a palm swell," he continues, "is a place for the meat of your thumb to rest comfortably. I like to hollow out a little spot for that when I build a custom stock, and kind of 'melt' the thumb into the pistol grip."

West favors a modified Etchen grip (named after shooting great Fred Etchen) with a slight hook at the bottom that helps lock the shooter into the gun.

"A pistol grip should feel good," West states. "When you slip your hand onto it, it should be like putting on a fine old glove.

"Fit," West concludes, "is critical with a shotgun. Some guns will fit you perfectly as they come from the factory and that gun will just flow to the target and break it without any real effort. If you ever find a gun like this, hang onto it for the rest of your life! If you don't have one of these, having a gun properly fitted can give you one. You can take a $500 shotgun, trick it up and make it fit you, and break as many targets—maybe more—with it than you can with a $10,000 shotgun. The shot all has to come out of the barrel, and if the barrel is looking where you are, you'll do just fine."

Master Eye

There are some shooters whom this approach will not help. Almost everybody has one eye that is slightly, or greatly, dominant. This eye often overpowers the other eye in vision decisions. If you are a right-hander and have a right dominant eye, you have a good situation. Left-handers with a left dominant

Lightweight shotguns are actually more difficult to shoot well on clay targets than are those guns in the 8-pound range. Serious competitors generally favor guns of about that weight, although some female shooters do well with 7½-pound guns on the Sporting Clays fields.

eye are equally fortunate. If you happen to have a dominant eye on the opposite side of your body, however, you can have problems. What happens is that the eye on the other side of your body is doing the looking, while the eye you have lined up on the rib is getting short-changed. Your gun will not shoot where you are looking.

Here's a quick test to see which is your master eye. With both eyes open, point your finger at a defined spot on a wall. Now close your left eye. If the finger stays on target your right eye is dominant. If the finger moves off target when you close your left eye, but stays on target when you close your right eye, the left eye is dominant.

Some right-handed people with a strongly left-dominant eye (or vice versa) simply cannot shoot a shotgun from their normal side. In the long run, the best solution is to learn to shoot from the same side as your dominant eye. Sometimes that doesn't work. For these shooters, the solution is a strange-looking contraption called a crossover stock. It features an extreme bend in the stock that, for a right-hander, will put the left eye in exact alignment with the barrel when the stock is shouldered on the right side. These are available from a number of stockmakers, but Reinhart Fajen Co. is among the best-known for this specialty.

It sometimes doesn't take much in the way of stock adjustment to get a gun to shoot where you look. The cure is often simple. I have a Franchi Prestige 12-gauge on which I slightly lengthened the stock, by changing the recoil pad. This is a sloping-comb field gun. Lengthening the stock moved my face

down the comb a bit, which caused the gun to shoot slightly low. An adjustable and detachable cheekpiece from Meadow Industries quickly corrected that. The pad attaches with Velcro strips and it raised the comb enough to return the gun to a 50-50 shooter (half the pattern above and half below the bead). The pad comes with inserts that can be quickly installed to raise the shot pattern in about 8-inch increments at 40 yards. This pad did not add any cast, so the lateral impact of the pattern stayed where it was supposed to. These pads are a simple way to make minor corrections, and there are a number of different models available.

Recoil Control

Once a gun is sighted-in, there are still a few things that can be done to fit it more comfortably to you. One area is in the control of recoil.

According to Newton's Third Law, for every action there is an opposite and equal reaction. No one has yet repealed that law, but they have found some interesting ways to amend it.

Shotguns kick. Some kick more than others, and that is not always dependent upon the gauge of the gun. I have seen some 20-gauge shotguns belt shooters harder than some 12s, and a few 28-gauges that would draw blood from the cheek.

Proper shotgun fit will aid immensely in reducing felt recoil by evenly distributing the recoil forces to those areas most capable of handling them. A correctly shaped comb (especially a padded one like the Jack West model) will further soften the blow. Too many shotguns seem to have combs designed to slice butter instead of cushion recoil. I've shot some, and, though I didn't feel the pain at the time, they sliced my cheek open like a razor!

Another way to reduce recoil is to add weight to the gun, and many gunsmiths do just that. A 12-gauge competition gun in the 9- to 10- pound range has little recoil with normal target loads. Many kick less than 20-gauge guns in the 6½- to 7- pound range. Weight added to the barrel helps keep the muzzle down on recoil and prevent cheek slap. If barrel weights make the gun too muzzle-heavy, adding some weight inside the buttstock will restore the balance.

Another way to cut punishment is to shoot a semi-auto. They can be set up with the same exact stock fit as any other shotgun, and their gas systems do make them noticeably softer to shoot.

You can add a recoil reduction device to the gun. There are a number of these on the market. You'll recognize them by brand names like Edwards, Bear Trap, Soft-Touch, etc. These are essentially "shock-absorbers" that use a spring-loaded or air/oil cushion device to slow the recoil impulse and turn it into a gentle push instead of a shove. They all add weight to the gun, and some smiths will tell you that the additional weight is what really does the job. Others will tell you they

work just as they are advertised. Regardless of the reason, they do work.

Another method of cutting recoil is porting the barrels. I have a ported gun, and it does cut muzzle jump slightly (an asset on a quick second shot), but does not seem to otherwise reduce recoil with target-level loads. I do use this gun for ducks, however, and the recoil reduction with stouter loads is noticeable.

Fit a gun properly, add whatever form of recoil reduction your gunsmith recommends, and you'll likely find that shooting is not nearly as punishing as it used to be. If you enjoy the sport, you owe it to yourself to make it fun!

The Trigger

One last thing you might want to consider is the gun's trigger. It is commonly accepted that shotgun triggers are stiff, gritty, and something no rifleman would tolerate. It's OK, though, because shotgun triggers are never "squeezed," they are "slapped." Therefore, it doesn't make any difference if they are miserable.

Bull again!

Shoot an 8-pound, squishy trigger, and then have a good smith tune it to a crisp 3.5- to 4-pound break, and watch the

There are a variety of shock-absorbing-type recoil reducing devices on the market. They all work, and one may be just right for you.

(Below) Meadow Industries' "Barrel Buddy" allows shooters to add as much as 8 ounces of weight to the barrel of the gun. Some shooters find that more weight forward promotes a smoother swing in many games, especially trap and Skeet.

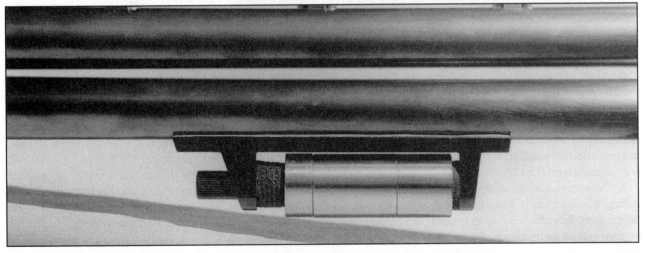

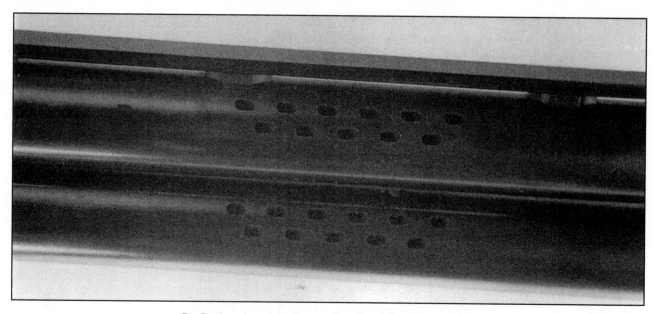

Pro-Porting a barrel creates a series of precise cuts through the barrel that direct propellant gases upward to reduce muzzle jump and some apparent recoil on each shot. For those who pursue clay target games where two targets are often engaged, it is a worthwhile modification.

difference it makes in your score! A good shotgun deserves a good trigger. The first time you try a good one on a shotgun, you will agree with me. The better shotgun smiths can tune yours, and it is well worth the time and money. There have been past (and current) champions that shot "custom" triggers in the 1-pound range. If they weren't an asset, do you think they would have used them?

There are some shooters who might need to get more radical than that, especially those afflicted with "trapshooter's flinch."

It is called that because that is the game in which it is most commonly observed, but it can affect any shooter. Basically, it is the inability of the shooter to pull the trigger. It is not a physical inability, but a mental one. You just can't make your finger trigger the round.

This has never happened to me, yet...but it could. In fact, it can crop up in any shooter. To the best knowledge of anyone I have yet discussed it with, it is a simple response by the body to the cumulative effects of recoil. The body just gets tired of taking a pounding and the subconscious says, "That's it, I ain't pullin' that trigger again!" The brain short-circuits the trigger finger. The subconscious has a lot of authority in those areas!

It sounds somewhat laughable, but once this happens to a shooter he is in big trouble. One remedy is to just stop shooting for awhile and let the subconscious get over its temper tantrum. Sometimes that works, just like laying off shooting in the middle of a slump will often help. Other times it won't, and one item that has proven to help shooters in this situation is a "release trigger."

A release trigger works in reverse of a conventional trigger: pulling the trigger sets it, releasing the trigger fires the gun. On double guns, they can be set up to function as a "release-pull" trigger—pull to set, release to fire the first barrel, pull to fire

the second. At least one Olympic trapshooter has used this in the Games because he felt it was the fastest way to get off two shots.

A number of gunsmiths do this work, but release triggers do have some controversy surrounding them. It's one of those subjects that few shooters seem to have a middle-of-the-road opinion on—you either love 'em or hate 'em!

I fall into a different group on that: I've played with them and don't like them, but if I had to use one I'm certain I could. They have extended the shooting careers of a number of competitors that would otherwise have had to quit.

I hate to sound like I'm whining, but "There oughta be a law" that every gun equipped with a release trigger of any configuration be so marked on the gun's buttstock in 1-inch neon fluorescent letters!

Release triggers are not inherently dangerous, not as long as the shooter knows what he has and understands how it works. They can be dangerous, however, if a shooter picks up the gun without realizing it has a release trigger.

You load a round, call for the bird, pull the trigger and nothing happens. You subconsciously think, "Darn! I've got a misfire." Then you release the trigger and the gun fires! Hopefully, safe gun-handling doctrine would have you pointing it down-range when you do. But it is most disconcerting and has the potential to be disastrous.

I'm well aware that range courtesy and common sense would preclude a shooter from picking up and firing a gun that wasn't his. I'm also aware that mistakes can happen. Release trigger guns should be marked.

Other than that, release triggers are a matter of personal preference and can help some shooters. For that matter, so is shotgun fitting, in the whole, and one reason why it is worth the time and trouble. Just turn your gun into your finger. It's not that hard to do.

Women and Shotgun Sports

SHOOTING IS OFTEN thought of primarily as a man's sport. In reality it is not theirs exclusively. One of the most famous shooters in history was a lady named Annie Oakley.

In more recent times, at the 1994 NSCA Florida State Championships, the runner-up shooter for High Overall was Bonnie McLaurin. The winner was her regular shooting partner, Bill Whitehurst, who is always quick to credit her coaching and advice with much of his success.

There are other examples as well, but the point should be made by now: There are plenty of good women shooters out there and their numbers are growing every year.

Distaff Needs

Unfortunately, the shooting industry has not been particularly quick in providing shooting equipment tailored to the needs of female shooters, as they have for their male counterparts. In years past, women shooters often had to make do with what was either "hand-me-down" gear or something made for short men. Neither approach was particularly satisfactory since no shooter, male or female, will perform their best with ill-fitting equipment. Here's a look at how female shooters might improve their game with equipment designed for their needs.

Clothing

"A lot of the shooting vests offered to women are nothing more than offshoots of men's vests," says Becky Bowen. "They make them the same way, just a little shorter and in pink or blue. That's not really women's shooting clothing...just short guy's clothing in different colors."

Bowen knows well of what she speaks. A veteran of the promotional side of the shooting sports industry, she, like a growing number of women, was bitten by the Sporting Clays bug some years back and quickly found that ill-fitting shooting vests do little toward helping your score, confidence and enjoyment of the game. So she did the logical thing by starting her own company, Lady Clays, in Shawnee Mission, Kansas.

U.S. women shooters fare very well in the no-holds-barred world of International competition. Three of our best lady trap shooters pose here with their awards for Singles trap at a June, 1994, meet in Colorado Springs. (Left to right) Corporal Theresa Wentzel, USAMU, 2nd place; Francis Strodtman, USST, 1st place; and Deena Julin, USST, 3rd place. Both Strodtman and Julin hold world records in International shotgun competition. (U.S. Army photo by Joseph J. Johnson)

Three-time National Ladies Sporting Clays champion Bonnie McLaurin is one of the top Sporting shooters in the country. She began her career as an International Skeet shooter on the U.S. Olympic Team.

Corporal Theresa Wentzel of the elite U.S. Army Marksmanship Unit spends her time in the "pits" servicing one of the Unit's Bunker traps. Female shooters perform the same tasks as men in this unit. (U.S. Army photo by Joseph J. Johnson)

"When I started shooting, my problem was that I could not find a shooting vest or shooting shirt that fit me," she says. "I figured if I and my female shooting partners were having that problem, then there had to be a lot of other ladies out there in the same boat."

Bowen sought the help of a professional pattern maker and over a period of eighteen months produced a system of measurements that would allow women to buy a custom-fitted shooting vest. There are no off-the-rack small, medium and large sizes. Each vest is essentially made to individual measurements. Bowen feels that is especially important for female shooters.

"Most men," she explains, "have larger shoulders than women, and vests made for them generally rely on those shoulders to fully support the vest. Women can't always be comfortable in that type of vest, because they don't have the shoulders. If you stick a box of shells in one side, the vest will ride up in the back, drop the pocket down around your knees, and generally make you look like you borrowed your husband's clothing. We use thirteen separate measurements that allow us to use the full female form to properly support the vest in a number of places. We combine that with elastic around the waist—more elastic for some women, less for others—that keeps the vest where it is supposed to be regardless of what is worn underneath it. With the elastic, there is enough 'give' for a comfortable fit while wearing a light T-shirt, sweatshirt or other garment."

The same exacting measurement requirements work equally well for men, as this writer can attest. (If men have a problem ordering a vest from a place called "Lady Clays" just put "Bec-Mar" on the address instead). I recently had one of their vests made for me, and the fit is precise and consistent regardless of which pockets I put shells in or how many shells I car-

Sporting Clays shooter Becky Bowen couldn't find a comfortable vest off the rack, so she started her own company to provide properly tailored shooting clothing for women.

ry. With one of their Sporting Clays vests, you have a lot of options in that area.

Their standard vest comes with double front pockets on each side. This provides a total of four shell pockets that keep different loads separated. That's a nice feature for Sporting shooters, who may often carry two, three or even four different loads to a shooting station. Also, it provides a convenient spot to stick the empty hulls until you get back to your shooting bag. A pocket for shooting glasses on the left breast is standard, and a choke tube pocket is available as an option.

I chose my vest with a full International-style shoulder pad on the shooting side, but abbreviated Skeet and trap pads are also available.

A very nice touch is the gun pad on the off shoulder. You spend a lot of time on a Skeet or Sporting range with your gun broken open over your shoulder and this extra pad keeps grease, crud and powder fouling from staining the vest, not to mention the damage the gun might do to the seams and fabric.

The gun mount pad also deserves some comment. Bowen does not believe in a thick shoulder pad.

"We make our vests for serious shooters," she explains, "shooters who already know the advantages of a properly fitted gun and what an excessively thick pad can do to the fit. We also pad women's vests differently than we do for men.

"Female shooters," she continues, "don't have the recoil forces restricted to the shoulder pocket. There can also be some blunt force trauma to the top and side of the breast, especially in the shooting sports that call for a low gun position, like Sporting Clays and International Skeet, where you cannot snuggle the gun precisely into the shoulder before you call for the bird. We add padding to cover both of those areas, and this actually forms a more consistent shoulder pocket for the gun."

Lady Clays vests can be made from material provided by them, or shooters can chose and supply their own. The latter option makes for some highly unconventional, yet quite attractive vests.

"One thing we like about our vests," says Bowen, "is that they are stylish and smart-looking. We don't claim that our vests will make you shoot better, but if you are wearing an ill-fitting vest that you don't like and you think looks ugly, you will probably shoot poorly. The better you look and feel, the better you are likely to shoot."

Bowen carries that one step further with matching hair barrettes.

"If you've got long hair," Bowen notes, "you learn to pull it back when you go to make the shot, and it didn't take me long to learn that if the hair gets away from you and gets caught between your cheek and the gun stock, it hurts. You do learn to keep your cheek to the stock when that happens, but it still hurts. So we began making hair bows in matching colors to the vests to positively hold that hair out of the way. They have become a popular item."

One additional bit of advice Bowen offers newer lady shooters is to invest in a couple of "shooting bras."

"An experienced shooter would know this," she states, "because they've shot enough to know that when the metal

Bec-Mar vests are custom tailored to the individual shooter, which provides a better fitting vest for many women.

adjustment fasteners are on the front of the bra, they can be driven right into the shoulder by the recoil of the gun. You may not realize this while you are shooting because you are so pumped up and concentrating on the shot, but you will when you get home and find a bruised and sometimes bloody shoulder. You can solve that problem quickly by just buying a couple of bras that have the adjustment fasteners in the back. A number of clothing manufacturers offer them—I get mine from Victoria's Secret—but there are others."

"It may sound like a small thing," she laughs, "but believe me it isn't. Wear the wrong bra and you'll have an unpleasant day."

Guns and Gun Fit

Anyone who has been around the shooting world for very long will no doubt recognize the name Reinhart Fajen. He was one of the premier custom stock makers in the world. Marty Fajen, his daughter, grew up in the business and is also an expert stock fitter, especially when it comes to fitting stocks to women.

"Shotgun fitting is shotgun fitting," she states, "and the process is no different for a man than it is for a woman. The point is to make the gun fit the body so perfectly that when it

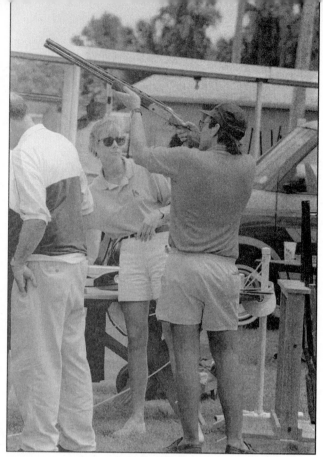

Women are taking a larger role in competitive shotgunning, largely due to the rise in popularity of Sporting Clays. This lady checks a potential customer's gun mount at the Kreigoff booth during the Florida State Sporting Clays Championships.

Marty Fajen learned the art of stock fitting from her father, one of the best in the business, and is convinced that women can benefit more from a properly fitted stock than men.

Skeet Hall of Fame member Mary Beverly (right) feels that getting a properly fitted shotgun is one of the most important things a woman can do to improve her game. That sentiment has been echoed by many top female shooters.

is brought to the shoulder the eye is centered on the rib and the gun positioned to the body the same way every time. But there are some areas of stock fitting, specific measurements, that are sometimes overlooked in men and cannot be overlooked in women.

"One thing we have found," she continues, "is that a far higher percentage of women will require some cast at toe. This just reflects the different body shape between men and women."

Cast at toe is the outward bending of the toe of the stock to move it away from the chest and more toward the lower portion of the shoulder pocket. Those shoulder pockets, on men and women, tend to run at an angle, while gun butts are made straight up and down. Men often can get away with a straight buttstock because they have heavier chest muscles to take the pounding, but women find that a stock with no cast at toe tends to punish the outer portion of the breast, and interferes with a consistent gun mount.

"Another difference we have found," says Fajen, "is that women are often more comfortable, and shoot better, with a

Small-framed female shooters often require a shorter stock, but simply cutting the stock down will not do the job. The comb height, cast and pitch must also be changed if the stock is to fit properly.

slightly higher comb and a bit more drop at heel than would be effective for a man. I think this has to do with the fact that many women tend to take at least some basic instruction and therefore learn to shoot with the head erect, bringing gun to cheek, not cheek to gun. That's understandable since many women lack the typical male history of shooting where they were just handed a gun and told to 'Go to it.' Men, by virtue of necessity and previous experience, have learned how to take an improperly fitted gun and just crawl around the stock until they get it in the right position. Women can benefit more from a properly fitted gun than many men can because they don't have the background in shooting and haven't learned how to crawl a stock to get the fit right."

Another area deals with cast-off, the amount the comb is moved into the gun and away from the shooter's face.

"Women's eyes tend to be closer together than men's," explains Fajen, "and because of that they often need more cast-off to get their master eye properly centered over the rib. We find that increased cast-off is often an asset to a female shooter."

One additional area Fajen pays particular attention to is the shape of the pistol grip on the shotgun.

"I think this is a very important and overlooked factor," Fajen claims, "because women just don't have the hand and wrist strength that men do. Their bones and muscles are smaller in that area and they require more positive support on the pistol grip hand than most men would. I am a firm believer that a properly fitted palm swell, one that positions the hand consistently on the pistol grip, is a significant advantage on a woman's gun, while it might be less important to a man."

Another important aspect of the pistol grip, for a woman, is the exact distance to the trigger. If that is not correct for the woman, she will often have to fight the trigger pull weight because she just doesn't have the hand strength to overcome a poor fit.

Fajen feels that women should avoid the straighter-type pistol grips found on most factory guns and opt for a "tear" grip, which has a thicker swell at the bottom of the grip, or the Etchen-style grip with an exaggerated hook at the bottom.

One last area that Fajen feels is often overlooked is the forend. Given a woman's smaller hand, she feels that the beefy forends found on many guns should be slimmed a bit to give the woman shooter more positive control with the leading hand.

When it comes to gun weight, Fajen is equally opinionated and speaks from hard-learned experience.

"A lot of women will shoot better with a lighter gun," she states. "In a 12-gauge, that means a gun in the 7- to 7$\frac{1}{2}$-pound range. When I first started shooting I chose a heavy gun of about 8$\frac{1}{2}$ pounds because that was what the 'experts' recommended to reduce recoil and improve my swing. After about 6 months, I got rid of it because it was killing me!

"I hate to admit it," she grins, "but women do get fatigued more quickly than men, and a heavy gun, or one with a lot of weight forward, is just too much weight to support for extended periods of time. This may not be real important in trap, where the round is over in less than fifteen minutes and you

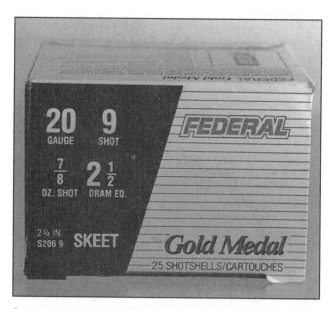

Some feel that the 20-gauge is the best choice for women because of its lower recoil, compared to the 12-gauge. Most of the top female shooters strongly disagree and point out that with light loads the 12-gauge won't kick any more than the 20 and will be more effective on clays.

can put the gun back into the rack, or in Skeet. But in Sporting Clays, where the round takes longer and you have a lot more walking, a gun that is too heavy will wear you down."

While many might feel a gun that light would produce excessive recoil, there are cures. One is to shoot any of the readily available 1-ounce loads, or the 24-gram International 12-gauge loads. It has been this writer's experience that they will deliver patterns every bit as good as any $7/8$-ounce 20-gauge load and usually better. They also will provide as much target breaking power out to 40 yards as an appropriately sized $1^1/8$-ounce 12-gauge load. And, they do it with extremely mild manners. I have shot a considerable number of Federal's 24-gram #$8^1/2$ International load and find it absolutely no handicap on a Skeet field, or for any Sporting Clays shot under 35 yards, which covers a lot of shots!

Ditto for the 1-ounce and 24-gram loads from Victory, Winchester, ACTIV and Fiocchi. If you miss the bird, don't blame the load. You would have missed it with a full 3-dram $1^1/8$-ounce load as well. With the 24-gram loads you pay a much smaller price at the shoulder, and that leads to better gun pointing for a longer period of time.

Combine a lighter gun with a lighter load, and most women will find their scores and their enjoyment of Sporting Clays going up.

As to what type of gun to select, Fajen has a strong opinion on that, as well.

Outdoor writer Carolee Boyles-Sprenkel (right) gets a few tips at wobble trap from instructor Mary Beverly. Many women are picking up shotguns for the first time and finding out what men have known for years—clay target games are fun!

Instructor Mary Beverly believes that women will learn shooting more readily if their initial instruction comes from a woman. Male instructors, she says, can then take over and improve the women's scores.

"It really irritates me when I see a husband start his wife out with an inexpensive gas-operated gun because he thinks it 'kicks less' and that's what women are supposed to shoot," she maintains. "That argument doesn't wash. If the gun is properly fitted, maybe with one of the easily obtained recoil reducing devices on the market, and lighter loads are used, an over/under isn't going to kick any more than a gas gun. The reliability factor and the ease of maintenance will make that O/U a much better choice for a woman. Too many women shooters are handicapped with discarded equipment that their husbands wouldn't use. How is a women supposed to shoot with that? Give them decent equipment and they'll be better shooters."

Getting Started

"Women who really want to learn to shoot are usually excellent students. They pay attention and absorb what you are trying to impart to them," says Mary Beverly. "The one thing that can often get in the way of the process is when they have their husband or boyfriend there to 'help them.' That situation places stresses on the female student that are best avoided."

That is not just Mary Beverly's opinion. After discussing the matter of new lady shooters with a number of lady shooters, and factoring in my own experience in firearms instruction, I have come to the conclusion that the worst thing a woman who truly wants to learn how to shoot can do is have her other half present at the time. It is not conducive to the learning process. It's better to get basic instruction before going to the range with a husband or boyfriend.

Mary Beverly speaks from a good deal of experience on that subject. She serves as an instructor in the Panhandle area of Florida and is especially well-known for her ability to handle new shooters, particularly women and children. Despite being a member of the National Skeet Shooting Hall of Fame, and the Florida Skeet Shooting Hall of Fame, as well as an active and accomplished Sporting Clays shooter, she resists the impulse to call herself a "Skeet" or "Sporting Clays" instructor. According to Beverly, she prefers to be considered as a basic shotgun instructor. She finds some of her most enjoyable moments coaching shooters with no previous experience, especially women.

"I see a lot of women who want to learn to shoot a shotgun," she says. "In some areas that interest is in Sporting Clays; in others it may be trap or Skeet. I think the initial preference is based more on what types of facilities are available locally than on the actual type of shotgun game itself. Sometimes they simply want to be able to enjoy time with a husband or boyfriend who shoots. That's how I got interested in Skeet many years ago. However, I have seen women come to the range who didn't have husbands or current boyfriends. They just wanted to start shooting."

Some female shooters find semi-auto shotguns more comfortable to shoot than fixed-breech firearms.

Florida shooter Lisa Sever began competitive trap shooting in college and competes throughout the state today. Many women shooters feel that college shooting programs for women are not being promoted adequately in today's academic environment.

Many instructors find most women make extremely good students because they have little background in shooting and fewer bad habits to break.

Beverly's approach, in this respect, is worth noting.

"I have found that women tend to look at things differently than men," she says. "I try to talk on that level and when I have a beginners class, especially if it is primarily women, I will just sit down and talk for about thirty minutes before we ever touch a shotgun. I talk about what they are going to see, how they are going to see it, and how they are going to perceive it.

"That approach," she continues, "can get them asking all sorts of questions about every aspect of the sport. They don't know the answers, and some are very simple. They might be hesitant to ask the questions of a male instructor because they don't want to appear stupid. I think that is one area where a female instructor can have a more positive effect on new women students than can a male.

"I've found that women are more concerned about the technical aspects of the game than many men are. They want to know what a choke is. How does it work? How is a shotshell constructed? What is a pattern? This is a different approach than many men will take because, for some reason, they assume that they are already supposed to know this and wouldn't ask any of these questions for fear of embarrassing themselves.

"I guess the best way to describe it is that women want to know the 'why' before they do it, and men just want to do it and don't give a hoot about the 'why.' I suppose that goes

Women can compete equally with men at any clay target game once they find a gun with which they are comfortable. The greater strength inherent in most men is not a factor in most shotgunning.

back to the days when their granddaddy handed them a gun and said 'Here son, come shoot with me.'

"Regardless of the why," Beverly has found, "it has been my experience that a brand-new female shooter is often best off to seek her initial instruction with a female teacher. There is a language-type thing there that is sometimes best served by a woman. After she receives the basics, then I would have to say that she might be better off going to one of the better male instructors in order to fine tune her game. There are some great ones out there."

Beverly benefited from that approach, having had the opportunity to receive instruction from the legendary Fred Missildine while she was on the southeastern Skeet circuit.

"He's the one who made it possible for me to be in the Skeet Hall of Fame," she claims. "He's the one who showed me how to use my abilities to the best advantage."

Like many top coaches, Beverly does not believe that you can clone shooters.

"You can't teach such a rigid doctrine that there is no room for the shooter to utilize his individual strengths," she feels. "This is one area where I feel husbands or boyfriends teaching girlfriends and wives makes for a disaster. The atmosphere is all wrong. The pressure is there to perform, and the poor shooter is forced to fit into some kind of mould.

"Shooters," she continues, "whether they be male or female, need to be able to utilize their individual strengths and abilities

in regard to speed, vision, reaction time and shooting style preference. The job of the instructor is to give the shooter the information needed for the shooter to make the determination as to what is best for them. Not simply to tell them, 'This is the only way to do it.' "

Beverly feels that this approach is doubly important for women, because they are not used to taking that type of rigid instruction to start with.

There are some other terribly wrong ways to start a new woman shooter, and some of these are terrible enough to make one truly wonder about the intentions of the instructor.

"I once saw a man hand his wife a lightweight side-by-side 12-gauge and a box of shells," Beverly remembers, "and told her, 'See if you can hit any of those targets.' Naturally, with a gun that light and hard-kicking, she didn't. I would be very surprised if she ever picked up a shotgun and fired at another clay target again. That's not the way to go about teaching a new shooter, especially a woman with no shooting background. You need to make those first experiences not only pleasurable but positive. That is what will bring new shooters back for more."

That is probably why the best shooting investment a new woman shooter can make is to seek good instruction right from the start. That, combined with a proper gun and shooting clothing that fits will go a long way toward bringing more ladies into contact with more clays.

chapter twenty-nine

Do You Need to Reload

NO MATTER HOW you slice it, clay target shooting is not the most inexpensive sport in the world. In addition to guns, range fees, travel and all the other associated costs, you have to factor in the shells you will use. There are only two ways to acquire those shells: You either buy factory fodder or roll your own. At some point, every clay target shooter will have to make the decision as to whether reloading is in his best interest. In some cases, it may not be.

It is commonly accepted that you can save considerable sums of money reloading your shells as compared to buying factory ammo. Your savings depend on how you buy those factory shells.

Walk into your local gun emporium and ask for a couple of boxes of target loads and you can generally expect to pay full list price. That doesn't mean the shop owner is deliberately gouging you. He has overhead, inventory costs and other expenses that must be recouped if he is to stay in business. He also doesn't have the buying power to make big lot purchases at lower prices. The larger discount chains do, and that's why you'll likely find the same shells for less there, assuming, of course, that the discount store carries the particular load you want. Very often they won't stock anything other than the lower-priced soft-shot field loads, unless there is strong clay target interest in their area and the store manager is smart enough to realize it. Don't count on the discount stores having a steady supply of target loads on hand when you need them.

Sometimes, however, those chains can have some very worthwhile buys. I remember a couple of years ago the local Wal-Mart somehow got hold of a large quantity of Remington's promotional loads. These normally wouldn't excite target shooters, but in this case (for some inexplicable reason) these shells were loaded in Remington's target-grade Uni-body hull, which is an excellent hull to reload. They cost only $80 a case, and the local Skeet shooters cleaned out the store! Not only did they get a case of shells to shoot, but also good hulls to reload, and at only a slight increase over what it would have cost them to reload that same case with their own components.

Sporting Clays shooters will find that keeping different loads separated is much easier if put in different hulls. It does require the loader stock more than one wad, but it is an easy way to achieve versatility.

Reloading a shotshell is nothing more than replacing those components expended upon firing and is an easy, and very safe, endeavor. Good hulls and proper reloading procedures will get you eight to ten reloads per hull.

This box of 28-gauge fired hulls is worth about $2.50 at most Skeet clubs. If it costs a shooter $2.50 to reload them, and a box of fresh shells could be purchased for $6.50, the amount the shooter saves by reloading the hulls is only $1.50 a box. Some shooters find that is not enough to justify the cost of the reloading equipment and components, nor the time to complete the task.

If you can find a bargain like that, it's worth buying as much ammo as you can afford.

Buy by the Case

The way most smart clay shooters buy factory shells is through their club in case lots. Most clubs will take orders for case lots from members whenever they restock on targets. That way they save a considerable amount on freight and can offer the shells at what amounts to wholesale cost.

At my club, as this is being written, top-grade target loads run about $100 a case for 12, 20 and 410, with the 28-gauge running about $120. That's about $5 per box for the first three and $6 for a box of 28. That represents what I would call an average best case price. That price can vary a bit around the country because of freight costs. Shotshells are heavy and expensive to ship. The farther you are from the manufacturer, the higher the cost will be.

Although $5 a box may sound cheap to someone buying retail one box at a time, you can cut that cost further by selling the empty hulls. Among Skeet shooters, the going prices for once-fired brand-name hulls are: 5¢ per 12-gauge; 6¢ per 20; 8-10¢ per 28; and 10¢ for the 410. Trap shooters have no interest in anything other than the 12, and most Sporting Clays shooters aren't enamored with the smaller gauges yet, so those prices are contingent on having a buyer.

What that means is that a full box of 410 shells costs $5 and the box of once-fired empty hulls is worth $2.50. Your cost to shoot factory 410s is around $2.50 per box. You can reload them for less than that, but not a lot.

The 28-gauge runs a buck a box more, and you can save money there. Even selling the empty hulls, you can realize a savings of $35 or more per case if you reload this gauge. The savings on 20-gauge shells is a bit less, while the 12-gauge will be similar in cost to the 20, unless empty 12-gauge hulls are worth more than 5¢ each in your area. At a trap range, that will likely be the case.

Another way to buy ammo, and a good one for the casual shooter, is to purchase it at the range. Many ranges operate under the assumption that they are there to sell clay targets, and that is where their profit is. Since it takes shells to shoot targets, they will often sell top quality target loads for about one dollar mark-up over their costs, which can be on the low end of the scale. Buying a single box of 28-gauge shells at my club (the most expensive shell they sell) runs $7, and the empties are worth about $2.50 a box. That brings the box cost to $4.50; and while you can reload them for about $2.50 a box, if you only shoot a dozen boxes a year, there is no point in it.

No, not every shooter needs to reload. In fact, some trap-shooters who belong to active clubs and can expect to be able to purchase a fresh case every month (and be assured of a market for selling their empties) have quit reloading. Why tie up the money in the equipment and components, not to mention the space it takes to set up and load, or the time required to do it, when each box of factory shells costs them only about $1.50 more?

Similarly, I know a number of Skeet shooters who reload the other gauges, but have stopped loading the 410. Why create extra work when the reward isn't worth it?

On the other hand (and it's a big hand!), circumstances may make reloading far more attractive. My situation is not unusual.

Reasons to Reload

I no longer shoot Skeet on a regular competitive basis, but still burn a lot of rounds at that game, in addition to trap. I also shoot a fair amount of Sporting Clays, primarily with the 12- and 28-gauges. In the case of the latter, reloading is mandatory if I want to realize the full potential of this gauge on the Sporting Clays course. That means I need a loading press, primers, shot in four sizes (#7$\frac{1}{2}$, 8, 8$\frac{1}{2}$ and 9) and a place to set up the press.

Adding the 12-gauge to that requires only a set of dies, a couple different cans of powder, some additional wads and, of course, some empty 12-gauge hulls. Everything else interchanges.

If you've already made the decision to load one gauge, then there's no reason not to load the rest, since you've already made the most significant investment on equipment for the first gauge.

Loading all of your own shells also simplifies things. I can purchase top-quality, nickel-plated, long-range Sporting Clays loads in 12-gauge. But if I only need three or four boxes a year (you don't use that many of these specialized long-range shells in an average round of Sporting Clays), why have a whole case sitting around? Ditto for the spreader loads; the #8$\frac{1}{2}$

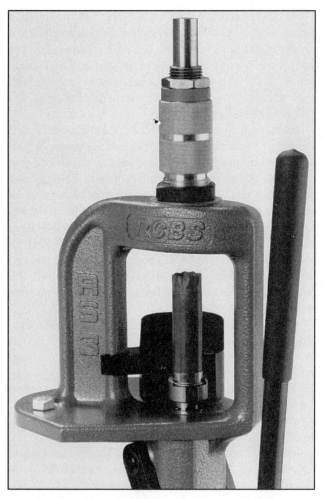

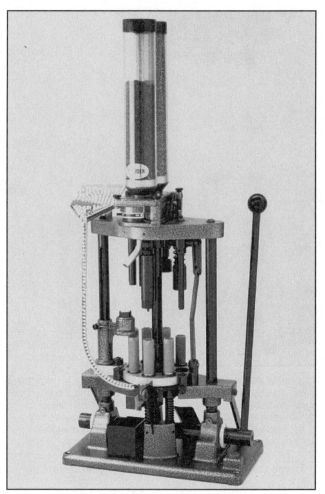

The simplest and least expensive option for the shotshell reloader is the RCBS die set that converts a standard metallic cartridge press to load shotshells. The only drawback is that they will produce very few shells per hour.

High-volume progressive reloading presses will allow you to produce a finished shell with each pull of the handle. They are the most popular choice in reloading equipment today.

load I like on the second shot of Skeet doubles; or any of the other non-standard loads that—while being a major asset when you need them—just aren't used that often. Nor do you suddenly find yourself out of a favorite load just before a match. You can always make more without having to wait for a bargain.

Yes, there are a number of shooters who do find reloading very worthwhile, both in terms of cost and shell performance. Rolling your own loads is not difficult.

Reloading Basics

As with metallic rounds, all the reloader is doing is sizing the hull back to factory specs to fit the chamber, and then replacing those components expended on firing. With a shotshell that means the primer, powder, wad and shot charge. Accomplishing this requires a loading press and a set of dies for that gauge.

A number of companies offer quality shotshell loading equipment. At the moment, the big players in the game are Hornady, MEC, Ponsness/Warren and Lee Precision. They're listed in our Directory at the back of this book. In years past, there have been a number of companies other than these, but they have either merged into larger companies or gone out of business. Some of their equipment is still around, and still in excellent operating condition. You can probably find some of it for sale on the used market at most any gun club or gun show, but I don't recommend it. Buying a loading press that is not currently manufactured can present a major problem if a part breaks and you need service. You may not be able to replace it, and if you can't have it custom-made, then your press is useless. You may as well make a lamp out of it. Parts break on occasion or just wear out, and if you can't fix it, there's not much point in buying it—no matter how attractive the price looks.

Expect to pay between $100 and $500 for a quality shotshell loader set up to load one gauge. Virtually all of them will offer interchangeable die capability, meaning that once you bite the bullet for the first purchase, adding other gauges is not expensive.

Press Types

There are essentially two different types of loading presses in use today, single stage and progressive.

The single stage requires that each hull be manually moved through each of the loading stations. On my no-longer-made

 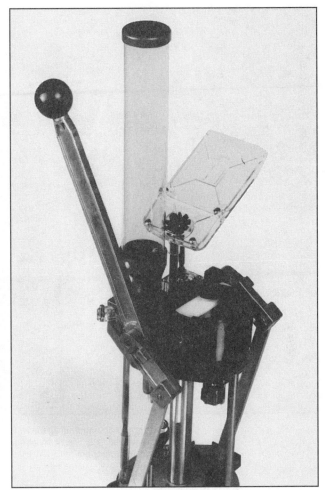

For those who need the maximum loaded-shell output, there are progressive presses that are power-operated and require the shooter do nothing more than insert shells and wads at the appropriate time.

Author does much of his reloading on the Hornady Apex progressive press. The innovative design allows a shell to be loaded with each pull of the handle, yet offers the ability to pull a shell from the machine at any step along the way for inspection. That saves a lot of 'bloop loads.'

Hornady 155, that means I move the shell to station one to de-prime and re-size it, station two to prime it, and station three to drop a powder charge, seat a wad and add the shot. At station four I start the crimp, while station five finishes it. It sounds slow, but it is not that bad. I can load fifty to sixty rounds per hour.

The advantage to the single stage press is that every loading operation is fully monitored and it is very hard to mess up. The quality of the ammunition loaded on this (or other single stage presses) is very high and uniform from shell to shell. I use this press a lot when making test rounds or when I just need to run off a couple boxes of specialty rounds. Another advantage to the single stage is that they fall into the lower end of the price spectrum, and changing to different gauge dies is a pretty simple affair. If you only shoot a couple hundred rounds a month and don't mind spending a few hours loading them, then a quality single stage press will serve you well.

If you need more shells in less time, the answer is a progressive press. Feed shells into station one and each time you cycle the handle it will automatically re-size, de-prime, move the shell, prime, drop powder and shot, and do all the other

things. All you have to do is feed in an empty hull, insert a wad, and you get one reloaded shell with each pull of the handle. They can crank out several hundred rounds per hour. Some of the expensive ones don't even require you to operate the handle.

The drawback to the progressive press, other than the cost and the fact it is not as easy to shift to other gauges, is that it requires a lot more attention on the operator's part. It is not difficult to forget to insert a wad, or drop shot, or leave out the powder, or forget something else. You'll find out quickly if you messed up on the range when a shell fails to fire. One wag once observed that shell knockers were invented by progressive press users who suffered from Attention Deficit Disorder!

All the different makers' presses do the same thing, just in a slightly different way. I happen to be very partial to Hornady and Ponsness/Warren equipment, but that's because their machines fit my style. All of them will work, and they come with complete instructions. In the case of the MEC equipment (whose instructions are so thorough that an engineering degree helps), they even have an information line to call for help when you need it.

Chronographing your loads in the only way to truly know how consistent they are. Many shooting clubs have a chronograph available for their members.

Heed the Data

Load data for shotshells is far more varied than for metallic rounds. With the latter, there are really only a half-dozen powder, bullet and primer combinations that will produce decent results with any given cartridge. Not the case here. Different makes and models of shotshells will have different internal volumes and shapes. These differences affect how they will react with any given wad and powder combination. For that reason, a lot of shooters like to standardize on just a couple of different hulls, since this cuts down the number of different wads they require. Put the wrong components in the hull and you can have, at best, a lousy load. At the worst, you can have a dangerous one! That was amply illustrated by a test done by Dave Fackler at Ballistic Products. He took six different hulls and used exactly the same wad, primer, powder charge and shot charge to load each. Here's what happened to velocities and pressures with these mid-range hunting loads.

Hull	Pressure (LUP)	Velocity (fps)
ACTIV All Plastic	9700	1320
Federal Gold Medal	8500	1290
Fiocchi Field	9000	1330
Remington Unibody	15,000	1385
Winchester Poly[1]	9000	1330
Winchester AA	10,800	1240

BPI PRESSURE TEST

[1] Plastic disc internal base.

Any pressure over 11,500 LUP (Lead Units of Pressure) is excessive in a 12-gauge shell. Any pressure under 6500 LUP may not let the shell fully perform by burning the powder charge properly and cleanly.

It is obvious from the test that not all hulls are created equal, and a combination of components that may produce a beautifully performing load in one can be hazardous in another. This is not a knock on any particular maker's shell, because all will work very nicely with the proper components and load data.

This test points out that anyone attempting to load shotshells should have current, tested data. That is very easy to get. Remington, Winchester, Federal, ACTIV, and other shell makers who also offer components have good loading data information that is yours for the asking. Companies like Ballistic Products, who sell components, have plenty of data on their loads. It's available for a phone call or letter. Don't start shotshell loading without good data. Otherwise you're asking for trouble.

Once you have the data that gives you the proper combination of wad, powder, primer and shot charge for a given hull, it is not advisable to deviate from it. Simply changing the make of primer can raise or lower pressure enough to turn a good load into a dog. You can, however, fine tune your gun's performance by picking the right load for the conditions, and one major factor in that respect is the temperature at which you will be using the load.

Shotshell Pressures

Each shotshell recipe provided by the ammo or component makers will provide the tested working pressure for that load, expressed in psi or LUP. These are the two ways of measuring shotshell pressure, and they are slightly different, but not enough to make much difference unless you are one of those who would rather pick nits than bust clays. As mentioned earlier, any pressure above 11,500 is excessive in a 12-gauge. It won't blow the gun, but it might well blow your pattern, and it will certainly increase the wear on your gun, not to mention your shoulder. Any pressure below 7500 (according to ballistic experts) will result in a shell that is not operating at full efficiency. I'm not sure I fully agree with that. At the risk of sounding like a nitpicker myself, I have found that 12-gauge loads can function nicely down to about 6500. The smaller gauges should be 8500 or above.

Within the acceptable pressure range, the higher the pressure, the more recoil and shot deformation, and the lower the pressure, the less. When I'm working with 12-gauge target loads, I prefer those that operate from 7500 to 9000 LUP. In the smaller gauges, I feel the range needs to be between 8500 and 10,000 LUP.

On the surface, that would seem to make it a simple matter to find a good load: Just follow the bouncing LUP! But it's not always that simple.

It is the accepted industry standard to pressure-test loads at a uniform 70 degrees F. temperature. The reason is that for each 10-degree rise (or fall) in ambient temperature, there will be a corresponding increase or decrease of 1000 LUP pressure.

In other words, select a load that pressure-tests at 10,500 LUP, and that's what you get at 70 degrees. But walk out onto a sweltering 95-degree Skeet field on a late August afternoon and you now have a load that is probably cracking 12,500 LUP! Not good. Not for your gun, your patterns or your shoulder. On the reverse side, select a conservative 7500 LUP load and shoot it in 40-degree weather and some of the rounds may not even ignite! They are called "bloop" loads because that's just what they sound like when they go off. When that happens, you tilt the barrel downward to pour out the shot that never left the barrel, drop a shell knocker down the barrel to remove the stuck wad (fail to do this and the next round disassembles your gun for you!), and then hope all that unburned powder won't find its way into the action and tie up your gun.

This is one area where reloaders have an advantage over factory-round shooters, because the factories must load to some uniform pressure, even though they have no idea at what temperature those shells will be shot. You know where you shoot and can load accordingly.

For cold weather 12-gauge loads, I pick one in the 10,500 LUP range. For hot weather conditions, I'll go with one in the 6000-7000 LUP range. By the time I actually get them on the range, they are at about the temperature and pressure I want them, a fact much appreciated by my gun, my shoulder and my scorecard.

Components

Another area where the reloader has a considerable amount of control is in the shot he elects to stuff into the shell.

Basically, the harder the shot, the better the load will pattern, and the shorter will be the shot string. The degree of pattern control a shooter can exercise by simply varying the type of shot is about 10 percent. That's about one full degree of choke.

Top-quality nickel-plated shot can tighten your patterns even more, a fact that has not been lost on World Class International trap competitors or clever Sporting Clays shooters.

If you want solid long-range patterns, go to hard shot. If you need to open a pattern quickly, use the cheap soft stuff. You can also open patterns by loading to higher velocity and pressure.

The type of powder you use can affect recoil and reliability. Some powders burn dirty. I won't shoot fast-burning flake powders like Red Dot because it gums up my gas guns. There are other powders that do the same. Sometimes you'll get them in factory loads. In fact, just a week ago I was running a very good make of factory ammo through my Franchi Prestige and the gun was a bit dirty. Early in the second round of Skeet the gun failed to feed a round. My Prestige just doesn't do that. It is one of the most reliable gas guns made. The culprit? Flake powder in the action temporarily bound up the shell carrier. Racking the action vigorously a few times cleared it and I was able to continue. In Sporting Clays that would have been a lost

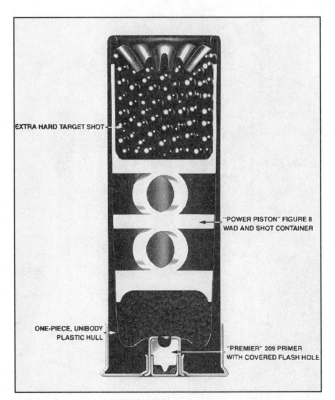

The components of a shotshell are pretty simple: shot, wad, powder and primer. Different wads, however, will work best in different hulls. The shooter must know what components are compatible if he is to make good loads, and there is a wealth of good reloading data available for the asking from the powder companies.

Red Dot is an inexpensive fast-burning powder that is popular with many shooters, but the author finds it is not clean-burning enough for his semi-autos, although it does a fine job in his over/unders.

Hi-Skor 800-X is an excellent choice for reloading the 20- and 28-gauge, but gives very poor results in 12-gauge target loads or the 410. If you are going to load several different gauges, you will have to acquire several different powders. There's no way around it.

Author is a big fan of Hodgdon's new Clays powder for 12-gauge target loads. It meters well and burns very cleanly while producing uniform velocities and excellent patterns.

When it comes to producing dense, yet even patterns, it pays to use a quality high-antimony shot, like Lawrence Brand Magnum. It costs little more than the softer chilled shot and produces much better results.

bird. Even on the Skeet range, where gun malfunctions are a legitimate excuse to reshoot, it was enough to interrupt my concentration.

IMR PB, Royal Scot, Hodgdon's new Clays and International Clays are all clean-burning powders. They load to target velocities beautifully and won't mess up a gas gun. In the smaller gauges, you can add 800-X to that list, although it does require a hot primer like the Federal 209A to light it off well in cool weather. With the 410, I consider H-110 to be the best bet, with Winchester 296 a good second choice.

These moderate-to-medium powders, PB and 800-X in particular, also seem to deliver more of a shove than a jolt. They are softer shooting at the same load velocity than many other powders.

One last advantage reloaders have is being able to create loads that don't exist in factory offerings. In past chapters I've mentioned some of the fast-opening loads that can be created using special wads from Ballistic Products, Inc., and the accompanying charts give some starting data on those, as well as on the tight-patterning nickel shot loads made with their International Target Driver Wad. I have listed just a few basic loads, but Dave Fackler will be happy to send you a couple of pounds of load data if you drop him a line.

There is no doubt that factory loads are good. In fact, reloaders will not be able to better the performance of many of them. That includes all established trap loads, many Skeet loads and some long-range International loads. But you can equal them, and do it for less money. You can also create loads that aren't available from the factory. As far as this shooter is concerned, those are more than enough reasons to spend time at the loading bench.

Pattern Testing

Testing what you have created requires patterning the gun and load combo. There really is no other way to be certain you're getting an effective load, because each shotgun barrel, even from the same maker, is its own "musical instrument"—a load that does a beautiful job in one gun can be a marginal performer in another. It is traditional to pattern the 12-, 20- and 28-gauges at 40 yards, with the 410 being shot at 30. I test them my own way.

I make up specific loads to operate with a specific choke tube within a specific range. That's where I pattern them—where I will be shooting them. It makes no sense, and provides no information, to test-pattern a 15-yard spreader load at 40 yards just because it happens to be a 12-gauge. Pattern it at 15 yards instead. The same holds true for a mid-range load or a high-performance nickel-plated long-range load. My procedure is to pattern spreader loads at 15 yards, Skeet or close-range Sporting loads at 21 yards, and 16-Yard trap loads (which are mid-range Sporting loads) at 30 yards. Handicap trap loads and other long-range loads get tested at 45 yards, although I might take a look at them at 55 yards as well. I may not be able to improve their performance, but at least I'll know what to expect of them.

That may be one of the biggest reasons I reload. I want to know what the load coming out of my barrel will do!

Author's Favorite Loads

These recipes can be adjusted for pattern density via the hardness of the shot used, and for their effective clay target breaking range via the size of the shot. Unless otherwise noted, they work equally as well with shot sizes #7½ through #9.

FAVORED LOADS

Load	Hull	Shot Wgt. (Oz.)	Primer	Powder Grains/Type	Wad	Velocity (fps)	Pressure (LUP)	Comments
12-Gauge Loads								
Ultra-light 1-ounce	Fed. Gold Medal or Field	1, high antimony	Fed. 209A	21.5/IMR PB	Fed. 12S0	1120	NA (under 8000)	A
Light 1⅛-ounce	Fed. Gold Medal, Field or ACTIV	1⅛	Fed. 209A	21.5/IMR PB	Fed. 12S3	1125	NA (under 8000)	B
3-dram	Fed. Gold Medal or ACTIV	1⅛	Fed. 209A	23.7/IMR PB	Fed. 12S3	1190	NA (under 9500)	C
Fackler's Long Range Smoker	ACTIV	1 1/16, #7½	Fio. 615	28.0/Scot Solo-1250	G/BP Int'l Target Driver	1260	7500	D
Fackler's Sporting Spreader	Fiocchi Purple Target	1 1/16, #9 (soft)	Fio. 615	27.0/Scot Solo-1250	G/BP Dispersor-X	1300	8900	E
20-Gauge Loads								
Basic ⅞-ounce	Fed. plastic target	⅞	Fed. 209A	17.5/800X	Fed. 20S1	1200	NA (under 9300)	F
Basic 1-ounce	Fed. plastic target	1	CCI 209M	18.0/Herco	Fed. 20S1	1210	9800	G
Brush Wad Spreader	Fed. plastic target	1	Fed. 209A	17.0/Herco	G/BP Brush Wad	1200	NA (under 9800)	H
28-Gauge Loads								
Basic ¾-ounce	Fed. Hi-Power	¾	CCI 209M	14.5/800X	Fed. 28S1	1210	8900	I
Spreader	Fed. Hi-Power	⅞, hard #9	CCI 209	13.0/Unique	G/BP Brush Wad	1150	NA	J
410-Bore Loads								
Basic ½-ounce	Fed. 2½" plastic	½, #8½ or #9, high antimony	Fed. 209A	15.0/H-110	Fed. 410SC	1175	NA	K
Close-range	Fed. 3" plastic	11/16, soft #9	CCI 209	14.0/H-110	Fed. 410SC	1130	NA	L

A—The softest 12-gauge load I have found that will function my Franchi Prestige gas-operated semi-auto. A real joy in an O/U! Excellent Skeet load.
B—Duplicates popular "Lite" target loads.
C—Great trap load with hard shot. Nickel shot makes a fine long-range load. Hard #8½ shot makes good mid-range load. Very versatile.
D—With nickel shot this is a real "Ma Bell" load. It will "reach out and touch" a 50-plus-yard bird! This same load in a Federal Gold Medal hull with 1⅛-oz. shot hits 1300+ fps and does just as good a job. Best at temps 75 to 90 degrees.
E—Very fast-opening load. Wide patterns at 15 yards. Best at that range or less. Reduce powder charge 1.0 grain and it loads well in Federal Gold Medal or ACTIV hull.
F—Good patterning load.
G—Good if you want to throw a heavier shot charge at close to medium range. The ⅞-oz. load with nickel shot seems to hold better patterns at longer range.
H—Very fast opening patterns for use under 15 yards.
I—A sweet little load that gets a lot from the 28-gauge. Not at its best at temps under 60 degrees.
J—Opens quickly; best at 15 yards and under.
K—About the best I can do in a 410 load that will pattern fairly well. Hard shot is a must. Prefer #8½ shot for ranges over 20 yards. Not recommended beyond 30 yards.
L—Opens very fast. Not worth a hoot beyond 15-18 yards, but does smoke the close ones.

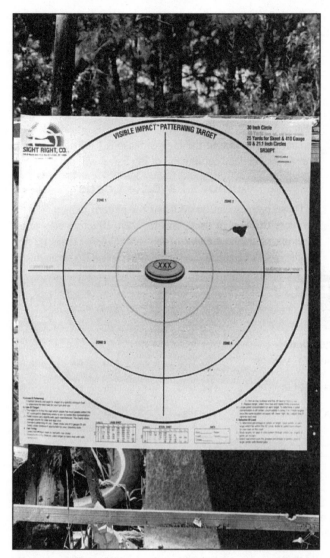

Not many shooters take the time to pattern their loads, but it is the best way to see if you have created the exact performance you want from that load. These Visible Impact targets make patterning your shotgun quick and inexpensive.

Thoughts on Spreaders

Most scattergunners want their shot patterns as dense and uniform as possible. But there are times when a very quick-opening pattern can be an asset.

This is especially true in the rapidly growing game of Sporting Clays. Here, shooters may be faced with a number of real "in-your-face" target presentations at ranges between 10 and 15 yards. Most of these shots will be at quick crossing birds, sometimes with a slight incoming or outgoing angle, and it doesn't take a Rhodes scholar to see that a shooter who can only generate a 10-inch-wide pattern at that range has to be far more precise with his aim than one who uses a load that gives a 20-inch diameter pattern. In fact, the larger pattern doesn't give you twice as much surface area to hit the target with, it gives four times as much. When you're swinging like crazy on an orange blur, that tends to help your score!

As a result, there has been a resurgence of interest in the 12-gauge "spreader" loads.

These loads have been around for a number of years. Gen-

erally, they haven't garnered much favor with competitive trap and Skeet shooters. They were primarily hunting fodder designed to open the shot charge from a Modified or Full choke to what might be achieved with an Improved Cylinder choking.

Often called "brush loads," they were intended to allow a shooter with a fixed choke (which was the rule rather than the exception just a decade ago) to have a quick and convenient way to open his patterns if he happened to wander temporarily into tight quarters. Hence the moniker "brush load."

There are a number of ways to open the pattern on a shotgun without changing the choke. Shooting softer chilled shot at high velocity will usually open a pattern one choke degree over harder shot at more moderate velocity. Wad inserts are also available to help spread the shot. These may be a simple X-divider or a post and base. They are placed into the wad prior to dropping the shot, or inserted into the shot charge after it has been dropped.

Gualandi recently produced a one-piece plastic wad with an X-spreader insert moulded in, and two side cup petals that instantly separate from the wad as it leaves the muzzle. These wads are available as reloading components from Ballistic Products.

The same wad is currently being loaded by ACTIV in their specially marked Sporting Clays loads. These use a light orange-colored hull and box instead of red. Available in sizes #9, #8 and #7$^1/_2$, they are, to the best of my knowledge, the only factory-loaded spreader target loads on the market at the moment. Will they add any birds to your Sporting Clays score? Maybe, maybe not.

The original intent of the spreader load was to turn a Full or Modified choke into an Improved Cylinder or Cylinder choke, and the Gualandi X-Spreader wad will certainly do that whether in the ACTIV factory loads or in your own reloads.

I tested the ACTIV load with #9 shot in my Ruger Red Label with Briley long choke tubes in Modified and Skeet 1. It showed that from the Modified tube it would produce patterns of almost identical dimensions and density to those achieved by a standard Federal #9 Skeet load from the Skeet-choked tube.

In short, it does just what a spreader load is intended to do. That makes the #7$^1/_2$ load a good item to have in your pocket in the hunting fields if you are using a more tightly choked barrel and suddenly find you need an open choke.

That makes spreader loads worthwhile additions to the contemporary factory shotshell lineup. A spreader load isn't needed in the field that often, and one box is likely to last for years. Competitive shooters may not find them that valuable, however, because of their quick-change choke options.

In doing some testing to find the best close-range load for my own Sporting Clays shooting, I tested the ACTIV load against several standard #9 Skeet loads that are not only less expensive, but more readily available. The results were eye-opening.

Patterning at 15 yards from the Briley Cylinder tube on my Red Label, I found that the ACTIV load produced a usable

Making fast-opening loads for those in-your-face Sporting Clays targets is easy with Ballistic Products X-Spreader wad (left) and their 12-gauge 'Brush Wad', far right. Either will produce usable patterns considerably larger than standard wads and can really boost your score on close, quick targets.

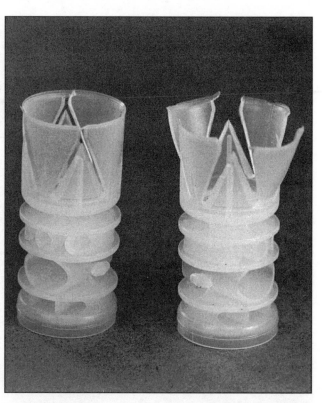

This BP Piston Skeet wad is a favorite of the author for producing wide, even patterns at ranges up to 25 yards. They are compatible with a number of different hulls and are very popular with European skeet shooters.

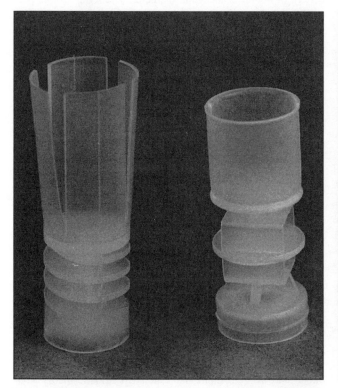

The sub-gauges can have their versatility greatly increased by reloading. These two wads (Federal on the left and BP 28-gauge Sporting on the right) allow the author to create quick-opening 28-gauge loads or stretch the little gauge for all it's worth... just by changing wad and shot size!

These BP Target Driver wads are intended to produce dense patterns at long range and offer reloaders a means to equal the performance of top-quality factory trap loads.

One-ounce 12-gauge loads offer better performance than any 20-gauge load and often produce less recoil. Many female shooters find them very pleasant to shoot.

High-speed 1-ounce loads of #9 shot are just the ticket for close-range Sporting Clays targets when combined with a Cylinder choke. They are easy to reload.

pattern of about 22 inches in diameter. The term "usable pattern" is a better reflection of the load's actual performance on targets than is a pellet count and pattern percentage figure. The usable pattern area is determined by simply using a felt marker to draw a circle around the portion of the pattern that is dense and evenly distributed enough to consistently break a target. Individual flier pellets, or small groups of two to four shot pellets outside this area, might possibly get you a target every now and then, but you can't count on them. So, they are not counted—just the "usable pattern area."

A 22-inch pattern at 15 yards is nothing to sneer at! That is 3 to 5 inches larger in diameter than you can get with a Skeet 1 choke, and twice as big as what you get with a Skeet 2 (Light Modified) choke. It is about as much as you can open a pattern at that range and still maintain enough density with $1 1/8$ ounces of shot to prevent a bird from slipping through. In short, the ACTIV spreader load is probably the best bet for "in-your-face" targets.

Patterning the Federal paper-hulled $2 3/4$-dram, $1 1/8$-ounce #9 Skeet load from the same Cylinder choke at the same range, I got a usable pattern of about 21 inches. That pattern was more evenly distributed than the ACTIV pattern, which had a couple of thin areas.

The next load I tested was the Federal plastic-hulled #9 Skeet load in the 3-dram size. Shotshell ballistic theory says that the heavier powder charge would tend to open the pattern a bit more quickly, and it did. The 3-dram, $1 1/8$-ounce load produced a pattern of almost 23 inches, and again it had better pellet distribution than the ACTIV load.

Sporting clays rabbit targets are constructed more stoutly than others and often take a heavier pellet to cleanly break. Many reloaders put up a pocket full of special loads to handle these.

Cobbling up a quick reload on my Hornady press using a Victory hull, 19 grains of Clays (about a 2³/₄-dram charge), Federal 209 primer and a purple PC wad (a 1-ounce wad that leaves about ¹/₈-inch of the shot charge unprotected) I got patterns that equaled the 3-dram Federal load, but with a bit less recoil. I could probably open that load a bit further by shifting to softer chilled shot, but I happened to be out of it at the time.

The results of my impromptu tests convinced me that, with my Briley Cylinder choke tube in place, an expensive spreader load is simply not necessary. I'm getting the same pattern diameter and slightly better density with either an easily available factory load or a quick and inexpensive reload.

Interestingly, shortly after these tests I ran into shooting champs Bill Whitehurst and Bonnie McLaurin at a local Sporting Clays range and asked them how they feel about spreaders. Their response? "Use a Cylinder choke and #9s and you get the same thing."

I wish I'd asked earlier. I could have saved some time!

There is one situation where I feel I would want to have a handful of the #9 ACTIV loads in one of my pockets. That is on those rare occasions when I shoot FITASC, the international version of Sporting Clays. It is rare for an American-style Sporting Clays range to throw targets that vary more than about one choke degree in range from the same stand. As a rule, when you step into the stand to shoot, if you have made a proper choke selection, you're OK. That's not necessarily so in FITASC. You may get a target that requires an Improved Modified or Full choke on one bird, and have that followed by a bird that fairly screams Improved Cylinder or Skeet 1. You

can't change choke tubes once you get onto the shooting stand, so you have a dilemma. The experienced shooter here would choke for the longer bird and plug in an ACTIV spreader load (or reload if rules allow) for the closer birds.

But that's a rare situation. For my money, when I have an "in-your-face" target, I'll stick with Cylinder chokes and #9s. That'll spread me as thin as I'm going to get.

Bigger Isn't Always Better

There is a definite and very noticeable trend among competitive 12-gauge shotgunners today, and that is a shift to high-speed 1-ounce and ⁷/₈-ounce loads for most shooting, reserving the traditional 1¹/₈-ounce loads only for longer ranges.

That trend began in a rather unusual way. Many years back, shooters competing in the demanding game of International (Bunker) trap were allowed to use full 3¹/₄-dram, 1¹/₄-ounce loads, and many did. This was rather punishing to the shooter because shooting two shots at a target is the rule, not the exception. Shooting seventy-five targets in a day means 150 shots with a heavy load.

The UIT Rules Committee decided to spice up the game a bit and changed the rules to allow a maximum of 1¹/₈ ounces of shot. That brought predictable howls from the competitors who were convinced that their scores would go down. But that didn't happen.

A few years later, they changed the rules to allow a maximum of 1 ounce of shot (28 grams). Again the howls, and again the same results. Scores did not go down...they went up!

How could a smaller shot charge improve scores? Take a

Shot size does count! These International targets show the effects of being hit with just a couple of pellets each. Larger shot might have resulted in a visible piece instead of a lost target. These were picked up on the range after sailing away as apparent misses.

look at the nearby table that shows the recoil produced by various powder and shot charge combinations in different gauges and gun weights and you'll see why—recoil!

Quite simply, the less punishment a shooter absorbs, the better he will shoot. The experience of the UIT Bunker trap shooters has proved this conclusively. In fact, when they made their most recent change to allow a maximum of 24 grams of shot (7/8-ounce) there were very few howls. The shooters had been educated.

Many of those same shooters have also realized that if an ounce of shot is enough to handle a high-speed, stoutly constructed Bunker trap target, it will certainly handle the slower standard targets. In fact, with only a few exceptions, almost every one of the top shooters I've interviewed during the course of this book has shifted to 1-ounce loads for trap, Skeet and Sporting Clays.

Earlier in this chapter, I provided loading data for a very mild, actually an ultra-light, 1-ounce, 12-gauge load that is an

Bunker trap is one of the most demanding games a shot load can be asked to handle. Yet, shooters found that rule changes restricting them to only 1 ounce of shot actually raised average scores!

RELATIVE RECOIL OF MODERN SHOT LOADS

Gauge	Shell Length	Gun Weight	Powder Dram Equivalent	Shot Weight (Oz.)	Recoil Energy (ft-lb.)
12	2³/₄	7 lb. 8 oz.	3	1	18
12	2³/₄	same	2³/₄	1¹/₈	19
12	2³/₄	same	3	1¹/₈	21
12	2³/₄	same	3¹/₄	1¹/₈	23
12	2³/₄	same	3¹/₄	1¹/₄	26
12	2³/₄	same	3³/₄	1¹/₄	32
12	2³/₄	same	Magnum	1¹/₂	45
12	3	8 lb. 12 oz.	4	1³/₈	32
12	3	same	4¹/₄	1⁵/₈	45
12	3	same	Magnum	1⁷/₈	54
16	2³/₄	6 lb. 8 oz.	2¹/₂	1	20
16	2³/₄	same	2³/₄	1¹/₈	24
16	2³/₄	same	3	1¹/₈	26
16	2³/₄	same	3¹/₄	1¹/₈	29
16	2³/₄	same	Magnum	1¹/₄	36
20	2³/₄	same	2¹/₄	7/8	16
20	2³/₄	same	2¹/₂	1	19
20	2³/₄	same	2³/₄	1	21
20	2³/₄	same	3	1¹/₈	25
20	3	6 lb. 12 oz.	Magnum	1¹/₈	28
20	3	same	Magnum	1³/₁₆	31

The gun weights shown are an average weight for each gauge. For a given load the recoil generated varies inversely with the gun weight. The heavier the gun, the less recoil produced. The lighter the load, the less recoil produced.

Young shooters can benefit greatly from the current crop of 1-ounce and ⁷/₈-ounce 12-gauge loads. The lack of recoil will aid their shooting.

excellent American Skeet load. Most of the 1-ounce shooters favor higher velocities. An increase in velocity provides an increase in the target breaking power of the individual pellets, which means you get a good break with fewer pellet hits. I have watched 1-ounce loads of #9 shot at 1300 fps absolutely crush the sturdy International Skeet targets, while an ultra-light load at 1100 fps would merely dust them, make them wobble a bit, but they wouldn't produce the visible piece required to score a hit. Higher speed is one of the keys to making 1-ounce loads effective beyond Skeet ranges, and loading data for these high-speed loads is now becoming available. Here's the data for some of the 1-ounce loads that I have found very effective.

With the Remington Unibody hull, load 22 grains of Hodgdon International powder and a Federal 209 primer. Use ⁷/₈-ounce of shot in the Federal 12SO wad or 1 ounce of shot in the purple PC wad. Velocity of both is in the 1280-1300 fps range and recoil is very mild. Either of these is an excellent close-range load with #9 shot, and my favorite for close Sporting Clays shots.

If you happen to prefer Green Dot powder, you get the same performance with 21.5 grains. If you use the Federal 209A primer, use 20.5 grains of Hodgdon International.

For ACTIV or Federal Gold Medal hulls, the Federal 12SO wad with the standard Federal 209 primer puts up a lovely 1-ounce load with the same powder charges listed above. It has low recoil and a velocity of about 1250-1280. I like this load very much with hard #8 shot as an all-round load. With a Modified choke, it is eminently suitable for 16-Yard and Double trap. Shift to an Improved Cylinder choke and it does a fine job on Sporting Clays targets to 35 yards. Switch to #8¹/₂ shot and it is a great International Skeet load, although not legal in sanctioned UIT matches. I'll use #7¹/₂ shot for Handicap trap and Bunker trap, not to mention dove, quail and woodcock. A very versatile little load.

Every now and then I run across a supply of Fiocchi hulls, and these create some logistics problems because they do not work well with the Federal wads I normally stock. However, they are good hulls and I want to use them. I use them to make an excellent 1-ounce load with the purple PC wad and 20-21 grains of Green Dot. An advantage here is that I can load these with a different shot size than my standard loads, say #7¹/₂, and use them when I want a little extra punch. Their distinctive color makes it impossible to confuse them with other loads in the heat of battle.

If you are used to shooting full 2³/₄- or 3-dram, 1¹/₈-ounce loads on a steady basis, the shift to 1-ounce loads will surprise you. They'll do pleasant things to your score, your cheek and shoulder as well. When it comes to busting clay targets, bigger isn't always better.

The Non-Toxic Alternative

A LOT OF clay target shooters aren't going to like what follows, but that doesn't make it any less true.

It is this writer's opinion that within ten years, lead shot will be a thing of the past. Banned. Outlawed. Prohibited.

If that sounds pessimistic, it is not. In fact, it is somewhat optimistic because many experts in the American ammunition industry feel that lead shot won't last even that long!

That is not particularly surprising, considering this decade of heightened environmental awareness. Lead is a proven health hazard. It is a poison that can cause physical damage when absorbed into the body through the skin, and it has adverse long-term effects. The assault on lead began with its use as a gasoline additive and continued into other common products like paint. There is a strong move afoot to ban lead from virtually every application, including its use in fishing sinkers! And that sentiment is on the increase. A number of gun clubs have already had to close their doors because their shotfall areas included wetlands and other environmentally sensitive areas. Like it or not, the future of clay target games is going to ride on non-toxic shot.

There are two non-toxic alternatives that appear likely to become major players—steel shot and Bismuth. Here's a look at what you can expect from them.

Steel Shot

It is safe to say that steel shot got off to a rocky start. Literally shoved down the throats of waterfowlers long before the technology was properly developed, steel shot earned what could only be described as a bad reputation.

Early steel shot loads suffered many ills. Chief among them was the fact that the shot pellets were extremely hard—hard enough to cause barrel scoring and choke damage. Steel shot does not deform upon firing like lead, nor does it flow as smoothly through a constriction point. Given the tight chokes favored by many waterfowlers, and the fact that some of the guns in use at the time had barrels of a softer steel than current models, the early steel shot loads would often peen the choke to a more open constriction. Steel shot also will rust, and more

Author has serious doubts that steel shot can be made to produce effective loads in his little Browning 28-gauge Citori. At the price of Bismuth, he may not be doing much shooting with it when lead passes from the scene.

Target ranges that have sensitive wetlands within their shotfall areas were the first to be forced to make the shift to steel target loads, but all ranges will ultimately be affected.

than one gunner found himself tossing a solid steel "slug" at a distant duck! Sometimes his choke tube went along with it.

The lack of pellet deformation also results in steel shot loads delivering tighter patterns than lead. Typically, steel will show a strong center density with a somewhat thin and inconsistent annular ring.

The biggest drawback to steel, however, is that it simply could not match the terminal ballistics of lead. Steel has 67 percent the density of lead. This results in a decrease in downrange striking energy when compared to a lead pellet of the same size, launched at the same velocity. Duck hunters quickly discovered that simply selecting the same size steel pellet

Lead is not a major concern in some areas where it can be conveniently reclaimed from the environment, like the International Shooting Park, in Colorado Springs, Colorado. But in some other areas, especially wetlands, momentum is growing to ban lead from shotshells. (U.S. Army photo by Joseph J. Johnson.)

Currently manufactured guns, like this Remington Peerless over/under, are perfectly capable of handling steel shot without problems. Some older guns with very lightweight barrels may not do as well, but they are not commonly seen in the hands of competitive clay target shooters.

Target-sized steel shot is not likely to cause damage to modern guns. Briley reports that their tests show it will not damage their sub-gauge insert tubes. Most reported steel shot gun damage has resulted from large hunting pellets, not the smaller target sizes.

what could only be described as perfect happiness if I selected a 1¼-ounce steel load of #3s to replace the 1¼-ounce load of lead #6s that I used over decoys. I went to a 1⅜-ounce load of #1 steel in a 3-inch magnum hull instead of the 1¼-ounce load of lead #4s that was my former long-range tool. With my new steel loads, the ducks dropped just as dead. The only other concession I had to make with steel was to open the choke constriction one degree. Instead of slipping Improved Cylinder and Modified tubes into my Ruger Red Label for decoy work, I changed to Skeet 1 and Improved Cylinder. Modified and Improved Cylinder became my pass-shooting tubes, replacing Modified and Full. It was not a traumatic experience. Shifting to steel shot will work well for a lot of popular clay target chores.

Many of the earlier problems with steel shot that earned it a poor reputation among waterfowlers have either been corrected or will have no effect on clay target gunners. You can pretty much forget any chance of barrel and choke damage. Contemporary steel shot pellets are made of softer material, and the majority of choke damage was the result of large shot pellets (BBs and up) anyway. The smaller pellets used on clays aren't going to pose any problems.

Rusting has also been brought under control by better weatherproofing of the shells and by adding rust-inhibiting compounds to the shot pellets. This technology is still relatively new and will no doubt improve. I'm not at all worried about shooting steel target loads in any smoothbore I own.

The only thing that really hasn't changed is the density difference between lead and steel, and steel's tendency to deliver tighter patterns. That's why the target loads of tomorrow will likely be different from those used today. To understand that a bit better, consider the following chart showing comparative pellet counts between lead and steel in target-sized shot:

COMPARATIVE PELLET COUNTS

Shot Size (inches)	Pellets per Ounce (steel)	Pellets per Ounce (lead)
#6 (0.110)	316	225
#7 (0.010)	420	300
#7½ (0.095)	490	350
#8 (0.090)	575	410
#9 (0.080)	not made	585

A look at the above chart will show that while the shot sizes in the steel target loads are larger than those found in lead loads, the increased number of steel shot pellets per ounce over that of lead will keep the total shot pellet count per load very similar. That's an important factor to keep in mind.

load as they had been using with lead resulted in very poor performance and a lot of crippled ducks.

What emerged was the "rule of two"—if you wanted to match the performance of a given lead shot size, you had to go two sizes larger with steel shot. In other words, if you had been happy with a load of lead #6, you would also be happy with a load of steel #4. That didn't work for me.

At the time steel shot became mandatory in my neck of the woods, I was mid-way through a six-year career as a duck hunting guide on Florida's Lake George. I had a lot of opportunity to directly compare the actual field performance of lead and steel, and I found that I had to go up *three* sizes with steel. After a lot of experimentation and test-patterning, I found

Author's tests of Winchester's new 1-ounce #7 steel target load showed it to be a sterling performer for Skeet and 16-Yard trap, with very modest recoil. He likes it!

Fiocchi's 24-gram steel shot target load is a 1400 fps screamer that is a joy to shoot. It crushes targets impressively at ranges out to 35 yards.

Remington offers the largest current lineup of steel shot target loads. Author found they performed well.

As mentioned earlier, I found that I had to use a steel pellet three sizes larger than lead to achieve the same down-range performance on ducks. Many others felt two sizes larger was adequate. If we apply the "rule of two" to the target range, we would replace #9 lead Skeet loads with #7 steel, and #7½ trap loads with #5½ steel. Fortunately, clay birds aren't ducks. They don't have to hit the water head-down-dead. All that is required here is a visible piece, and if my experience with the current crop of factory steel target loads is any indication, we are going to get that performance very easily from steel, at least in the 12- and 20-gauge loads I tested.

The loads I tried were the Winchester AASTL, a 3-dram load of 1-ounce of #7 steel; the Fiocchi 12ST78, a max-dram #7 load that is essentially a ⁷⁄₈-ounce International load at a listed velocity of 1440 fps; and four 12-gauge and one 20-gauge load from Remington. The latter had the largest steel shot target selection. They were RST12M (1¹⁄₈ oz., #6¹⁄₂); RSTL12M (1¹⁄₈ oz., #7); RSTL12L (1¹⁄₈ oz., #8); and the 20-

gauge RSTL20 (⁷⁄₈ oz., #8). These are the only steel shot loads currently manufactured as target loads, although many #6 steel hunting loads would have some application in the long-range arena.

Another aspect of steel worth remembering is the hardness of the individual pellets. Although I have no proof of it, I believe that hardness translates into a stronger blow on a brittle clay target and will result in a better break than a softer lead pellet with the same energy level. Part of that is based on my own experience, and part on the fact that the top International Skeet shooters in the world favor nickel-plated shot. That game doesn't require the tight-patterning characteristics of nickel, but International Skeet targets are made tougher than standard targets to take the more violent launch that gives them a higher velocity. Those International guys use nickel because those harder pellets break those tougher targets better than soft shot. Steel's not much different in the hardness area.

Both of the Remington loads with the #8 shot were wrung

One-ounce 12-gauge steel shot target loads carry almost as many pellets as a lead 1¹/₈-ounce load, but produce far less recoil. They are pleasant to shoot.

out on the Skeet range using a Skeet-choked barrel, and both gave performances virtually identical with what I would expect from standard 1¹/₈- and 1-ounce Skeet loads of #9 lead shot. There was no difference, not in the way the targets broke or in the way the gun felt. Nor was there any difference in the scores I normally would shoot in those gauges with lead shot. As Yogi Berra might sum it up, "If I hadn't known it was steel shot, I wouldn't have known it was steel shot."

The Winchester and Fiocchi #7 loads circled the field next, and there was a difference. Those loads pulverized targets with all the authority of a full 1¹/₈-ounce load of #8s, yet with the recoil I would expect from a 1-ounce 12-gauge load. They were more impressive than the Remington loads in terms of target breaks, but the scores were the same. All of the above shells did just as well as lead, and if I had to use them to shoot Skeet for the rest of my life I would have no complaints. They wouldn't change my average one iota.

Moving to the 16-Yard trap line, I ran the #7 loads from Winchester, Remington and Fiocchi through my Franchi Prestige with the same Modified choke tube I would use with the #8 lead loads I favor for that game. Again, if there was a difference, I couldn't see it.

Only when I moved back to the 27-yard Handicap position

did I begin to feel that the #7 steel loads might be running out of steam, and even a Full choke tube didn't help. The target breaks began to lack the explosive quality displayed at closer ranges. In fact, they behaved a lot like a 3-dram #8 trap load would at that range, which is on the outside of its positive break range. Cycling Remington's #6¹/₂ steel load through the gun got things back to normal. They worked just fine. The extra pellet weight was enough to get the job done, and this load compared very favorably to a 3-dram #7¹/₂ lead load. I have no doubt that a number of 12-gauge #6 steel shot hunting loads would do just as well, and I look forward to testing some on long-range shots on the Sporting Clays range.

Remember that steel shot target loads are still in their infancy, largely due to a lack of demand. The currently manufactured loads I tested worked very well, but I have no doubt that as lead fades from the scene we will see more research done in this area. We'll probably have a wider selection of loads like we now have in lead.

One problem that will have to be addressed is getting steel shot loads to open as quickly at close range as lead loads. Despite the fact that the loads I used on the Skeet range did a great job, I found that they exhibited the same tight patterning and strong center density that characterizes most steel loads. I

Trap shooters will find that #7 steel shot starts to run out of steam as you move back up the Handicap line. Remington offers a #6½ shot load that handles Handicap targets better. More work will no doubt have to be done in the area of long-range steel shot target loads.

feel that some enterprising individual will be able to develop a wad (maybe a spreader wad, like we now use with lead) that will give the quick and wide patterns needed on some Sporting Clays ranges. I'm sure if the demand is there, the need will be met by someone. In any case, I'm not worried about finding effective steel shot clay target loads in 12- and 20-gauge. Given the option of utilizing the 3-inch hull in both gauges (which would give the extra room required for the same weight of less-dense shot), I see no reason why we won't be able to use steel effectively in these two gauges for all target games.

I'm certain some sharp-eyed reader will be more than willing to point out that these loads of #7 and #6 shot are not "legal" shells for many games at the moment, and he would be quite right. But the only thing it takes to make them legal is a stroke of the Rules Committee's pen. And when lead goes the way of the passenger pigeon, all of their previously legal loads will then become illegal. They'll have to do something and my bet is these loads will suddenly become legal.

When it comes to the 28 and 410, however, I do have my doubts about the effectiveness of steel. These hulls lack capacity, and that limits the volume of steel shot that can fit into them. I suspect that a reasonably effective 28-gauge Skeet load

could be assembled with #8 shot—that size does seem to give about the same performance as lead #9—but the 410 could prove a problem.

At present, there is excellent load data available for steel shot in the 12-gauge hull, and any shooter intending to load his own steel shells will absolutely require it. You can't load safe steel shells with components designed for lead shot. Steel shot requires special wads and powders. One excellent source of both loading data and components is Steel Reloading Components Inc. Dave Fackler, at Ballistic Products Inc., is also working on a variety of steel shot loads. At present, you will find an adequate amount of data on the 12-gauge, not much on the 20, and virtually nothing on the 28 and 410. Of course, there is really no need for any now because lead is still legal, and there is no real advantage in trying to push steel through the 20, 28 and 410 until you have to.

There is one potential problem that could arise with steel shot, and I do not know if any research is being done in the area at the moment. It concerns the use of steel shot loads in the aluminum sub-gauge tubes commonly used by Skeet shooters. I know that steel shot in target sizes will not damage modern gun barrels and chokes, but aluminum is not steel.

Should the problem of steel shot in the 28-gauge, 410 and

aluminum tubes develop, one could turn to our second non-toxic alternative: Bismuth.

The Case for Bismuth

Bismuth is an elemental metal that lies between lead and polonium on the Periodic Table of the Elements. In its pure form, it is a crystalline substance that is quite brittle. In fact, it is much like antimony. It is a non-toxic substance that has already proven itself: Bismuth is a key ingredient in Pepto-Bismol and has long enjoyed FDA approval for human consumption.

Although bismuth is not currently approved for use on waterfowl, that fact is more the result of politics and bureaucratic red tape than common sense. It is currently approved for that use in Canada, England, Australia and elsewhere, but our bureaucrats don't seem to get it yet. There is some hope it may be approved in time for the 1994/1995 waterfowl season, and surely within the following year.

In its pure state, Bismuth is 86 percent as dense as lead. That's a considerable improvement over steel's paltry 67 percent. When alloyed with tin, however (an important step in producing a shotgun pellet from this material), bismuth improves to about 91 percent the density of lead.

In terms of hardness, the stuff measures about 18 on the Brinnell hardness scale. By comparison, soft lead shot measures about 10, pure copper around 40, and steel is too hard to measure on that scale. The actual hardness of Bismuth is about that of straight wheelweight alloy, a substance long favored by metallic cartridge shooters who cast their own bullets.

Bismuth is as hard as the very best grade of copper-plated lead shot and much softer than steel. That's a big plus. In fact, it makes Bismuth virtually the ballistic twin of premium-grade lead target shot.

I had the opportunity to pattern some of the first commercially available hunting loads using Bismuth shot. They performed as well as the best premium copper-plated, buffered, lead hunting loads available. The material is now being loaded into target ammunition, and their performance will equal that of lead target loads.

In terms of ballistic performance, Bismuth is identical to lead except for being 10 percent less dense. That means that a 1-ounce charge of Bismuth will contain about 10 percent more pellets than the same weight in lead. While steel shot requires heavier wads and slower-burning powders to make an effective shell, Bismuth can simply be substituted on a per volume basis in any lead shot target load recipe currently in use. The shot bushing that currently throws a 1^1/$_8$-ounce charge of lead will throw the same volume of Bismuth. The shot charge will weigh about 1^1/$_{16}$ ounces, but the pellet count will be comparable. The lighter shot weight gives a bit less pressure and recoil, and sometimes a slight increase in velocity.

For those who might seriously want to explore the reloading possibilities of Bismuth, the best loads will be produced if one abandons the fast-burning powders like Red Dot, 700-X, etc., and shifts to slightly slower-burning propellants. Green Dot and IMR PB generally give better results. Precise loading data on Bismuth was not available as of February, 1994, but is

Bismuth offers lead-like performance in a non-toxic package, but not many shooters will be able to afford it on a regular basis. The stuff ain't cheap!

expected by the fall of the year. Still, you can crank out some very effective non-toxic loads by keeping the above in mind.

Bismuth Negatives

Unfortunately, what often sounds too good to be true sometimes is. Although Bismuth is an excellent ballistic substitute for lead, it has some warts.

The first of these is a pellet-fracturing problem. Bismuth is a brittle substance, although alloying it with tin helps. Still, it is not a total cure. Bismuth pellets in sizes larger than #5 do exhibit a tendency to go to pieces on occasion. This may be a problem for waterfowl hunters (especially goose hunters) who might see this new material as a return to the glory days of lead when a stout load of #1s would cleanly tumble a Canada. Bismuth may not be the panacea they seek. That's one reason why slower-burning powders are recommended—a hard initial jolt can cause an increase in fracturing. This will not be a significant factor for target shooters, however, since they are unlikely to use pellets larger than #7^1/$_2$ or assemble loads with the belt of a 3-inch magnum. No, target shooters will have a different problem—affording the stuff!

High Cost

Bismuth is not cheap. Nor is it widely available. It is not a metal that is mined in the sense that others are. It is essentially a by-product of separate mining operations and, as such, the world's known supply is not overly large. Complicating that is the fact that much of that known supply is in Third World countries that could only charitably be described as "politically unstable." Adding to that is the fact that the Bismuth Cartridge Company has sole rights to distribution of Bismuth shot in the United States.

Contemporary 12- and 20-gauge steel shot loads will easily handle the close range targets found in Sporting Clays and Skeet. The picture isn't as bright for the 28-gauge and 410.

Skeet shooters are likely to be most affected by the shift to non-toxic shot since the 410 and 28-gauge are an important part of their game. Steel won't cut it in these gauges at the present level of technology.

When you have a material that is expensive to start with, not widely abundant, and is marketed through a company that has a monopoly on its sales and distribution...well, Economics 101 should indicate that the price is not likely to go down.

As of February, 1994, a case of Bismuth 410 shells had a basic wholesale price of $176.83. Add a bit of shipping and that's about twice what a case of lead 410 target loads will set you back. But that's not the worst part. A case of Bismuth target loads consists of only ten boxes, not the twenty boxes we're used to in a case of shells.

That means a single twenty-five round box of 410 Bismuth shells has a wholesale price of $17.63.

If you buy a box of lead factory 410s at a best case price of around $5 per box, and sell the hulls for 10¢ each, you shoot that box of shells for about $2.50. With Bismuth, it goes to about $15!

Loading your own isn't going to save much. At current prices, a 25-pound bag of lead shot is around $12. That works out to around $50 for 100 pounds of good lead shot. Top quality steel shot is running about $13 per 10-pound bottle, which means a 100-pound price of about $130. That's a little more than 2.5 times the cost of lead. A 12-pound bottle of bismuth will set you back about $58, so you wind up paying about $470 for 100 pounds of bismuth shot! That's 3.6 times the cost of steel shot.

I don't care how good the stuff shoots, this is one clay target shooter who is going to take a long, hard look at every possibility steel shot holds! Since I didn't come from a rich family, the only possibility I have of shooting a steady diet of Bismuth shot is to marry into money!

Steel's Future

Steel is a material that is readily available, lends itself well to large-scale manufacturing operations, and is in a competitive market. Back to Economics 101. We can expect the price of steel shot to drop somewhat as demand increases and economy of scale begins to exert itself. While steel shot is never likely to reach the current low price of lead, I can afford to shoot a helluva lot more steel than I can Bismuth.

To my way of thinking, basic economics is going to make steel shot the most significant material in the non-toxic future. Its performance from the 12- and 20-gauges is good enough that it is doubtful if any appreciable increase would be gained from switching to Bismuth. The jury is still out on the 28-gauge, and the prognosis is dim for the 410. It is possible that Bismuth may well be the way one has to go with these smaller bores. If there is a plus side to that, it's that neither of these consume the amounts of shot that the larger gauges do. If these gauges remain in the competitive arena (and there is no guarantee that they will if shooters have to fork over a minimum of $15 for ammo every time they bust twenty-five Skeet targets!), it is quite possible that their role will be reserved for competition only, which would cut down on the quantity of these shells expended, and thus make them somewhat more affordable. While some writers are waxing eloquent over the ballistic possibilities of Bismuth, I think that hard economic realities will result in its assuming a "niche" role—you shoot it when you can't get steel to do the same job as well!

No, shifting to non-toxic shot won't be a completely painless transition. We can expect to pay more for our shells whether we opt for steel or Bismuth. Other than that, about the only practical effects will be to give shotgun writers something new to write about, and shooters something new to complain about.

The targets will keep breaking, just like they always have.

Steel shot can be loaded on conventional loading equipment with nothing more than different bushings. Bismuth can be substituted on a volume-for-volume basis with no changes in equipment.

What It Takes To Win

The U.S. Shooting Team (now called USA Shooting) has been extremely successful in recent years under the coaching of Lloyd Woodhouse. In these pages, Author asks tough questions and gets good answers.(Photo courtesy USA Shooting.)

When playing the game is not enough and winning becomes the goal, good coaching combined with lots of practice and the proper mental attitude will take you there.

THERE IS A significant difference between being a good shooter and being one who can win in competition. Sometimes that difference has little to do with the relative shooting skills possessed by the shooters.

If you have been around shooting competition—rifle, pistol or shotgun—you have no doubt seen a shooter who has talent and can shoot good scores. Unfortunately, when the "Big Day" comes, that shooter is never able to put it all together well enough to win. By the same token, there are some shooters who always seem to be right up there among the leaders and are a threat to win any meet they enter. Yet, in informal practice, their shooting abilities seem no greater than those of other skilled shooters.

What do they have that the other shooters don't? And more importantly, what are they doing differently?

In an attempt to answer those questions, I was fortunate enough to be able to sit down for a lengthy conversation with Lloyd Woodhouse, the shotgun coach of our United States Shooting Team.

Woodhouse, who earned a solid reputation as a competitive shooter himself, is no stranger to coaching shotgunners. Assuming the role of Head Coach for the U.S. Air Force Skeet team in 1976, he held that position until 1985, when he joined the staff of the USST. During his tenure with the USST he has coached two Olympic teams, two Pan American teams, and six world championship teams. At the 1993 World Shotgun Championships his shooters won eleven medals, three individual world titles, and three Olympic country quota slots for the United States. Under Coach Woodhouse's direction, American shotgunners have earned the reputation as being among the best in the world.

Here's what the coach has to say about building winners.

Christian: *You have a lot more shooters competing for slots on the shotgun team than you have positions open. What do you look for in a shooter when you make the decision as to which shooters to accept?*

Woodhouse: That is a question I am asked frequently. I look for self-contained individual motivation, that burning

You cannot watch yourself perform. Many top coaches and shooters are adamant that shooters should not practice alone, because that might result in the shooter's developing some bad habits and then reinforcing them. That's how slumps get started. Lisa Sever practices under the watchful eye of Chris Pearce, himself a championship level International Skeet and trap shooter.

deep-down gut desire to achieve. That would be the most important thing I could find in an athlete—shooters are athletes—and it is sometimes a difficult thing to put your finger on. It is, at least to me, vitally important. The other things I look for are good hand/eye coordination, good biomechanics, and good motor skills. When you think about it, any athlete that is really good has all of that. Take Michael Jordan, for example. This guy is a great basketball player, an excellent golfer, and now he is becoming a solid professional baseball player. He has the desire and the physical skills to make it work.

Most of winning is self-drive. It's in the college student whom you don't have to tell to go to the library and study. It's in the student who does the research ahead of time and is prepared—self-motivation. A good competitive shooter is self-motivated.

Now, you do have to guide them and kick them in the butt every now and then, but you don't have to force them out there onto the practice range. They want to be there and they know how important that is.

I really don't think you can teach motivation. It's either there or it's not. It's something that has to come from within. The biggest heartbreak I have had as a coach is to see a young

kid who is tremendously talented, yet doesn't have motivation.

Christian: *You're talking about motivation on the practice field, where the shooter is preparing for a match. What do you look for to see if that inner drive is carrying over into the actual competition itself?*

Woodhouse: One thing to watch for is when the shooter winds up in what you might call an "easy match." If I have one of my top shooters go out and shoot against an average shooter, I expect him to win by fifteen or twenty targets. If they shoot against those who are not elite athletes and beat them by only one or two targets, I think that's just terrible! That athlete has let his standards relax. He shot only well enough to win. That's not right. You should perform to your best level every time you go out and not let your performance drop to the level of the shooters around you. When you get down to the end of a tight match and there are only ten targets left, you want to make that other shooter do his best to take them away from you. You don't want to give him any of them. Make him win, if he can, and don't beat yourself. If you let yourself get into the habit of shooting down to the level of the competition, you may suddenly find it difficult to shoot up to the competition when you have to.

Christian: *Regardless of how motivated a shooter is, there are still steps that must be taken to prepare for a match. One that I think is very important is the pre-match practice, basically the practice schedule that shooter adopts as his, or her, match preparation. I've seen some shooters that seem to go overboard on that. Is it possible to over-practice for a match? And how badly does that detract from a shooter's performance?*

Woodhouse: I think a lot of that depends on the shooter, on his or her individual mindset, and on what type of training regime they are following. There are some shooters—I have one now—who absolutely thrive, and shoot well, on a heavy pre-match practice schedule. That shooter is used to it. It's a part of the shooter's natural rhythm. You don't really want to break a shooter's rhythm before a match; let them do what they have done in training. But this is one of the few shooters I have seen who can benefit from a heavy pre-match practice schedule. Most can't.

I have a lot of shooters who try to cram in as much practice before a major match as they can, and all they are really doing is trying to compensate for the fact that they have not properly prepared earlier.

I think the people who win in June do so because their train- ing program in March and April prepared them to win. Good training takes time. The best preparation takes place months before the match, and you can't make up for it by shooting a lot of targets just before a match.

I have some people who are winners and will shoot just one round of pre-match practice. If things are going right for them, they'll stop and put their guns away. On the other hand, I have people who will get out on the practice field, shoot a good round, and then want to shoot another one, and they do. Then they'll shoot another one. Then they'll start to get a little tired, or just visually weary, and they won't shoot quite as well, so they want to shoot another round because the last one wasn't quite so good. Then the next round is worse and they just start digging themselves deeper and deeper into poor shooting. As a coach, I can see exactly what is happening, but it can be very hard to tell the shooter to stop.

Christian: *That surprises me. I would have thought you, as the coach, would be pretty much omnipotent in that area.*

Woodhouse: You have to be real careful as a coach not to damage a shooter's confidence. That is an essential ingredient of a winner. Telling a shooter that he is performing poorly, and you want him to stop, can do that. What I normally do is ask them if maybe they think they should just back off for a little

Any shooter can suffer a lapse in concentration and performance. The experienced ones, like Lisa Sever, know when it is time to mentally regroup, think about the basics, and not reinforce bad habits. When you reach the upper levels of shooting, winning is mostly mental.

Veteran coaches agree that you can't clone a shooter. Each shooter must find the exact form, within the proven basics, that produces best for him. USAMU Sgt. Shawn Dulohery shows excellent form on the Bunker trap range, and if the piles of spent hulls are any indication, he has spent plenty of time perfecting it! (U.S. Army photo by Joseph J. Johnson)

while, sort of a "save some of those great shots for the match" type of thing. I certainly don't want to tell the shooter that all he is doing is burning himself out, even though that is exactly what he is doing.

A lot of times, shooters perceive that they can build their confidence by shooting a lot of practice before a match. To my mind, that's not true. You don't build confidence by shooting at targets, you build confidence by hitting them. If you shoot yourself out and start getting tired, sloppy, and start missing targets, your confidence is going to suffer because you cannot build positive mental images from negative experiences.

The best shooters I have seen and have been around are those who, once they shoot just enough pre-match practice to get comfortable with the range and the background, don't need to shoot a lot of practice. Because they did that months before.

I'll give you a good example of that. I have a young shooter, Lance Bade, who won a silver medal in trap in the May, 1994, meet in Beijing, China. He worked very hard on his game and was shooting well. He was scheduled to shoot the Doubles trap event very shortly after that, but because he had won a medal he had to go in for the mandatory drug test. He got delayed in there and was in danger of missing his only chance to shoot a practice round of Doubles trap before the actual event. I scurried around and eventually got him a late slot on the practice field. It was rather hectic, and it probably would have bothered a lot of shooters. Not Bade, however. He told me he didn't feel he needed the practice round. He knew he was shooting well, and he was quite confident. So he shot the Doubles trap event cold—without shooting his allotted practice round—and wound up in a hard run for the gold medal. He won the silver medal, but he was right up there at the top of the pack! That's the kind of confident, self-assured shooter who will be a winner.

Christian: *Even the best shooter will get into an occasional shooting slump where nothing seems to go right and he can't figure out why. How do you deal with that with your shooters?*

Woodhouse: The whole question of shooting slumps, and how to deal with them, is a difficult one. As a general rule, it means that you are doing something different with your shooting form, and you have now done it often enough that you are reinforcing the bad habit every time you do it.

This is where a good coach, one who knows the shooter, can help. The coach can often spot the subtle changes in form that detract from a shooter's performance before they begin to become ingrained. We know for a fact that you can't watch yourself perform. Some shooters think they can, but they can't.

Good shooters generally get in a slump because they train or shoot by themselves.

Getting a shooter out of a slump is dependent on the communication between the shooter and the coach. That's the key, and sometimes it can be tough translating what the shooter is telling you. There is a need to establish the verbiage that will allow the communication of thoughts and concepts between

Shooters do not build confidence by shooting at targets—they build it by hitting them. That requires the shooter to develop proper form and reinforce it through quality practice. Here, Bob Lee works on his form for outgoing tower shots at Turkey Run Sporting Clays range in Alachua, Florida, one of the prettier Sporting courses in the state.

the shooter and the coach. That is critical in developing a world class shooter.

Christian: *A lot of competitive shotgunners hate high wind because it changes the targets and drops their scores. You'll probably hear more complaining about that than any other environmental factor. How do you deal with that?*

Woodhouse: We like to train in high winds sometimes. And in cold weather, hot weather, rain—you name it. We accept whatever the environment offers and go right out and

I have a young shooter named Connie Shiller who won a gold medal and set a new women's world record at an April, 1993, meet in Mexico City. That's normally a breezy time. She didn't really win that medal in Mexico, though. She won it in January and February in Colorado when she and I were out on the field in the cold, snow and freezing rain. She learned the mental discipline of focusing on the targets and putting the physical discomfort she was feeling out of her mind long enough to get the job done. That's what she was

Concentration and individual motivation are key ingredients in a winner and that is what any coach looks for. PFC Danny White of the U.S. Army Marksmanship Unit exemplifies the qualities that make winning shooters. (U.S. Army photo by Joseph J. Johnson)

work in it. That is the way you gain confidence to deal with those conditions when you are confronted by them during a match.

I don't advise my shooters to change anything about their shooting style under adverse weather conditions. You stay with what brought you here and take one target at a time. Practicing under adverse conditions—something many shooters don't like to do—is what will give you the confidence to win under those conditions.

there to do, and I told her I didn't want to hear any bellyaching about cold hands, cold nose, cold wind—nothing. Just total focus. We'd shoot a half-dozen targets and then go back inside to thaw out. Then we'd do it again. And again. And again. We did that for two months.

She had already accepted the fact that this training regime was what would put her into the winner's circle. It did, and she embraced it. That's the kind of motivation it takes to win.

chapter thirty-two

Accessories You'll Find Useful

AT ITS SIMPLEST, clay target shooting requires nothing more than a gun and shells; yet, you won't find a single experienced shooter on the line with such minimal gear. Invariably, they will have a number of accessory items with them and probably a few more in the car. Here's a look at some items that improve both safety and performance.

Ear Protection

Continued exposure to gunfire will cause hearing loss. Even brief exposure can make a shooter jumpy and can cause that shooter to flinch every time he pulls the trigger. Most people accept the fact that hearing protection is advisable, but many new shooters don't realize that good hearing protection will improve their scores.

Hearing protection is available in a variety of styles and levels of effectiveness. Every clay target range I have ever been on has invariably offered disposable foam ear plugs for sale. These are inexpensive and are simply rolled into a little tube with the fingers and inserted into the ear canal, where they expand. In terms of hearing protection, they are better than nothing, but they are not very durable, nor are they as effective as other types.

Another option are muff-type ear protectors. These are made by a number of companies and offer a very good level of hearing protection. The drawback to them is that many shooters cannot use them while they shoot because they interfere with the proper mounting of the gun. This is something shooters should check before they consider purchasing a set. For shooters who are extremely sensitive to gunfire, combining a set of foam ear plugs with the external muffs will provide a very high level of noise reduction.

One of the best bets, at least in this writer's opinion, are custom-made moulded ear plugs. These are made by actually making a mould of the shooter's ear and casting a plug from one of the silicon compounds, which thus produces a very precise fit. I had mine made at an NRA show a number of years ago. If I recall correctly, they set me back about $25. These are without doubt the most comfortable and effective set of ear

Ear protection is vital to a shooter for health and for top shooting performance. Author favors the custom moulded ear plugs (center), but often wears his Bilsom Compac electronic muffs when instructing, since they allow normal conversation while attenuating high sound levels. Inexpensive foam ear inserts are better than nothing, and readily available at most ranges.

plugs I have ever used, and they will likely last forever. The degree of noise reduction is such that I cannot hear normal conversation when wearing them.

Another option is any of the electronic ear plugs now on the market. These come in off-the-rack slip-in models or custom-fit versions that require a mould of the shooter's ear. In either case, they tend to amplify low-level sounds, and they have an automatic shut-off circuit that cuts out any noise level above 85 to 95 decibels.

Wearing these is quite interesting and sometimes a bit disconcerting. You can hear conversation very well—including what people behind you are saying about you! You can hear most, but not all, clay target traps when they release. I find this an advantage in International Skeet and Sporting Clays events where there is a variable delay of up to 3 seconds between the time the shooter calls for the target and the time it is released. In this situation, I use both vision and hearing to help me pick up the target.

Not all shooters agree with that. I have spoken with a number of shooters who have been classically trained in International competition who do not want to hear the traps, because there are some models of trap that are so quiet they can't be heard. A shooter who gets used to listening for the trap will be in trouble when he faces these quiet traps because his timing will be off.

Hearing protection is an individual choice that largely depends on the style and training of the shooter. It's a lot like brussels sprouts. Some love 'em and some hate 'em.

With both sides of that argument presented, let me relate my personal experiences with electronically activated hearing protection.

As a competitive pistol shooter and former instructor, I have a considerable amount of experience with electronic ear muffs. The Bilsom Compacs I use allow me to hear all range commands, or what students are muttering under their breath about my heavy-handed instructional tactics, but have a cut-off circuit that shuts out any sound levels high enough to be harmful to my hearing. They are very comfortable and quite effective. I have learned from conversations with Lloyd Woodhouse, Coach of the U.S. Olympic shotgun team, that he uses similar muffs on the range when instructing shooters. Unfortunately, I can't use them with a long gun because they interfere with the mounting of the gun.

Understanding the effectiveness of electronic hearing protection, I began looking around for some of the current "in the

ear" models that I could use in clay target games. My search lead me to Starkey Labs.

Starkey Labs is quite likely the leader in this new field. They make three distinctly different models of in-ear protection. The top of the line is a custom-moulded plug, like the silicon plugs I already owned, but with electronic circuitry incorporated. These require an ear mould be made, which involves stuffing your ear with wet silicon, laying on your side until it hardens, removing the plug, and sending it to them. Sounds worse than it is.

Once Starkey gets the moulds, they create a custom-fitted ear plug and add the electronic circuits to it. You can dial in amplification or turn the unit off and use them like regular plugs, which gives a protection level equivalent to my silicon moulded plugs.

Another model they offer is a behind-the-ear unit. In this one, the electronic circuitry is contained in a lightweight plastic unit that rides behind the ear, like some hearing aids, with a plastic tube connecting it to a foam plug fitting inside the ear. I have a set of these and find them to be just a touch awkward, although many people find them quite comfortable and capable.

The set I use most is the compact in-the-ear unit that has a very small electronic package with a foam insert threaded onto it. The unit comes with three sets of foam inserts, and they have lasted me a long time. Extra inserts are available very inexpensively, should you wear yours out.

The best way I can describe this particular unit is as a hearing aid with extreme noise protection.

Having had experience with electronic hearing protection, I knew they would amplify low-level sounds while cutting off all sound levels above 95 decibels, which is well below the level that causes pain or contributes to hearing loss. What I

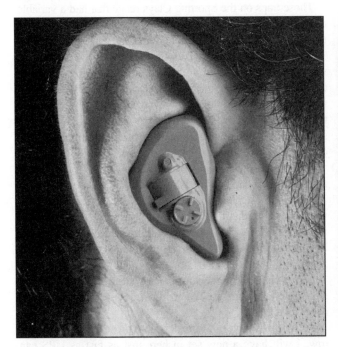

Custom-moulded electronic ear plugs from Starkey Labs provide excellent ear protection while amplifying low level sounds. Author favors them for games with a variable time delay on the target release.

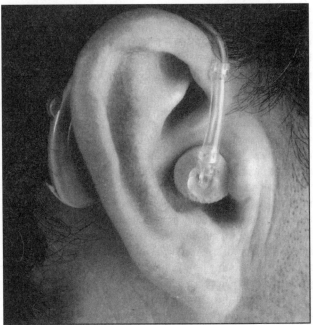

This behind-the-ear electronic plug from Starkey Labs is one of the more inexpensive ways to experience electronic hearing protection.

Recreational Hearing Health Care
The Human Ear

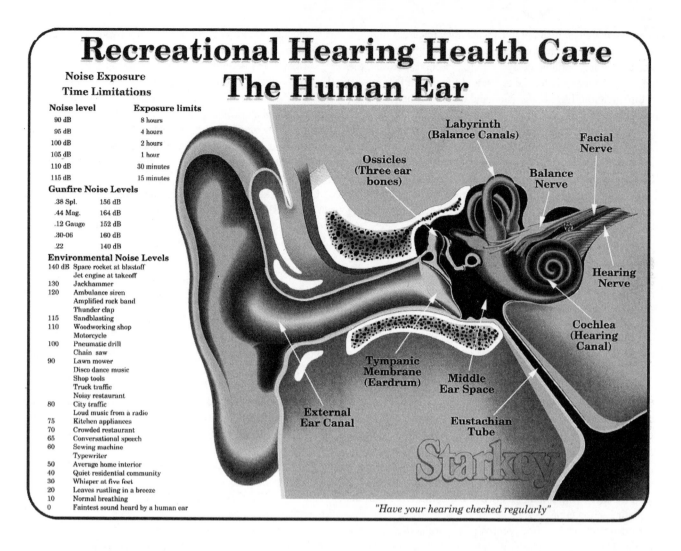

Noise Exposure Time Limitations

Noise level	Exposure limits
90 dB	8 hours
95 dB	4 hours
100 dB	2 hours
105 dB	1 hour
110 dB	30 minutes
115 dB	15 minutes

Gunfire Noise Levels

.38 Spl.	156 dB
.44 Mag.	164 dB
.12 Gauge	152 dB
.30-06	160 dB
.22	140 dB

Environmental Noise Levels

140 dB	Space rocket at blastoff
	Jet engine at takeoff
130	Jackhammer
120	Ambulance siren
	Amplified rock band
	Thunder clap
115	Sandblasting
110	Woodworking shop
	Motorcycle
100	Pneumatic drill
	Chain saw
90	Lawn mower
	Disco dance music
	Shop tools
	Truck traffic
	Noisy restaurant
80	City traffic
	Loud music from a radio
75	Kitchen appliances
70	Crowded restaurant
65	Conversational speech
60	Sewing machine
	Typewriter
50	Average home interior
40	Quiet residential community
30	Whisper at five feet
20	Leaves rustling in a breeze
10	Normal breathing
0	Faintest sound heard by a human ear

"Have your hearing checked regularly"

---

wasn't quite prepared for was the degree to which low-level sounds were amplified.

The first thing I did when I got the plugs was to grab the nosiest gun I had, a 2½-inch Ruger 357 Magnum, shove the hottest, noisiest loads in it that I had on hand, and head out to my backyard pond. I figured, if that gun didn't blow my ears off, then the plugs worked!

Out at the pond, I was amazed at what they allowed me to hear. The crackling of the cellophane on a pack of cigarettes was almost deafening. The click of the cylinder closing on the revolver was like somebody standing directly behind me slapping two pieces of metal pipe together!

Yet when I touched off the first round from the short barrel, my ears just smiled. The awesome blast of that little gun was nothing more than a muffled pop. Incredible!

Suffice it to say, all low-level sounds were amplified considerably, and all ear-damaging noise was muted to almost nothing. The panting of my dogs 30 feet behind me was more pronounced than the blast of the gun.

When I tried the ear plugs on a clay target range, it was a most interesting experience. I could easily hear every trap as it released. Even on a 5-Stand range that threw unknown targets, I could tell which trap released, immediately get onto the bird, and kick some serious clay target butt!

Those traps on the Sporting Clays range that had a variable delay were no problem. After I got used to the incredible level to which my hearing had been elevated, the game got easier.

There may be some makes of traps that you cannot hear with the naked ear, but with the gain in low-level hearing afforded me by the new ear plugs, I have yet to find one. That includes Beomats, LaPortes and every other popular electronic trap. The manual traps used on many Sporting Clays ranges sound like a Volkswagen falling off a bridge at midnight! You can hear them very well.

When I left the range after a day's shooting, my ears were fine. The plugs had provided the protection needed.

Do I use these plugs for all games? No. They are not needed with any game that throws a target upon command, and that includes all ATA trap, International trap, and American Skeet. For those games, I still rely on my old set of fitted silicon plugs.

I have come to the conclusion that those shooters who say electronic ear plugs are not worthwhile are those who have never tried them.

As for this shooter, if I break or lose those ear plugs tomorrow, I will have a new set in here just as fast as UPS can deliver them. Does that sum up my feelings on the Starkey Lab ear plugs?

Shooting Glasses

Any shooter or spectator who steps onto a Skeet, International Skeet, or a Sporting Clays range without some form of eye protection is foolish, period. No argument! A significant percentage of the targets shot in these games are moving toward the shooter. When they are broken, the pieces can keep on coming. One small piece of broken clay target traveling at 40 mph can cost you an eye!

In the trap games, the need for eye protection is not as great, since all targets are going away from the shooter. But the need is still there for eye protection. Ricocheting pellets, powder gases, unburned powder grains... all of these can be hazardous to your vision. Shooting glasses should be considered mandatory, and on many ranges they are.

Shooting Glasses can also aid your shooting by providing a crisper look at the bird through the use of colored lenses. Yellow is considered to be one of the best bets for cloudy or hazy days, since it improves the contrast between sky and target. Vermillion lenses were specifically developed for trap and Skeet shooters who usually shoot at orange-colored targets. They find this color makes them stand out better. Some Sporting Clays shooters like a moderate green shade, which often makes targets stand out better against a green vegetation background. Smoke or gray lenses are a good choice for bright sunlight and will result in less visual fatigue under those conditions.

A number of companies make shooting glasses with interchangeable lenses and offer a variety of colored inserts. It is worth a shooter's time to experiment with them. Backgrounds

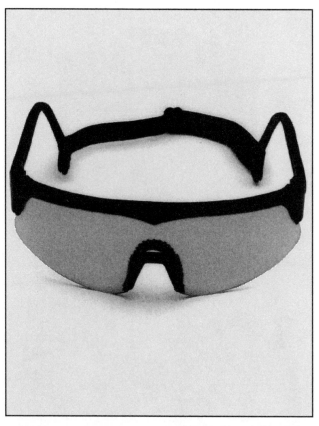

Inexpensive shooting glasses are readily available for those who do not require prescription lenses and should be worn anytime one is on a clay target range.

Different colored lenses can offer shooters a different and sometimes better view of the target. These Bushnell shooting glasses can be had in different lens tints, and ground to prescription.

A shooting vest is an asset for any clay target gunner and they are available in a number of types and styles. Shooters should pay attention to the construction of the vest, since some can be very uncomfortable in hot, humid weather. This Remington vest has a mostly mesh construction and is a good choice for hot weather shooting.

This El Gavilan shooting shirt is a comfortable and inexpensive alternative to a vest in hot weather.

at different clay target ranges vary, which change the target appearance. Some expert shooters will have slightly different tints in their lenses for just that reason. If you can't see the bird well, you'll have a tough time hitting it.

For prescription eyeglass wearers, it's best to have the lenses hardened or made of shatterproof material. A separate set of prescription shooting glasses is cheap insurance against the loss or injury of an eye.

An alternative is a set of good clip-on lenses. They're available in a number of colors and usually quite comfortable to wear.

Shooting Vests and Shirts

A good shooting vest is more than just a place to carry shells. It is actually a part of the shooting system that allows the shooter to achieve a consistent gun mount and gun placement into the shoulder pocket. A vest is not necessary to shoot, but I find my scores at low gun games are better when I wear my Bec-Mar vest with the full International-style gun pad than when I wear a plain hunting vest or just a light shirt. That full pad provides a slick, consistent surface for gun

mounting that gets the gun where it belongs, even if I am not in top form.

When selecting a vest, consider the shotgun games you shoot. Vests can be had with a small gun pad that is often favored by those who shoot trap and Skeet (where the gun is mounted before the bird is called for) or with a full front pad that is virtually mandatory in low gun games, because the gun butt can catch on an abbreviated pad. Many shooters today opt for the International-style pad. It works quite well at games where the gun is pre-mounted, as well as at low gun games.

If you are a Sporting Clays shooter, you may want to consider a vest with double divided shell pockets. This will allow you to keep track of up to four different loads quite easily. It is not uncommon to carry several different loads onto the shooting stand. Trap and Skeet shooters need just one big pocket for the shells and one for the fired hulls.

The construction of the vest is important. In the humid Southeast where I shoot, you will not see a full front- and back-cloth vest. They are too hot. They quickly become sweat-soaked and wind up about 10 pounds heavier than

This inexpensive Eagle Industries shooters bag is a handy place to store and tote ammo, and the numerous accessories scattergunners require.

when they started. That will exhaust you quickly. Southern shooters favor vests that are full mesh, except, of course, for the gun pad and pockets. Another option is a mesh in back and cloth face in front.

Shooters in more northerly climes often prefer a full vest simply for the warmth, because they'll probably be competing well into chilly weather.

There are many different styles of vests on the market today, and it is worth looking at a number of them before making a decision.

Sometimes it is just too hot for even the lightest vest, and on those days I wear an El Gavilan shooting shirt. This is a smartly styled, short sleeve, 100-percent cotton shirt with a very light, partial International-style gun pad. The shirt has a large upper pocket and a choke tube pocket below that. I have no use for choke tube pockets because I can't see any point in carrying all that weight, but this one allows me to slip in a couple of specialty loads for tough Sporting Clays stands and still has enough room for my ear plugs. It's a well-thought-out and very comfortable shirt. They are becoming quite popular with Sporting Clays shooters and are much less expensive than a quality vest.

With the shooting shirt, there are no shell pockets, so ammo is toted in a simple shell pouch. These are inexpensive ($15 or

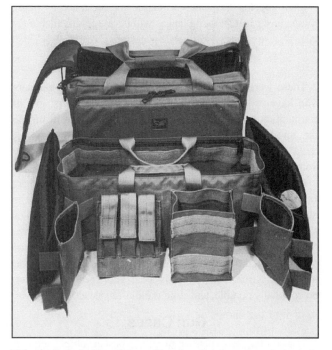

This Eagle Industries Deluxe Shooting Bag has enough pockets and places to tote just about anything a shooter might require on the range or for a round of Sporting Clays.

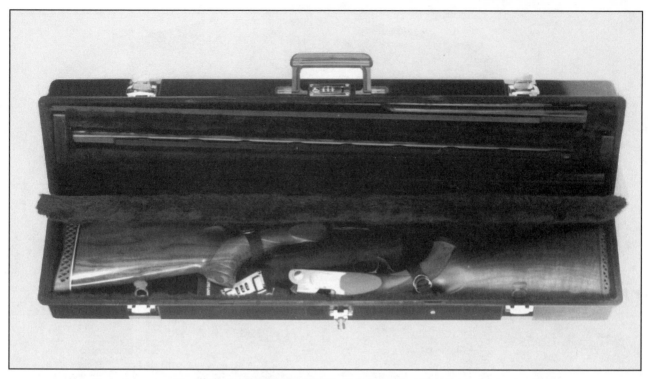

Top-quality gun cases like this John Hall design from Hastings are the best way to transport firearms via common carrier. Less expensive models will do a fine job of protecting your guns when you just toss 'em in a pickup truck and head for the range.

less) and have ample room to tote a hundred shells. The pouch belts on and, combined with the El Gavilan shirt, provides a lightweight and very comfortable alternative to a vest. That's generally what I wear during the most humid summer months here in Florida.

Shell pouches are widely available and are made by many companies. Most shooting ranges will have a few available for sale. They are a very worthwhile accessory.

Shooting Bags

These were originally developed for action pistol shooters who have to tote a couple of handguns, spare parts, lots of ammunition and a bunch of other stuff a long way from the car. Sporting Clays shooters, who carry ammo, a bunch of choke tubes, spare glasses and a lot of other stuff a long way from the car, embraced them quickly!

A good shooting bag should have enough separate pockets to handle choke tubes and lube, gun cloths, plenty of shells (with room for the empties) and whatever other gear a shooter will want to have along during a long round of Clays, and be sturdy enough to survive for years. There are a number of good ones on the market. I use one from Eagle Industries, who are probably the leaders in this area. Their gear has proven exceptionally durable, and mine is almost a decade old.

Gun Cases

Transporting an expensive firearm is best accomplished in a sturdy hard case. This will protect the gun from dings and dents, as well as from moisture. This is something that cannot

be accomplished with one of the soft, padded gun cases that I see all too many new shooters using. In fact, these cases cause more gun damage than they prevent because virtually all of them trap moisture, and that can quickly turn into rust.

A decent hard case for automobile travel is not expensive. Doskocil, Outers, Woodstream and others offer a number of inexpensive models in both full-length and take-down models that cost considerably less than a case of shells. I have a number of them.

If you intend to do much travel by airline, however, I can't really recommend them. Airline baggage handlers can break steel balls if they put their mind to it, and it takes a sturdy case to stand up to their tender ministrations. Briley and others offer some very heavy-duty aluminum take-down cases that will survive. And if you are shooting any type of quality shotgun, a good airline case is a smart investment regardless of your travel plans.

Choke Tube Equipment

Keeping a wide selection of choke tubes (some Sporting Clays shooters carry fifteen or more!) clean, protected and readily available requires more than simply using the little pill-bottle tubes they came in. I favor a five-slot plastic case that tucks into a side pocket of my shooting bag. Briley offers both a six-tube and three-tube case and they are very inexpensive.

If you change many choke tubes, you will soon come to dislike the skimpy tube wrenches supplied (seemingly as an afterthought) by the gunmakers. Accessory choke tube wrenches are available and very popular. B-Square makes one that I like, as do some others. One type I do not like are the battery-operated power wrenches. It is possible to get sloppy and cross-thread a tube, and that's bad news—and an expensive repair. I have also seen shooters unscrew the tubes so forcefully that they popped right up into the air and down onto the sandy ground, which required the shooter to thoroughly clean them before they could be used again.

I like to have with me a small can of Outers Metal Seal. This is very handy in a humid climate, and I usually apply a very light spray to the gun before I put it away at the end of a shooting season. "Finger rust" can develop just on the drive home. B-Square Choke Tube Lube is another small item always with me, since a tube without lube is going to get stuck at some point. A little 2-ounce bottle of Break-Free comes in handy, especially if you shoot a gas gun. A few quick squirts can often get a balky gun going again. One time, we had to use it just to free a rusted lock on one of the trap houses. Otherwise, we wouldn't have been able to shoot. Talk about a valuable accessory!

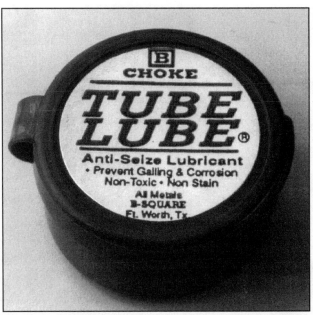

(Above) B-Square Choke Tube Lube is specially formulated to provide support for the tube threads and is a much better choice than light oils for lubricating interchangeable choke tubes.

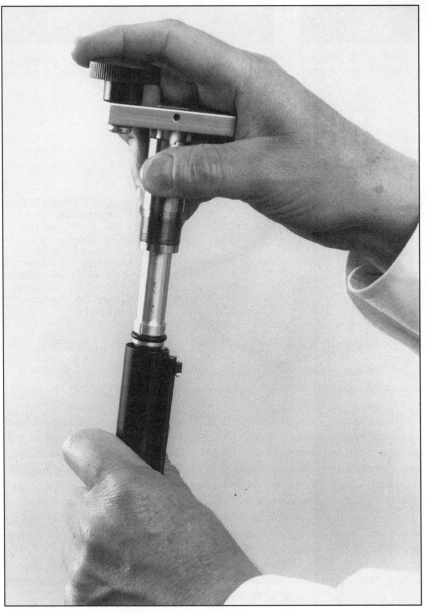

This B-Square choke tube tool makes short work of changing tubes. It's a major improvement over the skimpy little wrenches supplied by most gun makers.

For the truly jaded, several companies are now converting golf carts into gun carts! These are popular with those Sporting Clays shooters who can afford them!

Pull carts have been popular with clay target shooters for years, and they are an inexpensive way to tote all the gear required.

One of the best investments a clay target shooter can make is a portable trap like this Outers American Sporter. If a shooter has a place to set one up, it can duplicate virtually any shot you will see on a range.

One item a lot of Sporting Clays shooters will want to consider is a small portable target thrower. If you have the space to use it, it becomes a valuable training aid because it can be set to duplicate a greater variety of shots than can standard Skeet and trap machines. Some of the top Sporting Clays shooters in the country readily admit they use these to practice unusual and challenging shots.

Keeping fresh and alert during a long round of Sporting is important to a shooter's success, because a tired shooter seldom achieves his full potential. A number of companies now offer pull-carts that allow shooters to tote all their gear without having to pick it up. These are nothing more than modi-fied golf carts. I first encountered a homemade version on a Skeet range over ten years ago. For the really well-heeled, there are even electric golf carts modified for shooters, with their own little custom trailer that tows right behind the family sedan. I can attest that there is nothing so relaxing and conducive to good shooting as taking a trip around a Sporting Clays course via electric cart! It beats the heck out of lugging an 8-pound gun and another 10 to 15 pounds of shells on your back.

There are, of course, a number of other items that can aid your shooting. Remember, anything that improves your score is well worth having.

Section V
Appendices

Trap Rules

I
ORGANIZATION OF THE AMATEUR
TRAPSHOOTING ASSOCIATION

The following is an informative summary of the organization of the AMATEUR TRAP-SHOOTING ASSOCIATION OF AMERICA (A.T.A.). Complete details are contained in the Articles of Incorporation and the By-Laws of the Corporation which are contained in a separate booklet. The Official Trapshooting Rules of the A.T.A. govern the shooting of registered targets, the conduct of shooters and the duties of shoot management. The A.T.A. has the responsibility for the formulation, regulation and enforcement of these Rules. These Rules are contained in this booklet.

The A.T.A. reserves the right to make alterations in, or amendments to these Rules at any time, whenever it deems it to be in the best interest of the A.T.A.

A. PURPOSE OF THE A.T.A.

The purpose of the A.T.A. is to promote and govern the sport of amateur trapshooting throughout the world.

B. MEMBERSHIP

Membership is divided into two classes, both of which have full shooting rights and privileges. The membership year runs from October 1 through September 30.

LIFE MEMBERS. Only Life Members may hold office in the A.T.A. Life memberships are issued at a charge of **$300.00** but pay no annual dues.

ANNUAL MEMBERS. Annual Members pay annual dues of **$12.00**. They are entitled to vote for State Delegates and Alternate Delegates to the A.T.A. but may not hold those or other offices in the A.T.A.

C. STATE ORGANIZATIONS AND A.T.A. DELEGATE ELECTIONS

Shooters in the various states and provinces are organized into state and pro-vincial associations which control shooting in their own territories and conduct state and provincial championship tournaments. Such associations receive aid from the A.T.A. in the form of trophies and cash refunds. This aid is covered in a detailed set of written rules.

At each annual state or provincial championship tournament sanctioned by the A.T.A., there shall be held a business meeting on a date and time specified in the program for the tournament, which date must be one of the last three days of the tournament, and which time must be no earlier than 8:00 a.m. and no later than 9:00 p.m., except that if the meeting is held on the last day of the tournament, then it must commence no later than 12:00 noon, at which meeting all members of the A.T.A. residing in that State or Province, who are present in person at the meeting and are also members of their State Association, shall be entitled to vote for a State or Provincial Delegate and for not over two Alternate Delegates, all of whom shall be Life Members as a prerequisite to election. The criteria for election as a State Delegate or Alternate Delegate shall be actual physical residence within the boundaries of the state of representation, in receipt of life membership certificate from the A.T.A. and member in good standing of the State Association of the state of representation.

A.T.A. membership, Life and Annual, shall be evidenced by a membership card, the form of which shall be determined by the Board of Directors or Executive Committee. No membership shall be effective until after receipt of proper application at the General Office of the Corporation, approval of same, issuance of a membership card, and receipt of same by the member. A member shall not be qualified to cast a ballot for a State or Provincial Delegate or Alternate Delegates until properly qualified in accordance with this paragraph.

Selection of the State or Provincial Delegate, and the Alternate Dalegate(s) should be given the utmost consideration. As Delegates, in a properly called meeting, constitute the Board of Directors of the A.T.A. and as such have the responsibility of overseeing the operation of the Association, only those persons who are responsible dedicated individuals should be considered.

D. ZONES (DIVISIONS)

The zones are comprised of the following territories:

CENTRAL: Illinois, Indiana, Michigan, Iowa, Minnesota, Nebraska, North Dakota, Ohio, South Dakota, Wisconsin, and the provinces of Manitoba and Saskatchewan in Canada.

EASTERN: Connecticut, Delaware, Maine, Maryland, Massachusetts, New Hampshire, New York, Pennsylvania, Rhode Island, Vermont, New Jersey and the provinces of Ontario and Quebec, Canada, and the provinces in Canada lying east thereof.

SOUTHERN: Alabama, Florida, Georgia, Kentucky, Mississippi, North Carolina, South Carolina, Tennessee, Virginia, West Virginia, and the Canal Zone.

SOUTHWESTERN: Arkansas, Colorado, Kansas, Louisiana, Missouri, New Mexico, Oklahoma and Texas.

WESTERN: Alaska, Arizona, California, Hawaii, Idaho, Montana, Nevada, Oregon, Utah, Washington, Wyoming, and the provinces of Alberta and British Columbia.

E. EXECUTIVE COMMITTEE AND A.T.A. MANAGER

1. The Executive Committee consists of a representative from each of the five zones elected each year to the Executive Committee at the annual meeting of the Board of Directors. One member of the Executive Committee is designated President and the other four are designated Vice-Presidents.

2. The Board of Directors has delegated direction of the affairs of the A.T.A. between annual meetings to the Executive Committee.

3. The Executive Committee employs a manager to handle the daily affairs of the A.T.A. under its supervision. The A.T.A. Manager implements the policy set forth by the Board of Directors and/or the Executive Committee and follows their directions.

4. The main office and records of the A.T.A. are located at Vandalia, Ohio.

F. BOARD OF DIRECTORS

The Corporate Powers of the A.T.A. under Delaware law, are vested in the Board of Directors which consists of a Delegate from each State or Province. The Board of Directors meets annually during the Grand American World Trapshooting Tournament.

G. CONSTITUTION AND BYLAWS

The A.T.A. is organized under the Corporate Laws of the State of Delaware and has a Delaware charter and corporate By-laws formulated in accordance with Delaware laws.

H. JURISDICTION

The A.T.A. has jurisdiction over all affiliated associations regardless of location.

II
INFORMATION FOR NEW SHOOTERS
A. PROCEDURE FOR JOINING A.T.A.

1. ANNUAL MEMBERS

Application for Annual Membership may be made at any registered shoot by filling out an application and the payment of **$12.00** dues to the A.T.A. A temporary receipt will be given to the shooter, upon receipt of a proper application. The temporary receipt should be retained as evidence of payment and be used in lieu of a membership card until the membership card is received. The A.T.A. will issue an annual membership card in the usual course of business. This card will be marked to indicate the shooter's handicap yardage. Membership is effective upon receipt by the Member of the membership card.

Annual Members have all the shooting rights and privileges of Life Members, but may hold no office in the A.T.A. Annual Members are entitled to vote for the state delegate and alternates to represent their state, or province, at a meeting of the Board of Directors of the A.T.A. Annual Memberships are renewable by mail on or before October 1st. Send your complete name, address, including zip code, and **$12.00** to A.T.A., Vandalia, Ohio 45377, to renew, if you do not receive a renewal form from the A.T.A.

2. LIFE MEMBERSHIPS

Life Memberships are obtained by the submission of a proper application and the payment of **$300.00**. Upon approval of the application, the A.T.A. will issue a Life Membership Certificate, and Life Membership is effective upon the Member's receipt of same.

PLEASE NOTE: If you pay dues at a shoot, retain your receipt until you receive your A.T.A. membership card. Unless you can show evidence of memhership fee payment, you may have to pay again. Be sure you record all scores you have shot before you receive your A.T.A. card and then transfer these scores to your new card.

If you do not receive your A.T.A. card within four weeks, send a letter to the A.T.A., 601 West National Rd., Vandalia, Ohio 45377, advising the A.T.A. that you made application on certain date and give A.T.A. the name of the gun club where you made your application.

FROM THE **$12.00** ANNUAL MEMBERSHIP, **$2.00** IS RETURNED TO THE STATE ORGANIZATION.

FROM THE **$300.00** LIFE MEMBERSHIP, **$150.00** IS RETURNED TO THE STATE ORGANIZATION OVER A TEN (10) YEAR PERIOD AND PART IS RETAINED IN A SPECIAL A.T.A. EMERGENCY FUND.

FROM THE $1.50 DAILY FEE YOU PAY, TWENTY PERCENT (20%) IS RETURNED TO THE STATE ORGANIZATION.

B. TARGET AND MEMBERSHIP YEAR

The target year and Membership year runs from October 1st to September 30th; however, scores shot at any tournament ending after September 30, regardless of starting date, will be included in the following year's averages.

C. HANDICAP YARDAGE FOR A NEW A.T.A. SHOOTER

1. NEW LADY SHOOTER

New lady shooters will be assigned a handicap of 18.0 yards.

2. NEW SUB-JUNIOR SHOOTER

A shooter who has not reached his or her 15th birthday will be classified as a sub-junior and will be assigned a handicap of 18.0 yards.

3. NEW MALE JUNIOR SHOOTER

All male shooters between the age of 15 and 18 will be assigned a handicap of 19.0 yards.

4. NEW MALE SHOOTER

A new male shooter, 18 years of age or older, will be assigned a handicap of 20.0 yards.

5. A new member who had previously been a member of another trapshooting association (prior to current and previous years, see rule III,Q) must shoot their last assigned yardage in that association unless he has received an A.T.A. 1000 target review and been granted a reduction.

It will be the responsibility of the new member to notify the handicap committee of his last assigned yardage in that association.

D. CLASSIFICATION OF A NEW SHOOTER IN 16 YARDS AND DOUBLES EVENTS

A new shooter may be assigned to any class in 16 yards and doubles events until the shooter establishes his known ability.

E. RULES OF CONDUCT OF AN A.T.A. SHOOTER

Each member will be furnished a copy of these Official Trapshooting Rules, and it is assumed that the member will read and understand each Rule. Members are strongly encouraged to know these Rules and abide by them, both for their own benefit and for the benefit of other shooters.

1. By entering the competition, every contestant agrees to accept all official decisions and to abide by these Rules.

2. It is the duty of each A.T.A. member to have his or her Average Card punched if yardage is earned, and all wins and ties in 16 yard and doubles events shall be recorded on the Average Card. The Average Card must be punched to the correct earned yardage on the day the yardage is earned and before leaving the tournament grounds. If a member is required to leave the tournament grounds prior to the completion of a handicap event, it is the member's duty to determine if his or her score qualified for a yardage increase and to have his or her Average Card punched to the correct yardage prior to entering any other tournament. All 16 yard, handicap and doubles scores, and wins and ties in 16 yard and doubles events, are required to be correctly and legibly entered on each member's Average Card in the spaces provided at the completion of each tournament event. Failure of any member to strictly comply with this Rule may lead to penalty classification, disqualification and/or suspension from membership in the A.T.A.

3. When making your entry at any registered shoot, produce your plastic identification card and your Average Card so that your name, address, and membership number are properly noted and errors in records prevented. Shooters not having a plastic card should always list their entire name and address on the event cards.

The Average Card is intended for the purpose of providing the classification committees at the shoots with up-to-date data on your shooting ability. Shooters not having their Average Cards up to date may be put in a higher class or otherwise penalized.

Failure to accurately record scores, or the falsification of scores, can lead to suspension from the A.T.A.

4. Veterans are defined as male or female shooters 65 years of age or older. Sr. Veterans are 70 years of age or older. Sub-Juniors, Juniors and Veterans will be required to change their status on the date of their birth-day, e.g. on the day a Sub-Junior turns 15, any event shot on that day will be shot as a Junior. When a Junior reaches 18 on that day, he or she must shoot as an adult. Veterans will qualify for Veterans' races on their 65th birthday. The only exceptions are as follows:

a. When considering High-Overall or All-Around when there is a Sub-Junior, Junior or Veterans' trophy, the contestant's age on the first day that quali-fies him or her for said award must be utilized.

b. In the Grand American, when qualification for Sub-Junior or Junior is determined at the state level, he or she may be able to participate in the Champion of Champions event based on his or her age at the state shoot.

5. Contestants not timely reporting for competition, which shall include shootoffs, may be disqualified by shoot management.

6. A contestant may hold his gun in any position when it is his turn to shoot. He must in no manner interfere with the preceding shooter by raising his gun to point or otherwise create a distraction.

7. It is the duty of the contestant to see that his score as determined by the referee is correctly recorded. In case of error, it shall be the duty of the contestant to have that error corrected before he has fired the first shot at the succeeding position or before he leaves the trap if the target concerned was within the last five targets of that sub-event. Otherwise the score must stand as shown on the score sheet.

F. RENEWING MEMBERSHIP IN THE A.T.A.

Any shooter reapplying for membership in the A.T.A., who had been assigned a previous handicap yardage, shall resume shooting at that yardage. The only exception is if he or she was assigned a yardage based on age; because of present age, he may be required to shoot at a longer yardage. Failure of a shooter to shoot his previously assigned yardage will result in disqualification and the winning scores and prizes forfeited.

III
OFFICIAL RULES OF A.T.A. TOURNAMENTS

In these Rules the word "State" is intended to include Province or other similar territory having an affiliated association. The words "shoot" and "tournament" are intended to include "leagues" throughout these Official Rules with exceptions only as noted within same.

A. REGISTERED SHOOTS

The A.T.A. governs the conduct of all shoots registered with it. Only clubs affiliated with their state association will be permitted to hold registered shoots.

To constitute a registered shoot, at least five (5) or more persons must compete and complete each event, and provided that they first become members of A.T.A. and pay the registration fee of $1.50 for each day of competition at each shooting location, and such other state association fees and dues as may be charged.

No daily fee charges shall be permitted except those assessed by the A.T.A., the Zone, or the State in which the tournament is being held.

B. WHO MAY PARTICIPATE

Only Members in good standing who have paid their annual dues or are Life Members may participate in a registered A.T.A. Shoot.

C. EVENTS AND HOW SHOT

In official A.T.A. usage, a sub-event is any number of targets shot on any one field at one time, with one full rotation on all five stations by each shooter, such as 25 singles or handicap targets or in doubles 25 pairs, 15 pairs or 10 pairs. An event is the total targets of a specific type (16 yard, handicap, or doubles) such as 200 16-yard targets, 100 handicap targets, etc. for which separate entry is made. Therefore, an "event" consists of two or more "sub-events". It is not necessary to change traps after each sub-event. Events of less than 50 targets may not be registered.

1. 16 YARD SINGLES

This event must be shot 5 shots at each post from 16 yards (14.6m) with each shooter in order shooting at one target until all have shot five times, and then rotating in a clockwise manner to the next station.

2. HANDICAP TARGETS

This event must be shot 5 shots at each post from 17 to 27 yards (15.5-24.7m) with each shooter in order shooting at one target until all have shot five times, then rotating in a clockwise manner to the next station.

A contestant must stand on the highest whole yardage punched on his or her card. For example, if a card is punched at 20.5 yards, the shooter will stand on 20.0 yards. However, if one half yard is then earned, the card must be punched to 21.0 yards and the shooter must stand on the 21.0 yard line.

A shooter may not stand on a higher yardage than he is punched, unless assigned penalty yardage by the shoot handicap committee.

If there is a 200 target handicap event, the second 100 handicap event must not begin prior to the awarding of earned yardage based on the first 100 target event.

It is not permitted to have more than one 50 and/or 75 target handicap event in a registered tournament in any one day.

3. DOUBLES

This event must be shot from 16 yards (14.6m), with each shooter in order shooting at two targets thrown simultaneously from the trap house until all have shot the specified number of times, then rotating in a clockwise manner to the next station. (A doubles event will be shot by having each squad shoot successive alternating 15 pair and 10 pair sub-events on the trap or traps being utilized, or a club may elect to throw Doubles in sub-events of 25 pairs).

D. CLASSIFICATION, HANDICAPPING, AND SPECIAL DESIGNATION

1. For 16 yard targets and Doubles, shooters should be placed in 3 or more classes, according to their known ability.

a. To arrive at "known ability", the following should be taken into account as far as such information can be made available.

(1) Official registered targets (Abnormally low scores should be disregarded.) Averages of all registered shooters are compiled and published annually.

(2) Non-registered scores including shootoff scores, non-registered events, practice scores, etc.

(3) Any other information bearing on a shooter's ability to shoot and break targets.

b. For 16-yard events the following systems are suggested:

FIVE CLASSES

97% and over	AA
94% and under 97%	A
91% and under 94%	B
88% and under 91%	C
Under 88%	D

FOUR CLASSES

95% and over	A
92% and under 95%	B

| 89% and under 92% | C |
| Under 89% | D |

THREE CLASSES

95% and over	A
91% and under 95%	B
Under 91%	C

c. For Doubles events, the following systems are suggested:

FIVE CLASSES

93% and up	AA
89% and under 93%	A
85% and under 89%	B
78% and under 85%	C
Under 78%	D

FOUR CLASSES

90% and up	A
85% and under 90%	B
78% and under 85%	C
Under 78%	D

THREE CLASSES

89% and up	A
83% and under 89%	B
Under 83%	C

d. Any club desiring to use a different classification may do so by printing the desired classification in the program of the shoot.

e. For better classification of shooters it is suggested that the following method be used.

(1) If the shooter has less than 500 targets on current year's Average Card, use the previous year average and known ability.

(2) If the shooter has between 500 and 1,000 targets (inclusive) on his current year's Average Card, use the current average and known ability or the previous year's average and known ability, whichever is the higher.

2. RECORDING OF 16 YARD AND DOUBLES WINS AND TIES

a. Wins and ties in all 16 yard and doubles events, at all A.T.A. registered tournaments shall be recorded on each member's Average Card.

b. It is the duty of each A.T.A. member to assure that all wins and ties in 16 Yard and Doubles events are properly recorded on his or her Average Card prior to entering any A.T.A. tournament.

c. The intent of this Rule is to inform classification and handicap committees of prior wins and ties in 16 Yard and Doubles events.

3. A shooter will be handicapped between 17 and 27 yards at the highest yardage punched on his Average Card, unless he is required to shoot Penalty yardage. (Section 4.)

4. PENALTY CLASSIFICATION

The management of registered shoots may establish penalty yardage and penalty classification for 16 yard targets and doubles, if said conditions are printed in the program. In no event shall any shooter be assigned a classification of less than the minimum yardage appearing on his handicap card.

5. SPECIAL CATEGORIES

Ladies, Juniors, Sub-Juniors, Veterans, Sr. Veterans and Industry shooters shall be so designated.

a. All female shooters shall be designated as Ladies, though because of age they may also be designated as Juniors, Sub-Juniors, Veterans or Sr. Veterans.

b. A shooter who has not reached his or her 15th birthday will be designated as a Sub-Junior.

c. A male shooter upon reaching age 15 must shoot from a minimum handicap yardage of 19 yards unless he has already earned greater yardage.

d. A shooter who is 15 but has not reached his or her 18th birthday will be designated as a Junior.

e. A male shooter upon reaching age 18 must shoot from a minimum handicap yardage of 20 yards unless he has already earned greater yardage.

f. A male or female shooter who is 65 years or older will be designated as a Veteran.

g. A male or female shooter who is 70 years or older will be designated as a Sr. Veteran.

h. Industry personnel shall be so designated and may shoot for only those championships and trophies so designated.

i. All Ladies, Juniors, Sub-Juniors, Veterans, Senior Veterans and Industry shooters must declare their special category **at the time of their entry** in any registered event. Without such declaration, **at the time of their entry**, the shooter will not be allowed to compete for the applicable special category trophies. Shoot Management shall determine and shall conspicuously post a notice of at what point entry is considered completed for purpose of this Rule, and in all cases this point shall be prior to the time the shooter fires his/her first shot in the event. No shooter will be allowed to declare a special category after firing the first shot in the event. **No exceptions to this Rule are to be allowed.**

E. SQUADDING

1. In all A.T.A. events, contestants shall shoot in squads of five except:

a. When there are less than five contestants available for the last squad of any program.

b. When yardage differences in handicap events make it impossible or unsafe.

c. When there are withdrawals from a squad after the competition has begun and squads scheduled.

d. When, in the opinion of shoot management, the harmony of the shoot may be enhanced by squadding less than five contestants.

2. It is illegal for more than five shooters to be in a squad.

3. The squadding of practice shooters with those shooting registered events shall not be allowed, nor shall anyone be allowed to shoot registered events on a non-registered basis, except, however, this Rule shall not apply during Registered League Shooting.

4. The shooter in position 1 is the SQUAD LEADER and should:

a. ascertain that all members of the squad are ready before commencing the event or sub-event;

b. initial the score sheet at the end of each sub-event.

c. The Squad leader ONLY may call for one target before starting his squad to shoot in a regular or shootoff event.

5. If a broken or irregular target is thrown, the Squad leader may ask to see another target. If there is a delay due to trap or gun trouble, the contestant in turn may ask to see another target. If during a sub-event a contestant is consecutively thrown two illegal or broken targets, the contestant shall have the right to see a legal target before he resumes shooting.

F. OFFICIAL SCORING

1. PROCEDURE

a. The official score is the record kept by the scorer on the sheet furnished him by management for said purpose and shall show in detail the scores made in the event or sub-event for which furnished. It is recommended that the score sheet shall not be smaller than 10 inches by 28 inches and the box provided for each score not smaller than 3/4 by 3/4 of an inch. Score sheets on which more than one sub-event is recorded may be carried from trap to trap by the squad leader. Such score sheets must be left at the last trap to be handled by club personnel from that point.

b. The scorer shall keep an accurate record of each score of each contestant. If he calls dead or lost, the scorer shall promptly mark 1 for dead and zero for lost. His record of the competition shall be official and shall govern all awards and records of the competition to which it relates.

c. The scorer shall call all targets, or only the lost targets, as directed by the management.

d. Should more targets be fired in a sub-event than the event calls for, then the excess targets of the sub-event will not be scored.

e. It is the duty of the referee to see that the shooters change firing points at the proper time; however, any targets shot after failure to move at the proper time shall be scored.

f. The official score must be kept on a score sheet in plain view of the contestant. If contestant's view of the score sheet is obstructed for any reason, he may refuse to shoot until he has an unobstructed view of the score sheet.

g. It is an error if the scorer fails to properly mark the results of any shot in the section of the score sheet where the results should have been recorded. In such cases, it is the duty of that contestant to have any error corrected before he has fired **the first shot at the succeeding position or in the case of his last post before he leaves the trap.** Failing to do so he shall be held to the score as recorded. (Rule II,E.,7. Page 9; Rule V,C.,3. Page 45)

h. Every contestant in a squad shall be permitted to examine his score before the sheet is sent to the bulletin board or to the cashier's office. The score sheet should be initialed by the squad leader.

i. Errors in the details of the official score can only be corrected in strict accordance with the aforementioned rules, but an error made in totaling said details shall be corrected whenever same is discovered.

j. The referee shall distinctly announce "lost" when the target is missed and "no target" when a target is thrown broken.

2. BROKEN OR DEAD TARGET

A broken target (called dead) is one that has a visible broken piece from it; or one that is completely reduced to dust. The referee shall declare such target dead when it is so broken in the air. A "Dusted Target" is a target from which there is a puff of dust, but no perceptible piece is seen; it is not a broken target.

3. LOST TARGET

The referee shall rule "LOST":

a. When the contestant fires and fails to break the target whether missed completely or when ONLY DUST falls from it.

b. When a whole target appears promptly after a contestant's recognizable command and is within the legal limits of flight and the contestant voluntarily does not fire.

c. When an illegal target, a freak target, or a target of a markedly different color is fired at and missed. A contestant may refuse illegal, freak or off-colored targets, but if he fires at them the result must be scored.

d. When a contestant voluntarily withdraws from, or is disqualified from, and takes no further part in a sub-event after having fired at one (1) or more targets of said sub-event and thereby does not fire at the total number of targets comprising such sub-event, the referee shall rule all targets which the contestant did not fire at in the sub-event to be "LOST" targets and they shall be scored accordingly.

e. When a score sheet shall come into the office with one or more targets that are not scored either "DEAD" or "LOST," they shall be scored as "LOST" targets by shoot management.

f. All previous rules regarding flinches, defective or dud shells, safety on, unloaded gun or barrel, defective gun, broken gun, misfires, when all of the charge of shot or the wad remains in the barrel, malfunction of a gun or otherwise which previously entitled a contestant to re-shoot the target or to change guns or shells and continue the event without all subsequent misfires being called "LOST" are RESCINDED. **The following procedure shall hereafter be followed in all tournaments:**

(1) A contestant shall be allowed one (1) failure to fire, for any reason other than stated in Paragraph 3.b., above, during each sub-event in Singles and Handicap Events. When the first allowable failure to fire in any sub-event in Singles and Handicap Events occurs, the contestant shall be allowed to call for and fire at another target, and the result of the shot will be scored in accordance with these Official Rules.

(2) A contestant shall be allowed two (2) failures to fire, for any reason other than stated in Paragraph 3.b., above, during each sub-event of Double Events if the failure to fire occurs when the contestant attempts to shoot the first target of a Doubles pair, or when the contestant attempts to shoot the second target of a Doubles pair after the first target has been fired at and broken and would have been scored "DEAD". When the first target of a Doubles pair is fired at and missed and that target would be scored "LOST", there shall be no allowable failure to fire at the second target. When the first or second allowable failure to fire occurs in any Doubles sub-event, the contestant shall be allowed to call for and fire at another pair of targets and the result of the shots at the new pair will be scored in accordance with these Official Rules.

(3) Whenever an allowable failure to fire as provided in this Rule occurs, the scorekeeper shall mark a large legible F on the scoresheet in the space where that target is scored along with the score for that target, and also place the same mark beside the total sub-event score. After one (1) F is placed in the space where the individual target is scored in Singles and Handicap Events, and two (2) F in Doubles Events, any subsequent failure to fire in the same sub-event and for any reason, when a target is called and the target appears promptly and within legal limits of flight, shall be ruled "LOST" and shall be scored accordingly. Cumulative application of the Rule is pro-hibited, and "sub-event" shall be as defined by Official Rules III,C.,1.,2., and 3.

(4) SHOOT MANAGEMENT IS REQUIRED to examine each scoresheet before the score is posted, and any target scored which contains an F in the scoring space, other than for an allowable failure to fire as set forth above, shall be scored "LOST" whether originally scored as "LOST" by the scorekeeper or not, and the provisions of Official Rule III,F.,1.,g shall not restrict shoot management's duty under this Rule.

g. When a contestant deliberately fires at the same target twice in Doubles Events. This Rule is not applicable to a gun "doubling" or "machinegunning", these occurrences are included in Paragraph 3.,f., and 3.,f.,(2), above.

h. When a commonly called "soft load" occurs, and the shot is fired but no part of the over-powder wad or shot remains in the barrel and the target is missed.

i. THERE SHALL BE NO EXCEPTIONS TO THIS RULE.

4. NO TARGET

a. The referee shall rule "NO TARGET" and allow another target in the following instances in addition to those set forth in Paragraph 3.,f., above, ONLY:

(1) In single target events when the target is thrown broken, regardless of the result of any shot fired.

(2) When a contestant shoots out of turn.

(3) When two contestants fire at the same target.

(4) When the trap is sprung without any call of pull, or when it is sprung at any material interval of time before or after the call of the contestant, provided the contestant does not fire. If the contestant fires, the result must be scored.

(5) When two targets are thrown at the same time, in single target events, regardless of whether the contestant fires.

(6) When an "illegal" target is thrown, which is a target that is not within the prescribed angle or height limits for single target shooting, or that is known as a "flipper" or "freak" target is thrown, that may have slipped out of the carrier of the trap or one not properly placed on the trap, provided the contestant does not fire at it. If the contestant fires, the result must be scored.

(7) When a target whose color is markedly different from that of the others is thrown, and the contestant does not fire. If the contestant fires, the result must be scored.

(8) When firing, the contestant's feet must be behind the firing mark at sixteen (16) yards, or behind the mark for the handicap yardage assigned to him, depending upon the event being participated in. The contestant must stand with at least one foot on an imaginary line drawn through the center of the trap and continuing through the center of the firing point, or have one foot on each side of the line. Exceptions to the Rule contained in the second sentence of this paragraph may be granted by the referee due to inequalities in the shooting platform, and shall be granted for wheelchair contestants. Wheelchair contestants shall position their chair so that the center of mass of their body is over the place where they would stand as required by this Rule if no chair were used. If a contestant fails to follow this Rule in its entirety, the referee shall rule any target fired at and broken a "NO TARGET", but if fired at and missed, the referee shall rule the target "LOST".

b. In addition, in DOUBLES EVENTS, the referee shall rule "NO TARGET" and allow another pair of target in the following instances ONLY:

(1) When only one target is thrown.

(2) When more than two targets are thrown.

(3) When both targets are broken by one shot.

(4) When one or both targets are thrown broken even though the contestant fires at one or both targets.

(5) If one or both targets are not within the prescribed angle height limits and the contestant does not fire at either target. If the contestant fires at an illegal first target and the second target is legal, he must also fire at the second target, and if he fails to do so, the legal second target shall be ruled "LOST". A contestant is not required to fire at an illegal target, after he has fired at either a legal or illegal first target, but if he does fire, the result must be scored.

G. SHOOT OFFS

The management of a tournament may rule that ties shall be carried over to the first (or more if needed) sub-event of the next like event. However, when there are ties in a handicap event and any tying shooter earns yardage and consequently will be shooting farther back in the subsequent handicap event, all tying shooters must agree to the carry over.

All ties whenever possible shall be shot off and in such a manner as the management of the competition shall designate. Unless otherwise specified by the management, ties on single target events shall be shot off in 25 target events and doubles in 10 pair events.

Ties for All-Around championships shall be shot off on 20 singles, 10 handicap, and 5 pair of doubles. Ties for High-Overall shall be shot off in such a manner that the shoot off represents as closely as possible in the same proportion of singles, handicap and doubles targets as the High-Overall program contains but keeping the shoot off to 50 targets or less. The singles, handicap and doubles portion of the shoot off shall be in order that the event occurred in the program.

When squadding shooters for shoot offs for High-Overall and All-Around, the shooting order shall be in the order in which they shot in the last event involved except where such order would be inadvisable or dangerous because of yardage differences, and this order shall remain through each portion of the shoot off. In subsequent shoot offs, the position shall be rotated in a clockwise manner, with the shooter from position 1 advancing to poition 2 and the shooter from position 5 rotating to position 1 or to the position dictated by the number of shooters remaining, but always in clockwise rotation.

The following method shall be used for rotation of shooters: Starting firing points to be used shall be as follows-except where handicap yardage makes it unsafe.

If one shooter—firing point number 2.

If two shooters—firing points numbers 2 and 4.

If three shooters—firing points numbers 2, 3 and 4.

If four shooters—firing points numbers 2, 3, 4 and 5.

If five shooters—firing points numbers 1, 2, 3, 4 and 5.

If more than five shooters are involved in the tie, they shall be divided as equally as possible into two or more squads as directed by the management.

H. SAFETY

1. It is the shooter's responsibility and the shoot management's responsibility to conduct a shoot in a safe manner.

2. It is the shoot management's responsibility to remove any competitor who is conducting himself in an unsafe manner. (Repeat violators should be reported to the Executive Committee for further action.)

3. It is the shoot management's responsibility to instruct the trap help in the proper and safe conduct of their respective duties.

4. All trap help must have a flag or other warning device to warn of the trap boy's exit from the trap house.

5. Trap personnel should be totally instructed in the potential danger of the trap (particularly the target throwing arm).

6. Movement and exposure on adjacent traps should be kept to the minimum.

7. The practice of tracking targets behind a shooting squad is unsafe, disconcerting to the shooter, and is not permitted.

8. Alcohol and drugs impair judgement and the A.T.A. rules pertaining to alcohol and/or drugs must be enforced by club management. This rule shall be strictly complied with and shall apply to practice shooting as well as regular events.

9. In handicap there shall be no more than two (2) yards difference between adjacent shooters in the squad, AND NO MORE THAN A TOTAL DIFFERENCE OF THREE (3) YARDS IN A SQUAD. **When squadding 17, 18 and 19 yardages, there shall be no more than one yard difference between adjacent shooters in the squad, and no more than a total difference of two yards in a squad.**

10. A gun which for any reason fails to fire as intended must be promptly opened without any determination by the referee of the cause of the failure to fire.

11. All guns must have the action open and contain no live shell or empty shell at any time, except while the shooter is on the firing line. The gun's action may be closed when it is in a gun rack but it shall not contain a live shell or empty shell. Repeat violators of these Rules will be given a thirty (30) day suspension upon a second violation of these Rules; a third violation of these Rules will result in a ninety (90) day suspension; and further violations will be reviewed by the Executive Committee for further disciplinary action.

12. As a safety precaution, test shots will not be permitted.

13. A contestant shall place a live shell in his gun only when at a firing point facing the traps. In singles shooting he may place only one live shell in his gun at a time and must remove it or the empty shell(s) before moving from one position to another. In doubles shooting he may place two live shells in his gun at a time and must remove both live shells or the empty shells before moving from one position to another. In changing from one position to another, the shooter shall not walk in front of the other competitors.

14. Snap caps or recoil reduction devices may be excluded from the above only if colored a safety orange as to permanently identify them as not being a live shell or empty shell.

15. All guns used by contestants must be so equipped and so used as not to eject empty shells in a manner to substantially disturb or interfere with other contestants.

The management may disqualify a contestant for violation of these Rules.

I. GUNS AND AMMUNITION

A contestant cannot use:

1. A gun whose chamber is larger than 12 gauge. Only 12 gauge shotguns and ammunition may be used at the Grand American Tournament; guns of smaller gauges are permissible in other

registered shooting, but no consideration shall be given to that fact in handicap and classification.

2. Any load other than lead shot. This includes tracers, copper, and nickel coated shot.

3. Any load heavier than 3 drams equivalent of powder or containing more than $1^1/_8$ ounces of shot, or any load containing shot larger than number $7^1/_2$, all as defined by the Sporting Arms and Ammunition Manufacturers' Institute, Inc. specifications.

4. Any shell loaded with black powder.

Any shooter violating any of these rules shall be barred from competition. Any such violator shall be referred to the Executive Committee for possible further disciplinary action.

J. FIRING POSITION AND SHOOTING ORDER

1. There shall be 5 firing points, numbered 1 to 5, left to right, spaced 3 yards apart, and sixteen yards from Point B (Diagram I). At all positions, the contestant's feet must be behind the firing mark at sixteen (16) yards, or behind the mark for the handicap yardage assigned to him or her, depending on the event being participated in. The contestant must stand with at least one foot on an imaginary line drawn through Point B and continuing through the center of the firing point, or have one foot on each side of the line. Wheelchair contestants shall position their chair so that the center of mass of their body is over the place where they would stand as required by this Rule if no chair were used.

The 16 yard (14.6m) position shall be 16 yards behind Point B. The distance that the target shall be thrown shall also be measured from Point B.

2. All contestants must shoot in regular order or sequence according to his or her position in the squad. A contestant who does not shoot in regular order is "out of turn" and the results are not scored.

3. When the referee calls no target for any contestant, the next contestant is not in order until the preceding shooter has shot and the referee has ruled dead or lost.

4. The referee shall not throw a target unless all contestants are in the correct positions.

5. To preserve the harmony of the competition, no member of a squad shall move toward the next firing point until the last shot of the five target sequence has been fired.

6. At any registered trapshooting competition, no person shall be permitted to "shoot up"; that is, enter and take a part in any completed or partially completed event or events after Squad no. 1 shall have completed sub-event no. 1 of any new event to be shot on Trap no. 1.

7. At tournaments which are shot "section system", with several squads starting at the same time on several traps, such procedure shall be construed for purposes of this rule to be the same as if all squads started on Trap no. 1.

K. TRAP MACHINE

A trap **machine** which throws targets at an unknown angle shall be used. All trap **machines** used to throw A.T.A. registered targets shall be so manufactured, modified, or equipped as to interrupt irregularly the oscillation of the trap or otherwise assure the unpredictability of the flight of substantially all targets thrown.

Each gun club that throws A.T.A. registered targets must have on file in the A.T.A. main offices a signed Affidavit that the trap machines used to throw registered targets meet the requirements of this Rule. The State A.T.A. Delegate is responsible for the enforcement of this Rule.

L. TRAPHOUSES

Traphouses must adequately protect the trap loaders and shall not be higher than necessary for the purpose. Traphouses constructed after January 1, 1956 shall conform to the following specifications:

Length not less than 7 feet, 6 inches (2.3m), nor more than 8 feet, 6 inches (2.6m).

Width not less than 7 feet 6 inches (2.3m), nor more than 8 feet, 6 inches (2.6m).

Height not less than 2 feet, 2 inches (.7m), nor more than 2 feet, 10 inches (.9m), the height to be measured from the plane of the number 3 shooting position.

Firing Points. The firing points shall be three yards (2.7m) apart on the circumference of a circle whose radius is 16 yards (14.6m).

M. TARGETS

No target shall measure more than four and five-sixteenths ($4^5/_{16}$) inches (10.94cm) in diameter, not more than one and one-eighth ($1^1/_8$) inches (28.58mm) in height, and with an allowable variation of not more than five (5) percent from these specifications.

N. FLIGHTS AND ANGLES

Targets, whether single or doubles, shall be thrown not less than 48 yards (44m) nor more than 52 yards (47m) measured on level ground in still air.

Targets, whether single or doubles, shall be between 8 feet (2.4m) and 12 feet (3.7m) high, when ten yards from Point B. THE RECOMMENDED HEIGHT IS NINE FEET. The height at a point ten yards (9m) from Point B is to be understood to mean height above an imaginary horizontal straight line drawn through the firing point and Point B.

In singles shooting, the trap shall be so adjusted that within the normal distribution of angles as thrown by the trap, the right angle shall not be less than a straightaway from firing point 1 and the left angle shall not be less than a straightaway from firing point 5.

Under no circumstances shall a Standard Model 1524 trap be set in less than the #2 hole. Any other trap machine shall be adjusted so as to throw not less than equivalent angles. To help in determining legal angles, stakes should be placed on the arc of a circle whose radius is 50 yards (46m) and whose center is Point B. One stake should be placed where a line drawn through firing point 1 and Point B intersects this arc and another stake placed where a line drawn through firing point 5 and Point B intersects the arc. These lines and stakes will assist in determining the required angles, but it is to be understood that the angle specifications apply when the target is from 15 yards to 20 yards (14-18m) from the trap rather than where the target strikes the ground. However, no target is to be declared illegal unless it is more than 25 degrees outside the angles prescribed.

Distance handicaps, when used, shall be prolongations of the lines given in Diagram I, commonly known as fan shaped. The distance between firing points at 16 yards (14.6m) shall then be 3 yards (2.7m).

Should a trap be throwing targets that, although not necessarily illegal, appreciably vary from the legal targets as previously described, any shooter may request that management reset the trap even though prior squads have shot. The final decision as to whether or not a trap is to be reset will be made by shoot management.

O. TROPHIES, AIDS, AND REQUIREMENTS FOR STATES AND ZONES

1. RESIDENCE

No person, amateur or industry representative, may compete for A.T.A. Trophies or Titles in State or Zone tournaments, unless he or she, for the immediately preceding six (6) months, has been a bona fide resident of said State or Zone, and a member in good standing of the State Association of that person's residence. No person may compete for any such A.T.A. Trophies or Titles in more than one (1) State or Zone each target year. However, nothing shall preclude such person from returning to the former State or Zone residence and competing for trophies in the event he or she has not been a bona fide resident of another State or Zone for the immediate preceding six (6) month period prior to such competition.

In case there is a dispute with respect to the residence of a shooter attending a State or Zone tournament, it shall be the duty of the State Association or the Zone Officials, in which the shoot is being held, to rule as to said shooter's right to compete as a resident shooter. **The ruling of the State Association or Zone Officials shall be final.**

2. At all shoots where A.T.A. trophies are furnished, a line referee must be provided by the host club or State Association.

3. COMPULSORY PURSES

No compulsory purse and/or option of any type shall be permitted in any tour-naments in which A.T.A. trophies or A.T.A. added money are provided.

4. STATE AIDS

THE A.T.A. IN ITS PROGRAM OF BUILDING STRONG STATE ASSOCIATIONS AIDS THEM FINANCIALLY. FROM THE **$12.00** ANNUAL MEMBERSHIP, **$2.00** IS RETURNED TO THE STATE ORGANIZATION. FROM THE **$300.00** LIFE MEMBERSHIP, **$150.00** IS RETURNED TO THE STATE ORGANIZATION OVER A TEN (10) YEAR PERIOD AND PART IS RETAINED IN A SPECIAL A.T.A. EMERGENCY FUND. FROM THE $1.50 DAILY FEE YOU PAY, TWENTY PERCENT (20%) IS RETURNED TO THE STATE ORGANIZATION.

These are made to the state association ten days prior to the State Tournament, provided such tournament is held and provided the state turns in to the A.T.A. at least $200.00 from annual membership dues and registration fees. From this refund, there will be deducted an amount equal to that which is represented by "unpaid cards" of shooters from that state who shot in registered shoots without payment of annual membership dues, and any fines due because of late shoot reports. On or before January 1 of each year, the A.T.A. shall inform the secretary of each state of the approximate amount of refund to be paid to that State and **this information must be printed in the program for that annual State Tournament.**

5. STATE A.T.A. TROPHIES

The A.T.A. will also donate the following trophies to each state and provincial association:

Singles Champion	Handicap Champion
Singles Runner-up	Handicap Runner-up
Lady Singles Champion	Doubles Champion
Veteran Singles Champion	All-Around Champion
Senior Veteran Singles Champion	
Junior Singles Champion	
Sub-junior Singles Champion	

Singles Class Champions (AA, A, B, C, D) awarded in Class or Singles Champion-ship.

Only one A.T.A. trophy shall be awarded to any person in any separate event. A special category shooter is not disqualified from winning the special category trophy by entering in a shoot-off for any other trophy, and can fall back to the special category trophy if he is unsuccessful in the shoot-off. A shooter cannot win both an A.T.A. special category trophy and another championship A.T.A. trophy in the same event. Special awards that are not specific A.T.A. trophies mentioned above shall be exempt from this rule.

When a shooter's scores qualify for more than one A.T.A. trophy, the burden is on the shooter to make the choice. The shooter's failure to notify such persons as must be designated in the shoot program within 15 minutes after posting of the last event scores, gives management the right and the duty to make the determination and the choice of trophy for that shooter. Shoot management, when making this determination, is to consider special category championship trophies superior to class championship trophies.

HOWEVER, WHEN THERE ARE BOTH JUNIOR AND SUB-JUNIOR A.T.A. TROPHIES, THE JUNIOR MUST TAKE THE JUNIOR TROPHY, AND THE SUB-JUNIOR MUST TAKE THE SUB-JUNIOR TROPHY REGARDLESS OF THE HIGH SCORE BETWEEN THE TWO OF THEM. **THIS RULE ALSO APPLIES TO VETERANS AND SENIOR VETERANS.**

6. CHAMPIONSHIP EVENTS AT STATE TOURNAMENTS

The four state championships mentioned above shall be determined on the following:

Singles—200 targets

Doubles—50 pair

Handicap—100 targets

All-Around—the sum of the above, 400 targets

Ladies, Junior, Veterans, Sub-Junior, Senior Veterans and any other champion-ships not included in the five mentioned above may be determined on a lesser number of targets at the discretion of the state shoot management.

7. ZONE AIDS

The A.T.A. donates $3000.00 in added money to be awarded at each Zone tournament. ZONE OFFICIALS MAY DETERMINE THE DIVISION OF THE A.T.A. ADDED MONEY FOR ZONE TOURNAMENTS IN THE SINGLES AND DOUBLES CLASS CHAMPIONSHIPS AND IN THE CHAMPIONSHIP EVENTS OF SINGLES, HANDICAP, AND DOUBLES. IT SHALL BE MADE AVAILABLE TO ALL A.T.A. REGISTERED SHOOTERS REGARDLESS OF LOCATION UNLESS THE MONEY IS SPECIFICALLY RESTRICTED TO ZONE RESIDENTS AT THE DISCRETION OF THE VARIOUS A.T.A. ZONES AND IT MUST BE SO STATED IN THE ZONE PROGRAMS.

8. ZONE A.T.A. TROPHIES

The A.T.A. will donate the following trophies to each Zone for Zone Tournament:

Singles Champion   Handicap Champion

Lady Singles Champion Handicap Runner-up

Veteran Singles Champion   Doubles Champion

Senior Veteran Singles Champion   All-Around Champion

Junior Singles Champion

Sub-junior Singles Champion

Doubles Class Championship AA, A, B, C, D

Singles Championship AA, A, B, C, D

Singles Class Championship AA, A, B, C, D

Doubles Championship AA, A, B, C, D

Only one A.T.A. trophy shall be awarded to any person in separate event. A special category shooter is not disqualified from winning the special category by entering into a shoot-off for any other trophy, and can fall back to the special category trophy if he is unsuccessful in the shoot-off. A shooter cannot win both an A.T.A. special category trophy and another championship A.T.A. trophy in the same event. Special awards that are not specific A.T.A. trophies mentioned above shall be exempt from this rule.

When a shooter's scores qualify for more than one A.T.A. trophy, the burden is on the shooter to make the choice. The shooter's failure to notify such persons as must be designated in the shoot program within 15 minutes after posting of the last event scores, gives management the right and the duty to make the determination and the choice of trophy for that shooter. Shoot management when making this determination is to consider special category championship trophies superior to class championship trophies.

HOWEVER, WHEN THERE ARE BOTH JUNIOR AND SUB-JUNIOR A.T.A. TROPHIES, THE JUNIOR MUST TAKE THE JUNIOR TROPHY AND THE SUB-JUNIOR MUST TAKE THE SUB-JUNIOR TROPHY

REGARDLESS OF THE HIGH SCORE BETWEEN THEM. **THIS RULE ALSO APPLIES TO VETERANS AND SENIOR VETERANS.**

9. CHAMPIONSHIP EVENTS AT ZONE TOURNAMENTS

Zone championships shall be determined on the following:

Singles—200 targets

Doubles—5O pair

Handicap—100 targets

All-Around—the sum of the above, 400 targets

Class championships—a minimum of 100 targets (not to be shot concurrently with the Singles Championship).

Zone tournament programs shall call for a minimum of 600 registered targets.

P. GRAND AMERICAN QUALIFICATION

No shooter shall shoot Handicap events at the Grand American World Trapshooting Tournament (except Veterans, Sr. Veterans, Ladies, Juniors, and Sub-juniors) at less than 25.0 yards unless both of the following conditions are met: the shooter has registered a minimum of 1500 registered handicap targets during the current year and/or the previous two (2) years, and the shooter has registered at least 500 handicap targets since October 1 of the previous year and not later than the Friday preceding the first regular day of the Grand American of the current year. Shooters belonging to another trapshooting association must shoot their longest yardage either assigned by that trapshooting association or by the A.T.A.

Veterans, Ladies, Juniors and Sub-Juniors who have not met the minimum target requirements above may shoot in any Grand American Handicap event from their assigned yardage provided they forfeit all rights to trophies, options and purses.

No shooter shall shoot 16 yard events at the Grand American World Trapshooting Tournament in less than Class A unless he has a minimum of 1500 registered 16 yard targets recorded for that year and/or the previous two years of which at least 500 have been shot since October 1 of the previous year and not later than the Friday preceding the first regular day of the Grand American World Trapshooting Tournament of the current year.

No shooter shall shoot doubles events at the Grand American World Trapshooting Tournament in doubles classification less than Class A unless he has a minimum of 1000 registered doubles targets recorded for that year and/or the previous two years, of which 500 have been shot since October 1 of the previous year and not later than the Friday preceding the first regular day of the Grand American World Trapshooting Tournament of the current year.

It shall be the shooter's responsibility to inform the Handicap Committee as to his or her target eligibility.

Yardage earned for high score and all ties in any Grand American handicap event shot in the regular program (does not include preliminary events) may not be removed in part or whole by any committee action prior to the end of the Grand American tournament the following year.

Q. SPECIAL RULES FOR MEMBERS OF OTHER SHOOTING ORGANIZATIONS

If a shooter is a member of any other trapshooting association or was a member of such association the preceding year AND shot targets in such association in the current or preceding A.T.A. target year, he or she will shoot from the handicap yardage of whichever association shows the greater yardage.

A member who at any time has previously been a member of another trapshooting association, must shoot their last assigned yardage in that association (if it is greater) unless they have received an A.T.A. 1000 target review and receive a yardage reduction and have not shot that association's targets for the period of time prescribed in the above paragraph.

It will be the responsibility of the shooter to notify the shoot handicap committee if he or she holds or has held a card of another trapshooting association. Failure to notify the shoot handicap committee of another trapshooting association card may be cause for penalty action resulting in forfeiture of entry fees and all monies and possible suspension from all A.T.A. shoots for one year.

R. OPTIONS AND MONEY DIVISIONS

1. Added Money. No tournament promoter or other person responsible shall in any advertisement or program mention any purse or money in excess of the money actually added or guaranteed. Examples of money divisions may be included provided it is clearly stated that the amounts listed are examples and not guaranteed amounts. The word "example" must be included. **Failure to observe the above provisions shall be grounds for disciplinary action by the state association and/or by the Executive Committee.**

THE A.T.A. DOES NOT GUARANTEE AND IS NOT RESPONSIBLE FOR ACTUAL PAYMENT OF ADDED MONEY, GUARANTEED MONEY AND PRIZES ADVERTISED OR OFFERED AT ANY SHOOT EXCEPT THE MONEY, PRIZES AND TROPHIES DIRECTLY SUPPLIED BY A.T.A.

2. At every registered tournament, the cashier or other official in charge, is required to post on an outside bulletin board the names of all contestants who have entered any purse, options or any other monies, with each type of entry by each contestant noted. Purses, options, etc., may be entered by and for contestants only. **ANY CLUB OR CASHIER MAY DEDUCT UP TO ONE-HALF ($^{1}/_{2}$) OF ONE PERCENT OF THE GROSS AMOUNT OF PURSE AND OPTIONS TO HELP DEFRAY COSTS OF COMPUTATIONS. BREAKAGE ACCUMULATED BY ROUNDING OFF IS TO BE CONSIDERED PART OF THE ONE HALF ($^{1}/_{2}$) OF ONE PERCENT.** The one-half ($^{1}/_{2}$) of one percent may be deducted from the gross amount of monies collected from purses, options, Lewis Class purses, guaranteed purses, or otherwise, but in no event shall Hall of Fame contribution awards be included in the computation or deduction. The deductions mentioned above shall be made in such manner that no individual purse, option, Lewis class purse, guaranteed purse or otherwise shall be reduced in any amount greater than the percentage that particular item bears to the whole amount of monies collected, and all monies collected shall be returned to the shooters in the same event in which collected. This Rule shall not apply to any monies collected above the actual costs of any merchandise or other prizes, FOR WHICH A SEPARATE FEE IS CHARGED, and any excess monies of the type shall not be required to be returned to the shooters PROVIDED SPECIFIC NOTIFICATION of non-return of such monies shall be conspicuously inserted into each program where such monies will be collected.

The cashier shall have posted on the bulletin board the amount to be paid each purse or option winner. In the event payment is made by check, after the shoot is over, and the contestants have left the ground, a payoff sheet for unposted events must accompany each check showing the amount paid for each individual event or option included in the payment.

Any reasonable request to inspect the cashier sheets must be honored by the shoot management. **A shooter or a gun club must file a written complaint or contest any payoff or trophy award within 60 days after the competition or forfeit the right to do so.**

Failure to comply strictly with this rule shall result in disciplinary action by the State Association and/or the Executive Committee.

3. CALCUTTAS

The A.T.A. does not condone or encourage calcuttas at any registered A.T.A. Trapshoot.

S. PAYMENT AND OVERPAYMENTS

Anyone who presents a check at any shoot for fees and targets, or has or allows his or her fees and targets to be paid by such check, that is returned or dishonored for insufficient funds or any other reason, may not compete in any registered shoot until full payment has been made to the individuals or club to which it was presented; further, the provisions of Rule III,V,1,a, shall apply. Clubs receiving such a check shall report the name and address of the shooter or individual issuing the check to the A.T.A. along with a copy and a statement that the check was for registered targets and/or fees. After having been reimbursed, the club MUST immediately inform the A.T.A. so that rein-statement proceedings may be initiated.

Any A.T.A. member who has been suspended for presenting a check that is re-turned for insufficient funds or other causes and thereafter becomes eligible for reinstatement shall be required to pay the sum of $25.00 to the A.T.A. as a reinstatement fee.

Any club which conducts a registered tournament should make payment of all added money, purses, optionals, and other monies to the shooters as promptly as possible. **Failure to do so within 15 days result in the cancellation of registration privileges of that club for the remainder of the year, and no further registration shall be granted to that club until all monies due to shooters, the A.T.A. and state organizations have been paid. The persons responsible, and/or officers of such delinquent clubs, shall be barred from shooting registered targets until such payments have been made.**

Any competitor at a registered shoot who, through error, has been overpaid on any purse, added money, optional, or other awards, and who is notified of the overpayment by registered mail, must return the overpayment within 15 days. Failure to do so shall result in disbarment from all registered shoots until payment is made.

T. CHALLENGE AND PROTEST

Any contestant may challenge the load of any other contestant. On receipt of a challenge, the management shall obtain a shell or shells from the challenged party, and if after examination, the management finds the contestant violated the A.T.A. rule, he may be disqualified.

A protest concerning a score or scores must be made before or immediately after the close of the competition to which such scores relate. A protest may be made by a contestant.

U. DISQUALIFICATION

1. A shooter may be disqualified for an event or for a whole tournament **by Shoot Management at any time during a tournament, or at any time by the Executive Committee or such person as they shall designate** for that purpose whenever the following prohibited conduct is brought to their attention:

a. if, in the opinion of management or the Executive Committee, he disrupts the harmony of the shoot;

b. if he shoots at any place other than the regular firing line;

c. if he fails to shoot at his correct yardage;

d. if he has failed to have his card punched for earned yardage at a prior shoot, or fails to report earned yardage at the time of any subsequent registration;

e. if he behaves in an ungentlemanly or disorderly manner **such as physical or verbal abuse of shoot personnel, other competitors or spectators;**

f. if he interferes with the management's procedures in conducting the shoot;

g. if he does not respond and report to the firing line when his squad is called to shoot;

h. if he does not abide by the rules of the A.T.A., by the rules set out by management, and/or in the official program.

2. **IT IS THE RESPONSIBILITY AND THE REQUIRED DUTY** of shoot management to immediately remove and disqualify any contestant at any time during an A.T.A. sanctioned tournament:

a. who consumes any alcoholic beverages or drugs during participation in any event, sub-event or between sub-events, including shootoffs and practice, or;

b. who is under the obvious influence of alcohol or drugs before starting, or during any event, sub-event, shootoff or practice, or;

c. who handles a gun dangerously on or off the firing line, or;

d. who deliberately or carelessly violates gun safety precautions, Official Rules regarding Safety (Rule III, H.), or in any manner endangers contestants, spectators, or gun club personnel.

For purposes of this Rule, "drugs" shall mean any illegal drug, and shall also mean any prescription medication if that prescription medica-tion affects the judgement or conduct of the contestant to a degree that renders the contestant incapable of safely participating in the sport of trapshooting, whether during a registered tournament or practice.

3. Disqualification for a single event does not prevent a contestant from participating in other events in the same tournament and scores shot in other events are not affected; however, any disqualification pursuant to Rule 2., above, shall incude all events or practice on the same day after the time of disqualification.

4. If the infraction is severe, the management may disqualify the contestant for the entire tournament and require him to leave the grounds.

5. Disqualification for a tournament does not prevent a shooter from participating in other tournaments.

6. All entrance monies in events not competed in, as a result of disqualification, are to be returned in full. Events which have been started do not qualify for refunds due to disqualification.

7. Scores shot in an event or a tournament for which a shooter is disqualified will not be registered, and any trophies or monies which the contestant has received for an event for which he is disqualified MUST be returned. Any shooter who is disqualified from an event or tournament and fails to return any trophies or purses which the shooter received in that event or tournament remain disqualified and will be barred from shooting A.T.A. targets or otherwise participating in A.T.A. activities until all trophies and monies have been returned and written certification from the gun club involved is received at the A.T.A. Main Offices.

V. SUSPENSIONS, EXPULSIONS, AND REINSTATEMENT

1. The Executive Committee may at any time at its discretion suspend any member or discipline shoot management, in addition to any disqualification as provided in Rule III,U., who:

a. presents a check at any shoot for fees and targets, or has or allows his fees and targets to be paid by such check, that is returned or dishonored for insufficient funds or any other reason; further any person who presents such a check more than two (2) times shall be automatically suspended for a period of one (1) year; the Executive Committee may designate authority to the General Manager to suspend any member for presentation of dishonored checks, on first and second offenses, until the gun club where the check(s) was written has been reimbersed and reinstatement fee has been paid;

b. falsifies his scores;

c. fails to have his handicap card properly punched for earned yardage or fails to report earned yardage at the time of registration for any subsequent tournament;

d. fails to return any overpayment after proper notification;

e. is convicted of any gun or firearms violation;

f. willfully, deliberately, or repeatedly violates the rules of the A.T.A. as contained in the Official Rules Book;

g. encourages, participates in or allows a willful rule violation by any minor of which he or she is parent or for whom he or she is acting as legal or actual guardian, either temporary or permanent. For purposes of these rules only, a "minor" shall mean a person who has not attained his or

her 18th birthday, and "guardian" shall mean a person who has actual physical custody or control of a minor, either temporarily or permanently and custody or control for the purpose of attending a single registered trapshooting tournament shall satisfy that definition of "guardian" for the purpose of enforcement of this rule only;

h. engages in conduct or behavior which constitutes cause for suspension in the opinion of the Executive Committee.

2. A member who is suspended or disqualified is barred from shooting A.T.A. targets or otherwise participating in A.T.A. activities for the period of his suspension or disqualification.

3. If the Executive Committee feels the violations warrant suspension for longer than one year, or expulsion, the member shall have the right of appeal if he complies with the terms and provisions of the By-Laws.

4. The procedure for suspension or disciplinary action is as follows:

a. All complaints of violations of A.T.A. rules by individuals and/or gun clubs, whether made to the A.T.A. headquarters or to any A.T.A. official, shall be immediately called to the attention of the A.T.A. state or provincial delegate representing the state in which the alleged violation occurred.

b. The delegate shall then proceed to obtain such complaint in writing, specifying the exact rule(s) violated along with full details, including names and addresses of all witnesses. The delegate shall make an immediate investigation and confirm, to the best of his ability, the details of the incident in question.

c. Within ten (10) days of the first notice of the complaint, and after complying with paragraph (b), above, the delegate shall serve written notice of the complaint upon the alleged violator, by certified mail, return receipt requested, and require a written reply within ten (10) days of receipt. A copy of such notice of complaint shall at the same time be sent to the zone vice-president, along with a complete copy of the supporting file.

d. Upon receipt of any answer from the alleged violator, or if no such answer is received within the ten days, the delegate shall confer with such state officers as he deems necessary, and recommend appropriate action to the zone vice-president within seven (7) days; a copy of any response, answer, state- ment or other document relating to the complaint shall be provided to the zone vice-president at the time the delegate makes his recommendation.

e. The zone vice-president, upon receipt of the delegate's recommendation(s), shall review the entire file and write his own recommendations, with supporting facts, to all members of the Executive Committee within ten (10) days.

f. All other members of the Executive Committee will, within seven (7) days after their receipt of the zone vice-president's recommendations, advise the A.T.A. president of their agreement or disagreement with the recommendations of the zone vice-president;

g. The A.T.A. president will then immediately cause appropriate action to be taken in accordance with the majority vote of the Executive Committee. Suspensions and/or expulsions made under this section shall conform to the applicable provisions pertaining thereto as fully set forth in the Articles of Incorporation and By-laws of the Amateur Trapshooting Association of America.

5. REINSTATEMENT

Any A.T.A. member who has been suspended for any reason must pay a $25.00 reinstatement fee when his period of suspension is completed or when, in the case of returned checks, he has reimbursed the club where the check was written.

W. INDUSTRY PERSONNEL

Any person who (a) receives compensation for shooting or for the display or sale of the products or merchandise of any firm, company, corporation, or individual engaged in the manufacture, fabrications, importation, distribution, sale or servicing of arms, parts, ammunition, components, clay targets, or other products or services related to trapshooting or (b) received any allowance, remuneration (whether partial or total), or other consideration for attending, shooting at, or otherwise participating in trapshooting events, shall be deemed an Industry Representative upon receipt by the A.T.A. of his or her written declaration setting forth such relationship and expressing the intention to be designated an Industry Representative. No Industry Representative shall compete for money or trophies in registered tournaments, except those events especially provided for Industry Representatives. Exceptions to this rule are - tournaments sponsored by Indian, fraternal or similar organizations, registered leagues, and those events clearly designated as open to both Amateurs and Industry Representatives. An Industry Representative may regain amateur standing after termination of the relationship which qualified him for designation as an Industry Representative by furnishing written certification thereof to the A.T.A. via Registered or Certified Mail postpaid to the Manager, Vandalia, Ohio 45377. When he receives his new amateur card from A.T.A., he will then be classified as an amateur.

X. AMATEURS

Unless a shooter qualifies as "industry personnel", that shooter is considered an amateur and shall be entitled to all rights as set forth in these rules.

Y. ALL-AMERICA TEAM REQUIREMENTS

	16's	Hd	Dbls
Men	3000	2000	1000
Women, Juniors	2500	1500	750
Sub-Juniors, Veterans,			
Sr. Veterans, Industry	2000	1000	500

1. Men must have competed in at least three different states; other categories in at least two states.

2. A person's age on Monday of the Grand American determines category.

3. The proper form for team consideration may be submitted to the A.T.A. office before October 31st. This form is available at the Grand or by request from the A.T.A. office or TRAP & FIELD.

Z. REGISTERED LEAGUE SHOOTING

The following Rules shall apply to League Shooting only:

1. Registered League Shooting shall apply only to 16 yard single targets.

2. Registered League Shooting shall be subject to and governed by Official A.T.A. Rules. In the event of any conflict between any Registered League's Rules and any Official A.T.A. Rule, Official A.T.A. Rules shall take precedence and shall govern. All complaints of A.T.A. Rules violation or any Registered League's Rules violation, as a result of which any contestant or league is subject to possible disqualification, suspension or expulsion, shall be governed by the Rules and procedures contained in Official A.T.A. Rules III, T., U. and V.

3. The A.T.A. will maintain and publish Registered League Targets history, and all Registered League Targets shall be counted for purses of target attainment accomplishments.

4. All Registered League Targets shall be counted toward target requirements for the Grand American World Trapshooting Tournament and for all other A.T.A. Registered Tournaments.

5. Registered League Target Averages shall be reported in the annual TRAP & FIELD Average Book, separate from A.T.A. Target Averages, and shall be maintained on a separate column on the A.T.A. Average Card.

6. The following conditions are required to be met before any League Targets will be registered:

a. A League must elect to become a Registered League.

b. Any member of a Registered League electing to register his scores must be a Life or Annual Member of the A.T.A.

c. Application for Registered League Shooting must be made on application forms approved and supplied by the A.T.A., and each form must be fully completed before submission. An application fee of $25.00 for each Registered League must be paid at the time of submission of the application to the A.T.A. office. The application must be approved in writing by the State Association Secretary before the form is submitted to the A.T.A.

d. Each Registered League's total score will be registered upon payment of a fee equal to the standard A.T.A. Daily Fee charged for registered tournaments. Registration will be made when the designated League Representative provides shoot reports to the A.T.A. office containing the total number of targets thrown and broken for the League, and the total number of targets broken by each individual League participant, along with the required fee.

e. League shoot reports are required to be sent to the A.T.A. office within fifteen (15) days after the date of the last shoot of the League. Failure to comply with this deadline shall result in a penalty of $25.00 assessed against the defaulting League. In the event the penalty is not timely paid, the $25.00 penalty shall be deducted from the State Association's annual rebate.

f. In the event any League fails to comply with the requirements set forth in this Rule, League scores for the League and for individual participants in the League will not be registered.

IV
THE A.T.A. HANDICAP SYSTEM

The A.T.A. Handicap system is the method whereby shooters whose ability to win has been demonstrated and shooters whose ability is unknown are handicapped by shooting a greater distance from the trap house. The minimum handicap is 17.0 yards and the maximum is 27.0 yards. A shooter's yardage is determined by rules governing new shooters, by yardage earned, or by his established handicap yardage which is based on known ability and 1000 target reviews.

At each State or Provincial shoot, the handicapping and classifying shall be the responsibility of a committee appointed by the state association with the A.T.A. delegate as chairman.

A. CENTRAL HANDICAP COMMITTEE

1. The Central Handicap Committee, made up of a chairman and 5 or more members, is appointed by the Executive Committee.

2. It is the responsibility of the Central Handicap Committee to control yardage of all members of the A.T.A. Any Central Handicap Committee member may increase a shooter's yardage at his discretion when applying the known ability rule. The only others authorized to increase a shooter's yardage are members of the Executive Committee.

B. KNOWN ABILITY

Handicap and 16 yard averages and/or scores in both registered and non-registered shoots may be used as the basis for determining known ability. Scores abnormally low in relation to the remainder of the scores shot may be disregarded at the discretion of the handicap committee.

C. EARNED YARDAGE

1. Yardage will be automatically earned by shooters of high scores in all A.T.A. registered events, according to the table following. This additional yardage is indicated by punches on the shooter's handicap card.

EARNED YARDAGE TABLE

Number of Shooters	High Scores (and all ties)				
	1st	2nd	3rd	4th	5th
15-24	1/2 yd				
25-49	1 yd	1/2 yd			
50-124	1 yd	1/2 yd	1/2 yd		
125-249	1 yd	1 yd	1/2 yd		
250-499	11/2 yd	1 yd	1/2 yd	1/2 yd	
500-1499	2 yd	11/2 yd	1 yd	1/2 yd	
1500 and up	21/2 yd	2 yd	11/2 yd	1 yd	1/2 yd

2. Any score of 96 will automatically earn 1/2 yard provided it does not earn at least that much under the earned yardage table. Any score of 50x50 or 75x75 in events of that length will automatically earn 1/2 yard **provided it does not earn at least that much under the earned yardage table.**

3. The State Handicap Champion will automatically earn 1 yard.

4. Any score of 97, 98 and 99 will automatically earn 1 yard, and a score of 100 will automatically earn 1½ yard provided these scores do not earn at least that much under the earned yardage table.

5. The earned yardage table applies to events of 50, 75 or 100 handicap targets.

6. In case of handicap events of more than 100 targets, each 100 targets (or remaining part of 100 targets) shall constitute a separate event for earned yardage purposes and shall be reported as a separate event on the shoot report form.

7. A shooter's card will be punched from the yardage actually shot. IT IS THE SHOOTER'S RESPONSIBILITY TO SEE THAT HIS HANDICAP CARD IS PROPERLY PUNCHED BEFORE SHOOTING ANOTHER HANDICAP EVENT. FAILURE TO DO SO WILL MAKE HIM SUBJECT TO DISQUALIFICATION OR SUSPENSION.

8. Industry shooters and their scores shall be counted when determining the number of shooters in an event for earned yardage purposes and in applying the earned yardage table. The number of contestants starting the event will be the number used for the earned yardage table.

D. PENALTY YARDAGE

The management of registered shoots may establish penalty yardage if said conditions are printed in the program. In no event shall any shooter be assigned a handicap of less than the minimum yardage appearing on his handicap card.

E. SPECIAL HANDICAP RULES

1. A shooter must continue to shoot from the last yardage assigned or earned until he receives a target review, regardless of the length of time that has elapsed since that yardage was assigned or earned.

2. A shooter's handicap yardage may be reduced only as a result of a 1000 target review or a special review. No reduction may be made in the field.

3. A shooter's handicap yardage may be increased at any time during the year including immediately before and during the Grand American World Trapshooting Tournament:

a. because of earned yardage, or;

b. as a result of a review, or;

c. at the discretion of a member of the Central Handicap or Executive Committee.

4. A shooter at all times shall have the right to appeal any committee action to the Executive Committee.

5. Yardage earned for high score and ties in any Grand American handicap event in the regular program (does not include preliminary events) may not be removed in part or whole by any committee action prior to the end of the Grand American World Trapshooting Tournament in the following year.

6. If a shooter earns increased yardage while a reduction is in process, the reduction shall automatically be void.

7. When multiple 100 target handicap events (marathon) are shot in the same day, only two 100 target events may be considered as a maximum per day towards reduction. The two events considered out of the marathon must be those two in which the two highest scores are registered.

F. REVIEWS

1.—1000 TARGET REVIEW

The shooting record of each member will be automatically reviewed for possible yardage changes after each successive 1000 registered handicap targets shot in the current and previous year if no yardage was earned.

a. A shooter with a low purified handicap average accompanied by a relative 16 yard average will, with the approval of his state delegate, receive a one yard reduction, EXCEPT:

(1) No shooter will be reduced more than two yards in any target year.

(2) No male shooter eighteen (18) years of age or older will be handicapped below 20 yards without a special review; exceptions to this policy may be Sub-Juniors, Juniors, Veterans, Senior Veterans, and Ladies.

(3) The known ability rule will be used in assessing a shooter's record.

b. A shooter with a high purified handicap average will receive a "Special Review" for possible yardage increase.

c. If a yardage change is made, the shooter will receive by mail a new membership card with the new assigned yardage.

2.—SPECIAL REVIEW

A "Special Review" is an evaluation by the Central Handicap Committee generated by a high purified average on a 1000 target review or initiated by a shooter through his state delegate or the Central Handicap Committeeman. The results of a Special Review shall be agreed upon by the Central Handicap Committee and the shooter's State Delegate. If after a reasonable communication, a disagreement in yardage assignment exits between the State Delegate and the Central Handicap Committee, the matter may be directed to the Executive Committee. A Special Review may be used:

a. To determine possible yardage increases for shooters showing high purified handicap averages on a 1000 target review.

b. To determine possible yardage reduction for a shooter because of advancing age or physical disability. The review may be initiated by a shooter through his state delegate.

3.—ASSIGNED YARDAGE INCREASE

a. To consider appeals from increased yardage by assignment, a member may appeal an assigned yardage increase by writing to the A.T.A. office after having shot 500 targets at the assigned yardage. However, for any further reduction, 1000 additional handicap targets must be shot.

b. There will be no yardage increase by shooter request.

c. THE ONLY PERSONS AUTHORIZED TO DECREASE OR INCREASE A MEMBER'S HANDICAP YARDAGE ARE THE MEMBERS OF THE CENTRAL HANDICAP COMMITTEE AND THE EXECUTIVE COMMITTEE.

V
REQUIREMENTS AND RECOMMENDATIONS
FOR CONDUCTING A REGISTERED SHOOT OR REGISTERED LEAGUE
A. APPLICATION

Proper blank application forms, obtained from the A.T.A., or local state secretaries, should be filled out and mailed to the state secretary for approval. If there are club dues or other obligations in your State, these must be enclosed with applications. Registered league dues of $25.00 per league must be submitted with the appropriate league application.

If the application is in order, your state secretary will approve and forward it to the A.T.A. for the certification of registration.

Upon receipt of the approved application form, the A.T.A. will issue the registration certificate, provided all conditions of the application have been met and that the date requested will not conflict with the dates of a tournament granted to another club or association in close proximity. The question of close proximity is left to the judgment of the officials of the state association. In the event the state association is unable or unwilling to decide the question of close proximity, the question will be referred to the A.T.A. State Delegate who has the duty to make the decision, and whose decision is final. The A.T.A. State Delegate has no duty, responsibility or authority of the A.T.A. to decide any shoot dates until the question of close proximity has been referred to the A.T.A. State Delegate by the state association. A record of the issuance of the certificate of registration will be kept on file in the main office of the A.T.A, and prior to the holding of the tournament, necessary office supplies for the proper recording of scores will be sent the club or association.

B. PREPARATION AND PROGRAMS

1. Programs should be sent to an up-to-date list of shooters. It is recommended that the total amounts of money spent on trophies be included in the program.

2. IT IS REQUIRED THAT A.T.A. SHOOT PROGRAMS INDICATE THE SPECIFIC AMOUNT COLLECTED ON BEHALF OF THE A.T.A., AND IT IS FURTHER REQUIRED THAT SUCH FEES BE SET APART AS A SEPARATE FEE FROM ALL OTHER FEES AND CHARGES MADE BY SHOOT MANAGEMENT. No tournament promoter shall in any advertisement or program mention any purse or money in excess of the money actually added or guaranteed. Examples of money divisions may be included provided it is clearly stated that the amounts listed are examples and not guaranteed amounts. The word "example" must be included. Failure to observe the above provisions shall be grounds for disciplinary action by the state association and/or by the Executive Committee.

3. THE A.T.A. DOES NOT GUARANTEE AND IS NOT RESPONSIBLE FOR ACTUAL PAYMENTS OF ADDED MONEY, GUARANTEED MONEY AND PRIZES ADVERTISED OR OFFERED AT ANY SHOOT EXCEPT THE MONEY, PRIZES AND TROPHIES DIRECTLY SUPPLIED BY A.T.A.

4. The management should ascertain that the gun club facilities are in good condition prior to the shoot and that an adequate supply of such things as shells, targets, bulletin sheets, squad sheets, scoring crayons, thumb tacks, average books, change, and spare trap parts is on hand. Adequate toilet facilities should be provided for, as well as drinking water and lunch.

C. CHECKLIST FOR THE SHOOT

1. The management should arrange for

a. Capable classifying and handicapping committee.

b. Competent cashiers who will figure purses and options correctly and pay off as many events as possible before the close of the shoot.

c. Squadding personnel

(Note - At small shoots, all three of the above may be done by the same person or persons.)

d. Sufficient and trained trappers who are provided with a safety flag or other warning device to indicate when they are exiting from the traphouse.

e. Referees who know the A.T.A. rules and whose decision on whether a target is dead or lost is final, subject to review only by the shoot committee or other governing body.

f. Scorers who have been adequately trained to call all targets, or only the lost targets as directed, and to record the scores correctly on the sheets provided.

g. Pullers who must be provided with an unobstructed view of shooters. It is illegal at an A.T.A. shoot for shooters to supply their own pullers.

(Note—One person may serve as puller, scorer, and referee. If the person or persons serving in these capacities is negligent or inefficient, the management shall remove him or them.)

h. Any additional help needed to conduct the tournament efficiently, such as squad hustler, scoreboard recorder, score sheet runners, and enough personnel to property operate a shooting facility.

2. The management of any registered tournament, at its discretion, may reject any entry, or refund any entry. In all cases except as may be otherwise provided in these rules, the authority of the management of a registered shoot is supreme and all contestants must abide by its rulings.

3. The management shall appoint a judge or judges to be called upon for ruling on official complaints when the occasion arises. If a judge has not been appointed, the president of the club, or in his absence, the secretary shall act as judge. The scorer must call upon a judge to settle any controversy regarding a score or when he has made an error by being ahead or behind in his scoring.

THE OFFICIALS OF THE A.T.A. WILL NOT CHANGE THE DECISIONS OF THESE PERSONS MADE IN ACCORDANCE WITH THESE RULES, OR CHANGE THE REPORT OF ANY SHOOT HELD IN ACCORDANCE WITH THESE RULES.

4. At every registered tournament all targets on the official program shall be registered. Registered scores which have been made by any contestant as a result of duplicating any portion of the regularly advertised program will not be recorded. Special events may be held and the scores registered provided that shooters have been notified of such special events by shoot management, that the special event is announced and posted, and that at least five entries shoot and complete the special event.

5. The sponsors of registered tournaments are responsible for the payment of all added money, guaranteed money, purses, and/or prizes advertised or offered in their shoot programs. **If the management of a registered shoot does not meet the above obligations, the A.T.A. is not responsible for such payments and will not be liable.**

6. The management shall see that the cards of any shooters earning yardage are punched. If for any reason a card is not punched at the shoot, the gun club should immediately inform the A.T.A., the shooter, and the shooter's State A.T.A. Delegate in writing.

D. FOLLOW UP DUTIES

Following the conclusion of a tournament, the management is responsible or should delegate the responsibility for:

1. Completing and sending to the A.T.A. office:

a. The A.T.A. report form with complete names, addresses, A.T.A. card numbers, and accurate scores of all shooters.

b. The earned yardage report.

c. Names and addresses of those paying A.T.A. dues at the shoot.

d. A check for A.T.A. daily fees or league registration fees collected at the shoot or league.

e. One copy of the official shoot program or league rules. This must be done within 15 days following the last day of the registered shoot or league to avoid a $25.00 late shoot report fine which, if not paid, will be deducted from the state rebate in which the shoot is held.

2. Sending State fees collected to the State Association.

3. Sending a copy of the winners report to TRAP & FIELD.

4. Reporting shoot results to the local radio and TV stations and the local newspapers.

5. Making sure that scores are reported on any sub-events of 25 targets which is completed. In case the shooter is prevented by reasons beyond his control from completing a 25 target sub-event, the scores for that partial sub-event shall not be reported. Example: a shooter has shot 61 targets of a 100 target event when a storm permanently stops shooting. The management should report his scores for the first 50 targets only.

E. KEEPING SHOOT RECORDS

The tournament management is required to keep the records from all registered shoots for at least one year.

Skeet Rules

SECTION I - EQUIPMENT

A. TARGETS

Standard targets of good quality measuring no more than four and five-sixteenth ($4^5/_{16}$) inches in diameter nor more than one and one-eighth ($1^1/_8$) inches in height shall be used.

B. AMMUNITION

1. Gauge Specifications—Lead Shot Only

Shells commercially manufactured by reputable companies, which are clearly labeled and guaranteed as to lead shot sizes and weight are recommended for use in registered skeet shoots. However, the National Skeet Shooting Association will accept results of shoots and register scores where reloads have been used.

The National Skeet Shooting Association assumes no responsibility in connection with the use of reloads.

2. Reloads

a. The maximum load permissible is described below. This table makes ample allowance for manufacturing purposes, but the use of a proper shot bar is cautioned (a 12 gauge bar designed for $7^1/_2$ shot will weigh approximately 11 grains heavy when No. 9 shot is used).

Gauge	Ounce Lead	Grains Standard	Grains Maximum
12	$1^1/_8$	492.2	507
20	$^7/_8$	382.8	394
28	$^3/_4$	328.1	338
410	$^1/_2$	218.8	229

b. Any shooter may elect to have his shells weighed by management before entering an event. The shooter must submit all shells to be used in said event. After one shell is selected, weighed and approved by these standards, the balance of the shells shall be stamped, approved and sealed by some suitable method and not be opened until on the field where the event is to be shot in the presence of the field referee. Failure to have the field referee witness the breaking of the sealed boxes or containers on their respective fields shall necessitate the shooter using factory ammunition or risk having his score disqualified. Any shooter using approved and sealed ammunition shall be immune from further checking.

c. Challenge Rule: At shoots where shells have not been checked, any contestant may, upon formal challenge presented to shoot management, have the chief referee, who shall use timely discretion, select a shell from another contestant and have said shell checked against the standards listed in Rule 1-B-2-a. To prevent abuse of a shooter with this rule, shoot management shall make known the challenger and the individual challenged.

Entire groups or squads shall not be challenged for purposes of anonymity.

d. Shooters using reloads shall be required to furnish their own spares for defective ammunition.

3. Checking Factory Loads

Any shooter found to be using commercial loads heavier than the maximum grains permissible as listed in 1-B-2-a shall have his score disqualified for that event.

C. FIELD LAYOUT

It is recommended and desirable for all NSSA registered targets to be shot on fields constructed according to the following specifications and the diagram shown on the centerfold of this book.

Field Layout deviation will not affect NSSA's consideration of scores.

Under no circumstances will protests based on alleged irregularity of field layout be considered.

1. A skeet field shall consist of eight shooting stations arranged on a segment of a circle of twenty-one (21) yards radius, with a base cord exactly one hundred twenty (120) feet, nine (9) inches long, drawn six (6) yards from the center of the circle. The center of the circle is known as the target-crossing point and is marked by a stake. Station 1 is located at the left end of the base while standing on the periphery of the segment. Stations 2 to 6, inclusive, are located on the periphery at points equidistant from each other. The exact distance between Stations 1 and 2, 2 and 3, etc., is twenty-six (26) feet, eight and three-eighths ($8^3/_8$) inches. Station 8 is located at the center of the base chord.

a. Shooting Stations 1 and 7, each a square area three feet on a side, shall have two sides parallel to the base chord.

b. Shooting Stations 2 to 6, inclusive, each a square area, three feet on a side, shall have two sides parallel to a radius of the circle drawn through the station marker.

c. Shooting Station 8 is a rectangular area 3 feet wide by 6 feet long, with the long sides parallel to the base chord.

2. The location of each shooting station shall be accurately designated.

a. The marker for shooting Stations 1-7, inclusive, is on the center of the side nearest the target crossing point.

b. The marker for shooting Station 8 is on the center point of the base chord.

3. One target should emerge from a skeet house (called high house) at a point three (3) feet beyond Station Marker 1 (measured along the base chord extended), and ten (10) feet above the ground level. The other should emerge from a skeet house (called low house) at a point three (3) feet beyond Station Marker 7 (measure along the base chord extended), and two and one-half ($2^1/_2$) feet from the base chord extended (measure on side of target-crossing point), and three and one-haff ($3^1/_2$) feet above the ground.

4. Mandatory markers (where geographically possible) shall be placed at points 44 yards and 60 yards from both the high house and the low house to indicate the shooting boundary limit of 44 yards. These distances shall be measured along a line and the flight of a regular target 60 yards from the opening (where target emerges) in skeet house through the target-crossing point. The 60-yard distance markers must be suitably marked to indicate Station 8 ground level where geographically possible.

5. The target-crossing point must be marked in a visible manner where geographically possible.

6. It is recommended to remove posts or box stands tangent to the front of the stations interfering with the shooter.

7. It is recommended and desirable that the side of the skeet house, from the bottom of the chute to the top of the house, be very light color or painted white where feasible.

8. As a safety precaution, there shall be a barrier (wire, chain or rope) located between the shooting stations and the spectators. No spectators shall be allowed within this barrier and the referee shall be responsible for the enforcement of this rule. This barrier shall be mandatory at all state, zone, regional and world championship shoots.

9. Each skeet mount at world championships sites must be approved by a NSSA appointed representative. Unusual or undesirable field variations must be corrected before contract negotiations are completed.

D. MANDATORY POSITIONS FOR REFEREES

1. For shooting Station 1 (1R), stand six feet to the right and three feet back of the front of Station 1 where possible.

2. For shooting Station 2 (2R), stand six feet back and three feet to the right of Station 2.

3. For shooting Stations 3,4,5 and 6 (3-4-5-6R), stand six feet back and three feet to the left of the respective station.

4. For shooting Station 7 (7R), stand six feet to the left and three feet back of the front of Station 7 where possible.

5. For shooting Station 8 (8R), stand on center line of the field, not less than 6 feet from shooter (and not more than 10 feet).

6. During "Doubles" shooting, as shooters are coming back around the circle, referees should stand six feet back and three feet to the right of Stations 5,4 and 3.

Exception: A shooter may request the referee to move behind the station at Station 3 or 5.

E. RECOMMENDED POSITIONS FOR SHOOTERS

It is recommended for courtesy to team members that shooters do not advance more than one-third of the way to the next shooting station until all shooters on the squad have completed the station. Furthermore, shooters should stand a minimum of six feet outside the shooting circle while waiting to shoot.

F. RECOMMENDED PROCEDURE FOR SETTING DISTANCE ON TARGETS

It is recommended to adjust the skeet machine spring to a tension that will just reach the 60 yard stake, passing near dead center on the target setting hoop, under a "no wind" condition. Once this setting is made, it is unnecessary to change the spring tension during a tournament unless the spring becomes defective. The prevailing wind during a shoot may cause the targets to fall far short or long, but they are legal targets providing they pass through the setting hoop.

SECTION II—REGISTERED SHOOTS

A. GENERAL

1. Identification of Eligible Shooters

Members shall receive a new classification card as soon as possible after October 31.

a. This card will be of high quality paper and is to be used throughout the shooting year. Classification cards will be a different color each year for ease of identification. Replacement cards can be obtained from NSSA home office if lost or accidentally destroyed.

b. Presentation of a classification card, indicating a member's shooting reoord and paid membership status, and a plastic NSSA membership card is required for entry in a registered shoot.

c. Classification for the beginning of the year shall be indicated in the appropriate place on each classification shoot record card.

d. These cards also shall contain columns in which the holders are to keep their up-to-date running averages posted for each gun.

2. Open Shoot Registration

The term "open", as it may appear in any application for registration or sanction, or in the shoot program, if any, shall be deemed to mean "open to NSSA members without regard to residence."

3. Night Shooting

Registered shooting at night is permissible. All scores recorded for night registered shoots will receive the same treatment as any other registered shoot. Participants in night registered shoots must accept the conditions at the club where the shoot is held and no protest concerning shooting conditions, i.e., light conditions, natural or artificial, etc., will be allowed. *At night registered shoots, white targets will be used, unless otherwise published in the program.*

4. Shooting Order

The management shall determine the shooting order of the individuals in each squad at the beginning of the round, and the shooters shall adhere to this order. If the order is changed during any succeeding round of the same event, each squad member shall be responsible that his name be in the proper order on the respective score sheet, and that the change be plainly indicated for the attention of the final recorder.

Each squad shall report to the field at its appointed time. Upon failure of a shooter to appear at the appointed time, where a regular schedule has been posted in advance, or after proper call, the squad shall proceed without the absent shooter and the offender be dropped to the first vacancy in the schedule, or if there is no vacancy, to the bottom of the list. Weather conditions shall not be deemed sufficient excuse for delay in taking the field or proceeding with the round, unless all shooting has been officially suspended at the discretion of the management.

5. Squadding Restrictions

The squadding of practice shooting in a registered event shall not be allowed. Violations of this rule shall be sufficient cause for non-registration of all scores in the squad.

Exception: IF THERE SHOULD BE A SINGLE ENTRY IN THE LAST SQUAD OF ANY EVENT, SHOOT MANAGEMENT MAY ALLOW NO MORE THAN TWO ADDITIONAL SHOOTERS TO SHOOT FOR PRACTICE, BUT ONLY IF REQUESTED TO DO SO BY THE LONE ENTRY AND SAID LAST SQUAD. Pacer for lone participant on a field in shootoff shall not be permitted.

6. Checks—Payments, Over-Payments

Anyone who presents a check at any shoot that is returned for insufficient funds or other causes, may not compete in any registered shoot until full payment has been made to the individual or club to which it was presented. Any club receiving such a check shall report name and address of the shooter issuing the check to the NSSA and to its own state, territorial or district association.

Any competitor at a registered shoot who, through error, has been overpaid on any purse, added money, optional or other prize money and who is notified of the over-payment by registered mail, must return the over-payment within fifteen days. Failure to do so shall result in disbarment from all registered shoots until repayment is made.

7. Club Qualifications and Responsibilities

a. Only clubs affiliated with NSSA with affiliation fees currently paid up for the year concerned shall be eligible to conduct registered shoots. Evidence of club's status in this regard must be displayed in the form of official NSSA membership certificate for the appropriate year. Only clubs also affiliated and in good standing with their state or territorial association will be permitted to hold registered shoots in areas where such associations are active.

b. Where state or territorial associations exist, application for a registered shoot must be made through those bodies, which, in turn after giving approval, will submit application to NSSA. NSSA will then issue proper certification and supplies on which to report scores, winners and make financial reports. When an area association does not exist, clubs will make application directly to NSSA.

1) The application form furnished by NSSA shall include the scheduled shooting dates and may not be altered without 10 days notice. Shoot applications, property sanctioned, must be postmarked or received by NSSA at least 10 days prior to the shoot date.

2) Applications for night registered shoots must designate on the face of application that it will be a night shoot and all promotion by club shall clearly indicate that it is a night shoot.

c. Open shoots should be advertised to a majority of local contestants, and closed club shoots posted a minimum of seven days prior to the shoot data. Failure to so advertise, may result in a disqualification of shoot scores. Exception may, however, be granted by the Executive Director on merit.

d. It shall be the responsibility of the management of the club, association or other organization granted a certificate of registration, to see that each shoot is conducted in accordance with the official rules of the NSSA.

e. The group or club sponsoring the shoot shall check the NSSA membership of each shooter before accepting his entry and shall be responsible for the annual dues if they allow a participant to shoot when said participant's membership in NSSA has expired.

1) All individual shooters in all registered shoots must be members in good standing of the NSSA. IT SHALL BE THE RESPONSIBILITY OF THE CLUB HOLDING A REGISTERED SHOOT TO CHECK CARDS OF ALL PARTICIPANTS AND ENFORCE THIS RULE RIGIDLY.

2) Management will be billed by NSSA in all cases where expired members are allowed to shoot. Management may seek reimbursement from said shooters.

f. Management shall check the shooter's classification card to ascertain the proper classifications in which he should compete and enter on the shooter's classification card the classification in which it is entering him in each gun.

g. Class winners must be reported if they are to be reported in the magazine.

h. Scores in shoots on which complete records are not made by shoot management will not be recorded and the national association shall not be liable to refund fees received in such cases.

i. It is the shoot management's responsibility to appoint a chief referee.

j. In the interest of safety, interference and time, only the club management's personnel shall be permitted to pick up empty shells from the grounds during a registered shoot, and extreme care must be exercised to prevent interference with other squads shooting.

k. Shoot management shall determine the number of targets to be shot on a field. When shooting background is fairly uniform, it saves time to shoot 50 or 100 targets on the same field.

l. Shoot management has the right to determine the rotation and shooting sequence of events in their program, as well as shooting mixed guns in squads, unless their state association rules otherwise. When a participant is allowed to shoot an additional increment of targets (50 or 100 targets) above those shot in a program event, the first increment shot shall be the targets registered for the program event.

m. All two-man and five-man team events must be limited to club teams unless management exercises their prerogative of holding open or state team events duly announced in the program, or posted prior to acceptance of the first entry.

8. Individual Qualifications and Responsibilities

a. Residents of a state or territory must be members in good standing of their own state or territorial association before they can register targets shot in that state.

b. It shall be the sole responsibility of the shooters to see that they are entered into all the events desired. The official cashier sheet/entry form must be used. Once entered, clerical errors are the responsibility of shoot management.

c. Each shooter must verify his score and initial the official score sheet before leaving each field or accept it as the record. It shall be the responsibility of every shooter to enter in his proper class or classes at each shoot, including advancing himself in class when required by the rules based on averages at the completion of the regular string.

d. A shooter who fails to keep all of his correct scores posted on his card and shoots in a lower class than the one in which his record places him shall forfeit any winnings earned while shooting in the wrong class for the first offense, and for the second offense, shall forfeit all winnings and also be disbarred from registered competition for one year.

1) A shooter winning trophies or money by shooting in a lower class or *wrong class, including concurrent age groups* than the one in which he was entitled to shoot must return his winnings within 15 days after notification by NSSA headquarters that said winnings must be returned. Failure to comply within this 15 day period shall subject the shooter to suspension as an NSSA member and permanent disbarment from registered competition.

2) A shooter who enters, or allows himself to be entered in an event in a class lower than the class in which he was entitled to shoot forfeits all rights to any trophies or purses he would have earned shooting in his proper class unless the mistake is corrected prior to the distribution of such trophies or purse money.

e. It is the responsibility of the shooter to see that his safety is off and his gun is properly loaded with unfired shells of proper size and loaded before calling for a target (for safety purposes).

B. STANDARD EVENT SPECIFICATION

For the purpose of uniformity in records, averages, etc., the following provisions shall apply to all shoots registered or sanctioned by the NSSA.

1. Gauge Specifications

a. Twelve gauge events shall be open to all guns of 12 gauge or smaller, using shot loads not exceeding one and one-eighth ($1^1/_8$) ounces.

b. Twenty gauge events shall be open to all guns of 20 gauge or smaller, using shot loads not exceeding seven-eighths ($^7/_8$) of an ounce.

c. Twenty-eight gauge events shall be open to all guns of 28 gauge or smaller, using shot loads not exceeding three-quarters ($^3/_4$) of an ounce.

d. Four-ten events shall be open to all guns of .410 bore or smaller using shot not exceeding one-half ($^1/_2$) ounce.

e. A gun of larger gauge, which has been converted to take a smaller gauge shell may be used in an event for which it has been converted providing that the shell itself complies with the rule requirements for that event.

f. No shot smaller than No. 9 (2mm) or larger than $7^1/_2$ shall be used in any load.

2. Awards Eligibility

Anyone that participates in an event for a reduced entry fee (i.e., an N/C shooter or any shooter that shoots for targets only) shall not be eligible for tangible (i.e., purses, trophies) or intangible awards (i.e., event champion, sub-senior champion). Such shooter may not enter any concurrent events. An individual will not be required to participate in an OPTIONAL purse in order to win an honors award (i.e., event or class champion). This rule does not prohibit junior, sub-junior or collegiate shooter from participating in an event without paying that portion of an entry fee to be returned in the form of money, as outlined in ll-C-5-b. *Junior, sub-junior, and collegiate shooters who elect not to pay into an optional purse, or who elect not to pay that portion of the entry fee to be returned in the form of money, are still eligible to win intangible awards (listed above) and tangible awards, except money.*

3. Concurrent Events

a. Events designated for veterans, seniors, sub-seniors, sub-sub-seniors, women, juniors, sub-juniors, military service, two-man team or five-man team may be shot concurrently with the corresponding event on the regular program, or separately, at the discretion of the management.

b. NO JUNIOR, SUB-JUNIOR OR COLLEGIATE SHALL BE REQUIRED TO PAY ANY PART OF ENTRY FEE THAT IS TO BE RETURNED TO THE SHOOTERS IN THE FORM OF MONEY, INCLUDING OPEN PURSES AND CONCURRENT PURSES, BUT NOT TO INCLUDE TEAM EVENTS IF THE INVOLVED JUNIOR, SUB-JUNIOR OR COLLEGIATE IS SHOOTING AS PART OF AN OPEN TEAM.

4. Concurrent Event Awards

Any shooter charged an entry fee for a regiIar event and an additional entry fee for a concurrent event shall be eligible to win in both events unless clearly stipulated in the written program.

5. All-Around Titles

All-around titles must be an aggregate of all gauges offered in that registered tournament (preliminary events, Champion of Champions, not to be included) and will officially be recognized by the NSSA only when they include championships or title events in at least three of the four standard gauges and load divisions defined in paragraph No. 1 above and a total of at least 200 targets. Provided that the foregoing shall not be deemed to forbid local awards of special prizes for events of combination not recognized.

6. Minimum Number of Targets

No event of less than fifty (50) targets shall be designated as a championship or title event.

7. High Gun System

In explanation of the high gun system: If, for example, in a class, three should tie for high score and two tie for a second high score, the top three scores would divide evenly the monies for first, second and third places, and the two tying for second high score would divide evenly the monies for fourth and fifth places.

8. Method of Breaking Ties

In all registered NSSA tournaments, ties shall be decided in a uniform manner as prescribed in the following paragraph unless the shoot management gives due notice of any deviation in its published shoot programs. In the absence of a shoot program, notice of deviation must be posted conspicuously at the place of registration, thus informing all shooters of deviation before accepting entry fees.

a. Shoot management may elect to use regular skeet or a doubles event and shall follow NSSA rules for whichever event elected.

b. All ties for championship titles, such as event champion, two-man and five-man teams, veterans, seniors, sub-seniors, women, juniors, sub-juniors, junior women, military or any other concurrent title designated by the management, must be shot off by "miss-and-out" (sudden death).

WHEN THE SAME INDIVIDUALS ARE TIED FOR CONCURRENT TITLES, SUCH AS EVENT CHAMPION AND SENIOR CHAMPION, ONLY ONE SHOOTOFF WILL BE HELD TO DETERMINE BOTH TITLES UNLESS THE SHOOT MANAGEMENT ANNOUNCED IN ADVANCE OF THE FIRST SHOOTOFF THAT SEPARATE SHOOTOFFS WILL BE HELD. Management may combine other shootoffs only by approval of all the individuals involved in same.

c. After determining the position of all persons involved in shootoffs, all other awards shall be decided on the basis of the longest run in the event.

d. Long runs in an event shall be determined by using the shooter's FRONT or BACK Long Run (WHICHEVER IS LONGEST). If longest runs are tied, the Long Run from the opposite end shall be used to break the tie. If Long Runs are still tied, "miss-and-out" shootoffs must decide.

1) A shooters FRONT LONG RUN is figured by counting all targets shot in the event before the first miss.

2) To determine the BACK LONG RUN, count all targets broken after the shooter's last miss in the event. The optional shot must be counted in the proper sequence where it was fired.

e. Long runs for team scores shall be the total of targets broken by the members of the team combined up to the first miss by any member of the team; or the total number of targets broken by all members of the team after the last miss by any member of the team, whichever run is longest.

f. All ties for all-around championship must be decided by a miss-and-out shootoff commencing with the smallest gauge gun of which the all-around score is comprised. If a tie remains after this round, then the next larger gauge shall be employed for the next round. If a tie remains after all gauges have been employed, the shootoff shall revert back to the smallest gauge.

g. All other tied scores for all-around awards shall be decided on the basis of the longest run from front or rear (whichever is longest) in the smallest gauge event. If this also results in a tie, the same method shall be applied to the next larger gauge until the tie is broken.

h. Shootoffs take precedence over long runs, so all persons competing in a shootoff must continue to shoot off for all places beneath the event championship for which they may be tied.

9. NSSA Rules of Procedure for Shootoffs

NSSA rules shall apply subject to the following:

a. In employing doubles for shootoffs, a 50 target event is not required.

b. Doubles shootoffs shall be conducted doubles stations 3-4-5, miss and out by station. This means that a shooter must break both targets on a station in order to beat a shooter who only broke one target (i.e., if one shooter breaks the first target and another shooter breaks the second target, they are still tied).

c. If shoot management has elected to conduct shootoff using total score of a complete round, the shooter with the highest score shall be determined the winner. Tied high scores must continue to shoot complete rounds until the tie is broken and the winners determined. Lesser place winners shall be decided by the highest scores and if a tie exists, long run from the front shall determine these winners; if still tied, continue to shoot until the tie is broken.

d. In regular skeet "miss-and-out" shootoffs, long run from the front shall determine the winners. Ties shall continue to shoot the round until the tie is broken.

e. For Two and Five-Man Team Shootoff, management may combine or separate teams for shootoffs; and

1) regular skeet "miss-and-out" team winners shall be determined by the full team shooting until the first miss and comparing this long run with other squads involved. Any squads tied with long runs shall continue to shoot their rounds until the tie is broken.

2) If "total score", the total of the team scores shall determine the winner.

f. Shoot management shall post notice of time of shootoff as soon as possible during each event and shall also announce same by the public address system if possible.

g. Contestants involved in shootoffs forfeit all rights to the shootoff if absent or if they do not report within five minutes of the time the shootoff is called. However, any such person shall be entitled to any award he would have won by finishing last in the shootoff. It shall be the shooter's sole responsibility to determine the time of the shootoff before leaving the grounds. Shootoffs may not be held prior to the completion of an event (registration for the event has closed and no possible ties or winners left on the field) or of events of that day UNLESS ALL PARTIES INVOLVED AGREE.

h. If completion of shootoff is prevented by darkness, as defined in rule IV-C-4, the management and the contestants concerned shall determine the champion by a mutually agreeable method, but if no mutually agreeable method can be decided upon, then the shoot management shall determine in what manner the ties shall be decided. Management should make every effort to schedule the last squad of the day early enough to permit normal shootoffs.

i. If shooters involved in a shootoff offer management a mutually agreed upon method of determining the places, management may accept. If management does not accept, shootoffs must continue and any shooter or shooters who refuse to continue forfeits as in paragraph "f" above. Declaring of event co-champions at the world championship shall not be permitted. Contestants must continue to shoot or forfeit.

j. The shooting order for shootoffs shall be the sequence of finishing the event, where possible, and each lead-off man shall be dropped to last position on subsequent rounds.

k. Where shootoffs are held under lights, all white targets will be used unless otherwise published in the shoot program.

l. A shooter involved in a shootoff with a broken gun shall be allowed a ten minute time limit to repair or replace a broken gun, and then must continue in the shootoff.

C. ELIGIBILITY OF INDIVIDUALS

1. Membership

a. All competitors must be members of NSSA in good standing, with current dues paid.

b. Neither state champions nor provincial champions will be recognized by NSSA unless sanctioned by a state organization, or provincial organization, recognized with proper bylaws on record at NSSA.

2. Amateurs

Before participating in any events for money prizes, all shooters are warned of the following official rulings:

a. The United States Olympic Association and the Amateur Athletic Union both consider everyone who shoots for any money a professional and ineligible for all forms of athletic competition under their jurisdiction.

b. The National Athletic Association has ruled that shooting for money does not impair eligibility of the shooter to participate in other sports conducted under its jurisdiction.

c. Under the rules of the National Federation of State High School Associations, the problem is left up to the individual member state associations some of which will permit shooting for money. (Parents of prep school students are urged to ascertain the position of their own state high school association.)

d. Entries of minors in money events will be accepted only with the written consent of their parents or guardians. This written consent must be given to the NSSA and the scoreboard must carry the signatures of compliance.

3. Industry Shooters

a. Any employee of an arms, target, and/or ammunition company who services registered shoots in his assigned area at the direction of his superiors and whose job is to further the sales of his company's products and who is compensated for his shooting, traveling and entertaining expenses by his company, shall be considered an Industry Shooter and not eligible for amateur competition. Questionable cases shall be decided by the management of the company involved.

b. Former Industry Shooters are eligible to enter registered competition as amateurs after applying to NSSA with proof of job separation, or acceptable job description, provided such application is approved by the Executive Director. A waiting period of no more than 90 days may be required, if necessary.

4. Residency Requirements

a. An individual must be a bona fide resident (permanent abode) of a state to be eligible for state championships or to shoot as a state team member and must be a bona fide resident of a state within the zone to be eligible for closed zone championships or to shoot as a zone team member.

Persons with residence in more than one state must declare their eligibility by writing their state and club affiliation on the face of the current year membership card. Servicemen, by the same act, may choose their home state or the place in which they are permanently assigned for duty.

Persons who change their official abode shall become immediately eligible to shoot as an individual in the state or zone shoot. They should contact NSSA for new membership cards reflecting change of address and present same before entering the shoot.

An exception to the residency requirements may be allowed to the individual residency requirements, providing the following conditions are met:

1) The individual resides in a state without an association.

2) The individual joins the association of an adjacent state.

3) The state association agrees to accept non-bona fide residents into its association.

4) The state association notifies NSSA of these exceptions.

b. No person shall be eligible for more than one closed state or zone competition during the NSSA shooting year.

5. Concurrent Events

a. A shooter's eligibility for concurrent events which are based on age will be determined by his/her age on November 1. Their age on November 1 shall determine their eligibility for the entire upcoming shooting year. No contestant shall be eligible for more than one individual concurrent event based on age.

b. No junior, sub-junior or collegiate shall be required to pay any part of any entry fee that is to be returned to the shooter in the form of money.

c. Where shoot programs offer special concurrent events based upon age, shooter entering such special events must shoot in the one for which they are qualified by age, if such a class is available. Example: Seniors cannot enter a sub-senior event if a senior event is offered. However, sub-juniors can enter a juniors event if a sub-junior event is not available.

d. In parent and child events, unless specifically stated otherwise in the shoot program, the child must be of junior or sub-junior eligibility age.

e. A sub-junior is any person who has not reached their fourteenth birthday.

f. A junior is any person who has not reached their eighteenth birthday.

g. A collegiate shooter shall be defined as a full-time undergraduate student in an accredited degree oriented learning institution up to a maximum of four (4) years of eligibility. For one time only, a shooter is eligible to compete as a collegiate shooter prior to his freshman year as long as he produces a letter of acceptance from a degree oriented learning institution.

h. A sub-sub-senior is any person who has reached their fortieth birthday.

i. A sub-senior is any person who has reached their fiftieth birthday.

j. A senior is any person who has reached their sixtieth birthday.

k. A veteran is any person who has reached their seventieth birthday.

D. TEAM ELIGIBILITY

The spirit and intent of these rules shall be interpreted to include all bona fide teams properly organized in pursuance of club and/or domicile requirements, and to exclude all teams of makeshift or pick-up character, organized on the grounds and seeking to take advantage of technicalities either herein or in program stipulations or omissions.

1. Team Representation

a. The members of a team must be designated before the team begins the event.

b. Team members shall be accredited by NSSA to the state in which they reside, but irrespective of residence, team members must not have represented any other club in a team event in any NSSA registered shoot at any time during the current year. A shooter who shoots on one club team, either two-man or five-man, shall by that act elect that club as the only club he shall represent in club team events during the current year.

Exception: Service personnel who have, within this period, shot on teams sponsored by military organizations, such as division teams or teams representing specific departments of the same branch of the service, and have been required to do so as a duty assignment, may immediately shoot on teams representing individual military clubs, providing that said former teams have been definitely disbanded and also providing that they have been members in good standing of the clubs they are about to represent for a period of at least 90 days prior to the shoot.

c. No individual may shoot on more than one team in any one event, even though both teams represent the same club, except in re-entry events where the program states that it is permissible.

d. Team members shall not be eligible to shoot for any state champion-ships except in the state in which they reside.

2. State Teams

a. A state five-man team shall consist of five (5) individuals; a state two-man team, two (2) individuals.

b. Each member of a state team must have resided in the same state for at least ninety (90) days prior to the date of the shoot.

c. State teams may shoot in national competition, or in state shoots if approved by the state organization.

d. State Championship Team Events. Any out-of-state team whose membership complies with state residency requirements and Rule II-D-3-b and ll-D-3-d, may enter club team events but may be subject to a surcharge at the discretion of the state association.

3. Club Teams

a. A club five-man team shall consist of five (5) individuals; a club two-man team, two (2) individuals.

b. Team members must have been fully paid members of the club they represent for a period of at least 90 days prior to the date of the shoot (honorary, inactive, non-resident members, or members whose dues or assessments are in arrears are not eligible).

c. No person shall reside more than 100 miles from the club he represents unless he resides in the same state in which the club he represents is located.

d. The club represented must be affiliated and in good standing with the NSSA with dues currently paid.

4. Exceptions to Domicile and Club Membership Requirements

The provisions of domicile and club membership of individuals on club teams do not apply to:

a. Shooters who have affected a bona fide change in place of domicile with resultant change in club membership affiliation.

b. Clubs organized within less than 90 days prior to the date of the shoot, provided that members representing such clubs comply with II-D-1-b.

c. New members of any club who have never previously fired in a team event in an NSSA registered shoot.

d. Privately operated clubs, which require no paid membership, may with the approval of NSSA be represented by either two-man or five-man teams if the members of such teams meet all of the other requirements except those applying to club dues and club membership. Such team members must be certified by management of such club as having been active shooters of the club for a minimum of 90 days before they are eligible to shoot for that club.

e. Former members of college teams and school teams who have become members of senior clubs after their graduation.

5. Open Teams (Definition)

An open team is one which is composed of members with no restriction as to club or domicile. Records established by open teams shall not be accepted to establish official records.

6. Five-Man Teams

a. Five-man club teams and five-man state teams must shoot shoulder-to-shoulder, unless management publishes otherwise in their program or same is posted prior to accepting the first entry. To be eligible for tying or establishing world records, any five-man team MUST shoot shoulder-to-shoulder.

b. Each five-man club team and state team shall designate a team captain who shall be the team representative.

c. At the completion of each round, the shooters shall view their respective at scores and initial them. However, in the case of team shooting, the captain of the team may assume the responsibility for the shooters and sign for his entire squad.

7. Two-Man Teams

Two-man teams may shoot in separate squads.

8. Armed Forces Team Representation

For team representation, the domicile of members on active duty with the Army, Navy, Air Force and other military establishments shall be defined as the place at which they are permanently assigned for duty. Retired, reserve or National Guard personnel are not eligible for service team membership unless on active duty for a period in excess of 90 days.

9. NSSA World Championship Five-Man Teams

a. In the NSSA World Championships all members of a five-man team will shoot in the same squad through that particular event. If any team member fails to finish with his proper squad for any reason whatsoever, the team shall be disqualified as such but not the members as individual contestants.

b. Under no circumstances, however, will the provisions on broken gun and shooting up affect the requirement of shooting shoulder-to-shoulder throughout the five-man team competition at the NSSA World Championships.

c. MANAGEMENT MAY DEVIATE FROM THIS RULE IF THEY DEEM IT TO BE ADVISABLE TO CONDUCT FIVE-MAN TEAMS IN MORE THAN ONE SQUAD. FOR CONVENIENCE IN TABULATING TEAM SCORES, IT IS MORE DESIRABLE TO KEEP A FIVE-MAN TEAM IN ONE SQUAD.

E. PROTESTS

1. A Shooter May Protest:

a. If in his opinion the rules as herein stated have been improperly applied.

b. The conditions under which another shooter has been permitted to shoot.

c. Where he feels an error has been made in the compilation of a score.

2. How To Protest

A protest shall be initiated immediately when it is possible to do so upon the occurrence of the protested incident. No protest may be initiated by the shooter involved after thirty (30) minutes have elapsed after the occurrence of the incident for which a protest is desired to be made. Failure to comply with the following procedure will automatically void the protest.

A protest involving the scoring of a target, if filed immediately on the station, a second shot, or shots will be fired and the results recorded and noted as a protest. The protest shall proceed in the prescribed manner.

a. State the complaint verbally to the chief referee. If not satisfied with his decision, then:

b. File with the shoot management a protest in writing, stating all the facts in the case. Such protest must be filed within 12 hours after the occurrence of the protested incident. If not satisfied with the decision of the shoot management, then:

c. File with the NSSA a written appeal, stating all the facts. Such appeal must be filed within 12 hours after the decision of the shoot management has been made known to the shooter. Protests in team events must be made by the team captain. Team members who believe they have reason to protest will state the facts to their team captain, who will make the protest if he feels such action justified by the facts. The shoot management may appoint a shoot judge to handle protests referred to it which have been handled in the manner stated above.

F. DISQUALIFICATION AND EXPULSION

The shoot management shall upon proper evidence:

1. Disqualify any shooter for the remainder of the shoot program for willful or repeated violation of gun safety precautions which endanger the safety of shooters, field personnel and/or spectators.

2. Elect to refuse the entry or cause the withdrawal of any contestant whose conduct in the opinion of the shoot management is unsportsmanlike or whose participation is in any way detrimental to the best interests of the shoot.

3. Any shooter may be disqualified from a shoot for misrepresentation of his status under the eligibility rules.

4. Expel any shooter physically assaulting a referee or any shooter using extreme, abusive language to a referee upon adequate evidence presented by the chief referee.

5. The shoot management shall report to the NSSA all cases of disqualification and expulsion and the reasons for same. Subsequent action by the Executive Committee could result in being expelled and barred from further membership in the NSSA, after the shooter has had the opportunity to appear before the Executive Committee and present his case.

G. OFFICIAL SCORES

1. All scores or records, to be recognized as official, must be shot under the official NSSA rules.

2. All scores shall be recorded as having been shot with the gun in which event they shot, i.e., scores shot with a 20 gauge gun in a 12 gauge event must be recorded as 12 gauge scores. Such scores may not be included as part of a 20 gauge long run or average.

3. Only the scores shot on scheduled dates, approved by NSSA, shall be registered. Scores made in shootoffs shall not be registered, however, all NSSA rules shall apply in shootoffs.

4. No shooter will be permitted to enter the same event more than once, even though his score has been disqualified. When a participant is allowed to shoot an additional increment of targets (50 or 100 targets) above those shot in a program event, the first increment shot shall be the targets for the program event.

5. The scores of any shooter who takes part in a registered shoot shall be considered official, and shall be registered with the NSSA even though the shooter had given notice that it was not his intention to have his score recorded.

6. While the management may refund the entry fees and permit withdrawal of shooters who would be required to compete under drastically changed and clearly intolerable weather conditions or darkness not confronted by a majority of participants in an event, scores of all shooters who do if participate must be recorded. In the event of extreme weather conditions, power failure, trap failure, or unusually early darkness, the shoot management may elect to continue the event some other time (i.e., the next morning or the following weekend) but must immediately notify NSSA, with a full explanation, who will sanction the change, provided it is deemed in the best interest of skeet.

7. When a contestant stops or withdraws without finishing an event in which he has started, his partial scores shall be reported to the NSSA along with the other scores of the event.

8. If a contestant stops or withdraws voluntarily, or after disqualification by the management, his partial score for the round in which he is shooting shall be entered as his score of targets broken for that full round of twenty-five targets. He shall not be penalized, however, for any of the remaining full rounds of that particular event. Where such withdrawal is the result of sickness or injury, the shooter withdrawing shall be charged only with the targets actually fired upon in compiling and reporting his score.

9. The shoot management is responsible to see that each squad's scores are posted on the score boards, preferably by the referee, when feasible, or by an official score man, within thirty minutes of the time the squad finishes shooting.

H. REGISTERED SHOOT REPORTS

1. Reporting Requirements

It is the duty of each club or association holding a registered shoot to fulfill the following obligations. Payments and reports must be postmarked no more than 15 days after the last day of the shoot.

a. Make payments of all money, purses and options to the shooters.

b. Submit fees and reports due to state association.

c. Two reports (Financial and Registered Target Official Report) must be made to NSSA on all registered shoots. Standard forms available from NSSA headquarters must be used. Rules ll-H-3 and 4 outline required method of completing these reports.

2. Penalties

Failure to fulfill the reporting requirements shall carry the following penalties:

a. *All shoot reports and wrap-ups MUST be postmarked within 15 days of the last day of the shoot to qualify for printing in SKEET SHOOTING REVIEW. A $25.00 DELINQUENT FEE will be charged to all clubs that have not submitted a registered shoot report and financial report (including all payments due) within the postmarked date. First offense will be waived.*

b. Cancellation of all subsequent shoot dates for the offending club or association.

c. Denial of right to apply or reapply for any further registered shoot dates for a period of thirty (30) days in case of first offense, or ninety (90) days in case of second or subsequent offense or until obligations have been met.

d. Officers of any delinquent club or association shall be barred from shooting registered targets until all required obligations of said club association are met to the shooters, to the state association and to NSSA.

3. Financial Report

a. Daily Fees: List number of targets shot each day of shoot and remit to NSSA the required daily registration fee (in U.S. funds).

b. NSSA Dues Collected: Remittance (in U.S. funds) and duplicate copies of receipts for all types of NSSA memberships sold at your shoot must be attached. Membership applications must be completely and legibly filled out, including complete and accurate mailing address of purchaser.

(Shooter buying membership receives original receipt.)

4. Registered Target Official Report

An individual entry form/cashier sheet must be submitted on every shooter. These individual reports must include:

a. NSSA membership number

b. Full name or initials, corresponding to NSSA membership records

c. Member's complete address

Note: All of the above information is included on the plastic membership card. If an imprinter is not used, all information must be legibly written on individual shoot report form.

d. For each gauge in which the member participates (and HOA if appropriate) you must enter:

1) Number of targets shot at

2) Number of targets broke

3) Class in which member was entered (if member declares into a higher class at your shoot this information must be noted on shoot report form)

4) Awards won. Regardless of what method was used in making awards, winners must be determined and reported under NSSA classification system. This applies even if no awards are made. Do not list winners under class champions unless such awards were made.

5. Clubs are not REQUIRED to deliver or mail a copy of official shoot reports to the shooter. They are, however, required to retain copies of scoreboard and/or field score sheet on file for 90 days after the end of the applicable shooting year.

I. RECOGNITION AND AWARDS

1. High Average Leaders

a. For the purpose of determining yearly champions on the basis of average alone, leaders will be recognized if they have shot the following standard requirements of registered targets.

	.410	28	20	12
Open Team	1000	1000	1000	1200
All Concurrents	800	800	800	1000
Sub-Junior 400	400	500	700	

b. High All-Around Leaders will be recognized if they shot standard requirements in the four gauges listed above.

c. High Average Leaders in the Doubles Event will be recognized if they shot 500 registered doubles targets. For Sub-Junior, the requirements are 300 registered doubles targets.

2. All-American Team

Candidates for All-American selection must have shot standard target requirements as defined for High Average selection in II-I-1 in the .410, 28, 20, 12 and Doubles events.

3. Long Run Records

a. Only scores shot in registered events shall be included in official long runs. Scores shot with a smaller gun than the one for which the event is scheduled shall not be accredited as part of a long run with the smaller gun.

b. Shootoff targets and other non-registered targets shall not be counted as part of a long run.

c. All long runs shall be compiled in the order in which the scoring appears on the official score sheets except the optional shot shall be counted in the proper sequence where it was fired. The sequence in which the official score sheets are posted must coincide with the sequence in which the scores were broken.

4. High All-Around Averages

For purposes of determining yearly all-around averages, divide by 4 the total of a shooter's year end averages in all four gauges.

5. World Records

Current World Records are listed in the NSSA Record Annual each year. Any shooter, or team, who feels they have tied or broken an established World Record must follow the procedure outlined below for official recognition of a World Record score.

a. Establish that the event in which the record was tied or broken was a part of the shoot program and available to all eligible competitors.

b. Establish that the shooter or team properly entered the event prior to firing the record score.

c. Submit application for recognition to NSSA headquarters on the standard form which is available at NSSA member clubs. The form is also available from headquarters, upon request.

d. In the event that more than one shooter or team should break a world record score on the same calendar day, and provided they have correctly followed the outlined procedures, they shall become co-holders of that record.

6. Determination of Age Groups

A shooter's age on November 1 shall determine his eligibility for Recognition and Awards in any category based on age and all targets shot in that year.

SECTION III—SHOOTING PROCEDURE

A. DEFINITIONS

1. Shooting Positions

a. Shooter must stand with any part of both feet within the boundaries of the designated shooting station.

b. At Station 8, the designated shooting station is the half of the rectangular pad most distant from the respective high or low house.

c. Any shooter with one or both feet definitely off the shooting station should first be made to shoot over and, if he persists in standing off the station, he shall be penalized by loss of the target for each subsequent violation in that event.

However, if the shooter missed the target while committing the first violation of shooting position, the result shall be scored "lost".

2. Gun Position

Any safe position which is comfortable to the shooter.

3. No Bird

Any target thrown for which no score is recorded, or failure of a target to be thrown within the prescribed time limit of one second. This permits the throwing of instant targets, but gives a short time period in order to prevent a contestant from refusing a target which does not appear immediately after his call. If a shooter fires upon a target which appears after one second has elapsed between his call and the emergence of the target, and also before the referee calls "no bird", the result of his shot shall be scored. If he withholds his shot after such an alleged slow pull, the referee may declare the target "no bird" provided he, in his sole judgment, decides that the delay exceeded the one second time allowance. The pull is not required to be instantaneous.

4. Regular Target

A regular target is one that appears after the shooter's call and within a period not to exceed one (1) second, and **which passes within a three-foot circle centered at a point fifteen (15) feet above the target-crossing point.** The target-crossing point shall be measured from the level of Station 8. The target, in still air, must carry to a distance equivalent, on level ground, to 60 yards from the skeet house **when passing through the center of the hoop, with an allowance tolerance of plus or minus two yards.**

5.Irregular Target

a. An unbroken target that has not conformed to the definition of a regular target.

b. Two targets thrown simultaneously in singles.

However, if by error or for mechanical reasons doubles are thrown, and the shooter shoots and breaks or misses the correct target, it shall be scored as in singles. It shall be the shooter's prerogative to elect to shoot or withhold his shot when doubles are thrown in the calling of singles.

c. Target thrown broken. Under no circumstances shall the result of firing upon a broken target be scored.

6. Regular Double

A regular target thrown from each skeet house simultaneously.

7. Irregular Double

Either or both targets of a double thrown as irregular targets or only one target is thrown.

8. Proof Double

A repeat of a double.

9. Shooting Bounds

For Stations 1 to 7, inclusive, an area forty-four (44) yards in front of the skeet house from which the target is thrown. For Station 8, the distance from the skeet house to a point directly over a line with Station 4,8 and the target crossing point.

10. Balk

Failure to shoot at a regular target or double.

11. Malfunction of Gun

Failure of gun to operate or function through no fault of the shooter.

12. Defective Ammunition

Failure of ammunition to fire or function property.

a. Examples include, but are not limited to:

1) Failure to fire, provided firing pin indentation is clearly noticeable:

2) Firing of primer only, which will be characterized by a very weak report and absence of any noticeable recoil where powder charge has been omitted or not ignited:

3) Brass pulling off hull **between shots on doubles**:

4) Separation of brass from casing when gun is fired (usually accompanied by a "whistling" sound as the plastic sleeve leaves the barrel).

b. Components of the load remaining in barrel shall be considered as evidence of defective ammunition, but not a requirement.

c. Wrong size shells, empty shells and bloopers shall not be considered defective ammunition.

13. Blooper

Term used to describe an unusual burning of powder when a shell is fired,   and is distinguished by a louder than normal booming report. Usually occurs in reloads and caused by tilting of the over powder wad, incorrect pressures, or overload of powder. This cannot be considered defective ammunition.

14. Dead Target

A target from which in the sole judgment of the referee a visible piece is broken as a result of having been fired upon.

15. Lost Target

A target from which in the sole judgment of the referee no visible piece is broken as a result of having been fired upon.

16. Optional Shot

The shot fired after the first 24 targets have been scored dead in any one round (Station 8 low house only); or fired following the shooter's first lost target. In the latter instance, it must be fired from same station and at the same house as the one first missed.

17. Skeet Squad

a. A normal skeet squad is composed of five shooters.

b. Any five (5) shooters may designate themselves as a squad. All shooters shall be formed into squads of five (5) shooters each, as nearly as possible. Less than five (5) is permissible for expedience, but more than six (6) should not be squadded for safety reasons.

18. Round of Skeet

A round of skeet for one person consists of twenty-five (25) shots, the object being to score the greatest number of dead targets. Twenty-four shots are fired as described in III-B-1. The first shot scored lost in any round shall be repeated immediately and the result scored as the twenty-fifth shot. Should the first shot "lost" occur in a double, the lost target shall be repeated as a single with the result of this shot scored as the twenty-fifth shot.

If the first shot "lost" should be the first target of an irregular double, then a proof regular double shall be fired upon to determine the result of the second shot, and then the first target scored "lost" shall be repeated as a single and scored as the twenty-fifth shot.

Should the first twenty-four (24) targets of a round be scored "dead", the shooter shall take his optional shot at low house eight only.

19. Shooting Up

The procedure of a late shooter shooting out of turn to catch up with his squad (III-B-6).

B. GENERAL

1. Squad Shooting Procedure For A Round Of Skeet

a. A squad shall start shooting at Station 1 in the order in which the names appear on the score sheet. The first shot scored lost in the round shall be repeated immediately as the optional shot.

b. The first shooter shall start shooting singles at Station 1, shooting the high house target first and the low house target second. Then, loading two shells, he shall proceed to shoot doubles (shooting the first shot at the target from the nearest skeet house and the second shot at the target from the farthest skeet house) before leaving the station. The second shooter shall then proceed likewise followed by the other members of the squad in their turn.

c. Then the squad shall proceed to Station 2 and repeat the same sequence as on Station 1.

d. The squad shall then proceed to Station 3 where each shooter will shoot at a high house single target first and a low house single target second before leaving the shooting station.

e. The same procedure shall be followed at Stations 4 and 5.

f. Upon advancing to Station 6, the leadoff shooter will shoot singles in the same sequence as at the previous stations. Then, loading two shells, he shall shoot doubles by shooting at the low house target first and the high house target second before leaving the station. The other shooters will follow in their turn.

g. The same procedure will be followed on Station 7.

h. The squad will then advance to Station 8 where each shooter shall shoot at a target from the high house before any member of the squad shoots at a target from the low house.

i. The squad shall then turn to Station 8 low house and the leadoff shooter will shoot at the low house target.

j. The shooter shall repeat the low house target for his optional shot before leaving the station, provided he is still straight (no lost targets in the round). The other shooters will follow in turn.

k. At this time the shooter should verify his own score.

2. Rules and Procedures for Doubles Events

a. No less than a fifty (50) target event.

b. Shooting commences at Station 1 and continues through 7 and backwards from 6 through 5, 4, 3 and 2. Rounds 2 and 4 will end with doubles on Station 1 using the 25th shell from rounds 1 and 3. That is, rounds 1 and 3 will consist of 24 shots ending with doubles at Station 2, and rounds 2 and 4 will consist of 26 shots ending with doubles at Station 1.

c. When shooting doubles at Stations 1, 2, 3, 5, 6 and 7, shoot the first shot at the target from the nearest skeet house and the second shot at the target from the farthest skeet house.

When shooting doubles at Station 4, the shooter must shoot first at the high house target going around the stations from 1 through 7 and shoot at the low house 4 target first when coming back around the stations from 7 through 2 (or 1).

d. *The rules for doubles in a Doubles event are the same as the rules for doubles in a regular round of skeet.*

e. All other NSSA rules apply.

3. Shooters Right To Observe Targets

a. At the beginning of each round, the squad shall be entitled to observe two (2) regular targets from each skeet house and shall have the option of observing one regular target after each irregular target.

b. Shoot management, State Association, State Chief Referee and/or Zone Chief Referee shall have the right, where topographically possible, to make it mandatory to use a hoop or other suitable device whenever a target adjustment is necessary.

4. Progress From Station To Station

a. No member of the squad shall advance to the shooting station until it is his turn to shoot, and until the previous shooter has left the station. No shooter shall order any target or shoot at any target except when it is his turn. Targets fired upon while shooting out of turn, without permission of the referee, shall be declared "no bird".

b. No member of a squad, having shot from one station, shall proceed toward the next station in such a way as to interfere with another shooter. The penalty for willful interference in this manner shall be disqualification from the event.

c. No shooter shall unduly delay a squad without good and sufficient reason in the judgment of the referee in charge of his squad. A shooter who persists in deliberately causing inexcusable delays after receiving a first warning from the referee shall be subject to disqualification from the event.

5. Broken Gun

When a gun breaks in such a manner so as to render it unusable, the shooter has the option of using another gun if such gun can be secured without delay, or dropping out of the squad until the gun is repaired and finishing the event at a later time when a vacancy occurs or after all other contestants have finished the event.

Nothing shall prohibit the shooter from missing one round because of a broken gun, having the gun repaired and then rejoining the squad for all later rounds that the squad has not started. In that case the shooter will finish any or all rounds, starting with the shot where the breakdown occurred, that were not shot because of a broken gun, on the proper fields and in the first vacancy that may occur, or after the event has been finished by all other contestants.

6. Shooting Up

a. Where a shooter has registered in but does not show up to start an event with his squad, he will not be permitted to shoot up after the first man in the squad has fired a shot at Station 2.

b. He may join the squad for all later rounds, but the round missed because of lateness must be shot on the proper field in the first vacancy, or after all other contestants have finished.

c. In the interest of conserving time, the shoot management may modify this rule to meet special conditions, if it so desires.

7. Slow Squads

It is suggested that shoot management use substitute fields when breakdowns or unusually slow shooting squads are disrupting the normal sequence of squads. Under normal conditions, a squad should complete a round in 20 minutes. Squads desiring more time should not object to being transferred to a substitute field.

C. SCORING

1. The score in any one round shall be the total number of dead targets.

2. Targets declared "no bird" shall not be scored.

3. One "lost" target shall be scored on:

a. A balk or failure of gun to fire due to fault of shooter. Should this include both targets of a regular double, it shall be scored as first target lost, and a proof double shall be thrown to determine the result of the second shot only.

If a balk should occur, or his gun fail to fire because of the shooter's fault, when a proof double is thrown and the result of the first shot has already been scored, the second target shall be scored as "lost".

b. Each excessive malfunction or malfunctions of gun.

c. Doubles fired upon in reverse order.

d. Target broken after it is outside the shooting bounds.

e. Each target fired upon and allegedly missed because the shooter's gun had a bent barrel, or a bent compensator, or any other bent tube or accessory.

f. Each successive foot position violation.

g. Each successive time balk. It shall be considered a time balk if a shooter deliberately delays more than 15 seconds for each shot on a station and the referee shall warn him once each round without penalty.

4. A shot shall be repeated for each instance in which a target is missed due to defective ammunition.

5. If a shell having once misfired is used again, and fails to fire, the results shall be considered a fault on the part of the shooter and scored "lost".

6. No claim or irregularity shall be allowed, either on singles or doubles, where the target or targets were actually fired upon and alleged irregularity consists of deviation from the prescribed line of flight, or because of an alleged "quick pull" or "slow pull", unless the referee has distinctly called "no bird" prior to the firing of the shot. Otherwise, if the shooter fires, the result shall be scored. The referee shall have final say as to whether he called "no bird" before the shooter fired.

7. If the brass pulls off a hull between shots on doubles, score as defective ammunition but do not score, it as a gun malfunction.

8. During a regular round or a doubles event, if the brass pulls off a hull, or if a defective ammunition occurs between shots on doubles, the referee shall rule that if the first target was a "dead bird" nothing is established, and a proof double shall be fired upon to determine the result of both birds. However, if the first target was "lost", it shall be so established and a proof double shot to establish the second shot result.

D. GUN MALFUNCTIONS

The shooter must not be considered at fault if he has complied with the manu-facturer's operating instructions for loading the gun, and the gun does not fire. In the case of a gun going into battery (locking closed) for the first shot on doubles or any shot on singles, if the shooter as closed the action in accordance with the manufacturer's instructions, and if the bolt appears visually to be closed, the failure of a gun to fire shall be scored as malfunction.

1. Automatics

a. On an automatic, the shooter is not required to push forward or strike the breech bolt retraction lever to insure locking the gun. This is a normal gun function.

b. The shooter must load the shell or shells into the gun and see that the action appears closed. If he loads 2 shells on singles or doubles, and if the second shell fails to go into the chamber or is thrown out of the gun, it shall be scored a malfunction.

2. Pump Guns

a. The shooter is required to pump the gun, as recommended by the manu-facturer, on doubles and to close the action completely forward (visually) on singles.

b. If the shooter "short-shucks" the gun, the hammer will not be cocked, a fault of the shooter.

c. If the lifter throws the second shell out of the gun, it shall be a malfunction.

d. It shall be a malfunction, if between shots on singles or doubles, the gun returns the empty shell to the chamber provided the hammer is cocked.

e. The referee shall check for a malfunction as instructed under that title and shall then apply forward pressure on the forearm to see if the shell is lodged (a malfunction). However, if the gun closes smoothly, without jiggling, it is not a malfunction.

3. Double-Barreled Guns

a. The shooter is responsible for loading a shell in the proper barrel, or two shells for doubles.

b. The shooter must close the action in accordance with manufacturer's recommendations.

4. Shell Catching Devices

Where any device is attached to a shotgun which must be adjusted or removed to permit shooting doubles, it shall be the shooter's responsibility to perform such adjustment or removal.

Failure to fire a shot on doubles, due to such device, shall not be an allowable malfunction, and the bird shall be scored lost.

5. A target shall be repeated for each allowable malfunction.

6. Only No malfunctions of any one gun in the same round shall be allowable. The third and all subsequent malfunctions of the same gun shall be excessive. However, when more than one person is using the same gun in the same round, this rule shall apply to each person separately.

7. During the shooting of single targets, a shooter may load two shells except at Station 8 high house, or unless forbidden by club rules, and if the gun jams or malfunctions between shots, it shall be scored as a malfunction and the shooter permitted to shoot the target over. However, the shooter is still restricted to two allowable malfunctions with one gun in one round.

8. Malfunction on Singles or First Shot Doubles

To establish that a malfunction has occurred, the shooter must not open the gun or touch the safety before the referee's inspection.

a. If the shooter is holding the trigger pulled, the referee, after seeing that the gun is pointed in a safe direction, will place his finger over the shooter's and apply normal pressure.

b. If the shooter has released the trigger, the referee, after seeing that the gun is pointed in a safe direction, will exercise extreme caution not to jiggle or attempt to further close the action and will apply normal pressure to the trigger.

c. The target shall be scored "lost" if the gun fires or is opened before the referee's inspection. A malfunction will be ruled if it does not fire and the referee's examination for ammunition, safety, barrel selection, etc., establishes that the shooter had fulfilled required responsibilities.

9. Malfunction Between Shots on Doubles

If an apparent malfunction occurs between the first and second shot on doubles:

a. The referee shall apply the same procedures as listed under malfunction singles to determine if an allowable malfunction has occurred.

b. During a regular round or a doubles event, if an allowable malfunction has occurred, the referee shall rule if the first target was a "dead bird", nothing is established, and a proof double shall be fired upon to determine the result of both birds. However, if the first target was "lost" it shall be so established and a proof double shot to establish the second shot result.

c. If such malfunction is excessive (not allowable) and the first shot is a "dead bird", it shall be scored first bird "dead", second bird "lost" but, if the first bird is "lost" then both birds shall be scored "lost".

10. If a gun "doubles" or "fan-fires" while shooting singles or doubles, the referee shall rule a malfunction, and during a regular round or a doubles event, if the first target was a "dead bird", nothing established, and a proof single or double shall be fired upon to determine the results. However, if the first target was "lost", it shall be so established and a proof double shot to establish the second shot result.

E. DOUBLES OR PROOF DOUBLES

1. If the first target emerges broken, the doubles shall, in all cases, be declared "no bird" and a proof double shall be thrown to determine the result of both shots.

2. If a double is thrown but the targets collide, before the result of the first bird is determined, it shall be declared "no bird", and the result of a proof double shall determine the score of both shots.

3. If the first target of a double is thrown irregular, as to deviate from the prescribed line of flight, and is **not shot at**, a proof double shall determine the score for both shots, whether the second target is fired upon or not. The referee shall be the sole judge of irregularity.

4. If the first target of a double is thrown irregular, as to deviation from the prescribed line of flight, and is shot at, the result shall be scored for the first shot in accordance with lll-C-6 and if the shooter is deprived of a normal second shot for any of the reasons in lll-E-5, the second target only shall be declared "no bird" and a proof double shall be fired to determine the result of the second shot.

5. If the shooter is deprived of a normal second shot for any of the following reasons, the result of the first shot shall be scored, and the second target only shall be declared "no bird" and a proof double shall be fired to determine the result of the second shot.

a. The second target is thrown broken.

b. The second target is thrown irregular as to deviation from the prescribed line of flight and is **not shot at**.

c. The second target is not thrown at all.

d. The second target is not thrown simultaneously.

e. Both targets are broken with the first shot.

f. The wrong target is broken with the first shot. (For proof double ruling see paragraph 8 on the next page.)

g. The first shot is lost and a collision occurs before the result of the second shot is determined.

h. The second target collides with fragments of the first target property broken, before the result of the second target is determined.

i. The result of the first shot is determined, and interference occurs before the second shot is fired.

6. There shall be no penalty for withholding the first shot when either target of a double is irregular. A proof double shall determine the score of both shots thereafter.

7. If a double is thrown and an allowable malfunction occurs on the first shot, it shall be declared "no bird," and the result of a proof double shall determine the score of both shots. If such malfunction is excessive, (not allowable), the proof double shall be thrown to determine the result of the second shot only.

8. In shooting a proof double, after the first target (of a double) is "lost," if the shooter fires at, or breaks the wrong target first, said proof double shall be scored as both targets "lost." If, in such

a proof double after the first target (of a double) is "dead," the shooter fires at, or breaks, the wrong target first it shall be scored as first target "dead" and second target "lost."

F. INTERFERENCE

1. Any circumstance beyond the shooter's control which unduly affects his opportunity to break any particular target is interference.

a. If a shooter fires his shot, the appearance of a target, or a piece of target, from an adjoining field shall not be ruled as interference, unless such target, or piece of target strikes or threatens to strike the shooter or his gun. It shall be the final judgment of the referee to consider the evidence and determine whether a target or piece of target strikes or threatens to strike shooter or his gun.

b. If a shooter withholds his shot due to what he considers to be an interference, and if the cause is observed and ruled interference by the referee, the interference may be allowed.

c. If a shooter withholds a shot for safety purposes, the referee may give the shooter the benefit of the doubt and rule interference, providing he agrees safety was involved.

2. If the shooter shoots at a target, he accepts it. He must abide by the result unless the referee considers that there was legal interference. Following are a few illustrations of what may be considered legal interference.

a. A target box being thrown out the door in the shooter's line of vision between the time of the shooter's call and the firing of his shot.

b. Opening the skeet house door unexpectedly or suddenly under the same circumstances.

c. Any sudden disturbance or exceptionally loud noise, except an announcement over the loud speaker.

d. A bird flying directly across the target's line of flight just before it is fired upon.

e. A child or any other person or animal running out on the field suddenly in the shooter's line of vision.

f. A thrown object, or wind blown object, blown through the air so as to cause a conflict (a piece of paper being merely blown along the ground shall not qualify in this category).

g. All of these, and of course, a number of other occurrences can be allowed as interference if the referee, in his own judgment, feels there was sufficient interference to justify such a ruling.

h. The sun shall not be considered as interference. It must be accepted as a normal hazard.

G. SAFETY PRECAUTIONS

The safety of competitors, field personnel and spectators is of primary importance and requires continuous attention and self-discipline.

On any part of club grounds, as well as on the shooting field, particular attention must be given to the safety procedures outlined in the following paragraphs and to other safe gun handling techniques. Caution must also be used in moving about the field and club grounds.

Where self discipline and attention to safety procedures is lacking, it is the duty of the field personnel to enforce them and the duty of competitors to assist in such enforcement.

1. Eye and Ear Protection—All persons (including shooters, referees and trap personnel) must wear some form of eye and ear protection on a skeet range, at a shoot, sanctioned by NSSA.

2. No gun shall be loaded until the shooter is on the shooting station. Loading is considered as putting any part of a loaded shell in any part of the gun.

3. As a safety precaution, test shots will not be permitted without permission of the Field Referee. Such permission shall not unreasonably be withheld.

4. The loaded gun shall be kept pointed in a direction that will not endanger the lives of shooters, field personnel or spectators.

5. When not on the shooting station, the gun shall be carried with breech open. Pumps and automatics will have the bolt open. Fixed breech (double barrels including over and unders and side-by-sides) will be broken open.

6. When the shooter is on the shooting station and ready to shoot and a delay occurs, such as equipment breakdown, the gun shall be opened and all shells extracted.

7. During the shooting of single targets, the management may permit the loading of two shells at all stations except Station 8 high house. However, the management cannot compel the loading of two shells in the shooting of singles.

8. The loading of more than two shells in the gun shall not be allowed at any time.

9. A gun may not be used that will accept more than one (1) gauge of shells at the same time.

10. A shooter will not be permitted to use a gun with a "release-type" trigger unless the referee and the other members of the squad are notified. Extra caution must be exercised if the gun is given to a referee who is unfamiliar with its operation.

11. Any shooter whose gun accidentally discharges twice within one round for mechanical reasons shall be required to change guns or, if time permits, have his gun repaired, before continuing to shoot the round or subsequent rounds.

12. When a shooter intentionally fires a second time at the same target, he shall be warned by the referee. The second time the shooter intentionally fires a second shot at the same target in any event, the penalty shall be automatic disqualification from the event.

13. The placement of markers other than those specified in NSSA Rule Book shall be deemed illegal.

14. In the interest of safety, interference and time, only the club management's personnel shall be permitted to pick up empty shells from the grounds during a registered shoot, and extreme care must be exercised to prevent interference with other squads shooting.

15. There shall be a barrier (wire, chain or rope) located between the shooting stations and the spectators. No spectators shall be allowed within this barrier and the referee shall be responsible for the enforcement of this rule. This barrier shall be mandatory at all state, zone, regional and world championship shoots.

SECTION IV—REFEREES

A. LICENSED REFEREE

1. NSSA licensed referees shall pass prescribed written examinations (with the aid of a rule book) and also eye tests, using glasses if necessary. For the eye test, a visual card system will suffice and save cost of a professional eye examination.

a. These examinations will be given by their state associations or NSSA affiliated clubs.

b. Applications for official NSSA referee cards and emblems shall be approved by the applicant's state association, where one exists, or by an NSSA affiliated club where there is no state or district association.

c. It is recommended that all state organizations adopt the policy of using only NSSA licensed referees as chief referees.

d. All applicants for referee licenses must be paid up regular members of the NSSA.

2. Referees for NSSA World Championship Shoots

a. All applicants must be licensed NSSA referees for current year.

b. Each applicant must be recommended in writing by two current officers of his state association or by one NSSA director from his state or zone.

B. ASSOCIATE REFEREE

1. NSSA Associate Referees must meet all eligibility requirements specified for NSSA licensed referees (IV-A-1), with the exception of paid up membership in the NSSA.

2. An Associate Referee is eligible for an Associate Referee patch.

3. Application for Associate Referee status must be approved by applicant's state and/or zone Chief Referee.

4. An Associate Referee is not eligible to referee the World Championships.

C. CHIEF REFEREE

When shoot management designates a chief referee, he shall have general supervision over all other referees and shall be present throughout the shooting.

1. It shall be his responsibility to appoint the necessary assistant chief referees and all other referees shall meet with his approval.

2. The chief referee shall designate and assign the referees to the fields and shall be held responsible for their conduct at all times during the shoot.

3. It is recommended that the chief referee also have the responsibility of instructing all other referees and being certain they are acquainted with the rules and approved interpretations.

4. It shall be the chief referee and/or shoot management's responsibility to stop a shoot or shootoff when darkness or other conditions prevent a fair chance to shoot. This action **must carried out simultaneously on all fields.** Example: Use of public address system or the shutting off of power; or a suitable signal, the significance of which is known to all referees. Use of the referee's eye test card—$5/16$" dot at 21 yards—is MANDATORY.

5. Where practical, each state association should appoint a Chief Referee for its state. It is suggested that this chief referee be place in charge of all referees in the state and that he conduct training courses to develop better referees.

D. FIELD REFEREE

The field referee is responsible for the conduct of shooting on the field to which he has been assigned. On this field, he shall have jurisdiction over the area in rear of the field (that used by other shooters and spectators) as well as over the actual shooting area.

1. He shall be completely familiar with the shoot program and the NSSA rules.

2. He must be constantly alert, impartial and courteous (though firm) in the handling of shooters.

3. Upon protest, the referee shall rule upon the occurrence, and then without delay, proceed with the round as if nothing had happened. At the completion of the round, he shall notify the Chief Referee.

4. The referee shall distinctly announce all "lost" targets and all "no bird" targets.

5. The referee shall see that each shooter has a fair opportunity to shoot in his turn, and if in his sole opinion a shooter has been unduly interfered with while shooting, he shall declare "no bird" and allow the shooter another shot.

6. The referee shall declare "no bird" as soon as possible when:

a. The shooter's position is not according to the rules. The shooter shall be warned by the referee of his illegal shooter's position, but if he continues to violate the position, he shall be penalized by the by the loss of one target for each subsequent violation in that event.

b. Target does not emerge within the allowed time after the shooter's call.

c. Target emerges before shooter's call.

d. An irregular target is thrown in singles, doubles or proof doubles.

7. It shall be the referee's first duty after releasing the target to declare "no bird" as quickly as possible when he determines that an irregular target has been thrown.

a. If the shooter fires before the "no bird" call, the result of the shot shall be scored.

b. In the case of doubles or proof doubles during a regular round, if the referee's call of "no bird" occurs after the firing of the first shot (and said first shot was fired at a regular target), the result of the first shot shall be scored and a proof double shall be thrown to determine the result of the second shot only.

c. NO RESULT OF FIRING ON A BROKEN TARGET SHALL BE SCORED.

8. The result of shooting at a target after it has been declared "no bird" shall not be scored and the shot will be repeated in all instances.

9. Dusted targets or perforated targets that are retrieved after landing shall be declared "lost."

10. When the targets thrown from any machine are repeatedly irregular, the referee shall suspend shooting and order the machine adjusted or repaired. At shooter's request, after such repair or adjustment, the referee should allow shooter to observe a target, if such request is reasonable and not excessive.

11. The referee shall grant a shooter permission to shoot out of his regular turn where it is justified.

12. The referee shall disqualify, for the event:

a. A shooter who in his opinion has willfully interfered with another shooter while the latter is shooting.

b. Any shooter who repeatedly violates any of the safety precautions listed in Section III or for any act that in the referee's opinion endangers the safety of shooters, field personnel or spectators.

13. It shall also be the field referee's responsibility to supervise the keeping of correct scores and to see that all scores are verified by the respective shooters before the score sheet is taken from the field.

a. Every regular target fired upon shall be shown on the score pad and it is recommended that the mark "/" or "X" be used to signify "dead" and "0" to signify "lost."

b. If an error in scorekeeping is discovered on the field, the field referee shall remedy it promptly at the time of discovery.

c. In the event there is any question as to the correctness of a score after the score sheet leaves the field, shoot management shall check with the field referee and order the score corrected if it is determined that an error has been made.

d. The referee's responsibility in seeing that shooters verify their scores is to announce after each round, "Please check your scores."

14. The referee shall be the SOLE judge of decision of fact. For example, his decision as to whether a target is dead or lost shall be irrevocable, regardless of the opinion of spectators or other members of the squad.

15. It is better for a referee to continue to officiate at the same field.

a. Relief referees shall not take over the fields until the shooters have completed the round, except in cases of emergency, such as illness, etc.

b. No NSSA licensed referee may be disqualified in the middle of a round but he may choose to disqualify himself.

16. No member of a shooting squad may score or referee for other members of the squad.

SECTION V—NSSA CLASSIFICATION

A. DEFINITIONS

1. NSSA Shooting Year

The NSSA shooting year shall be any twelve month period running from November 1 through the following October 31.

2. Current Year

The twelve month period November 1 through October 31 of the year for which classification is being determined.

3. Previous Year

The twelve month period immediately preceding the current shooting year, i.e. November 1 - October 31.

4. Gauge

The term "gauge" used in this Classification Section includes International skeet and doubles as well as 12 gauge, 20 gauge, 28 gauge and .410.

5. Initial String

The required minimum number of registered targets necessary for an initial Classification is 200 for each gauge independent of each other gauge.

6. Regular String

The required minimum number of registered targets necessary for RECLASSIFICATION of a classified shooter is 300 for each gauge independent of each other gauge.

7. Initial Classification

The first classification of a newly classified shooter based on his INITIAL STRING of registered targets shot during the CURRENT year, or during the PREVIOUS year and the CURRENT year combined.

8. Regular Classification

a. The classification of a classified shooter at the beginning of the CURRENT year in each gauge will be based on all registered targets shot during the previous year, providing at least two hundred targets were shot.

b. The reclassification of a classified shooter based on his average for totals of all registered targets shot during the CURRENT YEAR.

9. Class Assigned

The class to which a shooter is assigned and would be required to shoot were he to compete in a subsequent shoot, whether or not he ever shot in that class.

10. Classification/Shoot Record Cards

a. As soon as possible after October 31 of each year, each PAID member will receive from NSSA a classification/shoot record card.

b. This classification/shoot record card shall include provisions for club designation, targets shot, targets broke, running average in each gauge and shall be imprinted with:

1) Member's name, address, membership expiration date and membership number.

2) Shooter's class for the start of the current year in each gauge in which he is a classified shooter, or NC if he shot less than 200 targets during previous year.

3) The number of targets shot at and broken in each gauge during previous year, if any.

4) The highest class in which shooter shot or was assigned during the previous year.

c. Any errors on shooter's new classification card, including those caused by failure of shoot reports to be received at NSSA headquarters in time to be included on new card, should be promptly reported to NSSA by the shooter so that a corrected card can be supplied and to insure proper inclusion in permanent record.

11. Classified Shooter

a. One who has fired at least the required INITIAL STRING of registered targets, or more, during the PREVIOUS year, or

b. One who has fired at least the required INITIAL STRING of registered targets, or more, during the CURRENT year, or

c. One who has fired at least the required INITIAL STRING of registered targets, or more during the PREVIOUS year and the CURRENT year combined.

12. Previously Classified Shooter (PC)

One who attained a classification during any of the three years prior to the current year but in the year immediately prior to the current year shot less than the 200 targets required for regular classification.

a. A PC shooter shall be solely responsible for his own record and, if requested by shoot management at the time of registration, be required to sign an affidavit attesting to his highest classification in the three years prior to current year. Falsification subjects shooter to action under II-A-8-d.

b. For classification procedures see V-B-4.

c. For classifying PC shooters in concurrent events see V-D-2-a.

13. Non-Classified Shooter (NC)

A new shooter or one whose record does not conform with any of the preceding requirements for Classified or Previously Classified shooters.

a. For classification procedures see V-B-4.

b. For classifying NC shooters in concurrent events see V-D-2-b.

B. PROCEDURES

1. Maintaining Shoot Record Card

a. Each shooter shall bear the responsibility of promptly and accurately entering his own score with the date, etcetera, in the proper gauge division at the conclusion of each registered EVENT in which he participates. Where a single EVENT extends more than one day, he should enter the total, not the day-to-day scores.

b. Shooter shall PROMPTLY have his classification changed in reclassification spaces on his classification/shoot record card whenever they have changed by averages on a regular string or cumulative regular stings, or because of class assigned.

c. The shooter is required to carry his card to each registered shoot and present it at registration.

1) A shooter failing to present his classification card, for any reason, MAY BE ASSIGNED CLASS AA AT THE DISCRETION OF SHOOT MANAGEMENT.

2) In the case of a lost card, or accidentally forgetting a card, the shooter may sign an affidavit attesting to his classification, subject to specified penalties. Such affidavit MUST be attached to the shoot report when it is forwarded to NSSA for tabulation.

NOTE: REPLACEMENT FOR A LOST CARD (INCLUDING REPORTED SCORES TO DATE) MAY BE OBTAINED FROM NSSA UPON REQUEST. IF THE ORIGINAL CARD IS LATER FOUND, THE SHOOTER SHOULD CAREFULLY CONSOLIDATE THE RECORD, THEN DESTROY THE EXTRA CARD.

d. In the space provided for club on his classification/shoot record card, each member shall designate, not later than his first competition in such events, the club he has elected to represent in club two-man and five-man team competition.

e. A shooter falsifying any entries or improperly using more than one card shall be disqualified and reported to NSSA for action according to section II-A-8-d.

2. Classification Review

A state association, director, club or shooter has the right to request a review of a shooter's record if it appears that he is unfairly competing in a class below his true level of ability. Upon review by a duly authorized national committee, the shooter may be assigned a higher class and may be required to disregard certain abnormally low scores for the purpose of classification and reclassification only.

3. Classification/Reclassification of Classified Shooter

Also see Reclassification Limitations.

a. Using the Universal Classification Tables, a classified shooter's class for the start of the current year shall be figured on the basis of his average on the total number of registered targets shot during the previous year, however, such class shall be no lower than:

1) One class below the HIGHEST class in which he shot during the PREVIOUS year, or

2) The class he was assigned if, because of a classification review, he

was required to move to a higher class than that required by average.

b. A shooter shall maintain throughout each shoot his classes and running averages as they were at the time of entry. A classified shooter shall not be subject to changes in classification during a shoot for any reason nor have his classification changed for a consolation event held after the regular shoot.

1) EXCEPTION: A non-classified or previously classified shooter who completes an INITIAL STRING of targets at the end of a preliminary event becomes classified for all remaining events of that gauge.

2) The total number of targets scheduled for an EVENT ARE TO BE USED IN DETERMINING STRINGS FOR CLASSIFICATION AND RECLASSIFICATION.

Example 1:

A non-classified or previously classified shooter has shot 150 registered 12 gauge targets and enters a 100 target 12 gauge event. He shall be classified on the total of 250 targets and NOT after shooting the first 50 targets of the event, which would total 200 targets.

Example 2:

A classified shooter has shot 550 registered 20 gauge targets and enters a 100 target 20 gauge event. He shall be reclassified on the total 650 targets and NOT after shooting the first 50 targets of the event, which would total 600.

c. A shooter who is classified at the beginning of the year on a class assigned or totals of targets shot during previous year will RECLASSIFY (**UPWARD ONLY**) at the end of his first REGULAR STRING and at the end of all succeeding regular strings shot during the CURRENT YEAR.

Example:

	SHOT	BROKE	AVERAGE	CLASS
CURRENT YEAR	100	XX		C
	100	XX		C
	100	XX		C
Reclassify on	300	XXX	XXXX	A
	100	XX		A
	100	XX		A
	100	XX		A
Reclassify on	600	XXX	XXXX	A
and again on	900, etc.			

d. Shooters must, however, always reclassify at the end of each regular string even though the correct number of targets for reclassification comes between the preliminary and the main event. Reclassification is not effective until **AFTER** the shoot, but must be accomplished on the correct number of targets.

Example:

	SHOT	BROKE	AVERAGE	CLASS
CURRENT YEAR	100	XX		C
	100	XX		C
*Preliminary	100*	XX		C
Reclassify on	**300**	**XXX**	**XXXX**	**A**
*Main Event	100*	XX		C*
of above shoot	100	XX		A
	200	XXX		A
Reclassify on	700	XXX	XXXX	A
	100	XX		A
	100	XX		A
	100	XX		A
Reclassify on	1000**	XXX	XXXX	AA

*Note that shooter must reclassify at the end of regular string EVEN THOUGH he does not CHANGE CLASS until **AFTER** the shoot:

**and that reclassification is at end of each regular string; not necessarily on multiples of 300.

e. A shooter who becomes a CLASSIFIED SHOOTER on combination of targets shot during the PREVIOUS year and CURRENT year shall be RECLASSIFIED on each succeeding REGULAR STRING of registered targets shot during the current year.

Example:

	SHOT	BROKE	AVERAGE	CLASS
PREVIOUS YEAR	100	XX		NC
CURRENT YEAR	100	XX		NC
CLASSIFY ON	**200**	**XXX**	**XXXX**	**D**
	100	XX		D
	100	XX		D
	100	XX		D
Reclassify on 400 shot in current year	400	XX	XXXX	B
	100	XX		B
	100	XX		B
	100	XX		B
Reclassify on 700 shot in current year	700	XXX	XXXX	B

NOTE: After Initial Classification, targets shot in PREVIOUS YEAR are not used in calculating averages.

f. A classified shooter who wishes to voluntarily declare himself up in class may do so. When he so elects, he must (at a registered shoot) have his card marked before competing in the event in the class for which he is declaring himself. His card shall be marked with the new classification by self-declaration in the class where he declared himself, and be entered on the Official Entry Form with notation "self-declared"

4. Classification of Previously Classified and Non-Classified Shooters

A shooter who has not attained a classification during the previous year will compete in a class determined by the following method for each individual gauge until he has shot an Initial String of 200 targets in that gauge.

a. Classes for each shoot, prior to attaining an initial string, are independent of other shoots entered. To determine class:

Drop the high score and low score rounds and classify on the total of the other rounds on a percentage basis. For 50 target events, use the entire 50 targets to calculate the percentage.

Example: In a 100 target 12 gauge event, shooter breaks 24-23-22-19. For purposes of determining class, disregard the 24 and 19. The remaining 2 rounds in this example total 45. As a percentage of 50, 45 is 90%—Class C (45 divided by 50). The shooter's ACTUAL score of 88 will be entered in Class C. **OR,**

In a 200 target 12 gauge event, scores of 24-23-22-19-24-23-23-22 would mean one of the 24's and the 19 would be disregarded. Score of remaining rounds totals 137 divided by 150 is .9133—Class C. This shooter's **ACTUAL** score of 180 will be entered in Class C.

OR,

For a 50 target event, a score of 42 is divided by 50 is 84%, Class E if the score was shot in a 12 gauge event.

b. Management may reserve the right to restrict PC and NC shooters from entering purses and/or class options but **MAY NOT REQUIRE** PC and/or NC shooters to pay any part of the entry fee that is to be returned to the shooters in the form of cash or other tangible awards.

NC or PC shooters will not be eligible for cash or tangible awards for which they have not paid the required entry fee prior to shooting the event.

c. Upon completing an Initial String in each individual gauge, the shooter will be given a classification based on average; however, a previously classified shooter may not be classed more than one class below the highest class he held in any of the 3 years immediately prior to the current year.

d. A PC or NC shooter who completes an INITIAL STRING of targets at the end of a preliminary event becomes classified for all remaining events of that gauge.

e. After this INITIAL CLASSIFICATION, a shooter will reclassify after each succeeding REGULAR STRING, using the total number of targets shot during the current year and will follow procedures as outlined in items b through f of this Classification/Reclassification of Classified Shooters.

f. A previously classified or a non-classified shooter who voluntarily wishes to declare himself classified, may do so provided he declares himself in Class AA. When he so elects, he must have his card marked (at a registered shoot) in AA before competing in the event for which he is declaring himself and Class AA must be entered on the Official Entry Form with notation "self-declared."

C. UNIVERSAL CLASSIFICATION TABLES

1. Use of the Universal Classification Tables shall be required for all registered shoots and shall be in accordance with the tables of averages shown below.

a. Shooter's correct class and average shall be posted on his shoot entry form.

b. Classification in each gauge gun is independent and shall be treated without regard to classification in any other gauge.

CLASSIFICATION TABLES FOR OPEN INDIVIDUAL CLASSES

Class 12 Gauge		**Class 20 Gauge**	
AAA	98.5 and over	AAA	98 and over
AA	97.5 to 98.49	AA	97 to 97.99
A	96 to 97.49	A	94.5 to 96.99
B	93.5 to 95.99	B	91 to 94.49
C	90 to 93.49	C	85.5 to 90.99
D	85.5 to 89.99	D	Under 85.5
E	Under 85.5		

Class 28 Gauge		**Class .410 Gauge**	
AAA	97.5 and over	AAA	95.5 and over
AA	96.5 to 97.49	AA	94.5 to 95.49
A	94 to 96.49	A	89.5 to 94.49
B	90.5 to 93.99	B	85 to 89.49
C	85.5 to 90.49	C	78.5 to 84.99
D	Under 85.5	D	Under 78.5

Class Doubles	
AAA	97 and over
AA	95 to 96.99
A	91 to 94.99
B	85 to 90.99
C	80 to 84.99
D	Under 80

*Class AAA attained only by average based on last reclassification.

2.Compulsory Classes

Only Classes AA, A, 8, C and D (and E in 12 Gauge) shall be compulsory.

a. Class AAA shall be optional and when AAA is not offered, Class AA shall include all shooters who would be in Class AAA if it were offered.®MDNM⁻

b. Class AAA is optional, however, it should be considered for use in any event where the number of entries exceeds 100, or where the number of entries eligible for AAA justifies doing so.

c. It shall be the sold responsibility of shoot management to determine whether Class AAA shall be offered and its decision shall be published in the shoot program or posted before the shoot.

3. High Overall

Unless otherwise published in the program or posted at the shoot, a shooter's HOA class will be based on his 4-gun average using the NSSA HOA Classification Table.

For shooters who have voluntarily declared into AA on any gun, or all guns, to calculate a HOA class, use the bottom percentage of AA in each respective self-declared gun. For a non-classified shooter, not wanting to voluntarily declare AA, who wishes to shoot HOA, use the highest percentage in "B" Class for any non-classified gun in calculating the shooters HOA, but not more than one class lower than their highest class in any one gun.

D. TEAM AND OTHER CONCURRENT EVENT CLASSIFICATIONS

1. Division of two-man team, five-man team, women, junior and other concurrent events into classes is NOT MANDATORY. In cases where shoot management should desire to establish classes in these events, they may do so.

When such classes are established, they should be designated by NUMBER rather than by letter, i.e., Class 1 (or I) XX—and over, Class 2 (or II) under XX.

2. Classification for team events shall be combined average of team mem-bers' scores, carried to the fourth decimal place at their initial or last reclassification (i.e.—.9525).

a. The average for a PREVIOUSLY CLASSIFIED shooter, competing in a team or other concurrent event that has been divided into classes, shall be his highest published average in the three years prior to the current year for the gauge entered.

b. The average for a NON-CLASSIFIED shooter competing in a team or other concurrent event shall be considered the highest percentage in "B" class of the gauge entered.

E. RECLASSIFICATION LIMITATIONS

1. DURING THE CURRENT YEAR a shooter is subject to reclassification **UPWARD ONLY.**

a. Reclassification **DOWN** will only be accomplished by NSSA headquarters at the beginning of the next skeet year; however,

b. Any shooter who believes he is entitled to compete in a lower class due to illness, accident, age, etcetera, may appeal to the Classification Committee of NSSA after prior approval of his request by his state association. In the absence of a state association in the shooter's state, his appeal may be made directly to the Classification Review Committee.

2. Each shooter classified at the beginning of the skeet year will shoot in that class or a higher class as determined by average or as assigned by the Classification Review Committee.

3. Reclassification in all cases shall be subject to the restriction and qualifications set out in this section and in the sections headed "Classification."

NSSA HOA Classification Tables

Use of this table is not mandatory. Clubs wishing to use some other method of determining HOA classes may do so as outlined in rule V-C-3. It is important for clubs to remember, however, that the method of determining HOA classification MUST be posted or published in the shoot program.

	4 Gun HOA	**5 Gun HOA**
AAA	97.5 & over	97.40 & over
AA	96 - 97.49	95.80 - 87.39
A	93.5 - 95.99	93.00 - 95.79
B	89.5 - 93.49	88.60 - 92.99
C	84.5 - 89.49	83.60 - 88.59
D	81 - 84.49	80.80 - 83.59
E	Under 81	Under 80.79

USE OF THIS TABLE IS NOT MANDATORY
It is an EXAMPLE - A GUIDE

SECTION VI—INTERNATIONAL SHOOTING

The NRA and the National Skeet Shooting Association (NSSA) have common goals concerning the support and growth of International Skeet. The major goal, after joint compliance with UIT rules and procedures, is one of congruent classification rules and procedures. Unfortunately, the two organizations have not yet achieved that goal; Therefore, NSSA members will use the following rules for classification and record keeping in NSSA registered International skeet events.

A. ELIGIBLE SHOOTERS

All competitors in NSSA registered International events must have a current NSSA membership.

B. CLASSIFICATION PROCEDURES

The classification rules and procedures for participation in NSSA registered International events are exactly the same as those set out in Section V of this rule book with one exception.

Exception: If there is a difference between a shooter's NSSA and NRA classifications, he will be required to use the higher of the two classifications in NSSA registered International events.

C. CLASSIFICATION TABLE FOR INTERNATIONAL EVENTS

Class	Averages
AA-Master	95 and over
A	87 to 94.99
B	81 to 86.99
C	75 to 80.99
D	Under 75

D. RECORDING SCORES

1. Only those scores shot in NSSA registered International events are to be used for determination of a shooter's NSSA International classification.

a. These are the only scores that will be included in NSSA records and publications.

b. These scores will NOT be included in NRA records unless the tournament has also been registered with NRA.

2. It is the responsibility of all shooters entering NSSA/NRA registered events to determine their correct classification according to NSSA/NRA rules.

E. REPORTING SCORES

Clubs registering International events with NSSA are subject to all requirements of Rule II-H, including payment of the required Daily Fees (in U.S. funds) for each target shot in the tournament.

F. RECOGNITION AND AWARDS

1. Scores shot and awards won by NSSA members in NRA and other UIT approved competitions will be recognized by NSSA for the purpose of All-American team selection, if in addition, the shooter has shot the NSSA standards of 1200 NSSA registered targets, provided such scores and awards can be substantiated by official records or published reports.

2. Candidates for All-American team selection must:

a. Shoot at least 1200 International NSSA registered targets during the NSSA shooting year.

b. Concurrent categories in International shooting will follow the 12 gauge NSSA standard registered targets subject to Rule II-I-1 (a) page 24.

PROTESTS

In order that protests may be more uniformly and fairly handled, the protesting shooter and the Protest Committee* should observe the following guidelines.

I. Record the exact time that:

A. The incident occurred.

B. A verbal protest was made to the field referee (if at all).

C. A verbal protest was made to the chief referee (if at all).

D. The chief referee ruled on the protest (if at all).

E. The Protest Committee's decision was made known to the protesting shooter.

II. Determine and record:

A. If there was a chief referee: Was the complaint brought to his attention by the protesting shooter?

B. Was the written protest tendered to Shoot Management within 12 hours of the protested incident?

C. Is the shooter not protesting a referee's decision of fact?

D. Is the shooter protesting: Improper application of the NSSA rules, or the conditions under which another shooter has been allowed to shoot or an error in scorekeeping?

III. If II-A through II-D above can all be answered "yes," the Protest Committee should then decide whether to grant or deny the protest. If the answer to any of the questions II-A through II-D above is "no," the protest is invalid.

IV. Any appeal to the NSSA of the Protest Committee's decision should include:

A. The facts outlined above.

B. A copy of the written protest.

C. A copy of the Protest Committee's decision.

V. Shoot Management should be prepared to provide the information in IV-A through IV-C above to the NSSA upon request.

*"Protest Committee" shall be defined as: Shoot Management, or a judge appointed by Shoot Management, or a panel of judges appointed by Shoot Management.

Sporting Clays Rules

NATIONAL SPORTING CLAYS ASSOCIATION
OFFICIAL RULES & REGULATIONS

ORGANIZATION OF THE NATIONAL SPORTING CLAYS ASSOCIATION

The National Sporting Clays Asssociation, a Division of the National Skeet Shooting Association, was formed in April 1989 to promote sporting clays in the United States and Canada.

The National Sporting Clays Association (NSCA) is a nonprofit organization owned and operated by and for its members. The primary objective of the NSCA is to promote the growth of sporting clays in a way which is beneficial to all who enjoy and participate in the game. The NSCA is guided by the Advisory Council comprised of range owners, both competitive and recreational shooters and the shooting industry.

The following is an informative summary of the organization of the National Sporting Clays Association. The Official National Sporting Clays Rules govern the shooting of registered targets, the conduct of shooters and the duties of shoot management. The NSCA has the responsibility for the formulation, regulation and enforcement of these rules. These rules are contained in this booklet.

The NSCA reserves the right to make alteration in, or amendments to these rules at any time, whenever it deems it to be in the best interest of the National Sporting Clays Association and its members.

GENERAL INFORMATION

A. PURPOSE OF NSCA

The purpose of the National Sporting Clays Association is to promote and govern the sport of sporting clays throughout the United States and Canada. The NSCA is dedicated to the development of the sport at all levels of participation. We vow to create an atmosphere of healthy and safe competition and meaningful fellowship within its membership.

B. MEMBERSHIP

Annual membership dues are $30.00 a year with a copy of the official magazine, Sporting Clays, "The Shotgun Hunters' Magazine." A $20.00 membership is available to dependents (no magazine).

Life Membership is available at $350, payable at full amount.

The membership and shooting year is from January 1 to December 31.

Application for annual membership may be made at any registered shoot by filling out an application or by contacting the NSCA for an application.

C. ADVISORY COUNCIL

The Advisory Council is comprised of NSCA members range owners, industry and shooters. Their primary function is to promote and guide the association.

I—CLASSIFICATION

A. CLASSIFICATION PROCEDURES

There are five classes that a shooter can classify into: AA - A - B - C - D.

1. Classification based on averages will no longer apply.

2. A shooter in the lower 50% of their class (according to their 1993 average) will move down one class (subject to review of wins).

3. A shooter who is assigned to a lower class may reject the class if the shooter wishes to remain in a higher class. To reject the assigned class, the shooter must sign the "refusal form" which will be included with the 1994 classification card, and return it to NSCA Headquarters immediately (within 7 days).

4. A shooter may also declare into a class higher than assigned; however, the shooter must stay in that class or higher for the entire year.

5. All new shooters in 1994 will be assigned a class. There will no longer be a non-classified (novice or hunter members class) for NSCA members registering targets.

To determine your assigned class:

a. A shooter who has never shot any registered clay targets will be assigned Class D.

b. A shooter who has shot registered targets with any clay target organization, other than a Sporting Clays Association (i.e., NSSA, ATA, NRA, International skeet or trap), will be assigned

into Class C or one class lower than his highest class attained in that clay target organization, whichever is greater.

c. A shooter from another sporting clays organization, (i.e., USSCA/SCA, CPSA, FITASC) will shoot their earned class or higher.

6. Shooters must win their way out of class which will be determined by:

a. Shooters who win their class in a major shoot* (100 or more participants), will move immediately into their next highest class.

b. Shooters who win two shoots* in their class with 50-99 participants will move immediately into their next highest class.

c. NSCA will review wins from small shoots (under 50 participants) to determine possible class increase.

d. Shoot Officials can place a shooter in a higher class based on known ability.

*When a shooter (in a class lower than AA) wins the open champion or any other title higher than his Class, the win is equivalent to a class win and is subject to move up in class determined by 6.a or 6.b. (as stated above).

7. It is the shooter's responsibility to follow these rules and declare himself/herself up in class at the appropriate time. Failure to do so will result in disqualification and return of all monies and prizes and/or suspension.

8. Classification carries over from one year to the next, however, the shooter can only be reclassified up or down at the end of the shooting year based on NSCA classification system.

9. During the current year, a shooter is subject to reclassify UPWARDS ONLY.

10. The shooter is responsible for entering his/her scores with the date and score shot on the back of this score card. It is also the duty of each NSCA member to assure that ALL wins are properly recorded on his/her score card at the conclusion of each NSCA tournament.

11. A classified shooter who wishes to voluntarily declare himself up in class may do so. When he so elects, he must (at a registered shoot) have his card marked before competing in the event in the class for which he is declaring himself. His card shall be marked with the new classification by self-declaration in the class where he declared, and be entered on the Official Entry Form with notation "self-declared."

12. A shooter may also be reclassified on his/her "known ability."

13. Reclassification for medical reasons shall be entertained on an individual bases by the NSCA Classification Review Committee.

14. Classification Review—The Advisory Council, club or shooter has the right to request a review of a shooter's record if it appears that he is unfairly competing in a class other than his true level of ability. Upon review by the committee, the shooter may be assigned a higher class.

B. RULES OF CONDUCT OF NSCA SHOOTER

Each member will be furnished a copy of these Official NSCA rules, with the understanding that the member will read and understand each rule. Members are strongly encouraged to know these rules and abide by them, both for their own benefit and for the benefit of other shooters and safety.

By entering the competition, every person agrees to accept all official decisions and to abide by these rules.

When making your entry at any registered shoot, produce your plastic identification card and your *classification* card so that your name, address and membership number are properly noted and errors in records are prevented. Shooters not having his/her plastic card should always list their NSCA number, entire name and address on the event cards.

It is the duty of each NSCA member to have his/her *classification* card updated at the end of each shoot.

The *classification* card is intended for the purpose of providing the shoot promoters with up-to-date *information*, proper classification and location of each shooter entering a classified event.

Failure to accurately record scores *and wins*, or the falsification of scores, can lead to suspension from the NSCA.

C. CONCURRENT EVENTS

A shooter's eligibility for concurrent events which are based on age will be determined by his/her age on January 1 of the shooting year.

Concurrent events will be offered in:

Lady

Sub-Junior—Any person who has not reached their 14th birthday.

Junior—Any person who has not reached their 18th birthday.

Senior—60 years and over.

D. TOURNAMENTS

Only clubs affiliated with NSCA shall be eligible to conduct registered shoots. See Section IV on rules for holding registered shoots.

Only members in good standing who have paid their annual dues may participate in registered NSCA shoots.

E. F.I.T.A.S.C.

F.I.T.A.S.C. (Federation Internationale de Tir aux Armes Sportives de Chasse) headquartered in Paris, France, has admitted the National Sporting Clays Association as the sole, exclusive association to govern Sporting Clays and Compak sporting in the United States. These targets will be registered separately under a special set of rules; however, all targets are included for total targets shot for the year.

II—DEFINITION OF TERMS

A. SHOOT PROMOTER

Individual(s) or entity which provides for the facilities and organization of the competition. Shoot Promoters may also act as Shoot Officials.

B. SHOOT OFFICIALS

Individual(s) appointed by the Shoot Promoter and responsible for course layout, target selection, and appointment of Field Judges. Shoot Officials shall be responsible for both layout and testing of the course for safety. Shoot Officials are responsible for ensuring that competitors are not allowed to test or preview the course prior to the competition.

C. FIELD JUDGE

Person of known ability assigned by the Shoot Officials to score targets and enforce the rules.

D. STATION

A shooting position from which one or more targets are attempted.

E. FIELD

A station or group of stations from which targets are attempted sequentially. Once a squad or individual checks into a "field," all "stations" and/or all targets on the "field" are attempted before moving to another "field." The Shoot Officials will provide direction for execution of shooting at each field.

F. REPORT PAIR

Report Pair are two sequential targets where the second target is launched at the sound of the gun firing at the first target. Targets may be launched from one or more traps.

G. FOLLOWING PAIR

Following Pair are two sequential targets where the second target is launched at the officials discretion after the first target. Targets may be launched from one or more traps.

H. SIMULTANEOUS PAIR

This is two targets launched simultaneously. Targets may be launched from one or more traps.

III—EQUIPMENT

A. TARGETS

Targets thrown in any event may include any or all of the following:

1. Regulation SKEET or TRAP targets as specified by ATA, NSSA or NSCA.

2. Mini, midi, batue, rocket, or rabbit targets as specified by NSCA.

3. Any sporting clays target approved by NSCA.

4. "Poison Bird" targets of a separate and clearly discernable appearance may be included at random. Shooters attempting shots at these targets shall be scored a "miss" or "lost bird." Shooters correctly refraining from attempting the "poison bird" (protected species) will be scored as a "hit" or "dead bird."

5. Target number and selection for any competition shall be at the discretion of the Shoot Officials. Target number and selection shall be the same for all shooters. It is recommended that 30% to 40% of targets for tournaments be speciality.

B. SHOTGUNS

1. Shotguns of 12 gauge or smaller, in safe working order, and capable of firing two shots are to be used in attempting all targets. Shooters *shooting registered targets* with a gauge other than 12 gauge **must** shoot **all** targets with that gauge for the remainder of the shooting year—and their classification card shall reflect that gauge on the front and back in ink. It shall be the responsibility of the shooter to inform the shoot official that he/she is shooting the tournament with a gauge other than 12 gauge. It shall be the shoot officials responsibility to mark the shooters score card with the declared gauge. It shall also be the shoot officials and the shooters responsibility to inform NSCA Headquarters in writing of the gauge he/she is shooting.

Procedures for changing a declared gauge to a larger gauge:

a.) A request in writing must be sent to NSCA Headquarters.

b.) The classification committee will review your current averages and assign a new class.

c.) Shooter will receive a new classification card from NSCA Headquarters reflecting classification change.

2. Shotguns fitted for multiple barrels (of various chokes and/or lengths) are permitted. The shooter is allowed to change barrels only between fields.

3. Shotguns with interchangeable or adjustable chokes are permitted at the shooter's discretion. Chokes can be changed or adjusted only between fields.

4. Competitors may enter a shoot with various guns and attempt targets at various fields with different guns, or the gun of another competitor. Guns may be changed only between fields except in case of malfunction (VIII-A-I-b).

5. Guns with release type triggers are allowed and *must be* clearly marked and shoot officials notified of their presence. *Safety stickers designating "release trigger," with instructions on placement, are available at no charge at NSCA office. Please send your request in writing.*

C. AMMUNITION

1. All shot shell ammunition including reloads may be used. Shoot Officials may limit the ammunition to commercially manufactured. *The National Sporting Clays Association assumes no responsibility in connection with the use of reloads.*

2. Loads for 12 gauge shall not exceed $1^1/_8$ ounce.

Maximum loads for any

Gauge	Ounce Lead
20	$^7/_8$
28	$^3/_4$
410($2^1/_2$")	$^1/_2$

3. Shot size shall not exceed U.S. #$7^1/_2$ (diameter 0.095").

4. Shot shall be normal production spherical shot. Plated shot is permitted.

D. THE COURSE

1. The course will provide for a predetermined number of shooting fields from which each competitor will attempt various targets. The number of "Stations" and the number and characteristics of targets from each station, on each field, will be determined by the Shoot Officials, and will be the same for all shooters. Changes in target trajectory, distance and/or velocity due to wind, rain, time of day or any other natural cause does not constitute a violation of this rule.

2. Targets will be propelled by, and launched from, any of a number of commercially produced, modified, or handmade devices which will propel an approved target in a manner to approach the characteristics (in the opinion of the Shoot Officials) of a game bird or animal typically taken by a sporting shotgun.

3. Launching devices which provide for targets traveling at varying angles and distances to the competitors are acceptable (i.e. wobble traps). No more than 20% of the targets shall be presented from such devices. No less than 80% of all targets in a shoot shall be presented with a reasonably consistent trajectory, distance and velocity to all shooters.

4. Devices which provide for propelling multiple targets are permitted.

5. Devices propelling targets of more than one type, and devices capable of providing targets at varying angles and distances, shall be employed such that the varying aspects of these devices will be the same for all shooters and will be free of all human element of selection.

6. Field Judges will be required at each station in sufficient number to competently enforce all "rules for the shooter," as well as, to score the attempts accurately. Numbers and positions for Field Judges shall be determined by the Shoot Officials.

IV—REGULATIONS FOR REGISTERED SHOOTS

A. CHECKS - PAYMENTS - OVERPAYMENTS

Anyone who presents a check at any shoot that is returned for insufficient funds, or other causes, may not compete in any registered shoot until full payment, plus penalty, has been made to the individual or club to which it was presented. Any club receiving such a check shall report name and address of the shooter issuing the check to the NSCA.

Any competitor at a registered shoot who, through error, has been overpaid on any purse, added money, optional or other prize money and who is notified of the overpayment by registered mail, must return the overpayment within fifteen days. Failure to do so shall result in disbarment from all registered shoots until repayment is made.

B. CLUB QUALIFICATIONS & RESPONSIBILITIES

Only clubs affiliated with NSCA with current fees paid shall be eligible to conduct registered shoots. Evidence of club's status in this regard must be displayed in the form of official NSCA membership certificate for the appropriate year. Only clubs in good standing will be permitted to hold registered shoots.

1. The application form furnished by NSCA shall include the scheduled shooting dates and may not be altered without 10 days notice. Shoot applications must be postmarked or received by NSCA at least 10 days prior to the shoot date. *Registered events are required to throw a minimum of 100 targets. Additional targets may be added to the event in increments of 50 targets, i.e. 150, 250.*

2. It shall be the responsibility of the management of the club to see that each shoot is conducted in accordance with the official rules of the NSCA.

3. The club sponsoring the shoot shall check the NSCA membership of each shooter before accepting his entry and shall be responsible for the annual dues if they allow a participant to shoot when said participant's membership in NSCA has expired.

a. All individual shooters in all registered shoots must be members in good standing of NSCA. IT SHALL BE THE RESPONSIBILITY OF THE CLUB HOLDING A REGISTERED SHOOT TO CHECK CARDS OF ALL PARTICIPANTS AND ENFORCE THIS RULE.

b. Management will be billed by NSCA in all cases where expired members are allowed to shoot. Management may seek reimbursement from said shooters, but must first abide by IV-B-3 above.

4. Management shall check the shooter's classification card to ascertain the proper classification for the event.

5. Class winners must be reported if they are to appear in the magazine.

6. Scores in shoots on which complete records are not made by shoot management will not be recorded and the national association shall not be liable to refund fees received in such cases.

7. It is the shoot management's responsibility to appoint a chief referee.

8. Shoot management shall determine the number of targets to be shot on a field.

9. *Clubs are required to retain copies of scoreboard and/or field score sheet on file for 90*

*days after the end of the applicable shooting year. **And for shooters reference, keep an accurate record of the number of entries at each and every registered event.***

C. SHOOTOFFS

In all registered NSCA tournaments, all ties shall be shot off unless otherwise specified by shoot management and published in the program or posted at the registration table. Recommended procedures for shootoffs and squads shall be posted prior to beginning of shoot.

D. INDIVIDUAL QUALIFICATIONS AND RESPONSIBILITIES

1. It shall be the sole responsibiliry of the shooters to see that they are entered into all the events desired. The official cashier sheet/entry form must be used. Once entered, clerical errors are the responsiblity of shoot management.

2. It shall be the shooter's responsibility to enter an event in the proper class.

3. A shooter who fails to keep all correct scores *and wins* posted on his card and shoots in a lower class than the one his record places him shall forfeit any winnings earned while shooting in the wrong class for the first offense, and for the second offense shall forfeit all winnings and also be disbarred from registered competition for one year.

a. A shooter winning trophies or money by shooting in a lower class than the one he was entitled to shoot must return his winnings within 15 days after notification by NSCA Headquarters that said winnings must be returned. Failure to comply within this 15 day period shall subject the shooter to suspension as an NSCA member and PERMANENT disbarment from registered competition.

b. A shooter who enters, or allows himself to be entered in an event in a class lower than the class he was entitled to shoot forfeits all rights to any trophies or purses he would have earned shooting in his proper class unless the mistake is corrected prior to the distribution of such trophies or purse money.

4. It is the responsibility of the shooter to see that his safety is off and his gun is properly loaded with unfired shells of proper size (and load) before calling for a target.

5. During a registered event, each shooter must verify his score before leaving the stand. Once the shooter has left the stand, his/her score is final.

E. RESIDENCY REQUIREMENTS

1. An individual must be a bonafide resident (permanent abode) of a state to be eligible for state championships or to shoot as a state team member and must be a bonafide resident of a state within the zone to be eligible for zone championships or to shoot as a zone team member.

Persons with residence in more than one state must declare their eligibility by writing their state affiliation on the face of the current year membership card. Serviceman, by the same act, may choose their home state or the place in which they are permanently assigned for duty and declare state on card.

Persons who change their official abode shall become immediately eligible to shoot as an individual in the state or zone shoot. They should contact NSCA for a new membership card reflecting change of address and present same before entering shoot.

2. No person shall be eligible for more than one closed state or zone competition during the NSCA shooting year.

F. CONCURRENT EVENTS

1. A shooter's eligibility for concurrent events which are based on age will be determined by his/her age on January 1. Their age on January 1 shall determine their eligibility for the entire upcoming shooting year. No contestant shall be eligible for more than one individual concurrent event based on age.

2. No junior or sub-junior shall be required to pay any part of entry fee that is to be returned to the shooter in the form of money.

G. ALL-AMERICAN CRITERIA

Open Team—Minimum 1,200 registered targets.

Lady and Senior Team—Minimum 1,000 registered targets.

Junior and Sub-Junior Team—Minimum 800 registered targets.

Mandatory attendance is a requirement at the National Championship for all categories.

Performance in U.S. Open, Zone, State and Feature shoots will be applied as additional criteria for All-American qualification.

H. DISQUALIFICATION AND EXPULSION

The shoot management shall upon proper evidence:

1. Disqualify any shooter for the remainder of the shoot program for willful or repeated violation of gun safety precautions which endanger the safety of shooters, field personnel and/or spectators.

2. Elect to refuse the entry or cause the withdrawal of any contestant whose conduct in the opinion of the shoot management is unsportsmanlike or whose participation is in any way detrimental to the best interests of the shoot.

3. Any shooter may be disqualified from a shoot for misrepresentation of his/her status under the eligibility rules (SAND-BAGGING).

4. Expel any shooter physically assaulting a referee or any shooter using abusive language to a referee upon sufficient evidence presented by the chief referee.

5. The shoot management shall report to NSCA all cases of disqualification and expulsion and the reasons for same. Subsequent action by the Advisory Council could result in being expelled and barred from further membership in the NSCA, after the shooter has had the opportunity to appear before the Advisory Council and present his/her case.

I. OFFICIAL SCORES

1. All scores or records, to be recognized as official, must be shot under the official NSCA rules.

2. Only the scores shot on scheduled dates, approved by NSCA, shall be registered. Scores made in shootoffs shall not be registered, however, all NSCA rules shall apply in shootoffs.

3. A maximum of 200 registered targets may be shot on one course in a single day without a change of target presentation. Only the first 100 targets qualify for prize awards. Shoot reports should be submitted as: "Main event (100 targets) and for classification purposes (100 targets)."

4. The scores of any shooter who takes part in a registered shoot shall be considered official, and shall be registered with the NSCA even though the shooter had given notice that it was not his intention to have his score recorded.

5. In the event of extreme weather conditions, power failure, trap failure, or unusually early darkness, the shoot management may elect to continue the event some other time (i.e., the next morning or the following weekend) but must immediately notify NSCA, with a full explanation, who will sanction the change, provided it is deemed in the best interest of sorting clays.

6. When a contestant stops or withdraws an event, without just cause, in which he has started, his partial scores shall be reported to the NSCA along with the other scores of the event.

7. If a competitor withdraws as the result of sickness or injury, the shooter withdrawing shall be charged only with the targets actually fired upon in reporting his score. Due to voluntary withdrawal, or if disqualification by the management, his partial score for the station (or stations) in which he is shooting shall be entered as his of targets broken for that station (or stations).

J. REGISTERED SHOOT REPORTS

1. Reporting Requirements—It is the duty of each club holding a registered shoot to fulfill the following obligations. Payments and reports must be postmarked no more than 15 days after the last day of the shoot.

a. Make payments of all money, purses and options to the shooters.

b. Shoot report and financial form must be made to NSCA on all registered shoots. Standard forms available from NSCA Headquarters must be used.

2. Penalties—Failure to fulfill the reporting requirements shall carry the following penalties:

a. Cancellation of all subsequent shoot dates for the offending club.

b. Denial of right to apply or reapply for any further registered shoot dates for a period of thirty (30) days in case of first offense, or ninety (90) days in case of second or subsequent offense or until obligations have been met.

c. Officers of any delinquent club shall be barred from shooting registered targets until all required obligations of said club are met to the shooters and to NSCA.

3. Financial Report

a. Daily Fees—List number of targets shot each day of shoot and remit to NSCA the required daily registration fee (in U.S. funds). Daily fees are $.02 per target.

b. NSCA dues collected—Remittance (in U.S. funds) and original copies of receipts for all NSCA memberships sold at your shoot must be attached. Membership applications must be completely and legibly filled out with name and address.

4. Shoot Report—An individual entry form/cashier sheet must be submitted on every shooter. These individual reports must include:

a. NSCA membership number

b. Member's full name

c. Member's complete address

d. Number of targets shot at

e. Number of targets broke

f. Class in which member was entered

g. Awards won. Winners must be determined and reported under NSCA classification system. This applies even if no awards are made. Do not list winners above class champions unless such awards were made.

5. Clubs are required to retain copies of scoreboard and/or field score sheet on file for 90 days after the end of the applicable shooting year.

K. SAFETY PRECAUTION

1. *Mandatory* Eye and Ear Protection—All persons, spectators, shooters, referees and trap personnel, must wear eye and ear protection on the course at a tournament sanctioned by NSCA.

2. *Trap Personnel Protection—All trap personnel in front of the line of fire must be out of sight with screen protection able to withstand the charge of shot at the given distance.*

3. *Shooting Stations—Walking, sitting or laying in/on a station including moving boats is not allowed during a registered event. All stations will be shot from a standing position only.*

V. EXECUTION OF THE SHOOT

A. SHOOTING ORDER

Contestants shall proceed through the course and competition in one of the following formats:

1. European Rotation

Individual competitors or groups of 2 through 5 competitors will proceed to the various stations. Groups may shoot in any order selected by the shooters. The squad or group shooting the stations of any field may be changed from field to field.

2. In European Rotation, a shoot start and shoot end time will be estabilshed. It will be the responsibility of each shooter to complete the entire event between these times.

3. Squading

At the discretion of the shoot officials, groups of 3 to 5 shooters will be formed to proceed from field to field in a fixed sequence.

4. In squading sequence, squads will be assigned a start time and it is the responsibility of each shooter to be ready on time, or within no more than 5 minutes of that time.

5. In either case, shots not attempted by the "shoot end time" (European Rotation), or shots not attempted by the shooter joining his squad after they have begun (squading), those targets not attempted will be scored as "lost." The Shoot Officials shall have the right to provide for make up targets if sufficient justification can be presented. Make up targets are provided solely at the discretion of the Shoot Officials.

6. Rotation of Order

In squads of shooters, rotation of shooting order is permitted between stations. Rotation may be formatted by Shoot Shoot Officials, order will be determined by shooters.

7. Shooters Viewing Targets

There will be no "view targets" for any shooter on station. In the instance of the commencement of shooting, or if no station has had a competitor on the line for 3 minutes or longer, targets may be presented for viewing from locations normally accessible to spectators, (not on the shooting station).

B. ATTEMPTING TARGETS

Targets will be presented for attempt at each station in one or more of the following formats.

1. Single Target/Single Shot

2. Single Target/Two Shots

The target will be scored "hit" or "dead" if successfully attempted on either shot.

3. Pairs/Two Shots

Pairs may be presented as Report, Following, or Simultaneous. In Simultaneous Pairs, the shooter has the right to shoot either of the targets first. If the shooter has missed the first target, he may fire the second cartridge at the same target.

When shooting Report or Following Pairs, the shooter will have the right, if missing the first target, to fire the second cartridge at the same target (the result being scored on the first target and the second target being scored as lost).

Should the shooter break both targets with either the first or the second shot, the result will be scored as two "kills".

4. Multiple Target/Two Shots

Two hits or dead birds minimum.

5. *Shooting Stations—Walking, sitting or laying in/on a station including moving boats is not allowed during a registered event. All stations will be shot from a standing position only.*

6. Time Reloads

Targets presented with set time periods for shooter to reload prior to the presentation of the subsequent targets are permitted. Five (5) seconds is the normal reload time but other intervals may be used at the discretion of the Shoot Official(s).

VI—RULES FOR THE SHOOTER

A. LOW GUN

Low Gun—The gun stock must be visible below the shooter's armpit.

The intersection of the comb and the heel of the stock must be held below the shooter's armpit. This point doesn't have to be "tucked" under the armpit nor does it have to be touching the armpit or any part of the body.

B. CALL FOR TARGET

Target will be launched immediately or with a delay of up to 3 seconds.

C. MOUNTING OF GUN

After calling for the target, shooter is to keep from mounting his gun until target is visible. If in the judgement of the Field Judge, the shooter moves to mount his gun prior to seeing the target, the target will be a "no bird" and the sequence and call will begin again. No penalty will be assessed the shooter. Excessive "no bird" (3 per day) can be construed as cause for scoring targets as lost.

D. SHOOTER'S RESPONSIBILITY

It will be the responsibility of each shooter to be familiar with these rules. Ignorance of the rules will not be a cause to "re-attempt" targets lost because of rule violations.

VII—SCORING

A. Targets shall be scored as "hit" or "killed" or "dead" and designated on score cards by an (X) when, in the opinion of the Field Judge, a visible piece has been broken from the target. Targets not struck and broken by the shooters shot shall be called "lost" or "missed" and designated on score cards by a (O).

B. The call of "lost" or "dead," "hit" or "miss" shall be announced by the Field Judge prior to recording the score on every target.

C. *Scoring Pairs—In the event of a "no bird" on any Report, True or Following Pair, nothing can be established. Two good targets must be presented to record the score. This will also apply for gun/ammo malfunctions while shooting pairs.*

D. If the shooter disagrees with the Field Judge's call, he must protest before firing at another sea of targets or before leaving that station. The Field Judge may poll the spectators and may reverse his original call. In all cases the final decision of the Field Judge will stand.

E. Each shooter will be assigned a score card to be presented to the Field Judges at the various stations or fields. Field Judges will score each shooter's attempts on the individual's score card. The total shall be tallied and the scores written in ink and initialed by the Field Judge.

F. Each shooter is responsible for his score card from assignment, at the start of the shoot, until the card is filed with the Shoot Officials at the end of each day's shooting.

G. Shooters are responsible for checking the Field Judge's totals of "hits and misses" at each station and/or field. (See IV-D-5)

VIII—MALFUNCTIONS

A. The shooter shall be allowed a combined total of three malfunctions per day attributed to either the shooters gun or ammo. Targets not attempted due to the fourth for latter malfunctions shall be scored as "lost." Targets not attempted on the three allowed malfunctions shall be treated as "no birds."

1. Gun Malfunctions

a. In the case of a gun malfunction, the shooter must remain in place, the gun pointed safely down range and must not open the gun or tamper with trigger, safety or barrel selector, until the field judge has determined the cause and made his ruling.

b. In the case of a broken gun, the shooter has the option to use another gun, if one is available, or he/she may drop out of competition until the gun is repaired. The shooter must however finish the event during the allotted schedule shooting time.

c. Targets shall be scored as lost if the shooter is unable to fire because of the following. Examples include but are not limited to:

1) Shooter has left the safety on.

2) Shooter has forgotten to load or properly cock the gun.

3) Shooter has forgotten to disengage the locking device from the magazine of an automatic weapon.

4) Shooter has not sufficiently released the trigger of a single trigger gun having fired the first shot.

d. If the shooter fails to comply with item VIII-A-I-a, the target or targets will be scored as "lost" or "missed."

2. Ammo Malfunctions

a. In the case of ammunition malfunction, the shooter must remain in place, the gun pointing safely down range and must not open the gun or tamper with the trigger, safery or barrel selector, until the Field Judge has determined the cause and made his ruling.

b. Examples include but are not limited to:

1) Failure to fire, providing firing pin indentation is clearly noticeable.

2) One in which the primer fires, but through failure of the shell or lack of components, and which, consequently leaves part of or all of the charge of shot or wad in the gun. A soft load in which the shot and wad leave the barrel, is not a misfire.

3) Brass pulling off hull between shots on pairs.

4) Separation of brass from casing when gun is fired (usually accompanied by a "whistling" sound as the plastic sleeve leaves the barrel).

c. If the shooter fails to comply with item VIII-A-2-a, the target or targets will be scored as "lost" or "missed."

B. TARGET MALFUNCTION

1. A target which breaks at launching shall be called a "no bird" and shooter will be provided a new target.

2. A target which is launched in an obviously different trajectory shall be called a "no bird" and the shooter will be provided a new target.

3. If a bad target or "no bird" is thrown during a timed reload sequence, the shooter will repeat the sequence beginning with the last target established.

The shooter must make an attempt at the *last* established target before proceeding with the remaining sequence. If the last established target occured before the timed reload, the shooter shall begin the sequence accordingly and proceed through the reloading again. The Field Judge shall enforce his judgement (either by implementing a suitable penalty, or allowing a repeat of the reloading sequence) to prevent a "no bird" or "bad target" thrown after either a successful or an unsuccessful reloading attempt from changing the results of the initial se-quence.

4. At a station of multiple targets (two or more—simultaneously launched), at least two good targets must be presented simultaneously or a "no bird" will be called and the multiple targets will be attempted again. Multiple targets shall be shot as "fair pair in the air," two new shots will be attempted and scored, no scores from previous "no bird" attempts will stand.

IX—PROTESTS

A. A shooter may protest if in his opinion the rules as stated herein are improperly applied.

B. There will be no protests concerning calls or scoring of hits or misses. The Field Judges final decision will stand.

C. Protests shall be made immediately upon completion of the shooting at a given field. Protest shall be made to the Shoot Official(s).

D. The Shoot Official(s) shall convene a predetermined "jury" of 3 to 5 Field Judges or competitors who are known to be representative of the shooters present and knowledgable about these rules. The jury will decide on the validity of the protest and the resolution of the case. They will prescribe penalties or award bonuses as they determine to be fair and in the spirit of the competition.

X—SAFETY SECTION

A. Safety is everyone's responsibility.

B. It is the shooters responsibility to report any unsafe shooting condition immediately to Shoot Officials.

C. *Mandatory Eye and Ear Protection—All persons, spectators, shooters, referees and trap personnel must wear eye and ear protection on the course at a tournament sanctioned by NSCA.*

D. *Trap Personnel Protection—All trap personnel in front of the line of fire must be out of sight with screen protection able to withstand the charge of shot at the given distance.*

E. *Shooting Stations—Walking, sitting or laying in/on a station including moving boats is not allowed during a registered event. All stations will be shot from a standing position only.* These stands all represent a simulated hunting situation; however, large crowds are not present during this type of hunting. SAFETY IS THE NUMBER ONE CONSIDERATION FOR ALL SPORTING CLAYS RANGES.

F. Shooters must have the direct permission of a Field Judge to test fire any gun. Other than on such permitted test firings, guns will be discharged only in attempt at competition targets.

G. Field Judges may be assisted by markers to record scores on the shooters' score cards.

H. It is the sole responsibility of the shooter to begin any event, station, and/or field with sufficient equipment and ammunition. Failure to do so, which in the opinion of the Field Judges will delay the shoot, will result in the loss of all targets as required to keep the shoot moving. Make-up targets will be provided only at the discretion of the shoot officials.

SAFETY FIRST - ACTIONS OPEN

Manufacturers' Directory

AMMUNITION, COMMERCIAL

ACTIV Industries, Inc., 1000 Zigor Rd., P.O. Box 339, Kearneysville, WV 25430/304-725-0451; FAX: 304-725-2080

Ballistic Products, Inc., 20015 75th Ave. North, Corcoran, MN 55340-9456/612-494-9237; FAX: 612-494-9236

Brenneke KG, Wilhelm, Ilmenauweg 2, D-30551 Langenhagen, GERMANY/0511/97262-0; FAX: 0511/9726262

Dynamit Nobel-RWS, Inc., 81 Ruckman Rd., Closter, NJ 07624/77-93-54-69; FAX: 77-93-57-98

Estate Cartridge, Inc., 2778 FM 830, Willis, TX 77378/409-856-7277; FAX: 409-856-5486

Federal Cartridge Co., 900 Ehlen Dr., Anoka, MN 55303/612-323-2300

Fiocchi of America, Inc., 5030 Fremont Rd., Ozark, MO 65721/417-725-4118; FAX: 417-725-1039

Gamo (See U.S. importer—Dynamit Nobel-RWS, Inc.)

GDL Enterprises, 409 Le Gardeur, Slidell, LA 70460/504-649-0693

Hirtenberger Aktiengesellschaft, Leobersdorferstrasse 31, A-2552 Hirtenberg, AUSTRIA/43(0)2256 81184; FAX: 43(0)2256 81807

Hornady Mfg. Co., P.O. Box 1848, Grand Island, NE 68801/800-338-3220, 308-382-1390

Omark Industries, Div. of Blount, Inc., 2299 Snake River Ave., P.O. Box 856, Lewiston, ID 83501/800-627-3640, 208-746-2351

Polywad, Inc., P.O. Box 7916, Macon, GA 31209/912-477-0669

Remington Arms Co., Inc., 1007 Market St., Wilmington, DE 19898/302-773-5291

RWS (See U.S. importer—Dynamit Nobel-RWS, Inc.)

Star Reloading Co., Inc., 5520 Rock Hampton Ct., Indianapolis, IN 46268/317-872-5840

Victory USA, P.O. Box 1021, Pine Bush, NY 12566/914-744-2060; FAX: 914-744-5181

Winchester Div., Olin Corp., 427 N. Shamrock, E. Alton, IL 62024/618-258-3566; FAX: 618-258-3599

AMMUNITION, CUSTOM

Ballistic Products, Inc., 20015 75th Ave. North, Corcoran, MN 55340-9456/612-494-9237; FAX: 612-494-9236

Cubic Shot Shell Co., Inc., 98 Fatima Dr., Campbell, OH 44405/216-755-0349; FAX: 216-755-0349

Estate Cartridge, Inc., 2778 FM 830, Willis, TX 77378/409-856-7277; FAX: 409-856-5486

Hirtenberger Aktiengesellschaft, Leobersdorferstrasse 31, A-2552 Hirtenberg, AUSTRIA/43(0)2256 81184; FAX: 43(0)2256 81807

Hornady Mfg. Co., P.O. Box 1848, Grand Island, NE 68801/800-338-3220, 308-382-1390

M&D Munitions Ltd., 127 Verdi St., Farmingdale, NY 11735/516-752-1038; FAX: 516-752-1905

AMMUNITION, FOREIGN

Ballistic Products, Inc., 20015 75th Ave. North, Corcoran, MN 55340-9456/612-494-9237; FAX: 612-494-9236

Cubic Shot Shell Co., Inc., 98 Fatima Dr., Campbell, OH 44405/216-755-0349; FAX: 216-755-0349

Dynamit Nobel-RWS, Inc., 81 Ruckman Rd., Closter, NJ 07624/77-93-54-69; FAX: 77-93-57-98

Estate Cartridge, Inc., 2778 FM 830, Willis, TX 77378/409-856-7277; FAX: 409-856-5486

Fiocchi of America, Inc., 5030 Fremont Rd., Ozark, MO 65721/417-725-4118; FAX: 417-725-1039

RWS (See U.S. importer—Dynamit Nobel-RWS, Inc.)

AMMUNITION COMPONENTS—BULLETS, POWDER, PRIMERS, CASES

Accurate Arms Co., Inc., Rt. 1, Box 167, McEwen, TN 37101/615-729-4207; FAX 615-729-4217

ACTIV Industries, Inc., 1000 Zigor Rd., P.O. Box 339, Kearneysville, WV 25430/304-725-0451; FAX: 304-725-2080

Ballistic Products, Inc., 20015 75th Ave. North, Corcoran, MN 55340-9456/612-494-9237; FAX: 612-494-9236

Bell Reloading, Inc., 1725 Harlin Lane Rd., Villa Rica, GA 30180

Brenneke KG, Wilhelm, Ilmenauweg 2, D-30551 Langenhagen, GERMANY/0511/97262-0; FAX: 0511/9726262

Brownells, Inc., 200 S. Front St., Montezuma, IA 50171/515-623-5401; FAX: 515-623-3896

CCI, Div. of Blount, Inc., 2299 Snake River Ave., P.O. Box 856, Lewiston, ID 83501/800-627-3640, 208-746-2351

DuPont (See IMR Powder Co.)

Federal Cartridge Co., 900 Ehlen Dr., Anoka, MN 55303/612-323-2300

Fiocchi of America, Inc., 5030 Fremont Rd., Ozark, MO 65721/417-725-4118; FAX: 417-725-1039

Hercules, Inc., Hercules Plaza, 1313 N Market St., Wilmington, DE 19894/800-276-9337

Hirtenberger Aktiengesellschaft, Leobersdorferstrasse 31, A-2552 Hirtenberg, AUSTRIA/43(0)2256 81184; FAX: 43(0)2256 81807

Hodgdon Powder Co., Inc., P.O. Box 2932, Shawnee Mission, KS 66201/913-362-9455; FAX: 913-362-1307

Hornady Mfg. Co., P.O. Box 1848, Grand Island, NE 68801/800-338-3220, 308-382-1390

IMR Powder Co., 1080 Military Turnpike, Suite 2, Plattsburgh, NY 12901

Lage Uniwad, Inc., P.O. Box 446, Victor, IA 52327/319-647-3232

Pattern Control, 114 N. Third St., Garland, TX 75040/214-494-3551

Polywad, Inc., P.O. Box 7916, Macon, GA 31209/912-477-0669

Precision Ballistics Co., P.O. Box 4374, Hamden, CT 06514/203-373-2293

Precision Components, 3177 Sunrise Lake, Milford, PA 18337/717-686-4414

Rainier Ballistics Corp., 4500 15th St. East, Tacoma, WA 98424/800-638-8722, 206-922-7589; FAX: 206-922-7854

Reloading Specialties, Inc., Box 1130, Pine Island, MN 55963/507-356-8500; FAX: 507-356-8800

Remington Arms Co., Inc., 1007 Market St., Wilmington, DE 19898/302-773-5291

Scot Powder Co. of Ohio, Inc., Box HD94, Only, TN 37140/615-729-4207; FAX: 615-729-4217

Shotgun Bullets Mfg., Rt. 3, Box 41, Robinson, IL 62454/618-546-5043

Taracorp Industries, Inc., 16th & Cleveland Blvd., Granite City, IL 62040/618-451-4400

Trico Plastics, 590 S. Vincent Ave., Azusa, CA 91702

Vihtavuori Oy, FIN-41330 Vihtavuori, FINLAND/358-41-3779211; FAX: 358-41-3771643

Vihtavuori Oy/Kaltron-Pettibone, 1241 Ellis St., Bensenville, IL 60106/708-350-1116; FAX: 708-350-1606

Winchester Div., Olin Corp., 427 N. Shamrock, E. Alton, IL 62024/618-258-3566; FAX: 618-258-3599

Windjammer Tournament Wads, Inc., 750 W. Hampden Ave. Suite 170, Englewood, CO 80110/303-781-6329

CHOKE DEVICES, RECOIL ABSORBERS AND RECOIL PADS

Action Products, Inc., 22 N. Mulberry St., Hagerstown, MD 21740/301-797-1414

Allen Sportswear, Bob, P.O. Box 477, Des Moines, IA 50302/515-283-2191; FAX: 515-283-0779

American Import Co., The, 1453 Mission St., San Francisco, CA 94103/415-863-1506; FAX: 415-863-0939

Answer Products Co., 1519 Westbury Drive, Davison, MI 48423/313-653-2911

Arms Ingenuity Co., P.O. Box 1, 51 Canal St., Weatogue, CT 06089/203-658-5624

Baker, Stan, 10,000 Lake City Way, Seattle, WA 98125/206-522-4575

Boyds', Inc., 3rd & Main, Geddes, SD 57342/605-337-2125; FAX: 605-337-3363

Briley Mfg., Inc., 1230 Lumpkin, Houston, TX 77043/800-331-5718, 713-932-6995; FAX: 713-932-1043

Butler Creek Corp., 290 Arden Dr., Belgrade, MT 59714/800-423-8327, 406-388-1356; FAX: 406-388-7204

C&H Research, 115 Sunnyside Dr., Box 351, Lewis, KS 67552/316-324-5445

Cation, 32360 Edward, Madison Heights, MI 48071/313-588-0160

Colonial Arms, Inc., P.O. Box 636, Selma, AL 36702-0636/205-872-9455; FAX: 205-872-9540

Danuser Machine Co., 550 E. Third St., P.O. Box 368, Fulton, MO 65251/314-642-2246; FAX: 314-642-2240

Dayson Arms Ltd., P.O. Box 217, Nashville, IN 47448-0217/812-988-0082; FAX: 812-988-0431

Delta Vectors, Inc., 7119 W. 79th St., Overland Park, KS 66204/913-642-0307

Dragun Enterprises, P.O. Box 222, Murfreesboro, TN 37133-2222/615-895-7373, 800-467-7375; FAX: 800-829-7536

Fabian Bros. Sporting Goods, Inc., 1510 Morena Blvd., Suite "G", San Diego, CA 92110/619-275-0816; FAX: 619-276-8733

FAPA Corp., P.O. Box 1439, New London, NH 03257/603-735-5652; FAX: 603-735-5154

Francesca, Inc., 3115 Old Ranch Rd., San Antonio, TX 78217/512-826-2584; FAX: 512-826-8211

Franchi S.p.A., Luigi, Via del Serpente, 12, 25020 Fornaci, ITALY

Frontier Arms Co., Inc., 401 W. Rio Santa Cruz, Green Valley, AZ 85614-3932

Galazan, Div. of Connecticut Shotgun Mfg. Co., P.O. Box 622, 35 Woodland St., New Britain, CT 06051-0622/203-225-6581; FAX: 203-832-8707

Gentry Custom Gunmaker, David, 314 N. Hoffman, Belgrade, MT 59714/406-388-4867

Graybill's Gun Shop, 1035 Ironville Pike, Columbia, PA 17512/717-684-2739

Great 870 Co., The, P.O. Box 6309, El Monte, CA 91734

Harper, William E. (See Great 870 Co., The)

Hastings Barrels, 320 Court St., Clay Center, KS 67432/913-632-3169; FAX: 913-632-6554

Holland's, Box 69, Powers, OR 97466/503-439-5155; FAX: 503-439-5155

I.N.C., Inc. (See Kick Eez)

Intermountain Arms & Tackle, Inc., 105 E. Idaho St., Meridian, ID 83642/208-888-4911; FAX: 208-888-4381

Jaeger, Inc./Dunn's, Paul, P.O. Box 449, 1 Madison Ave., Grand Junction, TN 38039/901-764-6909; FAX: 901-764-6503

Jenkins Recoil Pads, Inc., RR 2, Box 471, Olney, IL 62450/618-395-3416

KDF, Inc., 2485 Hwy. 46 N., Seguin, TX 78155/210-379-8141; FAX: 210-379-5420

Kick Eez, P.O. Box 12767, Wichita, KS 67277/316-721-9570; FAX: 316-721-5260

Kleen-Bore, Inc., 20 Ladd Ave., Northampton, MA 01060/413-586-7240; FAX: 413-586-0236

LaRocca Gun Works, Inc., 51 Union Place, Worcester, MA 01608/508-754-2887; FAX: 508-754-2887

Mag-Na-Port International, Inc., 41302 Executive Dr., Harrison Twp., MI 48045-3448//810-469-6727; FAX: 810-469-0425

Marble Arms Corp., 420 Industrial Park, P.O. Box 111, Gladstone, MI 49837/906-428-3710; FAX: 906-428-3711

Meadow Industries, P.O. Box 754, Locust Grove, VA 22508/703-972-2175; FAX: 703-972-2175

Menck, Thomas W., 5703 S. 77th St., Ralston, NE 68127-4201
Middlebrooks Custom Shop, 7366 Colonial Trail East, Surry, VA 23883/804-357-0881; FAX: 804-365-0442
Morrow, Bud, 11 Hillside Lane, Sheridan, WY 82801-9729/307-674-8360
Nelson/Weather-Rite, 14760 Santa Fe Trail Dr., Lenexa, KS 66215/913-492-3200
North Fork Custom Gunsmithing, James Johnston, 428 Del Rio Rd., Roseburg, OR 97470/503-673-4467
One Of A Kind, 15610 Purple Sage, San Antonio, TX 78255/512-695-3364
Pachmayr Ltd., 1875 S. Mountain Ave., Monrovia, CA 91016/818-357-7771, 800-423-9704; FAX: 818-358-7251
Palsa Outdoor Products, P.O. Box 81336, Lincoln, NE 68501/402-456-9281, 800-456-9281; FAX: 402-488-2321
PAST Sporting Goods, Inc., P.O. Box 1035, Columbia, MO 65205/314-445-9200
Pro-Port Ltd., 41302 Executive Dr., Harrison Twp., MI 48045-3448/810-469-7323; FAX: 810-469-0425
Protektor Model, 1-11 Bridge St., Galeton, PA 16922/814-435-2442
Ravell Ltd., 289 Diputacion St., 08009, Barcelona SPAIN
Shooter Shop, The, 221 N. Main, Butte, MT 59701/406-723-3842
Shotguns Unlimited, 2307 Fon Du Lac Rd., Richmond, VA 23229/804-752-7115
S.K. Guns, Inc., 3041A Main Ave., Fargo, ND 58103/701-293-4867; FAX: 701-232-0001
Stone Enterprises Ltd., Rt. 609, P.O. Box 335, Wicomico Church, VA 22579/804-580-5114; FAX: 804-580-8421
Trulock Tool, Broad St., Whigham, GA 31797/912-762-4678
Upper Missouri Trading Co., 304 Harold St., Crofton, NE 68730/402-388-4844

CUSTOM GUNSMITHS

A&W Repair, 2930 Schneider Dr., Arnold, MO 63010/314-287-3725
Accurate Plating & Weaponry, Inc., 1937 Calumet St., Clearwater, FL 34625/813-449-9112
Adair Custom Shop, Bill, 2886 Westridge, Carrollton, TX 75006
Ahlman Guns, Rt. 1, Box 20, Morristown, MN 55052/507-685-4243; FAX: 507-685-4247
Aldis Gunsmithing & Shooting Supply, 502 S. Montezuma St., Prescott, AZ 86303/602-445-6723; FAX: 602-445-6763
Alpine's Precision Gunsmithing & Indoor Shooting Range, 2401 Government Way, Coeur d'Alene, ID 83814/208-765-3559; FAX: 208-765-3559
American Custom Gunmakers Guild, P.O. Box 812, Burlington, IA 52601/319-752-6114
Amrine's Gun Shop, 937 La Luna, Ojai, CA 93023/805-646-2376
Answer Products Co., 1519 Westbury Drive, Davison, MI 48423/313-653-2911
Armament Gunsmithing Co., Inc., 525 Rt. 22, Hillside, NJ 07205/908-686-0960
Arms Craft Gunsmithing, 1106 Linda Dr., Arroyo Grande, CA 93420/805-481-2830
Arms Ingenuity Co., P.O. Box 1, 51 Canal St., Weatogue, CT 06089/203-658-5624
Arrieta, S.L., Morkaiko, 5, Elgoibar, E-20870, SPAIN/(43) 74 31 50; FAX: (43) 74 31 54
Art's Gun & Sport Shop, Inc., 6008 Hwy. Y, Hillsboro, MO 63050
Artistry in Wood, 134 Zimmerman Rd., Kalispell, MT 59901/406-257-9003
AWC Systems Technology, P.O. Box 41938, Phoenix, AZ 85080-1938/602-780-1050
Baity's Custom Gunworks, 414 2nd St., N. Wilkesboro, NC 28659/919-667-8785
Barta's Gunsmithing, 10231 US Hwy. 10, Cato, WI 54206/414-732-4472
Baron Technology, 62 Spring Hill Rd., Trumbull, CT 06611/203-452-0515; FAX: 203-452-0663
Baumannize Custom, 4784 Sunrise Hwy., Bohemia, NY 11716/800-472-4387; FAX: 516-567-0001
Bear Arms, 121 Rhodes St., Jackson, SC 29831/803-471-9859
Bear Mountain Gun & Tool, 120 N. Plymouth, New Plymouth, ID 83655/208-278-5221; FAX: 208-278-5221
Beaver Lodge (See Fellowes, Ted)
Beitzinger, George, 116-20 Atlantic Ave., Richmond Hill, NY 11419/718-847-7661
Belding's Custom Gun Shop, 10691 Sayers Rd., Munith, MI 49259/517-596-2388
Benchmark Guns, 12593 S. Ave. 5 East, Yuma, AZ 85365
Bengtson Arms Co., L., 6345-B E. Akron St., Mesa, AZ 85205/602-981-6375
Biesen, Al, 5021 Rosewood, Spokane, WA 99208/509-328-9340
Biesen, Roger, 5021 W. Rosewood, Spokane, WA 99208/509-328-9340
Billeb, Stephen L., 1101 N. 7th St., Burlington, IA 52601/319-753-2110
Billings Gunsmiths, Inc., 1940 Grand Ave., Billings, MT 59102/406-652-3104
Bolden's, P.O. Box 33178, Kerrville, TX 78029/210-634-2703
Bone Engraving, Ralph, 718 N. Atlanta, Owasso, OK 74055/918-272-9745
Borden Accuracy, RD 1, Box 244A, Tunkhannock, PA 18657/717-833-2234; FAX: 717-833-2382
Borovnik KG, Ludwig, 9170 Ferlach, Bahnhofstrasse 7, AUSTRIA/042 27 24 42; FAX: 042 26 43 49
Bowerly, Kent, HCR Box 1903, Camp Sherman, OR 97730/503-595-6028
Brace, Larry D., 771 Blackfoot Ave., Eugene, OR 97404/503-688-1278
Brgoch, Frank, 1580 S. 1500 East, Bountiful, UT 84010/801-295-1885
Brian, C.T., 1101 Indiana Ct., Decatur, IL 62521/217-429-2290
Briese Bullet Co., Inc., RR1, Box 108, Tappen, ND 58487/701-327-4578; FAX: 701-327-4579
Briganti & Co., A., 475 Rt. 32, Highland Mills, NY 10930/914-928-9573
Briley Mfg., Inc., 1230 Lumpkin, Houston, TX 77043/800-331-5718, 713-932-6995; FAX: 713-932-1043
Broken Gun Ranch, RR2, Box 92, Spearville, KS 67876/316-385-2587
Bruno Shooters Supply, 106 N. Wyoming St., Hazleton, PA 18201/717-455-2211; FAX: 717-455-2211
Buck Stix—SOS Products Co., Box 3, Neenah, WI 54956
Buckhorn Gun Works, 115 E. North St., Rapid City, SD 57701/605-787-6289
Budin, Dave, Main St., Margaretville, NY 12455/914-568-4103; FAX: 914-586-4105
Burgess & Son Gunsmiths, R.W., P.O. Box 3364, Warner Robins, GA 31099/912-328-7487
Burkhart Gunsmithing, Don, P.O. Box 852, Rawlins, WY 82301/307-324-6007
Burres, Jack, 10333 San Fernando Rd., Pacoima, CA 91331/818-899-8000
CAM Enterprises, 5090 Iron Springs Rd., Box 2, Prescott, AZ 86301/602-776-9640
Camilli, Lou, 4700 Oahu Dr. NE, Albuquerque, NM 87111/uquerque, NM 87111/505-293-5259
Campbell, Dick, 20,000 Silver Ranch Rd., Conifer, CO 80433/303-697-0150
Cannon's Guns, Box 1036, 320 Main St., Polson, MT 59860/406-887-2048
Carter's Gun Shop, 225 G St., Penrose, CO 81240/719-372-6240
Caywood, Shane J., P.O. Box 321, Minocqua, WI 54548/715-277-3866 evenings
Christman Jr., David, 937 Lee Hedrick Rd., Colville, WA 99114/509-684-5686 days; 509-684-3314 evenings
Chuck's Gun Shop, P.O. Box 597, Waldo, FL 32694/904-468-2264
Clark Firearms Engraving, P.O. Box 80746, San Marino, CA 91118/818-287-1652
Classic Arms Corp., P.O. Box 106, Dunsmuir, CA 96025-0106/916-235-2000
Classic Guns, Inc., Frank S. Wood, 3230 Medlock Bridge Rd., Suite 110, Norcross, GA 30092/404-242-7944
Clearview Products, 3021 N. Portland, Oklahoma City, OK 73107
Cloward's Gun Shop, 4023 Aurora Ave. N, Seattle, WA 98103/206-632-2072
Cochran, Oliver, Box 868, Shady Spring, WV 25918/304-763-3838
Cogar's Gunsmithing, P.O. Box 755, Houghton Lake, MI 48629/517-422-4591
Cole's Gun Works, Rt. 3, Box 159-A, Moyock, NC 27958/919-435-2345
Conrad, C.A., 3964 Ebert St., Winston-Salem, NC 27127/919-788-5469
Corkys Gun Clinic, 111 North 11th Ave., Greeley, CO 80631/303-330-0516
Costa, David, Island Pond Gun Shop, P.O. Box 428, Cross St., Island Pond, VT 05846/802-723-4546
Cox, C. Ed, RD 2, Box 192, Prosperity, PA 15329/412-228-4984
Creekside Gun Shop, Inc., Main St., Holcomb, NY 14469/716-657-6338; FAX: 716-657-7900
Curtis Custom Shop, RR1, Box 193A, Wallingford, KY 41093/703-659-4265
Custom Checkering Service, Kathy Forster, 2124 SE Yamhill St., Portland, OR 97214/503-236-5874
Custom Gun Products, 5021 W. Rosewood, Spokane, WA 99208/509-328-9340
Custom Gun Stocks, Rt. 6, P.O. Box 177, McMinnville, TN 37110/615-668-3912
Custom Gunsmiths, 4303 Friar Lane, Colorado Springs, CO 80907/719-599-3366
Custom Shop, The, 890 Cochrane Crescent, Peterborough, Ont. K9H 5N3 CANADA
D&D Gunsmiths, Ltd., 363 E. Elmwood, Troy, MI 48083/313-583-1512
D&J Bullet Co. & Custom Gun Shop, Inc., 426 Ferry St., Russell, KY 41169/606-836-2663; FAX: 606-836-2663
Dangler, Homer L., Box 254, Addison, MI 49220/517-547-6745
Darlington Gun Works, Inc., P.O. Box 698, 516 S. 52 Bypass, Darlington, SC 29532/803-393-3931
Davis Service Center, Bill, 10173 Croydon Way #9, Sacramento, CA 95827/916-369-6789
Dever Co., Jack, 8590 NW 90, Oklahoma City, OK 73132/405-721-6393
D.D. Custom Stocks, R.H. "Dick" Devereaux, 5240 Mule Deer Dr., Colorado Springs, CO 80919/719-548-8468
DGS, Inc., Dale A. Storey, 1117 E. 12th, Casper, WY 82601/307-237-2414
Dietz Gun Shop & Range, Inc., 421 Range Rd., New Braunfels, TX 78132/210-885-4662
Dilliott Gunsmithing, Inc., 657 Scarlett Rd., Dandridge, TN 37725/615-397-9204
Donnelly, C.P., 405 Kubli Rd., Grants Pass, OR 97527/503-846-6604
Dowtin Gunworks, Rt. 4, Box 930A, Flagstaff, AZ 86001/602-779-1898
Duffy, Charles E., Williams Lane, West Hurley, NY 12491/914-679-2997
Duncan's Gun Works, Inc., 1619 Grand Ave., San Marcos, CA 92069/619-727-0515
Dyson & Son Ltd., Peter, 29-31 Church St., Honley, Huddersfield, W. Yorkshire HDL7 2AH, ENGLAND/0484-661062; FAX: 0484 663709
Echols & Co., D'Arcy, 164 W. 580 S., Providence, UT 84332/801-753-2367
Eckelman Gunsmithing, 3125 133rd St. SW, Fort Ripley, MN 56449/218-829-3176
Eggleston, Jere D., 400 Saluda Ave., Columbia, SC 29205/803-799-3402
EGW Evolution Gun Works, 4050 B-8 Skyron Dr., Doylestown, PA 18901/215-348-9892; FAX: 215-348-1056
Ellicott Arms, Inc./Woods Pistolsmithing, 3840 Dahlgren Ct., Ellicott City, MD 21042/410-465-7979
Erhardt, Dennis, 3280 Green Meadow Dr., Helena, MT 59601/406-442-4533
Eyster Heritage Gunsmiths, Inc., Ken, 6441 Bishop Rd., Centerburg, OH 43011/614-625-6131
Fanzoj GmbH, Griesgasse 1, 9170 Ferlach, AUSTRIA 9170/(43) 04227-2283; FAX: (43) 04227-2867
Fautheree, Andy, P.O. Box 4607, Pagosa Springs, CO 81157/303-731-5003
Fellowes, Ted, Beaver Lodge, 9245 16th Ave. SW, Seattle, WA 98106/206-763-1698
Ferris Firearms, HC 51, Box 1255, Suite 158, Bulverde, TX 78163/210-980-4811
Fish, Marshall F., Rt. 22 N., P.O. Box 2439, Westport, NY 12993/518-962-4897
Fisher, Jerry A., 535 Crane Mt. Rd., Big Fork, MT 59911/406-837-2722
Fisher Custom Firearms, 2199 S. Kittredge Way, Aurora, CO 80013/303-755-3710
Flaig's, 2200 Evergreen Rd., Millvale, PA 15209/412-821-1717
Fleming Firearms, 9525-J East 51st St., Tulsa, OK 74145/918-665-3624
Flynn's Custom Guns, P.O. Box 7461, Alexandria, LA 71306/318-455-7130
Fogle, James W., RR 2, P.O. Box 258, Herrin, IL 62948/618-988-1795
Forster, Larry L., P.O. Box 212, 220 First St. NE, Gwinner, ND 58040-0212/701-678-2475
Forthofer's Gunsmithing & Knifemaking, 5535 U.S. Hwy 93S, Whitefish, MT 59937-8411/406-862-2674
Francesca, Inc., 3115 Old Ranch Rd., San Antonio, TX 78217/512-826-2584; FAX: 512-826-8211
Francotte & Cie S.A., Auguste, rue du Trois Juin 109, 4400 Herstal-Liege, BELIUM/41-48.13.18; FAX: 41-48.11.79
Frank Custom Gun Service, Ron, 7131 Richland Rd., Ft. Worth, TX 76118/817-284-4426; FAX: 817-284-9300
Frazier Brothers Enterprises, 1118 N. Main St., Franklin, IN 46131/317-736-4000; FAX: 317-736-4000
Fredrick Gun Shop, 10 Elson Dr., Riverside, RI 02915/401-433-2805
Fullmer, Geo. M., 2499 Mavis St., Oakland, CA 94601/510-533-4193
Gaillard Barrels, P.O. Box 21, Pathlow, Sask., S0K 3B0 CANADA/306-752-3769; FAX: 306-752-5969
Gander Mountain, Inc., P.O. Box 128, Hwy. "W", Wilmot, WI 53192/414-862-2331,Ext. 6425
Gator Guns & Repair, 6255 Spur Hwy., Kenai, AK 99611/907-283-7947
Genecco Gun Works, K., 10512 Lower Sacramento Rd., Stockton, CA 95210/209-951-0706
Gillmann, Edwin, 33 Valley View Dr., Hanover, PA 17331/717-632-1662
Gilman-Mayfield, Inc., 3279 E. Shields, Fresno, CA 93703/209-221-9415; FAX: 209-221-9419
Giron, Robert E., 1328 Pocono St., Pittsburgh, PA 15218/412-731-6041
Goens, Dale W., P.O. Box 224, Cedar Crest, NM 87008/505-281-5419
Goodling's Gunsmithing, R.D. #1, Box 1097, Spring Grove, PA 17362/717-225-3350
Goodwin, Fred, Silver Ridge Gun Shop, Sherman Mills, ME 04776/207-365-4451
Gordie's Gun Shop, 1401 Fulton St., Streator, IL 61364/815-672-7202
Grace, Charles E., 6943 85.5 Rd., Trinchera, CO 81081/719-846-9435
Graybill's Gun Shop, 1035 Ironville Pike, Columbia, PA 17512/717-684-2739
Green, Roger M., P.O. Box 984, 435 E. Birch, Glenrock, WY 82637/307-436-9804
Greg Gunsmithing Repair, 3732 26th Ave. North, Robbinsdale, MN 55422/612-529-8103
Griffin & Howe, Inc., 33 Claremont Rd., Bernardsville, NJ 07924/908-766-2287; FAX: 908-766-1068
Gun Shop, The, 5550 S. 900 East, Salt Lake City, UT 84117/801-263-3633
Gun Works, The, 236 Main St., Springfield, OR 97477/503-741-4118
Guns, 81 E. Streetsboro St., Hudson, OH 44236/216-650-4563
Gunsmithing Ltd., 57 Unquowa Rd., Fairfield, CT 06430/203-254-0436
H&L Gun Works, 817 N. Highway 90 #1109, Sierra Vista, AZ 85635/602-452-0702
Hallberg Gunsmith, Fritz, 33 S. Main, Payette, ID 83661
Hamilton, Alex B. (See Ten-Ring Precision, Inc.)
Hammans, Charles E., P.O. Box 788, 2022 McCracken, Stuttgart, AR 72106/501-673-1388
Hammond Custom Guns Ltd., Guy, 619 S. Pandora, Gilbert, AZ 85234/ert, AZ 85234/602-892-3437

Hank's Gun Shop, Box 370, 50 West 100 South, Monroe, UT 84754/801-527-4456

Hanson's Gun Center, Dick, 233 Everett Dr., Colorado Springs, CO 80911

Hardison, Charles, P.O. Box 356, 200 W. Baseline Rd., Lafayette, CO 80026-0356/303-666-5171

Hecht, Hubert J., Waffen-Hecht, P.O. Box 2635, Fair Oaks, CA 95628/916-966-1020

Heilmann, Stephen, P.O. Box 657, Grass Valley, CA 95945/916-272-8758

Hensler, Jerry, 6614 Country Field, San Antonio, TX 78240/210-690-7491

Hensley, Darwin, P.O. Box 329, Brightwood, OR 97011/503-622-5411

Heppler, Keith M., Keith's Custom Gunstocks, 540 Banyan Circle, Walnut Creek, CA, 4598/510-934-3509; FAX: 510-934-3143

High Bridge Arms, Inc., 3185 Mission St., San Francisco, CA 94110/415-282-8358

High Performance International, 5734 W. Florist Ave., Milwaukee, WI 53218/414-466-9040

Hill, Loring F., 304 Cedar Rd., Elkins Park, PA 19117

Hiptmayer, Klaus, RR 112 #750, P.O. Box 136, Eastman, Quebec J0E 1P0, CANADA/514-297-2492

Hoag, James W., 8523 Canoga Ave., Suite C, Canoga Park, CA 91304/818-998-1510

Hobaugh, Wm. H. (See Rifle Shop, The)

Hobbie Gunsmithing, Duane A., 2412 Pattie Ave., Wichita, KS 67216/316-264-8266

Hodgson, Richard, 9081 Tahoe Lane, Boulder, CO 80301

Hoelscher, Virgil, 11047 Pope Ave., Lynwood, CA 90262/310-631-8545

Hoenig & Rodman, 6521 Morton Dr., Boise, ID 83704/208-375-1116

Hofer Jagdwaffen, P., Buchsenmachermeister, Kirchgasse 24, A-9170 Ferlach, AUSTRIA/04227-3683

Holland, Dick, 422 NE 6th St., Newport, OR 97365/503-265-7556

Holland's, Box 69, Powers, OR 97466/503-439-5155; FAX: 503-439-5155

Hollis Gun Shop, 917 Rex St., Carlsbad, NM 88220/505-885-3782

Horst, Alan K., 3221 2nd Ave. N., Great Falls, MT 59401/406-454-1831

Huebner, Corey O., Box 6, Hall, MT 59837/406-721-1658

Hughes, Steven Dodd, P.O. Box 11455, Eugene, OR 97440/503-485-8869

Irwin, Campbell H., 140 Hartland Blvd., East Hartland, CT 06027/203-653-3901

Ivanoff, Thomas G. (See Tom's Gun Repair)

J&S Heat Treat, 803 S. 16th St., Blue Springs, MO 64015/816-229-2149; FAX: 816-228-1135

Jackalope Gun Shop, 1048 S. 5th St., Douglas, WY 82633/307-358-3441

Jaeger, Inc./Dunn's, Paul, P.O. Box 449, 1 Madison Ave., Grand Junction, TN 38039/901-764-6909; FAX: 901-764-6503

Jim's Gun Shop (See Spradlin's)

Johnston, James (See North Fork Custom Gunsmithing)

J.D. Jones (See SSK Industries)

Juenke, Vern, 25 Bitterbush Rd., Reno, NV 89523/702-345-0225

Jurras, L.E., P.O. Box 680, Washington, IN 47501/812-254-7698

K-D, Inc., Box 459, 585 N. Hwy. 155, Cleveland, UT 84518/801-653-2530

KDF, Inc., 2485 Hwy. 46 N., Seguin, TX 78155/210-379-8141; FAX: 210-379-5420

Ken's Gun Specialties, Rt. 1, Box 147, Lakeview, AR 72642/501-431-5606

Kimball, Gary, 1526 N. Circle Dr., Colorado Springs, CO 0909/719-634-1274

Klein Custom Guns, Don, 433 Murray Park Dr., Ripon, WI 54971/414-748-2931

Kleinendorst, K.W., RR #1, Box 1500, Hop Bottom, PA 18824/717-289-4687; FAX: 717-289-4687

Kneiper Custom Guns, Jim, 334 Summit Vista, Carbondale, CO 81623/303-963-9880

Knippel, Richard, 5924 Carnwood, Riverbank, CA 95367/209-869-1469

KOGOT, 410 College, Trinidad, CO 81082/719-846-9406

Kopp, Terry K., 1301 Franklin, Lexington, MO 64067/816-259-2636

Korzinek Riflesmith, J., RD #2, Box 73, Canton, PA 17724/717-673-8512

LaFrance Specialties, P.O. Box 178211, San Diego, CA 92117/619-293-3373

Lair, Sam, 520 E. Beaver, Jenks, OK 74037/918-299-2391

Lampert, Ron, Rt. 1, Box 177, Guthrie, MN 56461/218-854-7345

LaRocca Gun Works, Inc., 51 Union Place, Worcester, MA 01608/508-754-2887; FAX: 508-754-2887

Lawson Co., Harry, 3328 N. Richey Blvd., Tucson, AZ 85716/602-326-1117

Lebeau-Courally, Rue St. Gilles, 386, 4000 Liege, BELGIUM/041 52 48 43; FAX: 041 52 20 08

LeFever Arms Co., Inc., 6234 Stokes, Lee Center Rd., Lee Center, NY 13363/315-337-6722; FAX: 315-337-1543

Lind Custom Guns, Al, 7821 76th Ave. SW, Tacoma, WA 98498/206-584-6361

Lock's Philadelphia Gun Exchange, 6700 Rowland Ave., Philadelphia, PA 19149/215-332-6225; FAX: 215-332-4800

Long, George F., 1500 Rogue River Hwy., Ste. F, Grants Pass, OR 97527/503-476-7552

Mag-Na-Port International, Inc., 41302 Executive Dr., Harrison Twp., MI 48045-3448/810-469-6727; FAX: 810-469-0425

Makinson, Nicholas, RR 3, Komoka, Ont. N0L 1R0 CANADA/519-471-5462

Mandarino, Monte, 205 Fifth Ave. East, Kalispell, MT 59901/406-257-6208

Manley Shooting Supplies, Lowell, 3684 Pine St., Deckerville, MI 48427/313-376-3665

Marent, Rudolf, 9711 Tiltree St., Houston, TX 77075/713-946-7028

Martin's Gun Shop, 937 S. Sheridan Blvd., Lakewood, CO 80226/303-922-2184

Martz, John V., 8060 Lakeview Lane, Lincoln, CA 95648/916-645-2250

Masker, Seely, 54 Woodshire S., Getzville, NY 14068/716-689-8894

Mathews & Son, Inc., George E., 10224 S. Paramount Blvd., Downey, CA 90241/310-862-6719; FAX: 310-862-6719

Maxi-Mount, P.O. Box 291, Willoughby Hills, OH 44094-0291/216-946-3105

Mazur Restoration, Pete, 13083 Drummer Way, Grass Valley, CA 95949/916-268-2412

McCament, Jay, 1730-134th St. Ct. S., Tacoma, WA 98444/206-531-8832

MCRW Associates Shooting Supplies, R.R. #1 Box 1425, Sweet Valley, PA 18656/717-864-3967; FAX: 717-864-2669

MCS, Inc., 34 Delmar Dr., Brookfield, CT 06804/203-775-1013; FAX: 203-775-9462

Mercer Custom Stocks, R.M., 216 S. Whitewater Ave., Jefferson, WI 53549/414-674-3839, 800-704-4447

Mid-America Recreation, Inc., 1328 5th Ave., Moline, IA 52807/309-764-5089; FAX: 309-764-2722

Middlebrooks Custom Shop, 7366 Colonial Trail East, Surry, VA 23883/804-357-0881; FAX: 804-365-0442

Miller Co., David, 3131 E. Greenlee Rd., Tucson, AZ 85716/602-326-3117

Miller Custom, 210 E. Julia, Clinton, IL 61727/217-935-9362

Mills Jr., Hugh B., 3615 Canterbury Rd., New Bern, NC 28560/919-637-4631

Moeller, Steve, 1213 4th St., Fulton, IL 61252/815-589-2300

Morrow, Bud, 11 Hillside Lane, Sheridan, WY 82801-9729/307-674-8360

Mullis Guncraft, 3523 Lawyers Road E., Monroe, NC 28110/704-283-6683

Mustra's Custom Guns, Inc., Carl, 1002 Pennsylvania Ave., Palm Harbor, FL 34683/813-785-1403

Nelson, Stephen, 7365 NW Spring Creek Dr., Corvallis, OR 97330/503-745-5232

Nettestad Gun Works, RR 1, Box 160, Pelican Rapids, MN 56572/218-863-4301

New England Custom Gun Service, Brook Rd., RR2, Box 122W, W. Lebanon, NH 03784/603-469-3450; FAX: 603-469-3471

Newman Gunshop, 119 Miller Rd., Agency, IA 52530/515-937-5775

Nicholson Custom, Rt. 1, Box 176-3, Sedalia, MO 65301/816-826-8746

Nickels, Paul R., 4789 Summerhill Rd., Las Vegas, NV 89121/702-435-5318

Nicklas, Ted, 5504 Hegel Rd., Goodrich, MI 48438/810-797-4493

Nolan, Dave, Fox Valley Range, P.O. Box 155, Dundee, IL 60118/708-426-5921

North American Shooting Systems, P.O. Box 306, Osoyoos, B.C. V0H 1V0 CANADA/604-495-3131; FAX: 604-495-2816

North Fork Custom Gunsmithing, James Johnston, 428 Del Rio Rd., Roseburg, OR 97470/503-673-4467

Nu-Line Guns, Inc., 1053 Caulks Hill Rd., Harvester, MO 63304/314-441-4500; FAX: 314-447-5018

Oakland Custom Arms, Inc., 4690 W. Walton Blvd., Waterford, MI 48329/810-674-8261

Old World Gunsmithing, 2901 SE 122nd St., Portland, OR 97236/503-760-7681

Olson, Vic, 5002 Countryside Dr., Imperial, MO 63052/314-296-8086

Orvis Co., The, Rt. 7, Manchester, VT 05254/802-362-3622 ext. 283; FAX: 802-362-3525

Ottmar, Maurice, Box 657, 113 E. Fir, Coulee City, WA 99115/509-632-5717

Ozark Gun Works, 11830 Cemetery Rd., Rogers, AR 72756/501-631-6944; FAX: 501-631-6944

P&S Gun Service, 2138 Old Shepardsville Rd., Louisville, KY 40218/502-456-9346

Pace Marketing, Inc., 9474 NW 48th St., Sunrise, FL 33351-5137/305-741-4361; FAX: 305-741-2901

Pagel Gun Works, Inc., 1407 4th St. NW, Grand Rapids, MN 55744/218-326-3003

Pasadena Gun Center, 206 E. Shaw, Pasadena, TX 77506/713-472-0417; FAX: 713-472-1322

Paterson Gunsmithing, 438 Main St., Paterson, NJ 07502/201-345-4100

Pell, John T., 410 College, Trinidad, CO 81082/719-846-9406

PEM's Mfg. Co., 5063 Waterloo Rd., Atwater, OH 44201/216-947-3721

Penrod Precision, 312 College Ave., P.O. Box 307, N. Manchester, IN 46962/219-982-8385

Pentheny de Pentheny, 2352 Baggett Ct., Santa Rosa, CA 95401/707-573-1390; FAX: 707-573-1390

Peters & Hosea Gunmakers, 18255 Red Fox Dr., Beaver Creek, OR 97004/503-654-8532

Powell & Son (Gunmakers) Ltd., William, 35-37 Carrs Lane, Birmingham B4 7SX ENGLAND/21-643-0689; FAX: 21-631-3504

Pro-Port Ltd., 41302 Executive Dr., Harrison Twp., MI 48045-3448/810-469-7323; FAX: 810-469-0425

Quality Firearms of Idaho, Inc., 114 13th Ave. S., Nampa, ID 83651/208-466-1631

Ray's Gunsmith Shop, 3199 Elm Ave., Grand Junction, CO 81504/303-434-6162

Renfrew Guns & Supplies, R.R. 4, Renfrew, Ontario K7V 3Z7 CANADA/613-432-7080

Ridgetop Sporting Goods, P.O. Box 306, 42907 Hilligoss Ln. East, Eatonville, WA, 98328/206-832-6422

Ries, Chuck, 415 Ridgecrest Dr., Grants Pass, OR 97527/503-476-5623

Rifle Shop, The, Wm. H. Hobaugh, P.O. Box M, Philipsburg, MT 59858/406-859-3515

Rizzini Battista, Via 2 Giugno, 7/7Bis-25060 Marcheno (Brescia), ITALY

RMS Custom Gunsmithing, 4120 N. Bitterwell, Prescott Valley, AZ 86314/602-772-7626

Robar Co.'s, Inc., The, 21438 N. 7th Ave., Suite B, Phoenix, AZ 85027/602-581-2648; FAX: 602-582-0059

Roberts, J.J., 7808 Lake Dr., Manassas, VA 22111/703-330-0448

Robinson, Don, Pennsylvania Hse., 36 Fairfax Crescent, Southowram, Halifax, W. Yorkshire HX3 9SQ, ENGLAND/0422-364458

Rogers Gunsmithing, Bob, P.O. Box 305, 344 S. Walnut St., Franklin Grove, IL 61031/815-456-2685; FAX: 815-288-7142

Romain's Custom Guns, RD 1, Whetstone Rd., Brockport, PA 15823/814-265-1948

Ryan, Chad L., RR 3, Box 72, Cresco, IA 52136/319-547-4384

Sanders Custom Gun Service, 2358 Tyler Ln., Louisville, KY 40205/502-454-3338

Sandy's Custom Gunshop, Rt. #1, P.O. Box 4, Rockport, IL 62370/217-437-4241

Schiffman, Curt, 3017 Kevin Cr., Idaho Falls, ID 83402/208-524-4684

Schiffman, Mike, 8233 S. Crystal Springs, McCammon, ID 83250/208-254-9114

Schiffman, Norman, 3017 Kevin Cr., Idaho Falls, ID 83402/208-524-4684

Schumakers Gun Shop, William, 512 Prouty Corner Lp. #A, Colville, WA 99114/509-684-4848

Schwartz Custom Guns, Wayne E., 970 E. Britton Rd., Morrice, MI 48857/517-625-4079

Scott Fine Guns, Inc., Thad, P.O. Box 412, Indianola, MS 38751/601-887-5929

Scott, Dwight, 23089 Englehardt St., Clair Shores, MI 48080/313-779-4735

Scott, McDougall & Associates, 7950 Redwood Dr., Cotati, CA 94931/707-546-2264

Shaw, Inc., E.R. (See Small Arms Mfg. Co.)

Shay's Gunsmithing, 931 Marvin Ave., Lebanon, PA 17042

Shell Shack, 113 E. Main, Laurel, MT 59044/406-628-8986

Shooter Shop, The, 221 N. Main, Butte, MT 59701/406-723-3842

Shooters Supply, 1120 Tieton Dr., Yakima, WA 98902/509-452-1181

Shootin' Shack, Inc., 1065 Silver Beach Rd., Riviera Beach, FL 33403/407-842-0990

Shooting Specialties (See Titus, Daniel)

Shotgun Shop, The, 14145 Proctor Ave., Suite 3, Industry, CA 91746/818-855-2737; FAX: 818-855-2735

Shotguns Unlimited, 2307 Fon Du Lac Rd., Richmond, VA 23229/804-752-7115

Silver Ridge Gun Shop (See Goodwin, Fred)

Singletary, Kent, 7516 W. Sells, Phoenix, AZ 85033/602-849-5917

Sipes Gun Shop, 7415 Asher Ave., Little Rock, AR 72204/501-565-8480

Siskiyou Gun Works (See Donnelly, C.P.)

S.K. Guns, Inc., 3041A Main Ave., Fargo, ND 58103/701-293-4867; FAX: 701-232-0001

Skeoch, Brian R., P.O. Box 279, Glenrock, WY 82637/307-436-9804; FAX: 307-436-9804

Sklany, Steve, 566 Birch Grove Dr., Kalispell, MT 59901/406-755-4257

Slezak, Jerome F., 1290 Marlowe, Lakewood (Cleveland), OH 44107/216-221-1668

Small Arms Mfg. Co., 611 Thoms Run Rd., Bridgeville, PA 15017/412-221-4343; FAX: 412-221-8443

Smith, Art, P.O. Box 13, Hector, MN 55342/612-848-2760

Smith, Sharmon, 4545 Speas Rd., Fruitland, ID 83619/208-452-6329

Snapp's Gunshop, 6911 E. Washington Rd., Clare, MI 48617/517-386-9226

SOS Products Co. (See Buck Stix—SOS Products Co.)

Spencer Reblue Service, 1820 Tupelo Trail, Holt, MI 48842/517-694-7474

Sportsmen's Exchange & Western Gun Traders, Inc., 560 S. "C" St., Oxnard, CA 93030/805-483-1917

Spradlin's, 113 Arthur St., Pueblo, CO 81004/719-543-9462

SSK Industries, 721 Woodvue Lane, Wintersville, OH 43952/614-264-0176; FAX: 614-264-2257

Starnes, Ken, 32900 SW Laurelview Rd., Hillsboro, OR 97123/503-628-0705

Steelman's Gun Shop, 10465 Beers Rd., Swartz Creek, MI 48473/313-735-4884

Steffens, Ron, 18396 Mariposa Creek Rd., Willits, CA 95490/707-485-0873

Stiles Custom Guns, RD3, Box 1605, Homer City, PA 15748/412-479-9945, 412-479-8666
Stott's Creek Armory, Inc., RR1, Box 70, Morgantown, IN 46160/317-878-5489
Sullivan, David S. (See Westwind Rifles, Inc.)
Swann, D.J., 5 Orsova Close, Eltham North, Vic. 3095, AUSTRALIA/03-431-0323
S.W.I.F.T., 4610 Blue Diamond Rd., Las Vegas, NV 89118/702-897-1100
Swift River Gunworks, Inc., 450 State St., Belchertown, MA 01007/413-323-4052
Szweda, Robert (See RMS Custom Gunsmithing)
Talmage, William G., RR16, Box 102A, Brazil, IN 47834/812-442-0804
Taylor & Robbins, P.O. Box 164, Rixford, PA 16745/814-966-3233
Tennessee Valley Mfg., P.O. Box 1175, Corinth, MS 38834/601-286-5014
Ten-Ring Precision, Inc., Alex B. Hamilton, 1449 Blue Crest Lane, San Antonio, TX 78232/512-494-3063; FAX: 512-494-3066
300 Gunsmith Service, Inc., 6850 S. Yosemite Ct., Englewood, CO 80112/303-773-0300
Thurston Sports, Inc., RD 3 Donovan Rd., Auburn, NY 13021/315-253-0966
Titus, Daniel, Shooting Specialties, 872 Penn St., Bryn Mawr, PA 19010/215-525-8829
Tom's Gun Repair, Thomas G. Ivanoff, 76-6 Rt. Southfork Rd., Cody, WY 82414/307-587-6949
Tooley Custom Rifles, 516 Creek Meadow Dr., Gastonia, NC 28054/704-864-7525
Trevallion Gunstocks, 9 Old Mountain Rd., Cape Neddick, ME 03902/207-361-1130
T.S.W. Conversions, Inc., E. 115 Crain Rd., Paramus, NJ 07650-4017/201-265-1618
Van Epps, Milton, Rt. 69-A, Parish, NY 13131/315-625-7251
Van Horn, Gil, P.O. Box 207, Llano, CA 93544
Van Patten, J.W., P.O. Box 145, Foster Hill, Milford, PA 18337/717-296-7069
Vest, John, P.O. Box 1552, Susanville, CA 96130/916-257-7228
Vic's Gun Refinishing, 6 Pineview Dr., Dover, NH 03820-6422/603-742-0013
Vintage Arms, Inc., 6003 Saddle Horse, Fairfax, VA 22030/703-968-0779; FAX: 703-968-0780
Waffen-Weber Custom Gunsmithing, #4-1691 Powick Rd., Kelowna, B.C. CANADA V1X 4L1/604-762-7575; FAX: 604-861-3655
Walker Arms Co., Inc., 499 County Rd. 820, Selma, AL 36701/205-872-6231
Wardell Precision Handguns Ltd., 48851 N. Fig Springs Rd., New River, AZ 5027, 8513/602-465-7995
Weaver's Gun Shop, P.O. Box 8, Dexter, MO 63841/314-568-3101
Weems, Cecil, P.O. Box 657, Mineral Wells, TX 76067/817-325-1462
Wells, Fred F., Wells Sport Store, 110 N. Summit St., Prescott, AZ 86301/602-445-3655
Wells Custom Gunsmith, R.A., 3452 1st Ave., Racine, WI 53402/414-639-5223
Welsh, Bud, 80 New Road, E. Amherst, NY 14051/716-688-6344
Werth, T.W., 1203 Woodlawn Rd., Lincoln, IL 62656/217-732-1300
Wessinger Custom Guns & Engraving, 268 Limestone Rd., Chapin, SC 29036/803-345-5677
West, Robert G., 3973 Pam St., Eugene, OR 97402/503-344-3700
Westchester Carbide, 148 Wheeler Ave., Pleasantville, NY 10570/914-769-1445
Westwind Rifles, Inc., David S. Sullivan, P.O. Box 261, 640 Briggs St., Erie, CO 80516/303-828-3823
Wiebe, Duane, 3715 S. Browns Lake Dr. 106, Burlington, WI 53105-7931
Williams Gun Sight Co., 7389 Lapeer Rd., Box 329, Davison, MI 48423/810-653-2131, 800-530-9028; FAX: 810-658-2140
Williams Shootin' Iron Service, The Lynx-Line, 8857 Bennett Hill Rd., Central Lake, MI 49622/616-544-6615
Williamson Precision Gunsmithing, 117 W. Pipeline, Hurst, TX 76053/817-285-0064; FAX: 817-285-0064
Winter, Robert M., P.O. Box 484, Menno, SD 57045/605-387-5322
Wise Guns, Dale, 333 W. Olmos Dr., San Antonio, TX 78212/210-828-3388
Wisner's Gun Shop, Inc., 287 NW Chehalis Ave., Chehalis, WA 98532/206-748-8942; FAX: 206-748-7011
Wood, Frank (See Classic Guns)
Yankee Gunsmith, 2901 Deer Flat Dr., Copperas Cove, TX 76522/817-547-8433
Yavapai College, 1100 E. Sheldon St., Prescott, AZ 86301/602-776-2359; FAX: 602-776-2193
Zeeryp, Russ, 1601 Foard Dr., Lynn Ross Manor, Morristown, TN 37814/615-586-2357

GUN PARTS, U.S. AND FOREIGN

Ad Hominem, RR 3, Orillia, Ont. L3V 6H3, CANADA/705-689-5303
Ahlman Guns, Rt. 1, Box 20, Morristown, MN 55052/507-685-4243; FAX: 507-685-4247
Amherst Arms, P.O. Box 1457, Englewood, FL 34295/813-475-2020
Bear Mountain Gun & Tool, 120 N. Plymouth, New Plymouth, ID 83655/208-278-5221; FAX: 208-278-5221
Bob's Gun Shop, P.O. Box 200, Royal, AR 71968/501-767-1970
Briese Bullet Co., Inc., RR1, Box 108, Tappen, ND 58487/701-327-4578; FAX: 701-327-4579
British Arms Co. Ltd., P.O. Box 7, Latham, NY 12110/518-783-0773
Can Am Enterprises, 350 Jones Rd., Fruitland, Ont. LOR ILO, CANADA/416-643-4357
Cape Outfitters, Rt. 2, Box 437C, Cape Girardeau, MO 63701/314-335-4103; FAX: 314-335-1555
Chuck's Gun Shop, P.O. Box 597, Waldo, FL 32694/904-468-2264
Colonial Repair, P.O. Box 372, Hyde Park, MA 02136-9998/617-469-4951
Costa, David, Island Pond Gun Shop, P.O. Box 428, Cross St., Island Pond, VT 05846/802-723-4546
Defense Moulding Enterprises, 16781 Daisey Ave., Fountain Valley, CA 92708/714-842-5062
Delta Arms Ltd., P.O. Box 68, Sellers, SC 29592-0068/803-752-7426, 800-677-0641; 800-274-1611
Dibble, Derek A., 555 John Downey Dr., New Britain, CT 06051/203-224-2630
Duffy, Charles E., Williams Lane, West Hurley, NY 12491/914-679-2997
E&L Mfg., Inc., 39042 N. School House Rd., Cave Creek, AZ 85331/602-488-2598; FAX: 602-488-0813
Eagle International, Inc., 5195 W. 58th Ave., Suite 300, Arvada, CO 80002/303-426-8100
EMF Co., Inc., 1900 E. Warner Ave. Suite 1-D, Santa Ana, CA 92705/714-261-6611; FAX: 714-956-0133
FAPA Corp., P.O. Box 1439, New London, NH 03257/603-735-5652; FAX: 603-735-5154
First Distributors, Inc., Jack, 1201 Turbine, Rapid City, SD 57701/605-343-8481
Fleming Firearms, 9525-J East 51st St., Tulsa, OK 74145/918-665-3624
Forrest, Inc., Tom, P.O. Box 326, Lakeside, CA 92040/619-561-5800; FAX: 619-561-0227
Greider Precision, 431 Santa Marina Ct., Escondido, CA 92029/619-480-8892
Gun Parts Corp., The, 226 Williams Lane, West Hurley, NY 12491/914-679-2417; FAX: 914-679-5849
Gun Shop, The, 5550 S. 900 East, Salt Lake City, UT 84117/801-263-3633
Gun-Tec, P.O. Box 8125, W. Palm Beach, FL 33407
Hastings Barrels, 320 Court St., Clay Center, KS 67432/913-632-3169; FAX: 913-632-6554
High Performance International, 5734 W. Florist Ave., Milwaukee, WI 53218/414-466-9040
Irwin, Campbell H., 140 Hartland Blvd., East Hartland, CT 06027/203-653-3901
Jaeger, Inc./Dunn's, Paul, P.O. Box 449, 1 Madison Ave., Grand Junction, TN 38039/901-764-6909; FAX: 901-764-6503

Johnson Gunsmithing, Inc., Neal G., 111 Marvin Dr., Hampton, VA 23666/804-838-8091; FAX: 804-838-8157
K&T Co., Div. of T&S Industries, Inc., 1027 Skyview Dr., W. Carrollton, OH 45449/513-859-8414
K.K. Arms Co., Star Route Box 671, Kerrville, TX 78028/210-257-4718; FAX: 210-257-4891
Markell, Inc., 422 Larkfield Center #235, Santa Rosa, CA 95403/707-573-0792; FAX: 707-573-9867
McCormick Corp., Chip, 1825 Fortview Rd., Ste. 115, Austin, TX 78704/800-328-CHIP, 512-462-0004; FAX: 512-462-0009
Merkuria Ltd., Argentinska 38, 17005 Praha 7, CZECH REPUBLIC/422-875117; FAX: 422-809152
Moreton/Fordyce Enterprises, P.O. Box 940, Saylorsburg, PA 18353/717-992-5742; FAX: 717-992-8775
Morrow, Bud, 11 Hillside Lane, Sheridan, WY 82801-9729/307-674-8360
North American Specialties, 25442 Trabuco Rd., 105-328, Lake Forest, CA 92630/714-837-4867
Nu-Line Guns, Inc., 1053 Caulks Hill Rd., Harvester, MO 63304/314-441-4500; FAX: 314-447-5018
Oakland Custom Arms, Inc., 4690 W. Walton Blvd., Waterford, MI 48329/810-674-8261
Pace Marketing, Inc., 9474 NW 48th St., Sunrise, FL 33351-5137/305-741-4361; FAX: 305-741-2901
Pachmayr Ltd., 1875 S. Mountain Ave., Monrovia, CA 91016/818-357-7771, 800-423-9704; FAX: 818-358-7251
Parts & Surplus, P.O. Box 22074, Memphis, TN 38122/901-683-4007
Pennsylvania Gun Parts, 638 Whiskey Spring Rd., Boiling Springs, PA 17007/717-258-5683
Perazzi USA, Inc., 1207 S. Shamrock Ave., Monrovia, CA 91016/818-303-0068
Quality Firearms of Idaho, Inc., 114 13th Ave. S., Nampa, ID 83651/208-466-1631
Randco UK, 286 Gipsy Rd., Welling, Kent DA16 1JJ, ENGLAND/44 81 303 4118
Rizzini Battista, Via 2 Giugno, 7/7Bis-25060 Marcheno (Brescia), ITALY
Rutgers Gun & Boat Center, 127 Raritan Ave., Highland Park, NJ 08904/908-545-4344; FAX: 908-545-6686
Sarco, Inc., 323 Union St., Stirling, NJ 97980/908-647-3800
Shell Shack, 113 E. Main, Laurel, MT 59044/406-628-8986
Sheridan USA, Inc., Austin, P.O. Box 577, Durham, CT 06422
Sherwood Intl. Export Corp., 18714 Parthenia St., Northridge, CA 91324/818-349-7600
Smires, C.L., 28269 Old Schoolhouse Rd., Columbus, NJ 08022/609-298-3158
Southern Ammunition Co., Inc., Rt. 1, Box 6B, Latta, SC 29565/803-752-7751; FAX: 803-752-2022
Southern Armory, The, Rt. 2, Box 134, Woodlawn, VA 24381/703-236-7835; FAX: 703-236-3714
Sportsmen's Exchange & Western Gun Traders, Inc., 560 S. "C" St., Oxnard, CA 93030/805-483-1917
Tradewinds, Inc., P.O. Box 1191, 2339-41 Tacoma Ave. S., Tacoma, WA 98401/206-272-4887
Twin Pine Armory, P.O. Box 58, Hwy. 6, Adna, WA 98522/206-748-4590; FAX: 206-748-7011
Vintage Arms, Inc., 6003 Saddle Horse, Fairfax, VA 22030/703-968-0779; FAX: 703-968-0780
Vintage Industries, Inc., 781 Big Tree Dr., Longwood, FL 32750/407-831-8949; FAX: 407-831-5346
Walker Arms Co., Inc., 499 County Rd. 820, Selma, AL 36701/205-872-6231
Wardell Precision Handguns Ltd., 48851 N. Fig Springs Rd., New River, AZ 85027-8513/602-465-7995
Weaver's Gun Shop, P.O. Box 8, Dexter, MO 63841/314-568-3101
Westfield Engineering, 6823 Watcher St., Commerce, CA 90040/FAX: 213-928-8270
Wilson's Gun Shop, Box 578, Rt. 3, Berryville, AR 72616/501-545-3635; FAX: 501-545-3310
Wisner's Gun Shop, Inc., 287 NW Chehalis Ave., Chehalis, WA 98532/206-748-8942; FAX: 206-748-7011
W.C. Wolff Co., P.O. Box I, Newtown Square, PA 19073/610-359-9600, 800-545-0077

GUNS, FOREIGN—IMPORTERS (Manufacturers)

Alessandri and Son, Lou, 24 French St., Rehoboth, MA 02769/508-252-3436, 800-248-5652; FAX: 508-252-3436 (Battista Rizzini)
American Arms, Inc., 715 E. Armour Rd., N. Kansas City, MO 64116/816-474-3161; FAX: 816-474-1225 (Luigi Franchi S.p.A.; Grulla Armes)
Armas Kemen S.A., Box 228, Alpha Terrace, Glendale, CA 91208-2137/310-809-1999, 818-956-0722; FAX: 818-956-5512
Armes de Chasse, P.O. Box 827, Chadds Ford, PA 19317/215-388-1146; FAX: 215-388-1147 (AYA; Auguste Francotte & Cie S.A.)
Bell's Legendary Country Wear, 22 Circle Dr., Bellmore, NY 11710/516-679-1158 (B.C. Miroko/Charles Daly; William Powell & Son Ltd.)
Beretta U.S.A. Corp., 17601 Beretta Drive, Accokeek, MD 20607/301-283-2191 (Pietro Beretta Firearms)
British Sporting Arms, RR1, Box 130, Millbrook, NY 12545/914-677-8303 (B.C. Miroku/Charles Daley)
Browning Arms Co. (Parts & Service), 3005 Arnold Tenbrook Rd., Arnold, MO 63010-9406/314-287-6800; FAX: 314-287-9751
Cape Outfitters, Rt. 2, Box 437C, Cape Girardeau, MO 63701/314-335-4103; FAX: 314-335-1555 (San Marco; Societa Armi Bresciane Srl.; Westley Richards & Co.)
County, 11020 Whitman Ln., Tamarac, FL 33321/305-720-2066; FAX: 305-722-6353
Dynamit Nobel-RWS, Inc., 81 Ruckman Rd., Closter, NJ 07624/201-767-1995; FAX: 201-767-1589 (Wilhelm Brenneke KG)
Galaxy Imports Ltd., Inc., P.O. Box 3361, Victoria, TX 77903/512-573-4867; FAX: 512-576-9622 (Laurona Armas S.A.)
Giacomo Sporting, Inc., Delta Plaza, Rt. 26N, Rome, NY 13440 (Renato Gamba S.p.A.)
Griffin & Howe, Inc., 33 Claremont Rd., Bernardsville, NJ 07924/908-776-2287; FAX: 908-776-1068 (John Rigby & Co.)
GSI, Inc., 108 Morrow Ave., P.O. Box 129, Trussville, AL 35173/205-655-8299; FAX: 205-655-7078 (Merkel Freres)
G.U., Inc., 4325 S. 120th St., Omaha, NE 68137/402-330-4492 (SKB Arms Co.)
Heckler & Koch, Inc., 21480 Pacific Blvd., Sterling, VA 20166/703-450-1900; FAX: 703-450-8160 (Benelli Armi S.p.A.)
Hi-Grade Imports, 8655 Monterey Rd., Gilroy, CA 95021/408-842-9301; FAX: 408-842-2374 (Arrieta, S.L.)
Ithaca Acquisition Corp., Ithaca Gun Co., 891 Route 34B, King Ferry, NY 13081/315-364-7171; FAX: 315-364-5134 (Fabarm S.p.A.)
JagerSport, Ltd., One Wholesale Way, Cranston, RI 02920/800-426-3089, 401-944-9682; FAX: 401-946-2587 (Friedrich Wilh. Heym GmbH & Co.)

Jansma, Jack J., 4320 Kalamazoo Ave., Grand Rapids, MI 49508/616-455-7810; FAX: 616-455-5212 (Arrieta, S.L.)

K.B.I., Inc., P.O. Box 5440, Harrisburg, PA 17110-0440/717-540-8518; FAX: 717-540-8567 (Baikal)

Krieghoff International, Inc., 7528 Easton Rd., Ottsville, PA 18942/215-847-5173; FAX: 215-847-8691 (H. Krieghoff Gun Co.)

London Guns Ltd., Box 3750, Santa Barbara, CA 93130/805-683-4141; FAX: 805-683-1712

Mandall Shooting Supplies, Inc., 3616 N. Scottsdale Rd., Scottsdale, AZ 85252/602-945-2553; FAX: 602-949-0734 (Arizaga; Bretton; Hermanos Crucelegoi; Techni-Mec; Ignacio Ugartechea S.A.; Pietro Zanoletti)

MEC-Gar U.S.A., Inc., Box 112, 500B Monroe Turnpike, Monroe, CT 06468/203-635-8662; FAX: 203-635-8662 (MEC-Gar S.R.L.)

Moore & Co., Wm. Larkin, 31360 Via Colinas, Suite 109, Westlake Village, CA 91361/818-889-4160 (FERLIB; Armas Urki Garbi; Piotti; Rizzini)

New England Arms Co., Box 278, Lawrence Lane, Kittery Point, ME 03905/207-439-0593; FAX: 207-439-6726 (Arrieta, S.L.; FERLIB; Renato Gamba S.p.A.; Rizzini)

Orvis Co., The, Rt. 7, Manchester, VT 05254/802-362-3622 ext. 283; FAX: 802-362-3525 (Arrieta, S.L.)

Pachmayr Ltd., 1875 S. Mountain Ave., Monrovia, CA 91016/818-357-7771, 800-423-9704; FAX: 818-358-7251 (FERLIB)

Perazzi USA, Inc., 1207 S. Shamrock Ave., Monrovia, CA 91016/818-303-0068 (Perazzi m.a.p. S.P.A.)

Precision Sales International, Inc., P.O. Box 1776, Westfield, MA 01086/413-562-5055; FAX: 413-562-5056 (Marocchi F.lli S.p.A.)

Quality Arms, Inc., Box 19477, Dept. GD, Houston, TX 77224/713-870-8377; FAX: 713-870-8524 (Arrieta, S.L.; FERLIB)

Sile Distributors, Inc., 7 Centre Market Pl., New York, NY 10013/212-925-4389; FAX: 212-925-3149 (Benelli Armi S.p.A.; Marocchi F.lli S.p.A.)

Stoeger Industries, 55 Ruta Ct., S. Hackensack, NJ 07606/201-440-2700, 800-631-0722; FAX: 201-440-2707 (IGA; Tikka)

Turkish Firearms Corp., 8487 Euclid Ave., Suite 1, Manassas Park, VA 22111/703-369-6848; FAX: 703-257-7709

Weatherby, Inc., 3100 El Camino Real, Atascadero, CA 93422/805-466-1767; FAX: 805-466-2527 (Weatherby, Inc.)

GUNS, FOREIGN—MANUFACTURERS (Importers)

Arizaga (Mandall Shooting Supplies, Inc.)

Arrieta, S.L., Morkaiko, 5, Elgoibar, E-20870, SPAIN/(43) 74 31 50; FAX: (43) 74 31 54 (Hi-Grade Imports; Jack J. Jansma; New England Arms Co.; The Orvis Co.; Quality Arms, Inc.)

AYA (Armes de Chasse)

Baikal (K.B.I., Inc.)

Benelli Armi, S.p.A., Via della Stazione, 61029 Urbino, ITALY/39-722-328633; FAX: 39-722-327427 (E.A.A. Corp.; Heckler & Koch, Inc.; Sile Distributors)

Beretta Firearms, Pietro, 25063 Gardone V.T., ITALY (Beretta U.S.A. Corp.)

Brenneke KG, Wilhelm, Ilmenauweg 2, D-30551 Langenhagen, GERMANY/0511/97262-0; FAX: 0511/9726262 (Dynamit Nobel-RWS, Inc.)

Bretton, 19, rue Victor Grignard, F-42026 St-Etienne (Cedex 1) FRANCE/77-93-54-69; FAX: 77-93-57-98 (Mandall Shooting Supplies, Inc.)

Browning Arms Co. (Parts & Service), 3005 Arnold Tenbrook Rd., Arnold, MO 63010-9406/314-287-6800; FAX: 314-287-9751

Cosmi Americo & Figlio s.n.c., Via Flaminia 307, Ancona, ITALY I-60020/071-888208; FAX: 071-887008 (New England Arms Co.)

Crucelegui Hermanos (Mandall Shooting Supplies, Inc.)

FERLIB, Via Costa 46, 25063 Gardone V.T. (Brescia) ITALY/30 89 12 586; FAX: 30 89 12 586 (Wm. Larkin Moore & Co.; New England Arms Co., Pachmayr Co.; Quality Arms, Inc.)

Franchi S.p.A., Luigi, Via del Serpente, 12, 25020 Fornaci, ITALY (American Arms, Inc.)

Francotte & Cie S.A., Auguste, rue du Trois Juin 109, 4400 Herstal-Liege, BELGIUM/41-48.13.18; FAX: 41-48.11.79 (Armes de Chasse)

Gamba S.p.A., Renato, Via Artigiani, 93, 25063 Gardone V.T. (Brescia), ITALY (Giacomo Sporting, Inc.; New England Arms Co.)

Garbi, Armas Urki, #12-14, 20.600 Eibar (Guipuzcoa) SPAIN/43-11 38 73 (Wm. Larkin Moore & Co.)

Grulla Armes, Apartado 453, Avda Otaloa, 12, Eiber, SPAIN (American Arms, Inc.

Heym GmbH & Co. KG, Friedrich Wilh, Coburger Str.8, D-97702 Muennerstadt, GERMANY (JagerSport, Ltd.)

IGA (Stoeger Industries)

Krieghoff Gun Co., H., Bosch Str. 22, 7900 Ulm, GERMANY (Krieghoff International, Inc.)

Lanber Armes S.A., Calle Zubiaurre 5, Zaldibar, SPAIN/34-4-6827702; FAX: 34-4-6827999

Laurona Armas S.A., P.O. Box 260, 20600 Eibar, SPAIN/34-43-700600; FAX: 34-43-700616 (Galaxy Imports Ltd., Inc.)

Marocchi F.lli S.p.A., Via Galileo Galilei, I-25068 Zanano di Sarezzo, ITALY (Sile Distributors)

MEC-Gar S.R.L., Via Madonnina 64, Gardone V.T. (BS), ITALY 25063/39-30-8911719; FAX: 39-30-8910065 (MEC-Gar U.S.A., Inc.)

Merkel Freres, Strasse 7 October, 10, Suhl, GERMANY (GSI, Inc.)

Miroku, B.C./Daly, Charles (Bell's Legendary Country Wear; British Sporting Arms)

Perazzi m.a.p. S.P.A., Via Fontanelle 1/3, 1-25080 Botticino Mattina, ITALY (Perazzi USA, Inc.)

Perugini Visini & Co. s.r.l., Via Camprelle, 126, 25080 Nuvolera (Bs.), ITALY

Piotti (Wm. Larkin Moore & Co.)

Powell & Son (Gunmakers) Ltd., William, 35-37 Carrs Lane, Birmingham B4 7SX ENGLAND/21-643-0689; FAX: 21-631-3504 (Bell's Legendary Country Wear)

Rigby & Co., John, 66 Great Suffolk St., London SE1 0BU, ENGLAND (Griffin & Howe, Inc.)

Rizzini, Battista, Via 2 Giugno, 7/7Bis-25060 Marcheno (Brescia), ITALY (Lou Alessandri & Son)

Rizzini, F.LLI (Wm. LarkinMoore & Co.; New England Arms Co.)

San Marco (Cape Outfitters)

SKB Arms Co., C.P.O. Box 1401, Tokyo, JAPAN (G.U., Inc.)

Societa Armi Bresciane Srl., Via Artigiani 93, Gardone Val Trompia, ITALY 25063/30-8911640, 30-8911648 (Cape Outfitters)

Techni-Mec, Via Gitti s.n., 25060 Marcheno, ITALY (Mandall Shooting Supplies, Inc.)

Tikka (Stoeger Industries)

Ugartechea S.A., Ignacio, Chonta 26, Eibar, SPAIN 20600/43-121257; FAX: 43-121669 (Mandall Shooting Supplies, Inc.)

Weatherby, Inc., 3100 El Camino Real, Atascadero, CA 93422/805-466-1767; FAX: 805-466-2527 (Weatherby, Inc.)

Westley Richards & Co., 40 Grange Rd., Birmingham, ENGLAND B29 6AR/010-214722953 (Cape Outfitters)

Zabala Hermanos S.A., P.O. Box 97, Eibar, SPAIN 20600/43-768085, 43-768076; FAX: 43-768201 (American Arms, Inc.)

Zanoletti, Pietro, Via Monte Gugielpo, 4, I-25063 Gardone V.T., ITALY (Mandall Shooting Supplies, Inc.)

Zoli, Antonio, Via Zanardelli 39, Casier Postal 21, I-25063 Gardone V.T., ITALY

GUNS, U.S.-MADE

Beretta U.S.A. Corp., 17601 Beretta Drive, Accokeek, MD 20607/301-283-2191

Browning Arms Co. (Parts & Service), 3005 Arnold Tenbrook Rd., Arnold, MO 63010-9406/314-287-6800; FAX: 314-287-9751

Connecticut Valley Classics, P.O. Box 2068, 12 Taylor Lane, Westport, CT 06880/203-435-4600

Galazan, Div. of Connecticut Shotgun Mfg. Co., P.O. Box 622, 35 Woodland St., New Britain, CT 06051-0622/203-225-6581; FAX: 203-832-8707

H&R 1871, Inc., 60 Industrial Rowe, Gardner, MA 01440/508-632-9393; FAX: 508-632-2300

Ithaca Aquisition Corp., Ithaca Gun Co., 891 Route 34B, King Ferry, NY 13081/315-364-7171; FAX: 315-364-5134

Ljutic Industries, Inc., 732 N. 16th Ave., Yakima, WA 98902/509-248-0476; FAX: 509-457-5141

Maverick Arms, Inc., 7 Grasso Ave., P.O. Box 497, North Haven, CT 06473/203-230-5300; FAX: 203-230-5420

Mossberg & Sons, Inc., O.F, 7 Grasso Ave., North Haven, CT 06473/203-288-6491; FAX: 203-288-2404

New England Firearms, 60 Industrial Rowe, Gardner, MA 01440/508-632-9393; FAX: 508-632-2300

Remington Arms Co., Inc., 1007 Market St., Wilmington, DE 19898/302-773-5291

Savage Arms, Inc., Springdale Rd., Westfield, MA 01085/413-568-7001; FAX: 413-562-7764

Sporting Arms Mfg., Inc., 801 Hall Ave., Littlefield, TX 79339/806-385-5665; FAX: 806-385-3394

Sturm, Ruger & Co., Inc., Lacey Place, Southport, CT 06490/203-259-7843

Tar-Hunt Custom Rifles, Inc., RR3, Box 572, Bloomsburg, PA 17815/717-784-6368; FAX: 717-784-6368

U.S. Repeating Arms Co., Inc., 275 Winchester Ave., New Haven, CT 06511/203-789-5000; FAX: 203-789-5071

GUNSMITH SUPPLIES, TOOLS, SERVICES

Aldis Gunsmithing & Shooting Supply, 502 S. Montezuma St., Prescott, AZ 86303/602-445-6723; FAX: 602-445-6763

Atlantic Mills, Inc., 1325 Washington Ave., Asbury Park, NJ 07712/201-774-4882

Badger Shooters Supply, Inc., 202 N. Harding, Owen, WI 54460/715-229-2101; FAX: 715-229-2332

Bear Mountain Gun & Tool, 120 N. Plymouth, New Plymouth, ID 83655/208-278-5221; FAX: 208-278-5222

Bengtson Arms Co., L., 6345-B E. Akron St., Mesa, AZ 85205/602-981-6375

Biesen, Al, 5021 Rosewood, Spokane, WA 99208/509-328-9340

Biesen, Roger, 5021 W. Rosewood, Spokane, WA 99208/509-328-9340

Birchwood Casey, 7900 Fuller Rd., Eden Prairie, MN 55344/800-328-6156, 612-937-7933; FAX: 612-937-7979

Blue Ridge Machinery & Tools, Inc., P.O. Box 536-GD, Hurricane, WV 25526/800-872-6500; FAX: 304-562-5311

Briley Mfg., Inc., 1230 Lumpkin, Houston, TX 77043/800-331-5718, 713-932-6995; FAX: 713-932-1043

Brownells, Inc., 200 S. Front St., Montezuma, IA 50171/515-623-5401; FAX: 515-623-3896

B-Square Company, Inc., P.O. Box 11281, 2708 St. Louis Ave., Ft. Worth, TX 76110/817-923-0964, 800-433-2909; FAX: 817-926-7012

Can Am Enterprises, 350 Jones Rd., Fruitland, Ont. LOR ILO, CANADA/416-643-4357

Carbide Checkering Tools, P.O. Box 11, 200 Lyons Hill Rd., Athol, MA 01331/508-249-9241

Chapman Manufacturing Co., 471 New Haven Rd., P.O. Box 250, Durham, CT 06422/203-349-9228; FAX: 203-349-0084

Chem-Pak, Inc., 11 Oates Ave., P.O. Box 1685, Winchester, VA 22601/800-336-9828; FAX: 703-722-3993

Choate Machine & Tool Co., Inc., P.O. Box 218, Bald Knob, AR 72010/501-724-6193, 800-972-6390; FAX: 501-724-5873

Chopie Mfg., Inc., 700 Copeland Ave., LaCrosse, WI 54603/608-784-0926

Clymer Manufacturing Co., Inc., 1645 W. Hamlin Rd., Rochester Hills, MI 48309-3312/810-853-5555; FAX: 810-853-1530

Crouse's Country Cover, P.O. Box 160, Storrs, CT 06268/203-429-4715

Cumberland Arms, Rt. I, Box 1150 Shafer Rd., Blantons Chapel, Manchester, TN 37355

Custom Checkering Service, Kathy Forster, 2124 SE Yamhill St., Portland, OR 97214/503-236-5874

Custom Gun Products, 5021 W. Rosewood, Spokane, WA 99208/509-328-9340

D&J Bullet Co. & Custom Gun Shop, Inc., 426 Ferry St., Russell, KY 41169/606-836-2663; FAX: 606-836-2663

Davidson Products, 2020 Huntington Dr., Las Cruces, NM 88801/505-522-5612

Decker Shooting Products, 1729 Laguna Ave., Schofield, WI 54476/715-359-5873

Dem-Bart Checkering Tools, Inc., 6807 Hwy. #2, Bickford Ave., Snohomish, WA 98290/206-568-7356; FAX: 206-568-3134

Dremel Mfg. Co., 4915-21st St., Racine, WI 53406

Duffy, Charles E., Williams Lane, West Hurley, NY 12491/914-679-2997

Du-Lite Corp., 171 River Rd., Middletown, CT 06457/203-347-2505

Dutchman's Firearms, Inc., The, 4143 Taylor Blvd., Louisville, KY 40215/502-366-0555

Echols & Co., D'Arcy, 164 W. 580 S., Providence, UT 84332/801-753-2367

Ed's Gun House, Rt. 1, Box 62, Minnesota City, MN 55959/507-689-2925

EGW Evolution Gun Works, 4050 B-8 Skyron Dr., Doylestown, PA 18901/215-348-9892; FAX: 215-348-1056

Eilan S.A.L., Paseo San Andres N8, Eibar, SPAIN 20600/(34)43118916; FAX: (34)43 114038

Faith Associates, Inc., 1139 S. Greenville Hwy., Hendersonville, NC 28739/704-692-1916; FAX: 704-697-6827

Ferris Firearms, HC 51, Box 1255, Suite 158, Bulverde, TX 78163/210-980-4811

First Distributors, Inc., Jack, 1201 Turbine, Rapid City, SD 57701/605-343-8481

Fisher, Jerry A., 535 Crane Mt. Rd., Big Fork, MT 59911/406-837-2722

Forgreens Tool Mfg., Inc., P.O. Box 990, Robert Lee, TX 76945/915-453-2800

Frazier Brothers Enterprises, 1118 N. Main St., Franklin, IN 46131/317-736-4000; FAX: 317-736-4000

G.B.C. Industries, Inc., P.O. Box 1602, Spring, TX 77373/713-350-9690; FAX: 713-350-0601

Grace Metal Products, Inc., P.O. Box 67, Elk Rapids, MI 49629/616-264-8133

GRS Corp., Glendo, P.O. Box 1153, 900 Overlander St., Emporia, KS 66801/316-343-1084

Gunline Tools, P.O. Box 478, Placentia, CA 92670/714-528-5252; FAX: 714-572-4128

Gun-Tec, P.O. Box 8125, W. Palm Beach, FL 33407

Hastings Barrels, 320 Court St., Clay Center, KS 67432/913-632-3169; FAX: 913-632-6554

Henriksen Tool Co., Inc., 8515 Wagner Creek Rd., Talent, OR 97540/503-535-2309

Hoehn Sales, Inc., 75 Greensburg Ct., St. Charles, MO 63304/314-441-4231

Hoelscher, Virgil, 11047 Pope Ave., Lynwood, CA 90262/310-631-8545

Holland's, Box 69, Powers, OR 97466/503-439-5155; FAX: 503-439-5155

Hoppe's Div., Penguin Industries, Inc., Airport Industrial Mall, Coatesville, PA 19320/251-384-6000

Huey Gun Cases, Marvin, P.O. Box 22456, Kansas City, MO 64113/816-444-1637

Iosso Products, 1485 Lively Blvd., Elk Grove Villiage, IL 60007/708-437-8400

Ivanoff, Thomas G. (See Tom's Gun Repair)

Jantz Supply, P.O. Box 584, Davis, OK 73030/405-369-2316; FAX: 405-369-3082

JGS Precision Tool Mfg., 1141 S. Summer Rd., Coos Bay, OR 97420/503-267-4331; FAX:503-267-5996

K&M Services, 5430 Salmon Run Rd., Dover, PA 17315/717-764-1461

Kasenit Co., Inc., 13 Park Ave., Highland Mills, NY 10930/914-928-9595; FAX: 914-928-7292

KenPatable Ent., Inc., P.O. Box 19422, Louisville, KY 40259/502-239-5447

Kimball, Gary, 1526 N. Circle Dr., Colorado Springs, CO 80909/719-634-1274

Kleinendorst, K.W., RR #1, Box 1500, Hop Bottom, PA 18824/717-289-4687; FAX: 717-289-4687

Koppco Industries, 1301 Franklin, Lexington, MO 64067/816-259-3239

Korzinek Riflesmith, J., RD #2, Box 73, Canton, PA 17724/717-673-8512

LaRocca Gun Works, Inc., 51 Union Place, Worcester, MA 01608/508-754-2887; FAX: 508-754-2887

Lea Mfg. Co., 237 E. Aurora St., Waterbury, CT 06720/203-753-5116

Lee Supplies, Mark, 9901 France Ct., Lakeville, MN 55044/612-461-2114

London Guns Ltd., Box 3750, Santa Barbara, CA 93130/805-683-4141; FAX: 805-683-1712

Mag-Na-Port International, Inc., 41302 Executive Dr., Harrison Twp., MI 48045-3448/810-469-6727; FAX: 810-469-0425

Marsh, Mike, Croft Cottage, Main St., Elton, Derbyshire DE4 2BY, ENGLAND/0629 650 669

MCRW Associates Shooting Supplies, R.R. #1 Box 1425, Sweet Valley, PA 18656/717-864-3967; FAX: 717-864-2669

Menck, Thomas W., 5703 S. 77th St., Ralston, NE 68127-4201

Metalife Industries, Box 53 Mong Ave., Reno, PA 16343/814-436-7747; FAX: 814-676-5662

Michael's Antiques, Box 591, Waldoboro, ME 04572

Milliron Custom Machine Carving, Earl, 1249 NE 166th Ave., Portland, OR 97230/503-252-3725

Morrow, Bud, 11 Hillside Lane, Sheridan, WY 82801-9729/307-674-8360

Mowrey's Guns & Gunsmithing, RR1, Box 82, Canajoharie, NY 13317/518-673-3483

N&J Sales, Lime Kiln Rd., Northford, CT 06472/203-484-0247

Nitex, Inc., P.O. Box 1706, Uvalde, TX 78801/512-278-8843

Palmgren Steel Products, 8383 S. Chicago Ave., Chicago, IL 60617/312-721-9675; FAX: 312-721-9739

PanaVise Products, Inc., 1485 Southern Way, Sparks, NV 89431/702-353-2900; FAX: 702-353-2929

PEM's Mfg. Co., 5063 Waterloo Rd., Atwater, OH 44201/216-947-3721

Penguin Industries, Inc., Airport Industrial Mall, Coatesville, PA 19320/215-384-6000

Practical Tools, Inc., Div. Behlert Precision, 7067 Easton Rd., P.O. Box 133, Pipersville, PA 18947/215-766-7301; FAX: 215-766-8681

Precision Metal Finishing, John Westrom, P.O. Box 3186, Des Moines, IA 50316/515-288-8680; FAX: 515-244-3925

Precision Specialties, 131 Hendom Dr., Feeding Hills, MA 01030/413-786-3365; FAX: 413-786-3365

Pro-Port Ltd., 41302 Executive Dr., Harrison Twp., MI 48045-3448/810-469-7323; FAX: 810-469-0425

Ravell Ltd., 289 Diputacion St., 08009, Barcelona SPAIN

Reardon Products, P.O. Box 126, Morrison, IL 61270/815-772-3155

Rice, Keith (See White Rock Tool & Die)

Riggs, Jim, 206 Azalea, Boerne, TX 78006/210-249-8567

Roto Carve, 2754 Garden Ave., Janesville, IA 50647

Scott, McDougall & Associates, 7950 Redwood Dr., Cotati, CA 94931/707-546-2264

Sharp Shooter, Inc., P.O. Box 21362, St. Paul, MN 55121/612-452-4687

Sheridan USA, Inc., Austin, P.O. Box 577, Durham, CT 06422

Shirley Co. Gun & Riflemakers Ltd., J.A., P.O. Box 368, High Wycombe, Bucks. HP13 6YN, ENGLAND/0494-446883; FAX: 0494-463685

Shooter's Choice, 16770 Hilltop Park Place, Chagrin Falls, OH 44023/216-543-8808; FAX: 216-543-8811

S.K. Guns, Inc., 3041A Main Ave., Fargo, ND 58103/701-293-4867; FAX: 701-232-0001

Smith Whetstone Co., Inc., 1700 Sleepy Valley Rd., P.O. Box 5095, Hot Springs, AR 71902-5095/501-321-2244; FAX: 501-321-9232

Stalwart Corporation, P.O. Box 357, Pocatello, ID 83204/208-232-7899; FAX: 208-232-0815

Starrett Co., L.S., 121 Crescent St., Athol, MA 01331/617-249-3551

Stoney Point Products, Inc., 124 Stoney Point Rd., P.O. Box 5, Courtland, MN 56021-0005/507-354-3360; FAX: 507-354-7236

Stuart Products, Inc., P.O. Box 1587, Easley, SC 29641/803-859-9360

Sullivan, David S. (See Westwind Rifles, Inc.)

Sure Shot of LA, 103 Coachman Dr., Houma, LA 70360/504-876-6709

TDP Industries, Inc., 603 Airport Blvd., Doylestown, PA 18901/215-345-8687

Texas Platers Supply Co., 2453 W. Five Mile Parkway, Dallas, TX 75233/214-330-7168

Tom's Gun Repair, Thomas G. Ivanoff, 76-6 Rt. Southfork Rd., Cody, WY 82414/307-587-6949

Trulock Tool, Broad St., Whigham, GA 31797/912-762-4678

Turnbull Restoration, Doug, 6426 County Rd. 30, Bloomfield, NY 14469/716-657-6338

Venco Industries, Inc. (See Shooter's Choice)

Washita Mountain Whetstone Co., P.O. Box 378, Lake Hamilton, AR 71951/501-525-3914

Weaver's Gun Shop, P.O. Box 8, Dexter, MO 63841/314-568-3101

Welsh, Bud, 80 New Road, E. Amherst, NY 14051/716-688-6344

Wessinger Custom Guns & Engraving, 268 Limestone Rd., Chapin, SC 29036/803-345-5677

Westfield Engineering, 6823 Watcher St., Commerce, CA 90040/FAX: 213-928-8270

Westrom, John (See Precision Metal Finishing)

Westwind Rifles, Inc., David S. Sullivan, P.O. Box 261, 640 Briggs St., Erie, CO 80516/303-828-3823

White Rock Tool & Die, 6400 N. Brighton Ave., Kansas City, MO 64119/816-454-0478

Will-Burt Co., 169 S. Main, Orrville, OH 44667

Williams Gun Sight Co., 7389 Lapeer Rd., Box 329, Davison, MI 48423/810-653-2131, 800-530-9028; FAX: 810-658-2140

Wilson's Gun Shop, Box 578, Rt. 3, Berryville, AR 72616/501-545-3635; FAX: 501-545-3310

HEARING PROTECTORS

Behlert Precision, P.O. Box 288, 7067 Easton Rd., Pipersville, PA 18947/215-766-8681; FAX: 215-766-8681

Bilsom Intl., Inc., 109 Carpenter Dr., Sterling, VA 20164/703-834-1070

Blount, Inc., Sporting Equipment Div., 2299 Snake River Ave., P.O. Box 856, Lewiston, ID 83501/800-627-3640, 208-746-2351

Brown Co., E. Arthur, 3404 Pawnee Dr., Alexandria, MN 56308/612-762-8847

Browning Arms Co. (Parts & Service), 3005 Arnold Tenbrook Rd., Arnold, MO 63010-9406/314-287-6800; FAX: 314-287-9751

Clark Co., Inc., David, P.O. Box 15054, Worcester, MA 01615-0054/508-756-6216; FAX: 508-753-5827

Cobra Gunskin, 133-30 32nd Ave., Flushing, NY 11354/718-762-8181; FAX: 718-762-0890

Dragun Enterprises, P.O. Box 222, Murfreesboro, TN 37133-2222/615-895-7373, 800-467-7375; FAX: 800-829-7536

E-A-R, Inc., Div. of Cabot Safety Corp., 5457 W. 79th St., Indianapolis, IN 46268/800-327-3431; FAX: 800-488-8007

Fitz Pistol Grip Co., P.O. Box 610, Douglas City, CA 96024/916-623-4019

Flents Products Co., Inc., P.O. Box 2109, Norwalk, CT 06852/203-866-2581; FAX: 203-854-9322

Hoppe's Div., Penguin Industries, Inc., Airport Industrial Mall, Coatesville, PA 19320/251-384-6000

Kesselring Gun Shop, 400 Hwy. 99 North, Burlington, WA 98233/206-724-3113; FAX: 206-724-7003

Marble Arms Corp., 420 Industrial Park, P.O. Box 111, Gladstone, MI 49837/906-428-3710; FAX: 906-428-3711

North American Specialties, 25442 Trabuco Rd., 105-328, Lake Forest, CA 92630/714-837-4867

North Specialty Products, 2664-B Saturn St., Brea, CA 92621/714-524-1665

Paterson Gunsmithing, 438 Main St., Paterson, NJ 07502/201-345-4100

Peltor, Inc., 41 Commercial Way, E. Providence, RI 02914/401-438-4800; FAX: 800-EAR-FAX1

Penguin Industries, Inc., Airport Industrial Mall, Coatesville, PA 19320/215-384-6000

R.E.T. Enterprises, 2608 S. Chestnut, Broken Arrow, OK 74012/918-251-GUNS; FAX: 918-251-0587

Rutgers Gun & Boat Center, 127 Raritan Ave., Highland Park, NJ 08904/908-545-4344; FAX: 908-545-6686

Safariland Ltd., Inc., 3120 E. Mission Blvd., P.O. Box 51478, Ontario, CA 91761/909-923-7300; FAX: 909-923-7400

Safesport Manufacturing Co., 1100 W. 45th Ave., Denver, CO 80211/303-433-6506; FAX: 303-433-4112

Silencio/Safety Direct, 56 Coney Island Dr., Sparks, NV 89431/800-648-1812, 702-354-4451; FAX: 702-359-1074

Smith & Wesson, 2100 Roosevelt Ave., Springfield, MA 01102/413-781-8300

Stock Shop, The, 134 Zimmerman Rd., Kalispell, MT 59901/406-257-9003

Tyler Mfg.-Dist., Melvin, 1326 W. Britton Rd., Oklahoma City, OK 73114/405-842-8044

Valor Corp., 5555 NW 36th Ave., Miami, FL 33142/305-633-0127

Willson Safety Prods. Div., P.O. Box 622, Reading, PA 19603-0622/610-376-6161; FAX: 610-371-7725

LABELS, BOXES, CARTRIDGE HOLDERS

Accuracy Products, S.A., 14 rue de Lawsanne, Brussels, 1060 BELGIUM/32-2-539-34-42; FAX: 32-2-539-39-60

Advance Car Mover Co., Rowell Div., P.O. Box 1, 240 N. Depot St., Juneau, WI 53039/414-386-4464; FAX: 414-386-4416

Anderson Manufacturing Co., Inc., P.O. Box 2640, 2741 N. Crosby Rd., Oak Harbor, WA 98277/206-675-7300; FAX: 206-675-3939

Ballistic Products, Inc., 20015 75th Ave. North, Corcoran, MN 55340-9456/612-494-9237; FAX: 612-494-9236

Berry's Mfg., Inc., 401 North 3050 East, St. George, UT 84770

Del Rey Products, P.O. Box 91561, Los Angeles, CA 90009/213-823-0494

Fitz Pistol Grip Co., P.O. Box 610, Douglas City, CA 96024/916-623-4019

Flambeau Products Corp., 15981 Valplast Rd., Middlefield, OH 44062/216-632-1631; FAX: 216-632-1581

Hornady Mfg. Co., P.O. Box 1848, Grand Island, NE 68801/800-338-3220, 308-382-1390

J&J Products, Inc., 9240 Whitmore, El Monte, CA 91731/818-571-5228; FAX: 818-571-8704

King & Co., Box 1242, Bloomington, IL 61701/309-473-3964

Lakewood Products, Inc., P.O. Box 1527, 1445 Eagle St., Rhinelander, WI 54501/715-369-3445

Loadmaster, P.O. Box 1209, Warminster, Wilts. BA12 9XJ ENGLAND/(0985)218544; FAX: (0985)214111

Lyman Products Corp., Rt. 147 West St., Middlefield, CT 06455/203-349-3421; FAX: 203-349-3586

Midway Arms, Inc., P.O. Box 1483, Columbia, MO 65205/800-243-3220, 314-445-6363; FAX: 314-446-1018

MTM Molded Products Co., Inc., 3370 Obco Ct., Dayton, OH 45414/513-890-7461; FAX: 513-890-1747

Precision Reloading, Inc., P.O. Box 122, Stafford Springs, CT 06076/203-684-7979; FAX: 203-684-6788

Ravell Ltd., 289 Diputacion St., 08009, Barcelona SPAIN

Scharch Mfg., Inc., 10325 Co. Rd. 120, Unit C, Salida, CO 81201/719-539-7242

LOAD TESTING AND PRODUCT TESTING, (Chronographing, Ballistic Studies)

Ammunition Consulting Services, Inc., P.O. Box 701084, San Antonio, TX 78270-1084/201-646-9624; FAX: 210-646-0141

Arms, Peripheral Data Systems, P.O. Box 1526, Lake Oswego, OR 97035/800-366-5559, 503-697-0533; FAX: 503-697-3337

A-Square Co., Inc., One Industrial Park, Bedford, KY 40006-9667/502-255-7456; FAX: 502-255-7657

Ballistic Research, 1108 W. May Ave., McHenry, IL 60050/815-385-0037
Bestload, Inc., P.O. Box 4354, Stamford, CT 06907/FAX: 203-978-0796
Briese Bullet Co., Inc., RR1, Box 108, Tappen, ND 58487/701-327-4578; FAX: 701-327-4579
Buck Stix—SOS Products Co., Box 3, Neenah, WI 54956
Bustani Appraisers, Leo, P.O. Box 8125, W. Palm Beach, FL 33407/305-622-2710
Clerke Co., J.A., P.O. Box 627, Pearblossom, CA 93553-0627/805-945-0713
D&H Precision Tooling, 7522 Barnard Mill Rd., Ringwood, IL 60072/815-653-4011
Dever Co., Jack, 8590 NW 90, Oklahoma City, OK 73132/405-721-6393
Farr Studio, Inc., 1231 Robinhood Rd., Greeneville, TN 37743/615-638-8825
Fusilier Bullets, 10010 N. 6000 W., Highland, UT 84003/801-756-6813
Hank's Gun Shop, Box 370, 50 West 100 South, Monroe, UT 84754/801-527-4456
Hensler, Jerry, 6614 Country Field, San Antonio, TX 78240/210-690-7491
High Performance International, 5734 W. Florist Ave., Milwaukee, WI 53218/414-466-9040
Hoelscher, Virgil, 11047 Pope Ave., Lynwood, CA 90262/310-631-8545
Jackalope Gun Shop, 1048 S. 5th St., Douglas, WY 82633/307-358-3441
Jensen Bullets, 86 North, 400 West, Blackfoot, ID 83221/208-785-5590
J.D. Jones (See SSK Industries)
Jurras, L.E., P.O. Box 680, Washington, IN 47501/812-254-7698
Lachaussee, S.A., 29 Rue Kerstenne, Ans, B-4430 BELGIUM/041-63 88 77
Lomont Precision Bullets, 4236 W. 700 South, Poneto, IN 46781/219-694-6792; FAX: 219-694-6797
Maionchi-L.M.I., Via Di Coselli-Zona Industriale Di Guamo, Lucca, ITALY 55060/011 39-583 94291
McMurdo, Lynn (See Specialty Gunsmithing)
Multiplex International, 26 S. Main St., Concord, NH 03301/FAX: 603-796-2223
Neutralizer Police Munitions, 5029 Middle Rd., Horseheads, NY 14845-9568/607-739-8362; FAX: 607-594-3900
Oil Rod and Gun Shop, 69 Oak St., East Douglas, MA 01516/508-476-3687
Pace Marketing, Inc., 9474 NW 48th St., Sunrise, FL 33351-5137/305-741-4361; FAX: 305-741-2901
Pejsa Ballistics, 2120 Kenwood Pkwy., Minneapolis, MN 55405/612-374-3337; FAX: 612-374-3337
Ransom International Corp., P.O. Box 3845, 1040-A Sandretto Dr., Prescott, AZ 86302/602-778-7899; FAX: 602-778-7993
R.I.S. Co., Inc., 718 Timberlake Circle, Richardson, TX 75080/214-235-0933
Romain's Custom Guns, RD 1, Whetstone Rd., Brockport, PA 15823/814-265-1948
RPM, 15481 N. Twin Lakes Dr., Tucson, AZ 85737/602-825-1233; FAX: 602-825-3333
Rupert's Gun Shop, 2202 Dick Rd., Suite B, Fenwick, MI 48834/517-248-3252
SOS Products Co. (See Buck Stix—SOS Products Co.)
Specialty Gunsmithing, Lynn McMurdo, P.O. Box 404, Afton, WY 83110/307-886-5535
SSK Industries, 721 Woodvue Lane, Wintersville, OH 43952/614-264-0176; FAX: 614-264-2257
Stock Shop, The, 134 Zimmerman Rd., Kalispell, MT 59901/406-257-9003
Tioga Engineering Co., Inc., P.O. Box 913, 13 Cone St., Wellsboro, PA 16901/717-724-3533, 717-662-3347
Vulpes Ventures, Inc., Fox Cartridge Division, P.O. Box 1363, Bolingbrook, IL 60440-7363/708-759-1229
White Laboratory, Inc., H.P., 3114 Scarboro Rd., Street, MD 21154/410-838-6550; FAX: 410-838-2802
Whitestone Lumber Corp., 148-02 14th Ave., Whitestone, NY 11357/718-746-4400; FAX: 718-767-1748
X-Spand Target Systems, 26-10th St. SE, Medicine Hat, AB T1A 1P7 CANADA/403-526-7997; FAX: 403-526-7997

RELOADING TOOLS AND ACCESSORIES

American Products Co., 14729 Spring Valley Road, Morrison, IL 61270/815-772-3336; FAX: 815-772-7921
Ammo Load, Inc., 1560 East Edinger, Suite G., Santa Ana, CA 92705/714-558-8858; FAX: 714-569-0319
AMT, 6226 Santos Diaz St., Irwindale, CA 91702/818-334-6629; FAX: 818-969-5247
ASI, 6226 Santos Dias St., Irwindale, CA 91706/818-334-6629
Ballistic Products, Inc., 20015 75th Ave. North, Corcoran, MN 55340-9456/612-494-9237; FAX: 612-494-9236
Barlett, J., 6641 Kaiser Ave., Fontana, CA 92336-3265
Berry's Mfg., Inc., 401 North 3050 East, St. George, UT 84770
Blount, Inc., Sporting Equipment Div., 2299 Snake River Ave., P.O. Box 856, Lewiston, ID 83501/800-627-3640, 208-746-2351
Buck Stix—SOS Products Co., Box 3, Neenah, WI 54956
C&D Special Products (Claybuster), 309 Sequoya Dr., Hopkinsville, KY 42240/800-922-6287, 800-284-1746
CCI, Div. of Blount, Inc., 2299 Snake River Ave., P.O. Box 856, Lewiston, ID 83501/800-627-3640, 208-746-2351
Chem-Pak, Inc., 11 Oates Ave., P.O. Box 1685, Winchester, VA 22601/800-336-9828; FAX: 703-722-3993
Coats, Mrs. Lester, 300 Luman Rd., Space 125, Phoenix, OR 97535/503-535-1611
D.C.C. Enterprises, 259 Wynburn Ave., Athens, GA 30601
Denver Instrument Co., 6542 Fig St., Arvada, CO 80004/800-321-1135, 303-431-7255; FAX: 303-423-4831
Dever Co., Jack, 8590 NW 90, Oklahoma City, OK 73132/405-721-6393
E&L Mfg., Inc., 39042 N. School House Rd., Cave Creek, AZ 85331/602-488-2598; FAX: 602-488-0813
Engineered Accessories, 1307 W. Wabash Ave., Effingham, IL 62401/217-347-7700; FAX: 217-347-7737
Enguix Import-Export, Alpujarras 58, Alzira, Valencia, SPAIN 46600/(96) 241 43 95; FAX: (96) 241 43 95
Fisher Enterprises, 655 Main St. #305, Edmonds, WA 98020/206-776-4365
Flambeau Products Corp., 15981 Valplast Rd., Middlefield, OH 44062/216-632-1631; FAX: 216-632-1581
4-D Custom Die Co., 711 N. Sandusky St., P.O. Box 889, Mt. Vernon, OH 43050-0889/614-397-7214; FAX: 614-397-6600
Goddard, Allen, 716 Medford Ave., Hayward, CA 94541/510-276-6830
Graphics Direct, 18336 Gault St., Reseda, CA 91335/818-344-9002
Hoelscher, Virgil, 11047 Pope Ave., Lynwood, CA 90262/310-631-8545
Hollywood Engineering, 10642 Arminta St., Sun Valley, CA 91352/818-842-8376
Hondo Ind., 510 S. 52nd St.,#I04, Tempe, AZ 85281
Hornady Mfg. Co., P.O. Box 1848, Grand Island, NE 68801/800-338-3220, 308-382-1390
Huntington Die Specialties, 601 Oro Dam Blvd., Oroville, CA 95965/916-534-1210; FAX: 916-534-1212

K&M Services, 5430 Salmon Run Rd., Dover, PA 17315/717-764-1461
Lachaussee, S.A., 29 Rue Kerstenne, Ans, B-4430 BELGIUM/041-63 88 77
LAP Systems Groups, N.A., P.O. Box 162, arietta, GA 30061
Lee Precision, Inc., 4275 Hwy. U, Hartford, WI 53027/414-673-3075
MCS, Inc., 34 Delmar Dr., Brookfield, CT 06804/203-775-1013; FAX: 203-775-9462
MEC, Inc., 715 South St., Mayville, WI 53050/414-387-4500
Midway Arms, Inc., P.O. Box 1483, Columbia, MO 65205/800-243-3220, 314-445-6363; FAX: 314-446-1018
Miller Engineering, R&D Engineering & Manufacturing, P.O. Box 6342, Virginia Beach, VA 23456/804-468-1402
Mountain South, P.O. Box 381, Barnwell, SC 29812/FAX: 803-259-3227
MTM Molded Products Co., Inc., 3370 Obco Ct., Dayton, OH 45414/513-890-7461; FAX: 513-890-1747
Multi-Scale Charge Ltd., 3269 Niagara Falls Blvd., N. Tonawanda, NY 14120/905-566-1255; FAX: 416-276-6295
OK Weber, Inc., P.O. Box 7485, Eugene, OR 97401/503-747-0458; FAX: 503-747-5927
Omark Industries, Div. of Blount, Inc., 2299 Snake River Ave., P.O. Box 856, Lewiston, ID 83501/800-627-3640, 208-746-2351
Pattern Control, 114 N. Third St., Garland, TX 75040/214-494-3551
Ponsness/Warren, P.O. Box 8, Rathdrum, ID 83858/208-687-2231; FAX: 208-687-2233
Precision Reloading, Inc., P.O. Box 122, Stafford Springs, CT 06076/203-684-7979; FAX: 203-684-6788
Protector Mfg. Co., Inc., The, 443 Ashwood Place, Boca Raton, FL 33431/407-394-6011
Ravell Ltd., 289 Diputacion St., 08009, Barcelona SPAIN
RCBS, Div. of Blount, Inc., 605 Oro Dam Blvd., Oroville, CA 95965/800-533-5000, 916-533-5191
R.E.I., P.O. Box 88, Tallevast, FL 34270/813-755-0085
Rice, Keith (See White Rock Tool & Die)
Riebe Co., W.J., 3434 Tucker Rd., Boise, ID 83703
Scot Powder Co. of Ohio, Inc., Box HD94, Only, TN 37140/615-729-4207; FAX: 615-729-4217
Sierra Specialty Prod. Co., 1344 Oakhurst Ave., Los Altos, CA 94024
Slipshot MTS Group, P.O. Box 5, Postal Station D, Etobicoke, Ont., CANADA M9A 4X1/FAX: 416-762-0962
Speer Products, Div. of Blount, Inc., P.O. Box 856, Lewiston, ID 83501/208-746-2351; FAX: 208-746-2915
Stalwart Corporation, P.O. Box 357, Pocatello, ID 83204/208-232-7899; FAX: 208-232-0815
Star Machine Works, 418 10th Ave., San Diego, CA 92101/619-232-3216
Taracorp Industries, Inc., 16th & Cleveland Blvd., Granite City, IL 62040/618-451-4400
Webster Scale Mfg. Co., P.O. Box 188, Sebring, FL 33870/813-385-6362
Westfield Engineering, 6823 Watcher St., Commerce, CA 90040/FAX: 213-928-8270
White Rock Tool & Die, 6400 N. Brighton Ave., Kansas City, MO 64119/816-454-0478
Whitestone Lumber Corp., 148-02 14th Ave., Whitestone, NY 11357/718-746-4400; FAX: 718-767-1748
William's Gun Shop, Ben, 1151 S. Cedar Ridge, Duncanville, TX 75137/214-780-1807

SHOTGUN INSTRUCTION

Beverly, Mary, 3201 Horseshoe Trail, Tallahassee, FL 32312

STOCKS (Commercial and Custom)

Accuracy Unlimited, 16036 N. 49 Ave., Glendale, AZ 85306/602-978-9089
Ajax Custom Grips, Inc., Div. of A. Jack Rosenberg & Sons, 9130 Viscount Row, Dallas, TX 75247/214-630-8893; FAX: 214-630-4942
Amrine's Gun Shop, 937 La Luna, Ojai, CA 93023/805-646-2376
Angelo & Little Custom Gun Stock Blanks, Chaffin Creek Rd., Darby, MT 59829/406-821-4530
Arms Ingenuity Co., P.O. Box 1, 51 Canal St., Weatogue, CT 06089/203-658-5624
Armurier Hiptmayer, RR 112 #750, P.O. Box 136, Eastman, Quebec J0E 1P0, CANADA/514-297-2492
Artistry in Wood, 134 Zimmerman Rd., Kalispell, MT 59901/406-257-9003
Bain & Davis, Inc., 307 E. Valley Blvd., San Gabriel, CA 91776-3522/818-573-4241, 213-283-7449
Balickie, Joe, 408 Trelawney Lane, Apex, NC 27502/919-362-5185
Barnes Bullets, Inc., P.O. Box 215, American Fork, UT 84003/801-756-4222; FAX: 801-756-2465
Barta's Gunsmithing, 10231 US Hwy. 10, Cato, WI 54206/414-732-4472
Bartlett, Don, 3704 E. Pine Needle Ave., Colbert, WA 99005/509-467-5009
Barton, Michael D. (See Tiger-Hunt)
Bear Arms, 121 Rhodes St., Jackson, SC 29831/803-471-9859
Beitzinger, George, 116-20 Atlantic Ave., Richmond Hill, NY 11419/718-847-7661
Belding's Custom Gun Shop, 10691 Sayers Rd., Munith, MI 49259/517-596-2388
Bell & Carlson, Inc., 509 N. 5th St., Atwood, KS 67730/800-634-8586, 913-626-3204; FAX: 913-626-9602
Benchmark Guns, 12593 S. Ave. 5 East, Yuma, AZ 85365
Biesen, Al, 5021 Rosewood, Spokane, WA 99208/509-328-9340
Biesen, Roger, 5021 W. Rosewood, Spokane, WA 99208/509-328-9340
Billeb, Stephen L., 1101 N. 7th St., Burlington, IA 52601/319-753-2110
B.M.F. Activator, Inc., 803 Mill Creek Run, Plantersville, TX 77363/409-894-2005, 800-527-2881
Bob's Gun Shop, P.O. Box 200, Royal, AR 71968/501-767-1970
Boltin, John M., P.O. Box 644, Estill, SC 29918/803-625-2185
Bowerly, Kent, HCR Box 1903, Camp Sherman, OR 97730/503-595-6028
Boyds', Inc., 3rd & Main, Geddes, SD 57342/605-337-2125; FAX: 605-337-3363
Brace, Larry D., 771 Blackfoot Ave., Eugene, OR 97404/503-688-1278
Brgoch, Frank, 1580 S. 1500 East, Bountiful, UT 84010/801-295-1885
Brown Co., E. Arthur, 3404 Pawnee Dr., Alexandria, MN 56308/612-762-8847
Buckhorn Gun Works, 115 E. North St., Rapid City, SD 57701/605-787-6289
Bullberry Barrel Works, Ltd., 2430 W. Bullberry Ln. 67-5, Hurricane, UT 84737/801-635-9866
Burkhart Gunsmithing, Don, P.O. Box 852, Rawlins, WY 82301/307-324-6007
Burres, Jack, 10333 San Fernando Rd., Pacoima, CA 91331/818-899-8000
Butler Creek Corp., 290 Arden Dr., Belgrade, MT 59714/800-423-8327, 406-388-1356; FAX: 406-388-7204
Cali'co Hardwoods, Inc., 1648 Airport Blvd., Windsor, CA 95492/707-546-4045; FAX: 707-546-4027
Camilli, Lou, 4700 Oahu Dr. NE, Albuquerque, NM 87111/505-293-5259
Campbell, Dick, 20,000 Silver Ranch Rd., Conifer, CO 80433/303-697-0150
Cape Outfitters, Rt. 2, Box 437C, Cape Girardeau, MO 63701/314-335-4103; FAX: 314-335-1555

Caywood, Shane J., P.O. Box 321, Minocqua, WI 54548/715-277-3866 evenings

Cherokee Gun Accessories (See Glaser Safety Slug, Inc.)

Chicasaw Gun Works (See Cochran, Oliver)

Christman Jr., David, 937 Lee Hedrick Rd., Colville, WA 99114/509-684-5686 days; 509-684-3314 evenings

Chuck's Gun Shop, P.O. Box 597, Waldo, FL 32694/904-468-2264

Churchill, Winston, Twenty Mile Stream Rd., RFD P.O. Box 29B, Proctorsville, VT 05153/802-226-7772

Clifton Arms, Inc., P.O. Box 1471, Medina, TX 78055/210-589-2666; FAX: 210-589-2661

Cloward's Gun Shop, 4023 Aurora Ave. N, Seattle, WA 98103/206-632-2072

Cochran, Oliver, Box 868, Shady Spring, WV 25918/304-763-3838

Coffin, Charles H., 3719 Scarlet Ave., Odessa, TX 79762/915-366-4729

Coffin, Jim, 250 Country Club Lane, Albany, OR 97321/503-928-4391

Colonial Repair, P.O. Box 372, Hyde Park, MA 02136-9998/617-469-4951

Conrad, C.A., 3964 Ebert St., Winston-Salem, NC 27127/919-788-5469

Costa, David, Island Pond Gun Shop, P.O. Box 428, Cross St., Island Pond, VT 05846/802-723-4546

Crane Sales Co., George S., P.O. Box 385, Van Nuys, CA 91409/818-505-8337

Creedmoor Sports, Inc., P.O. Box 1040, Oceanside, CA 92051/619-757-5529

Custom Checkering Service, Kathy Forster, 2124 SE Yamhill St., Portland, OR 97214/503-236-5874

Custom Gun Products, 5021 W. Rosewood, Spokane, WA 99208/509-328-9340

Custom Gun Stocks, Rt. 6, P.O. Box 177, McMinnville, TN 37110/615-668-3912

D&D Gunsmiths, Ltd., 363 E. Elmwood, Troy, MI 48083/313-583-1512

D&J Bullet Co. & Custom Gun Shop, Inc., 426 Ferry St., Russell, KY 41169/606-836-2663; FAX: 606-836-2663

Dahl's Custom Stocks, N2863 Schofield Rd., Lake Geneva, WI 53147/414-248-2464

Dangler, Homer L., Box 254, Addison, MI 49220/517-547-6745

D.D. Custom Stocks, R.H. "Dick" Devereaux, 5240 Mule Deer Dr., Colorado Springs, CO 80919/719-548-8468

de Treville & Co., Stan, 4129 Normal St., San Diego, CA 92103/619-298-3393

Dever Co., Jack, 8590 NW 90, Oklahoma City, OK 73132/405-721-6393

DGS, Inc., Dale A. Storey, 1117 E. 12th, Casper, WY 82601/307-237-2414

Dillon, Ed, 1035 War Eagle Dr. N., Colorado Springs, CO 80919/719-598-4929; FAX: 719-598-4929

Dowtin Gunworks, Rt. 4, Box 930A, Flagstaff, AZ 86001/602-779-1898

Dragun Enterprises, P.O. Box 222, Murfreesboro, TN 37133-2222/615-895-7373, 800-467-7375; FAX: 800-829-7536

Dressel Jr., Paul G., 209 N. 92nd Ave., Yakima, WA 98908/509-966-9233; FAX: 509-966-3365

Duane Custom Stocks, Randy, 110 W. North Ave., Winchester, VA 22601/703-667-9461; FAX: 703-722-3993

Duncan's Gun Works, Inc., 1619 Grand Ave., San Marcos, CA 92069/619-727-0515

Dutchman's Firearms, Inc., The, 4143 Taylor Blvd., Louisville, KY 40215/502-366-0555

Echols & Co., D'Arcy, 164 W. 580 S., Providence, UT 84332/801-753-2367

Eggleston, Jere D., 400 Saluda Ave., Columbia, SC 29205/803-799-3402

Emerging Technologies, Inc., P.O. Box 3548, Little Rock, AR 72203/501-375-2227; FAX: 501-372-1445

Erhardt, Dennis, 3280 Green Meadow Dr., Helena, MT 59601/406-442-4533

Eversull Co., Inc., K., 1 Tracemont, Boyce, LA 71409/318-793-8728; FAX: 318-793-5483

Fajen, Inc., Reinhart, 1000 Red Bud Dr., P.O. Box 338, Warsaw, MO 65355/816-438-5111; FAX: 816-438-5175

Farmer-Dressel, Sharon, 209 N. 92nd Ave., Yakima, WA 98908/509-966-9233; FAX: 509-966-3365

Fibron Products, Inc., 170 Florida St., Buffalo, NY 14208/716-886-2378; FAX: 716-886-2394

Fisher, Jerry A., 535 Crane Mt. Rd., Big Fork, MT 59911/406-837-2722

Flaig's, 2200 Evergreen Rd., Millvale, PA 15209/412-821-1717

Folks, Donald E., 205 W. Lincoln St., Pontiac, IL 61764/815-844-7901

Forster, Larry L., P.O. Box 212, 220 First St. NE, Gwinner, ND 58040-0212/701-678-2475

Frank Custom Gun Service, Ron, 7131 Richland Rd., Ft. Worth, TX 76118/817-284-4426; FAX: 817-284-9300

Gaillard Barrels, P.O. Box 21, Pathlow, Sask., S0K 3B0 CANADA/306-752-3769; FAX: 306-752-5969

Game Haven Gunstocks, 13750 Shire Rd., Wolverine, MI 49799/616-525-8257

Gene's Custom Guns, P.O. Box 10534, White Bear Lake, MN 55110/612-429-5105

Gervais, Mike, 3804 S. Cruise Dr., Salt Lake City, UT 84109/801-277-7729

Gilman-Mayfield, Inc., 3279 E. Shields, Fresno, CA 93703/209-221-9415; FAX: 209-221-9419

Giron, Robert E., 1328 Pocono St., Pittsburgh, PA 15218/412-731-6041

Glaser Safety Slug, Inc., P.O. Box 8223, Foster City, CA 94404/800-221-3489, 415-345-7677; FAX: 415-345-8217

Goens, Dale W., P.O. Box 224, Cedar Crest, NM 87008/505-281-5419

Golden Age Arms Co., 115 E. High St., Ashley, OH 43003/614-747-2488

Gordie's Gun Shop, 1401 Fulton St., Streator, IL 61364/815-672-7202

Goudy Classic Stocks, Gary, 263 Hedge Rd., Menlo Park, CA 94025-1711/415-322-1338

Grace, Charles E., 6943 85.5 Rd., Trinchera, CO 81081/719-846-9435

Grace Tool, 3661 E. 44th St., Tucson, AZ 85713/602-747-0213

Green, Roger M., P.O. Box 984, 435 E. Birch, Glenrock, WY 82637/307-436-9804

Greene, M.L., 17200 W. 57th Ave., Golden, CO 80403/303-279-2383

Greenwood Precision, P.O. Box 468, Nixa, MO 65714-0468/417-725-2330

Griffin & Howe, Inc., 33 Claremont Rd., Bernardsville, NJ 07924/908-766-2287; FAX: 908-766-1068

Gun Shop, The, 5550 S. 900 East, Salt Lake City, UT 84117/801-263-3633

Guns, 81 E. Streetsboro St., Hudson, OH 44236/216-650-4563

Gunsmithing Ltd., 57 Unquowa Rd., Fairfield, CT 06430/203-254-0436

Hallberg Gunsmith, Fritz, 33 S. Main, Payette, ID 83661

Halstead, Rick, RR4, Box 272, Miami, OK 74354/515-236-5904

Hank's Gun Shop, Box 370, 50 West 100 South, Monroe, UT 84754/801-527-4456

Hanson's Gun Center, Dick, 233 Everett Dr., Colorado Springs, CO 80911

Harper's Custom Stocks, 928 Lombrano St., San Antonio, TX 78207/512-732-5780

Hastings Barrels, 320 Court St., Clay Center, KS 67432/913-632-6554

Hecht, Hubert J., Waffen-Hecht, P.O. Box 2635, Fair Oaks, CA 95628/916-966-1020

Heilmann, Stephen, P.O. Box 657, Grass Valley, CA 95945/916-272-8758

Hensley, Darwin, P.O. Box 329, Brightwood, OR 97011/503-622-5411

Heppler, Keith M., Keith's Custom Gunstocks, 540 Banyan Circle, Walnut Creek, CA 94598/510-934-3509; FAX: 510-934-3143

Heydenberk, Warren R., 1059 W. Sawmill Rd., Quakertown, PA 18951/215-538-2682

Hillmer Custom Gunstocks, Paul D., 7251 Hudson Heights, Hudson, IA 50643/319-988-3941

Hiptmayer, Klaus, RR 112 #750, P.O. Box 136, Eastman, Quebec J0E 1P0, CANADA/514-297-2492

Hoelscher, Virgil, 11047 Pope Ave., Lynwood, CA 90262/310-631-8545

Hoenig & Rodman, 6521 Morton Dr., Boise, ID 83704/208-375-1116

Huebner, Corey O., Box 6, Hall, MT 59837/406-721-1658

Hughes, Steven Dodd, P.O. Box 11455, Eugene, OR 97440/503-485-8869

Intermountain Arms & Tackle, Inc., 105 E. Idaho St., Meridian, ID 83642/208-888-4911; FAX: 208-888-4381

Ivanoff, Thomas G. (See Tom's Gun Repair)

Jackalope Gun Shop, 1048 S. 5th St., Douglas, WY 82633/307-358-3441

Jaeger, Inc./Dunn's, Paul, P.O. Box 449, 1 Madison Ave., Grand Junction, TN 38039/901-764-6909; FAX: 901-764-6503

Jamison's Forge Works, 4527 Rd. 6.5 NE, Moses Lake, WA 98837/509-762-2659

Johnson Gunsmithing, Inc., Neal G., 111 Marvin Dr., Hampton, VA 23666/804-838-8091; FAX: 804-838-8157

Johnson Wood Products, RR #1, Strawberry Point, IA 52076/319-933-4930

Ken's Rifle Blanks, Ken McCullough, Rt. 2, P.O. Box 85B, Weston, OR 97886/503-566-3879

Kilham & Co., Main St., P.O. Box 37, Lyme, NH 03768/603-795-4112

Klein Custom Guns, Don, 433 Murray Park Dr., Ripon, WI 54971/414-748-2931

Klingler Woodcarving, P.O. Box 141, Thistle Hill, Cabot, VT 05647/802-426-3811

Knippel, Richard, 5924 Carnwood, Riverbank, CA 95367/209-869-1469

Laseraim Arms, Inc., Sub. of Emerging Technologies, Inc., P.O. Box 3548, Little Rock, AR 72203/501-375-2227; FAX: 501-372-1445

Lawson Co., Harry, 3328 N. Richey Blvd., Tucson, AZ 85716/602-326-1117

Lind Custom Guns, Al, 7821 76th Ave. SW, Tacoma, WA 98498/206-584-6361

Lynn's Custom Gunstocks, RR 1, Brandon, IA 52210/319-474-2453

Mandarino, Monte, 205 Fifth Ave. East, Kalispell, MT 59901/406-257-6208

Masen Co., John, P.O. Box 5050, Suite 165, Lewisville, TX 75057/817-430-8732

Mathews & Son, Inc., George E., 10224 S. Paramount Blvd., Downey, CA 90241/310-862-6719; FAX: 310-862-6719

McCament, Jay, 1730-134th St. Ct. S., Tacoma, WA 98444/206-531-8832

McCullough, Ken (See Ken's Rifle Blanks)

McDonald, Dennis, 8359 Brady St., Peosta, IA 52068/319-556-7940

McFarland, Stan, 2221 Idella Ct., Grand Junction, CO 81505/303-243-4704

McGuire, Bill, 1600 N. Eastmont Ave., East Wenatchee, WA 98802/509-884-6021

Meadow Industries, P.O. Box 754, Locust Grove, VA 22508/703-972-2175; FAX: 703-972-2175

Mercer Custom Stocks, R.M., 216 S. Whitewater Ave., Jefferson, WI 53549/414-674-3839, 800-704-4447

Mid-America Recreation, Inc., 1328 5th Ave., Moline, IL 52807/309-764-5089; FAX: 309-764-2722

Miller Co., David, 3131 E. Greenlee Rd., Tucson, AZ 85716/602-326-3117

Miller Gun Woods, 1440 Peltier Dr., Point Roberts, WA 98281/206-945-7014

Monell Custom Guns, Red Mill Road, Pine Bush, NY 12566/914-744-3021

Morrow, Bud, 11 Hillside Lane, Sheridan, WY 82801-9729/307-674-8360

MPI Stocks, P.O. Box 8363, Portland, OR 97283-0266/503-226-1215; FAX: 503-216-2661

Muzzlelite Corp., P.O. Box 987, DeLeon Springs, FL 32130

Nettestad Gun Works, RR 1, Box 160, Pelican Rapids, MN 56572/218-863-4301

New England Arms Co., Box 278, Lawrence Lane, Kittery Point, ME 03905/207-439-0593; FAX: 207-439-6726

New England Custom Gun Service, Brook Rd., RR2, Box 122W, W. Lebanon, NH 03784/603-469-3450; FAX: 603-469-3471

Nickels, Paul R., 4789 Summerhill Rd., Las Vegas, NV 89121/702-435-5318

Norman Custom Gunstocks, Jim, 14281 Cane Rd., Valley Center, CA 92082/619-749-6252

North American Shooting Systems, P.O. Box 306, Osoyoos, B.C. V0H 1V0 CANADA/604-495-3131; FAX: 604-495-2816

Oakland Custom Arms, Inc., 4690 W. Walton Blvd., Waterford, MI 48329/810-674-8261

Oil Rod and Gun Shop, 69 Oak St., East Douglas, MA 01516/508-476-3687

Old World Gunsmithing, 2901 SE 122nd St., Portland, OR 97236/503-760-7681

One Of A Kind, 15610 Purple Sage, San Antonio, TX 78255/512-695-3364

Or-šn, Tahtakale Menekse Han 18, Istanbul, TURKEY 34460/90212-522-5912; FAX: 90212-522-7973

Orvis Co., The, Rt. 7, Manchester, VT 05254/802-362-3622 ext. 283; FAX: 802-362-3525

Pagel Gun Works, Inc., 1407 4th St. NW, Grand Rapids, MN 55744/218-326-3003

Paulsen Gunstocks, Rt. 71, Box 11, Chinook, MT 59523/406-357-3403

PEM's Mfg. Co., 5063 Waterloo Rd., Atwater, OH 44201/216-947-3721

Pentheny de Pentheny, 2352 Baggett Ct., Santa Rosa, CA 95401/707-573-1390; FAX: 707-573-1390

Perazzi USA, Inc., 1207 S. Shamrock Ave., Monrovia, CA 91016/818-303-0068

R&J Gun Shop, 133 W. Main St., John Day, OR 97845/503-575-2130

Reiswig, Wallace E., Claro Walnut Gunstock Co., 1235 Stanley Ave., Chico, CA 95928/916-342-5188

Richards Micro-Fit Stocks, 8331 N. San Fernando Rd., P.O. Box 1066, Sun Valley, CA 91352/818-767-6097

RMS Custom Gunsmithing, 4120 N. Bitterwell, Prescott Valley, AZ 86314/602-772-7626

Robinson, Don, Pennsylvania Hse., 36 Fairfax Crescent, Southowram, Halifax, W. Yorkshire HX3 9SQ, ENGLAND/0422-364458

Robinson Firearms Mfg. Ltd., RR2, Suite 51, Comp. 24, Winfield, B.C. CANADA V0H 2C0/604-766-5353

Romain's Custom Guns, RD 1, Whetstone Rd., Brockport, PA 15823/814-265-1948

Roto Carve, 2754 Garden Ave., Janesville, IA 50647

Royal Arms, 5126 3rd Ave. N., Great Falls, MT 59405/406-453-1149

Ryan, Chad L., RR 3, Box 72, Cresco, IA 52136/319-547-4384

Sanders Custom Gun Service, 2358 Tyler Ln., Louisville, KY 40205/502-454-3338

Saville Iron Co. (See Greenwood Precision)

Schiffman, Curt, 3017 Kevin Cr., Idaho Falls, ID 83402/208-524-4684

Schiffman, Mike, 8233 S. Crystal Springs, McCammon, ID 83250/208-254-9114

Schwartz Custom Guns, David W., 2505 Waller St., Eau Claire, WI 54703/715-832-1735

Sherk, Dan A., 1311-105 Ave., Dawson Creek, B.C. V1G 2L9, CANADA/604-782-3720

Sile Distributors, Inc., 7 Centre Market Pl., New York, NY 10013/212-925-4389; FAX: 212-925-3149

Skeoch, Brian R., P.O. Box 279, Glenrock, WY 82637/307-436-9804; FAX: 307-436-9804

Smith, Art, P.O. Box 13, Hector, MN 55342/612-848-2760

Smith, Sharmon, 4545 Speas Rd., Fruitland, ID 83619/208-452-6329

Snider Stocks, Walter S., Rt. 2 P.O. Box 147, Denton, NC 27239

Speedfeed, Inc., P.O. Box 258, Lafayette, CA 94549/510-284-2929; FAX: 510-284-2879

Speiser, Fred D., 2229 Dearborn, Missoula, MT 59801/406-549-8133

Stiles Custom Guns, RD3, Box 1605, Homer City, PA 15748/412-479-9945, 412-479-8666

Stock Shop, The, 134 Zimmerman Rd., Kalispell, MT 59901/406-257-9003

Storey, Dale A. (See DGS, Inc.)

Strawbridge, Victor W., 6 Pineview Dr., Dover, NH 03820/603-742-0013

Swann, D.J., 5 Orsova Close, Eltham North, Vic. 3095, AUSTRALIA/03-431-0323

Szweda, Robert (See RMS Custom Gunsmithing)

Talmage, William G., RR16, Box 102A, Brazil, IN 47834/812-442-0804

Tecnolegno S.p.A., Via A. Locatelli, 6, 10, 24019 Zogno, ITALY/0345-91114; FAX: 0345-93254

T.F.C. S.p.A., Via G. Marconi 118, B, Villa Carcina, Brescia 25069, ITALY/030-881271; FAX: 030-881826

Tiger-Hunt, Michael D. Barton, Box 379, Beaverdale, PA 15921/814-472-5161

Tirelli, Snc Di Tirelli Primo E.C., Via Matteotti No. 359, Gardone V.T., Brescia, ITALY 25063/030-8912819; FAX: 030-832240

Tom's Gun Repair, Thomas G. Ivanoff, 76-6 Rt. Southfork Rd., Cody, WY 82414/307-587-6949

Tom's Gunshop, 3601 Central Ave., Hot Springs, AR 71913/501-624-3856

Trevallion Gunstocks, 9 Old Mountain Rd., Cape Neddick, ME 03902/207-361-1130

Tucker, James C., P.O. Box 15485, Sacramento, CA 95851/916-923-0571

Vest, John, P.O. Box 1552, Susanville, CA 96130/916-257-7228

Vic's Gun Refinishing, 6 Pineview Dr., Dover, NH 03820-6422/603-742-0013

Vintage Industries, Inc., 781 Big Tree Dr., Longwood, FL 32750/407-831-8949; FAX: 407-831-5346

Waffen-Weber Custom Gunsmithing, #4-1691 Powick Rd., Kelowna, B.C. CANADA V1X 4L1/604-762-7575; FAX: 604-861-3655

Walnut Factory, The, 235 West Rd. No. 1, Portsmouth, NH 03801/603-436-2225; FAX: 603-433-7003

Weatherby, Inc., 3100 El Camino Real, Atascadero, CA 93422/805-466-1767; FAX: 805-466-2527

Weems, Cecil, P.O. Box 657, Mineral Wells, TX 76067/817-325-1462

Wells Custom Gunsmith, R.A., 3452 1st Ave., Racine, WI 53402/414-639-5223

Wenig Custom Gunstocks, Inc., 103 N. Market St., Lincoln, MO 65338/816-547-3334; FAX: 816-547-2881

Werth, T.W., 1203 Woodlawn Rd., Lincoln, IL 62656/217-732-1300

West, Jack L., 1220 W. Fifth, P.O. Box 427, Arlington, OR 97812

West, Robert G., 3973 Pam St., Eugene, OR 97402/503-344-3700

Western Gunstock Mfg. Co., 550 Valencia School Rd., Aptos, CA 95003/408-688-5884

Williamson Precision Gunsmithing, 117 W. Pipeline, Hurst, TX 76053/817-285-0064; FAX: 817-285-0064

Windish, Jim, 2510 Dawn Dr., Alexandria, VA 22306/703-765-1994

Winter, Robert M., P.O. Box 484, Menno, SD 57045/605-387-5322

Wright's Hardwood Sawmill, 8540 SE Kane Rd., Gresham, OR 97080/503-666-1705

Yee, Mike, 29927 56 Pl. S., Auburn, WA 98001/206-839-3991

York M-1 Conversions, 803 Mill Creek Run, Plantersville, TX 77363/800-527-2881, 713-477-8442

Zeeryp, Russ, 1601 Foard Dr., Lynn Ross Manor, Morristown, TN 37814/615-586-2357

TARGETS AND CLAYBIRD TRAPS

American Target, 1328 S. Jason St., Denver, CO 80223/303-733-0433; FAX: 303-777-0311

American Whitetail Target Systems, P.O. Box 41, 106 S. Church St., Tennyson, IN 47637/812-567-4527

A-Tech Corp., P.O. Box 1281, Cottage Grove, OR 97424

Ballistic Products, Inc., 20015 75th Ave. North, Corcoran, MN 55340-9456/612-494-9237; FAX: 612-494-9236

Barsotti, Bruce (See River Road Sporting Clays)

Birchwood Casey, 7900 Fuller Rd., Eden Prairie, MN 55344/800-328-6156, 612-937-7933; FAX: 612-937-7979

Blount, Inc., Sporting Equipment Div., 2299 Snake River Ave., P.O. Box 856, Lewiston, ID 83501/800-627-3640, 208-746-2351

Blue and Gray Products, Inc. (See Ox-Yoke Originals, Inc.)

Caswell International Corp., 1221 Marshall St. NE, Minneapolis, MN 55413/612-379-2000; FAX: 612-379-2367

Champion Target Co., 232 Industrial Parkway, Richmond, IN 47374/800-441-4971

Champion's Choice, Inc., 201 International Blvd., LaVergne, TN 37086/615-793-4066; FAX: 615-793-4070

Clay Target Enterprises, 300 Railway Ave., Campbell, CA 95008/408-379-4829

Cunningham Co., Eaton, 401 Superior St., Kansas City, MO 64106/816-842-2600

Dapkus Co., J.G., P.O. Box 293, Durham, CT 06422

Datumtech Corp., 2275 Wehrle Dr., Buffalo, NY 14221

D.C.C. Enterprises, 259 Wynburn Ave., Athens, GA 30601

Diamond Mfg. Co., P.O. Box 174, Wyoming, PA 18644/800-233-9601

Dutchman's Firearms, Inc., The, 4143 Taylor Blvd., Louisville, KY 40215/502-366-0555

Epps "Orillia" Ltd., Ellwood, RR 3, Hwy. 11 North, Orillia, Ont. L3V 6H3, CANADA/705-689-5333

Federal Champion Target Co., 232 Industrial Parkway, Richmond, IN 47374/800-441-4971; FAX: 317-966-7747

G.H. Enterprises Ltd., Bag 10, Okotoks, Alberta T0L 1T0 CANADA/403-938-6070

Hiti-Schuch, Atelier Wilma, A-8863 Predlitz, Pirming Y1 AUSTRIA/0353418278

Hoppe's Div., Penguin Industries, Inc., Airport Industrial Mall, Coatesville, PA 19320/251-384-6000

Hornady Mfg. Co., P.O. Box 1848, Grand Island, NE 68801/800-338-3220, 308-382-1390

Hunterjohn, P.O. Box 477, St. Louis, MO 63166/314-531-7250

Innovision Enterprises, 728 Skinner Dr., Kalamazoo, MI 49001/616-382-1681; FAX: 616-382-1830

Jackalope Gun Shop, 1048 S. 5th St., Douglas, WY 82633/307-358-3441

Kennebec Journal, 274 Western Ave., Augusta, ME 04330/207-622-6288

Littler Sales Co., 20815 W. Chicago, Detroit, MI 48228/313-273-6888; FAX: 313-273-1099

M&D Munitions Ltd., 127 Verdi St., Farmingdale, NY 11735/516-752-1038; FAX: 516-752-1905

National Target Co., 4690 Wyaconda Rd., Rockville, MD 20852/800-827-7060, 301-770-7060; FAX: 301-770-7892

North American Shooting Systems, P.O. Box 306, Osoyoos, B.C. V0H 1V0 CANADA/604-495-3131; FAX: 604-495-2816

Nu-Teck, 30 Industrial Park Rd., Box 37, Centerbrook, CT 06409/203-767-3573; FAX: 203-767-9137

Old Western Scrounger, Inc., 12924 Hwy. A-l2, Montague, CA 96064/916-459-5445; FAX: 916-459-3944

Outers Laboratories, Div. of Blount, Inc., Route 2, Onalaska, WI 54650/608-781-5800

Ox-Yoke Originals, Inc., 34 Main St., Milo, ME 04463/800-231-8313; FAX: 207-943-2416

Parker Reproductions, 124 River Rd., Middlesex, NJ 08846/908-469-0100; FAX: 908-469-9692

Pease Accuracy, Bob, P.O. Box 310787, New Braunfels, TX 78131/210-625-1342

Penguin Industries, Inc., Airport Industrial Mall, Coatesville, PA 19320/215-384-6000

Protektor Model, 1-11 Bridge St., Galeton, PA 16922/814-435-2442

Quack Decoy & Sporting Clays, 4 Ann & Hope Way, P.O. Box 98, Cumberland, RI 02864/401-723-8202; FAX: 401-722-5910

Red Star Target Co., 4519 Brisebois Dr. NW, Calgary AB T2L 2G3 CANADA/403-289-7939; FAX: 403-289-3275

Remington Arms Co., Inc., 1007 Market St., Wilmington, DE 19898/302-773-5291

Richards Classic Oil Finish, John, Rt. 2, Box 325, Bedford, KY 40006/502-255-7222

River Road Sporting Clays, Bruce Barsotti, P.O. Box 3016, Gonzales, CA 93926/408-675-2473

Rockwood Corp., Speedwell Division, 136 Lincoln Blvd., Middlesex, NJ 08846/908-560-7171

Schaefer Shooting Sports, 2280 Grand Ave., Baldwin, NY 11510/516-379-4900; FAX: 516-379-6701

Seligman Shooting Products, Box 133, Seligman, AZ 86337/602-422-3607

Shooters Supply, 1120 Tieton Dr., Yakima, WA 98902/509-452-1181

Shooting Arts Ltd., Box 621399, Littleton, CO 80162/303-933-2539

Shotgun Shop, The, 14145 Proctor Ave., Suite 3, Industry, CA 91746/818-855-2737; FAX: 818-855-2735

Stoney Baroque Shooters Supply, John Richards, Rt. 2, Box 325, Bedford, KY 40006/502-255-7222

Stoney Point Products, Inc., 124 Stoney Point Rd., P.O. Box 5, Courtland, MN 56021-0005/507-354-3360; FAX: 507-354-7236

Thompson Target Technology, 618 Roslyn Ave., SW, Canton, OH 44710/216-453-7707; FAX: 216-478-4723

Trius Traps, P.O. Box 25, 221 S. Miami Ave., Cleves, OH 45002/513-941-5682; FAX: 513-941-7970

Verdemont Fieldsports, 3035 Jo An Dr., San Bernardino, CA 92407-2022/714-880-8255; FAX: 714-880-8255

White Flyer, Div. of Reagent Chemical & Research, Inc., 9139 W. Redfield Rd., Peoria, AZ 85381/800-647-2898

White Flyer Targets, 124 River Rd., Middlesex, NJ 08846/908-469-0100; FAX: 908-469-9692

TRAP AND SKEET SHOOTER'S EQUIPMENT

Allen Sportswear, Bob, P.O. Box 477, Des Moines, IA 50302/515-283-2191; FAX: 515-283-0779

Baker, Stan, 10,000 Lake City Way, Seattle, WA 98125/206-522-4575

Ballistic Products, Inc., 20015 75th Ave. North, Corcoran, MN 55340-9456/612-494-9237; FAX: 612-494-9236

Blount, Inc., Sporting Equipment Div., 2299 Snake River Ave., P.O. Box 856, Lewiston, ID 83501/800-627-3640, 208-746-2351

C&H Research, 115 Sunnyside Dr., Box 351, Lewis, KS 67552/316-324-5445

Clymer Manufacturing Co., Inc., 1645 W. Hamlin Rd., Rochester Hills, MI 48309-3312/810-853-5555; FAX: 810-853-1530

Crane & Crane Ltd., 105 N. Edison Way #6, Reno, NV 89502-2355/702-856-1516; FAX: 702-856-1616

D&H Prods. Co., Inc., 465 Denny Rd., Valencia, PA 16059/412-898-2840

Ganton Manufacturing Ltd., Depot Lane, Seamer Rd., Scarborough, North Yorkshire, Y012 4EB ENGLAND/0723-371910; FAX: 0723-501671

G.H. Enterprises Ltd., Bag 10, Okotoks, Alberta T0L 1T0 CANADA/403-938-6070

Great 870 Co., The, P.O. Box 6309, El Monte, CA 91734

Hafner Creations, Inc., Rt. 1, P.O. Box 248A, Lake City, FL 32055/904-755-6481

Harper, William E. (See Great 870 Co., The)

Hastings Barrels, 320 Court St., Clay Center, KS 67432/913-632-3169; FAX: 913-632-6554

K&T Co., Div. of T&S Industries, Inc., 1027 Skyview Dr., W. Carrollton, OH 45449/513-859-8414

Lynn's Custom Gunstocks, RR 1, Brandon, IA 52210/319-474-2453

Mag-Na-Port International, Inc., 41302 Executive Dr., Harrison Twp., MI 48045-3448/810-469-6727; FAX: 810-469-0425

Maionchi-L.M.I., Via Di Coselli-Zona Industriale Di Guamo, Lucca, ITALY 55060/011 39-583 94291

Meadow Industries, P.O. Box 754, Locust Grove, VA 22508/703-972-2175; FAX: 703-972-2175

Moneymaker Guncraft Corp., 1420 Military Ave., Omaha, NE 68131/402-556-0226

MTM Molded Products Co., Inc., 3370 Obco Ct., Dayton, OH 45414/513-890-7461; FAX: 513-890-1747

Nielsen Custom Cases, P.O. Box 26297, Las Vegas, NV 89126/800-377-1341, 702-878-5611; FAX: 702-877-4433

Noble Co., Jim, 1305 Columbia St., Vancouver, WA 98660/206-695-1309

Outers Laboratories, Div. of Blount, Inc., Route 2, Onalaska, WI 54650/608-781-5800

PAST Sporting Goods, Inc., P.O. Box 1035, Columbia, MO 65205/314-445-9200

Perazzi USA, Inc., 1207 S. Shamrock Ave., Monrovia, CA 91016/818-303-0068

Pro-Port Ltd., 41302 Executive Dr., Harrison Twp., MI 48045-3448/810-469-7323; FAX: 810-469-0425

Protektor Model, 1-11 Bridge St., Galeton, PA 16922/814-435-2442

Ravell Ltd., 289 Diputacion St., 08009, Barcelona SPAIN

Remington Arms Co., Inc., 1007 Market St., Wilmington, DE 19898/302-773-5291

Rhodeside, Inc., 1704 Commerce Dr., Piqua, OH 45356/513-773-5781

Shootin' Accessories, Ltd., P.O. Box 6810, Auburn, CA 95604/916-889-2220

Shooting Specialties (See Titus, Daniel)

Shotgun Shop, The, 14145 Proctor Ave., Suite 3, Industry, CA 91746/818-855-2737; FAX: 818-855-2735

Speer Products, Div. of Blount, Inc., P.O. Box 856, Lewiston, ID 83501/208-746-2351; FAX: 208-746-2915

10-X Products Group, 2915 Lyndon B. Johnson Freeway, Suite 133, Dallas, TX 75234/214-243-4016

Daniel Titus, Shooting Specialties, 872 Penn St., Bryn Mawr, PA 19010/215-525-8829

Trius Traps, P.O. Box 25, 221 S. Miami Ave., Cleves, OH 45002/513-941-5682; FAX: 513-941-7970

Universal Clay Pigeon Traps, Unit 5, Dalacre Industrial Estate, Wilbarston, ENGLAND LE16 8QL/011-44536771625; FAX: 011-44536771625

X-Spand Target Systems, 26-10th St. SE, Medicine Hat, AB T1A 1P7 CANADA/403-526-7997; FAX: 403-526-7997